HOME
AND
AWAY

A COMPLETE RECORD OF AUSTRALIAN CRICKET TOURS

HOME AND AWAY

Statistics by Ross Dundas

Foreword by Geoff Lawson, OAM

JACK POLLARD

Published by ABC Books for the
AUSTRALIAN BROADCASTING CORPORATION
GPO Box 9994 Sydney NSW 2001

Copyright © Jack Pollard 1995

First published November 1995

All rights reserved. No part of this publication
may be reproduced, stored in a retrieval system or
transmitted in any form or by any menas, electronic,
mechanical, photocopying, recording or otherwise,
without the prior written permission of the
Australian Broadcasting Corporation.

National Library of Australia
Cataloguing-in-Publication entry
Pollard, Jack, 1926–
    Home and away: a complete record of Australian cricket tours.
    ISBN 0 7333 0449 4.

    1. Cricket—Australia—History. 2. Cricket—
    Australia—History—Pictorial works. 3. Cricket—
    Australia—Records. 4. Cricket—Tournaments—
    Australia—History. 5. Test matches (Cricket)—
    Australia—History. I. Australian Broadcasting
    Corporation. II. Title.

796.358650994

Designed by Howard Binns-McDonald
Statistics set in 6.5/7.5 Gill Sans by
Midland Typesetters, Maryborough, Victoria
Printed in Australia by
Australian Print Group, Maryborough, Victoria

3995-3.5

5 4 3 2 1

CONTENTS

Foreword	vii
Introduction	1
BEFORE TEST MATCHES BEGAN	3
SONS OF CONVICTS	17
INTERNATIONAL TOURS ESTABLISHED	35
THE AMERICAN INVOLVEMENT	55
SOUTH AFRICAN CHALLENGE	61
GOING HOME	81
THE SERVICES XIs	95
TELEVISION TO THE RESCUE	101
MCC IN AUSTRALIA	115
ASIA AWAKES	127
WEST INDIAN FIGHT-BACK	149
THE PACKER REVOLT AND OTHER REBELLIONS	169
THE OLD ENEMY	173
CHAMPION AUSTRALIAN STATE TEAMS	189
SPECIAL PURPOSE XIs	201
LIMITED OVER CRICKET	211
THE GREATEST TRIP	215
THE VERDICT	229
APPENDIX	235

FOREWORD

'It's remarkable how great a grip cricket's got over so many parts of the Commonwealth, and not merely on people of European stock. I can't help thinking that there's some connection between a liking for democratic ideals and the game of cricket. Both require patience, tolerance and understanding. Both are not as spectacular as many forms of government or forms of games, and are only appreciated when the finer points are grasped.'

Those were the words of former England captain R.E.S. Wyatt in 1951 when the Empire was still basically intact and the British influence still strong. The Commonwealth chugs along with many republics in tow and perhaps more to come in the changing face of world politics. The number of nations that play cricket continues to grow and Bob Wyatt's outline on ideals could never be more true. Cricket is an international game played in the most unlikeliest of conditions by peoples with extremely diverse customs and cultures.

This authoritative work by the prolific and respected Jack Pollard gives the history of cricket tours through the ages. The format of commentary and statistics on each page allows an insight into every overseas tour involving Australia by major teams since 1868, accompanied by a unique collection of team, individual and action photographs. The book is principally a pictorial history and allows the reader an easy browse through any chapter. Open it at any page at any time and your attention is captured. All 35 of Australia's Test tours to the Old Dart, including the 1993 Ashes battle, are presented along with the 38 visits by England to Australia's shores with full statistics courtesy of the Australian Cricket Board's statistician, Ross Dundas.

Jack Pollard has had to dig deep to find the material on games such as the 'Men versus Women' match in which the men were handicapped by batting with broom-handles (not even a thought of a sweep shot here). The first-class fixture which would be of particular interest to modern day players, administrators and legislators could be the 'Smokers v Non-Smokers' clash at Lord's in 1884 in which victory went to the Non-Smokers by nine wickets and raised 561 pounds 15 shillings and sixpence for the Cricketers' Fund Friendly Society. The return clash in 1887 in Melbourne saw the Non-Smokers amass a record 803 as the Smokers ran out of puff but failed to press home the victory when time was up and only five wickets were needed. These teams consisted of English and Australia Test players joining together. One wonders just what the dressing-room banter would have been in light of English cricket supremo of the last century, Lord Hawke's view of smoking: 'Let me say, however, that I never smoked until my day's cricket was done. . . I do not think that I am a bit old-fashioned in my opinion that there is too much smoking amongst those actually playing first-class cricket. It is not good for the nerves—and nerves play more havoc than even the most devastating fast bowler on the other side.' Perhaps this reflects in the results of those two fixtures.

The fortunes of the Test-playing nations and the lesser lights of the cricket-playing fraternity are followed through their developmental years and one wonders what would have become of cricket in the USA if they had continued on from the conquest of Australia in 1893 in Philadelphia. Jack Blackham's team made no excuses for an innings loss to the Yanks at the Germantown cricket club. The Americans scored 525

FOREWORD

in their only innings which still stands as their highest score in American first-class games. Australia's other significant loss to one of the less recognised cricket nations occurred in the Netherlands when Bob Simpson's 1964 tourists were beaten on the 'mat' at The Hague Cricket Club by just four runs. The rise of the West Indies is chronicled and the elevation of New Zealand, Sri Lanka and Zimbabwe from the 'Second Division' to their current status in the Test-playing ranks.

Despite recent moves to have many of the 'Rebel' tours to South Africa dismissed from official records they have been quite rightly included in this volume. Statistics and photographs from those tours and Kerry Packer's World Series Cricket years appear along with Jack's description of events. It would be a slur on the term 'first class' and the calibre of player and contest if these performances were not included in the all-time records.

The collection of photographs has come largely from the players actually involved on the tours or from their relatives and the many State and national cricket associations around the globe. Unfortunately no pictorial record could be found of the Echuca 'Wharfies' or the Lindfield 'Funnelwebs' but there is a priceless shot of the 'One-Armed' players versus the 'One-Legged' players clash. The progress of cricket is reflected in the advancement of photography as the type and style of photograph changes with the period from the sepia tones and posed 'action shots' to the magnificent colour recreations of night cricket and multicoloured clothes. It would be somewhat anachronistic however, if the heroes of the 19th and early half of the 20th centuries were portrayed in anything but black and white.

The international teams are supplemented with Champion State Teams, Special Purpose XIs, the Services XIs and the latter development of world cricket of limited over games. In short, a lot of teams and matches feature in this important work.

If the British 'sphere of influence' referred to the cricket ball then we have been fortunate indeed to have been touched. This volume goes a long way to capturing the essence of that sphere.

GEOFF LAWSON, O.A.M.

INTRODUCTION

Although they cannot provide a precise date of origin, cricket historians agree the game derived from folk games such as club-ball, creag, crosse, gate ball and stool ball, popular in Europe in the 13th century. In some of these, one player armed with a crooked staff or club defended the stump of a tree or a low kneeling-stool known as a 'krickstoel' and used in Dutch churches. His opponent threw selected round stones, later replaced by hidebound balls filled with cork. Runs were scored by hitting the ball past certain points and recorded by scorers who cut notches in sticks.

The equipment used and the rules of the game were refined and developed by Englishmen, who not only gave it a fascination akin to chess but also provided it with a code of ethical conduct that has endured. The present-day bat evolved from a simple club. Tree stumps were replaced by a wicket or gate formed by two sticks and a crosspiece along the top known as a bail. Pads, originally for one leg only, were introduced around 1800 by 'Long Bob' Robinson of Farnham, Surrey, and shin pads in the 1830s, like those worn by modern hockey players. Gloves for batting—kid gloves with rubber strips glued on the top of each finger—were introduced by Blackheath schoolmaster and Kent, Surrey and All-England cricketer, Nicholas Wanostrocht, known as Felix, around 1825. From 1776, when 'Lumpy' Stevens bowled a ball three times through a gap in the two-pronged wicket of John Small, a third stump was introduced.

Cricket's written history dates from the middle of the 16th century, but there is ample evidence of its existence far earlier than that. Cricket was played at the 'Free School' in the Borough of Guildford in the late 1550s. By 1598 the game had won enough recognition to earn a place in an Italian dictionary. In 1611, Randle Cotgrave's English–French dictionary defined 'crosse' as a bishop's staff, also 'a cricket staffe, or the crooked staffe wherewith boys play cricket'.

Oliver Cromwell was criticised in 1621 for playing cricket in his youth, but in 1656 Cromwell made amends for his roisterous teens by ordering all 'krickett sticks' and balls in Ireland to be burned by the common hangman. Cromwell's action temporarily killed cricket in Ireland but had little effect on the subsequent establishment of the Hambledon Club, the Star and Garter Club, or other English strongholds of the game.

Cricket had a set of rules by 1700 but the earliest known code was drawn up in 1744 by a group of noblemen who used the Artillery Ground in London and called themselves the London Club. These laws were revised in 1755 by a group of London clubs, with the Star and Garter Club in Pall Mall playing a leading role.

The laws called for two wickets, each nine inches wide (21.6 cm) and 22 yards (20.12 m) apart. Between the stumps was a hole large enough to accommodate the ball. If the fieldsmen could pop the ball into the hole before the batsman reached it with the tip of his bat, the batsman was out. This later developed from a hole into the popping crease, which was marked four feet (1.22 m) in front and parallel to the bowling crease. The popping crease had to be at least 12 feet (3.66 m) in length.

Apart from fascinating laws such as this, cricket developed a wide range of expressions that delighted its adherents as much as it perplexed newcomers to the game. An over of four, six or eight deliveries—according to the conditions agreed on for certain matches—from which no run was scored was called a 'Maiden'. A player who batted defensively, primarily to prevent his dismissal

INTRODUCTION

rather than score runs, blocking like a stone wall, was labelled a 'stonewaller'. Harry Jupp, the Surrey right-hand opening batsman, was known as 'Young Stonewall' because of his defensive powers. Fieldsmen who ventured so close to the ball they were considered foolhardy were said to be at 'silly mid-off', 'silly point', or 'silly leg'.

I believe the most significant development of all, however, was cricket's adoption of a numbering system used in France that provided for contests between teams of eleven players. This strange eleven players-a-side system transformed cricket from a single wicket game, allowed for teams from neighbouring villages to meet, but above all, gave entire communities a compact, practical group they could support.

From matches between villages, cricket spread to matches between wandering clubs in the mid-19th century, sides like William Clarke's All England Eleven and the United North of England XI and United Yorkshire, groups that were just big enough to provide a range of colourful personalities but not so big as to confuse cricket addicts. Helped by the introduction of railways, these mainly professional touring teams helped popularise cricket among people who had never seen cricket at its best. This paved the way for county cricket and eventually for international cricket.

Cricket has provided a marvellous array of individual heroes, witty, colourful figures, who have enriched the game just as much as the brilliant run-scorers and wicket-takers. Yet when you get right down to it, cricket matches are contests between teams of eleven players, the French baker's ten plus a bonus of one for those who bought ten loaves. Players are called on to channel their individual talents into achievements that benefit the team and often have to sacrifice individual honours in the team's cause. Rodney Marsh offered no complaint when his captain Bill Lawry declared Australia's innings closed on 9 for 493 against Ray Illingworth's English team at Melbourne in 1970–71, with Marsh on 92 not out and eight short of becoming the first Australian wicket-keeper to score a Test century. For Marsh knew that in cricket, team objectives transcend those of individuals.

The aim of this book is to assemble the records of all the best cricket teams, looking back on the long history of cricket around the world. Down the years some fascinating elevens—again I marvel at that number—have emerged and made significant contributions in the game's progress. They deserve a place alongside the achievements of the great England, Australian, West Indian, Indian, Pakistani, South African, and New Zealand teams.

All the major cricket tours involving Australia, including Australian visits to England, New Zealand, South Africa, West Indies, India, Pakistan, Sri Lanka and Zimbabwe, and Australian tours by all these countries have been covered in the text. But tours not regarded as major ventures, involving one or two matches for celebratory games or exclusively limited over matches can be found in the Appendix.

In the early days MCC teams captained by Archie MacLaren (1922–23), Harold Gilligan (1929–30), and Errol Holmes (1935–36) popped in for a few games on their way to longer itineraries in New Zealand. The boom in the popularity of limited over cricket has produced tours to Australia by all Australia's rival cricket nations, usually without involving the tourists in a Test. The English county teams Worcestershire (1988–89) and Lancashire (1989–90 and 1990–91) and the champion Sri Lankan club Tamil Nadu (1988–89). Unless their tours were rated a major feature of the Australian summer, their visits are recorded in the Appendix.

The same applies for Australia's overseas tours exclusive for limited over cricket such as the World Cups in England and India and Pakistan. None of the results of World Series Cricket matches in the two years of the Packer revolt are recorded. Complete results of the two South African tours in 1985–86 and 1986–87 by Australian teams captained by Kim Hughes are provided in the Away section of the Appendix, although the Australian Cricket Board refused to include the players' performances on those tours in their first-class records.

In 127 years of Australian cricketers on tour, the overall judgment remains firmly based on how the team as a unit fared. Australia's 364 Test players have had to meet changes in playing hours, four-ball, six-ball and eight-ball overs, 'sticky' wickets when pitches were uncovered, the partial covering of pitches where bowlers operated, and finally the total covering of the wicket area. The height of the stumps was altered, the follow-on law amended, and new balls became available to captains at varying marks, now after not less than 85 overs. By the end of the century I suspect that high-tech balls that can be seen at night under lights will allow Tests to proceed after dark. Statisticians limited now to night-time limited over matches with two white balls will have a new entry for their ledgers—hat-tricks or centuries recorded after sundown. Let's hope the number of players in a team never changes, for it is one feature of a wonderful game the founders got just right.

CHAPTER ONE

BEFORE TEST MATCHES BEGAN

International cricket began on 24 and 25 September 1844, nearly twenty years before the American Civil War and seven years after Queen Victoria ascended the throne, when a Canadian team met the United States on a site that later became the New York University Medical Centre. This was seven years after the first recorded match in New York, and four years after members of the New York St George Club made an abortive trip to play Toronto in Toronto, only to find that the letter setting down their travel plans had not been delivered. Formal apologies were tendered and the New Yorkers won a hastily arranged pickup match by ten wickets.

The Americans should have won the initial international match, as cricket had been played in American colonies since 1709 when English migrants influenced staging of matches in Philadelphia and Pennsylvania. American cricket was regarded as the strongest outside England and a high proportion of the $100,000 bet on the match was said to have come from US supporters. Both teams were heavily loaded with English migrants, accustomed to the betting that accompanied cricket back in their homeland. After all, if it was good enough for the Reverend Lord Frederick Beauclerk (a great grandson of Charles II and Nell Gwynne) to wager a thousand guineas on a match at Lord's, then surely it was justifiable for them to invest a few hundred dollars of their American profits on the cricket.

More than 5000 people watched the match start, with Canada scoring 82 in their first innings by 2 p.m. on the first afternoon. The United States replied with 64. Canada scored only 63 at their second attempt, leaving the US to make 82 to win. Despite their first innings failure this appeared an easy task, as the Americans had James Turner to open their batting. Turner had reached 120 for the Union CC of Camden, New Jersey, earlier that year, the first century recorded in North America. He followed his seven runs in the first innings with 14 in the second and Canada bundled the US out for 58 to win by 33 runs.

After Canada had won the first three matches there was high drama in the fourth when Samuel Dudson, of Philadelphia, bowled a ball which Canada's John Helliwell hit high in the air. Dudson set himself for the catch but was shocked to see Helliwell running full tilt towards him. Dudson took Helliwells's charge head-on and lay on the ground in pain for several minutes. Then he got up and threw the ball at Helliwell. After players subdued them Helliwell claimed the rules allowed him to charge the bowler. This had been permissible until 1787 when the laws of cricket were revised. One of the laws of the game in 1702 allowed:

> ...either of ye strikers may hinder ye catcher in his running ground or if she is hit directly across ye wickets yet other player may place his body anywhere within ye swing of his bat so as to hinder ye bowler from catching her, but he must neither strike nor touch at her with his hands.

Helliwell's explanation, that such charges with the bat raised in the air like a lance were within the laws, was 140 years out of date and when the Americans took their places in the field to resume play the Canadians refused to continue batting. The Americans claimed the match and local newspapers reported that Canada had forfeited. The Americans claimed all bets, but some Canadians paid up sourly. The animosity the affair created resulted in suspension of America–Canada matches for seven years.

The first overseas tour by an English team should have

occurred in 1789, when a visit to France was arranged by the English Ambassador to Paris, the Duke of Dorset. The English players travelled to Dover but before they boarded the ship to cross the Channel, they met a flustered Duke of Dorset, who was fleeing from the French Revolution. Names of the players who cancelled their trip to Paris remain unknown.

Cricket's popularity spread all over England in the first half of the 1800s, and by 1841 the British army had become a valuable source of talent when it issued an order that all barracks should have a cricket ground. Introduction of penny postage speeded up the arrangement of match fixtures and reports of results to newspapers.

A major advance came in 1846 when William Clarke, born on 24 December 1798, in Nottingham, founded the All England Eleven. Clarke followed his father into bricklaying but found the life of a publican more convivial. In his 39th year he married the widowed landlady of the Trent Bridge Inn. He developed the paddock next to the pub into the Trent Bridge cricket ground, where he perfected the under-arm bowling that had just become fashionable. Derek West, in his absorbing book, *The Elevens of England*, published in London in 1988, said:

Approaching the wicket at a gentle trot, Clarke bent back his elbows at the last moment to bowl from under his right armpit, making the ball lift steeply from the ground. At times, he delivered from the level of the hip, propelling the ball in the style of a man tossing a quoit. He varied his length and action as much as his pace, which was generally slow, with the occasional faster ball, and on pitching the 'leather sphere' moved sharply from leg to off. The twist was so prodigious that he preferred bowling from the Pavilion end against the slope at Lord's.

Clarke was virtually unknown in the south of England until he helped a North of England team defeat South of England at Lord's in 1836 by six wickets. Ten years later he made his first appearance for the Players against the Gentlemen at the age of 47. He was only 5ft 9in (175 cm) tall and 14 st (88.9 kg), but compensated for his bulk with a sharp wit dedicated to deluding batsmen. West says, to his contemporaries Clarke was 'a crafty, fox-headed cricketer who always expected to get a wicket in the next over'. Even the loss of an eye in an accident playing fives did not lessen Clarke's passion for cricket.

He founded his All England Eleven in 1846, the same year as he became a ground bowler at Lord's, reasoning

The All England XI in 1847: J. Guy, G. Parr, W. Martingell, A. Mynn, W. Denison, J. Dean, W. Clarke, N. Felix, O.C. Pell, W.R. Hillyer, F.W. Lillywhite, W. Dorrinton, F. Pilch and T. Ewell sen. *From the watercolour by Nicholas Felix*

that publicans all over England would welcome an elite eleven playing against the best locals, usually on grounds near their pubs. His choice of name was an inspiration, for it immediately conveyed a hint of excellence that only fine players could produce. The inaugural match was played at Sheffield between 31 August and 2 September, with the All England XI fielding a team which included noted amateurs and professionals and historic figures such as Fuller Pilch, Alfred Mynn, and the Oxford University star the Reverend Villiers Shallet Charnock Smith. Clarke was captain and sponsor–manager of a side that soon became famous.

Scores in the England Eleven's matches were low, even though they often took on teams of 18 and 22 players, because the pitches were uneven and furrowed. Batting for the All England XI in 1848, George Parr, then rated the best batsman in England, took six hours to score 25 in a rain-interrupted innings. James Grundy remained unbeaten against a team of 16 in 1857, scoring 51 in 5 hours 15 minutes.

Clarke's program of matches expanded rapidly and he recruited all the best players as they were developed, including John Wisden, nicknamed 'The Little Wonder' and later 'The Cardinal', a bowler of pace and accuracy whose batting became valuable to the All England XI. Although he only had one eye, Clarke used it unerringly in spotting talent.

The Eleven of England attracted audiences cricket had never had before because Clarke insisted on enclosed arenas where spectators would be forced to pay to watch, with marquees for serving food. Cricket for profit cost the hosts £56 to £80 and the takings belonged to Clarke, and local businessmen and publicans jumped at the idea. Clarke paid agreed amounts to his players, an agreed sum for the rental of the venues, and took as much of the gatemoney as he could.

The idea worked well until the players rebelled in a Kerry Packer–style chase for a better share of the profits. A number of leading players voted in September 1852 not to play for or against any team in which Clarke had management control. It did not matter that less than half the players who agreed to this had played for Clarke's team, but the concept of one elite team disappeared with the formation of sides variously known as the United Eleven and the United All England Eleven, and the emergence of a United South of England Eleven.

Clarke's greed destroyed a concept that served cricket well, but it also made good cricketers ambitious and boosted the entire concept of touring and this in turn encouraged them to look at the next most powerful cricketing nation at the time, the United States. Meanwhile in Australia intercolonial cricket had begun and immediately established a rivalry between the major colonies, Victoria and New South Wales, that would endure.

Before intercolonial cricket began in Australia in 1851, however, some marvellous teams emerged. In Western Australia, a clergyman named Lefroy from New Norcia, north of Perth, toured the State with teams of Aboriginal players recruited from the mission where they had been taught cricket fundamentals. In Ballarat, the locals fielded a team dominated by Aborigines. Australia's warm reception of cricket inspired a London magazine to publish a picture of settlers riding on horseback to a match. In Victoria, the potential of Aboriginal cricketers had excited John Conway's Clarke-like interest in making money out of touring cricket teams. All the colonies were having trouble establishing their authority over club teams and their leading players, but the touring opportunities become more obvious to good players after the first inter-colonial match between Tasmania and Victoria in 1851.

The Canada v. USA series was revived in 1853 when the US won a low-scoring match by 34 runs and that night entertained their opponents at Delmonico's

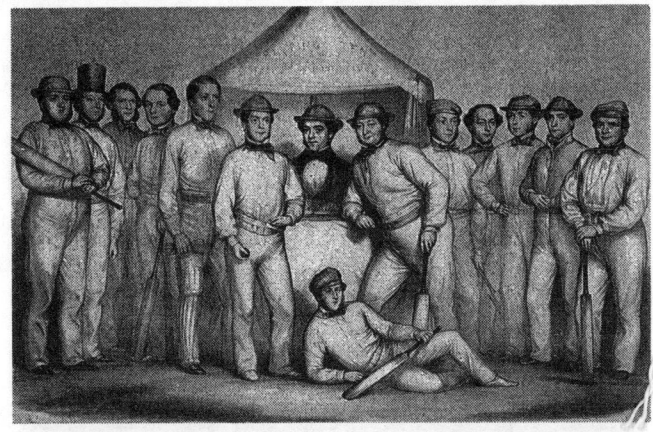

The United Eleven of All England in 1852: T. Hunt, G.H. Wright, T.M. Adams, W. Mortlock, T. Lockyer, J. Wisden, F. Lillywhite, J. Lillywhite, J. Dean, W. Caffyn, J. Grundy, W. Martingell, T. Sherman and H. Sampson. They were promoted with names Kerry Packer would have envied: 'Star of The North' (Hunt), 'Old Stonewall' (Mortlock), 'The Little Wonder' (Wisden), 'Joyous Jemmy' (Dean), 'The Surrey Pet' (Caffyn). *Lord's Library*

A drawing by Henry S. Glover of the intercolonial match between New South Wales and Victoria in Melbourne in January 1858. *Melbourne Cricket Club Library*

restaurant. The ill-feeling between the countries that was apparent in the initial matches disappeared and has never revived.

In 1858 at Sheffield, Heathfield Harman Stephenson, playing for an All England XI that had declined in prestige against Twenty-Two of Hallam and Staveley took three wickets in three balls. Team-mates rewarded him with a new hat, the first recorded 'hat-trick'. Stephenson was destined for higher honours.

On 7 September 1859, 15 years after the first matches between Canada and the US began, the first English team to go overseas went to North America under the captaincy of the 'Lion of the North', George Parr, the finest batsman in England, who included only professionals in his 12-man party. Parr was then 33 years old. His team played five matches, none of them rated first-class. W.P. Pickering, a former Cambridge blue and a foundation member of the Surrey county team, arranged the tour and paid all the team's expenses from the £1300 sterling he received in grants from sponsors in Canada and the US. This was the first of all international cricket touring teams, and what a challenging future they opened up!

The Englishmen reached Quebec on 22 September and played their first match against Twenty-Two of Lower Canada on 24 and 26 September. They won by eight wickets, Parr taking 6 for 8 and 10 for 19 with his roundarm lobs and John Jackson, the Nottinghamshire fast roundarm bowler, 7 for 21 and 6 for 20. Lower Canada made 85 and 63; Parr's XI made 117 and 2 for 32. Their supremacy established, the Englishmen applied themselves to enjoying lavish hospitality in Montreal, Hoboken, Philadelphia, Hamilton and Rochester, rounding off their unbeaten tour with a 68-run victory over Twenty-Two of Canada and the US. After covering all their costs, the team's only hardship of the tour came on the voyage home when a gale struck their ship. William Caffyn later wrote in his book, *Seventy-One Not Out*:

> Jemmy Grundy declared we would never see land again; poor George Parr was almost out of his mind; old Jackson dropped to his knees; and indeed our situation was a critical one. Our jib-boom broke and one member of the crew had both legs broken while he and other members of the crew were trying to set matters right.

Aborigines took to cricket from the arrival of the first settlers in Australia in 1788 and for years helped out white farmers' teams by filling in when they were short of players. They had exceptional whip in their throwing arms, wiry legs that seldom tired, and overcame the affront of not being asked to bowl, but recognised that the game built up friendliness among farm workers.

The centre of Aboriginal cricket in the first half of the 18th century was at Edenhope and Harrow in Victoria, where Aboriginal teams often defeated all-white sides. The skill of the black cricketers around Edenhope overshadowed the commendable exploits of the Aboriginal cricketers from the New Norcia mission north of Perth, and the Aboriginal elevens in Queensland and northern New South Wales and in coastal regions of Tasmania.

An Aboriginal team attracted 10,000 spectators to Melbourne Cricket Ground on Boxing Day 1866, and some of the players in that match went to England in 1868, ten years before the first white Australian team. To get away to England, the Aboriginal team had to overcome objections that they would be prone to disease in northern hemisphere weather, and assertions from the Aboriginal Protection Board that they were being exploited. To avoid demonstrations they slipped away from Sydney in a ship bound for London via Hong Kong.

The Aborigines attracted crowds of more than 5000 often enough for the MCC committee to reverse its decision not to invite them to appear at Lord's. An MCC team which included an earl, a viscount, a lieutenant-colonel, and a captain, scored 164 and 120, with Cuzens taking 10 for 117 in the match. The Aborigines led on the first innings with a total of 185, but collapsed in their second innings for 45. Johnny Mullagh, star of the tour, scored 12 of the 45 runs, Cuzens 21. The accepted tour figures follow.

The first overseas touring team on the deck of the ship that took them from Liverpool, England, to America: *Back row* R. Carpenter, W. Caffyn, T. Lockyer, J. Wisden, H.H. Stephenson, G. Parr, J. Grundy, J. Caesar, T. Hayward, J. Jackson; *front row* A.J. Diver, J. Lillywhite. They were all professionals but the trip was arranged by W.P. Pickering, a Cambridge Blue.

BEFORE TEST MATCHES BEGAN

THE ABORIGINAL TOUR OF ENGLAND 1868

First-class Results					All Matches				
Matches	Won	Lost	Drawn	Tied	Matches	Won	Lost	Drawn	Tied
–	–	–	–	–	47	14	14	19	–

All Matches not First-class

Date	Venue	Opponent	Results for Australians
May 25	The Oval	*Surrey Club	Lost by an inns & 7 runs
May 29	Maidstone	*Mote Park	Drawn
Jun 2	Gravesend	*Gentlemen of Kent	Lost by an inns & 69 runs
Jun 5	Richmond	*Richmond	Drawn
Jun 8	Hove	*Gentlemen of Sussex	Lost by 9 wkts
Jun 10	Ladywell	*Gentlemen of Lewisham	Won by 6 wkts
Jun 12	Lord's	*MCC	Lost by 55 runs
Jun 15	Southsea	*East Hampshire	Lost by an inns & 9 runs
Jun 19	Bishop Stortford	*Bishop Stortford	Lost by 8 wkts
Jun 22	Hastings	*Hastings	Drawn
Jun 26	Halifax	*Gentlemen of Halifax	Won by 7 wkts
Jun 29	Blackburn	*East Lancashire	Drawn
Jly 2	Rochdale	*Rochdale	Lost by 77 runs
Jly 6	Swansea	*Gentlemen of Swansea	Won by an inns & 33 runs
Jly 10	Bradford	*Bradford	Drawn
Jly 13	York	*Gentlemen of Yorkshire	Lost by an inns & 51 runs
Jly 16	Longsight	*Longsight	Lost by 4 wkts
Jly 20	Bury	*Vulcan United & Bury Clubs	Drawn
Jly 23	Lakenham	*Carrow	Won by an inns & 52 runs
Jly 27	Keighley	*Keighley	Drawn
Jly 30	Bootle	*Bootle	Won by 9 wkts
Aug 3	Nottingham	*Nottingham Commercial	Drawn
Aug 7	Longsight	*Longsight	Won by 107 runs
Aug 10	Bramall Lane	*Gentlemen of Sheffield	Drawn
Aug 13	Dewsbury	*Saville Club	Lost by an inns & 58 runs
Aug 17	North Shields	*Tynemouth	Won by 2 wkts
Aug 21	Newcastle	*Northumberland	Drawn
Aug 24	Middlesbrough	*Middlesbrough	Drawn
Aug 27	Scarborough	*Scarborough	Won by 10 wkts
Aug 31	Hunslet	*Hunslet	Won by 7 wkts
Sep 2	Derby	*Derbyshire	Lost by 139 runs
Sep 4	Lincoln	*Lincoln	Lost by 10 runs
Sep 7	Burton-on-Trent	*Burton-on-Trent	Won by 69 runs
Sep 10	Bootle	*Bootle	Won by 154 runs
Sep 14	Witham	*Witham	Won by an inns & 43 runs
Sep 17	Hove	*Gentlemen of Sussex	Drawn
Sep 21	Blackheath	*Blackheath	Lost by 13 runs
Sep 23	Islington	*Gentlemen of Middlesex	Drawn
Sep 25	The Oval	*Gentlemen of Surrey Club	Drawn
Sep 28	Maidstone	*The Press	Drawn
Sep 30	Eastbourne	*Eastbourne	Drawn
Oct 2	Hammersmith	*Turnham Green	Drawn
Oct 5	Southsea	*East Hampshire	Won by an inns & 71 runs
Oct 7	Southampton	*Gentlemen of Hampshire	Drawn
Oct 9	Reading	*Reading	Won by 218 runs
Oct 12	Godalming	*Godalming	Drawn
Oct 15	The Oval	*Gentlemen of Surrey Club	Lost by 9 wkts

The Aboriginal cricket team organised by Tom Wills, one of the inventors of Australian Rules football (top left), photographed during a match at Ballarat, Victoria, in January 1867.

All Matches Averages

Player	M	Inn	NO	Runs	HS	50	100	Avrge	Overs	Mdns	Runs	Wkts	Avrge	5wi	10wm	Best
Bullocky	39	61	3	579	64*	1	–	9.33	22.0	7	46	4	11.50	–	–	–
Cuzens, J	46	72	8	1358	87	8	–	19.90	868.0	361	1296	114	11.37	3	–	5/28
Dick-a-Dick	45	66	5	356	42	–	–	5.26	35.0	6	96	5	19.20	–	–	–
Charlie Dumas	44	53	13	218	17*	–	–	4.60	–	–	–	–	–	–	–	–
Jim Crow	13	15	4	37	12	–	–	2.70	–	–	–	–	–	–	–	–
King Cole	7	10	2	75	18	–	–	7.50	14.0	4	34	1	34.00	–	–	–
Lawrence, C (Capt)	40	57	12	1156	63	3	–	20.16	1579.0	451	3022	250	12.09	28	5	8/48
Norton, WS	1	2	–	11	11	–	–	5.50	–	–	–	–	–	–	–	–
Mosquito	34	49	24	77	8*	–	–	3.17	–	–	–	–	–	–	–	–
Mullagh, J	45	71	4	1698	94	6	–	23.65	1877.0	831	2489	245	10.16	17	4	8/9
Peter	42	59	7	284	30	–	–	4.48	–	–	–	–	–	–	–	–
Red Cap	47	73	3	630	56	1	–	8.46	366.0	141	576	54	10.66	5	–	7/34
Shepherd, W	7	11	–	66	11	–	–	6.00	56.0	14	124	6	20.66	–	–	–
Shum-Storey, GH	1	1	–	16	16	–	–	16.00	–	–	–	–	–	–	–	–
Sundown	2	3	–	1	1	–	–	0.33	–	–	–	–	–	–	–	–
Tiger	47	69	5	431	32	–	–	6.17	–	–	–	–	–	–	–	–
Twopenny	46	70	6	589	35*	–	–	8.29	176.0	78	242	35	6.91	3	2	9/9

The Aboriginal cricket team that went overseas in 1868, ten years before the first white tour: *back row* Tarpot, T.W.Wills, Mullagh; *front* King Cole, Dick-a-Dick, Jellico, Peter, Red Cap, Harry Rose, Bullocky, Cuzens.

Most of the players came from the Madimadi or Wutjubaluk tribes and underwent extensive coaching from Tom Wills before they left. William Shepherd, a white professional on Surrey's books, umpired for the Aborigines and acted as scorer or captain when manager Lawrence needed a rest. The Aborigines all wore white shirts known as Garibaldis, with coloured neckties, hat-ribbons and sashes to help spectators identify them, with merino undershirts to help them keep warm. For displays of spear-throwing and boomerang-throwing, they wore possum and kangaroo skins across their loins.

The Aboriginal pioneers of Australian cricket tours defied the forecasts that they would be left penniless and hungry, and proved a reasonable investment for the former Mayor of Sydney, George Smith, who shared John Conway's view that they would attract big crowds. Smith paid the team's fares and hotel bills and although most of the players did not play cricket of a first-class standard,

The All-Aboriginal team organised by Alfred Lefroy at the New Norcia Mission in Western Australia in the 1870s. Lefroy is seated in the centre, holding the ball.

their displays of spear-throwing and boomerang-throwing earned Smith enough money for him to bring several splendid racehourses back to Australia. The team travelled home in comfortable cabins without being forced to work for their passages as critics predicted. The tour proved of little benefit for Australian cricket, however, as only two of the team, Twopenny and Johnny Mullagh, went on to play first-class cricket. Mullagh left a hotel where the Victorian team stayed, preferring to sleep in the open after the proprietor made disparaging comments about his colour.

After the revival of the Canada versus USA matches in 1853, cricket enjoyed an upsurge in popularity in north America. The outstanding allrounders John M. Laing (Canada) and John Barton King (US) emerged in the 1890s. Laing appeared 13 times for Canada against teams from the US, Australia and England, and took 77 wickets. He once made 249 in a Chicago club match, and hit the northern American record of 344 not out for Belmont against Marion. King, a great inswing bowler, toured England three times. The best English cricketers still regarded a trip to America as more attractive than other overseas tours, but perhaps because of the wild voyages he had coped with to and from America in 1859, George Parr refused to join the first English team to Australia.

The Melbourne restaurateurs Spiers and Pond, searching for a promotion that would boost trade at their theatre–restaurants and hotels, at first invited novelist Charles Dickens to visit Australia and give lectures at their expense. Dickens did not reply (the most recent scholarly research indicates he never received the invitation).

Dickens' silence, and the upsurge in cricket's popularity in the burgeoning colonies, persuaded Spiers and Pond to send their energetic Mr Mallam to England

The United States team that played the seventh match against Canada in 1856, winning by nine wickets: G. Wheatcroft (umpire), Barlow, A. Marsh, H. Sharpe, S. Wright, A.H. Gibbes, J. Higham, Hon. H. Bingham, Cuyp, R. Waller, W. Wilby, T. Senior.
John I. Marder Collection

to collect a team of English cricketers to replace Dickens. Young Mallam arrived in England in the declining years of William Clarke's All England Eleven and found that all the best players were in Birmingham for a match between North and South. He jumped on a train and on his first night in Birmingham entertained the players to dinner.

Mallam outlined the proposition that players who joined the Australian tour would all receive £150 and have their fares and expenses paid. Parr said that on his experience on the American trip, when all the players received £250, the guarantee was completely inadequate. Parr's northern teammates agreed. Back in London Mallam received unexpected help from the Surrey club secretary, William Burrup, who knew how important it was for professional English cricketers to find winter jobs. Together they persuaded Heathfield Stephenson, who had been in Parr's side in the US, to lead a team to Australia.

The team included the 'Surrey Pet' William Caffyn, the Surrey allrounder Tom Sewell, and the big-hitting Surrey left-hander George Griffith. Mallam tried to coax Richard Daft, the finest batsman in England, to join the side in Australia but failed. The prospect of a boisterous sea voyage to a remote part of the world frightened players like Daft, but those who were not matching his earnings took the risk. As they left for Australia, relatives who feared they might not see them again cried unrestrainedly on the wharf, while Caffyn played his cornet to get the tour started on a melodious note.

Mallam was successful in recruiting George ('Tiny') Wells, noted Sussex bowler who could alternate with round-armers of medium pace or underarm slows, George ('Farmer') Bennett who specialised in high-flighted round-armers for Kent, Yorkshire allrounder Roger Iddison and his team-mate Edwin Stephenson. The 12-man team was completed with Middlesex stalwart Tom Hearne, Surrey opening batsman William Mortlock, his team-mate William Mudie, an allrounder, and Charles Lawrence, an allrounder who had played for Surrey, Middlesex, Scotland, All England and the United Ireland XI. Mallam had to make a special trip to Ireland, where Lawrence worked as secretary to the United Ireland XI, to get his agreement to tour.

ENGLAND IN AUSTRALIA 1862

HH STEPHENSON'S TEAM

First-class Results					All Matches				
Matches	Won	Lost	Drawn	Tied	Matches	Won	Lost	Drawn	Tied
–	–	–	–	–	14	6	3	5	–

Date	Venue	Opponent	Results for Touring Team
Jan 1	Melbourne	*XVIII of Victoria	Won by an inns & 96 runs
Jan 9	Beechworth	*XXII of the Ovens	Won by an inns & 191 runs
Jan 17	Melbourne	*XXII of NSW & Victoria	Drawn
Jan 20	Geelong	*XXII of Geelong	Won by 9 wkts
Jan 29	Sydney	*XXII of New South Wales	Won by 49 runs
Feb 6	Bathurst	*XXII of Bathurst	Drawn
Feb 13	Sydney	*XXII of NSW & Victoria	Lost by 13 wkts
Feb 21	Hobart (LRG)	*XXII of Tasmania	Won by 4 wkts
Feb 24	Hobart (LRG)	*E Stephenson's XI	Drawn
Mar 1	Melbourne	The World	Lost by 6 wkts
Mar 6	Ballarat	*XXII of Ballarat	Drawn
Mar 11	Bendigo	*XXII of Bendigo	Won by an inns & 63 runs
Mar 14	Castlemaine	*XXII of Castlemaine	Lost by 3 wkts
Mar 20	Melbourne	*XXII of Victoria	Drawn

The first England cricket team in Australia in 1862: George Wells, George Bennett, William Mortlock, Roger Iddison, William Caffyn, Tom Sewell, George Griffiths, William Mudie, Ed Stephenson, Charles Lawrence, Tom Hearne. The captain, H.H. Stephenson, is seated centre on the chair. Sponsors Spiers and Pond are behind the players to the left and right, with their Mr Mallam behind Stephenson.

Player	M	Inn	NO	Runs	HS	50	100	Avrge	Ct/St	Overs	Mdns	Runs	Wkts	Avrge	5wi	10wm	Best
Bennett, G	1	1	–	72	72	1	–	72.00	4	58.0	17	115	14	8.21	2	1	7/30
Caffyn, W	1	2	1	88	75*	1	–	88.00	–	29.0	7	74	2	37.00	–	–	2/63
Griffith, G	1	2	–	52	39	–	–	26.00	–	51.1	19	89	7	12.71	1	–	5/52
Hearne, T	1	2	–	6	5	–	–	3.00	–	–	–	–	–	–	–	–	–
Iddison, R	1	1	–	28	28	–	–	28.00	1	66.0	23	118	3	39.33	–	–	2/65
Lawrence, C	1	2	–	15	15	–	–	7.50	1	19.0	6	34	1	34.00	–	–	1/29
Mortlake, W	1	2	–	19	15	–	–	9.50	–	5.0	–	13	–	–	–	–	–
Mudie, W	1	2	–	27	14	–	–	13.50	2	1.0	–	3	–	–	–	–	–
Sewell, T	1	2	–	14	10	–	–	7.00	–	8.0	3	25	–	–	–	–	–
Stephenson, E	1	2	–	6	4	–	–	3.00	1/1	–	–	–	–	–	–	–	–
Stephenson, HH (Capt)	1	2	–	7	4	–	–	3.50	1/1	9.0	–	32	1	32.00	–	–	1/32
Wells, G	1	2	1	75	48	–	–	75.00	–	4.0	–	10	–	–	–	–	–

This all-professional team was a strong, experienced combination but was far from the best English side available. No less than ten players refused invitations to join the tour because of the terms offered. They were Parr, Daft, Willsher, Lockyer, Jackson, Carpenter, Hayward, Anderson, Grundy and Caesar. Wells travelled ahead of the team with his wife. The rest attended a farewell banquet in London before sailing from Liverpool on 20 October 1861 in the steamship *Great Britain*. The *Great Britain* weighed only 2000 tonnes but carried 687 passengers and long before the calm, monotonous eight-week voyage ended the cricketers complained of boredom.

This changed dramatically when they docked in Melbourne. They found 3000 people on the wharf to welcome them and a further 10,000 lining the streets through which they travelled by coach to Spiers and Pond's pride and joy, the Café de Paris, in Bourke Street. Every window and verandah near the cafe was crammed with people waving streamers and flags. For the next ten weeks the Englishmen became accustomed to champagne breakfasts and long, expensive dinners. The venues of their practice sessions had to be kept secret to curb the crowds that wanted to meet them.

The Englishmen were amazed by the support for cricket in Australia. By then intercolonial cricket flourished in Sydney and Melbourne, after surviving a shaky start in Hobart in 1851 when the Gentlemen of Van Diemen's Land (Tasmania) met a Victorian team from Port Phillip. Free settlers and Australian-born players had taken over from the soldiers who had introduced cricket to Australia. Matches between Victorian and New South Wales teams had already become bitter grudge fights that captivated the populations of Sydney and Melbourne. There were 70 cricket clubs in Victoria, 80 in New South Wales, with South Australia, Tasmania, and Queensland clubs striving to match them. There were more Aborigines reported to be doing well at the game on outlying properties. On the goldfields, to which thousands of Europeans had been lured in the 1840s and 1850s, regular cricket matches were still held among teams who used the names of their native counties or English universities.

Stephenson was wary of what the Englishmen had let themselves in for and tried to have the number of their opposition for the first match cut from Twenty-Two of Victoria to Fifteen. Spiers and Pond compromised by reducing the Victorian side to eighteen. More than 15,000 people watched the start of this historic match on the Melbourne Cricket Ground which lasted from 1 to 4 January 1862. Spiers and Pond made enough during those four days to cover their expenses for the entire tour. The flair they showed in this promotion (for example, they provided each English player with a coloured sash and a matching ribbon for his hat) was matched by rousing tunes from a large band. More than 5000 cases of beer disappeared in the brightly coloured refreshment marquees, and when England won by an innings and 96 runs before lunch on the fourth day, Spiers and Pond sent a hot air balloon aloft to entertain spectators.

The Englishmen did not meet defeat until their seventh match when they lost to Twenty-Two of New South Wales and Victoria on the Sydney Domain by 13 wickets. George Moore, who ran a confectionary store at West Maitland, 195 kilometres north of Sydney, took ten wickets for the winners, including 6 for 29 in England's first innings. The Moores were a mighty source of fine cricketers. George's father and grandfather played cricket in England, George's brother James and James' sons Leon and William Moore all played for New South Wales. George's grandson, Charlie Macartney, also born in West Maitland, became one of Australia's greatest Test batsmen. Charlie's cousin, Frank Cummins, a nephew of L. and W.H. Moore, made 11 appearances for New South Wales between 1925–26 and 1932–33. George kept playing for New South Wales until 1872–73, making his last appearance at 52 years 325 days, which made him the second oldest first-class Australian cricketer behind the Tasmanian, John Marshall, who was 58 when he played against Victoria in 1853–54.

Spiers and Pond paid each man a 100 sovereign bonus. Caffyn headed the tour averages with 419 runs at 23.27. Caffyn and Iddison did most of the bowling, delivering more than 400 overs each. Caffyn had 80 wickets at 6.18, Iddison 103 at 6.61. Spiers and Pond, who made a profit of £11,000 on the tour, offered the England team an extra £1200 to stay a further month but the team had commitments in England. Lawrence accepted an offer of £200-a-year to coach the Albert Club in Sydney and did not return home.

Despite the enormous progress cricket had made in England, there was little development on the Continent outside Holland and Denmark. A national administrative body, the Dutch Cricket Association, was formed in 1883 and remains the oldest surviving cricket control body. Led by the famous Rood en Wit cricket club of Haarlem, the Dutch attained a high standard of club cricket and were the first outside the British Empire to send players on tour to England. One Dutch player, C.J. Posthuma, was good enough for Dr W.G. Grace to take him to London to play for his London County team.

Ten clubs formed the Dansk Boldspil Union to organise Danish cricket in 1889. In Denmark, the locals played a side from the Royal High School, Edinburgh, Denmark drawing on the enthusiasm of English engineers who were building their railways. The fairytale writer Hans Christian Andersen was among Danish cricketers.

Heathfield Harman Stephenson, captain of the first English cricket team in Australia in 1862.

HOME AND AWAY

ENGLAND IN AUSTRALIA 1863–64

G PARR'S TEAM

First-class Results					All Matches				
Matches	Won	Lost	Drawn	Tied	Matches	Won	Lost	Drawn	Tied
–	–	–	–	–	14	7	2	5	–

Date	Venue	Opponent	Results for Touring Team
Jan 1	Melbourne	*XXII of Victoria	Drawn
Jan 7	Bendigo	*XXII of Bendigo	Won by 144 runs
Jan 11	Ballarat	*XXII of Ballarat	Won by an inns & 12 runs
Jan 14	Ararat	*XXII of Ararat	Won by an inns & 68 runs
Jan 19	Maryborough	*XXII of Maryborough	Won by an inns & 77 runs
Mar 2	Campbell's Creek	*XXII of Castlemaine	Won by an inns & 37 runs
Mar 5	Melbourne	G Anderson's Team	Lost by 4 wkts
Mar 16	Sydney	*XXII of New South Wales	Won by 4 wkts
Mar 26	Sydney	*XXII of New South Wales	Drawn
Apr 2	Sydney	*XXII of New South Wales	Won by 1 wkt
Apr 12	Geelong	*XXII of Geelong	Drawn
Apr 14	Maryborough	*G Anderson's Team	Lost by 56 runs
Apr 18	Ballarat	*XXII of Ballarat	Drawn
Apr 21	Melbourne	*XXII of Victoria	Drawn

Player	M	Inn	NO	Runs	HS	50	100	Avrge	Ct/St	Overs	Mdns	Runs	Wkts	Avrge	5wi	10wm	Best
Anderson, G	1	2	–	43	38	–	–	21.50	1	–	–	–	–	–	–	–	–
Caeser, J	1	2	–	9	9	–	–	4.50	–	–	–	–	–	–	–	–	–
Caffyn, W	1	2	–	74	40	–	–	37.00	–	43.1	22	40	4	10.00	–	–	2/14
Carpenter, R	1	2	–	22	22	–	–	11.00	1	–	–	–	–	–	–	–	–
Clarke, A	1	2	1	46	40	–	–	46.00	1	–	–	–	–	–	–	–	–
Grace, EM	1	2	–	21	21	–	–	10.50	2	41.0	13	69	9	7.67	1	–	5/33
Hayward, T	1	2	–	18	17	–	–	9.00	1	53.0	22	77	4	19.25	–	–	3/38
Jackson, J	1	2	–	24	12	–	–	12.00	–	64.0	34	77	3	25.67	–	–	2/60
Lockyer, T	1	2	1	84	44	–	–	84.00	–/2	–	–	–	–	–	–	–	–
Parr, G (Capt)	1	2	1	30	26*	–	–	30.00	–	–	–	–	–	–	–	–	–
Tarrant, G	1	2	–	26	17	–	–	13.00	–	77.0	33	113	5	22.60	–	–	4/63
Tinley, RC	1	2	–	37	24	–	–	18.50	1	60.2	15	97	7	13.86	1	–	7/76

The Melbourne Cricket Club took over the organisation of England's second tour of Australia in 1863–64. This time George Parr had no qualms about making the long voyage. He chose a team thoroughly representative of English cricket, comprising ten seasoned professionals and the amateur Dr E.M. Grace, one of the famous family, who had become a formidable figure in England in 1862 by scoring 192 not out and taking ten wickets in an innings for MCC against the Gentlemen of Kent, a feat even his brother, W.G. Grace, would have envied.

Caffyn was on his second trip to Australia and his third overseas tour, having gone to America with the first English team in 1859. The voyage from Liverpool to Melbourne took 61 days, and George Anderson, a poor sailor, spent much of that time in his bunk. The Melbourne Cricket Club allowed the side a fortnight to practise and this helped build public interest in the first match against Twenty-Two of Victoria, which was watched by more than 40,000 people. Tinley's lobs proved troublesome to the local players right from the start and his 11 for 52 and 8 for 63 enabled England to have by far the best of the match. The Victorian Twenty-Two scored 146 and 143, England 176 and 4 for 105, before the umpires promptly at 6 p.m. drew stumps amid protests from spectators. With England only nine short of victory most of the crowd thought the umpires should have let the match finish.

Parr then took his players on a six-day voyage to New Zealand, where he was perturbed by a local Maori chief, who apparently took a fancy to him and followed him everywhere. The English players enjoyed their captain's discomfort. Back in Australia the Englishmen had three interesting matches against Twenty-Twos of New South Wales coached by Charles Lawrence. They won the first by four wickets, drew the second after the local captain George Gilbert took 5 for 58, and won the third, the most exciting of the tour, by one wicket. George Tarrant's pace bowling had the large crowds at these matches awed to silence and had a profound effect on an 11-year-old boy in the audience, Frederick Spofforth, who vowed to emulate Tarrant.

On the way to Melbourne after this narrow victory, the ship carrying the Englishmen, the *Wonga Wonga*, was badly holed when it collided with a yacht, the *Viceroy*. The *Viceroy* sank before some of the players were out of their bunks in the *Wonga Wonga*, which had to return to Sydney. The players boarded another ship for Melbourne two days later for the final matches of the tour. The English players each received £250 for the tour. When they sailed for Bombay on 26 April 1864 they left behind Dr E.M. Grace, who wanted to visit friends, and William Caffyn, who remained to join the Melbourne Cricket Club as their £300-a-year professional.

The coaching of the two players left behind after the

The second English team to Australia which toured in 1864 under the captaincy of the Nottinghamshire star, George Parr, the 'Lion Of The North'. *National Library of Australia*

first two English tours of Australia, Charles Lawrence and William Caffyn, brought rapid improvement in Australian cricket. They not only lifted the playing skills of their pupils but provided invaluable advice on the preparation of pitches. Their success also encouraged other English professionals to visit Australia, among them the Sussex pro Jesse Hide, who was curator–coach at Adelaide Oval for five years.

Hide pointed out that wooden rollers had little effect on flattening turf pitches, which needed several days' preparation and could not be selected on the day matches began. Fences were superior to the chains used in England to define boundaries, and the outfield needed to be cut to ensure fieldsmen did not totter in the long grass.

INTERCOLONIAL CRICKET

The Melbourne Cricket Ground on New Year's Day 1864, during the match between Parr's team and Twenty-Two of Victoria.

The discovery of gold had seen Australia's population multiply dramatically in the 1850's. Ships laden with Irish and English prospectors barely had time to tie up at the wharves in Australia's south-east before their passengers headed for the goldfields. Some of them were cricketers and in between working their claims they engaged in some tense matches that established the boisterous atmosphere of Australian cricket.

Intercolonial cricket began in Launceston in 1851 with a match between Tasmania and Victoria which has been accepted as Australia's initial first-class match. Cricket in Tasmania was dominated by single wicket matches or matches with only five men on each side but by combining players based in Hobart with the best of those who lived around Launceston in the north, Tasmania managed to beat the Victorians by three wickets.

The first New South Wales v. Victoria match followed in Melbourne in March 1856. Victoria initiated this by challenging any team in the Australian colonies to play the Melbourne Cricket Club for £500 a side. New South Wales had trouble raising the money for return fares to Melbourne and only made the trip because barrister Richard Driver put in £60 of his own money when the trip was in jeopardy. Driver was not among the players chosen but was then invited to join the team.

The Melbourne *Argus* praised the New South Welshmen for refusing to play for the advertised £500 a side stake and added that the honour of playing was enough. (In reality, the New South Wales players could not have raised the £500 for the bet.) The lack of stake money did not stop bookmakers from appearing at the match, where bets of 2-to-1 against New South Wales were freely taken. The underarm grubber bowler John McKone won the match for New South Wales by taking 5 for 11 in Victoria's second innings. Set to score 15 to win, New South Wales lost seven wickets getting them.

The return match in Sydney in January 1857 created tremendous interest, and more than 15,000 spectators attended the second day. New South Wales introduced Captain Edward Ward, who ran the Sydney Mint and usually batted wearing a monocle. and Victoria brought in Tom Wills, the experienced English-educated allrounder. New South Wales won by 65 runs, chiefly because of Ward's round-armers. He took 27 wickets in four matches, averaging 7.6 per wicket, letting the ball go with a decidedly jerky action.

After losing these first two matches, Victoria defeated New South Wales five times in a row, using an attack including Gideon Elliott, Sam Cosstick and Wills. In the 1859 match Wills took 11 for 49, and in 1860 he had 9 for 39. His 1859 coup was all the more remarkable, as he broke the middle finger of his bowling hand during the match. Tom Horan, writing as 'Felix' in *The Australasian*, described Wills as the 'W.G. Grace of Australia, as well known for his good nature as he was for his skill as a player'.

New South Wales quickly advanced under coaches Charles Lawrence and William Caffyn, who had transferred to Sydney after serving a year of his contract with the Melbourne Cricket Club. Both played only five matches in inter-colonial cricket for New South Wales but they were gifted instructors in the game, as their rising young pupils demonstrated.

ENGLAND IN AUSTRALIA 1873-74

WG GRACE'S TEAM

	First-class Results					All Matches			
Matches	Won	Lost	Drawn	Tied	Matches	Won	Lost	Drawn	Tied
–	–	–	–	–	15	10	3	2	–

Date	Venue	Opponent	Results for Touring Team
Dec 26	Melbourne	*XVIII of Victoria	Lost by an inns & 21 runs
Jan 1	Ballarat	*XXII of Ballarat	Drawn
Jan 8	Stawell	*XXII of Stawell	Lost by 10 wkts
Jan 14	Warrnambool	*XXII of Warrnambool	Won by 9 wkts
Jan 24	Sydney	*XVIII of New South Wales	Lost by 8 wkts
Jan 31	Bathurst	*XXII of Bathurst	Won by 8 wkts
Feb 5	Sydney	*XV of Victoria & NSW	Won by 218 runs
Feb 12	Sandhurst	*XXII of Sandhurst	Won by 7 wkts
Feb 17	Castlemaine	*XXII of Castlemaine	Won by 5 wkts
Feb 19	Melbourne	*XV of Victoria	Won by 7 wkts
Feb 26	Launceston	*XXII of Northern Tasmania	Won by an inns & 32 runs
Mar 3	Hobart (LRG)	*XXII of Southern Tasmania	Won by 8 wkts
Mar 12	Melbourne	*XVIII of Victoria	Drawn
Mar 23	Kadina	*XXII of Yorke's Peninsula	Won by an inns & 9 runs
Mar 26	Adelaide	*XXII of South Australia	Won by 7 wkts

The third England cricket team in Australia in 1873-74 was captained by the most famous English player of his time, Dr W.G. Grace, noted gamesman and wine-expert.

The Melbourne Cricket Club failed with an offer to Dr W.G. Grace to bring a team to Australia in 1872, but the club succeeded the following year with a better offer. Grace was only 25 but was already the best known English cricketer of his time, a striking athlete, with a heavy black beard, wide shoulders and a magnificent eye. His combative nature, high scores, and round-arm bowling brought success that revolutionised English cricket. Although he was a medical practitioner, he earned most of his annual income from appearance fees, despite his amateur status. He was guaranteed £1500, plus all expenses for his wife and himself for the 1873-74 Australian tour. The professionals in his team received £170 each for the tour. The East Melbourne and South Melbourne Cricket Clubs between them put up £1750 of the required guarantee, and the Melbourne Cricket Club £2000.

Alfred Shaw, the outstanding English bowler of the time, refused the terms offered for the tour. Oscroft, Greenwood, McIntyre and Southerton supplemented their tour guarantees by selling bats to Australian players. The organisers did little for team unity by providing the professionals with second-class passages to and from Australia and lodging them in inferior hotels, whereas Grace and the other amateurs went first-class all the way.

The improved technique among Australian cricketers emerged from the first match in which Eighteen of Victoria defeated Grace's XI by an innings and 21 runs. The Victorians reached 266 in their first innings, largely because of 84 by Bransby Beauchamp Cooper, formerly of Middlesex and Kent, who was born in India and educated at Rugby. Cooper had once shared a partnership of 283 with W.G. for the Gentlemen of the South against Players of the South. John Conway, 32 and Harry Boyle, 30, made useful contributions to the Victorian score, and W.G. had the best bowling analysis with 10 for 49.

The Eighteen of Victoria which defeated Grace's 1873 touring team by an innings and 21 runs: *top* B.B. Cooper, S. Costick, G. Gibson, H.G. Wyndham; *second row* B. McGan, G. Hedley, G.P. Robertson (capt.), J. Conway; *third row* L. Goldsmith, J. Coates, H.F. Boyle, C. Carr; *fourth row* W. Midwinter, F. Allan, T.J.D. Kelly, T. Horan; *bottom* W.W. Gaggin, Colonel Ward (umpire), H. Bishop.

Frank Allan, a 6 ft 2 in (188 cm) tall left-arm fast-medium bowler whom many give credit for pioneering swing bowling in Australia, opened the bowling with Harry Boyle, a heavily bearded right-arm roundarm bowler of brisk pace. They were well supported by Sam Cosstick, the Melbourne CC's ground bowler, who had learned to bowl at his birthplace, Croydon, in Surrey. Between them they had Grace's XI out for 110. Forced to follow on, Grace's side made only 132 at their second attempt. W.G. made 23 and 51 but could not prevent his team's ignominious defeat before an aggregate crowd of 40,000, most of whom paid half a crown for admission.

The one-sidedness of Victoria's win, the first in Melbourne over an English touring team, brought pleas for a match on level terms against Grace's team. The *Australasian* scoffed at the idea. 'Any numbskull who talks about Eleven Victorian Natives playing this Eleven of England are prattling about what they don't understand,' the paper said. But there was no doubt that the gap between English and Australian standards had narrowed.

At Ballarat in their second match W.G. Grace made 126, his brother G.F. Grace 112, but the English total of 470 did not prevent Twenty-Two of Ballarat securing a draw. The horses pulling the Englishmen's coach laboured up to their hocks in dust to get them to Ballarat and a further horrendous coach trip took them the 123 kilometres to Stawell for their third match, with the opposition Twenty-Two strengthened by the inclusion of John Conway and Sam Cosstick from Melbourne.

On a disgraceful pitch that was little more than a dust bowl, the Englishmen were further harassed by a plague of flies. England were dismissed for 43 and 91, with Cosstick taking 6 for 18 in the first innings, Conway 6 for 47 in the second. Twenty-Two of Stawell had scored 71 and 11 for 64 to win by ten wickets. W.G. immediately issued an angry warning to all his players against drinking during their matches.

After the luxury and comfort he had experienced on his trip to America in 1872, W.G. found travelling in Australia harsh and primitive but he took it in good humour and even developed a deep fondness for the Australian bush. 'The way the stockmen ride when kangaroo hunting is a revelation,' he wrote later. 'Some of us stood aghast at the recklessness with which they dashed through the bush.'

The Albert Ground at Redfern had replaced Hyde Park and the Domain as the venue for Sydney's big cricket matches and there, from 24 to 27 January 1874, Grace's XI met Eighteen of New South Wales and Grace had his first encounter with Fred Spofforth, cricket's original demon bowler. Spofforth acquitted himself admirably but it was Joseph Coates, the left-hand medium-pace round-armer born in Huddersfield, who baffled the English batsmen, taking 6 for 29 in an innings of 92. Grace's cousin William Pocock, who played for the Warwick club in Sydney, was one of the best New South Wales batsmen, for whom Dave Gregory topscored with a gritty 32. New South Wales took a lead of 35 runs, despite W.G.'s 11 for 69, after they dismissed Grace's XI for 90 in their second innings and required only 56 to win. They got them for the loss of half their wickets. There was unbridled jubilation each time W.G. was dismissed.

That was the tourists' last defeat in a program that took them from Sydney, over the mountains to Bathurst, back to Sydney, into Victoria for three matches, across to Hobart and Launceston, back to Melbourne for the third time, and finally to South Australia for the two matches that wound up the tour. The Kadina match against Twenty-Two of Yorke Peninsula was an amazing affair, with the local association putting up the £800 Grace asked for, while the South Australian Cricket Association wavered about raising the money. They had to sweep a bushel of pebbles from the pitch before play began, and even then W.G. had trouble finding it when he went out to toss.

Kadina struggled to 43 after their first six wickets fell for two runs. McIntyre took 9 for 4, Southerton 11 for 29, for Grace's XI who were all out for 64 by the end of the first day. Kadina made only 13 in their second knock, with 11 batsmen recording ducks and the only eight runs coming from the bat. McIntrye took 16 wickets for 5 runs, while Lillywhite had 13 for 7 from his 84 balls. Tom Wills, who had gone to Kadina to coach and strengthen the local side, secured spectacles, both clean-bowled.

The farcical Kadina match ended Grace's arrangements with the Melbourne syndicate but he agreed to play a a further match in Adelaide for £110 and half the gate receipts. The syndicate protested but when Grace pointed out that his tour program was for 14 matches only, they soon dropped claims for a share of the Adelaide gate, the first major match on Adelaide Oval and the first appearance of an overseas side there.

The South Australian Cricket Association persuaded the colony's administrators to declare a half-holiday for the second day of match, for which the admission charge was half a crown. The association made £300 profit, which made the SACA solvent for the first time. The Twenty-Two of South Australia made 63 and 82, Grace's XI 108 and 3 for 38, to win by seven wickets. Encouraged by the financial success of the match the SACA staged the first inter-colonial match on Adelaide Oval in December 1874 between South Australia and Victoria.

Grace's team went home after playing 15 matches before large, enthusiastic audiences. They won ten, lost three, and had two draws, with the opposing sides always outnumbering them. The skills displayed by Grace's players left dozens of young Australians keen to play like them, but did not daunt Australia's older players. Sam Cosstick summed up: 'Bar W.G., we Australians are as good as they are, and some day we'll lick 'em with eleven.'

CHAPTER TWO

SONS OF CONVICTS

Financial success of the first England teams in Australia helped solve a major problem for English cricket professionals. They previously lacked the security of winter pay and when their five months with a county club ended they had to find casual work as waiters, gardeners, road-menders, warehousemen or whatever job was available. Some Yorkshire and Lancashire players returned to mines or knitting mills.

In the 30 years to 1903 when the MCC took control of Australian tours, 13 teams visited Australia. Four of the first six tours were financed by leading English professionals Alfred Shaw, James Lillywhite and Arthur Shrewsbury and several of the first 13 teams were predominantly professionals.

These were arduous trips involving rough sea voyages, followed by long, dusty overland coach journeys and wild trips in flimsy coastal vessels. The touring teams played at least 30 matches, most of them against Fifteens, Eighteens, and Twenty-Twos. Introduction of inter-colonial steam trains reduced the hardship by replacing trips in horse-drawn carriages, but the tours were notorious for their frequent champagne dinners and heavy drinking interrupted by boring speeches. George Ulyett estimated he travelled 160,000 miles on five trips within Australia.

The great Nottinghamshire bowler Alfred Shaw, enthusiastic promoter of Australian tours, made it clear in his memoirs, *Forty Seasons Of First-Class Cricket*, that the English professionals made far less out of Australian trips than Australians who toured England. Shaw said with reasonable caution English professionals could return home with £100 to £150 profit from half a year away. But this was rarely achieved by players who treated Australian junkets as a drinking holiday and mismanaged their money. The majority returned home with little to show from the cricket, but with a philosophical attitude to the wonderful weeks with a 'great bunch of drinking men'. Some of them became great traders in cricket bats, autographed photographs, and everything from porcelain mugs to colourful ties and caps, all scarce in Australia. Shrewsbury sold bats he made in Nottingham in all the colonies.

By contrast most of the Australians who regularly toured England received several hundred pounds from their tours, enough to set themselves up in business or buy a good house. Alick Bannerman made six trips to England between 1880 and 1893, Jack Blackham went on all the first eight tours, Harry Boyle went on five plus one as manager, and Joey Palmer on four. They tended to make the Australian team an exclusive club, with membership difficult to secure.

James Lillywhite junior, the Sussex slow-medium left-arm bowler and lower order left-hand batsman who had toured North America in 1868 with Willsher's team, and Australia in 1873–74 with W.G. Grace's side, arranged, captained and managed the fourth English team to Australia in 1876–77. He decided on an all-professional party, reasoning that the differences between the amateurs and professionals had caused most of the problems on the third tour three seasons earlier.

ENGLAND IN AUSTRALIA 1876-77

J LILLYWHITE'S TEAM

First-class Results					All Matches				
Matches	Won	Lost	Drawn	Tied	Matches	Won	Lost	Drawn	Tied
3	1	1	1	–	15	5	4	6	–

Date	Venue	Opponent	Results for Touring Team
Nov 16	Adelaide	*XXII of South Australia	Won by an inns & 46 runs
Dec 7	Sydney	*XV of New South Wales	Lost by 2 wkts
Dec 12	Newcastle	*XXII of Newcastle	Won by 74 runs
Dec 20	Goulburn	*XXII of Goulburn	Won by 95 runs
Dec 26	Melbourne	*XV of Victoria	Lost by 31 runs
Jan 1	Ballarat	*XXII of Ballarat	Drawn
Jan 5	Geelong	*XXII of Geelong	Won by an inns & 103 runs
Jan 12	Sydney	*XV of New South Wales	Lost by 13 wkts
Jan 15	Redfern	New South Wales	Drawn
Mar 15	Melbourne	AUSTRALIA (1st Test)	Lost by 45 runs
Mar 20	Bendigo	*XXII of Bendigo	Drawn
Mar 23	Ballarat	*XXII of Ballarat	Drawn
Mar 26	Ararat	*XXII of Ararat	Drawn
Mar 31	Melbourne	AUSTRALIA (2nd Test)	Won by 4 wkts
Apr 14	Adelaide	*XXII of South Australia	Drawn

Player	M	Inn	NO	Runs	HS	50	100	Avrge	Ct/St	Overs	Mdns	Runs	Wkts	Avrge	5wi	10wm	Best
Armitage, T	3	4	–	33	21	–	–	8.25	–	12.0	3	42	1	42.00	–	–	1/11
Charlwood, HRJ	3	5	–	81	36	–	–	16.20	–	–	–	–	–	–	–	–	–
Emmett, T	3	5	–	91	48	–	–	18.20	5	29.0	15	52	–	–	–	–	–
Greenwood, A	3	5	–	86	49	–	–	17.20	2	–	–	–	–	–	–	–	–
Hill, A	3	5	2	103	49	–	–	34.33	1	135.0	63	190	11	17.27	–	–	4/27
Jupp, H	2	4	–	68	63	1	–	17.00	2/–	–	–	–	–	–	–	–	–
Lillywhite, J jr (Capt)	3	4	1	29	13	–	–	9.67	1	125.0	50	176	10	17.60	–	–	4/70
Pooley, E	1	1	–	36	36	–	–	36.00	–/1	–	–	–	–	–	–	–	–
Selby, J	3	5	–	85	38	–	–	17.00	1/–	–	–	–	–	–	–	–	–
Shaw, A	3	5	1	36	23	–	–	9.00	1	260.3	153	200	17	11.76	2	–	5/19
Southerton, J	3	4	2	23	16*	–	–	11.50	3	65.3	30	107	7	15.29	–	–	4/46
Ulyett, G	3	5	–	243	94	3	–	48.60	1	86.1	39	133	6	22.16	–	–	3/39

Lillywhite's team included the finest bowlers in England, the outstanding wicket-keeper in Edward Pooley, but lacked strength in batting because of the absence of Richard Daft, Arthur Shrewsbury and Ephraim Lockwood. The team reached Adelaide on 6 November, after six weeks at sea, and had nine days to practise before the first match against Twenty-Two of South Australia on Adelaide Oval. Southerton spent a week before the match preparing the pitch. John Selby set up a win for Lillywhite's XI by scoring 59 in their first innings of 153. Shaw demoralised the opposition by taking 14 wickets for 12 runs. The South Australians managed only 53 in their second innings, to lose by an innings and 46 runs.

Public agitation that local players should be allowed to test themselves on level terms against Lillywhite's team increased when Fifteen of New South Wales beat the Englishmen by two wickets in Sydney. Edwin Evans, a right-arm slow-medium bowler who varied his flight with great judgment, gave the New South Wales XV the advantage when he took 5 for 37 in England's second innings of 106. This gave the locals a target of 151 to win which they achieved for the loss of 12 wickets. Wins over Twenty-Twos of Newcastle and Goulburn did nothing to dissipate the view that England could be beaten on level terms, an idea that dominated public-house bars when Fifteen of Victoria defeated the English in Melbourne by 31 runs. The Victorian XV had Lillywhite's XI out for 135 (F.E. Allan 5 for 44) and 129 (W.E. Midwinter 7 for 54).

Spofforth and Evans routed the Englishmen in their eighth tour match, in which Fifteen of New South Wales defeated Lillywhite's XI by 13 wickets. The margin of victory inspired New South Wales officials to challenge the visitors to a match on level terms. This was a crucial match for the future of international cricket, although it failed to produce a result. The Englishmen scored 270, Ulyett contributing 94, Evans taking 5 for 96. New South Wales followed on after scoring 82 in their first innings and were 6 for 140 when time ran out.

This moral victory convinced Lillywhite's players they could beat Australia's best on level terms, and when their tour manager John Conway suggested that an Australia v. England match be added to the tour programme Lillywhite agreed. The Englishmen then went off for eight matches in New Zealand while Conway made arrangements for what became the first of all Test matches.

Conway ignored the Victorian Cricketers' Association and the New South Wales Cricket Association in the selection of the Australian team. He had discussions with

The Fourth England team in Australia in 1876-77, captained by James Lillywhite, introduced Test cricket. The team: *back row* H. Jupp, T. Emmett, R. Humphrey, A. Hill, T. Armitage, G. Ulyett; *middle* E. Pooley, J. Southerton, James Lillywhite, A. Shaw, A. Greenwood; *front* H. Charlwood, J. Selby. *Lord's Library*

George S. Coppin, president of the Richmond Victoria CC and the most successful Australian theatrical entrepreneur of the 19th century, on the composition of the team but mainly backed his own judgment. Spofforth refused to play unless Billy Murdoch, his Balmain clubmate and wicket-keeper for New South Wales, kept wicket. Conway refused to include Murdoch, having decided Jack Blackham was Australia's best keeper. Blackham earlier had failed to win a place in Carlton's first XI and been forced to join South Melbourne.

Frank Allan sent Conway a telegram regretting he could not play because the dates for the Test coincided with the Warrnambool Agricultural Show, where he loved to mingle with old friends. Edwin Evans said he could not play because of his new job as an inspector of land set aside for selection farmers.

After a rough voyage back to Australia from New Zealand, Lillywhite's team arrived the day before the first Test without Edward Pooley, widely respected as the best wicket-keeper in England. Pooley was in gaol in Christchurch, charged with causing malicious damage to a local pub, and John Selby had to substitute for him as England's keeper in the big match.

Conway picked an unknown left-arm medium-pace bowler, John Robart Hodges, to replace Allan in the Australian XI. Hodges had only just won promotion from a junior team, Capulet, into Richmond's first grade team and had never played for Victoria. Melbourne cricket fans scoffed at his selection and, because of all the changes in the side Conway originally picked, gave Australia no chance of victory. Less than 1000 spectators watched the start of play on 15 March 1877. Dave Gregory, who had won a dressing-room election for captain just before play began, won the toss and sent in Charles Bannerman, born in Kent 25 years earlier, to face the first ball in Test cricket. Bannerman blocked the first delivery from Alfred Shaw, but called his partner Nat Thomson through for a single off the second ball. Thomson was out for one, clean bowled by Allen Hill, the Yorkshire fast round-armer.

When he was 10 Bannerman dollied up a simple catch for Tom Armitage but to the disappointment of bowler Alfred Shaw the ball hit Armitage on the stomach without him getting a hand to it. By the close of play that day Bannerman was 126 not out, with Australia 6 for 126. Bannerman, a fierce front-foot driver coached by Billy Caffyn, went on to 165 before a ball from Ulyett split a finger and he had to retire. Australia made 245 and 104, leaving England, whose first innings yielded 196, to score 154 to win. Kendall took 7 for 55 with his left-arm spinners to make sure they did not get them, Australia winning by 45 runs.

England won the return Test a fortnight later in Melbourne by four wickets, to leave the Test series one–all. Murdoch and Spofforth made their debuts in this match without distinguishing themselves. The excitement all came from Thomas Joseph Dart Kelly, renowned for the spectacular blazers he wore to the cricket, who made eight successive strokes for four for Australia, also in his debut match. This match ended Lillywhite's career as a player but he later accompanied four more teams to Australia, often acting as umpire. He was regularly asked to instruct Australian umpires and arbitrate on points of law.

Lillywhite's team, the fourth English squad to tour Australia, played 15 matches, three against eleven, one of which they won, one they lost and the third finishing as a draw. Of the matches against the odds, they won four, drew five and lost three. Pooley did not show up for the second Test, preferring to go home to England.

The New Zealand public were sympathetic and raised his fare home. He spent his final years in the Lambeth workhouse. Each of the English players who completed the tour received £300, double their original guarantee and they travelled first-class all the way.

Apart from the customary champagne breakfasts and dinners, Australian cricket had impressed the Englishmen with a big advance in playing standards. They recognised that Spofforth, Blackham, Charles Bannerman and Billy Murdoch were as good as any players in England, with a crop of other players not far behind their level of performance. Sydney and Melbourne, it seemed, could be relied on to yield big match profits of around £3000, which was better than most English grounds attracted at that time.

Australia's egalitarian approach to cricket teams and the realisation that the tours offered a break from harsh winters and the strictures of life as a professional cricketer proved highly attractive to England's most talented players. The amateurs from exclusive schools and universities who ran England's cricket also enjoyed the prospect of several months in the sun with the professionals handling the hard work and from the time of the First Test in Melbourne invitations to tour Australia were eagerly sought.

Establishment of international cricket through regular tours to Australia excited the hierarchy at Lord's and in 1878 one of the Marylebone Cricket Club's most influential members brought the first all-amateur team to Australia. This was the Honorable George Robert Canning, who had become the fourth Lord Harris in 1872. After an education at Eton, he won blues at Oxford University for cricket in 1871, 1872, and 1874, as a right-arm fast round-arm bowler and right-hand middle order batsman.

Lord Harris virtually controlled the Kent county club, which appointed him captain in 1871 and saw an immediate improvement in its fortunes. He took over as president of Kent in 1875 and became a noted advocate of sustaining cricket's highest ethical standards and a strict application of the Laws of Cricket. He showed his fairmindedness in working for a fairer deal for county professionals.

The Melbourne Cricket Club, founded in 1838, was eager to take over control of Australian cricket and emulate the MCC and it invited Lord Harris to bring a team to Australia at its expense. At the last moment His Lordship found he could not comply with the Melbourne club's request for an all-amateur side and was forced to include professional bowlers George Ulyett and Tom Emmett in place of amateur bowlers of lesser stature who could not spare the six months for the trip. Lord Harris's side arrived in Adelaide as the first Australian team to tour England arrived back in Sydney.

ENGLAND IN AUSTRALIA 1978-79

LORD HARRIS'S TEAM

First-class Results					All Matches				
Matches	Won	Lost	Drawn	Tied	Matches	Won	Lost	Drawn	Tied
5	2	3	–	–	13	5	3	5	–

Date	Venue	Opponent	Results for Touring Team
Dec 12	Adelaide	*XVIII of South Australia	Won by 3 wkts
Dec 26	Melbourne	*XV of Victoria	Drawn
Jan 2	Melbourne	AUSTRALIA (Only Test)	Lost by 10 wkts
Jan 9	Hobart (TCA)	*XVIII of Southern Tasmania	Won by 6 wkts
Jan 13	Launceston	*XVIII of Northern Tasmania	Drawn
Jan 24	Sydney	New South Wales	Lost by 5 wkts
Jan 31	Bathurst	*XVIII of Bathurst	Drawn
Feb 7	Sydney	New South Wales	Won by an inns & 41 runs
Feb 17	Yarra Bend	*XV of the Bohemian Club	Drawn
Feb 21	Melbourne	Victoria	Lost by 2 wkts
Feb 26	Sandhurst	*XXII of Bendigo	Drawn
Mar 1	Ballarat	*XXII of Ballarat	Won by an inns & 48 runs
Mar 7	Melbourne	Victoria	Won by 6 wkts

Player	M	Inn	NO	Runs	HS	50	100	Avrge	Ct/St	Overs	Mdns	Runs	Wkts	Avrge	5wi	10wm	Best
Absolom, CA	5	8	–	128	52	1	–	16.00	3	71.0	30	98	3	32.67	–	–	2/37
Emmett, T	5	8	2	110	41	–	–	18.33	2	482.1	255	512	44	11.63	6	2	8/47
Harris, Lord (Capt)	5	9	–	289	67	2	–	32.11	2	3.0	–	14	–	–	–	–	–
Hone, L	5	8	1	58	22	–	–	8.29	6/2	–	–	–	–	–	–	–	–
Hornby, AN	5	9	–	167	67	2	–	18.56	2	79.0	48	79	4	19.75	–	–	2/9
Lucas, AP	5	9	1	158	51	1	–	19.75	3	239.1	105	347	14	24.79	–	–	3/32
Mackinnon, FA	3	6	3	37	15*	–	–	12.33	–	–	–	–	–	–	–	–	–
Penn, F	2	3	–	87	56	1	–	29.00	2	3.0	1	3	–	–	–	–	–
Royle, VPFA	5	8	–	214	75	2	–	26.63	11	4.0	1	6	–	–	–	–	–
Schultz, SS	5	8	2	46	20	–	–	7.67	1	81.0	27	174	4	43.50	–	–	2/8
Ulyett, G	5	9	–	306	71	3	–	34.00	3	230.0	104	367	11	33.36	–	–	4/13
Webbe, AJ	5	9	1	101	27	–	–	12.63	7	–	–	–	–	–	–	–	–

Lord Harris 1878-79 English team, the fifth to visit Australia, played only one Test, which they lost. The team and wives: *back row* R.D. Walker, F. Penn, Lord Harris, L. Hone, F.A. Mackinnon; *centre* A.P. Lucas, S.S. Schultz, Mrs Hornby, Lady Harris, H.D. Maul, C.A. Absolom; *front* A.N. Hornby, Miss Ingram, V. Royle, A.J. Webbe. *MCC Library*

Lord Harris's team easily defeated Eighteen of South Australia, but were held to a draw by Fifteen of Victoria, for whom Donald Campbell scored a commendable 128. Lord Harris was surprised by the public support for his team's matches and the eagerness with which Australians awaited the scheduled special match—not yet called a 'Test'—between his team and the best Australians. This match began dramatically when England slumped to 4 for 26. Spofforth, the tall, lean pace bowler from Balmain in Sydney, then performed a hat-trick to send England to 7 for 26. A big-hitting innings of 52 from Lord Harris's Kent team-mate Charles Absolom helped boost England's total to 113.

Australia replied with 256, despite seven consecutive overs of grubbers from 'Monkey' Hornby, all maidens. Spofforth exploited Australia's advantage by taking 7 for 62, to finish with match figures of 13 for 110, Australia winning by 10 wickets. Spofforth dismissed Francis MacKinnon, 35th Chieftain of the Scottish clan MacKinnon, in both England innings.

Lord Harris was impressed by the umpiring of young Victorian football hero George Coulthard in this match, now recognised as the third of all Tests. Coulthard, famous among Melburnians as a Carlton footballer, agreed to leave his duties as a ground bowler at the Melbourne Cricket Ground and accompany Lord Harris's team to Sydney. He was then 22.

Coulthard umpired matches between New South Wales and England in Sydney, where the home side won by five wickets, and between Eighteen of Bathurst and the tourists in Bathurst, which ended in a draw. The return match in Sydney against New South Wales proved one of the most controversial in history and almost snuffed out the concept of international cricket before it was properly established.

Coulthard upset the *Sydney Morning Herald* with some of his decisions on the first day when England reached 267. The *Herald* complained that betting, banned by signs around the Sydney Cricket Ground, was carried on with impunity. New South Wales followed-on after scoring 177 on the second day and appeared to be recovering when Coulthard ruled the State captain Billy Murdoch run out.

Hooting among gamblers in the stands began as a bit of fun, but with a well known bookmaker urging on the hecklers, built up into a deafening reaction to Coulthard's decision. The great Australian writer Banjo Paterson said he enjoyed jumping the fence and joining his pals out in the centre, but Lord Harris was not amused. He defended Coulthard when a spectator attacked him, only to be struck across the shoulders by a larrikin with a stick. 'Monkey' Hornby dragged Lord Harris's assailant from the ground and in the scuffle had his shirt torn from his back.

The New South Wales captain Dave Gregory, who a few months earlier had led the first Australian team in England, refused to send in a batsman to replace Murdoch. With the Englishmen holding their positions and Lord Harris determined to remain for fear Gregory would claim a forfeit, the demonstrators had half an hour of mayhem. Twice they were cleared from the ground but each time they stormed back and play had to be abandoned for the day.

Sydney papers blamed English players for arousing the crowd with comments all could hear about 'sons of convicts', and editorials questioned the lack of policemen or official attempts to prevent the gamblers openly taking bets. England refused to replace Coulthard. Well aware of Dave Gregory's record of persistently challenging umpiring decisions, Lord Harris's players said he could have prevented the assault on their boss. While the chief offenders were in court being fined on Monday morning, England coasted to an easy victory.

The tour schedule called for a Test in Sydney, but Lord Harris refused to remain and took his side back to Melbourne. They played five further matches, two against Victoria on the MCG and three in country centres, before the Melbourne Club gave them a farewell dinner, and they went off to New Zealand and the US for two further matches before returning to Lord's.

Lord Harris was an affable figure at the farewell dinner, but back in England he bitterly attacked the Sydney rioters, Dave Gregory, and the excessive gambling permitted at Australian cricket. He disagreed with the Australian view that amateur umpires were more honest than paid umpires, but did concede that Australia's bowlers were superior to their English opponents.

ENGLAND IN AUSTRALIA 1881–82

A SHAW'S TEAM

First-class Results					All Matches			
Matches	Won	Lost	Drawn	Tied	Matches	Won	Lost	Drawn	Tied
7	3	2	2	–	18	8	3	7	–

Date	Venue	Opponent	Results for Touring Team
Nov 25	Maitland	*XXII of Northern District	Drawn
Nov 25	Newcastle	*XXII of Newcastle	Drawn
Nov 29	Orange	*XXII of Orange	Won by an inns & 88 runs
Dec 2	Bathurst	*XXII of Bathurst	Won by 76 runs
Dec 7	Parramatta	*XXII of Cumberland	Lost by 5 wkts
Dec 9	Sydney	New South Wales	Won by 68 runs
Dec 14	Cootamundra	*XVI of Cootamundra	Won by 75 runs
Dec 16	Melbourne	Victoria	Won by 18 runs
Dec 23	Adelaide	*XV of South Australia	Drawn
Dec 31	Melbourne	AUSTRALIA (1st Test)	Drawn
Feb 14	Stanmore	*XVIII of Stanmore	Drawn
Feb 17	Sydney	AUSTRALIA (2nd Test)	Lost by 5 wkts
Feb 22	Windsor	*XXII of Hawkesbury	Won on 1st innings
Feb 24	Melbourne	Victoria	Won by 8 wkts
Mar 3	Sydney	AUSTRALIA (3rd Test)	Lost by 6 wkts
Mar 10	Melbourne	AUSTRALIA (4th Test)	Drawn
Mar 15	Dunolly	*XXII of Dunolly	Won by an inns & 13 runs
Mar 17	Ballarat	*XX of Ballarat	Drawn

Billy Midwinter

Player	M	Inn	NO	Runs	HS	50	100	Avrge	Ct/St	Overs	Mdns	Runs	Wkts	Avrge	5wi	10wm	Best
Barlow, RG	7	14	1	391	75	3	–	30.08	3	94.2	38	147	3	49.00	–	–	1/4
Bates, W	7	13	1	349	84	3	–	29.08	3	403.0	208	520	30	17.33	1	–	5/17
Emmett, T	7	12	–	109	27	–	–	9.08	9	162.0	88	274	10	27.40	–	–	3/27
Midwinter, WE	7	12	–	166	48	–	–	13.83	8	301.0	128	435	13	33.46	–	–	4/81
Peate, E	7	13	7	104	33*	–	–	17.33	1	494.3	234	522	30	17.40	2	–	6/30
Pilling, R	7	13	3	87	23	–	–	8.70	12/6	–	–	–	–	–	–	–	–
Scotton, WH	7	12	1	228	50*	1	–	20.73	3	–	–	–	–	–	–	–	–
Selby, J	7	13	1	312	70	3	–	26.00	1	–	–	–	–	–	–	–	–
Shaw, A (Capt)	7	12	–	137	40	–	–	11.42	5	191.0	120	171	8	21.38	–	–	3/5
Shrewsbury, A	7	12	2	382	82	3	–	38.20	8	–	–	–	–	–	–	–	–
Ulyett, G	7	14	–	549	149	3	1	39.21	5	138.1	45	257	10	25.70	–	–	2/11

Alfred Shaw's sixth England team to Australia, an all-professional combination, included Billy Midwinter, a remarkable renegade who played in seven first-class matches against his former Australian team-mates. Shaw's team: *back row* G. Ulyett, R. Pilling, J. Lillywhite (umpire), J. Conway (manager), W. Midwinter, W. Bates; *centre* A. Shrewsbury, A. Shaw, T. Emmett, E. Peate; *front* R.G. Barlow, W.H. Scotton, J. Selby.

The sixth English team to tour Australia was all-professional, and quickly discovered that Lord Harris's antagonism towards Australians was ill-founded. The Australian cricket fans responded warmly to the splendid standard achieved by Albert Shaw's players, but were very surprised by the inclusion in the touring team of Billy Midwinter, who must rate as one of sport's great renegades.

Smiling Billy remains the only player to have appeared for and against Australia, a right-hand batsman of extreme guile, a medium-pace right-arm round-arm bowler, an outfielder with a marvellous pick-up and throw, a successful quarter-mile runner, outstanding marksman, and a billiards player many men regretted challenging. He was born in St Briavels in the Forest of Dean, Gloucestershire, in 1851, and came to Australia in 1861 when his family could not find work. He married, sired two children, and sustained the hope of getting rich with a big strike at Sandhurst, before it changed its name to Bendigo.

Midwinter played cricket as a young boy with Harry Boyle, who helped him clear a pitch out of the bush at Sydney Flat. The Midwinters lived in a shack at California Gully and in between his butcher's rounds his father practised with him and Harry. At 13, Billy left the Sydney Flat team to play for what became known as Bendigo United. Billy and his pal Harry made a big impression when Melbourne's Carlton club visited Bendigo, and in 1871 they both played in a Bendigo side that defeated New South Wales as they passed through on their way to a match against Victoria.

In the summer of 1873–74, Midwinter and Boyle were invited to play for Victoria against W.G. Grace's visiting English team. W.G. soon discovered that Midwinter was Gloucestershire-born, although Billy only made seven. Later that season Billy clean bowled W.G. and his brother G.F. Grace, which aroused close inspection of Billy's 6 ft 3 ins (190 cm), 14 stone (89 kg) technique. From then on, until his death in Kew Asylum, Melbourne, after the tragic deaths of his wife and children had deranged him, Billy travelled back and forth to England, and ended up playing eight Tests for Australia and four for England. He remains the only cricketer to play for both sides.

The Honorable Francis Walter Bligh, captain of the England team to Australia, was a charmer. He was born at Bruton Street, London, on 13 March 1859, and like his elder brother Lord Edward Clifton was educated at Eton. He had won a place in the Kent XI before he graduated from Cambridge and returned to live in the family home at Puckle Hill at Cobham. He was a tall, right-hand opening batsman, speedy outfield, and good enough to win his blue in all his four years at university.

Bligh played in the Cambridge University XI that defeated Australia in 1878 and in 1880 he hit a brilliant century for Kent against Surrey at The Oval. He had tremendous appeal for the ladies being extremely handsome, but he was not favoured by good health.

He looked a bit pale at the end of the 1882 English summer in which Australia created The Ashes legend by bundling England out for 77 in the final innings and colleagues at Lord's suggested he take a team to Australia to get the wretched things back. Bligh did not play in The Ashes match at The Oval in which 'Monkey' Hornby captained England but he regarded The Ashes as jolly good fun and agreed to go.

HOME AND AWAY

ENGLAND IN AUSTRALIA 1882-83

HON IFW BLIGH'S TEAM

First-class Results					All Matches				
Matches	Won	Lost	Drawn	Tied	Matches	Won	Lost	Drawn	Tied
7	4	3	–	–	17	9	3	5	–

Date	Venue	Opponent	Results for Touring Team
Nov 10	Adelaide	*XV of South Australia	Drawn
Nov 17	Melbourne	Victoria	Won by 10 wkts
Nov 22	Sandhurst	*XXII of Sandhurst	Drawn
Nov 24	Castlemaine	*XXII of Castlemaine	Drawn
Dec 1	Sydney	New South Wales	Won by an inns & 144 runs
Dec 6	Maitland	*XVIII of Maitland	Won by an inns & 15 runs
Dec 8	Newcastle	*XVIII of Newcastle	Drawn
Dec 26	Ballarat	*XVIII of Ballarat	Drawn
Dec 30	Melbourne	AUSTRALIA (1st Test)	Lost by 9 wkts
Jan 8	Launceston	*XVIII of Northern Tasmania	Won by an inns & 75 runs
Jan 12	Hobart (TCA)	*XVIII of Southern Tasmania	Won by 7 wkts
Jan 19	Melbourne	AUSTRALIA (2nd Test)	Won by an inns & 27 runs
Jan 26	Sydney	AUSTRALIA (3rd Test)	Won by 69 runs
Feb 2	Brisbane	*XVIII of Queensland	Won by an inns & 154 runs
Feb 8	Maryborough	*XVIII of Maryborough	Won by an inns & 58 runs
Feb 17	Sydney	AUSTRALIA (4th Test)	Lost by 4 wkts
Mar 9	Melbourne	Victoria	Lost by an inns & 73 runs

Player	M	Inn	NO	Runs	HS	50	100	Avrge	Ct/St	Overs	Mdns	Runs	Wkts	Avrge	5wi	10wm	Best
Barlow, RG	7	12	2	281	80	1	–	28.10	7	376.0	203	473	23	20.57	1	–	7/40
Barnes, W	7	11	1	113	32	–	–	11.30	5	199.2	75	306	12	25.50	1	–	5/70
Bates, W	7	11	1	271	55	1	–	27.10	6	312.0	150	429	24	17.88	2	1	7/28
Bligh, Hon IFW (Capt)	5	9	1	64	19	–	–	8.00	7	–	–	–	–	–	–	–	–
Leslie, CFH	7	11	1	310	144	2	1	31.00	2	43.0	19	61	4	15.25	–	–	3/31
Morley, F	5	7	3	9	3	–	–	2.25	2	187.0	105	197	8	24.63	–	–	4/47
Read, WW	7	11	–	291	75	2	–	26.45	1	53.0	18	92	5	18.40	–	–	4/28
Steel, AG	7	11	1	415	135*	2	1	41.50	7	283.0	123	401	24	16.71	1	–	5/32
Studd, CT	7	11	–	253	56	1	–	23.00	4	194.2	118	174	10	17.40	–	–	3/28
Studd, GB	7	12	2	40	9	–	–	4.00	10	–	–	–	–	–	–	–	–
Tylecote, EFS	7	11	–	209	66	1	–	19.00	10/6	–	–	–	–	–	–	–	–
Vernon, GF	4	6	1	60	24	–	–	12.00	1	–	–	–	–	–	–	–	–

The Melbourne Cricket Club agreed to organise a tour by the seventh English team, which included four professionals, Morley, Barnes, Bates and Barlow for the hard work and eight amateurs, Bligh, Steel, C.T. and G.B. Studd, G.F. Vernon, C.F.H. Leslie, Walter Read, and the Kent wicket-keeper Edward Tylecote, whose middle name was Ferdinando. Tylecote wore a thick black moustache like nearly all his team-mates except the clean-shaven Charles Leslie, and in 1868 had hit 404 not out for Classical v. Modern at Clifton College, at that time a world record for any match.

The tour had historical significance not lost on Bligh or his mainly aristocratic team and in a speech before they sailed Bligh pledged that he would bring back The Ashes. The tour itinerary at that stage included three Tests against the Australians who had humbled England and were still touring England.

The team sailed from England in the *Peshawar* in October 1882, before Murdoch's men returned home on a voyage that proved highly eventful. At night on a moonlit deck Bligh often chatted with Florence Rose Morphy, daughter of a Beechworth, Victoria, magistrate whose early death confined her to an upbringing of genteel poverty. Florence was returning to Melbourne with the Clarkes, a family of graziers and bankers whose children she tutored.

About 560 kilometres after leaving Colombo, a full-rigged barque, later identified as the *Glenroy*, bore down on the *Peshawar* and crashed into her sides, ripping a huge hole amidships. The captain shouted to his crew to lower the lifeboats but fortunately the sea remained calm and the *Peshawar* did not sink. Fred Morley was knocked out and lay on the deck with a badly smashed rib. The *Peshawar* limped back to Colombo with a gaping hole just above the waterline, with the English cricketers watching the sharks in the sea below it.

This mishap delayed the Englishmen's arrival in Australia until early November, but they still arrived ahead of Murdoch's team, who docked to a heroes' welcome. For the next month the Australians were feted in the capital cities. Each player received a medal, there was a torchlight procession, and cricket fans sat back and waited for them to repeat the dose against Bligh's outfit.

Fred Morley was virtually useless, and he stayed in humble hotels with his fellow professionals in accommodation far inferior to that enjoyed by Bligh's amateurs. Bligh's hand had been injured in the *Peshawar* collision and forced him to miss the team's first six matches.

(*Opposite*) The seventh England team in Australia: *back row* W. Barnes, F. Morley, C.T. Studd, G.F. Vernon, W.W. Read; *centre* C.B. Studd, E.F.S. Tylecote, Hon. Ivo Bligh (capt.), A.G. Steel, C.F.H. Leslie; *front* R.G. Barlow, W. Bates. They helped further The Ashes legend.

The beautiful Australian Florence Morphy, who became Ivo Bligh's wife. She and her lady friends burnt the stump or bails to provide the ashes, depositing them in an urn because the velvet bag designed by a Sydney woman did not appear grand enough for such a trophy.

Midwinter had returned to the Victorian team after appearing in 30 matches for the fourth Australian team in England. He announced that his investments in mining shares had prospered and allowed him to change status from professional to amateur cricketer while he ran the first of his Melbourne pubs. The *Sydney Mail* was unimpressed. 'Are we to have another season of vagueness from this very slippery cricketer?' asked the paper. 'One day he is an Australian and the next he is an English man.' Another paper suggested he be called an Anglo-Australian but Midwinter objected, arguing that he was 'Australian to the core'.

The three days of the First Test in Melbourne elated the Melbourne Cricket Club's treasurer by attracting 54,000 spectators. Australia won by nine wickets against an English team that had six newcomers to international matches, Bligh, Leslie, Read, Tylecote, Vernon and G.B. Studd. Joey Palmer took 10 for 126 for Australia. Morley was still in bed, but Bligh played, despite his hand injury.

England won the Second Test in Melbourne, where Billy Bates dismissed McDonnell, Giffen and Bonnor to achieve the first hat-trick by an Englishman in Tests. England won by an innings and 27 runs before a stunned crowd. Bates' figures: 7 for 28 and 7 for 74. He also made 55 with the bat.

With the series level, the Sydney Cricket Ground curator prepared two pitches for the decisive Third Test, each captain having the choice on which to bat. Almost 23,000 watched the first day. Tylecote appeared set to become the first keeper to score a Test century when he was run out for 66. Morley returned to take six important wickets, including Alick Bannerman when he was 94, and England won by 69 runs.

Bligh stayed with the Fletcher family in Ocean Street, Woollahra, while he was in Sydney and, after England won the Third Test, Annie Fletcher, a splendid needleworker, suggested that she should make a velvet bag in which Bligh could keep the ashes. Bligh accepted her bag but when the Englishmen returned to Melbourne Florence Morphy and her lady friends complained that the bag was not grand enough for such a celebrated trophy. The ladies went away and bought a silver urn and burnt a stump or some bails to fill it.

The Englishmen considered that they had completed their mission by regaining The Ashes, but agreed to add a further Test to their tour. Australia brought back Midwinter for this match and he bowled 70 overs, compared with 67 from Palmer. The captains experimented by using fresh pitches for all four innings. Bonnor, who had made a brilliant 85 in the First Test, this time reached 87, thanks to eight dropped catches. This offset the advantage A.G. Steel had given England with 135 not out and Australia went on to win by four wickets.

Bligh was reported to have taken The Ashes and the urn with him when he went home with his team but it is more likely that he left them with Florence Morphy in Melbourne. The Melbourne Cricket Club paid the professionals £220 each and put the amateurs in first-class hotels with all the wine they could drink. Without W.G. Grace, Hornby and Lucas, England did not field her strongest eleven and those who appeared in the Tests often carried injuries. Morley never complained of pain when bowling with the cracked rib but within 18 months died of congestion of the lungs. The only dispute on a happy tour came in the Third Test when the Australians protested that Barlow was running on the pitch while bowling. Bligh replied that Spofforth always did this.

Once he had followed protocol and informed his father of his intentions, Bligh returned to Melbourne and married Florence Morphy. Their first child was born in

Melbourne before they returned to live at Puckle Hill and revitalise the Cobham Park family estate. Bligh became the eighth Earl Darnley in 1900 and when he died in 1927 he did not mention The Ashes in his will, but the Countess of Darnley presented the urn to the Marylebone Cricket Club, which has retained them in a display cabinet at Lord's. There are two urns, one of pottery, the other of gold. Dozens of replicas have been made over the years throughout the cricket world, but the originals have remained at Lord's, along with the scorecard of the Ashes Test and Annie Fletcher's velvet bag.

Rowland Bowen, the notoriously vituperative editor of England's *Cricket Quarterly*, suggested in one issue that The Ashes legend was a stale joke that should be allowed to die, but the public and the media disagree. Articles continue to appear attempting to solve the riddle of whether the Melbourne ladies burned a bail or a stump. When Bob Radford, chief executive of the New South Wales Cricket Association, achieved the impossible by persuading the MCC to allow The Ashes urn to leave the Imperial Cricket Museum at Lord's and be flown to Sydney for the Test to celebrate Australia's Bicentenary in 1988, he had to provide a special RAAF aircraft and a police motorcycle escort to bring the urn to and from Lord's.

The *Cricketer* magazine, then edited by Christopher Martin-Jenkins, ran a story in 1982 which exposed a cleaning accident in which one of Earl Darnley's servants upset the urn and spilt the contents across the carpet. He burnt some twigs to replace them. The MCC refused to comment on the authenticity of the ashes in the urn.

Bligh played no more first-class cricket after the Australian tour, retiring with four Tests and 47 matches for Kent to his credit. He scored 2734 first-class runs at 20.71, with two centuries. He also caught 81 batsmen. His best season was 1880 when he hit 1013 runs at 30.69. He and his brothers remained staunch Kent supporters and were largely responsible for the rich traditions the county enjoys. He and his wife always celebrated Kent triumphs. During World War I they entertained a lot of Australian servicemen on leave at Cobham, surprising them with a knowledge of tennis at which Bligh represented Cambridge.

Romance also influenced the cricket career of Billy Murdoch, who married and retired from big cricket for a time to build a future for his family as a lawyer in the country at Cootamundra. *Cricket* magazine's Charles Alcock, a respected authority, reported that both Murdoch and Spofforth had succumbed to the charms of Derbyshire maidens on their visits to England and were engaged to these lasses. Spofforth, 23, went back to Derbyshire and married 22-year-old Phillis Cadman, whose father set him up in a plum job in the Star Tea Company he owned. When Spofforth died in 1926, he left a massive £164,000 in his will.

Murdoch forgot his Derbyshire fiancée, however, when he met Jemima Watson, an amateur actress and heiress, on the 48-day voyage back to Australia in 1884. Jemima shone in all shipboard activities, according to author Ray Robinson, and the Australian captain found her irresistible. They married at Fitzroy in December that year with George Bonnor as best man, after the marriage had been approved by Jemima's father, John Watson, a Bendigo gold-mining tycoon who struck it rich on a quartz reef at Paddy's Gully. They went to Adelaide for their honeymoon so Billy could play in the First Test against the England team led by Arthur Shrewsbury.

Australian cricket at the time was in turmoil because of the demands of the best players for a big share of the gate takings. The touring England teams' managers could not agree to the Australians' terms and considered them extortionate, considering the co-operation Australian teams received in England. Finally the South Australian Cricket Association had to take over the match and guarantee each side £450. Murdoch played but his absence from practice was noted.

When the entire Australian team rebelled again and refused to accept the terms offered for the next Test in Melbourne, the 1884 tourists were sacked and an entirely new Australian side was named, nine of them newcomers to Tests. Rather than take sides Murdoch, then 30 years old, retired to his legal practice in Cootamundra after 16 successive Tests, 13 as captain, and was absent from the Australian XI for the next 15 Tests, including two tours of England. He appeared occasionally for New South Wales in that period and in benefit matches for old team-mates, sometimes travelling to and from Sydney in late hour milk trains.

Murdoch must have itched to return to Test cricket as he dug into court cases about sheep stealing, breaches of covenants, and actions against fence-building. Magistrates on country benches stretched his goodwill and he often wrote to his brother Gilbert in Balmain about the old fossils he encountered on the bench and how he loved to 'warm their tails for them'.

ENGLAND IN AUSTRALIA 1884–85

A SHREWSBURY'S TEAM

Matches	First-class Results				All Matches				
	Won	Lost	Drawn	Tied	Matches	Won	Lost	Drawn	Tied
8	6	2	–	–	33	16	2	15	–

Date	Venue	Opponent	Results for Touring Team
Nov 1	Adelaide	*XV of South Australia	Won by 3 wkts
Nov 6	Norwood	*XVIII of South Australia	Drawn
Nov 14	Melbourne	Victoria	Won by 118 runs
Nov 21	Sydney	New South Wales	Won by 4 wkts
Nov 26	Windsor	*XXII of Hawkesbury	Drawn
Nov 28	Parramatta	*XVIII of Cumberland	Won by 9 wkts
Dec 1	Grafton	*XXII of Clarence River	Won by 8 wkts
Dec 12	Adelaide	AUSTRALIA (1st Test)	Won by 8 wkts
Dec 20	Maryborough	*XXII of Maryborough	Drawn
Dec 23	Sandhurst	*XVIII of Bendigo	Drawn
Dec 26	Ballarat	*XXII of Ballarat	Drawn
Dec 29	Benalla	*XXII of Benalla	Drawn
Jan 1	Melbourne	AUSTRALIA (2nd Test)	Won by 10 wkts
Jan 7	Wagga Wagga	*XXII of Wagga Wagga	Won by 2 wkts
Jan 9	Wollongong	*XXII of Wollongong	Won by an inns & 62 runs
Jan 12	Candelo	*XXII of Candelo	Won by an inns & 12 runs
Jan 16	Nowra	*XXII of Shoalhaven	Drawn
Jan 20	Yass	*XXII of Yass	Drawn
Jan 21	Moss Vale	*XXII of Moss Vale	Drawn
Jan 24	Sydney	New South Wales	Won by an inns & 37 runs
Jan 31	Brisbane	*XXII of Brisbane	Won by 9 wkts
Feb 5	Maryborough	*XXII of Maryborough	Won by 129 runs
Feb 7	Gympie	*XXII of Gympie	Won by 8 wkts
Feb 14	Maitland	*XXII of Maitland	Drawn
Feb 17	Singleton	*XXII of Singleton	Drawn
Feb 20	Sydney	AUSTRALIA (3rd Test)	Lost by 6 runs
Feb 27	Narrabri	*XXII of Narrabri	Won by an inns & 44 runs
Mar 2	Armidale	*XXII of Armidale	Drawn
Mar 5	Ashfield	*XVIII of Jnr Cricket Assn	Drawn
Mar 9	Wellington	*XXII of Wellington	Drawn
Mar 14	Sydney	AUSTRALIA (4th Test)	Lost by 8 wkts
Mar 21	Melbourne	AUSTRALIA (5th Test)	Won by an inns & 98 runs
Apr 2	Adelaide	*XV of South Australia	Drawn

Player	M	Inn	NO	Runs	HS	50	100	Avrge	Ct/St	Overs	Mdns	Runs	Wkts	Avrge	5wi	10wm	Best
Attewell, W	8	11	2	108	30	–	–	12.00	6	527.1	332	428	28	15.29	1	–	5/19
Barnes, W	8	13	1	520	134	4	1	43.33	15	282.1	148	344	26	13.23	1	–	6/31
Bates, W	8	12	–	363	68	3	–	30.25	4	176.1	96	206	14	14.71	2	–	5/24
Briggs, J	8	12	1	216	121	–	1	19.64	5	8.0	3	13	–	–	–	–	–
Flowers, W	8	13	–	189	56	1	–	14.54	–	298.2	158	332	22	15.09	2	–	8/31
Hunter, J	8	11	4	97	39*	–	–	13.86	11/6	–	–	–	–	–	–	–	–
Peel, R	8	11	4	84	21*	–	–	12.00	8	663.2	346	673	35	19.23	2	–	7/27
Read, JM	8	12	1	178	56	1	–	16.18	5	–	–	–	–	–	–	–	–
Scotton, WH	8	14	1	224	82	1	–	17.23	4	–	–	–	–	–	–	–	–
Shrewsbury, A (Capt)	8	14	3	440	105*	2	1	40.00	12	–	–	–	–	–	–	–	–
Ulyett, G	8	12	–	136	68	1	–	11.33	4	249.0	126	361	20	18.05	–	–	4/52

Alfred Shaw, Arthur Shrewsbury and James Lillywhite jointly funded the eighth tour of Australia by an England team in 1884–85. Lillywhite toured as the team's umpire, with what Shaw regarded as the strongest side ever to visit Australia, an all-professional combination carefully selected by men with experience of Australian conditions. They were a mentally tough side. On the way out Shaw engaged two Arabs to row him and Ulyett back to their ship after sightseeing on the Nile. The Arabs stopped rowing halfway to the ship and refused to go further without more cash. Ulyett threw one Arab into the sea and rowed the boat the rest of the way himself, with the former oarsman swimming alongside.

In Melbourne, Victorian members of the Australian side that had just returned from England refused to appear for Victoria on the terms offered but their claims were rejected out of hand and England beat a patched-up Victorian XI easily. In Sydney, the New South Wales members of the team that had just returned from England took the same stand and they, too, were rebuffed. Despite their lack of hard matches, England won the First Test in Adelaide, the most important match played in that city at the time, by eight wickets and the Second Test in Melbourne by 10 wickets, before Paddy Horan's 6 for 40 and Spofforth's 6 for 90 gave Australia a thrilling six-run win in the Third Test in Sydney. Australia drew level at two-all by winning the Fourth Test in Sydney, after Spofforth's 5 for 30 skittled England for 77 in their second innings. The decider in Melbourne went to England because of Shrewsbury's 105 not out.

The close tussles in the series proved a big attraction and it was played out before big audiences. The three sponsors were elated by the financial return after enduring dust storms, flooded pitches, rows over umpires, repeated demands for more pay from their Australian rivals, and injuries to key players like Billy Bates, who was kicked by a horse and had a pipe he was smoking rammed through his mouth.

The eighth England team in Australia, a speculative venture by three former tourists: *back row* W. Barnes, J. Hunter, W. Attewell, J. Lillywhite, J.M. Read, W. Bates; *centre* R. Peel, A. Shrewsbury (capt.), A. Shaw, W. Scotton; *front* W. Flowers, G. Ulyett, J. Briggs.

ENGLAND IN AUSTRALIA 1886-87

A SHREWSBURY'S TEAM

First-class Results					All Matches				
Matches	Won	Lost	Drawn	Tied	Matches	Won	Lost	Drawn	Tied
10	6	2	2	–	30	12	2	16	–

Date	Venue	Opponent	Results for Touring Team
Oct 30	Adelaide	*XV of South Australia	Drawn
Nov 6	Melbourne	Victoria	Drawn
Nov 12	Parramatta	*XVIII of Parramatta	Won by 23 runs
Nov 19	Sydney	New South Wales	Lost by 6 wkts
Nov 26	Goulburn	*XVIII of Goulburn	Won by an inns & 59 runs
Nov 29	Cootamundra	*XXII of Cootamundra	Won by 10 wkts
Dec 3	Sydney	*XVIII Sydney Juniors	Won by an inns & 130 runs
Dec 8	Lithgow	*XXII of Lithgow	Won by 77 runs
Dec 10	Sydney	New South Wales	Won by 9 wkts
Dec 17	Melbourne	Australian XI	Won by 57 runs
Dec 23	Geelong	*XVIII of Geelong	Drawn
Dec 27	Ballarat	*XX of Ballarat	Won by an inns & 13 runs
Jan 1	Melbourne	Australian XI	Drawn
Jan 7	Sydney	Australian XI	Won by 9 wkts
Jan 14	Bathurst	*XVIII of Bathurst	Drawn
Jan 17	Orange	*XXII of Orange	Drawn
Jan 23	Bowral	*XXII of Bowral	Drawn
Jan 25	Camden	*XXII of Camden	Drawn
Jan 28	Sydney	AUSTRALIA (1st Test)	Won by 13 runs
Feb 4	Narrabri	*XXII of Narrabri	Drawn
Feb 7	Armidale	*XXII of Armidale	Drawn
Feb 10	Newcastle	*XVIII of Newcastle	Drawn
Feb 14	Singleton	*XVIII of Singleton	Drawn
Feb 18	Sydney	New South Wales	Lost by 122 runs
Feb 25	Sydney	AUSTRALIA (2nd Test)	Won by 71 runs
Mar 4	Melbourne	Victoria	Won by 9 wkts
Mar 11	Melbourne	*XV of East Melbourne	Drawn
Mar 15	Sandhurst	*XVIII of Sandhurst	Drawn
Mar 17	East Melbourne	Non Smokers v Smokers	Drawn
Mar 24	Adelaide	*XV of South Australia	Drawn

(Note: The Non Smokers v Smokers game was a mixture of Australian players and the touring England Team.)

The same combination of cricketer-entrepreneurs took a third side to Australia, the ninth England tourists, in 1886–87. The team: *back row* W. Flowers, A. Shrewsbury, G.A. Lohmann, W. Gunn, W. Barnes, J.M. Read; *seated* W. Bates, A. Shaw, J. Lillywhite (umpire), M. Sherwin, W.H. Scotton, R.G. Barlow; *front* J. Briggs.

Player	M	Inn	NO	Runs	HS	50	100	Avrge	Ct/St	Overs	Mdns	Runs	Wkts	Avrge	5wi	10wm	Best
Barlow, RG	11	19	3	339	86	1	–	21.19	9	374.2	182	439	18	24.39	–	–	4/43
Barnes, W	8	12	1	319	109	1	1	29.00	8	382.2	228	352	25	14.08	2	1	7/51
Bates, W	11	18	–	383	86	1	–	21.28	6	436.4	198	558	28	19.93	1	–	6/73
Briggs, J	11	17	–	319	86	3	–	18.76	7	637.4	316	808	34	23.76	2	–	5/42
Flowers, W	11	17	3	286	69	2	–	20.43	3	403.2	209	438	24	18.25	2	–	5/21
Gunn, W	11	17	1	473	150	1	1	29.56	13	18.0	9	28	1	28.00	–	–	–
Lohmann, GA	11	17	2	212	40*	–	–	14.13	12	811.2	390	1028	59	17.42	8	3	8/35
Read, JM	11	17	–	266	53	1	–	15.65	3	54.0	23	76	2	38.00	–	–	1/14
Scotton, WH	11	18	1	192	43*	–	–	11.29	4	26.0	4	82	–	–	–	–	–
Sherwin, M	11	17	9	113	25	–	–	14.13	22/9	–	–	–	–	–	–	–	–
Shrewsbury, A (Capt)	11	19	4	721	236	2	2	48.07	17	1.0	–	–	–	–	–	–	–
Wood, R	3	5	1	26	10*	–	–	6.50	1	8.0	5	8	–	–	–	–	–

After a rugged voyage that saw several players tormented by sea-sickness, in 1886–87 the ninth England touring team reached Adelaide for their opening match to find that a splendid pitch had been prepared. Shrewsbury began with a century but Fifteen of South Australia held England to a draw. Victoria also made a draw of the second match and for the first time the tourists went to Sydney by train instead of the customary wild trip by sea. Trapped on a sticky wicket, England lost in two days to New South Wales in Sydney and were completely routed by Turner and Ferris. They played 18 matches in all before the First Test at Sydney, where both sides were baffled by a sodden pitch. England won by 13 runs after scoring only 45 in their first innings and Turner taking 6 for 15. Charles Bannerman umpired in this match, with his brother Alick at one stage taking an hour to add to his score.

England also won the other Test in the series, thanks to some solid team batting against Turner and Ferris, Lohmann taking 8 for 35 in Australia's first innings of 84. A third Test against Australia had been planned in Melbourne but after a match against Victoria had been ruined by a rival race meeting the Englishmen found the New South Wales players could not get to Melbourne. A match between Smokers and Non-Smokers was substituted for the Test. Only a few hundred people watched some of the brightest batting ever in Melbourne, with the Non-Smokers scoring 803 at 100-an-hour. The match ended in confusion with Scotton, who was batting for the Smokers, picking up the ball as a souvenir and being given out 'handled the ball'.

ENGLAND IN AUSTRALIA 1887-88

GF VERNON'S TEAM

	First-class Results				All Matches			
Matches	Won	Lost	Drawn	Tied	Matches	Won	Lost	Drawn	Tied
8	6	1	1	–	27	12	1	14	–

Date	Venue	Opponent	Results for Touring Team
Oct 28	Adelaide	South Australia	Won by 71 runs
Nov 9	Melbourne	Victoria	Won by an inns & 18 runs
Nov 14	Castlemaine	*XXII of Castlemaine	Drawn
Nov 16	Sandhurst	*XVIII of Sandhurst	Drawn
Nov 18	Ballarat	*XVIII of Ballarat	Drawn
Nov 25	Sydney	New South Wales	Lost by 9 wkts
Dec 2	Parramatta	*XVIII of Parramatta	Drawn
Dec 5	Richmond	*XXII of Hawkesbury	Drawn
Dec 7	Manly	*XVIII of Manly	Drawn
Dec 10	Melbourne	*XVIII Melbourne Juniors	Drawn
Dec 14	Maryborough	*XXII of Maryborough	Drawn
Dec 19	Sale	*XXII of Gippsland	Won by an inns & 3 runs
Dec 24	Adelaide	South Australia	Drawn
Dec 31	Melbourne	Australian XI	Won by an inns & 78 runs
Jan 5	Yarra Bend	*XV of Yarra Bend	Won by 129 runs
Jan 13	Launceston	*XVIII of Northern Tasmania	Drawn
Jan 17	Latrobe	*XXII of North West Coast	Won by an inns & 108 runs
Jan 20	Hobart (TCA)	*XVII of South Tasmania	Drawn
Jan 26	Hobart (TCA)	*XV of Tasmania	Drawn
Feb 2	Benalla	*XVIII of Benalla	Won by an inns & 53 runs
Feb 7	Cootamundra	*XXII of Cootamundra	Drawn
Feb 10	Sydney	AUSTRALIA (Only Test)	Won by 126 runs
Feb 17	Sydney	New South Wales	Won by 8 wkts
Feb 24	Goulburn	*XXII of Goulburn	Drawn
Feb 28	Wagga Wagga	*XVIII of Wagga Wagga	Won by an inns & 5 runs
Mar 2	Melbourne	Australian XI	Won by 87 runs
Mar 9	Melbourne	Victoria	Won by 282 runs

(Note: The Test against AUSTRALIA was a mixture of GF Vernon's and A Shrewsbury's touring England Teams.)

The tenth England team in Australia: *back row* J.T. Rawlin, M.P. Bowden, G.F. Vernon, Sir T.C. O'Brien, J. Beaumont; *centre* A.E. Newton, W. Bates, Lord Hawke, W. Attewell, R. Peel; *front* A. Abel, W.W. Read, and A.E. Stoddart. Vernon took over the captaincy after Lord Hawke had to return home because of the death of his father.

Player	M	Inn	NO	Runs	HS	50	100	Avrge	Ct/St	Overs	Mdns	Runs	Wkts	Avrge	5wi	10wm	Best
Abel, R	8	14	1	320	95	2	–	24.62	8	28.0	9	46	1	46.00	–	–	1/23
Attewell, W	9	14	3	212	43	–	–	19.27	9	736.2	425	590	54	10.93	4	2	7/15
Bates, W	3	5	–	59	28	–	–	11.80	1	137.3	55	194	9	21.56	–	–	3/36
Beaumont, J	8	12	5	40	16	–	–	5.71	3	479.0	247	667	22	30.32	–	–	3/34
Bowden, MP	6	10	3	99	35*	–	–	14.14	6/5	–	–	–	–	–	–	–	–
Hawke, Hon MB	3	5	–	76	48	–	–	15.20	1	–	–	–	–	–	–	–	–
Newton, AE	8	12	1	264	77	2	–	24.00	7/2	–	–	–	–	–	–	–	–
O'Brien, TC	7	10	–	186	45	–	–	18.60	7	–	–	–	–	–	–	–	–
Peel, R	9	15	2	449	55	3	–	34.54	11	744.2	371	822	49	16.78	2	–	5/18
Rawlin, JT	8	12	1	193	78*	1	–	17.55	5	244.1	134	221	5	44.20	–	–	2/87
Read, WW	8	13	2	610	183	1	3	55.45	13	21.0	5	52	2	26.00	–	–	1/16
Stoddart, AE	9	15	–	450	94	4	–	30.00	8	113.0	45	187	7	26.71	–	–	2/31
Vernon, GF (Capt)	6	9	–	155	50	1	–	17.22	3								

The tenth England team to Australia, captained by G.F. Vernon and sponsored by the prestigious Melbourne Cricket Club, toured Australia in the summer of 1887–88 at the same time as the eleventh England team to Australia, captained by C.A. ('Round The Corner') Smith and sponsored once again by Shaw and Shrewsbury. The folly of two English teams touring at the same time proved a financial disaster for both. The Melbourne Cricket Club went ahead with their tour after trying to persuade Shaw and Shrewsbury to postpone their tour but they refused. Both sides travelled to Australia in the same ship, the S.S. *Iberia*, and Vernon took over the captaincy of the Melbourne club's side after the original captain, Lord Hawke, was forced to return home following the death of his father. Further confusion was created by injuries in both groups and the usual demands from the best Australians about higher pay for Tests.

The two England teams combined to play the only Test of the season in mid-February but rain ruined any chance this had of success. England were dismissed for 113 after being sent in by Australian captain Percy McDonnell, Shrewsbury batting superbly on a gluepot for 44. This proved a match-winning innings when Australia were out for only 42, their lowest total for any Test in Australia. The bowlers took all the honours in a match England won by 126 runs, Lohmann taking 5 for 17 and 4 for 35 and Peel 5 for 18 and 4 for 40. Turner's 12 for 87 remains the best analysis for a Sydney Test.

Vernon's team were handicapped by the loss of Bates who lost an eye when he was hit in a net practice at Melbourne. The team played well throughout but poor attendances cost the Melbourne Cricket Club a reported £2000 on the promotion. The other England team

A SHREWSBURY'S TEAM

First-class Results					All Matches				
Matches	Won	Lost	Drawn	Tied	Matches	Won	Lost	Drawn	Tied
7	5	2	–	–	23	15	2	6	–

Date	Venue	Opponent	Results for Touring Team
Nov 4	Parramatta	*XVIII of Parramatta	Drawn
Nov 10	Sydney	New South Wales	Lost by 10 wkts
Nov 18	Brisbane	*XVIII of Queensland	Won by 10 wkts
Nov 23	Maryborough	*XXII of Maryborough	Won by an inns & 21 runs
Nov 25	Gympie	*XXII of Gympie	Won by an inns & 145 runs
Dec 2	Brisbane	*XVIII of Queensland	Won by 114 runs
Dec 9	Sydney	New South Wales	Won by 10 wkts
Dec 16	Melbourne	Victoria	Won by an inns & 456 runs
Dec 24	Ballarat	*XXII of Ballarat	Won by 8 wkts
Dec 31	Sandhurst	*XVIII of Bendigo	Drawn
Jan 6	North Fitzroy	*XVIII Melbourne Juniors	Drawn
Jan 10	Bowral	*XXII of Bowral	Won by an inns & 27 runs
Jan 13	Sydney	New South Wales	Lost by 153 runs
Jan 20	Bourke	*XXII of Bourke	Drawn
Jan 27	Orange	*XXII of Orange	Won by an inns & 80 runs
Feb 3	Sydney	Combined XI	Won by 5 wkts
Feb 10	Sydney	AUSTRALIA (Only Test)	Won by 126 runs
Feb 16	Newcastle	*XVIII of Newcastle	Drawn
Feb 21	Tamworth	*XXII of Tamworth	Won by 9 wkts
Feb 24	Sydney	Australian XI	Won by an inns & 42 runs
Mar 2	Sydney	*XVIII Sydney Juniors	Drawn
Mar 6	Bathurst	*XVIII of Bathurst	Won by 8 wkts
Mar 9	Sydney	Australian XI	Won by 158 runs

(Note: The Test against AUSTRALIA was a mixture of A Shrewbury's and GF Vernon's touring England Teams.)

The England team captained by C. Aubrey Smith made an 1887–88 visit in competition with the team led by G.F. Vernon, with unhappy results. Smith's team: *back row* G. Brann, R.L. Docker, J. Lillywhite, M. Read, R. Pougher; *middle* G. Ulyett, R. Pilling, C.A. Smith (capt.), A. Shrewsbury, G. Lohmann; *front* E.M. Preston, J. Briggs, W. Newham.

Player	M	Inn	NO	Runs	HS	50	100	Avrge	Ct/St	Overs	Mdns	Runs	Wkts	Avrge	5wi	10wm	Best
Brann, G	5	8	2	158	118	–	1	26.33	4	–	–	–	–	–	–	–	–
Briggs, J	8	13	1	229	75	2	–	19.08	7	377.1	215	436	30	14.53	2	1	6/40
Docker, LC	7	11	1	138	48	–	–	13.80	6	–	–	–	–	–	–	–	–
Lohmann, GA	8	13	–	173	39	–	–	13.31	10	666.3	364	755	63	11.98	7	2	7/43
Newham, W	7	12	–	146	53	1	–	12.17	6	–	–	–	–	–	–	–	–
Pilling, R	8	12	5	48	10	–	–	6.85	16/6	–	–	–	–	–	–	–	–
Pougher, AD	6	9	2	107	25*	–	–	15.29	5	157.1	79	189	12	15.75	–	–	4/40
Preston, JM	7	10	1	81	27	–	–	9.00	3	225.2	92	307	17	18.06	–	–	4/16
Read, JM	8	13	–	218	39	–	–	16.77	3	–	–	–	–	–	–	–	–
Shrewsbury, A (Capt)	8	14	1	766	232	2	2	58.92	14	–	–	–	–	–	–	–	–
Smith, CA	6	8	–	197	68	2	–	24.63	4	124.0	57	153	7	21.86	–	–	3/11
Ulyett, G	6	10	1	201	72	1	–	22.33	3	22.0	5	49	1	49.00	–	–	1/32

travelled to remote country towns and to New Zealand for matches in an effort to improve their financial return but Shaw and Shrewsbury lost £2400 each on the venture and their partner Lillywhite failed to meet his share of the loss. Shrewsbury kept most of his players in Australia to play rugby football in the hope that this would prove a rewarding speculation but this, too, failed to pay.

The abject failure of the dual tours ushered in a slump in public support for cricket and in a decline of the Australian Test team's competence. The 1888 side in England lost the Test rubber by two–one, the 1890 team two–nil. At the centre of Australia's problems was a bitter fight between the Melbourne Cricket Club and colonial associations trying to form an Australian control body. The Melbourne Club wanted to administer all Australian cricket as the Marylebone Club did in England but the colonies believed that would end in the club taking tour profits that should go towards helping hard-pressed district clubs.

After four years without an English tour, the critics and the feuding Melbourne and Sydney factions knew another tour was urgently needed to revive Australian cricket, but neither party in the dispute could afford to sponsor one. Finally, Henry Holroyd North, the third Earl of Sheffield, Viscount Pevensey, Baron Sheffield of Roscommon, Ireland, and Baron Sheffield of Sheffield Park in East Sussex, who lavishly entertained Australian teams in England, agreed to finance a tour. He was one of the great benefactors of English cricket, a London-born Eton-educated cricket-lover who had served in the diplomatic service before his election to Parliament as the member for East Sussex. He had little skill as a player but had achieved spectacles in his sole first-class match for Gentlemen of Sussex against the Gentlemen of Kent in 1856.

There is evidence to suggest that Lord Sheffield visited Australia at the urging of a friend in the diplomatic service worried about British investments in Australia at a time when several Australian banks were foundering in the 1890 Depression. The delays in achieving

Federation certainly were alarming to British investors and it is likely his Lordship decided to combine cricket with a close-up look at Australian business. He took expert cricket advice from Alfred Shaw and Arthur Shrewsbury, both of whom strongly recommended that he include W.G. Grace in his touring team because of Grace's tremendous crowd-pulling powers. Shrewsbury went so far as to draw up a projected balance sheet for the trip in which he calculated that expenses for 13 men would come to £6632, which included laundry bills, fares, tips for ship's stewards, advertising, and payments to the bands that played at England's matches.

Initially, Grace refused Lord Sheffield's invitation to captain a team to Australia. He would turn 43 in July 1891, and wanted to build up his medical practice, and insisted that his fee would be too high. But Lord Sheffield agreed to pay Grace £3000 to tour, plus all expenses for Grace's wife and two children, plus the cost of employing a locum to look after Grace's patients while he was away. The tour proceeded in the southern summer of 1891–92, but immediately Lord Sheffield viewed the program on the team's arrival he handed over all the speech-making to Grace, who said he should have asked for more money.

ENGLAND IN AUSTRALIA 1891-92

LORD SHEFFIELD'S TEAM

First-class Results					All Matches				
Matches	Won	Lost	Drawn	Tied	Matches	Won	Lost	Drawn	Tied
8	6	2	–	–	27	12	2	13	–

Date	Venue	Opponent	Results for Touring Team
Nov 20	Adelaide	South Australia	Won by an inns & 62 runs
Nov 27	Melbourne	Victoria	Won by an inns & 107 runs
Dec 4	Sydney	New South Wales	Won by 4 wkts
Dec 9	Parramatta	*XX of Cumberland	Drawn
Dec 11	Camden	*XXII of Camden	Won by an inns & 43 runs
Dec 15	Bowral	*XXIV of Bowral	Won by 67 runs
Dec 18	Goulburn	*XXII of Goulburn	Won by an inns & 16 runs
Dec 22	Melbourne	*XVI of Melbourne Club	Drawn
Dec 26	Ballarat	*XX of Ballarat	Won by an inns & 134 runs
Jan 1	Melbourne	AUSTRALIA (1st Test)	Lost by 54 runs
Jan 7	East Melbourne	*XVI of East Melbourne	Drawn
Jan 9	Melbourne	*XVI of South Melbourne	Drawn
Jan 13	Williamstown	*XXII of Williamstown	Drawn
Jan 15	Bairnsdale	*XXII of Bairnsdale	Won by an inns & 98 runs
Jan 21	Malvern	*XXII of Malvern	Drawn
Jan 23	Melbourne	*XX Melbourne Juniors	Drawn
Jan 29	Sydney	AUSTRALIA (2nd Test)	Lost by 72 runs
Feb 5	Newcastle	*XX of Newcastle	Drawn
Feb 11	Manly	*XXII of Manly	Drawn
Feb 12	Sydney	*XXII Sydney Juniors	Drawn
Feb 16	Penrith	*XXIII of Nepean	Drawn
Feb 19	Sydney	New South Wales	Won by 7 wkts
Feb 26	Wollongong	*XXII of Illawarra	Drawn
Mar 4	Hobart (TCA)	*XV of Southern Tasmania	Won by an inns & 39 runs
Mar 10	Launceston	*XVIII of Northern Tasmania	Drawn
Mar 17	Melbourne	Victoria	Won by 9 wkts
Mar 24	Adelaide	AUSTRALIA (3rd Test)	Won by an inns & 230 runs

The team W.G. Grace led on his second visit to Australia in 1891-92 under Lord Sheffield's sponsorship: *back row* R. Carpenter (umpire), W. Attewell, G.A. Lohmann, J.M. Read, G. Bean, J.W. Sharpe, R.A. Thoms (umpire); *seated* J. Briggs, G. MacGregor, W.G. Grace, R. Peel, A.E. Stoddart, R. Abel; *absent* Manager Alfred Shaw, H. Philipson, O.G. Radcliffe and Lord Sheffield.

Player	M	Inn	NO	Runs	HS	50	100	Avrge	Ct/St	Overs	Mdns	Runs	Wkts	Avrge	5wi	10wm	Best
Abel, R	8	12	2	388	132*	–	1	38.80	10	–	–	–	–	–	–	–	–
Attewell, W	8	11	3	126	43*	–	–	15.75	7	2858	241	573	44	13.02	4	1	6/34
Bean, G	7	11	1	178	50	1	–	17.80	5	–	–	–	–	–	–	–	–
Briggs, J	8	13	–	262	91	1	–	20.15	8	1212	71	420	32	13.13	4	1	6/49
Grace, WG (Capt)	8	11	1	448	159*	2	1	44.80	17	385	21	134	5	26.80	–	–	3/64
Lohmann, GA	8	11	1	222	102	–	1	22.20	9	2390	178	640	40	16.00	3	1	8/58
McGregor, G	7	9	2	101	31	–	–	14.43	10/2	–	–	–	–	–	–	–	–
Peel, R	7	11	2	229	83	1	–	25.44	8	1116	83	283	15	18.87	–	–	4/50
Phillipson, H	2	2	1	16	15*	–	–	16.00	2/3	–	–	–	–	–	–	–	–
Radcliffe, OG	2	3	–	31	18	–	–	10.33	–	–	–	–	–	–	–	–	–
Read, JM	8	11	–	328	106	2	1	29.82	3	–	–	–	–	–	–	–	–
Sharpe, JW	7	9	3	63	23	–	–	10.50	5	1645	113	508	17	29.88	2	–	6/40
Stoddart, AE	8	12	–	450	134	2	1	37.50	5	54	3	22	–	–	–	–	–

More than 20,000 spectators turned up at the Melbourne Cricket Ground for each of the first two days of the First Test and more than 10,000 on both the third and fourth days. The ascendancy swung back and forth until Australia won by 54 runs, thanks to great bowling by Robert McLeod (5 for 53) and Turner (5 for 51). Lord Sheffield went off to Tasmania, saying the mainland heat was too much for him, leaving Grace to run the team and handle persistent newspaper comments about Grace's bulk and lack of athleticism. Grace took it in good part but refused to allow Australia to replace the injured Harry Moses in the Second Test at Sydney. Grace was within his rights, as he had warned Australia he would take this step if they insisted on going into the match knowing Moses had a leg injury. Finally, after being hooted by spectators, Grace relented and allowed the agile Syd Gregory to field for Moses, after Lord Sheffield had ordered him to do so. Australia won the match by 72 runs to clinch the series and although England gained some solace for a big win in the Third Test in Melbourne, the aims of the tour were achieved.

Satisfied that the tour had revived Australian cricket, Lord Sheffield went home pleased that the takings of £14,000 odd left him only £2000 out of pocket, a loss Shrewsbury said could be attributed 'to all the wine Grace and his amateurs drank'. When the ship carrying the Englishmen docked in Naples, his Lordship sent a cheque back to Ben Wardill, secretary of the Melbourne Cricket Club, thanking him for the warm reception of his team and suggesting the £150 cheque be spent on the development of Australian cricket. After much dithering among colonial administrators it was spent on the Sheffield Shield.

ENGLAND IN AUSTRALIA 1894-95

AE STODDART'S TEAM

First-class Results					All Matches				
Matches	Won	Lost	Drawn	Tied	Matches	Won	Lost	Drawn	Tied
12	8	4	–	–	23	9	4	10	–

Date	Venue	Opponent	Results for Touring Team
Nov 3	Gawler	*XVIII of Gawler	Drawn
Nov 9	Adelaide	South Australia	Lost by 6 wkts
Nov 16	Melbourne	Victoria	Won by 145 runs
Nov 23	Sydney	New South Wales	Won by 8 wkts
Nov 30	Armidale	*XXII of New England	Drawn
Dec 5	Toowoomba	*XVIII of Toowoomba	Drawn
Dec 7	Brisbane	Queensland	Won by an inns & 274 runs
Dec 14	Sydney	AUSTRALIA (1st Test)	Won by 10 runs
Dec 21	Sydney	*XVIII Sydney Juniors	Drawn
Dec 29	Melbourne	AUSTRALIA (2nd Test)	Won by 94 runs
Jan 5	Ballarat	*XVIII of Ballarat	Drawn
Jan 11	Adelaide	AUSTRALIA (3rd Test)	Lost by 382 runs
Jan 18	Broken Hill	*XVIII of Broken Hill	Won by an inns & 8 runs
Jan 25	Dandenong	*XVIII of Dandenong	Drawn
Feb 1	Sydney	AUSTRALIA (4th Test)	Lost by an inns & 147 runs
Feb 9	Armidale	*XVIII of New England	Drawn
Feb 15	Brisbane	Queensland & NSW XI	Won by 278 runs
Feb 22	Newcastle	*XVIII of Newcastle	Drawn
Mar 1	Melbourne	AUSTRALIA (5th Test)	Won by 6 wkts
Mar 9	Launceston	*XVIII of Northern Tasmania	Drawn
Mar 14	Hobart (TCA)	*XV of Southern Tasmania	Drawn
Mar 21	Melbourne	Victoria	Lost by 7 wkts
Mar 28	Adelaide	South Australia	Won by 10 wkts

Officials in Sydney and Melbourne joined to sponsor the thirteenth England team to Australia in 1894–95 under the captaincy of Andrew Stoddart, who had made two previous tours of Australia (with Vernon in 1887–88 and Grace in 1891–92). By then there was great enthusiasm for big cricket in Australia and the tour was a huge financial success. Australia lost the First Test when they were caught on a rain-soaked pitch in Sydney, and in the Second Test at Melbourne Stoddart played a wonderful innings for 173, which led to a second England win. Australia responded with a thrilling win in the Third Test in Adelaide where Albert Trott took 8 for 43 in his debut, and Frank Iredale made 140.

At Sydney in the Fourth Test Albert Trott hit a dazzling 85 not out after Harry Graham's 105 to give Australia another win and square the series. Vast crowds attended the deciding Fifth Test in Melbourne, with Australia appearing certain to win until J.T. Brown strode to the crease and scored 140 in 145 minutes to swing the rubber. Little wonder with such champagne cricket that the tour made a profit of £7000 from takings of more than £18,000.

Player	M	Inn	NO	Runs	HS	50	100	Avrge	Ct/St	Overs	Mdns	Runs	Wkts	Avrge	5wi	10wm	Best
Briggs, J	12	20	1	360	57	1	–	18.95	6	375.4	75	1057	44	24.02	1	–	5/97
Brockwell, W	12	22	1	504	81	1	–	24.00	11	121.5	38	336	7	48.00	–	–	3/33
Brown, JT	12	21	2	825	140	1	4	43.42	10	–	–	–	–	–	–	–	–
Ford, FGJ	11	20	1	508	106	2	1	26.74	6	45.2	8	159	1	159.00	–	–	1/47
Gay, LH	6	11	5	186	39*	–	–	31.00	9/5	–	–	–	–	–	–	–	–
Humphreys, W	4	7	3	42	18*	–	–	10.50	4	112.0	12	314	6	52.33	–	–	2/69
Lockwood, WH	10	14	2	224	39	–	–	18.67	5	285.4	66	791	18	43.94	–	–	4/54
MacLaren, AC	11	20	3	804	228	1	3	47.29	4	–	–	–	–	–	–	–	–
Peel, R	12	21	1	421	73	4	–	21.05	10	661.2	175	1441	57	25.28	3	–	6/67
Philipson, N	9	15	1	187	59	1	–	13.36	15/3	–	–	–	–	–	–	–	–
Richardson, T	11	19	5	114	20	–	–	8.14	1	614.5	148	1616	68	23.76	7	1	8/52
Stoddart, AE (Capt)	10	18	1	870	173	4	3	51.18	7	3.0	–	31	1	31.00	–	–	1/31
Ward, A	12	22	–	916	219	1	3	41.64	6	–	–	–	–	–	–	–	–

ENGLAND IN AUSTRALIA 1897–98

AE STODDART'S TEAM

First-class Results					All Matches				
Matches	Won	Lost	Drawn	Tied	Matches	Won	Lost	Drawn	Tied
12	4	5	3	–	22	6	5	11	–

Date	Venue	Opponent	Results for Touring Team
Oct 28	Adelaide	South Australia	Drawn
Nov 6	Melbourne	Victoria	Won by 2 wkts
Nov 12	Sydney	New South Wales	Won by 8 wkts
Nov 19	Newcastle	*XVIII of Newcastle	Drawn
Nov 22	Glen Innes	*XXII of Glen Innes	Won by an inns & 117 runs
Nov 26	Brisbane	*XIII of Queensland & NSW	Drawn
Nov 30	Toowoomba	*XVIII of Toowoomba	Drawn
Dec 3	Armidale	*XXII of New England	Drawn
Dec 13	Sydney	AUSTRALIA (1st Test)	Won by 9 wkts
Dec 27	Bendigo	*XVIII of Bendigo	Won by 10 wkts
Jan 1	Melbourne	AUSTRALIA (2nd Test)	Lost by an inns & 55 runs
Jan 7	Ballarat	*XVIII of Ballarat	Drawn
Jan 10	Stawell	*XXII of Stawell	Drawn
Jan 14	Adelaide	AUSTRALIA (3rd Test)	Lost by an inns & 13 runs
Jan 21	Hamilton	*XXII of Western District	Drawn
Jan 29	Melbourne	AUSTRALIA (4th Test)	Lost by 8 wkts
Feb 5	Sydney	New South Wales	Lost by 239 runs
Feb 12	Sydney	*XII of Sydney & Melbourne Uni's	Drawn
Feb 19	Brisbane	Combined Qeensland & Victorian XI	Drawn
Feb 26	Sydney	AUSTRALIA (5th Test)	Lost by 6 wkts
Mar 11	Melbourne	Victoria	Won by 7 wkts
Mar 19	Adelaide	South Australia	Drawn

Andrew Stoddart's second Australian tour as England's captain met far stronger opposition than the first. His team: *standing* J.T. Hearne, A.C. MacLaren, T.W. Hayward, J. Briggs, G.H. Hirst, A.E. Stoddart. A. Priestly (team supporter), N.F. Druce, E. Wainwright, J.R. Mason, W. Storer; *seated* Visitor, J.H. Board, K.S. Ranjitsinhji, their host, Ben Wardill (Melbourne Cricket Club), T. Richardson.

Stoddart's insistence on attractive cricket and his own big-hitting made him such a popular figure in Australia that Sydney and Melbourne officials had no hesitation in inviting him to captain the fourteenth England team to Australia in 1897–98. Stoddart's mother died in England just before the First Test and he was so grief-stricken he could not leave his hotel room, let alone play cricket. Archie MacLaren took over as England captain, and in his first Test in the job hit a match-winning 109. Joe Darling matched it by becoming the first left-hander

Player	M	Inn	NO	Runs	HS	50	100	Avrge	Ct/St	Overs	Mdns	Runs	Wkts	Avrge	5wi	10wm	Best
Board, JH	4	6	–	140	59	1	–	23.33	5/2	1.0	1	0	–	–	–	–	–
Briggs, J	8	12	3	165	46*	–	–	18.33	1	294.0	79	779	12	64.92	–	–	3/96
Druce, NF	11	18	1	473	109	1	1	27.82	8	1.0	–	1	–	–	–	–	–
Hayward, TW	12	21	3	693	96	5	–	38.50	4	195.0	40	645	15	43.00	1	–	5/66
Hearne, JT	12	18	10	87	31*	–	–	10.88	5	559.0	186	1307	44	29.70	4	–	6/98
Hirst, GH	11	17	1	342	85	2	–	21.38	11	230.4	62	682	9	75.77	–	–	4/66
MacLaren, AC	11	20	1	1037	142	3	5	54.58	4	–	–	–	–	–	–	–	–
Mason, JR	12	21	1	516	128*	2	1	25.80	12	181.1	48	502	20	25.10	1	–	5/41
Ranjitsinhji, KS	12	22	3	1157	189	6	3	60.89	7	19.4	5	58	–	–	–	–	–
Richardson, T	11	15	3	105	25*	–	–	8.75	7	524.2	107	1594	54	29.52	4	1	8/94
Stoddart, AE (Capt)	7	11	–	206	40	–	–	18.73	3	31.0	7	104	3	34.67	–	–	2/50
Storer, W	11	17	1	604	84	4	–	37.75	22	73.3	8	284	6	47.33	–	–	4/79
Wainwrigt, E	10	17	–	456	105	2	1	26.82	5	72.0	14	249	1	249.00	–	–	1/32

to score a Test century but after Prince Ranjitsinghji had backed up MacLaren with an innings of 175, Darling's display was to no avail. This was the Test in which Charlie McLeod was run out after leaving his crease when he was bowled by a no-ball. McLeod was deaf and did not hear the umpire's call.

McLeod had his revenge in the Second Test when he made 112 and set Australia on the way to a total of 520, enough to win by an innings. Stoddart returned to his captain's post for the Third Test in Adelaide, where Darling's 178, his second century of the series, led to another Australian triumph. Not to be outdone, another South Australian left-hander, Clem Hill, made 188 to give Australia victory and the series in the Fourth Test. Hill's score remains the best by a batsman under 21—he was 20 years 317 days old—in England–Australia Tests. Darling got his third 100 of the rubber (160) in the Fifth Test, reaching three figures in only 91 minutes. Australia's four–one success was marred only by the calling of fast bowler Ernie Jones for throwing by Australian umpire James Phillips.

ENGLAND IN AUSTRALIA 1901–02

By the time MacLaren brought the fifteenth England side to Australia in 1901–02, Jones had gained better control of his action and he had little trouble satisfying umpires. He no longer tried to bowl every delivery at express speed but he was still very fast indeed. Darling had taken over then as Australia's captain and he won Jones's respect by overpowering him in a light-hearted dressing-room wrestle. Jones, a former miner of immense strength, had never previously been thrown. Darling shrewdly got an extra effort from Jones by asking keeper Kelly to stand up on the stumps when Jones's pace slowed. This annoyed Jones so much the following deliveries hurtled past startled batsmen or into their stumps.

Darling had drilled a talented group into a splendid cricket team and even when England won the First Test because of a MacLaren century (116) and the mastery of the great Sydney Francis Barnes (5 for 65 and 1 for 74) the Australians did not lose their composure. Hugh Trumble and Monty Noble bowled superbly to win the Second Test for Australia and when Barnes broke down in the Third Test, England's hopes disappeared. Hill had an amazing run of 99, 98 and 97 in successive Test innings to give birth to the expression 'nervous nineties' but Australia still went on to a four–one series win. Typical of a breezy, entertaining series was Bill Howell's 35 in 14 minutes in the Fourth Test, when he was out to the fifteenth ball he received. He hit 23 off the first eight balls. Victorian Jack Saunders took nine wickets on debut in this Test, only to find himself dropped from the Fifth Test. In such a strong Australian team, Saunders' omission caused little complaint.

AC MACLAREN'S TEAM

	First-class Results				All Matches			
Matches	Won	Lost	Drawn	Tied	Matches	Won	Lost	Drawn	Tied
11	5	6	–	–	22	8	6	8	–

Date	Venue	Opponent	Results for Touring Team
Nov 9	Adelaide	South Australia	Lost by 233 runs
Nov 15	Melbourne	Victoria	Won by 118 runs
Nov 22	Sydney	New South Wales	Lost by 53 runs
Nov 29	West Maitland	*XVIII of West Maitland	Drawn
Dec 2	Glen Innes	*XVIII of Glen Innes	Won by an inns & 89 runs
Dec 4	Armidale	*XVIII of Armidale	Drawn
Dec 7	Newcastle	*XV of Newcastle	Drawn
Dec 13	Sydney	AUSTRALIA (1st Test)	Won by an inns & 124 runs
Dec 20	Goulburn	*XVIII of Goulburn	Won by 6 wkts
Dec 26	Bendigo	*XVIII of Bendigo	Drawn
Jan 1	Melbourne	AUSTRALIA (2nd Test)	Lost by 229 runs
Jan 8	Stawell	*XVIII of Stawell	Drawn
Jan 10	Ballarat	*XVII of Ballarat	Drawn
Jan 17	Adelaide	AUSTRALIA (3rd Test)	Lost by 4 wkts
Jan 25	Melbourne	*XVI of Country	Won by 10 wkts
Jan 31	Sydney	New South Wales	Won by an inns & 128 runs
Feb 7	Bathurst	*XVIII of Western District	Drawn
Feb 14	Sydney	AUSTRALIA (4th Test)	Lost by 7 wkts
Feb 22	Melbourne	Victoria	Won by 8 wkts
Feb 28	Melbourne	AUSTRALIA (5th Test)	Lost by 32 runs
Mar 11	Broken Hill	*XVIII of Broken Hill	Drawn
Mar 14	Adelaide	South Australia	Won by 6 wkts

Player	M	Inn	NO	Runs	HS	50	100	Avrge	Ct/St	Overs	Mdns	Runs	Wkts	Avrge	5wi	10wm	Best
Barnes, SF	6	10	2	90	26*	–	–	11.25	5	281.4	55	676	41	16.49	5	2	7/38
Blythe, C	8	14	6	62	20	–	–	7.75	3	298.5	100	711	34	20.91	1	–	5/45
Braund, LC	11	19	5	404	103*	1	1	28.86	24	623.5	144	1779	61	29.16	7	1	6/90
Garnett, HG	4	6	1	41	17	–	–	8.20	4/1	–	–	–	–	–	–	–	–
Gunn, J	9	16	2	154	30	–	–	11.00	6	307.3	94	769	29	26.52	2	–	5/73
Hayward, TW	11	19	1	701	174	4	1	38.94	5	71.1	18	208	10	20.80	–	–	4/22
Jessop, GL	10	18	–	359	87	1	–	19.94	5	118.4	30	397	12	33.08	–	–	4/68
Jones, AO	11	19	1	229	44	–	–	12.72	13	49.0	8	161	3	53.67	–	–	1/24
Lilley, AFA	11	18	–	406	84	2	–	22.56	20/5	–	–	–	–	–	–	–	–
MacLaren, AC (Capt)	10	16	–	929	167	4	3	58.06	19	–	–	–	–	–	–	–	–
McGahey, CP	7	12	2	210	57	1	–	21.00	3	60.3	13	165	7	23.57	–	–	3/58
Quaife, WG	11	19	1	440	68	2	–	24.44	6	5.0	–	18	–	–	–	–	–
Robson, C	1	2	1	24	17*	–	–	24.00	–/3	–	–	–	–	–	–	–	–
Tyldesley, JT	11	19	–	696	142	3	2	36.63	5	–	–	–	–	–	–	–	–

CHAPTER THREE

INTERNATIONAL TOURS ESTABLISHED

The early England tours by Australian teams established their captains as the most important figures in Australian sport. From the first tour in 1878 under Dave Gregory's leadership, the captaincy held a status no other sporting job matched. Gregory and his successors, Billy Murdoch in 1880, 1882, 1884, and 1890, Dr Henry Scott in 1886, Percy McDonnell in 1888, Jack Blackham in 1893, and Harry Trott in 1896, became more famous than Melbourne Cup winners, champion boxers or oarsmen. Their progress was more avidly followed than political campaigns, and when their teams defeated England, rivalry between the independent colonies disappeared and Australia became one nation.

The Australian captaincy has remained a prestigious, but demanding job. The incumbents need to be witty speechmakers, shrewd arbitrators in dressing-room disputes, socially graceful, able to mix with wharfies and royalty, tactically innovative, consistently sportsmanlike, and worthy of their team places as batsmen or bowlers. Only one wicket-keeper, Blackham, has ever led an Australian team to England.

The cricketers who gave the Australian captaincy this exalted position were successful in their chosen vocations. Dave Gregory was not an outstanding player but good enough to command respect with his right-hand middle order batting and his right-arm fast-medium round-arm bowling. Dave was one of 13 children, seven of them boys. He was born at Fairy Meadow, NSW, educated at St James' Church of England School in Sydney, where he won a medal for a good pass in an exam. When the governor went to the school to present it to him, he offered Dave a job. Dave called on the governor to make good his promise immediately he left school and went to work in the accounts section at Government House.

Dave played cricket on Sydney's Domain with his brothers Ned, Walter, Charlie and Arthur, on a pitch laid out with a spirit-level by members of the National Club, who played matches against pub teams or sides organised by garrison soldiers and naval officers.

At a time when Victoria dominated inter-colonial cricket through the skill of Tom Wills, John Conway and Sam Cosstick, Sydney cricket fans persuaded the Gregorys to form a team to play the Victorians in what was called a single-wicket match. The Gregorys practised every morning for the match against a Victorian team that had won all the prizemoney in similar matches. More than 5000 spectators turned up at the Albert Ground to see the Gregorys defeat the Victorians after a dispute over a Victorian umpire no-balling Dave for throwing. William Caffyn, the former Surrey star, replaced the umpire and found no reason to no-ball Dave again.

The Gregorys' victory established the family reputation and assisted Dave and Edward ('Ned') Gregory win places in the Australian team that opposed the All-England XI in the first Test at Melbourne in March 1877. On the morning of the match the players chosen by John Conway—he ignored the existing colonial administrative bodies—held a dressing-room election for the captaincy and gave Dave Gregory the job. He was a man of commanding presence, with a thick, shiny black beard, popular with women, and known to his colleagues as 'Handsome Dave'. He was extremely erect in bearing, 6 ft 2 in tall, 14 st 4 lb, and careful about liquor, though he enjoyed it after matches. His batting lacked style or polish but was very safe and calm. He was a model fieldsman in the slips at a time when that position was new to many Australians. Above all, he could be relied on in a crisis.

His strength was in lifting his team's performance in the field, carrying out advice from Caffyn on pressuring batsmen with timely bowling changes, arranging drills to improve gathering and throwing, and instructing his players to watch him for signals on their field positions.

Gregory's triumph with a team that had to be introduced to each other before the first Test in Melbourne made him an automatic choice to lead the first white Australian team to tour England. This 1878 venture went ahead only 27 years after the first intercolonial match despite opposition from the colonial cricket associations. Players were invited to go in letters from Conway, and each man had to deposit cash in advance for the team's expenses, with the promise that they would share in tour profits. They arrived in England nine years after the collapse of the All England Eleven, which had lost its elite status after the death of founder William Clarke in 1856, aged 57. Teams with names like United North and United South of England attempted a revival but foundered, partly because too many players appeared for several itinerant representative sides.

James Lillywhite, England's captain in the 1876–77 Tests, acted as advance agent for the Australians but could offer only limited financial assistance. Tom Wills, the Victorian educated at Rugby, who had played for Cambridge University and Kent, could not tour because of ill health but made a donation towards tour funds. To secure further cash, the team played warm-up matches around the eastern colonies. Left-arm bowler Tom Kendall, a match-winner in the first Test, played in these matches but was dropped from the tour, allegedly for excessive drinking, before the team sailed.

AUSTRALIA IN ENGLAND 1878

	First-class Results					All Matches			
Matches	Won	Lost	Drawn	Tied	Matches	Won	Lost	Drawn	Tied
15	7	4	4	–	37	18	7	12	–

Date	Venue	Opponent	Results for Australians
May 20	Nottingham	Nottinghamshire	Lost by an inns & 14 runs
May 27	Lord's	MCC	Won by 9 wkts
May 30	Huddersfield	Yorkshire	Won by 6 wkts
Jun 3	The Oval	Surrey	Won by 5 wkts
Jun 6	Elland	*XVIII of Elland	Won by 80 runs
Jun 10	Batley	*XVIII of Batley	Drawn
Jun 13	Longsight	*XVIII of Longsight	Lost by 2 wkts
Jun 17	Chelsea	Gentlemen of England	Lost by an inns & 1 run
Jun 20	Lord's	Middlesex	Won by 98 runs
Jun 24	Bournbrook	*XXII of Birmingham	Drawn
Jun 27	Hunslet	*XVIII of Hunslet	Drawn
Jly 1	Sheffield	Yorkshire	Lost by 9 wkts
Jly 4	Stockport	*XVIII of Stockport	Won by 149 runs
Jly 8	Twickenham	The Orleans Club	Drawn
Jly 10	Swansea	*XVIII of South Wales	Won by an inns & 37 runs
Jly 12	Oldham	*XVIII of Werneth and Oldham	Drawn
Jly 15	Leicester	*Leicestershire	Won by 8 wkts
Jly 18	Hull	*Hull	Won by 10 wkts
Jly 22	Lord's	Cambridge University	Lost by an inns & 72 runs
Jly 26	Crewe	*XXII of Crewe	Won by 99 runs
Jly 29	Keighley	*XVIII of Keighley	Won by 7 wkts
Aug 1	Rochdale	*XVIII of Rochdale	Drawn
Aug 5	Buxton	*XXII of Buxton	Drawn
Aug 7	Burnley	*XVIII of Burnley	Drawn
Aug 8	Liverpool	*XVIII of Stanley CC	Won by an inns & 71 runs
Aug 12	Dudley	*XVIII of Dudley	Drawn
Aug 15	Manchester	Lancashire	Drawn
Aug 19	Yeadon	*XVIII of Yeadon	Lost by 24 runs
Aug 22	Scarborough	*XVIII of Scarborough	Won by an inns & 46 runs
Aug 26	Hastings	*XVIII fo Hastings & District	Won by an inns & 47 runs
Aug 29	Hove	Sussex	Won by 7 wkts
Sep 2	The Oval	Players of England	Won by 8 runs
Sep 5	Clifton	Gloucestershire	Won by 10 wkts
Sep 9	Scarborough	Gentlemen of England	Drawn
Sep 11	Chelsea	Players of England	Drawn
Sep 13	Partick	*XII of yWest of Scotland	Won by an inns & 84 runs
Sep 16	Sunderland	*XVII of Sunderland	Lost by 71 runs

Australia's first cricket captain, Dave Gregory.

Player	State	M	Inn	NO	Runs	HS	50	100	Avrge	Ct/St	Overs	Mdns	Runs	Wkts	Avrge	5wi	10wm	Best
Allan, FE	VIC	15	24	6	129	33	–	–	7.17	7	348.3	159	513	25	20.52	1	–	6/76
Bailey, GH	TAS	12	21	4	254	40	–	–	14.94	5	10.0	3	17	1	17.00	–	–	1/9
Bannerman, AC	NSW	15	26	3	260	71*	1	–	11.30	8	–	–	–	–	–	–	–	–
Bannerman, C	NSW	15	28	1	567	61	4	–	21.00	13	–	–	–	–	–	–	–	–
Blackham, JM	VIC	13	20	8	179	30*	–	–	14.92	8/3	–	–	–	–	–	–	–	–
Boyle, HF	VIC	14	21	5	98	18	–	–	6.13	11	362.0	144	484	51	9.49	3	–	7/48
Garrett, TW	NSW	15	25	1	265	43	–	–	11.04	5	256.2	130	318	32	9.94	2	1	7/38
Gregory, DW (Capt)	NSW	15	22	1	207	57	1	–	9.86	11	–	–	–	–	–	–	–	–
Horan, TP	VIC	15	27	1	290	69	1	–	11.15	2	35.3	8	100	7	14.28	1	–	5/30
Midwinter, WE	VIC	5	10	2	124	32	–	–	15.50	4	65.2	33	58	8	7.25	–	–	4/14
Murdoch, WL	NSW	15	25	4	274	49	–	–	13.05	11/7	22.0	6	46	2	23.00	–	–	2/46
Spofforth, FR	NSW	15	25	1	304	56	1	–	12.67	7	658.1	248	1067	97	11.00	11	5	9/53
Tennant, HN	TAS	1	2	–	7	6	–	–	3.50	–	–	–	–	–	–	–	–	–

The first Australian cricket team to tour England in 1878, ten years after the first Aboriginal side: *back row* Tom Horan, Fred Spofforth, John Conway (manager), Frank Allan; *middle row* George Bailey, Tom Garrett, Dave Gregory (capt.), Alick Bannerman, Harry Boyle; *front* Charles Bannerman, Billy Murdoch, Jack Blackham.

The first Australian tourists left without fanfare, snubbed by the public and cricket officials, with some players so unconfident of the prospects they paid their return fares in advance, expecting the tour to go broke. Kendall's sacking, a sad duty for Conway and Gregory, meant the team relied heavily on Billy Midwinter joining them in England as he had promised.

Cricket statisticians disagree on the number of matches the first team played, but there appears no reason to doubt Conway's figures of 41 games. The discrepancy probably arose when four of the programmed 37 matches finished early, and rather than disappoint crowds additional matches were organised. The team played 15 first-class matches, 2 others against teams of eleven, and 22 against the odds or exhibition matches. They won 18, lost 7 and had 12 draws.

The Australians impressed English newspapers with their fielding and the keenness they showed in quickly moving into position between overs. Their throwing and catching was splendid and every man remained alert for Gregory's waved instructions. With Jack Blackham proving a class above any English keeper, they were a polished outfit to watch, with four outstanding bowlers in Spofforth, Boyle, Garrett and Allan. Their weakness was in batting and one newspaper commented that there were seven players in the side who were 'worth only about 30 runs between them'.

Gregory made only one major tactical mistake, though he showed an unnecessary tendency to challenge umpiring decisions. At Lord's when Edward Lyttelton made the only century scored against them on tour with an innings of 113, Gregory failed to cover the area around point. This allowed Lyttelton to score repeated boundaries with the square cut, but Middlesex only totalled 186 runs and Australia won by 98 runs.

The tour started badly, with defeat by an innings by Nottinghamshire. This was in bitterly cold conditions, foreign to players in thin shirts and no sweaters, who had had little time to practise after their long journey by sea to San Francisco, across America by train, and again by sea to Liverpool. The players barely had time to think about their good fortune in securing leave from their jobs for 12 months before the wind sent them to shops for heavy shirts and sweaters. Some of them spent much of the tour huddled around heaters or fires in dressing-rooms while they awaited their turn to bat.

They recovered brilliantly from their initial upset by beating the MCC, Yorkshire and Surrey, all powerful sides, in successive matches. Their victory over the MCC at Lord's shocked English cricket followers, quite unprepared for such a result. Opposed to the best cricketers in England, they swept to a handsome nine-wicket win in only 3 hours 40 minutes, dismissing a team led by W.G. Grace, and including noted players like A.J. Webbe, A.N. Hornby, Alfred Shaw, G.F. Vernon and G.G. Hearne, for only 33 and 19. Spectators laughed when Grace hit the first ball of the match for four, expecting more of the same, but Midwinter, stealing round from fine leg caught the doctor off the second ball on the square leg boundary. Midwinter had joined the team when they arrived at Liverpool and his knowledge of English batsmen and their favourite strokes seemed likely to prove invaluable. There were six MCC ducks in the first innings and seven in the second and Boyle or Spofforth knocked back the stumps 14 times.

Australia made only 41 in their first innings, which gave them a lead of eight runs, but only had to score 12 runs to win in their second innings. There were few spectators present when play began, but the ground kept filling up as word spread around London of the startling cricket produced by the Australians. About 5000 were present at the finish, but a lot more did not get there in time. Spofforth had 10 for 20 (6 for 4 and 4 for 16) and Boyle 9 for 17 (3 for 14 and 6 for 3) in the match, with Allan, the other wicket-taker, 1 for 14.

This amazing victory was more important to Australian cricket on a tour that lacked a Test fixture than any of the international matches that have followed. The bowlers dismissed the MCC's best batsmen one after another as if they were novices. W.G. Grace was out second ball in each innings, seven others went first ball, and four to second balls. There was a feeling that the MCC's first innings' collapse, eight wickets for six runs, was a fluke, but by repeating their triumph in the second innings Australia established her reputation and completely destroyed the notion that English cricketers were the world's best. London's *Punch* magazine said:

The Australians came down like a wolf on the fold,
The Marylebone stars for a trifle were bowled.
Our Grace before dinner was very soon done,
And Grace after dinner did not get a run.

Big audiences watched whenever the Australians appeared for the rest of the tour. In one afternoon, Boyle and Spofforth had ensured all who invested in the tour a profit. They did not disappoint their new-found admirers either, dismissing the crack Yorkshire XI for 72 and 73 at Huddersfield in the next match to win by six wickets, and beating Surrey by five wickets at The Oval, where they had the opposition out for 107 and 80. More than 40,000 spectators attended the two days of the Surrey match and the two gatekeepers on duty could not cope with the crowds that finally spilled on to the field. Conway grabbed a top hat and collected entrance money in it, but most of the crowd still got in free.

An oil painting, now in the pavilion at Lord's, showing the first Australian team playing the Gentlemen of Kent and Surrey.

At Elland against a local Eighteen, Boyle dismissed seven batsmen in eight deliveries, which Frank Allan said was worth two hats or a full suit of clothes. Wickets fell so fast, batsmen could not pad up fast enough and spectators shouted 'send a man in', and then 'send in three or four—one's no use'. Not to be outdone by Boyle's first innings coup, Spofforth took 10 wickets in Elland's second innings, scattering the stumps eight times.

Although the matches against the odds were designed as social games, distinguished English batsmen kept bobbing up among the opposition. Players like Lord

Harris, the Hon. Ivo Bligh, Frank Penn and Charles Absolom from the Kent XI and James and Harry Phillips from the Sussex XI tried to get practice that would allow them to solve the problems the Australian bowlers presented. The Eighteen of Yeadon and District at Yeadon included the England players Edmund Peate and Richard Barlow, and the Eighteen of Longsight, a Manchester club, included G.F. Grace and Walter Gilbert, who had toured Australia with W.G. Grace's team in 1873–74.

The biggest setback of the tour came before the start of the match at Lord's against Middlesex. Charles Bannerman and Billy Midwinter were padded up ready to open Australia's innings when W.G. Grace burst into the dressing-room and grabbed Midwinter, who he said was contracted to play for his native Gloucestershire across the Thames at The Oval against Surrey. W.G. persuaded Midwinter to accompany him in a coach and although Conway, Gregory and Midwinter's lifelong friend Harry Boyle gave chase in another carriage, they were held back at The Oval gates where in a nasty scene W.G. called the Australians 'a damn lot of sneaks'.

Conway pointed out that Midwinter had promised to join the Australian team before they left home and because of this they did not bring another player. W.G. refused to let Midwinter rejoin the tourists and they returned to Lord's. Frank Allan replaced Midwinter and bowled Australia to victory by taking 6 for 76 in Middlesex's second innings, after Garrett had taken 7 for 38 in Middlesex's first innings. The Australians did not see the sad, confused Midwinter again on the tour.

For weeks heated letters were exchanged between the Australians and Gloucestershire until W.G. finally apologised for his rude words, which he said were induced by a report that the Australians had offered Midwinter more money to remain with them than Gloucestershire could pay. The fact was that nobody in the Australian team knew at that stage of the tour how much tour players would receive. When a match between Australia and Gloucestershire was played near the end of the tour, Midwinter did not play, saying he was unfit.

The 'kidnapping' of Midwinter left the Australians without a twelfth man, but they stubbornly refused to borrow fieldsmen from their opponents. Gregory knew he could win matches through his formidable bowling lineup, with Spofforth dismissing batsmen almost at will, and Boyle, Allan and Garrett strongly supporting him. Charles Bannerman, who had made a wonderful century in the first Test match in Melbourne the previous year, scored a chanceless 133, the first tour century among the Australians, at Leicester against Leicestershire. Left to score 209 to win, the Australians got off to an exciting start when Bannerman hit three fours in the first over. He hit 97 of his runs in boundaries with 23 fours and a five and a win that appeared unlikely at the start of the day was achieved with 65 minutes to spare, Australia winning by eight wickets.

The snowy-haired Tasmanian banker, George Bailey, later emulated Bannerman's feat by scoring 106 against Eighteen of Hastings at Hastings. This allowed Australia to defeat a spirited Hastings lineup by an innings and 47 runs, Billy Murdoch chiming in with 73 and Spofforth taking 12 for 39 in Hastings' second innings.

When Conway objected to the payment of £60 each to W.G. Grace and his relative W.G. Gilbert (who appeared in the Gentlemen XI that defeated Australia at Prince's), he was told they were always paid these sums just for appearing and regardless of their scoring. Later members of a Professional XI that opposed Australia at The Oval refused to play for their customary fee of £10. The Englishmen were resentful of the big gates they believed the Australians were grabbing and demanded £20 each. Conway refused to pay on the advice of the Surrey committee and a second-string side took the field against the Australians.

The match attracted large crowds. When the Professionals needed 19 runs with five wickets left, Australia appeared certain of defeat but Spofforth then took three wickets in an over to set up an Australian triumph by eight runs. A meeting of the Australian team then agreed to pay their opponents £20 apiece anyway, and handed Edward Barratt, the Surrey bowler, a bonus of £5 for taking all ten wickets in Australia's first innings.

The batting of the Bannerman brothers captivated English fans. Charles was a match-winner, driving fiercely and cutting with precision and at his best could score at better than one run a minute. His younger brother Alick (by three years) was one of Australia's original stonewallers, a batsmen of dour, stubborn defensive method who had not played in a first-class match when

Charles Bannerman.

he was hastily added to the side just before it sailed from Sydney. He wore down opposing attacks by seldom offering a stroke, just a dead bat, and this paved the way for the attacking shotmakers who followed to build a promising total. Paradoxically, he occasionally hit out to take three or four from the first over before settling down to half an hour of scoreless defence.

The most polished batsman in the first Australian team to England was Murdoch, who scored only 274 runs in 25 first-class innings, highest score 49, average 13.05. Murdoch was a man of great charm, a cheery-natured right-hand batsman of limited height who skipped down the pitch to drive with impressive footwork. He could cut superbly and found the wet wickets that prevailed on his first tour of England did not suit him. His mastery emerged with the sun.

Murdoch was born at Sandhurst, Victoria, home town to Midwinter and Boyle, but moved to Sydney before Sandhurst changed its name to Bendigo. He went to Sydney University to read law while living in the Balmain district where his brother Gilbert Murdoch became Mayor. Billy and Gilbert played cricket on the old Pigeon Ground, haunt of crack Sydney shotgunners, later known as Gladstone Park. He was good enough as a wicket-keeper for his mate Fred Spofforth to refuse to play in the First Test at Melbourne in March 1877 because Blackham was chosen as the keeper ahead of Murdoch. Faced with Blackham's dazzling success behind the stumps, Billy concentrated on his batting, a windfall for Australian cricket.

He remained a valuable member of the first Australian side despite his disappointments with the bat and his good humour helped his team-mates enjoy their successful financial venture. They returned home via America where they played six lucrative matches and survived umpires who applauded American boundaries and gave Australians out when they considered they had had their share of batting.

The tourists received a noisy welcome when they returned home in December. They had been away since April, and now dozens of launches and small boats accompanied their ship as it steamed up Sydney Harbour. Clapping crowds lined the wharves, where a band played, and they were driven in decorated coaches through streets lined with flags and flowers to the Town Hall, where the Mayor and his aldermen applauded each player as he went up the Town Hall steps. Similar welcomes greeted them in Melbourne and Adelaide where they played their last matches before disbanding.

All the players were paid £750 for the tour, according to reports at the time, enough to buy a fine home in a well-to-do suburb, but some years later it was disclosed that the players and manager Conway received £1040 apiece and that Conway had been paid a bonus on top of that because of his tireless work in negotiating matches. Dave Gregory, Charles Bannerman and Tom Garrett applied to the government departments that employed them for full pay for the time they had been away but the Colonial Secretary, Henry Parkes, rejected their applications. They had brought honour to the colony but he did not want to set a precedent, he told them.

AUSTRALIA IN ENGLAND 1880

Matches	First-class Results				Matches	All Matches			
	Won	Lost	Drawn	Tied		Won	Lost	Drawn	Tied
9	4	2	3	–	37	21	4	12	–

Date	Venue	Opponent	Results for Australians
May 13	Southampton	*XVIII of St Luke's Club	Won by an inns & 22 runs
May 17	Derby	Derbyshire	Won by 8 wkts
May 20	Longsight	*XVIII of Longsight	Won by 10 wkts
May 27	Rochdale	*XVIII of Rochdale	Won by an inns & 26 runs
May 31	Keighley	*XVIII of Keighley	Drawn
Jun 3	Burnley	*XVIII of Burnley	Won by an inns & 27 runs
Jun 7	Malton	*XVIII of Malton	Won by 4 wkts
Jun 10	Dewsbury	Yorkshire	Won by 5 wkts
Jun 14	Belfast	*XVIII of North of Ireland	Won by 9 wkts
Jun 17	Dublin	*XVIII of Dublin	Drawn
Jun 21	Birmingham	*XVIII of Birmingham	Won by an inns & 9 runs
Jun 24	Northampton	*XVIII of Northampton	Won by 8 wkts
Jun 28	Harrogate	*XVIII of Harrogate	Won by 10 wkts
Jly 1	Newcastle	*XVIII of Newcastle-on-Tyne	Drawn
Jly 5	Middlesbrough	*XVIII of Middlesbrough	Won by an inns & 26 runs
Jly 8	Manchester	*XVIII of Broughton	Drawn
Jly 12	Leicester	*Leicestershire	Drawn
Jly 16	Oldham	*XVIII of Werneth	Won by an inns & 21 runs
Jly 19	Crystal Palace	*XVIII of Crystal Palace	Won by 10 wkts
Jly 22	Huddersfield	Yorkshire	Drawn
Jly 26	Hull	*XVIII of Hull Town	Drawn
Jly 29	Crewe	*XVIII of Crewe	Drawn
Aug 2	Clifton	Gloucestershire	Won by 68 runs
Aug 5	Hunslet	*XVIII of Hunslet	Won by 8 wkts

The second Australian team to England which introduced Test cricket there in 1880, wore specially designed blazers that looked more like artists' smocks: *standing* G.E. Palmer, W.H. Moule, G. Bonnor, G. Alexander (manager), T. Groube; *seated* F.R. Spofforth, H.F. Boyle, W.L. Murdoch, P.S. McDonnell, A.C. Bannerman; *front* A.H. Jarvis, J. Slight, J.M. Blackham.

INTERNATIONAL TOURS

Date	Venue	Opponent	Results for Australians
Aug 9	Bradford	*XVIII of Bradford	Won by 10 wkts
Aug 12	Sunderland	*XVIII of Sunderland	Won by an inns & 38 runs
Aug 19	Scarborough	*XVIII of Scarborough	Lost by 90 runs
Aug 23	Yeadon	*XVIII of Yeadon	Won by an inns & 65 runs
Aug 26	Stockport	*XVIII of Stockport	Lost by 100 runs
Aug 30	Hastings	*XVIII of Hastings	Drawn
Sep 6	The Oval	ENGLAND (Only Test)	Lost by 5 wkts
Sep 10	Glasgow	*XVIII of Clydesdale CC	Drawn
Sep 13	Hove	Sussex	Drawn
Sep 16	Edinburgh	*Gentlemen of Scotland	Won by 6 wkts
Sep 20	Bradford	North of England	Drawn
Sep 23	Nottingham	Nottinghamshire	Lost by 1 wkt
Sep 27	Crystal Palace	Players of England	Won by 2 wkts

Player	State	M	Inn	NO	Runs	HS	50	100	Avrge	Ct/St	Overs	Mdns	Runs	Wkts	Avrge	5wi	10wm	Best
Alexander, G	VIC	9	12	1	130	40	–	–	11.81	7	121.0	58	162	5	32.40	–	–	2/18
Bannerman, AC	NSW	6	10	1	165	38	–	–	18.33	3	58.0	13	126	3	42.00	–	–	3/111
Blackham, JM	VIC	9	14	2	168	42*	–	–	14.00	5/6	–	–	–	–	–	–	–	–
Bonnor, GJ	VIC	9	14	1	123	35	–	–	9.46	5	–	–	–	–	–	–	–	–
Boyle, HF	VIC	9	14	3	157	69	1	–	17.44	13	422.1	197	493	31	15.90	3	2	6/70
Groube, TU	VIC	9	15	2	129	61	1	–	9.92	1	–	–	–	–	–	–	–	–
Jarvis, AH	SA	6	7	–	82	38	–	–	11.71	2/4	3.0	–	5	–	–	–	–	–
McDonnell, PS	NSW	9	15	1	391	79	1	–	27.92	4	7.0	3	20	–	–	–	–	–
Moule, WH	VIC	5	8	2	73	34	–	–	12.16	4	39.3	15	66	4	16.50	–	–	3/23
Murdoch, WL (Capt)	NSW	9	15	1	339	153*	–	1	24.21	10	–	–	–	–	–	–	–	–
Palmer, GE	VIC	9	11	5	81	23	–	–	13.50	2	594.3	278	772	66	11.69	9	1	7/44
Slight, J	VIC	3	5	–	41	21	–	–	8.20	1	–	–	–	–	–	–	–	–
Spofforth, FR	NSW	5	7	1	115	44	–	–	19.16	6	207.0	74	336	40	8.40	6	3	8/61

Dave Gregory declined to join the second Australian team to England in 1880. At 35, he believed he owed it to his wife to stay home and concentrate on his work with government accounts. He was to sire 16 children, 13 by his first wife, Mary Ann Hitchings, who died in 1890, and three by his second wife, Lily MacMillan, whom he married in 1892. When Lily died in 1910, he married Ellen Hillier. He was in turn Inspector of Accounts and Paymaster to the Treasury and lived in the Sydney suburbs of Paddington, Neutral Bay, and finally Turramurra, where he indulged his fondness for bushwalking. He died at 74, with all his teeth intact, carriage ramrod straight to the last, never having worn glasses in his life, the winner of two of the three Tests played while he was Australia's captain.

Harry Boyle took over from Conway as organiser of Australia's second England tour in 1880. Fixtures were difficult to arrange in England because of the Sydney riot in which Lord Harris and his players had been booed and forced to wrestle with demonstrators. Boyle found intense bitterness in England because of that riot and the English establishment's abhorrence of the idea of cricketers touring for profit. Lord Harris said he would try to set up matches in London providing the Australians declared they were appearing solely for pleasure and agreed to only accept their expenses. Boyle politely declined.

The Australians left home with the public expecting Boyle to be appointed captain. He was popular, known for his toughness and his habit of sitting out with the drivers on coach trips in snow or rain, and he was an important foil to Spofforth. He had taken 197 wickets at an average of only 7.43 in all games with his right-arm round-arm medium-pacers on the first tour and been the star of matches that shaped big cricket's future, but on the voyage to England the players by-passed him and elected the more affable Murdoch. The players knew they would need a good-humoured diplomat like Murdoch rather than a taciturn figure like Boyle in the difficult tour that lay ahead.

Murdoch had a very difficult job but after a match series confined mainly to the north of England, the Australians were granted fixtures in the south towards the end of their tour. Murdoch and Percy McDonnell both made more than 1000 runs in all games on the tour, Alick Bannerman was his customary rock-like self opening the innings, and the towering giant George Bonnor proved a crowd-pleasing long hitter. But the Victorian batsman James Slight, of whom heavy scoring was expected, had to have a fistula operation in London and played only six innings, forcing manager George Alexander to make frequent appearances.

England won the initial Test on English soil, despite Murdoch's 153 when the Australians were without their demon bowler Spofforth through injury. Murdoch's charm and witty speechmaking eased the bitterness the Sydney riot and the money-grabbing of the first Australian team had created. The second Australian team to England won 21 of their 37 matches (including non first-class), lost four, and left 12 unfinished. They lost the match that counted, but they earned their tour dividends by healing old wounds and assuring the future of international cricket.

AUSTRALIANS IN ENGLAND 1882 and 1884

1882 AUSTRALIANS

	First-class Results				All Matches			
Matches	Won	Lost	Drawn	Tied	Matches	Won	Lost	Drawn	Tied
33	18	4	11	–	38	23	4	11	–

Date	Venue	Opponent	Results for Australians
May 15	Oxford	Oxford University	Won by 9 wkts
May 17	Hove	Sussex	Won by an inns & 355 runs
May 22	Twickenham	The Orleans Club	Drawn
May 25	The Oval	Surrey	Won by 6 wkts
May 29	Cambridge	Cambridge University	Lost by 6 wkts
Jun 1	Manchester	Lancashire	Won by 4 wkts
Jun 5	Bradford	Yorkshire	Drawn
Jun 8	Nottingham	Nottinghamshire	Drawn
Jun 12	Derby	Derbyshire	Won by an inns & 109 runs
Jun 19	Sheffield	Yorkshire	Won by 6 wkts
Jun 22	The Oval	Gentlemen of England	Won by an inns & 1 run
Jun 26	Chichester	South of England	Won by an inns & 263 runs
Jun 29	Leicester	*Leicestershire	Won by 74 runs
Jly 3	Northampton	*Northamptonshire	Won by an inns & 80 runs
Jly 6	Lord's	Middlesex	Won by 8 wkts
Jly 10	Lord's	MCC	Drawn
Jly 13	Dewsbury	Yorkshire	Drawn
Jly 17	Bradford	Yorkshire	Won by 47 runs
Jly 20	Middlesborough	Yorkshire	Won by 7 wkts
Jly 24	Newcastle	*Northumberland	Won by an inns & 95 runs
Jly 27	Edinburgh	*Gentlemen of Scotland	Won by an inns & 18 runs
Jly 31	Liverpool	Liverpool & Districts	Drawn
Aug 3	Clifton	Gloucestershire	Won by an inns & 159 runs
Aug 7	Canterbury	Kent	Won by 7 wkts
Aug 10	The Oval	Players of England	Lost by an inns & 34 runs
Aug 14	Derby	England XI	Drawn
Aug 17	Portsmouth	Cambridge University	Lost by 20 runs
Aug 21	Taunton	Somerset	Won by an inns & 19 runs
Aug 25	Clifton	Gloucestershire	Drawn
Aug 28	The Oval	ENGLAND (Only Test)	Won by 7 runs
Aug 31	Tunbridge Wells	The United XI	Drawn
Sep 4	Nottingham	Nottinghamshire	Won by 184 runs
Sep 7	Scarborough	I Zingari	Drawn
Sep 11	Leeds	A Shaw's XI	Won by 89 runs
Sep 14	Manchester	North of England	Lost by 10 wkts
Sep 18	The Oval	A Shaw's XI	Drawn
Sep 21	Glasgow	*Scotland	Won by an inns & 23 runs
Sep 23	Harrogate	England XI	Won by 4 wkts

The 1882 Australians in England wore blazers of a better cut: *standing* H.H. Massie, G. Bonnor, S.P. Jones, F.R. Spofforth; *seated* C.W. Beal (manager), J.M. Blackham, G. Giffen, W.L. Murdoch (capt.), A.C. Bannerman, P.S. McDonnell; *front* G.E. Palmer, T.W. Garrett.

Player	State	M	Inn	NO	Runs	HS	50	100	Avrge	Ct/St	Overs	Mdns	Runs	Wkts	Avrge	5wi	10wm	Best
Bannerman, AC	NSW	31	52	2	1144	120*	5	1	22.88	27	67.0	26	112	4	28.00	–	–	2/20
Beal, CW	NSW	1	1	–	5	5	–	–	5.00	–	–	–	–	–	–	–	–	–
Blackham, JM	VIC	27	38	6	577	62	3	–	18.03	26/13	–	–	–	–	–	–	–	–
Bonnor, GJ	VIC	25	41	7	749	122*	2	1	22.03	23/1	–	–	–	–	–	–	–	–
Boyle, HF	VIC	27	42	13	283	39*	–	–	9.76	28	1101.2	488	1523	125	12.18	13	3	7/32
Garrett, TW	NSW	30	42	5	368	41	–	–	9.95	13	1167.3	474	1694	118	14.36	10	1	7/49
Giffen, G	SA	30	46	4	799	81	3	–	19.02	12	365.3	113	697	32	21.78	3	1	8/49
Horan, TP	VIC	28	46	4	986	141*	3	2	23.48	8	–	–	–	–	–	–	–	–
Jones, SP	NSW	18	28	1	336	59	2	–	12.44	18	40.0	10	85	1	85.00	–	–	1/22
Massie, HH	NSW	33	57	4	1360	206	6	1	25.66	16	6.0	1	18	–	–	–	–	–
McDonnell, PS	VIC	30	49	3	794	82	3	–	17.26	16	36.0	11	60	2	30.00	–	–	1/7
Murdoch, WL (Capt)	NSW	32	55	5	1582	286*	7	2	31.64	30/3	16.0	3	47	1	47.00	–	–	1/22
Palmer, GE	VIC	21	27	5	224	35	–	–	10.18	21	1032.3	440	1535	100	15.35	7	1	8/84
Spofforth, FR	NSW	30	41	11	263	37	–	–	8.77	17	1470.0	646	2079	157	13.24	16	4	9/51

Murdoch's outstanding leadership continued on the third and fourth Australian tours of England in 1882 and 1884. The 1882 team proved one of the best Australia ever sent to England, comparable with the 1905, 1921 and 1948 sides. They went ten weeks without defeat, after beating Oxford University by nine wickets in the opening match when Massie made 206 out of the 265 scored in three hours. They thrashed the strong Sussex combination by an innings and 355 runs, Palmer securing a hat-trick and Murdoch scoring 286 not out in a total of 643.

Their first setback came against Cambridge University, for whom C.T. Studd made a century and the Queenslander R.C. Ramsay took 12 wickets. A splendid sequence of 14 wins in 19 matches followed. The Gentlemen were beaten by an innings, George Giffen taking 8 for 49. Horan made centuries against Gloucestershire and a United XI, and against Cambridge Past and Present George Bonnor hit 66 out of the 79 scored in the half hour he was at the crease.

The only Test on the third team's itinerary was an historic thriller. Murdoch won the toss at The Oval on 28 August 1882, but his batsmen always struggled against the bowling of Peate and Barlow. Spofforth restricted England's lead to 38 by taking 7 for 46, but Australia managed only 122 at their second attempt, but even this was due to an heroic 55 from Massie in less than an hour.

W.G. Grace angered all the Australians when he ran out the 20-year-old Sam Jones after Jones grounded his bat inside the crease and then moved out along the pitch to do some gardening. Jones was given out when W.G. broke down the wicket, but W.G.'s lack of sportsmanship at a tense moment in the match irritated the Australians and their fans. Although England only required 85 to win in the final innings Spofforth kept telling his team-mates Australia could still win.

be cremated and shipped to Australia, and The Ashes legend was born. Spofforth, first bowler to take 14 wickets in a Test, conceded only one scoring stroke while dismissing four batsmen for two runs in his last 11 overs in the first innings, a spell that included the first Test hat-trick. In the second innings he bowled 10 maidens in his last 11 overs and took four wickets for two runs. One spectator died in the excitement and another gnawed the handle off his umbrella. Horan said men who could normally be relied on in a crisis walked past him towards the crease with ashen faces, trembling.

The rest of the tour was an anti-climax, but the tour was a triumph for manager Charles Beal and for

An artist's impression of spectators jumping the fence to cheer the 1882 Australians after they defeated England by seven runs at The Oval.

England reached 4 for 65 and suddenly a new phase entered the game. The batsmen could not get the ball past the fieldsmen. Spofforth bowled his break-backs at tremendous speed and Boyle was a model of accuracy at the other end. Blackham took every ball that passed the stumps with matchless skill and every fieldsman lifted his effort. A dozen overs passed without a run being scored as the intensity of the struggle pervaded the thousands of spectators.

By arrangement the Australians allowed England a single so that Spofforth could bowl at Lyttelton and after four further maidens Spofforth bowled him. With five wickets left, England needed only 19 runs at 5 for 66. Lucas struck Boyle for four and Spofforth immediately hit back dismissing Steel and Read in one over. Seven for 70 and 15 required. A two and three byes followed before Spofforth dismissed Lucas, who was replaced by C.T. Studd. Boyle then had Barnes caught off his glove by Murdoch. Peate, the last man in, swished at the first ball and got two from the shot, flukily played the next one, and then was bowled swinging at a delivery from Boyle.

Australia's seven-run win over a carefully chosen full-strength England XI inspired the mock obituary in the Sporting Times that the body of English cricket would

Murdoch, who at 30 was at the peak of his power. The 1882 team won 18 of its 33 first-class matches, lost 4, and played 11 draws. They played 38 matches in all for 23 wins, 4 losses and 11 draws.

Murdoch returned to England for his fourth trip and his third in a row as captain in 1884 after playing out the eventful series at home against the Hon. Ivo Bligh's seventh England touring team in 1882–83. This was another outstanding Australian team but with Garrett missing and Boyle past his best at 37 was thin on bowling. The team, chosen by manager George Alexander, showed its batting strength by scoring 619 in a warm-up match in Melbourne against The Rest of Australia, Murdoch contributing 279 not out, McDonnell 111. In the return match in Sydney, George Giffen took all ten wickets to bundle The Rest out for 113.

1884 AUSTRALIANS

First-class Results					All Matches				
Matches	Won	Lost	Drawn	Tied	Matches	Won	Lost	Drawn	Tied
31	17	7	7	–	32	18	7	7	–

Date	Venue	Opponent	Results for Australians
May 12	Uckfield	Lord Sheffield's XI	Won by an inns & 6 runs
May 15	Oxford	Oxford University	Lost by 7 wkts
May 19	The Oval	Surrey	Won by 8 wkts
May 22	Lord's	MCC	Lost by an inns & 115 runs
May 26	Birmingham	England XI	Won by 4 wkts
May 29	Lord's	Gentlemen of England	Lost by 4 wkts
Jun 2	Derby	Derbyshire	Won by an inns & 40 runs
Jun 5	Manchester	Lancashire	Drawn
Jun 9	Bradford	Yorkshire	Won by 3 wkts

Continued

Date	Venue	Opponent	Results for Australians
Jun 12	Nottingham	Nottinghamshire	Won by 3 wkts
Jun 16	Cambridge	Cambridge University	Won by an inns & 81 runs
Jun 19	Manchester	North of England	Lost by an inns & 22 runs
Jun 23	Liverpool	Liverpool & Districts	Won by 1 wkt
Jun 26	The Oval	Gentlemen of England	Won by 46 runs
Jun 30	Sheffield	Players of England	Won by 6 wkts
Jly 3	Huddersfield	England XI	Drawn
Jly 11	Manchester	ENGLAND (1st Test)	Drawn
Jly 14	Leicester	*Leicestershire	Won by 10 wkts
Jly 17	Lord's	Middlesex	Won by an inns & 29 runs
Jly 21	Lord's	ENGLAND (2nd Test)	Lost by an inns & 5 runs
Jly 24	Hove	Sussex	Drawn
Jly 31	The Oval	Players of England	Won by 9 wkts
Aug 4	Canterbury	Kent	Lost by 96 runs
Aug 7	Clifton	Gloucestershire	Drawn
Aug 11	The Oval	ENGLAND (3rd Test)	Drawn
Aug 18	Cheltenham	Gloucestershire	Won by an inns & 136 runs
Aug 21	Nottingham	Nottinghamshire	Drawn
Aug 25	Hove	Cambridge University	Won by 142 runs
Aug 28	Gravesend	South of England	Won by an inns & 107 runs
Sep 1	Nottingham	North of England	Lost by 170 runs
Sep 4	Scarborough	I Zingari	Won by 8 wkts
Sep 11	The Oval	South of England	Won by an inns & 5 runs

The 1884 Australian team to England: *back row* J.M. Blackham, H.J. Scott, umpire, W.E. Midwinter, P.S. McDonnell, W.H. Cooper; *seated* G. Giffen, H.F. Boyle, W.L. Murdoch (capt.), G. Bonnor, G.E. Palmer; *front* A.C. Bannerman, F.R. Spofforth.

Player	State	M	Inn	NO	Runs	HS	50	100	Avrge	Ct/St	Overs	Mdns	Runs	Wkts	Avrge	5wi	10wm	Best
Alexander, G	VIC	5	5	1	20	10*	–	–	5.00	4	18.0	7	24	2	12.00	–	–	2/24
Bannerman, AC	NSW	31	51	2	959	94	1	–	19.57	24	22.0	10	32	2	16.00	–	–	2/15
Blackham, JM	VIC	28	43	4	690	69	3	–	17.69	23/16	3.0	–	8	1	8.00	–	–	1/8
Bonnor, GJ	VIC	31	50	2	905	95*	4	–	18.85	31	95.0	25	229	6	38.16	–	–	3/34
Boyle, HF	VIC	27	37	14	243	48	–	–	10.57	28	719.1	283	1118	62	18.03	5	1	6/42
Cooper, WH	VIC	5	8	5	28	8*	–	–	9.33	3	130.0	26	309	6	51.50	–	–	3/79
Giffen, G	SA	31	50	1	1036	124	2	1	21.14	21	816.0	282	1588	81	19.60	6	2	7/69
McDonnell, PS	VIC	31	52	1	1190	103	5	1	23.33	22	10.0	4	27	–	–	–	–	–
Midwinter, WE	VIC	30	45	4	748	67	3	–	18.24	10	268.2	116	440	15	29.33	–	–	4/41
Murdoch, WL (Capt)	NSW	30	50	5	1377	211	6	2	30.60	22/4	5.0	–	25	–	–	–	–	–
Palmer, GE	VIC	30	46	10	483	68*	2	–	11.89	16	1214.3	446	2099	130	16.14	13	5	7/74
Scott, HJH	VIC	31	50	7	966	102	6	1	22.46	24	56.0	9	157	3	52.33	–	–	1/10
Spofforth, FR	NSW	31	45	6	464	54	1	–	11.89	16	1538.2	646	2564	201	12.75	24	11	8/62

Facing a schedule that included three Tests for the first time, the Australians lost three of their first six matches. The First Test at Old Trafford was drawn, with play washed out, England won the Second Test, the first ever staged at Lord's, after Murdoch fielded as a substitute for the injured W.G. Grace and caught team-mate 'Tup' Scott. Cambridge graduate and Lancashire star Alan G. Steele's 148 set up victory by an innings and five runs. The Third Test at The Oval was drawn after Murdoch scored the first double century, 211, in Test cricket.

The tour was notable for Lord Harris's action in refusing to play for England in the First Test because of the selection of noted 'chucker' John Crossland. Several counties followed his Lordship's lead and refused to play Lancashire if they picked Crossland, who finally was forced out of the Lancashire side when it was discovered he lacked the necessary residential qualification.

All 31 matches Australia played on the tour were 11-a-side for the first time. Australia was unlucky to lose the series after having by far the best of the two drawn Tests. The tour ended with the famous Smokers versus Non-Smokers match in which the top England and Australian players were in each side. Bonnor made 124 out of the 156 added while he was at the crease, hitting 16 fours and a six off Spofforth to show why Australians rated him their greatest hitter.

AUSTRALIA IN ENGLAND 1886

First-class Results					All Matches			
Matches	Won	Lost	Drawn	Tied	Matches	Won	Lost	Drawn	Tied
37	9	7	21	–	39	9	8	22	–

Date	Venue	Opponent	Results for Australians
May 13	Uckfield	Lord Sheffield's XI	Lost by 8 wkts
May 18	Nottingham	Nottinghamshire	Drawn
May 20	The Oval	Surrey	Lost by 3 wkts
May 24	Lord's	MCC	Abandoned
May 27	Oxford	Oxford University	Won by 25 runs
May 31	Manchester	North of England	Drawn
Jun 3	Lord's	Gentlemen of England	Won by 7 wkts
Jun 7	Derby	Derbyshire	Won by 6 wkts
Jun 10	Cambridge	Cambridge University	Drawn

The 1886 Australian team's England tour was sponsored by the Melbourne Cricket Club, who appointed Dr H.J.H. Scott as captain despite his modest record. *back row* J. McIlwraith, H. Trumble, A.H. Jarvis, W. Bruce, S.P. Jones, G.E. Palmer, F.R. Spofforth; *front* Ben Wardill (manager), J. Blackham, E. Evans, 'Tup' Scott, G. Bonnor, T.W. Garrett, G. Giffen.

INTERNATIONAL TOURS

Date	Venue	Opponent	Results for Australians
Jun 14	Manchester	Lancashire	Won by an inns & 12 runs
Jun 17	The Oval	Gentlemen of England	Drawn
Jun 21	Nottingham	Players of England	Drawn
Jun 24	Lord's	Middlesex	Won by 1 wkt
Jun 28	Chichester	Lord March's XI	Won by 8 wkts
Jly 2	Chiswick Park	CI Thornton's XI	Drawn
Jly 5	Manchester	ENGLAND (1st Test)	Lost by 4 wkts
Jly 8	Nottingham	Nottinghamshire	Drawn
Jly 12	Sheffield	Yorkshire	Won by 6 wkts
Jly 16	Liverpool	Liverpool & Districts	Drawn
Jly 19	Lord's	ENGLAND (2nd Test)	Lost by an inns & 106 runs
Jly 22	Huddersfield	Yorkshire	Drawn
Jly 26	Stoke-on-Trent	England XI	Drawn
Jly 29	The Oval	Surrey	Lost by an inns & 209 runs
Aug 2	Canterbury	Kent	Lost by 10 wkts
Aug 5	Clifton	Gloucestershire	Drawn
Aug 9	Edgbaston	*Warwickshire	Drawn
Aug 12	The Oval	ENGLAND (3rd Test)	Lost by an inns & 217 runs
Aug 16	Cheltenham	Gloucestershire	Won by 26 runs
Aug 19	Portsmouth	GN Wyatt's XI	Won by 7 wkts
Aug 23	Leyton	Cambridge University	Drawn
Aug 26	Hove	Sussex	Drawn
Aug 30	Gravesend	South of England	Drawn
Sep 2	Scarborough	Lord Londesborough's XI	Drawn
Sep 6	Bradford	Players of England	Drawn
Sep 9	Hove	South of England	Drawn
Sep 19	Lord's	England XI	Drawn
Sep 16	Hastings	South of England	Drawn
Sep 20	Skegness	*XVI of Skegness & Visitors	Lost by 9 wkts
Sep 24	Birmingham	England XI	Drawn
Sep 27	Harrogate	England XI	Drawn

Bulletin cartoonist Phil May showed the 1886 Australians arriving home, injuries still mending, a sick and sorry lot.

Player	State	M	Inn	NO	Runs	HS	50	100	Avrge	Ct/St	Overs	Mdns	Runs	Wkts	Avrge	5wi	10wm	Best
Blackham, JM	VIC	32	49	5	731	71	3	–	16.59	27/15	21.0	9	36	–	–	–	–	–
Bonnor, GJ	VIC	20	34	2	581	49	–	–	18.16	17	–	–	–	–	–	–	–	–
Bruce, W	VIC	33	47	3	704	106	2	1	16.00	27	329.0	112	620	13	47.69	–	–	3/27
Evans, E	NSW	28	40	15	336	74*	1	–	13.44	19	490.2	246	588	28	21.00	1	–	5/36
Garrett, TW	NSW	34	47	8	550	49*	–	–	14.10	11	1654.1	778	2221	123	18.06	5	1	6/22
Giffen, G	SA	35	61	8	1424	119	10	1	26.87	20	1673.2	710	2673	154	17.36	13	5	9/60
Hardie, JR		1	1	–	0	0	–	–	0.00	–	–	–	–	–	–	–	–	–
Hyslop, HH		1	1	–	1	1	–	–	1.00	1	–	–	–	–	–	–	–	–
Jarvis, AH	SA	33	50	6	780	96*	4	–	17.73	23/8	9.0	2	24	1	24.00	–	–	1/9
Jones, SP	NSW	35	62	2	1497	151	8	2	24.95	22	149.0	52	297	7	42.43	–	–	2/53
McIlwraith, J	VIC	27	37	5	520	62*	1	–	16.25	13	–	–	–	–	–	–	–	–
Palmer, GE	VIC	33	54	4	972	94	5	–	19.44	30	1393.0	552	2306	101	22.83	6	1	7/84
Pope, RJ	NSW	4	6	4	30	12	–	–	15.00	3	–	–	–	–	–	–	–	–
Scott, HJH (Capt)	VIC	36	63	5	1278	123	6	1	22.03	22	9.0	4	12	1	12.00	–	–	1/2
Spofforth, FR	NSW	20	29	8	163	37*	–	–	7.76	8	930.3	372	1528	89	17.17	7	2	9/18
Trumble, JW	VIC	34	51	8	823	56*	1	–	19.14	17	483.3	182	803	30	26.77	2	1	6/90
Wardill, BJ		1	1	–	17	17	–	–	17.00	1	–	–	–	–	–	–	–	–

The Melbourne Cricket Club paid all expenses for Australia's 1886 England tour and appointed a popular club member, Dr Henry James Herbert Scott as captain. All four Australian teams that preceded it were sponsored by the players, assisted by private entrepreneurs. Murdoch, Boyle, McDonnell and Alick Bannerman were unavailable and the side included four newcomers to England in Edwin Evans, Billy Bruce, John Trumble and John McIlwraith.

Scott and manager Ben Wardill, secretary of the Melbourne Club, soon had problems settling disputes between the players. Scott, nicknamed 'Tup' because of his liking for sightseeing tuppeny (twopenny) bus rides round London, found his batting affected by the team's quarrelling and lacked the firmness demanded to discipline the trouble-makers. His team played bravely in the First Test before England won by four wickets but were overwhelmed in the next two Tests. Loss of Spofforth with an injured hand badly wounded Australia, and England's leading batsmen had a picnic. Arthur Shrewsbury made 164 in the Second Test, and W.G. Grace hit 170 in the Third to pave the way to England's win by an innings.

The team won only nine of their 37 matches, lost 7 and left 21 drawn, but the Australians attracted large crowds which made the tour financially lucrative. George Giffen was a major success, heading both batting (1424 runs at 26.82) and bowling (154 wickets at 17.36) averages. Sam Jones played the innings of his life with 151 against The Gentlemen at The Oval. Australians who watched this knock presented him with a gold watch as a reward.

The Australians were surprised that the Hon. Ivo Bligh, who had led England in the previous series in Australia, did not appear in the Tests. Ivo had played a big part in fostering The Ashes legend and had married an Australian girl, installing her in the family mansion at Cobham in Kent where he set about restoring the family fortunes, an act he had already achieved for English cricket in Australia.

AUSTRALIA IN ENGLAND 1888

First-class Results					All Matches				
Matches	Won	Lost	Drawn	Tied	Matches	Won	Lost	Drawn	Tied
37	17	13	7	–	40	19	14	7	–

Date	Venue	Opponent	Results for Australians
May 7	Surrey	CI Thornton's XI	Won by 6 wkts
May 11	Edgbaston	*Warwickshire	Won by an inns & 150 runs
May 14	The Oval	Surrey	Won by an inns & 154 runs
May 17	Oxford	Oxford University	Won by an inns & 19 runs
May 21	Sheffield	Yorkshire	Won by an inns & 64 runs
May 24	Manchester	Lancashire	Lost by 23 runs
May 28	Lord's	Gentlemen of England	Drawn
May 31	The Oval	Players of England	Lost by 10 wkts
Jun 4	Nottingham	Nottinghamshire	Lost by 10 wkts
Jun 7	Cambridge	Cambridge University	Drawn
Jun 11	Leyton	Oxford University	Won by 74 runs
Jun 14	Lord's	Middlesex	Won by 8 wkts
Jun 18	Birmingham	England XI	Won by 10 wkts
Jun 21	Lord's	MCC	Won by 14 runs
Jun 25	Bradford	Yorkshire	Drawn
Jun 28	Manchester	North of England	Won by 5 wkts
Jly 3	Liverpool	Liverpool & Districts	Won by 130 runs
Jly 5	Leicester	*Leicestershire	Lost by 20 runs
Jly 9	Derby	*Derbyshire	Won by an inns & 79 runs
Jly 12	Stoke-on-trent	England XI	Won by an inns & 135 runs
Jly 16	Lord's	ENGLAND (1st Test)	Won by 61 runs
Jly 19	Hove	Sussex	Lost by 58 runs
Jly 23	Leyton	Cambridge University	Drawn
Jly 26	Huddersfield	Yorkshire	Drawn
Jly 30	The Oval	Surrey	Drawn
Aug 3	Hastings	England XI	Won by an inns & 27 runs
Aug 6	Canterbury	Kent	Won by 81 runs
Aug 9	Clifton	Gloucestershire	Lost by 257 runs
Aug 13	The Oval	ENGLAND (2nd Test)	Lost by an inns & 137 runs
Aug 16	Nottingham	Nottinghamshire	Lost by an inns & 199 runs
Aug 20	Cheltenham	Gloucestershire	Lost by 8 wkts
Aug 23	Crystal Palace	England XI	Lost by 78 runs
Aug 27	Portsmouth	Oxford & Cambridge University	Drawn
Aug 30	Manchester	ENGLAND (3rd Test)	Lost by an inns & 21 runs
Sep 3	Harrogate	England XI	Won by 56 runs
Sep 6	Scarborough	Lord Londesborough's XI	Lost by 155 runs
Sep 10	Holbeck	A Shrewsbury's XI	Lost by 4 wkts
Sep 13	Manchester	A Shrewsbury's XI	Lost by 9 wkts
Sep 17	Hastings	South of England	Won by 9 wkts
Sep 20	The Oval	Surrey	Won by 34 runs

Percy McDonnell, the only Greek scholar to captain Australia, with the 1888 Australians, the sixth to tour England: *back row* J.M. Blackham, J. Worrall, A.H. Jarvis, G.H.S. Trott, C.T.B. Turner, H.F. Boyle; *seated* C.W. Beal (manager), A.C. Bannerman, P.S. McDonnell, G. Bonnor, J.J. Ferris, J.D. Edwards. They had to call on expatriate Australian Sammy Woods to help them in the Tests.

Player	State	M	Inn	NO	Runs	HS	50	100	Avrge	Ct/St	Overs	Mdns	Runs	Wkts	Avrge	5wi	10wm	Best
Bannerman, AC	NSW	33	59	7	887	93*	3	–	17.06	28	53.0	20	117	3	39.00	–	–	3/103
Blackham, JM	VIC	35	55	1	447	37	–	–	8.28	26/20	12.0	4	26	1	26.00	–	–	1/14
Bonnor, GJ	NSW	36	60	3	1155	119	5	2	20.26	32	31.0	12	66	2	33.00	–	–	1/26
Boyle, HF	VIC	17	25	8	101	22	–	–	5.94	10	126.1	64	158	10	15.80	–	–	2/18
Edwards, JD	VIC	33	52	11	484	50*	1	–	11.80	8	9.0	–	40	1	40.00	–	–	1/23
Ferris, JJ	NSW	37	57	16	489	39	–	–	11.93	16	2080.1	937	2934	199	14.74	17	3	8/41
Jarvis, AH	SA	31	48	3	569	39	–	–	12.64	14/13	–	–	–	–	–	–	–	–
Jones, SP	NSW	12	20	2	303	61	1	–	16.83	3	68.3	19	134	10	13.40	–	–	4/19
Lyons, JJ	SA	24	39	6	466	84	1	–	14.12	9	229.0	54	514	18	28.56	–	–	4/97
McDonnell, PS (Capt)	NSW	35	58	1	1331	105	6	1	23.35	14	8.0	2	28	–	–	–	–	–
Trott, GHS	VIC	36	61	2	1081	73	5	–	18.32	25	479.0	138	1111	43	25.84	–	–	4/28
Turner, CTB	NSW	36	56	2	789	103	1	1	14.61	17	2427.2	1127	3307	283	11.69	31	12	9/15
Woods, SMJ		6	10	–	54	18	–	–	5.40	2	158.0	59	298	11	27.09	–	–	4/44
Worrall, J	VIC	36	57	10	517	46	–	–	11.00	17	253.0	98	449	24	18.71	1	–	5/20

The weaknesses in Percy McDonnell's sixth Australian team to England were apparent before they left home. They lost all three matches before they sailed but McDonnell's reputation as a batsman of rare fighting quality gave fans hope that he could revive the side. Only Boyle, who was far past his best, remained of the bowlers who had established Australia's international reputation, and a tremendous work-load fell on Turner and Ferris. There was nobody else who could bowl straight or to a length, with McDonnell's sole choice of variation resting on Harry Trott's leg-breaks.

Turner took 314 wickets in all matches on the tour with his right-arm fast-medium off-breaks, favouring an open, front-on delivery stride from which he made the ball turn sharply if pitches suited him. Ferris, a former Sydney bank clerk, opened the bowling with left-arm medium pace swinging deliveries, and when the shine left the ball, bowled accurate spinners that enabled him to take 220 wickets in all games. Harry Trott's subtle but sometimes wayward spinners accounted for some quality batsmen but his all up bag of 48 wickets was a long way behind those of Turner and Ferris.

Australia won the First Test but lost the other two Tests by an innings, with the batsmen lacking the ability to adapt to English conditions. Claude Beale, returning for his second tour as manager, again gave an impressive show of tact and diplomacy and managed to conceal the extent of Sam Jones' illness. Had it become known that Jones had smallpox, the entire tour would have been in jeopardy. McDonnell, Bonnor and Trott did well to score more than 1000 runs in all their games on the 40-match tour, 19 of which were won, 14 lost and 7 drawn, and Alick Bannerman was a persistent frustration to opposing bowlers with stonewalling that brought him 943 runs, top score 93 not out.

AUSTRALIA IN ENGLAND 1890

First-class Results					All Matches				
Matches	Won	Lost	Drawn	Tied	Matches	Won	Lost	Drawn	Tied
34	10	16	8	–	38	13	16	9	–

Date	Venue	Opponent	Results for Australians
May 8	Sheffield Park	Lord Sheffield's XI	Won by an inns & 34 runs
May 13	Edgbaston	*Warwickshire	Won by 132 runs
May 15	Wiltshire	WH Laverton's XI	Lost by 181 runs
May 20	Oxford	Oxford University	Won by an inns & 61 runs
May 22	The Oval	Surrey	Won by 8 wkts
May 26	Sheffield	Yorkshire	Lost by 7 wkts
May 29	Manchester	Lancashire	Won by an inns & 155 runs
Jun 2	Lord's	MCC	Lost by 7 wkts
Jun 5	Cambridge	Cambridge University	Drawn
Jun 9	Lord's	Middlesex	Drawn
Jun 12	Nottingham	Nottinghamshire	Lost by an inns & 26 runs
Jun 16	The Oval	South of England	Lost by 97 runs
Jun 19	Lord's	Players of England	Lost by an inns & 263 runs
Jun 23	Bradford	Yorkshire	Lost by 8 wkts
Jun 26	Manchester	North of England	Drawn
Jun 30	Derby	*Derbyshire	Drawn
Jly 3	Stoke-on-Trent	A Staffordshire's XI	Won by 88 runs
Jly 7	Leicester	*Leicestershire	Won by an inns & 64 runs
Jly 10	Perth	Gloucestershire	Drawn
Jly 14	Sheffield	Players of England	Lost by 9 wkts
Jly 17	The Oval	Surrey	Drawn
Jly 21	Lord's	ENGLAND (1st Test)	Lost by 7 wkts
Jly 24	Hove	Sussex	Won by an inns & 45 runs
Jly 28	Maidstone	Kent	Won by 9 wkts
Jly 31	Barnes	The Lyric Club	Lost by 96 runs
Aug 4	Canterbury	Kent	Lost by 108 runs
Aug 7	Leyton	Cambridge & Oxford University	Drawn
Aug 11	The Oval	ENGLAND (2nd Test)	Lost by 2 wkts
Aug 14	Portsmouth	Oxford & Cambridge University	Drawn
Aug 18	Nottingham	Nottinghamshire	Lost by 20 runs
Aug 21	Cheltenham	Gloucestershire	Won by 8 wkts
Aug 25	Manchester	ENGLAND (3rd Test)	Abandoned
Aug 29	Stoke-on-Trent	*Staffordshire	Won by an inns & 28 runs
Sep 1	Leeds	North of England	Won by 160 runs
Sep 4	Scarborough	Lord Londesborough's XI	Won by 8 runs
Sep 8	Lord's	MCC	Lost by 4 wkts
Sep 11	East Molesey	Hurst Park Club	Lost by 34 runs
Sep 15	Hastings	South of England	Lost by 10 wkts
Sep 18	Manchester	England XI	Drawn

Murdoch was persuaded to come out of retirement to lead this Australia team to England in 1890: *back row* J.M. Blackham, H. Trumble, S.P. Jones, J.E. Barrett, F.H. Walters, H.F. Boyle (manager); *seated* P.S. Charlton, J.J. Ferris, W.L. Murdoch, J.J. Lyons, C.T.B. Turner, G.H.S. Trott; *front* K.E. Burn, S.E. Gregory.

Murdoch was persuaded to come out of retirement and leave his law practice in Cootamundra to captain the seventh Australians, but no amount of persuasion could coax George Giffen to temporarily forsake his duties as an Adelaide postman unless his brother Walter accompanied the side. Unfortunately, Walter was below the standard required. Bonnor, Alick Bannerman, Harry Moses, and Robert McLeod, one of a remarkable family

Player	State	M	Inn	NO	Runs	HS	50	100	Avrge	Ct/St	Overs	Mdns	Runs	Wkts	Avrge	5wi	10wm	Best
Barrett, JE	VIC	32	58	7	1227	97	9	–	24.06	9	38.0	15	89	6	14.83	1	–	6/68
Blackham, JM	VIC	28	47	5	655	75	3	–	15.60	38/27	16.0	4	37	–	–	–	–	–
Boyle, HF	VIC	1	1	–	3	3	–	–	3.00	–	10.0	4	17	–	–	–	–	–
Burn, EJK	TAS	21	37	4	344	35*	–	–	10.42	15								
Charlton, PC	NSW	26	43	9	450	41	–	–	13.24	23	395.3	144	772	42	18.38	3	–	5/27
Ferris, JJ	NSW	30	50	13	613	54*	1	–	16.57	15	1545.2	628	2657	186	14.28	15	5	7/16
Gregory, SE	NSW	33	55	13	501	59*	2	–	11.93	20	3.0	–	21	–	–	–	–	–
Jones, SP	NSW	19	30	1	328	98	1	–	11.31	4	2.0	–	16	–	–	–	–	–
Lyons, JJ	SA	33	59	1	1029	99	5	–	17.74	9	404.4	112	979	43	22.77	5	–	5/30
Murdoch, WL (Capt)	NSW	33	59	2	1394	158*	6	2	24.46	21/2	–	–	–	–	–	–	–	–
Pope, RJ	NSW	3	4	–	6	6	–	–	1.50	4	2.0	–	19	–	–	–	–	–
Trott, GHS	VIC	33	59	1	1211	186	2	2	20.88	30	188.0	34	578	20	28.90	–	–	3/20
Trumble, H	VIC	28	44	10	288	34*	–	–	8.47	50	483.4	158	1131	52	21.75	2	–	5/77
Turner, CTB	NSW	31	54	–	854	59	2	–	15.81	22	1500.1	652	2526	178	14.19	16	4	7/23
Walters, FH	VIC	23	38	3	351	53*	1	–	10.03	15	–	–	–	–	–	–	–	–

of seven cricketing brothers, all declined to tour. This denied Australians the chance to assess the quality of Moses' left-hand batting, which W.G. Grace and others said needed to be tested in England.

This was the team for which the senior players picked Tasmanian Ken Burn as Blackham's wicket-keeping understudy, only to find when Burn joined the team in Adelaide on its way to England that he had never kept wicket in his life. Of the newcomers, Burn, Syd Gregory, and Francis Walters were failures, Ferris and Turner again saving Australia's prestige by taking 215 wickets each in all matches. Hugh Trumble, the next highest wicket-taker, took 53 wickets. Gregory and Trumble were to give Australia exceptional service as a result of this experience, but Walters failed to develop as hoped.

Dr John Barrett, who played for Victoria at 17 in 1883, finished second to Murdoch on the tour first-class batting averages with 1227 runs. His highest scores were 97 and 73 not out against an England XI at Manchester, and 96 against a combined Oxford and Cambridge XI. He became the first Australian to bat through an innings with 67 not out in the Lord's Test. He cost Australia The Oval Test, however, when he threw wildly for overthrows with both batsmen stranded in mid-pitch. A calm throw could have run out either batsman, but England won by two wickets. The versatile Sammy Woods, the Australian pace bowler living in England, had to be co-opted to help the team, but failed to take the wickets expected of him in the Tests. 'Roley' Pope, who had played for Australia in 1885 in Melbourne and became a favoured 'team traveller', played in three matches when injuries depleted the side without success.

AUSTRALIA IN ENGLAND 1893

First-class Results					All Matches				
Matches	Won	Lost	Drawn	Tied	Matches	Won	Lost	Drawn	Tied
31	14	10	7	–	36	18	10	8	–

Date	Venue	Opponent	Results for Australians
May 8	Uckfield	Lord Sheffield's XI	Lost by 8 wkts
May 11	Birmingham	*Warwickshire	Won by 10 wkts
May 15	Perth	Gloucestershire	Drawn
May 18	Lord's	MCC	Drawn
May 22	Sheffield	Yorkshire	Lost by 64 runs
May 25	Manchester	Lancashire	Won by an inns & 14 runs
May 29	The Oval	Surrey	Lost by 58 runs
Jun 1	Oxford	Oxford University	Won by 19 runs
Jun 5	Bradford	Yorkshire	Drawn
Jun 8	Cambridge	Cambridge University	Won by 117 runs
Jun 12	Lord's	MCC	Lost by 7 wkts
Jun 15	The Oval	South of England	Lost by 10 wkts
Jun 19	Lord's	Players of England	Won by 6 wkts
Jun 22	Gravesend	Kent	Won by 1 run
Jun 26	Nottingham	A Shrewsbury's XI	Lost by an inns & 153 runs
Jun 29	Manchester	North of England	Won by 3 wkts
Jly 3	Derby	*Derbyshire	Won by an inns & 71 runs
Jly 6	Leicester	*Leicestershire	Won by an inns & 51 runs
Jly 10	Leeds	Yorkshire	Won by 145 runs
Jly 13	Hove	Sussex	Won by 8 wkts
Jly 17	Lord's	ENGLAND (1st Test)	Drawn
Jly 20	Taunton	Somerset	Won by 6 wkts
Jly 24	Lord's	Middlesex	Won by 390 runs
Jly 27	The Oval	Surrey	Lost by 2 wkts
Jly 31	Portsmouth	Oxford & Cambridge University	Drawn
Aug 3	Leyton	*Essex	Drawn
Aug 7	Canterbury	Kent	Lost by 36 runs
Aug 10	Liverpool	Liverpool & Districts	Won by an inns & 34 runs
Aug 14	The Oval	ENGLAND (1st Test)	Lost by an inns & 43 runs
Aug 17	Cheltenham	Gloucestershire	Won by 8 wkts
Aug 21	Birmingham	Second Class Counties	Won by 4 wkts
Aug 24	Manchester	ENGLAND (3rd Test)	Drawn
Aug 28	Blackpool	*XVI of Blackpool & District	Won by 79 runs
Aug 31	Nottingham	Nottinghamshire	Won by an inns & 154 runs
Sep 4	Scarborough	Cl Thornton's XI	Drawn
Sep 7	Hastings	South of England	Lost by 6 wkts

The eighth Australian team, with plenty of old faces, that toured England in 1893 under Jack Blackham, still the only wicket-keeper to lead an Australian team on an overseas tour: *back row* R.W. McLeod, J.J. Lyons, H. Trumble, W. Bruce, G.H.S. Trott; *middle* A. Coningham, G. Giffen, J. Blackham, C.T.B. Turner, W. Giffen; *front* A.H. Jarvis, A.C. Bannerman, S.E. Gregory, H. Graham.

Player	State	M	Inn	NO	Runs	HS	50	100	Avrge	Ct/St	Overs	Mdns	Runs	Wkts	Avrge	5wi	10wm	Best
Bannerman, AC	NSW	28	47	1	1061	133	4	1	23.07	7	–	–	–	–	–	–	–	–
Blackham, JM (Capt)	VIC	20	31	12	283	42	–	–	15.42	26/16	–	–	–	–	–	–	–	–
Bruce, W	VIC	31	53	4	1227	191	6	1	25.04	24	288.4	79	718	33	21.76	1	–	6/29
Coningham, A	NSW	12	18	2	213	46	–	–	13.31	6	208.1	65	497	27	18.41	2	–	6/41
Giffen, G	SA	29	50	1	1133	180	2	2	23.12	28	906.4	257	2247	118	19.04	12	2	8/98

▶

Player	State	M	Inn	NO	Runs	HS	50	100	Avrge	Ct/St	Overs	Mdns	Runs	Wkts	Avrge	5wi	10wm	Best
Giffen, WF	SA	10	15	1	170	62	1	–	12.14	3	–	–	–	–	–	–	–	–
Graham, H	VIC	29	48	3	1119	107	5	1	24.87	25	4.0	–	22	–	–	–	–	–
Gregory, SE	NSW	29	48	4	1022	112	7	1	23.23	22	9.0	1	40	1	40.00	–	–	1/17
Jarvis, AH	SA	11	16	4	47	10	–	–	3.92	11/8	–	–	–	–	–	–	–	–
Lyons, JJ	SA	29	50	1	1377	149	8	1	28.10	14	17.0	3	61	–	–	–	–	–
McLeod, RW	VIC	27	44	11	593	47*	–	–	17.97	15	510.1	197	1031	43	23.98	2	1	7/24
Trott, GHS	VIC	31	54	2	1269	145	7	1	24.40	15	296.3	64	907	38	23.87	2	–	5/27
Trumble, H	VIC	29	46	11	774	105	2	1	22.11	52	834.1	274	1794	108	16.61	9	3	7/31
Turner, CTB	NSW	26	40	4	475	66	1	–	13.19	9	1079.0	413	2018	148	13.64	16	5	8/95

Blackham's long experience and his vigorous leadership of Victoria won him a unique place in Australia's cricket history as the only keeper to take a touring team overseas when he captained the 1893 party. He proved a highly temperamental captain whose torment in a crisis affected his entire team. He disappeared into the corners of the dressing-room, towel over his head, when matches got close or took a ride in a horse-drawn cab if the strain became unbearable. He could not be blamed for failures due largely to the lack of a pace bowler on pitches that were becoming increasingly fast. Turner was not the force he had been on previous tours, George Giffen probably had left it too late to show his best on tour at 32, Hugh Trumble was still developing, and Harry Trott's leg-breaks remained costly even if they secured 60 wickets in all matches.

Two of the three Tests were narrowly saved and ended in draws. The other was lost to a fine England team, which like most of the other leading teams Australia encountered was well served by fast bowlers. Lyons, Graham, Trott, Bannerman, Giffen, Bruce, and Syd Gregory all made 1000 runs and scored centuries. At Oxford, against Oxford and Cambridge Past and Present, Australia scored 843, then a world record total for a first-class match. On the way home, a disappointing tour culminated with defeat by The Gentlemen of Philadelphia.

AUSTRALIA IN ENGLAND 1896

	First-class Results					All Matches			
Matches	Won	Lost	Drawn	Tied	Matches	Won	Lost	Drawn	Tied
34	20	6	8	–	34	20	6	8	–

Date	Venue	Opponent	Results for Australians
May 11	Uckfield	Lord Sheffield's XI	Drawn
May 14	Leyton	Essex	Won by 7 wkts
May 18	Crystal Palace	CE De Trafford's XI	Won by an inns & 221 runs
May 21	Eastbourne	South of England	Won by an inns & 8 runs
May 25	Sheffield	Yorkshire	Drawn
May 28	Manchester	Lancashire	Won by 154 runs
Jun 1	Oxford	Oxford University	Won by 7 wkts
Jun 4	Perth	Gloucestershire	Won by an inns & 91 runs
Jun 8	Wembly Park	Wembly Park XI	Won by 135 runs
Jun 11	Lord's	MCC	Lost by an inns & 18 runs
Jun 15	Leeds	Yorkshire	Drawn
Jun 18	Birmingham	Midlands Counties XI	Lost by 4 wkts
Jun 22	Lord's	ENGLAND (1st Test)	Lost by 6 wkts
Jun 25	Nottingham	Nottinghamshire	Won by 6 wkts
Jun 29	Bradford	Yorkshire	Won by 140 runs
Jly 2	Manchester	North of England	Won by 42 runs
Jly 6	Southampton	Hampshire	Won by an inns & 125 runs
Jly 9	Leyton	Players of England	Won by an inns & 137 runs
Jly 13	Leicester	Leicestershire	Won by an inns & 317 runs
Jly 16	Manchester	ENGLAND (2nd Test)	Won by 3 wkts
Jly 20	Derby	Derbyshire	Drawn
Jly 23	Lord's	MCC	Drawn
Jly 27	The Oval	Surrey	Won by 7 wkts
Jly 30	Bexhill	Earl de La Warr's XI	Lost by 4 wkts
Aug 3	Birmingham	Warwickshire	Won by an inns & 60 runs
Aug 6	Canterbury	Kent	Won by 176 runs
Aug 10	The Oval	ENGLAND (3rd Test)	Lost by 66 runs
Aug 13	Hove	Sussex	Won by 6 wkts
Aug 17	The Oval	Surrey	Drawn
Aug 20	Cheltenham	Gloucestershire	Won by an inns & 54 runs
Aug 24	Taunton	Somerset	Drawn
Aug 27	Liverpool	Lancashire	Won by 217 runs
Aug 31	Scarborough	CI Thornton's XI	Lost by an inns & 38 runs
Sep 3	Hastings	South of England	Drawn

Harry Trott always looked mournful but his players rated him the shrewdest of all Australian captains. This was the team he led in England in 1896: *back row* F. Lemmon (scorer), A.E. Johns, E.J. Eady, J. Darling, H. Donnan, J. McKibbin, H. Graham, H. Musgrove (manager); *centre* H. Trumble, E. Jones, G.H.S. Trott, G. Giffen, F.A. Iredale; *front* J.J. Kelly, S.E. Gregory, C. Hill.

Player	State	M	Inn	NO	Runs	HS	50	100	Avrge	Ct/St	Overs	Mdns	Runs	Wkts	Avrge	5wi	10wm	Best
Darling, J	SA	32	53	1	1555	194	6	3	29.90	13	7.0	2	28	1	28.00	–	–	1/5
Donnan, H	NSW	28	44	1	1009	167	5	1	23.46	12	100.0	35	231	5	46.20	–	–	2/56
Eady, CJ	TAS	17	24	3	290	42	–	–	13.81	18	201.0	74	408	16	25.50	–	–	4/6
Giffen, G	SA	32	49	1	1208	130	6	2	25.17	20	865.2	219	2257	117	19.29	7	1	8/30
Graham, H	VIC	20	32	2	547	96	4	–	18.23	10	4.0	2	19	1	19.00	–	–	1/19
Gregory, SE	NSW	31	48	2	1464	154	10	3	31.82	11	–	–	–	–	–	–	–	–
Hill, C	SA	31	46	3	1196	130	5	2	27.81	14/1	2.0	–	4	–	–	–	–	–
Iredale, FA	NSW	32	51	3	1328	171	4	4	27.67	36	5.0	–	18	–	–	–	–	–
Johns, AE	VIC	10	12	6	84	31*	–	–	14.00	17/7	–	–	–	–	–	–	–	–
Jones, E	SA	29	41	6	482	40	–	–	13.77	18	868.3	282	1940	121	16.03	7	1	8/39
Kelly, JJ	NSW	25	38	8	490	45	–	–	16.33	37/22	–	–	–	–	–	–	–	–
McKibbin, TR	NSW	22	34	11	175	28*	–	–	7.61	13	647.1	198	1441	101	14.27	7	3	7/11
Musgrove, HA	VIC	2	3	–	4	2	–	–	1.33	2	4.0	–	18	–	–	–	–	–
Trott, GHS (Capt)	VIC	33	54	5	1297	143	8	3	26.47	20	339.4	66	928	44	21.09	1	–	5/66
Trumble, H	VIC	30	43	11	628	45*	–	–	19.63	39	1140.1	380	2340	148	15.81	11	5	7/67

Lugubrious George Henry Stevens ('Harry') Trott defied forecasts by captaining the 1896 team with such flair team-mates like Hugh Trumble later rated him among Australia's greatest captains. George Giffen said Harry was the best allrounder cricketer Victoria ever sent to England. Clem Hill ranked Harry the best tactician in his experience of big cricket. Sadly historians have not been kind to Harry, who remains virtually neglected when discussions occur on our finest leaders. The Trotts, in fact, have a sad history, with two of the eight children born in Collingwood, both gifted players, meeting untimely deaths, Harry in a mental asylum at 51, Albert by shooting himself in a London boarding house at 41. Albert's big-hitting is part of cricket legend but Harry's fine achievement in winning five of the eight Tests in which he was Australia's captain is forgotten.

He was a cricketer of adaptability who tailored his performance with bat or ball to suit prevailing conditions, one of the few Australians who excelled on wet or muddy pitches. His carefully considered handling of newcomers Clem Hill, Joe Darling and Tom McKibbin boosted their careers and allowed Trumble to achieve his always rich potential. Trott's big advantage compared with previous captains was the fearsome bowling of Ernie Jones, a tearaway prone to inaccuracy, whose pace had even great batsmen backing away. Trott's cunning with the temperamental Jones brought Jones 121 wickets on the tour at 16.03 apiece. Jones' bag was inferior to Trumble's 148 tour wickets at 15.81 but he gave Australia's bowling a hostility it had not had since the Spofforth era.

The team started well, winning seven of their first nine matches, with two drawn. Lack of experience in their batting was then exposed when they were heavily defeated by MCC at Lord's, where they collapsed for 18 in their first innings, when the Leicestershire medium-pacer Dick Pougher took 5 for 0 from three overs and Jack Hearn took 4 for 4, with the first three Australian batsmen scoring the runs and the rest all falling for ducks.

The Tests were tremendous tussles, England winning the first by dismissing Australia for 53 in the first innings when Tom Richardson took 6 for 39, hitting the stumps each time. Trott and Syd Gregory put on 221 in 161 minutes for the fourth wicket in Australia's second innings, a record for any wicket in Tests, but could not prevent England winning by six wickets, Richardson

Dick Pougher.

taking a further six wickets and hitting the stumps three times. 'Ranji', or Kumar Shri Ranjitsinhji, made his debut in the second Test, scoring 154 not out in England's innings before Australia won by three wickets. Ranji, the first Indian to appear in Tests, scored 100 of his runs before lunch on the third day, also the first player to do so. England clinched the rubber by winning the third Test by 66 runs when Australia failed to pass 44 in the chase for the 11 runs needed to win on a difficult pitch.

Trott's benevolent captaincy and theatrical director Harry Musgrove's management regained prestige Australian cricket had lacked for a decade. Trott allowed himself only one game off in his team's 34 first-class matches in England, and was on the field for all 11 games in the US and New Zealand on the way home, ensuring that even when they did not win his band were competitive and happy. His life as a postman was never quite the same when he returned home and he could not understand why families arrived outside his weatherboard house in Albert Park and insisted on wishing him well. Inadvertently, his sportsmanship in agreeing to Ranji's inclusion in the England team, at a time when there was no Test cricket in India, created a precedent that was to persistently worry administrators.

AUSTRALIA IN ENGLAND 1899

	First-class Results					All Matches			
Matches	Won	Lost	Drawn	Tied	Matches	Won	Lost	Drawn	Tied
35	16	3	16	–	35	16	3	16	–

Date	Venue	Opponent	Results for Australians
May 8	Crystal Palace	South of England	Drawn
May 11	Leyton	Essex	Lost by 126 runs
May 15	The Oval	Surrey	Won by an inns & 71 runs
May 18	Eastbourne	England XI	Won by 172 runs
May 23	Sheffield	Yorkshire	Drawn
May 25	Manchester	Lancashire	Won by an inns & 84 runs
May 29	Oxford	Oxford University	Drawn
Jun 1	Nottingham	ENGLAND (1st Test)	Drawn
Jun 5	Lord's	MCC	Won by 8 wkts
Jun 8	Cambridge	Cambridge University	Won by 10 wkts
Jun 12	Bradford	Yorkshire	Drawn
Jun 15	Lord's	ENGLAND (2nd Test)	Won by 10 wkts
Jun 19	Portsmouth	Oxford University	Won by 10 wkts
Jun 23	Leicester	Leicestershire	Won by 248 runs
Jun 26	Derby	Derbyshire	Won by an inns & 249 runs
Jun 29	Leeds	ENGLAND (3rd Test)	Drawn
Jly 3	Nottingham	Nottinghamshire	Drawn
Jly 7	Truro	England XI	Won by 8 wkts
Jly 10	Birmingham	Midlands Counties XI	Won by 44 runs
Jly 13	Perth	Gloucestershire	Won by 6 wkts
Jly 17	Manchester	ENGLAND (4th Test)	Drawn
Jly 20	Crystal Palace	WG Grace's XI	Drawn
Jly 24	The Oval	Surrey	Lost by 103 runs
Jly 27	Hove	Sussex	Drawn
Jly 31	Lord's	MCC	Won by 9 wkts
Aug 3	Southampton	Hampshire	Drawn
Aug 7	Birmingham	Warwickshire	Won by 9 wkts
Aug 10	Canterbury	Kent	Lost by 2 wkts
Aug 14	The Oval	ENGLAND (5th Test)	Drawn
Aug 17	Cheltenham	Gloucestershire	Drawn
Aug 21	Lord's	Middlesex	Won by an inns & 230 runs
Aug 24	Taunton	Somerset	Drawn
Aug 28	Liverpool	Lancashire	Drawn
Aug 31	Scarborough	Cl Thornton's XI	Drawn
Sep 4	Hastings	South of England	Won by 110 runs

Joe Darling's 1899 team to England played five Tests for the first time: *back row* J.J. Kelly, M.A. Noble, H. Trumble, C.E. McLeod, Ben Wardill (manager); *seated* E. Jones, F. Laver, J.J. Darling, S.E. Gregory, A.E. Johns, W.P. Howell; *front* C. Hill, V.T. Trumper, F.A. Iredale; *absent* J. Worrall.

Player	State	M	Inn	NO	Runs	HS	50	100	Avrge	Ct/St	Overs	Mdns	Runs	Wkts	Avrge	5wi	10wm	Best
Darling, J (Capt)	SA	35	56	9	1941	167	8	5	41.30	32	3.0	–	10	–	–	–	–	–
Gregory, SE	NSW	32	49	6	1181	124	3	3	27.47	9	19.0	3	73	–	–	–	–	–
Hill, C	SA	16	23	1	879	160	2	3	39.95	11	5.0	–	16	1	16.00	–	–	1/16
Howell, WP	NSW	32	40	11	307	49*	–	–	10.58	29	1119.4	426	2381	117	20.35	6	2	10/28
Iredale, FA	NSW	27	38	3	1039	115	4	2	29.68	20	5.0	1	11	1	11.00	–	–	1/11
Johns, AE	VIC	8	8	3	50	27*	–	–	10.00	5/1	–	–	–	–	–	–	–	–
Jones, E	SA	28	35	4	552	55	4	–	17.81	24	1163.2	331	2849	135	21.10	10	4	7/31
Kelly, JJ	NSW	30	39	6	768	103	3	1	23.27	39/3	3.0	–	16	–	–	–	–	–
Laver, F	VIC	27	38	10	859	143	3	1	30.68	12	243.1	79	619	23	26.91	1	–	4/27
McLeod, CE	VIC	28	38	7	544	77	1	–	17.55	14	776.2	270	1860	81	22.96	5	2	7/57
Noble, MA	NSW	33	50	7	1608	156	9	3	37.39	23	744.5	254	1878	82	22.90	5	1	7/15
Trumble, H	VIC	32	51	8	1183	100	5	1	27.51	49	1246.3	432	2618	142	18.44	10	3	8/35
Trumper, VT	NSW	33	48	3	1556	300*	9	3	34.58	15	7.0	1	29	1	29.00	–	–	1/10
Worrall, J	VIC	24	39	5	1202	128	7	3	35.35	12	31.0	2	104	1	104.00	–	–	1/59

Joe Darling, who scored more runs than any of his colleagues in 1896, took over from Trott as captain of the 1899 Australian team to England, ushering in cricket's Golden Age. Darling headed the batting averages with almost 2000 runs and seldom failed, demonstrating his claims to ranking among the great left-handers. He made five centuries, top score 167. Syd Gregory, Monty Noble, Jack Worrall, Hugh Trumble, Frank Iredale, and Victor Trumper also scored more than 1000 runs, with Trumper pleasing the purists most.

Trumper missed selection in the original team but after watching him make 75 in the last of three warm-up matches for the team before they sailed selectors and Trumble realised they had erred and invited Trumper to join the team, but on a bonus of £200 compared with the £700 guaranteed the rest of the team. Trumper was clean bowled in five of his first seven innings but impressed Darling enough to win a place in the First Test at Trent Bridge. Hearne bowled him for a duck in the first innings, and Jackson bowled him for 11 in the second. Darling stuck with his judgement of what he saw in the nets and in the Second Test at Lord's Trumper scored a chanceless 135 not out, at the age of 21. All who saw him in the next 10 years agreed he was the most brilliant of all Australian batsmen.

Darling was dour but capable of flashes of magnificent

hitting, Hill disheartened bowlers by continually thumping them from wide of the off stump to the leg boundary, and Noble was at his best in a crisis. Iredale was a copy-book cutter and driver, Worrall stubborn in defence but prepared to hit, and with Trumper always capable of destroying an attack, as he did with an innings of 300 not out against Sussex at Brighton, the Australian batting was very strong. They were supported by wise captaincy, particularly in the management of ex-bee-keeper Bill Howell's off-breaks, Noble's swing, and Trumble's subtle spin.

Most of all, Darling fashioned this Australian team into one of the best ever with his clever handling of Ernie Jones, the former miner with the physique of a Greek Adonis, converting him from a rough and ready demon who exhausted himself in a few overs into a coordinated paceman who kept going for hours. Joe Kelly kept wicket splendidly and the team's fielding reached a high standard. Strong in every department, the team regained The Ashes, lost only three of their 35 matches, won 16 and played 16 draws. Australia won one Test and had the better of the four draws in a series that saw the end of W.G. Grace's Test career at the age of 50 years 320 days. Grace made 28 and 1 and did not take a wicket with his roundarmers, but realised his fielding was deplorable. 'It's not good—I can't bend down to them,' he said, acknowledging later that Australia's challenge to England's supremacy had kept him playing first-class cricket long after his planned retirement.

AUSTRALIA IN ENGLAND 1902

	First-class Results					All Matches			
Matches	Won	Lost	Drawn	Tied	Matches	Won	Lost	Drawn	Tied
37	21	2	14	–	39	23	2	14	–

Date	Venue	Opponent	Results for Australians
May 5	Crystal Palace	London County	Drawn
May 8	Nottingham	Nottinghamshire	Won by an inns & 4 runs
May 12	The Oval	Surrey	Won by an inns & 78 runs
May 15	Leyton	Essex	Drawn
May 19	Leicester	Leicestershire	Won by 7 wkts
May 22	Oxford	Oxford University	Won by an inns & 54 runs
May 26	Lord's	MCC	Drawn
May 29	Birmingham	ENGLAND (1st Test)	Drawn
Jun 2	Leeds	Yorkshire	Lost by 5 wkts
Jun 5	Manchester	Lancashire	Drawn
Jun 9	Cambridge	Cambridge University	Won by an inns & 183 runs
Jun 12	Lord's	ENGLAND (2nd Test)	Drawn
Jun 16	Eastbourne	England XI	Won by 131 runs
Jun 19	Derby	Derbyshire	Won by 8 wkts
Jun 23	Bradford	Yorkshire	Won by 44 runs
Jun 26	Bradford	England XI	Won by 7 wkts
Jun 30	Edinburgh	*An Eleven of Scotland	Won by an inns & 104 runs
Jly 3	Sheffield	ENGLAND (3rd Test)	Won by 143 runs
Jly 7	Birmingham	Warwickshire	Drawn
Jly 10	Worcester	Worcestershire	Won by 174 runs
Jly 14	Perth	Gloucestershire	Won by an inns & 222 runs
Jly 17	Taunton	Somerset	Drawn
Jly 21	The Oval	Surrey	Drawn
Jly 24	Manchester	ENGLAND (4th Test)	Won by 3 runs
Jly 28	Leyton	Essex	Drawn
Jly 31	Hove	Sussex	Drawn
Aug 4	Cardiff	*Glamorgan & Wiltshire	Won by 6 wkts
Aug 7	Southampton	Hampshire	Won by an inns & 79 runs
Aug 11	The Oval	ENGLAND (5th Test)	Lost by 1 wkt
Aug 14	Lord's	MCC	Won by an inns & 34 runs
Aug 18	Cheltenham	Gloucestershire	Won by an inns & 10 runs
Aug 21	Canterbury	Kent	Won by 89 runs
Aug 25	Lord's	Middlesex	Won by 6 wkts
Aug 28	Liverpool	Lancashire	Won by 18 runs
Sep 1	Harrogate	Players of England	Won by an inns & 47 runs
Sep 4	Scarborough	CI Thornton's XI	Drawn
Sep 8	Hastings	South of England	Drawn
Sep 11	Bournemouth	South of England	Won by 61 runs
Sep 15	The Oval	Players of England	Drawn

Joe Darling's tact and the diplomacy of manager Ben Wardill in 1902 helped overcome lingering English misgivings about the commercial attitude of the Australians, although they insisted on being known simply as cricketers and not as amateurs or professionals. Noble took the allround honours in a champion team but with the bat it was Trumper who 'entranced the eye, inspired the side, demoralised his opponents, and made run-getting appear the simplest thing in the world', as Neville Cardus wrote. Trumper's modesty often prevented him going on beyond 100, by which time he believed it was only fair to give a team-mate a hit, and he often threw his hand away after compiling one of his 11 tour centuries. He scored 2570 runs in 36 matches at 48.49.

The team improved on the record of the previous tourists and must rate among the top three or four sides produced by Australia. They batted more aggressively than earlier Australian teams, with a surfeit of big hits, and tried to win every match, undeterred by an exceptionally wet English summer. Their crowd appeal meant that Australia's matches overshadowed county matches, though they were of a high standard, and the outcome of the five-Test rubber completely outshone the county championship.

Darling recognised Trumper's contribution to all this, and never let the coach carrying the team leave their hotel until he was sure Trumper was aboard. Trumper in turn regarded Darling as a very special captain from the day on the previous tour when Darling told him that he had asked the other players to grant Trumper the same share of the tour bonus as they all received. Trumper's health was never robust and he was grateful for the consideration Darling showed when he had influenza or caught a cold. Trumper hated self-promotion and chastised team-mates who hogged the strike or deprived colleagues in the pavilion of a chance to bat.

Player	State	M	Inn	NO	Runs	HS	50	100	Avrge	Ct/St	Overs	Mdns	Runs	Wkts	Avrge	5wi	10wm	Best
Armstrong, WW	VIC	36	50	10	1084	172*	2	1	27.10	32	674.3	203	1374	74	18.56	3	–	8/47
Carter, H	NSW	16	18	4	105	31	–	–	7.50	19/5	1.0	–	7	–	–	–	–	–
Darling, J (Capt)	SA	36	51	5	1113	128	4	2	24.19	26	–	–	–	–	–	–	–	–
Duff, RA	NSW	38	57	5	1501	183	5	2	28.86	23	20.0	4	53	4	13.25	–	–	3/17
Gregory, SE	NSW	35	50	6	955	86	3	–	21.70	18	4.0	–	21	–	–	–	–	–
Hill, C	SA	36	50	1	1555	136	7	4	31.73	28	19.5	4	59	4	14.75	–	–	3/30
Hopkins, AJY	NSW	38	53	7	1147	105*	5	1	24.93	22	242.1	67	669	38	17.60	2	–	7/10
Howell, WP	NSW	20	24	6	95	16	–	–	5.28	15	497.0	148	1215	68	17.87	5	1	6/33
Jones, E	SA	21	19	1	215	40	–	–	11.94	13	542.2	142	1438	70	20.54	3	–	6/26
Kelly, JJ	NSW	25	31	7	326	75	2	–	12.53	22/13	4.0	–	13	2	6.50	–	–	2/13
Noble, MA	NSW	34	47	5	1416	284	7	3	33.71	29	710.0	205	1870	94	19.89	5	2	8/48
Pope, RJ	NSW	1	1	1	2	2*	–	–	–	–	–	–	–	–	–	–	–	–
Saunders, JV	VIC	26	33	9	84	9*	–	–	3.50	14	713.0	160	2092	123	17.00	10	3	6/9
Trumble, H	VIC	20	28	6	389	68	2	–	17.68	18	912.0	292	1921	137	14.02	13	7	9/39
Trumper, VT	NSW	36	53	–	2570	128	11	11	48.49	24	152.3	43	415	20	20.75	2	–	5/19

The eleventh Australian team in England in 1902: *back row* C. Hill, H. Trumble, W.P. Howell, E. Jones, Ben Wardill (manager), W.W. Armstrong, J.V. Saunders, J.J. Kelly; *seated* R.A. Duff, M.A. Noble, J.J. Darling (capt.), A.J. Hopkins, V.T. Trumper; *front* H. Carter, S.E. Gregory.

Hugh Trumble, the bony, long-limbed off-spinner whom 'Plum' Warner called 'a great camel', took the bowling honours with 137 victims at 14.02 apiece, but Noble, Jones and Warwick Armstrong, on his initial English tour, were not far behind him. The entire side fielded brilliantly and the Tests between Australia and one of the most powerful of all English teams developed into epic struggles, decided by touches of genius. At Old Trafford, for example, when England was eight runs short of winning and had two wickets in hand, Clem Hill sprinted more than 30 metres round the square leg boundary to hold a magnificent catch. On the strength of that catch Australia won by three runs when the Victorian left-arm googly bowler Jack Saunders dismissed the last English batsman.

This dramatic victory gave Australia The Ashes, although England won the last Test at The Oval. England's last pair were at the crease with 15 runs required to win and decided 'to get them in singles'. They edged closer to the target despite Darling's pressure and as they scored the winning runs and left the field torrential rain fell to end a memorable series. There was scarcely a failure in a team in which seven players made centuries and Australians made 24 centuries in all, with only six scored against them. Six Australians took more than 50 wickets in the 38 matches, Australia winning 21, drawing 14, and losing only two.

Darling kept spirits high despite the depressing weather and Trumper did a lot for morale when he flatly rejected an offer to quit Australian cricket and play for an English county. Despite the physical strain of a tour that lasted from May to September, the players were all pleased to stop off on the way home for the first visit by an Australian team to South Africa.

CHAPTER FOUR

THE AMERICAN INVOLVEMENT

Although they continued their matches against Canada until 1912, America's leading cricketers looked forward more to visits from English touring teams. The main aim of US players was to tour England, and the confrontations with Canada were treated as a preparation for the trips to Britain.

Six years after the Australian Aboriginal team visited England, a team of American baseballers, organised by the sports goods manufacturer A.G. Spalding, arrived in 1874 with divided aims. They played a series of baseball matches to satisfy the first task of promoting their sport but combined them with cricket matches to popularise their sport among Britons. Their hosts were generous in allowing them to field teams of 18 or 22 players for their six matches in England and in the match against Ireland in Dublin they had 21 players. The Americans defeated Prince's Club, Sheffield, Manchester and Ireland, and played draws against MCC, Richmond and Surrey, to complete their three week tour unbeaten.

A Canadian cricket team played 17 matches, none of them first-class, in Britain in 1880 over three months. English cricket historian Peter Wynne-Thomas reported in his book a sensational development just after the fifth match of the Canadians' tour when their captain T. Jordan was arrested on suspicion of being the military deserter T. Dale. This allegation proved true and he was sent to prison. The Reverend T.D. Phillips was sent from Canada to replace Jordan/Dale, but did not arrive until the tour was almost over and had virtually collapsed. The tour came to an abrupt end when the tourists ran out of money. The Canadians co-opted six English players to help lift their performance, including Walter Wright, a Notts professional who later became a bowler of quality. Wynne-Thomas said that among the Canadians D.J. Smith, W. Pinckney, and A.H. Lemmon proved useful batsmen and J.S. Gilean an effective fast bowler.

The Canadians won five matches, drew five and had seven losses. They played 14 of their matches on level terms but in the other three were allowed additional players because of the strength of the opposition. Their best win probably was against Surrey at The Oval, where they played 15 players. Dismissed for 41 in their first innings, they sent back Surrey for 67 and 36 and scored 171 in their second innings to win by 110 runs.

PHILADELPHIA IN ENGLAND 1884

An all-amateur 'Gentlemen of Philadelphia' team toured England for nine matches in 1884 on an $8000 guarantee. They played a three-day match in New York to prepare for the tour but this did not help lift their performance enough for them to attract crowds in England.

The tour began with matches against Dublin University, which the Philadelphians left drawn, and against the Gentlemen of Ireland, which the Philadelphians won by six wickets, and good wins over the Gentlemen of Scotland in Edinburgh and Scarborough in Scarborough. This took the Philadelphians to the most important match of their tour, against a powerful MCC XI at Lord's. MCC scored 406 all out in this match, thanks to an innings of 106 by C.T. Studd,

The Philadelphian team that toured England in 1884: *back row* J.B. Thayer jnr, W. Brockie jnr, E.W. Clark jnr, C.A. Newhall, H. McNutt, J.A. Scott, W.C. Lowry; *front* W.C. Morgan jnr, R.S. Newhall (capt.), F.E. Brewster, H. Brown (kneeling), S. Law, D.P. Stoever, T. Robins (scorer). *University of Pennsylvania Press*

who had toured Australia two years earlier with Ivo Bligh's team. The Philadelphians responded with 174, C.T. Studd taking 6 for 78, and 61 in their second innings when forced to follow-on, to lose by an innings and 171 runs.

Three of the Philadelphian batsmen, J.A. Scott, R.S. Newhall and J.B. Thayer, scored more than 800 runs on the tour at around 30 an innings, but the best player was the left-arm bowler W.C. Lowry, who took 110 wickets in the nine matches at an average of 12.73 apiece. The Americans returned home convinced they would have put up a better showing had D.S. Newhall, star of a noted cricket family, been able to get leave from his job to join them.

AUSTRALIA IN THE US 1878-96

Australian cricketers first encountered American cricketers at the end of the initial white tour of England in 1878 when Dave Gregory took his pioneering team to Philadelphia for the first of six matches they had arranged in the US on their way home. The Australians were rushed on to a train when their ship docked in New York and took the field the next day. They were shocked by the umpires, who clapped every run by Philadelphia and were almost ecstatic when Robert Newhall made 84 in a total of 196. The umpiring became so farcical that wicket-keeper Jack Blackham threw the ball to Gregory in disgust when he had a stumping appeal rejected with the batsman metres out of his crease.

Gregory agreed the umpiring was intolerable and led the Australians from the field. In the dressing-room Philadelphian officials threatened to stop payment on a cheque they had given manager John Conway for their guaranteed expenses unless Gregory took his players back on to the field. The Australians reluctantly trooped out and continued the match. The team that had defeated the powerful MCC at Lord's a few months earlier had to settle for a draw after they trailed on the first innings by 46 runs. This was the first match in America in which the locals met international visitors on level terms, and the result was hailed as a landmark that established the reputation of American cricket.

The Australians won four of their matches in the US and drew the other two, quickly learning to laugh at the opposition's non-conformist behaviour. They won their first match in Canada against Twenty-Two of Ontario by 10 wickets on 8 and 9 October 1878, scoring 123 and 0 for 31 against Ontario XXII's 100 and 154. Charles Bannerman, already the first Australian to score a Test century, the first to score 100s in New Zealand and England, added another record to his collection by compiling 125 in the second Canadian match, against Twenty-Two of Montreal. Despite Bannerman's batting and some marvellous bowling by Spofforth (8 for 39) and Allan (9 for 24), the match was a tragedy for the Australians who had their cash and precious souvenirs from the England tour stolen by a dressing-room thief while they were on the field.

In California American batsmen called for lemonade after every few runs. Gregory suggested they might like to place a jug of it behind the stumps. When a new batsman came in and immediately ran two, Charles Bannerman told him: 'Better suck a lemon. Hot work you know.'

Billy Murdoch took the third team to America on their way home from England in 1882. They played two matches, both against the odds, and won them both, and by their presence encouraged American players who made their second tour of England in 1889. All the 12 non first-class matches were on level terms, and the Americans fared well by winning four, drawing five, and losing only three. At the end of the tour they gave all their gate receipts to the Cricketers' Fund Friendly Society.

Jack Blackham took the eighth Australian team to England to Philadelphia on their way home in 1893. Philadelphia scored 525 in the first match, the highest score by an American team in first-class cricket, and dismissed Australia for 199 and 258 to win by an innings and 68 runs. The Australians made no excuse for their shock defeat, although they had been rushed from their ship, the *Germanic*, straight to Philadelphia in a private railway car after a boisterous seven-day crossing of the Atlantic.

Three years later Harry Trott's ninth Australian team to England played three matches on level terms in Philadelphia. Australia won the first two convincingly, but Philadelphia staged a remarkable revival by winning the third by an innings and 99 runs. This triumph stimulated the Philadelphians to make a far more ambitious tour of England in 1897. All the Philadelphian cricket clubs banded together to raise $US8000 to pay

(*Top*) J. Barton King, who topped the English first-class bowling averages on the last of his three tours of Britain.

Australian Sammy Woods toured the US in 1899 with this team led by Prince Ranjitsinhji: *back row* G. Woolley (umpire), S.M.J. Woods, B.J.T. Bosanquet, A. Priestley, unidentified, F. Luffman (umpire); *centre* G. Brann, A.C. MacLaren, K.S. Ranjitsinhji, A.E.Stoddart, C. Robson; *front* G.L. Jessop, C.B. Llewellyn, W.P. Robertson, C.L. Townsend.

for the tour, a magnificent effort considering the fundraising came from only 250 active cricketers and their supporters.

The Philadelphian team included the finest of all American cricketers, John Barton King, a match-winning allrounder born in Philadelphia in 1873 who bowled right-arm at a brisk pace and swung the ball prodigiously. He also scored 2047 runs in his limited first-class career at an average of 20.16, with a topscore of 113 not out. He began the first of his three tours of England as a 20-year-old novice but grew in stature with every match and was largely responsible for Philadelphia's defeat of Warwickshire and Sussex, who included Ranji in their batting lineup. King took 5 for 95 and 7 for 72 against Warwickshire and against Sussex relished the sea breeze that whipped across the Hove pitch, taking 7 for 13 and 6 for 102 after contributing 58 with the bat. The Philadelphians won three, lost eight and drew four matches.

Although their record was unimpressive the 1897 team's overall displays never fell below first-class and officials in Philadelphia believed that with more frequent international competition they could match England's best teams. They invited Prince Ranjitsinghi to take a team for a five-match tour of the US and Canada in 1899 and limited his choice to amateurs, but unfortunately Ranji's team had too many dominant players for their opponents. The tourists won three of their five matches by wide margins with the other two drawn. Archie MacLaren made 149 in the major match of the tour, Gilbert Jessop 64 in 35 minutes, Ranji 57, Stoddart 56 and Ranji's side won by an innings and 173 runs by running up a total of 436.

English cricket was very strong when the fourth Philadelphians, again with John King, had a 17-match tour in 1903, but the Americans managed to win seven matches, losing six, and leaving four unfinished. Percy Clark, a right-arm fast medium bowler from Germantown, and the captain, Haverford-born John Lester who bowled right-arm slows, gave King the backing he lacked on the previous tour and between them they made batsmen earn their runs. Lester was a delightful stroke-maker in a stubborn batting lineup. The Philadelphians could be particularly proud of their nine-wicket defeat of the powerful Lancashire XI, King taking 5 for 46 and 9 for 62.

Australian googly bowler Herbert Hordern toured England in matches against the major public schools with a Pennsylvania University team in 1907, and five years later Syd Gregory's 14th Australian team lost an exciting match to Philadelphia by six runs on their way home from their English tour. Five of the 1912 team declined to tour America, Bardsley, Jennings, Hazlitt, Macartney and Minnett preferring to go home separately through the Suez Canal. This left Syd with ten tourists and he was forced to make up the side in America with manager G.S. Crouch and the Sydney visitor Andrew Hume.

AUSTRALIA IN THE US AND CANADA 1912 AND 1913

The 1912 Australians played six matches in America, only two of which were first-class. They won four and drew one and lost one. They found John Barton King, then in his last season of first-class cricket, still a formidable rival. King had excelled himself in England in 1908, by topping the first-class averages with 87 wickets at 11.01 on his final overseas tour, and in 1909 had achieved the unusual feat of clean bowling all eleven batsmen in an Irish Gentlemen's XI, including the eventual not out batsman G.A. Morrow whom he skittled with a no-ball. In the second innings of that match King took a hat-trick.

The Australians learned that when King's club, Belmont, played Trenton, the Trenton captain arrived at the crease after King had dismissed the ninth Trenton batsman, full of apologies for missing his train. Trenton would not have been in a such a disastrous position, said the captain, had he arrived earlier. Affronted by this King ordered all his fieldsmen from the field, including the wicket-keeper. The Trenton captain protested but the umpires said King was within his rights. After further argument King said he did need one fieldsman and positioned a man 20 metres behind the stumps and four metres to the leg. He then bowled his inswinger, which clipped the Trenton captain's stumps, and watched as the ball trickled to the lone fieldsman.

A strong Australian team organised by the noted wheeler-dealer Edgar Richard Mayne, otherwise known as 'Ernie', made an unofficial tour of America in 1913–14. Mayne, who had hailed from Jamestown, South Australia, had been approached in America on his visit with Syd Gregory's team the previous year by an entrepreneur named R.B. Benjamin, who promised an all-expenses-paid American and Canadian junket for a first-class Australian side. Mayne tried to secure Australian Board of Control approval for the trip but finally decided to tour without it.

The team held the election for captain that had always been customary in Australia on the voyage to America and picked Austin Diamond, the Sydney right-hand batsman born in Huddersfield, Yorkshire, widely respected for his knowledge of cricket. His team comprised: Sid Emery, Arthur Mailey, Charlie Macartney, Herbie Collins, Warren Bardsley, Les Cody, and Percy Arnott, from New South Wales, and the South Australians Granville Down, Gordon Campbell, and Surrey expatriate Jack Crawford. Six of them bowled spinners and Campbell kept wicket, the role he performed for the South Australian team. Crawford swung the ball each way at a fast-medium pace.

Diamond's XI played 53 matches, five of them first-class, and had 49 wins, three draws and only one loss. They opened their tour with nine matches in Canada, eight of which they won by wide margins. Rain washed out the other match after Eighteen of Edmonton had reached 15 for 111. Eight Australians made more than

The Gentlemen of Philadelphia XI that defeated the Australian team captained by Austin Diamond at the Germantown CC in Germantown in August 1913, 'redeeming the reputation of Philadelphia cricket': *back row* R.L. Pearson, T. Irving (umpire), J.H. Savage, A.G. Priestman, R.P. Anderson, F.H. Tripp, G. Woolley (umpire), F.A. Greene; *centre* P.A. Clarke, W.P. O'Neill (capt.), W.P. Newhall; *front* G.M. Graham, J.R. Stewart, H.S. Harned. Arthur Mailey said the Australians' defeat was due to Percy Clark's ten slips catches. The previous year Philadelphia beat Syd Gregory's official Australian XI on the same ground. *Roger Mann*

Australians in America and Canada, 1913: *standing* S.H. Emery, A.A. Mailey, J.N. Crawford, P.S. Arnott, W. Bardsley, G.C. Campbell; *seated* L.A. Cody, A. Diamond (capt.), R.B. Benjamin (manager), E.R. Mayne, C.G. Macartney; *front* G.S. Downs, H.L. Collins.

1000 runs, with Arnott's 101 in 45 minutes against Saskatchewan the fastest of the side's 24 tour centuries. In a team in which it was obligatory to lash out at every ball after reaching 100, Macartney's 186 against Combined Canada and the United States at Toronto was the highest score.

The Australian Board of Control blocked a second American tour in 1913 despite protests from Diamond, who said: 'The Board should remember that it was private tours which were the genesis of international cricket. The Board should encourage cricket in those parts of north America where there are thousands of Englishmen, because of the chance of developing cricket there as has been achieved in South Africa.' The Board said that a second American tour would clash with a scheduled official visit to South Africa, but World War I prevented this trip.

AUSTRALIA IN THE US AND CANADA 1932

Since 1918 dozens of Australian clubs and societies have played in north America, but only one team had Board of Control involvement. This was the 51-match tour organised in 1932 by Arthur Mailey, who was helped by Canadian Pacific Railways, shipping lines, American tourist interests, and the Canadian Cricket Board. The Board approved the tour after Mailey guaranteed that none of the tourists would receive more than £100 from tour profits, and promised detailed tour accounts.

The Board lifted their ban on wives accompanying Australian teams to allow Bradman's wife of 26 days, Jessie, to go on what was virtually a honeymoon trip. She acted as hostess at team receptions. Mailey originally planned to include Clarrie Grimmett on a tour which meant 1000 batsmen would have to be dismissed in 100 days, and when Grimmett withdrew, hurriedly replaced him with Fleetwood-Smith, who subsequently took 238 wickets at 7.5 runs apiece. Mailey, who at 42 was 20 years older than Fleetwood-Smith, took 203 wickets at 8.6 runs each. Bradman was the star of the trip, however, with 49 appearances in the 51 matches, during which he made 18 centuries. Statistician Irving Rosenwater said Bradman's 260 against Eighteen of Western Ontario was then the highest score ever made in Canada. On strange pitches with bizarre umpiring at Kicking Horse Falls, Moose Jaw, Medicine Hat and other colourful venues, captain Vic Richardson made sure everyone had a good time, including the opposition. When Mailey bowled a batsman at Saskatoon, he whispered to the umpire to call 'No-ball', because the batsman hadn't scored. In this spirit, the Australians had 44 wins, one loss and six draws.

Canada versus United States matches were closely contested until 1912. They were revived in 1964, and since 1980 have been played every two years. No US or Canadian team has toured Australia or New Zealand, a dream Austin Diamond nurtured before World War I.

NOTE: The statistics for the matches in this chapter can be found in the appendix.

The Australian team that toured America and Canada in 1932 with official sanction: *back row* S.J. McCabe, E.K. Tolhurst, E.F. Rofe, W.F. Ives, L.O'B. Fleetwood-Smith, P.H. Carney; *centre* A.F. Kippax, A.A. Mailey, V.Y. Richardson, D.G. Bradman; *front* H. Carter, R.N. Nutt. Jesse Bradman acted as the team's hostess.

The United States team photographed before the start of their annual match against Canada at Toronto in July 1888. These contests are still played every two years.

HOME AND AWAY

A team of veterans who played matches in Kimberley in 1878 about the time Australia met England in the first-ever Test in Melbourne: *back row* J. Vivian; J.P. Ablett, Major T. Maxwell, C.E. Nind, M.B. Beevor, W.F. Sheasby; *centre* W. Ling, A.F. Tancred, H.B. Roper; *front* P. Sim, W.W. Graham, G.S. Chandler. *South African Cricket Union*

The first South African team to go overseas photographed in England in 1894: *back row* W.V. Simkins (manager), C.O.H. Sewell, G.S. Kempis, D.C. Davey, F. Hearne, C.H. Mills, J. Middleton, A.W. Seccull; *seated* T.W. Routledge, G. Cripps, H.H. Castens (capt.), C.L. Johnson, A.E. Halliwell; *front* G.A. Rowe, D.C. Parkin, G.K. Glover. They won 12 of their 24 matches, none of them first-class. *South African Cricket Union*

CHAPTER FIVE

SOUTH AFRICAN CHALLENGE

Cricket began in South Africa with the missionaries, soldiers, and schoolmasters who arrived when English migration began in 1820 after the Cape came under the British flag. They had been preceded by the original Dutch, Huguenot, and German settlers who came to the region in 1652 and from whom the Afrikaners stemmed. English cricket historian Harry Altham said that a year after the occupation of Natal in 1843, the 45th Foot played the game in Pietermaritzburg and shortly afterwards British settlers at Bloemfontein started a club. Discovery of diamonds in 1867 and gold in 1886 accelerated migration from Britain and brought a dramatic increase in the number of cricket clubs.

For almost three decades, however, the standard remained low, until in 1888–89 Major Wharton, encouraged by the founder of the Castle shipping line Sir Donald Currie, arranged the visit of the first English team. This team was captained by Charles Aubrey ('Round The Corner') Smith, an old Carthusian and Cambridge blue who had played four times in the University match against Oxford. Smith's team was not strong or truly representative of English cricket but they easily won most of their matches and overwhelmed South Africa in the two Tests. Altham reported that the batting of Bobby Abel, the wicket-keeping of Monty Bowden and Harry Wood, and the bowling of Johnny Briggs was a revelation to South Africans. Briggs had an incredible tour, taking almost 300 wickets at five runs apiece, and dismissing 27 batsmen for 23 runs in one match.

In 1891–92 the Surrey schoolmaster Walter Read, who had toured Australia in 1887–88, took a much stronger side to South Africa. Despite an influx of English professionals like Frank Hearne, whose coaching had vastly improved standards, Read's team went through their tour unbeaten. Three Hearne brothers and Australians Jack Ferris and Billy Murdoch played in the only Test for England, who won by an innings and 189 runs in three days, with Harry Wood scoring the first century (134) by a keeper in Test cricket. Ferris took 13 wickets for 91 runs. Two days after this Test at Cape Town ended, Australia began the Third Test at Adelaide Oval against Lord Sheffield's England side.

The first South African team toured England in 1894, exciting little interest in a fixture list that comprised mainly matches against second-class sides. South African cricket officials succumbed to pressure to exclude hostile fast bowler 'Krom' Hendricks because he was of Malay extraction. The South Africans started as modestly as Australia had done but defeated a strong MCC XI captained by W.G. Grace at Lord's by 11 runs. Star of the Springbok team was wicket-keeper Ernest Halliwell, who proved as good as England's best if not as good as Australia's Jack Blackham. Halliwell returned to England with South Africa in 1901 and 1904. Halliwell was noted for his taking of the very fast deliveries of Johannes Jacobus ('Kodgee') Kotze, who took 348 first-class wickets at 17.86.

South Africa's rapid advance was demonstrated in 1895–96 when Lord Hawke, the Yorkshire captain and an influential figure in cricket policy-making at Lord's, took a carefully selected England side to the Cape. The

The Boer war prisoners and the Colombo Colts, who won their match in Ceylon in front of the British governor. P.H. deVilliers, the prisoners' captain, who figured in peace time matches against Lord Hawke's English tourists, is in the middle of the front row, hatless and with his arms folded. *Roger Mann*

England team included Charles Fry and Arthur Hill, Lord Hawke outstanding amateurs, plus the professional talent of Surrey's George Lohmann and batsman Tom Hayward, who was an automatic selection for England for 13 years. Australian-born Sammy Woods began the tour with a shoulder injury that stopped him bowling and then suffered a leg strain. The team played 18 matches, losing the first two to Fifteen of Western Province, but recovering to win the Tests handsomely. Lohmann's right-arm medium pace was too subtle for the South Africans and he took 35 Test wickets on matting pitches at 5.80 apiece, including 15 for 45 (7 for 38 and 8 for 7) at Port Elizabeth. Lohmann had spent most of his time since January 1893 in South Africa for the rain-free, dry air which he hoped would help his fight against tuberculosis. Lohmann took eight wickets in an innings 20 times in his career and when he died in South Africa at 36 five years later had an amazing total of 1841 first-class wickets to his credit.

The Boer War disrupted arrangements for this tour but when the Englishmen were held up by an armed posse of Boers they were treated cordially and parted on friendly terms. When Lord Hawke returned in 1898–99, with a team that included the Australian allrounder Albert Trott, a locust plague and a crash involving the train in which they were travelling from Kimberley to Matjesfontein were the major hazards. Despite these diversions and the ease with which their team won most of the matches on level terms the Englishmen were impressed by the improvement in South African cricket. England won the First Test at Johannesburg by 32 runs after 'Plum' Warner made 132 not out and Albert Trott took 5 for 49, and the Second Test at Cape Town by 210 runs when Johnny Tyldesley hit 112 and Schofield Haigh accounted for six batsmen for only 11 runs. It was clear, as South Africa prepared for the first visit by Australia, that given more international cricket South Africa would emerge as a nation that could take on the best.

Star of the 1898–99 England team in South Africa was Australian Albert Trott, shown next to his captain Lord Hawke. The team: *back row* G.A. Lohmann (manager), W.R. Cuttell, F. Mitchell, F.W. Milligan, A.G. Archer, A.A. White (umpire); *seated* S. Haigh, H.R. Bromley-Davenport, Lord Hawke, A.E. Trott, J.H. Board; *front* J.T. Tyldesley, C.E.M. Wilson, P.F. Warner. *South African Cricket Union*

AUSTRALIA IN SOUTH AFRICA 1902

	First-class Results					All Matches			
Matches	Won	Lost	Drawn	Tied	Matches	Won	Lost	Drawn	Tied
4	3	–	1	–	6	3	–	3	–

Date	Venue	Opponent	Results for Australians
Oct 11	Johannesburg	SOUTH AFRICA (1st Test)	Drawn
Oct 15	Johannesburg	*Transvaal	Drawn
Oct 18	Johannesburg	SOUTH AFRICA (2nd Test)	Won by 159 runs
Oct 25	Durban	*Natal XV	Drawn
Nov 5	Cape Town	Western Province	Won by 282 runs
Nov 8	Cape Town	SOUTH AFRICA (3rd Test)	Won by 10 wkts

Player	State	M	Inn	NO	Runs	HS	50	100	Avrge	Ct/St	Overs	Mdns	Runs	Wkts	Avrge	5wi	10wm	Best
Armstrong, WW	VIC	4	7	1	294	159*	1	1	49.00	4	27.0	5	162	2	81.00	–	–	2/24
Carter, H	NSW	1	2	–	26	25	–	–	13.00	–	–	–	–	–	–	–	–	–
Darling, J (Capt)	SA	4	7	–	91	61	1	–	13.00	5	–	–	–	–	–	–	–	–
Duff, RA	NSW	4	8	2	270	82*	1	–	45.00	1	–	–	–	–	–	–	–	–
Gregory, SE	NSW	4	7	–	68	21	–	–	9.71	2	–	–	–	–	–	–	–	–
Hill, C	SA	4	7	1	362	142	2	1	60.33	–	–	–	–	–	–	–	–	–
Hopkins, AJY	NSW	4	7	–	118	39	–	–	16.86	2	28.0	2	129	8	16.13	–	–	3/39
Howell, WP	NSW	3	5	1	88	57*	1	–	22.00	2	90.3	22	228	31	7.35	3	1	9/23
Jones, E	SA	1	1	–	0	0	–	–	0.00	2	28.0	8	100	4	25.00	–	–	3/78
Kelly, JJ	NSW	3	4	–	51	25	–	–	12.75	4/4	–	–	–	–	–	–	–	–
Noble, MA	NSW	4	7	1	125	53*	1	–	20.83	1	49.0	8	186	6	31.00	–	–	3/75
Saunders, JV	VIC	3	5	2	5	4	–	–	1.67	1	60.3	10	214	15	14.27	1	–	7/34
Trumble, H	VIC	1	2	1	13	13	–	–	13.00	–	34.0	4	127	–	–	–	–	–
Trumper, VT	NSW	4	8	1	307	70	2	–	43.86	4	33.0	2	175	6	29.17	–	–	3/60

Despite their impressive performance in England against powerful opposition the 1902 Australian team—the first fully representative side to visit South Africa—was expected to be extended. South Africa had improved since their visits to England in 1894 and 1901, both financial failures, and at home on matting pitches at 6000 feet above sea level, were keen to boost their international prestige. Billy Murdoch, who had shared the wicket-keeping for an England XI against South Africa in 1891–92, was among those who forecast a difficult time for the Australians.

Some majestic batting by Hill, Trumper, Duff and Armstrong, supported by fine bowling by Howell and Saunders, proved the predictions wrong. The Australians were rushed to the Old Wanderers' ground in Johannesburg for the First Test as soon as their ship from England berthed. South Africa won the toss and batted and were soon on their way to a massive total, with deliveries that beat the bat passing over the top of the stumps. Transvaal opening batsman Louis Tancred, one of five notable brothers in South African cricket, reached 97 before Reggie Duff caught him off Trumper. Tancred put on 173 for the second wicket with Charlie ('Buck') Llewellyn, who made 90 and then took 6 for 92 in Australia's first innings.

With a first innings lead of 158, South African captain Harry Taberer, in his only Test, enforced the follow-on under the laws that then applied. Hill saved the match for Australia by scoring 142, including a century before lunch on the third day, the first time this had been done in Tests for Australia. Australia declared at 7 for 372, leaving South Africa to chase 214 for victory. They were

The 1902 Australian team in South Africa: *backrow* umpire F. Hearne, E. Jones, W.P. Howell, M.A. Noble, W.W. Armstrong, J.V. Saunders, umpire W.H. Creese, H.S. Carter; *seated* C. Hill, A.J. Hopkins, J. Darling (capt.), R.A. Duff, J.J. Kelly; *front* V.T. Trumper, S.E. Gregory; *absent* H. Trumble.

4 for 101, 114 short of their target with six wickets left, when the three days allotted to the Test ran out.

After this escape the Australians adapted to the strange conditions. Trumper scored a classic 218 not out against Fifteen of Transvaal at Pretoria immediately after the Test. Darling accepted Farmer Bill Howell's pleas that he was an accomplished matting wicket bowler because of his experience in New South Wales country cricket and promoted him to the teams for the second and third Tests. Howell took five wickets in the Second Test at

Johannesburg, but it was Saunders who won the match for Australia with 7 for 34 in South Africa's second innings. Armstrong became the second Australian to bat through an innings—after Dr John Barrett—with 159 not out in Australia's second innings. Howell was again given a long bowl in the Third Test at Cape Town and took 4 for 18 and 5 for 81. Australia won by ten wickets despite a whirlwind 104 in only 80 minutes by Jimmy Sinclair, who hit ten sixes and eight fours. This is still the fastest Test century for South Africa, and came in a total of only 225.

Sinclair was a remarkably tough and colourful character, renowned for his big hitting and his 104 in Cape Town followed 101 in Johannesburg in the second Test. He was taken prisoner by the Boers in the war but escaped and made the safety of the British lines just in time for South Africa's 1901 tour of England. On that tour he twice took 13 wickets in a match with his fast bowling. He hit Wilfred Rhodes out of the Harrogate ground so hard he knocked a cabbie off his cab.

Sinclair's pace bowling and prodigious hitting far from overshadowed the feats of coloured professional 'Buck' Llewellyn, a Welshman of English extraction, born in Pietermaritzburg. He played for Natal at 18 and after his Test debut against England in 1895-96 in Johannesburg played regularly for Hampshire. He scored his career highest, 216, for Hampshire against South Africa in 1901 at Southampton. He was among the 14 players from whom England picked the team for the first Test against Australia but missed out. He had previously hit 72 and 21 and taken 8 for 132 against the 1899 Australian tourists for Hampshire. His left-arm spin claimed 25 wickets in the three Tests against the Australians and cost only 17.92 runs each. Llewellyn played in 15 Tests for South Africa, five against England and ten against Australia. Taunts about his colour forced Llewellyn to take refuge in toilets, and lock himself in. His chief tormentor was Jimmy Sinclair.

For Australia, a high spot of the South African venture was Howell's feat in taking three wickets in four balls in the first innings of the Cape Town Test and three wickets in five balls in the second innings. Australia won one and drew two of the three matches against the odds in South Africa, and in their fourth first-class match defeated Western Province by 282 runs at Cape Town, Howell taking 17 wickets for 54 runs.

Australia did not encounter South Africa again until the fourteenth team to England played in the 1912 Triangular Tournament, which involved two Tests against England and two against the Springboks. Although this was widely regarded as the weakest team Australia has ever sent to England, following the withdrawal of Trumper, Carter, Cotter, Ransford Armstrong and Hill who could not accept the Australian Board's terms, Australia won both the matches with South Africa comfortably.

World War I prevented Australia's scheduled tour of South Africa proceeding in 1913-14. Players originally selected for this trip were T.J.E. Andrews, W.W. Armstrong (Capt.), E.P. Barbour, W. Bardsley, F. Baring, W. Carkeek, G.R. Hazlitt, C. Kelleway, C.G. Macartney, E.R. Mayne, A.G. Moyes, J. Ryder and W.J. Whitty, with G.C. Campbell as manager. Hill, Massie, Hordern, Ransford, and Trumper were unavailable. Bert Folkard went into the team when Hazlitt dropped out and later Roy Park replaced Barbour. The First AIF team played nine matches in South Africa on their way home, eight of them first-class, but it was not until 1921-22 that the second official Australian team visited South Africa.

South Africa at Lord's during the Triangular tournament with England and Australia, 1912: *back row* C. Stricker, R.O. Schwartz, R. Beaumont, T. Campbell, G.P.O. Hartigan, J.D. Cox; *centre* S.J. Pegler, L.J. Tancred, F. Mitchell (capt.), G. Faulkner, S.J. Snooke, A.D. Nourse; *front* H.W. Taylor, T.A. Ward, C.P. Carter.

The AIF team in South Africa in 1919: *back row* C.E. Pellew, C.B. Willis, C.S. Winning, J.M. Gregory, E.A. Bull, J.T. Murray, A.W. Lampard, E.J. Long, W.S. Stirling; *seated* J.M. Taylor, W.L. Trenerry, E.J. Cameron (manager), H.L. Collins (capt.), W.A. Sewell (South African liaison officer), C.T. Docker, W.A. Oldfield. *Les Hill Collection*

AUSTRALIA IN SOUTH AFRICA 1921–22

	First-class Results					All Matches			
Matches	Won	Lost	Drawn	Tied	Matches	Won	Lost	Drawn	Tied
6	4	–	2	–	6	4	–	2	–

Date	Venue	Opponent	Results for Australians
Oct 22	Johannesburg	Transvaal	Won by 9 wkts
Oct 29	Durban	Natal	Won by 194 runs
Nov 5	Durban	SOUTH AFRICA (1st Test)	Drawn
Nov 12	Johannesburg	SOUTH AFRICA (2nd Test)	Drawn
Nov 19	Cape Town	Western Province	Won by 8 wkts
Nov 26	Cape Town	SOUTH AFRICA (3rd Test)	Won by 10 wkts

Player	State	M	Inn	NO	Runs	HS	50	100	Avrge	Ct/St	Overs	Mdns	Runs	Wkts	Avrge	5wi	10wm	Best
Andrews, TJE	NSW	6	8	1	104	35*	–	–	14.86	6	3.0	–	20	–	–	–	–	–
Bardsley, W	NSW	5	9	2	190	66	1	–	27.14	3	–	–	–	–	–	–	–	–
Carter, H	NSW	4	7	3	55	31*	–	–	13.75	2/3	–	–	–	–	–	–	–	–
Collins, HL (Capt)	NSW	6	11	2	548	203	1	2	60.89	7	43.0	22	50	3	16.67	–	–	2/6
Gregory, JM	NSW	5	6	–	266	119	2	1	44.33	9	179.3	39	445	30	14.83	3	1	6/57
Hendry, HSTL	NSW	5	7	2	126	57*	1	–	25.20	8	85.0	21	193	6	32.17	–	–	3/13
Macartney, CG	NSW	5	9	2	492	135	2	2	70.29	4	138.3	62	240	14	17.14	2	–	5/40
Mailey, AA	NSW	6	7	2	32	14	–	–	6.40	7	275.5	48	802	35	22.91	2	1	6/88
Mayne, ER	SA	4	6	–	111	43	–	–	18.50	5	1.0	–	1	–	–	–	–	–
McDonald, EA	VIC	4	4	1	20	9*	–	–	6.66	1	175.0	55	445	13	34.23	–	–	3/53
Oldfield, WAS	NSW	3	3	1	26	17*	–	–	13.50	1/3	–	–	–	–	–	–	–	–
Pellew, CE	SA	2	2	–	26	20	–	–	13.00	1	–	–	–	–	–	–	–	–
Ryder, J	VIC	6	8	1	468	142	5	1	66.86	3	97.0	29	180	8	22.50	–	–	3/24
Taylor, JM	NSW	5	7	–	62	18	–	–	8.86	3	11.0	4	19	–	–	–	–	–

Warwick Armstrong, overweight and shin-sore after the arduous tour of England in which his team beat England three–nil and played their way through 38 matches, handed over the captaincy to Herbie Collins for the brief tour of South Africa on the way home. The Australians played six first-class matches, three of them Tests, won four, and drew two. They began by defeating the Transvaal by nine wickets at Johannesburg and Natal by 194 runs at Durban.

The First Test at Durban was drawn despite a marvellous innings of 116 by Macartney after his first innings 59. Collins scored the first double century by an Australian against South Africa in the Second Test at Johannesburg, only to have his 203 overshadowed by Jack Gregory's century in 70 minutes on his way to 117, but this Test was also drawn. Gregory's century remained the fastest in Tests in terms of balls received (67) until Viv Richards made a century against England at St John's in 11 fewer balls (56) in 1985–86. Gregory's century was in stark contrast to Charlie Frank's 152 in 518 minutes to save the Test for South Africa after they followed-on 207 behind. Frank, badly gassed in World War I, also scored 108 for South Africa against the First AIF XI in Johannesburg in 1919–20. Australia won the Third Test at Cape Town by 10 wickets when Ryder made 142, showing how badly neglected he had been in England. Macartney took 5 for 44 with his left-arm slows. All the Australians' matches were on matting, with the Tests extended to four days.

AUSTRALIA IN SOUTH AFRICA 1935–36

Vic Richardson took over the Australian captaincy vacated by Bill Woodfull for Australia's first full scale tour of South Africa, with Bradman unable to tour through illness. Australia triumphed in one of the happiest of tours because of brilliant batting by Stan McCabe, Jack Fingleton, Arthur Chipperfield, Len Darling and Leo O'Brien, smart fielding dictated by Bert Oldfield's polished keeping, and persistently penetrative bowling from Clarrie Grimmett, Bill O'Reilly, Ernie McCormick, and to a lesser extent 'Chuck' Fleetwood-Smith.

They received only one big setback—in the Second Test when Dudley Nourse scored 231, the highest score by a South African in Tests. Australia had outplayed Natal, Western Province, and Transvaal in the lead-up to the Tests. O'Reilly clinched a nine-wicket win in the First Test by taking 5 for 49 in South Africa's second innings after centuries by McCabe, 149, and Chipperfield. After Nourse's long innings in the Second Test, McCabe led the way in a spirited Australian chase for the 299 runs required for victory. He scored his first 50 in 40 minutes and hit the ball so hard that when storm clouds arrived South Africa's captain, Herbie Wade, appealed to the umpires to go off on the grounds that his fieldsmen were in danger. McCabe was on 189 not out after hitting a

HOME AND AWAY

Matches	First-class Results Won	Lost	Drawn	Tied	Matches	All Matches Won	Lost	Drawn	Tied
16	13	–	3	–	16	13	–	3	–

Date	Venue	Opponent	Results for Australians
Nov 23	Durban	Natal	Won by an inns & 26 runs
Nov 30	Cape Town	Western Province	Won by an inns & 44 runs
Dec 7	Johannesburg	Transvaal	Won by 10 wkts
Dec 14	Durban	SOUTH AFRICA (1st Test)	Won by 9 wkts
Dec 24	Johannesburg	SOUTH AFRICA (2nd Test)	Drawn
Jan 1	Cape Town	SOUTH AFRICA (3rd Test)	Won by an inns & 78 runs
Jan 7	Port Elizabeth	Eastern Province	Won by an inns & 144 runs
Jan 11	East London	Border	Won by an inns & 14 runs
Jan 18	Bloemfontein	Orange Free State	Won by an inns & 146 runs
Jan 25	Johannesburg	Transvaal	Won by an inns & 31 runs
Jan 31	Kimberley	Griqualand West	Won by an inns & 105 runs
Feb 8	Bulawayo	Southern Rhodesia	Drawn
Feb 15	Johannesburg	SOUTH AFRICA (4th Test)	Won by an inns & 184 runs
Feb 22	Durban	Natal	Drawn
Feb 28	Durban	SOUTH AFRICA (5th Test)	Won by an inns & 6 runs
Mar 14	Cape Town	Western Province	Won by 8 wkts

Player	State	M	Inn	NO	Runs	HS	50	100	Avrge	Ct/St	Overs	Mdns	Runs	Wkts	Avrge	5wi	10wm	Best
Barnett, BA	VIC	9	11	–	155	41	–	–	14.09	4/9	–	–	–	–	–	–	–	–
Brown, WA	NSW	15	19	2	1065	148	9	2	62.64	6	1.0	–	2	–	–	–	–	–
Chipperfield, AG	NSW	14	15	4	655	109	1	4	59.54	14	114.4	23	297	12	24.75	–	–	4/53
Darling, LS	VIC	15	16	1	711	108	3	2	47.40	2	4.0	1	15	1	15.00	–	–	1/13
Fingleton, JHW	NSW	15	19	4	1192	167	4	6	79.16	14	1.0	–	3	–	–	–	–	–
Fleetwood–Smith, LO	VIC	7	4	1	18	12	–	–	6.00	–	265.4	59	770	25	30.80	2	1	7/71
Grimmett, CV	SA	12	11	2	125	30*	–	–	13.88	6	663.1	229	1362	92	14.80	9	4	7/40
McCabe, SJ	NSW	13	16	2	800	189*	1	4	57.14	3	150.0	34	376	7	53.71	–	–	2/30
McCormick, EL	VIC	13	11	4	36	13	–	–	5.14	5	344.2	88	885	49	18.06	1	–	5/29
O'Brien, LPJ	VIC	12	13	2	523	113	1	2	47.54	4	9.0	1	44	1	44.00	–	–	1/33
O'Reilly, WJ	NSW	15	13	3	168	56*	1	–	16.80	9	662.5	250	1289	95	13.56	11	3	8/73
Oldfield, WAS	NSW	13	12	2	343	132	–	1	34.30	9/14	–	–	–	–	–	–	–	–
Richardson, VY (Capt)	SA	14	14	1	443	84	3	–	34.07	26	–	–	–	–	–	–	–	–
Sievers, MW	VIC	9	9	2	294	72	2	–	42.00	4	136.1	29	299	7	42.71	–	–	2/22

century before lunch when a heavy storm ended the match. Australia were then 125 runs from victory with eight wickets left.

Fingleton began a wonderful sequence by scoring 112 in the Third Test at Cape Town, adding 233 for the first wicket with Brown, 121. Grimmett took ten wickets in the match, and Australia won by an innings and 78 runs. Between Tests the Australians outclassed Eastern Province, Border, Orange Free State and Basutoland, Transvaal, Griqualand West, and drew with Rhodesia when rain interrupted play. Fingleton hit another century, 108, in the Fourth Test at Johannesburg, where Grimmett took another ten wickets to give Australia an innings and 184-run win. At Durban in the Fifth Test, Fingleton made his third century in three Test innings, 118, and Richardson held a record five catches in South Africa's second innings. This time Grimmett took 13 for 173 to finish the rubber with 44 wickets at 14.59. Fingleton made 1192 runs at 79.16 on the tour and Grimmett took 92 wickets at 14.80, O'Reilly 95 wickets at 13.56. Wade also achieved a landmark by ending his career after captaining South Africa in all his ten Tests.

Australians in South Africa, 1935–36: *back row* E.L.L. McCormick, M.W.S. Sievers, W.J. O'Reilly, J.H. Fingleton, B.A. Barnett; *centre* W.F. Lambrechts (manager), L.P. O'Brien, W.A. Brown, S.D.H. Rowe (manager), L.O.B. Fleetwood-Smith, A.G. Chipperfield, W. Ferguson (scorer); *front* C.V. Grimmett, S.J. McCabe, V.Y. Richards (capt.), W.A. Oldfield, L.S. Darling. *Les Hill Collection*

AUSTRALIA IN SOUTH AFRICA 1949-50

	First-class Results					All Matches			
Matches	Won	Lost	Drawn	Tied	Matches	Won	Lost	Drawn	Tied
21	14	–	7	–	25	18	–	7	–

Date	Venue	Opponent	Results for Australians
Oct 21	Eshowe	*Zululand	Won by an inns & 280 runs
Oct 28	Durban	Natal	Drawn
Nov 5	Benoni	NE Transvaal	Won by 10 wkts
Nov 11	Bulawayo	Southern Rhodesia	Won by an inns & 161 runs
Nov 19	Salisbury	South Africans	Won by an inns & 72 runs
Nov 26	Bloemfontein	Orange Free State	Won by an inns & 139 runs
Dec 2	Cape Town	Western Province	Drawn
Dec 6	Wellington	*W Province Country Districts	Won by an inns & 54 runs
Dec 10	Johannesburg	Transvaal	Won by 15 runs
Dec 16	Durban	South Africans	Drawn
Dec 24	Johannesburg	SOUTH AFRICA (1st Test)	Won by an inns & 85 runs
Dec 31	Cape Town	SOUTH AFRICA (2nd Test)	Won by 8 wkts
Jan 7	Port Elizabeth	Eastern Province	Won by an inns & 39 runs
Jan 14	East London	Border	Won by an inns & 293 runs
Jan 20	Durban	SOUTH AFRICA (3rd Test)	Won by 5 wkts
Jan 27	Johannesburg	Transvaal	Won by 7 wkts
Feb 1	Witbank	*NE Transvaal Country Districts	Won by an inns & 170 runs
Feb 4	Pretoria	NE Transvaal	Won by an inns & 165 runs
Feb 10	Johannesburg	SOUTH AFRICA (4th Test)	Drawn
Feb 17	Kimberley	Griqualand West	Drawn
Feb 22	Ladysmith	*Natal Country Districts	Won by 129 runs
Feb 24	Pietermaritzburg	Natal	Drawn
Mar 3	Port Elizabeth	SOUTH AFRICA (5th Test)	Won by an inns & 259 runs
Mar 10	Cape Town	Western Province	Drawn
Mar 17	Johannesburg	South Africans	Won by an inns & 88 runs

Australia in South Africa, 1949–50: *back row* R.N. Harvey, J.R. Moroney, K.A. Archer, K.R. Miller, G. Noblet, W.A. Johnton, R.R. Lindwall, S.J.E. Loxton, A.K. Walker; *seated* W. Ferguson (scorer), G.R.A. Langley, R.A. Saggers, A.L. Hassett (capt.), E.A. Dwyer (manager), A.R. Morris, I.A. Johnson, C.L. McCool, C. Cartledge (South African liaison officer).

Player	State	M	Inn	NO	Runs	HS	50	100	Avrge	Ct/St	Overs	Mdns	Runs	Wkts	Avrge	5wi	10wm	Best
Archer, KA	QLD	15	21	5	698	134	4	1	43.62	8/1	6.0	–	30	–	–	–	–	–
Harvey, RN	VIC	19	25	5	1526	178	4	8	76.30	10	28.0	3	104	3	34.66	–	–	2/46
Hassett, AL (Capt)	VIC	15	16	3	889	167	5	4	68.38	14	10.0	2	29	1	29.00	–	–	1/13
Johnson, IW	VIC	18	18	2	360	70	2	–	22.50	10	426.4	75	1329	79	16.82	3	–	6/22
Johnston, WA	VIC	13	6	5	29	24*	–	–	29.00	6	335.2	77	770	56	13.75	3	–	6/20
Langley, GRA	SA	6	4	–	72	58	1	–	18.00	16/6	–	–	–	–	–	–	–	–
Lindwall, RR	NSW	16	14	2	150	28	–	–	12.50	5	289.7	53	738	49	15.06	2	–	5/25
Loxton, SJE	VIC	18	23	3	809	101	6	1	40.45	5	89.0	23	217	12	18.08	–	–	4/32
McCool, CL	QLD	18	20	5	438	100*	–	1	29.20	15	316.2	57	980	51	19.21	1	–	5/41
Miller, KR	NSW	13	18	3	577	131	4	1	38.46	10	258.0	42	728	44	16.54	2	–	6/35
Moroney, JR	NSW	18	27	3	1331	160*	5	6	55.45	5/1	–	–	–	–	–	–	–	–
Morris, AR	NSW	18	27	3	1411	157	1	8	58.79	5	9.0	–	48	–	–	–	–	–
Noblet, G	SA	15	11	5	138	55*	1	–	23.00	8	307.4	88	557	38	14.65	–	–	4/11
Saggers, RA	NSW	14	11	3	111	33	–	–	13.87	30/20	–	–	–	–	–	–	–	–
Walker, AK	NSW	15	11	2	89	25*	–	–	9.88	2	210.5	43	506	25	20.24	–	–	4/22

Lindsay Hassett took over the Australian captaincy for this tour after Bradman's retirement. Keith Miller, rated the finest allrounder in the world after his postwar exploits in England, was omitted from the original party—newspapers claimed in punishment for bowling bouncers in Bradman's Testimonial match—but was flown in as a replacement when Bill Johnston was hurt in a car accident. Miller played in all five Tests, hit a century and four fifties and took 44 wickets on the tour at an average cost of 16.54, including 5 for 40 in the First Test. Transvaal had a rare chance to beat Australia before the Tests began but collapsed for 53 chasing 69. Ian Johnson took 6 for 22.

Australia won the series four–nil, with the other Test drawn and throughout the tour were brilliantly led by Hassett whenever defeat threatened. His team remained unbeaten largely because Neil Harvey scored eight centuries, four of them in Tests, compiling 1526 runs at 76.30. Arthur Morris hit nine centuries, two of them in Tests, Jack Moroney seven centuries, with one in Tests, and altogether the Australians hit 33 centuries. Only four centuries were made against them, two by Dudley Nourse, and one each by Athol Rowan and Owen Wynne.

Australia won the First Test at Johannesburg by an innings and 85 runs, the Second Test at Cape Town by eight wickets, thanks to Harvey's 178, the first of his four in successive Tests. The Third Test at Durban produced some diabolically cunning captaincy by Hassett that gave Australia victory despite a disastrous first innings of 75, their lowest-ever total in South Africa. For some inexplicable reason Nourse, with a lead of 236, chose to bat on. Miller turned an off-break almost the width of the pitch in the first over and immediately Hassett realised the pitch remained hazardous (18 wickets had fallen for 146 runs on the second day). Australia's bowlers were told not to get the South Africans out but not to concede boundaries while the pitch dried out. Veterans in the crowd realised what was going on when the Australians did not bowl at the stumps and fieldsmen retreated to cut off fours, but Nourse did not declare. South Africa's innings ended at 99 leaving Australia to score 336 in 435 minutes. They got them with 25 minutes to spare, Harvey contributing 151 not out.

After this celebrated victory, Australia drew the Fourth Test at Johannesburg, where Moroney made centuries in each innings, 118 and 101 not out, and Harvey made an even 100. By the Fifth Test at Port Elizabeth all the Australian batsmen were in superb form. Morris, 157, Harvey, 116, and Hassett, 167, lifted Australia's first innings total to 549 and this proved enough to win by an innings and 259 runs. This was South Africa's sixth series against Australia without a win. Ron Saggers, Tallon's understudy the previous year in England, kept wicket efficiently throughout the rubber. Harvey scored 660 runs in the Tests at an average of 132.00.

AUSTRALIA IN SOUTH AFRICA 1957-58

First-class Results					All Matches				
Matches	Won	Lost	Drawn	Tied	Matches	Won	Lost	Drawn	Tied
20	11	–	9	–	22	11	–	11	–

Date	Venue	Opponent	Results for Australians
Oct 19	Kitwe	*Northern Rhodesia	Drawn
Oct 25	Salisbury	Rhodesia	Won by an inns & 14 runs
Nov 1	Bulawayo	Rhodesia	Won by 10 wkts
Nov 8	Johannesburg	Transvaal	Won by 9 wkts
Nov 15	Pretoria	South Africans	Won by an inns & 30 runs
Nov 22	Durban	Natal	Drawn
Nov 29	East London	Border	Won by an inns & 6 runs
Dec 6	Port Elizabeth	Eastern Province	Won by an inns & 81 runs
Dec 12	Cape Town	Western Province	Won by 10 wkts
Dec 20	Benoni	NE Transvaal	Drawn
Dec 23	Johannesburg	SOUTH AFRICA (1st Test)	Drawn
Dec 31	Cape Town	SOUTH AFRICA (2nd Test)	Won by an inns & 141 runs
Jan 7	Pretoria	*South African Country Districts	Drawn
Jan 10	Johannesburg	Transvaal	Drawn
Jan 17	Pietermaritzburg	Natal	Drawn
Jan 24	Durban	SOUTH AFRICA (3rd Test)	Drawn
Jan 31	Bloemfontein	Orange Free State	Drawn
Feb 7	Johannesburg	SOUTH AFRICA (4th Test)	Won by 10 wkts
Feb 14	Kimberley	Griqualand West	Drawn
Feb 21	Cape Town	Western Province	Won by an inns & 50 runs
Feb 28	Port Elizabeth	SOUTH AFRICA (5th Test)	Won by 8 wkts
Mar 8	Cape Town	South African University	Drawn

Australia in South Africa, 1957-58: *standing* L.E. Favell, A.T.W. Grout, R.B. Simpson, I. Meckiff, N.J.N. Hawke, K.D. Mackay, L.F. Kline, B.N. Jarman; *seated* J. Norton (manager), P.J.P. Burge, R. Benaud, R.N. Harvey, I.D. Craig (capt.), C.C. McDonald, A.K. Davidson, J.W. Burke, M. McLennan (baggage master).

Player	State	M	Inn	NO	Runs	HS	50	100	Avrge	Ct/St	Overs	Mdns	Runs	Wkts	Avrge	5wi	10wm	Best
Benaud, R	NSW	18	20	4	817	187	–	4	51.06	18	742.7	187	2056	106	19.39	11	2	7/46
Burge, PJP	QLD	12	12	3	441	111*	2	1	49.00	10	–	–	–	–	–	–	–	–
Burke, JW	NSW	16	19	3	1041	189	5	4	65.06	7	191.0	53	468	21	22.28	1	–	6/40
Craig, ID (Capt)	NSW	16	17	1	591	113	2	2	36.93	5	–	–	–	–	–	–	–	–
Davidson, AK	NSW	17	17	2	813	129	2	4	54.20	14	430.1	101	1090	72	15.13	6	–	6/34
Drennan, J	SA	11	7	4	56	31*	–	–	18.66	2	197.4	42	587	26	22.57	2	–	5/43
Favell, LE	SA	13	14	–	660	190	2	2	47.14	6	10.0	1	64	2	32.00	–	–	1/7
Gaunt, RA	WA	7	5	2	12	8*	–	–	4.00	3	161.4	18	488	12	40.66	–	–	3/26
Grout, ATW	QLD	12	12	3	341	95	3	–	37.88	35/12	1.0	–	2	–	–	–	–	–
Harvey, RN	VIC	14	15	–	759	173	5	2	50.60	10	45.5	11	148	2	74.00	–	–	1/17
Jarman, BN	SA	9	11	5	174	30*	–	–	29.00	19/10	2.0	–	9	–	–	–	–	–
Kline, LF	VIC	17	13	5	68	16*	–	–	8.50	4	422.1	119	1104	54	20.44	2	–	6/65
Mackay, KD	QLD	16	18	5	739	113	8	1	56.84	7	269.4	74	519	17	30.52	–	–	3/29
McDonald, CC	VIC	14	19	2	609	99	5	–	35.82	4	10.0	1	35	2	17.50	–	–	1/14
Meckiff, I	VIC	12	10	3	154	48	–	–	22.00	6	308.0	77	762	33	23.09	2	–	6/29
Simpson, RB	WA	16	18	4	671	150*	2	2	47.92	26	31.0	4	111	2	55.50	–	–	1/34

The heroes who had served Australian cricket so well immediately after World War II disappeared from Test cricket after losing The Ashes to England in 1956. Hassett, Morris and Barnes had retired earlier but now they were joined by Ian Johnson, Keith Miller, Ray Lindwall and Gil Langley, leaving 22-year-old Ian Craig, Australia's youngest-ever captain, to take the team to South Africa. Facing a relatively untried side, the South Africans were optimistic they could win their first Test against Australia and perhaps even take the rubber. Craig's team crushed those hopes by going through the 22-match tour unbeaten and winning the Test series three-nil with two draws.

The patience the selectors had shown with Benaud finally paid off after regular failures. Benaud took 106 tour wickets with leg-breaks, top-spinners and googlies and headed the batting averages with 817 runs at 51.06, including four centuries. Alan Davidson also developed into a top-class allrounder, with 813 runs at 54.20 and four centuries, plus 72 wickets at 15.13. Lindsay Kline's left-arm spin also made a valuable contribution. Wally Grout grabbed the chance he had been waiting for after years as Tallon's deputy. Only Benaud and Jimmy Burke made Test centuries. Simpson, McDonald and Mackay consistently scored well, compensating for the disappointing run-getting of Harvey and Craig. South Africa often showed signs of panic against wrist spin and only the opening bowlers Adcock and Heine showed any hostility.

South Africa began well with an opening stand of 176 by McGlew (108) and Goddard (90) at Johannesburg but Australia fought back splendidly and with Grout taking a record six catches in the second innings a draw looked a fair result. Australia won the Second Test at Cape Town by an innings and 141 runs after Burke (189) and McDonald (99) put on 190 for the first wicket, Kline ending the match with a hat-trick. The Third Test at Durban was also drawn, following another century by McGlew (105) and 134 from Waite. Australia saved the match despite succumbing to Adcock (6 for 43) in their first innings of 163. Australia won the Fourth Test in Johannesburg by 10 wickets after Benaud scored 100 and took nine wickets in the match. The Fifth Test at Port Elizabeth ended in an eight-wicket win for Australia after Davidson took 4 for 44 and 5 for 38, Benaud rounding off a personal triumph with 5 for 82 in the second innings. Craig may have disappointed with the bat but he led the team with flair and could be proud that such an inexperienced side was unconquered.

AUSTRALIA IN SOUTH AFRICA 1966-67

Australia in South Africa, 1966-67: *back row* G. Watson, N.J. Hawke, D. Renneberg, J. Hubble, I.R. Redpath; *centre* M. McLennan (scorer), G. Becker, H.B. Taber, K.R. Stackpole, I.M. Chappell, G. Thomas; *front* J.W. Martin, T.R. Veivers, W.M. Lawry, W.S. Jacobs (manager), R.B. Simpson (capt.), G.D. McKenzie, R.M. Cowper.

First-class Results					All Matches				
Matches	Won	Lost	Drawn	Tied	Matches	Won	Lost	Drawn	Tied
17	7	5	5	–	24	11	6	7	–

Date	Venue	Opponent	Results for Australians
Nov 2	Bulawayo	*Matabelaland	Drawn
Nov 5	Salisbury	Rhodesia	Won by 8 wkts
Nov 11	Johannesburg	Transvaal	Lost by 76 runs
Nov 16	Stilfontein	*Transvaal Country Districts	Won by 10 wkts
Nov 18	Cape Town	Western Province	Won by an inns & 108 runs
Nov 23	Wellington	*Western Province Cntry Districts	Won by 8 wkts
Nov 25	Port Elizabeth	Eastern Province	Won by 6 wkts
Nov 30	Grahamstown	*Eastern Province Cntry Districts	Won by 8 wkts
Dec 2	East London	South Africans	Lost by 190 runs
Dec 9	Durban	Natal	Won by 67 runs
Dec 15	Harmony	*Orange Free State Cntry Districts	Won by 7 wkts

Date	Venue	Opponent	Results for Australians
Dec 17	Pretoria	South African Universities	Drawn
Dec 23	Johannesburg	SOUTH AFRICA (1st Test)	Lost by 233 runs
Dec 31	Cape Town	SOUTH AFRICA (2nd Test)	Won by 6 wkts
Jan 7	East London	Norder	Won by 10 wkts
Jan 13	Bloemfontein	Orange Free State	Drawn
Jan 20	Durban	SOUTH AFRICA (3rd Test)	Lost by 8 wkts
Jan 27	Pretoria	NE Transvaal	Drawn
Jan 31	Benoni	*South African Country	Drawn
Feb 3	Johannesburg	SOUTH AFRICA (4th Test)	Drawn
Feb 10	Kimberley	Griqualand West	Won by 376 runs
Feb 17	Pietermaritzburg	South Africans	Drawn
Feb 24	Port Elizabeth	SOUTH AFRICA (5th Test)	Lost by 7 wkts
Mar 4	Johannesburg	*South African XI	Lost by 3 wkts

Player	State	M	Inn	NO	Runs	HS	50	100	Avrge	Ct/St	Overs	Mdns	Runs	Wkts	Avrge	5wi	10wm	Best
Becker, GC	WA	5	7	1	68	16	–	–	11.33	10/4	–	–	–	–	–	–	–	–
Chappell, IM	SA	15	27	4	868	164	2	2	37.73	12	407.5	115	1154	35	32.97	1	–	5/53
Cowper, RM	VIC	14	25	2	1116	201*	5	2	48.52	10	272.1	103	610	27	22.59	–	–	4/8
Hawke, NJN	SA	11	15	6	163	27*	–	–	18.11	6	273.3	75	761	20	38.05	–	–	2/19
Hubble, JM	WA	8	7	1	45	20	–	–	7.50	6	153.5	34	440	18	24.44	1	–	5/74
Lawry, WM	VIC	13	22	–	858	107	5	1	39.00	2	2.0	–	17	1	17.00	–	–	1/17
Martin, JW	NSW	11	13	–	299	60	2	–	23.00	5	297.3	83	862	42	20.52	3	1	7/30
McKenzie, GD	WA	11	18	4	224	35	–	–	16.00	6	501.2	137	1125	44	25.56	4	–	5/46
Redpath, IR	VIC	13	23	3	1045	154	5	2	52.25	12	4.0	–	13	–	–	–	–	–
Renneberg, DA	NSW	13	17	7	42	22	–	–	4.20	5	347.2	70	1001	35	28.60	1	–	5/97
Simpson, RB (Capt)	NSW	14	26	4	1344	243	5	3	61.09	26	256.1	72	734	24	30.58	–	–	3/74
Stackpole, KR	VIC	13	21	2	740	138*	2	2	38.94	5	109.0	34	279	3	93.00	–	–	1/14
Taber, HB	NSW	12	17	3	162	30	–	–	11.57	32/2	–	–	–	–	–	–	–	–
Thomas, G	NSW	10	15	–	485	134	2	1	32.33	11/2	2.0	–	10	–	–	–	–	–
Veivers, TR	QLD	14	21	2	703	109	4	1	37.00	6	213.1	63	509	5	101.80	–	–	2/50
Watson, GD	VIC	10	15	2	295	118*	1	1	22.69	5	128.1	29	364	13	28.00	–	–	3/12

After 64 years and 22 attempts South Africa won their first Test at home against Australia. They set up a 233-run victory by scoring 620 in the second innings of the First Test at Johannesburg over Christmas 1966. Wicket-keeper Dennis Lindsay, who in 1961 against Essex hit five successive sixes to give his side a win, this time took 274 minutes to contribute 182 to South Africa's highest Test score. Lindsay had quite a match as he had earlier equalled the world's record by dismissing six Australian batsmen in their first innings. Brian Taber, who had never previously attended a Test, dismissed eight batsmen on his debut for Australia.

Australia fought back to level the series with a six-wicket win in the Second Test at Cape Town, with Simpson, 153, and Stackpole, 134, lifting the first innings total to 542. Graeme Pollock made 209 of South Africa's 353 total in reply. Perth fast bowler Graham McKenzie's match return of 8 for 132 was a major contribution to Australia's triumph. Simpson won the toss and sent South Africa in at Durban in the Third Test and appeared to have acted wisely when Eddie Barlow went first ball, but South Africa reached 300, to which Australia could only respond with 147. Following-on Australia made 334 after Bill Lawry had ten stitches inserted in his head after missing a hook shot against Peter Pollock. South Africa made the 185 needed to win, for the loss of only two wickets. Rain prevented a result in the Fourth Test at Johannesburg after Lindsay's third century (131) of the rubber, and South Africa then clinched their first series win over Australia by winning the Fifth Test at Port Elizabeth by seven wickets. Peter Pollock became the third South African to take 100 Test wickets, which his brother Graeme celebrated with 105, his sixth Test 100 on his 23rd birthday.

This was an outstanding South African XI, which had shared the series in Australia in 1963–64, and defeated England in 1965 for the first time in 30 years. Bob Simpson led an Australian side that contained five newcomers to Tests as well, but could not overcome the lack of bowling strike power to support McKenzie. Lawry, Thomas, Cowper and Stackpole all disappointed. Graeme Watson flopped as a replacement for Doug Walters, who missed the tour because of his Army call-up. In most of Australia's 17 matches Simpson had the job of covering up a six- or seven-man tail and the tour produced only seven Australian wins.

AUSTRALIA IN SOUTH AFRICA 1969-70

SOUTH AFRICAN CHALLENGE

First-class Results					All Matches				
Matches	Won	Lost	Drawn	Tied	Matches	Won	Lost	Drawn	Tied
12	4	4	4	–	12	4	4	4	–

Date	Venue	Opponent	Results for Australians
Jan 6	Pretoria	NE Transvaal	Won by 10 wkts
Jan 10	Kimberley	Griqualand West	Won by an inns & 1 run
Jan 16	Port Elizabeth	Eastern Province	Drawn
Jan 22	Cape Town	SOUTH AFRICA (1st Test)	Lost by 170 runs
Jan 30	Johannesburg	Transvaal	Drawn
Feb 5	Durban	SOUTH AFRICA (2nd Test)	Lost by an inns & 129 runs
Feb 13	East London	Border	Won by 2 wkts
Feb 19	Johannesburg	SOUTH AFRICA (3rd Test)	Lost by 307 runs
Feb 27	Durban	Natal	Drawn
Mar 5	Port Elizabeth	SOUTH AFRICA (4th Test)	Lost by 323 runs
Mar 13	Cape Town	Western Province	Drawn
Mar 19	Bloemfontein	Orange Free State	Won by an inns & 185 runs

Player	State	M	Inn	NO	Runs	HS	50	100	Avrge	Ct/St	Overs	Mdns	Runs	Wkts	Avrge	5wi	10wm	Best
Chappell, IM	SA	10	16	1	503	108	2	2	33.53	9	12.4	5	41	2	20.50	–	–	2/11
Connolly, AN	VIC	9	11	3	107	36	–	–	13.37	4	371.5	117	882	38	23.21	2	–	6/47
Freeman, EW	SA	6	11	2	232	67	2	–	25.77	5	150.2	27	490	12	40.83	–	–	4/39
Gleeson, JW	NSW	9	11	3	111	24	–	–	13.87	4	502.0	181	1150	59	19.40	5	1	6/46
Irvine, JT	WA	6	8	1	241	56	1	–	34.42	7	–	–	–	–	–	–	–	–
Jordan, RC	VIC	6	5	3	101	31*	–	–	50.50	9/6	–	–	–	–	–	–	–	–
Lawry, WM (Capt)	VIC	10	15	5	545	157*	2	1	54.50	10	–	–	–	–	–	–	–	–
Mallett, AA	SA	7	6	1	62	20	–	–	12.40	2	348.5	121	1042	33	33.09	1	–	5/126
Mayne, LC	WA	9	9	–	132	41	–	–	14.66	4	310.1	82	799	28	28.53	1	–	5/26
McKenzie, GD	WA	9	9	1	49	19	–	–	6.12	4	271.5	71	651	10	65.10	–	–	2/33
Redpath, IR	VIC	11	17	2	748	152	5	2	49.86	10	4.0	1	22	–	–	–	–	–
Sheahan, AP	VIC	11	16	3	648	93	6	–	49.84	6	–	–	–	–	–	–	–	–
Stackpole, KR	VIC	11	17	2	564	123	2	1	37.60	9	66.4	15	191	8	23.87	–	–	2/0
Taber, HB	NSW	8	12	4	196	46	–	–	24.50	25/2	3.0	2	6	–	–	–	–	–
Walters, KD	NSW	10	17	1	473	109	3	1	29.56	10	103.0	22	296	9	32.88	–	–	2/16

With players' tempers frayed by two months of argument and gastric troubles in Ceylon and India, Bill Lawry's team took a sorry beating in a four-Test series that ended three years of isolation from big cricket. Lawry, on his seventh overseas tour at the age of 32, completely failed to lift the spirit of his team, and the South African bowlers made nonsense of his tour forecasts. South Africa won the First Test at Cape Town by 170 runs after Barlow scored his fourth 100 against Australia. Barry Richards made a superb 140 in only his second Test to give South Africa a fine start in the Second Test at Durban, but even this innings was overshadowed by Graeme Pollock's 274. Pollock hit a five and 43 fours in 417 minutes batting. Australia responded to South Africa's 622, their best in Test cricket, with a paltry 157. Following-on, they managed 336, but still lost by an innings and 129 runs.

By then Australia's morale was at an all-time low, with the Victorians supporting Lawry scornful of their New South Wales team-mates, and the South Africans disappointed that they saw so little of Lawry off the field. Gleeson took 8 for 186, fine match figures against such a powerful batting lineup in the Third Test at Johannesburg, but could not prevent another decisive South African triumph, this time by a record run margin of 307 after another century (110) by Barlow. At Port Elizabeth centuries from Richards (126) and left-hander Lee Irvine (102) enabled South Africa to complete a four-nil drubbing, their record margin after 172 Tests.

South Africa's dominance attracted jubilant, sell-out crowds, and when officials proposed that a Fifth Test be added to Australia's itinerary, vice-captain Ian Chappell told a team meeting that they should take the chance to show what Test appearances were worth by asking for $500 a man for the extra Test. South Africa agreed, but the ACB, who paid $180 for Tests in Australia at the time, refused, offering the players $200 for a fifth Test. The Test was never played although the affluent Wanderers' Club was ready to make up the difference between the ACB offer and the $500 sought by the Australians. The Australian Board's attitude to Test payments was one of the grievances that led to the Packer-funded rebellion seven years later.

(*Opposite*) Australia in South Africa, 1969–70: *standing* L.C. Mayne, E.W. Freeman, A.N. Connolly, A.A. Mallett, A.P. Sheahan, J.T. Irvine, J.W. Gleeson, M. McLennan (scorer); *seated* K.D. Walters, I.R. Redpath, G.D. McKenzie, I.M. Chappell, F.W. Bennett (manager), W.M. Lawry (capt.), K.R. Stackpole, H.B. Taber, R.C. Jordon.

AUSTRALIA IN SOUTH AFRICA 1994

	First-class Results					All Matches			
Matches	Won	Lost	Drawn	Tied	Matches	Won	Lost	Drawn	Tied
6	3	1	2	–	16	7	5	4	–

Date	Venue	Opponent	Results for Australians
Feb 10	Randjiesfontein	*Nici Oppenheimer XI	Drawn
Feb 12	Verwoerdburg	Northern Transvaal	Won by 249 runs
Feb 17	Potchefstroom	*President's XI	No result
Feb 19	Johannesburg	*South Africa (L/O Intl)	Lost by 5 runs
Feb 20	Verwoerdburg	*South Africa (L/O Intl)	Lost by 56 runs
Feb 22	Port Elizabeth	*South Africa (L/O Intl)	Won by 88 runs
Feb 24	Durban	*South Africa (L/O Intl)	Lost by 7 wkts
Feb 26	Bloemfontein	Orange Free State	Won by 60 runs
Mar 4	Johannesburg	SOUTH AFRICA (1st Test)	Lost by 197 runs
Mar 12	Stellenbosch	Boland	Drawn
Mar 17	Cape Town	SOUTH AFRICA (2nd Test)	Won by 9 wkts
Mar 25	Durban	SOUTH AFRICA (3rd Test)	Drawn
Apr 2	East London	*South Africa (L/O Intl)	Won by 7 wkts
Apr 4	Port Elizabeth	*South Africa (L/O Intl)	Lost by 26 runs
Apr 6	Cape Town	*South Africa (L/O Intl)	Won by 36 runs
Apr 8	Bloemfontein	South Africa (L/O Intl)	Won by 1 run

The Australian team in South Africa, 1994: *back row* M.L. Hayden, S.K. Warne, S.R. Waugh, T.B.A. May, M.J. Slater; *centre* L.J. Trigar (physiotherapist), C.J. McDermott, G.D. McGrath, M.G. Hughes, P.R. Reiffel, D.M. Jones; *front* M.E. Waugh, M.A. Taylor, R.B. Simpson (coach), A.R. Border (capt), C. Battersby (manager), D.C. Boon, I.A. Healy.

Player	State	M	Inn	NO	Runs	HS	50	100	Avrge	Ct/St	Overs	Mdns	Runs	Wkts	Avrge	5wi	10wm	Best
Boon, DC	TAS	6	11	1	392	96	3	–	39.20	6/–	–	–	–	–	–	–	–	–
Border, AR (Capt)	QLD	3	5	1	152	45	–	–	38.00	4/–	9.0	4	17	–	–	–	–	–
Hayden, ML	QLD	3	6	1	151	50	1	–	30.20	3/–	–	–	–	–	–	–	–	–
Healy, IA	QLD	6	10	3	276	61	2	–	39.42	20/2	–	–	–	–	–	–	–	–
Hughes, MG	VIC	5	5	1	71	30	–	–	17.75	1/–	161.0	27	563	17	33.12	–	–	4/127
Jones, DM	VIC	2	3	–	168	85	2	–	56.00	–/–	2.0	–	6	1	6.00	–	–	1/6
McDermott, CJ	QLD	3	4	–	48	31	–	–	12.00	–/–	128.2	26	370	7	52.86	–	–	3/63
McGrath, GD	NSW	4	3	2	5	4	–	–	5.00	–/–	145.1	34	348	14	24.86	–	–	4/38
Reiffel, PR	VIC	4	5	1	53	22	–	–	13.25	5/–	116.1	24	320	14	22.86	–	–	4/27
Slater, MJ	NSW	6	12	1	548	105	3	1	49.82	1/–	–	–	–	–	–	–	–	–
Taylor, MA	NSW	5	10	–	373	75	4	–	37.30	4/–	–	–	–	–	–	–	–	–
TBA May	SA	3	3	1	14	11	–	–	7.00	–/–	143.1	33	437	12	36.42	1	–	5/98
Warne, SK	VIC	5	8	1	85	34	–	–	12.14	1/–	278.0	96	552	24	23.00	–	–	4/86
Waugh, ME	NSW	6	10	2	573	154	–	3	71.63	3/–	39.0	9	119	–	–	–	–	–
Waugh, SR	NSW	5	7	1	400	102	3	1	66.67	7/–	89.5	31	157	11	14.27	1	–	5/28

Their careers ruined by the apartheid ban, all of the great players who inflicted the shattering four–nil defeat on Australia in 1969–70 had retired when Australia returned 24 years later. Now Allan Border's team sought to regain prestige on strange pitches before surprisingly hostile crowds against opponents who had already proved resolute and well-organised. The six-Test programme designed to restore South Africa's first-class status had the teams level with one win apiece after the first half in Australia.

Australia began well in the First Test at Johannesburg, but the loss of Mark Waugh and Allan Border through run-outs allowed South Africa to recover. Australia's performance was marred on the third day by the appalling behaviour of Shane Warne and Merv Hughes. Warne lifted his arm and waved Andrew Hudson to the dressing-room after clean bowling him; Hughes lashed out with his bat at a spectator who abused him as he left the field — ugly, stupid incidents shown on TV sets around the world. Both players were fined $450 by the match referee and a further $4000 by the Australian Cricket Board. A fighting 122 by Hansie Cronje set up South Africa's victory by 197 runs.d

One Test down and lagging 1–3 in the eight-match limited over series, Australia found key players under censure or fighting off illness or injury. Worse still, Hansie Cronje appeared to have bested Shane Warne, with 251 in a dazzling knock for Orange Free State, followed by his Test century. To their credit, the Australians rallied to win the Second Test at Cape Town by nine wickets, sharing the series with a draw in the Third Test at Durban, and then won three of the last four one day matches to share the honours in the limited overs series.

Four Australian batsmen averaged more than 50 in the tests, Steve Waugh (65.00), Mark Waugh (58.25), David Boon (55.40) and Michael Slater (50.20), but only one South African, Andrew Hudson (58.60). Shane Warne regained his composure to finish Australia's best bowler with 15 wickets at 22.40 which gave him 51 wickets from the 500 overs he bowled in nine Tests in the 1993–94 season. Ian Healy, who had dropped 11 catches in international matches in Australia during the summer, returned to his best in South Africa with 22 tour dismissals. A month after the South Africa tour ended Allan Border retired as Australian captain, with 11 174 runs at 50.56 to his name from 156 Tests, 93 as captain.

Four South African teams toured Australia before they were ex-communicated from world cricket because of their government's apartheid policies. None of those teams won a series, although the fourth team might easily have done so but for a last-wicket stand of 45 runs in 75 minutes by Tom Veivers and Neil Hawke in the Fifth Test in 1963–64. The South Africans were frustrated, on 0 for 75, chasing 171 in 85 minutes to win, when time ran out. Of the 20 Tests played between the countries in Australia, Australia won 12, South Africa four, and four were drawn. The matches were always entertaining and friendly. Only the 1931–32 rubber, which Australia won five–nil, was one-sided. South Africa's improvement since then suggested she had players who could avenge past defeat when the Tests between the countries lapsed. South Africa returned to Australia for the 1992 World Cup, unluckily missing a place in the final won by Pakistan.

SOUTH AFRICA IN AUSTRALIA 1910-11

Matches	First-class Results				Matches	All Matches			
	Won	Lost	Drawn	Tied		Won	Lost	Drawn	Tied
15	6	7	2	–	22	12	7	3	–

Date	Venue	Opponent	Results for Touring Team
Nov 5	Adelaide	South Australia	Won by 281 runs
Nov 11	Melbourne	Victoria	Lost by 5 wkts
Nov 18	Sydney	New South Wales	Lost by 3 wkts
Nov 25	Brisbane	Queensland	Won by 122 runs
Nov 30	Toowoomba	*Toowoomba	Won by an inns & 11 runs
Dec 2	Brisbane	Australian XI	Drawn
Dec 9	Sydney	AUSTRALIA (1st Test)	Lost by an inns & 114 runs
Dec 16	Newcastle	*XV of Newcastle & District	Won by 5 wkts
Dec 21	Sydney	*Combined Universities	Drawn
Dec 26	Bendigo	*XV of Bendigo	Won by an inns & 41 runs
Dec 31	Melbourne	AUSTRALIA (2nd Test)	Lost by 89 runs
Jan 7	Adelaide	AUSTRALIA (3rd Test)	Won by 38 runs
Jan 17	Launceston	Tasmania	Won by 209 runs
Jan 20	Hobart (TCA)	Tasmania	Drawn
Jan 27	Hamilton	*XVI of Hamilton	Won by an inns & 30 runs
Jan 30	Ballarat	*XV of Ballarat	Won by an inns & 206 runs
Feb 3	Melbourne	Victoria	Won by 8 wkts
Feb 17	Melbourne	AUSTRALIA (4th Test)	Lost by 530 runs
Feb 24	Sydney	New South Wales	Lost by 44 runs
Mar 3	Sydney	AUSTRALIA (5th Test)	Lost by 7 wkts
Mar 10	Adelaide	South Australia	Won by 6 wkts
Mar 15	Broken Hill	*XVIII of Broken Hill	Won by an inns & 278 runs

South Africa in Australia, 1910-11: *back row* S.J. Pegler, T. Campbell, L. Stricker, C.B. Lewellyn, G.C. Pearse, A.D. Nourse; *centre* G.A. Faulkner, S.J. Snooke, R.P. Fitzgerald (manager), P.W. Sherwell (capt.), R.O. Schwartz, M. Hathorn; *front* M. Commaille, J.W. Zulch, A.E. Vogler.

Player	M	Inn	NO	Runs	HS	50	100	Avrge	Ct/St	Overs	Mdns	Runs	Wkts	Avrge	5wi	10wm	Best
Campbell, T	5	9	4	57	32	–	–	11.40	6/6	–	–	–	–	–	–	–	–
Commaille, JMM	6	12	1	99	29	–	–	9.00	1	–	–	–	–	–	–	–	–
Faulkner, GA	14	27	1	1534	204	12	4	59.00	9	353.3	36	1254	49	25.59	4	2	7/26
Hathorn, M	2	4	–	29	15	–	–	7.25	1	–	–	–	–	–	–	–	–
Llewellyn, CB	12	22	1	553	88*	3	–	26.33	8	219.5	18	854	30	28.47	1	1	7/50
Nourse, AD	15	29	5	1454	201*	5	5	60.58	8	199.2	38	651	16	40.69	1	–	5/47
Pearse, COC	11	21	3	380	54	2	–	20.00	4	59.0	4	244	8	30.50	–	–	3/56
Pegler, SJ	11	19	2	229	50	1	–	13.47	5	235.5	27	848	27	31.41	1	–	5/54
Schwarz, RO	12	22	3	380	64	3	–	20.00	9	389.3	45	1475	59	25.00	4	1	6/47
Sherwell, PW (Capt)	13	24	6	540	144	2	1	30.00	17/20	–	–	–	–	–	–	–	–
Sinclair, JH	11	21	3	419	66*	3	–	23.28	3	280.4	33	948	24	39.50	–	–	4/53
Snooke, SJ	15	27	–	609	103	4	1	22.56	15	55.3	7	170	1	170.00	–	–	1/2
Stricker, LA	14	28	2	667	146	3	1	25.65	3	42.0	4	178	3	59.33	–	–	1/30
Vogler, AEE	11	20	4	145	41	–	–	9.60	12	309.3	40	1197	31	38.61	1	–	5/104
Zulch, JW	13	25	1	724	150	3	2	30.17	3	4.0	–	28	–	–	–	–	–

Percy Sherwell, born in Natal but educated in Bedfordshire, his parents' birthplace, was a compact, gusty wicket-keeper reliable in a crisis. He brought to Australia a great batsman in Aubrey Faulkner who also bowled the new delivery called the googly, a masterly allrounder in 'Buck' Llewellyn, and two other leading exponents of the googly, Reggie Schwartz and Bert Vogler. Unfortunately, they encountered Trumper, Hill, Bardsley and Armstrong in outstanding form in a team that could afford to bat the accomplished left-hander Vernon Ransford at No. 6.

Australia's batting power showed early in the First Test at the SCG in December 1910 after Trumper had been run out for 27. Bardsley and Hill then put on 224 before another wicket fell, attacking the spinners from the moment they took guard. At the end of the first day Australia were 6 for 494, still the best first day score in Tests, and next morning Australia reached 528, Bardsley scoring 132, Hill 191. Express bowler 'Tibby' Cotter and left-arm speedster Bill Whitty then took eight wickets each to dismiss South Africa for 174 and 240, Australia winning by an innings and 114 runs. Faulkner made South Africa's first double century in Tests (204) in the Second Test in Melbourne but could not prevent an Australia triumph by 89 runs. Trumper made 159 and Whitty took 6 for 17 in South Africa's second innings of 80.

The six days of the Third Test at Adelaide proved a run feast which South Africa eventually won by 38 runs. Both sides joined the heavy scoring, Billy Zulch made 105, Sibley ('Tip') Snooke 103 in South Africa's first innings of 482. Australia responded with 465, Trumper scoring 214 not out. Faulkner made 115 in South Africa's second innings of 360 and on the last day helped bowl Australia out for 339, taking the vital wicket of Trumper (28). Australia brought in their own googly expert 'Ranji' Hordern for the last two Tests. Ironically, considering the practice the South Africans had against googlies, he bowled Australia to victory in the last two Tests, Australia winning by 530 runs in Melbourne following 100s by Hill (100) and Armstrong (132), and by seven wickets in Sydney, where Macartney hit 137. Hordern took 14 wickets in these two matches, assisting Australia to a four–one series success. Schwartz's 25 wickets in the five Tests cost 26.04 runs each, but Faulkner and Vogler took a hammering. Faulkner's 10 Test wickets cost 51.40 and Vogler's four wickets 44.00 apiece.

SOUTH AFRICA IN AUSTRALIA 1931-32

The 1931-32 South Africans in Australia: *back row* S. Steyn, S. Tandy (manager), X. Balaskas; *middle row* A.J. Bell, A.J. Christy, N. Quinn, S. Curnow, K. Viljoen, B. Mitchell, L.S. Brown; *front row* E.L. Dalton, C.L. Vincent, D.P.B. Morkel, H.B. Cameron (capt.), H.W. Taylor, E.A. v.d. Merwe, Q. McMillan.

	First-class Results				All Matches				
Matches	Won	Lost	Drawn	Tied	Matches	Won	Lost	Drawn	Tied
16	4	6	6	–	18	6	6	6	–

Date	Venue	Opponent	Results for Touring Team
Oct 22	Perth	Western Australia	Drawn
Oct 30	Adelaide	South Australia	Won by 192 runs
Nov 6	Melbourne	Victoria	Lost by 87 runs
Nov 13	Sydney	New South Wales	Drawn
Nov 20	Brisbane	Queensland	Drawn
Nov 27	Brisbane	AUSTRALIA (1st Test)	Lost by an inns & 163 runs
Dec 5	Sydney	New South Wales	Drawn
Dec 11	Newcastle	*Combined Country XI	Won by 163 runs
Dec 18	Sydney	AUSTRALIA (2nd Test)	Lost by an inns & 155 runs
Dec 26	Geelong	*Combined Victorian Country XI	Won by an inns & 246 runs
Dec 31	Melbourne	AUSTRALIA (3rd Test)	Lost by 169 runs
Jan 8	Launceston	Tasmania	Drawn
Jan 15	Hobart (TCA)	Tasmania	Won by 4 wkts
Jan 22	Adelaide	South Australia	Won by 7 wkts
Jan 29	Adelaide	AUSTRALIA (4th Test)	Lost by 10 wkts
Feb 6	Melbourne	Victoria	Drawn
Feb 12	Melbourne	AUSTRALIA (5th Test)	Lost by an inns & 72 runs
Mar 19	Perth	Western Australia	Won by 242 runs

Player	M	Inn	NO	Runs	HS	50	100	Avrge	Ct/St	Overs	Mdns	Runs	Wkts	Avrge	5wi	10wm	Best
Balaskas, X	6	7	–	132	61	1	–	18.85	7	349	2	236	8	29.50	–	–	3/48
Bell, AJ	13	18	12	34	10	–	–	5.67	4	2853	62	1273	51	24.96	3	–	5/69
Brown, LS	6	6	2	33	11	–	–	8.25	3	1288	30	533	14	38.07	–	–	4/26
Cameron, HB (Capt)	15	24	3	642	74	4	–	30.57	20/11	16	–	13	–	–	–	–	–
Christy, JAJ	14	24	1	909	119	5	3	39.52	6	242	4	135	3	45.00	–	–	1/9
Curnow, SH	13	23	2	599	81*	4	–	28.52	8	–	–	–	–	–	–	–	–
Dalton, EL	9	15	2	405	100	3	1	31.15	5	8	–	2	–	–	–	–	–
McMillan, Q	13	21	2	298	46	–	–	15.68	5	2171	15	1469	51	28.80	3	1	9/53
Mitchell, B	15	26	–	715	125	5	–	27.50	20	142	–	73	2	36.50	–	–	2/15
Morkel, DPB	14	24	2	577	150*	3	1	26.22	10	1311	19	637	27	23.59	1	–	8/13
Quinn, NA	12	18	3	61	24	–	–	4.06	–	2809	88	1003	42	23.88	1	–	5/36
Steyn, SSL	3	5	1	48	19*	–	–	12.00	1	8	–	8	–	–	–	–	–
Taylor, HW	13	25	2	813	124	6	1	35.34	2	8	–	2	–	–	–	–	–
Van Der Merwe, EA	3	3	–	62	35	–	–	20.67	5/3	–	–	–	–	–	–	–	–
Viljoen, KG	13	21	1	438	111	1	1	21.90	5	–	–	–	–	–	–	–	–
Vincent, CL	14	21	5	415	83	1	–	25.93	15	2875	88	1186	33	35.94	2	–	5/59

Bradman repeated the heavy punishment Trumper, Hill, Bardsley and Ransford had handed out 20 years earlier when Horace Brakenridge ('Jock') Cameron brought a South African team to Australia shortly after Bradman's triumphant first tour of England. Bradman's Test scores were 226, 112, 2, 167, and 299 not out. He did not bat in the last Test after twisting his ankle in the dressing-room. Cameron impressed behind the stumps, and Jim

Christy, Ken Viljoen, and Bruce Mitchell scored well against the states, but found Clarrie Grimmett and Bert Ironmonger too crafty in the Tests, all of which Australia won decisively. The states also extended South Africa, who ended the tour with only nine wins from 21 matches. They fared better in New Zealand, winning both Tests on their first visit.

Bradman had a Test average of 201.50, Woodfull, the next best Australian 70.16, whereas Mitchell averaged only 32.20 in heading the South African batting averages. Ironmonger's 31 wickets at 9.67 came from only four Tests and included 5 for 6 and 6 for 18 in the Fifth Test at Melbourne when South Africa were out for 36 and 45, batting on a vicious 'sticky' wicket which restricted the match to 5 hours 53 minutes play. Grimmett, who had dominated South Africa's batsmen in all their tour meetings, did not get a bowl in this Test, but ended with 33 wickets at 16.87 from the series. Australians made 12 centuries, six of them from Bradman, against South Africa, who managed ten 100s between them, three of them by Christy.

SOUTH AFRICA IN AUSTRALIA 1952-53

First-class Results					All Matches				
Matches	Won	Lost	Drawn	Tied	Matches	Won	Lost	Drawn	Tied
16	4	3	9	–	23	7	3	13	–

Date	Venue	Opponent	Results for Touring Team
Oct 18	Northam	*Northam & District	Drawn
Oct 24	Perth	Western Australia	Drawn
Oct 31	Adelaide	South Australia	Drawn
Nov 7	Melbourne	Victoria	Drawn
Nov 14	Sydney	New South Wales	Lost by 5 wkts
Nov 21	Newcastle	*New South Wales Country XI	Won by 7 wkts
Nov 25	Bundaberg	*Queensland Country XI	Drawn
Nov 28	Brisbane	Queensland	Drawn
Dec 5	Brisbane	AUSTRALIA (1st Test)	Lost by 96 runs
Dec 12	Sydney	Australian XI	Drawn
Dec 19	Ballarat	*Victorian Country XI	Drawn
Dec 24	Melbourne	AUSTRALIA (2nd Test)	Won by 82 runs
Jan 1	Sydney	New South Wales	Drawn
Jan 6	Orange	*New South Wales Country XI	Drawn
Jan 9	Sydney	AUSTRALIA (3rd Test)	Lost by an inns & 38 runs
Jan 16	Hobart (TCA)	*Tasmania	Won by an inns & 122 runs
Jan 19	Launceston	Tasmania	Won by an inns & 98 runs
Jan 24	Adelaide	AUSTRALIA (4th Test)	Drawn
Jan 31	Melbourne	Victoria	Drawn
Feb 6	Melbourne	AUSTRALIA (5th Test)	Won by 6 wkts
Feb 14	Adelaide	South Australia	Drawn
Feb 20	Port Lincoln	*South Australian Country XI	Won by an inns & 316 runs
Mar 26	Perth	Western Australia	Won by 175 runs

South Africa in Australia, 1952-53: *back row* H.J. Tayfield, J.C. Watkins, A.R.A. Murray, M.G. Melle; *centre* W. Ferguson (scorer), K.J. Funston, H.J. Keith, E.B. Norton, G. Innes, E.R. Fuller; *front* J.H.B. Waite, P.N.F. Mansell, J.E. Cheetham (capt.), K.G. Viljoen (manager), D.J. McGlew, W.R. Endean, R.A. McLean.

Player	M	Inn	NO	Runs	HS	50	100	Avrge	Ct/St	Overs	Mdns	Runs	Wkts	Avrge	5wi	10wm	Best
Cheetham, JE (Capt)	12	19	4	601	83	6	–	40.07	6	1.0	–	5	–	–	–	–	–
Endean, WR	14	27	3	1281	181*	9	2	53.38	24	–	–	–	–	–	–	–	–
Fuller, ERH	9	12	5	40	9	–	–	5.71	2	247.1	38	852	32	26.63	2	–	6/38
Funston, KJ	10	17	1	602	92	4	–	37.63	5	–	–	–	–	–	–	–	–
Innes, G	7	12	2	307	109	2	1	30.70	3	2.0	–	6	–	–	–	–	–
Keith, HJ	12	20	4	563	113*	3	2	35.19	5	128.0	28	380	4	95.00	–	–	2/54
Mansell, PNF	12	18	1	310	57	3	–	18.24	20	249.0	19	1029	25	41.16	1	–	6/53
McGlew, DJ	13	23	1	815	182	3	2	37.05	7	6.0	–	22	1	22.00	–	–	1/5
McLean, RA	15	29	2	712	89	5	–	26.37	7	1.1	–	11	–	–	–	–	–
Melle, MG	13	17	7	79	32*	–	–	7.90	5	340.5	35	1274	40	31.85	2	1	9/22
Murray, ARA	11	19	2	377	51	2	–	22.18	4	340.1	93	1015	33	30.76	2	–	5/118
Norton, EB	8	13	–	185	58	1	–	14.23	3	–	–	–	–	–	–	–	–
Tayfield, HJ	14	20	2	232	40	–	–	12.89	13	604.4	123	1954	70	27.91	5	1	7/71
Waite, JHB	14	26	1	726	90	5	–	29.04	20/4	–	–	–	–	–	–	–	–
Watkins, JC	12	21	2	581	92	4	–	30.58	15	256.0	74	623	16	38.94	–	–	4/41

The Australian Board of Control, mindful of the deficit from the West Indian tour the previous summer, were worried about likely losses when Jack Cheetham's South African side visited Australia. Critics unanimously forecast an overwhelming series win for Australia, who had not lost a rubber since the 1932-33 Bodyline Tests. The South African Cricket Board ultimately ensured that the tour went ahead by offering to bear the first £10,000 lost by 'an educational tour' which they hoped would develop future heroes. Cheetham prepared his inexperienced players like boxers, ordering early morning calisthenics and drills that transformed them into one of the finest fielding sides that ever visited Australia. They confounded the experts by sharing the series and went home with £3000 profit.

The Test result was all the more unforeseen because South Africa won only two of their matches against the states. They lacked bowlers of Miller and Lindwall's strike power. Russell Endean was the sole century-maker in the Tests, whereas Australians made six Test 100s. Without Nourse, the Rowan brothers, van Ryneveld, and McCarthy, who had been the strength of their team on previous postwar tours, they lacked established players to put in against seasoned, highly experienced Australians who had dominated their English, West Indian and New Zealand contemporaries.

Australia won the First Test at Brisbane by 96 runs thanks to 109 and 52 run out from Harvey and intelligent bowling by Ring (6 for 72) and Lindwall (5 for 60). South Africa had their first win over Australia since 1910–11 and only their second in the 31 Tests between the countries by winning the Second Test at Melbourne by 82 runs. Endean set up this shock by scoring 162 not out in 45 minutes, supported by wonderful catching. Tayfield, who took 13 for 165 with off-spinners, took one catch when he dived metres to hold a full-blooded drive from Morris that rebounded off Cheetham at silly mid-off. Endean sprinted right round the boundary to catch a Miller shot that otherwise would have brought six. Harvey's 190 in the Third Test at Sydney brought up his 1000 runs in eight Tests against South Africa and gave Australia victory by an innings and 38 runs. Miller and Lindwall took 13 wickets in South African totals of 173 and 232. South Africa forced a draw in the Fourth Test at Adelaide despite centuries by McDonald (154) and Hassett (163) in Australia's first innings of 530, and 116 from Harvey in the second innings.

Ian Craig became Australia's youngest Test player at 17 years 239 days in the Fifth Test at Melbourne. Facing Australia's first innings total of 520, South Africa pulled off a stunning win by six wickets. Harvey's 205 gave him 834 runs for the rubber at 92.66. Craig, who had made an exciting 213 not out for New South Wales against the tourists, scored 100 runs (53 and 47), but without Miller and Lindwall, who had both broken down in the Fourth Test, Australia could not confine Roy McLean, whose dazzling 76 not out sealed South Africa's win, and levelled the series at two victories apiece.

SOUTH AFRICA IN AUSTRALIA 1963-64

First-class Results					All Matches				
Matches	Won	Lost	Drawn	Tied	Matches	Won	Lost	Drawn	Tied
14	5	3	6	–	28	16	4	8	–

Date	Venue	Opponent	Results for Touring Team
Oct 25	Perth	Western Australia	Won by 5 wkts
Oct 30	Cunderdin	*Western Australian Country XI	Won by 178 runs
Nov 1	Perth	Combined XI	Drawn
Nov 8	Adelaide	South Australia	Lost by 8 wkts
Nov 13	Whyalla	*South Australian Country XI	Won by 10 wkts
Nov 15	Melbourne	Australian XI	Won by 3 wkts
Nov 22	Sydney	New South Wales	Won by an inns & 101 runs
Nov 27	Ipswich	*Queensland Country XI	Won by an inns & 41 runs
Nov 29	Brisbane	Queensland	Lost by an inns & 73 runs
Dec 4	Southport	*Queensland Country XI	Won by 7 wkts
Dec 6	Brisbane	AUSTRALIA (1st Test)	Drawn
Dec 13	Toowoomba	*Australian Universities	Drawn
Dec 16	Lismore	*New South Wales Country XI	Won by 121 runs
Dec 18	Benalla	*Victorian Country XI	Won by 10 wkts
Dec 20	Launceston	Tasmania	Won by an inns & 147 run
Dec 24	Devonport	*Tasmanian Country XI	Won by 32 runs
Dec 26	Hobart (TCA)	Combined XI	Drawn
Dec 30	Geelong	*Victorian Country XI	Won by 5 wkts
Jan 1	Melbourne	AUSTRALIA (2nd Test)	Lost by 8 wkts
Jan 8	Parkes	*New South Wales Country XI	Won by 10 wkts
Jan 10	Sydney	AUSTRALIA (3rd Test)	Drawn
Jan 17	Melbourne	Victoria	Drawn
Jan 22	Warrnambool	*Victorian Country XI	Won by 9 wkts
Jan 24	Adelaide	AUSTRALIA (4th Test)	Won by 10 wkts
Jan 31	Newcastle	*New South Wales Country XI	Drawn
Feb 3	Canberra	*Prime Minister's XI	Lost by 4 runs
Feb 4	Cooma	*New South Wales Country XI	Won by 7 wkts
Feb 7	Sydney	AUSTRALIA (5th Test)	Drawn

Brian Booth at short mid-off dislocates finger stopping a Peter Van Der Merwe drive in the first Australia v. South Africa Test at Brisbane in 1963-64. The injury put Booth out of the match after he had scored 169 in Australia's first innings.

Player	M	Inn	NO	Runs	HS	50	100	Avrge	Ct/St	Overs	Mdns	Runs	Wkts	Avrge	5wi	10wm	Best
Barlow, EJ	14	25	2	1523	209	4	6	66.21	11	187.6	25	765	23	33.26	–	–	3/6
Bland, KC	10	15	2	539	126	4	1	41.46	5	61.0	7	214	3	71.33	–	–	2/115
Carlstein, PR	8	13	1	450	123	3	1	37.50	8	1.0	–	7	–	–	–	–	–
Farrer, WS	7	12	–	293	107	1	1	24.41	2	0.3	–	2	–	–	–	–	–
Goddard, TL (Capt)	12	20	3	1054	194	7	1	62.00	13	286.5	58	752	22	34.18	1	–	5/60

Player	M	Inn	NO	Runs	HS	50	100	Avrge	Ct/St	Overs	Mdns	Runs	Wkts	Avrge	5wi	10wm	Best
Halse, CG	10	11	6	57	19*	–	–	11.40	4	235.3	14	937	18	52.05	–	–	3/50
Lindsay, D	8	11	2	379	104	2	1	42.11	15/4	–	–	–	–	–	–	–	–
Partridge, JT	11	11	3	74	12	–	–	9.25	5	433.5	65	1410	50	28.20	3	–	7/91
Pithey, DB	8	13	3	193	40	–	–	19.30	8	209.4	33	703	16	43.93	–	–	4/39
Pithey, AJ	11	19	1	667	170	4	1	37.05	5	–	–	–	–	–	–	–	–
Pollock, RG	14	20	1	1018	175	1	5	53.57	19	85.3	8	383	12	31.91	–	–	3/46
Pollock, PM	9	9	2	96	27*	–	–	13.71	3	251.3	23	1049	40	26.22	2	–	6/95
Seymour, MA	12	14	3	135	62	1	–	12.27	3	385.3	63	1117	32	34.90	1	–	5/65
Van Der Merwe, PL	10	15	2	448	114	1	1	34.46	8	19.1	1	78	–	–	–	–	–
Waite, JHB	10	13	4	449	115*	3	1	49.88	20/2	–	–	–	–	–	–	–	–

Trevor Goddard's team arrived with Australian cricket in turmoil. Hassett, Miller, Johnston, Lindwall, Ring, McCool, Morris and other outstanding players just after World War II, had departed, and in rebuilding Australia had been accused of using alleged chuckers like Ian Meckiff and Gordon Rorke, whose drag compounded his problems and made English critics more vociferous. The Meckiff problem was resolved in the First Test when Meckiff was no-balled four times for throwing by umpire Col Egar. This was a shameful episode in Australian cricket, which left lovers of the game concerned that a player had been allowed to go so far before he was humiliated. Richie Benaud handed over the Australian captaincy after that Test to Bob Simpson but played in the last three Tests.

South Africa shared the rubber, each side winning one Test, with three drawn. The Pollock brothers, Graeme, the forceful, shot-making left-handed batting maestro, and Peter, with his splendid right-hand batting and lively fast medium bowling, were South Africa's stars, but Goddard, Eddie Barlow and Colin Bland were not far behind them and keeper John Waite was a capable rival for Wally Grout. Australia's win came at Melbourne in the Second Test when Bill Lawry (157) and Ian Redpath (97) added 219 for the first wicket in the first innings. McKenzie, Hawke, and Connolly restricted the South African batsmen and Australia only needed 136 to win by eight wickets. The Third Test at Sydney was drawn despite Graeme Pollock's 122 at the age of 19 years 318 days.

South Africa levelled the series by winning the Fourth Test in Adelaide by ten wickets thanks to Barlow's 201 and Graeme Pollock's 175 in a 341-run third wicket stand. In the drawn Fifth Test Joe Partridge's 7 for 91 in Australia's first innings endangered Australia until Veivers and Hawke's last-ditch partnership delayed them just long enough to produce a draw, and leave South Africa still without a series win in Australia.

SOUTH AFRICA IN AUSTRALIA 1993-94

	First-class Results					All Matches			
Matches	Won	Lost	Drawn	Tied	Matches	Won	Lost	Drawn	Tied
5	1	2	2	–	17	6	9	2	–

Date	Venue	Opponent	Results for Touring Team
Dec 2	Canberra	*Prime Minister's XI	Lost by 4 runs
Dec 4	Melbourne	Victoria	Lost by 6 wkts
Dec 9	Melbourne	*Australia (L/O Intl)	Won by 7 wkts
Dec 11	Adelaide	*New Zealand (L/O Intl)	Abandoned
Dec 14	Sydney	*Australia (L/O Intl)	Lost by 103 runs
Dec 18	Hobart (Bel)	*New Zealand (L/O Intl)	Lost by 4 wkts
Dec 20	Brisbane	Queensland	Drawn
Dec 26	Melbourne	AUSTRALIA (1st Test)	Drawn
Jan 2	Sydney	AUSTRALIA (2nd Test)	Won by 5 runs
Jan 8	Brisbane	*New Zealand (L/O Intl)	Lost on run rate
Jan 9	Brisbane	*Australia (L/O Intl)	Lost by 48 runs
Jan 14	Perth	*New Zealand (L/O Intl)	Won by 5 wkts
Jan 16	Perth	*Australia (L/O Intl)	Won by 82 runs
Jan 18	Sydney	*New South Wales Invitation XI	Won by 19 runs
Jan 21	Melbourne	*Australia (L/O Intl)	Won by 28 runs
Jan 23	Sydney	*Australia (L/O Intl)	Lost by 69 runs
Jan 25	Sydney	*Australia (L/O Intl)	Lost by 35 runs
Jan 28	Adelaide	AUSTRALIA (3rd Test)	Lost by 191 runs

Player	M	Inn	NO	Runs	HS	50	100	Avrge	Ct/St	Overs	Mdns	Runs	Wkts	Avrge	5wi	10wm	Best
Callaghan, DJ	2	4	1	52	24*	–	–	17.33	3	7.0	1	20	1	20.00	–	–	1/13
Cronje, WJ	5	9	–	357	145	1	1	39.67	2	38.0	10	96	–	–	–	–	–
Cullinan, DJ	4	7	–	139	113	–	1	19.86	–	–	–	–	–	–	–	–	–
De Villiers, PS	4	5	1	56	30	–	–	14.00	2	169.4	44	398	16	24.88	1	1	6/43
Donald, AA	5	6	3	22	10	–	–	7.33	–	193.1	39	552	17	32.47	–	–	4/83
Hudson, AC	4	7	1	273	105	2	1	45.50	2	–	–	–	–	–	–	–	–
Kirsten, G	4	7	–	207	67	1	–	29.57	2	32.0	8	99	3	33.00	–	–	2/19

Continued

Player	M	Inn	NO	Runs	HS	50	100	Avrge	Ct/St	Overs	Mdns	Runs	Wkts	Avrge	5wi	10wm	Best
Kirsten, PN	1	2	–	121	79	1	–	60.50	–	4.0	–	17	–	–	–	–	–
Matthews, CR	4	5	2	61	42*	–	–	20.33	–	112.0	33	257	8	32.13	–	–	3/68
McMillan, BM	2	4	–	67	55	1	–	16.75	1	53.1	5	148	7	21.14	–	–	3/26
Rhodes, JN	4	7	2	191	76*	2	–	38.20	3	–	–	–	–	–	–	–	–
Richardson, DJ	4	6	–	77	26	–	–	12.83	13/2	–	–	–	–	–	–	–	–
Rundle, DB	2	4	1	52	29	–	–	17.33	2	66.0	13	180	5	36.00	–	–	3/51
Snell, RP	2	4	–	42	16	–	–	10.50	1	61.0	13	168	3	56.00	–	–	2/38
Stewart, ELR	1	2	–	13	7	–	–	6.50	3	–	–	–	–	–	–	–	–
Symcox, PL	3	4	–	44	18	–	–	11.00	1	92.5	21	209	5	41.80	–	–	2/49
Wessels, KC (Capt)	4	7	1	164	63*	1	–	27.33	2	–	–	–	–	–	–	–	–

After a fighting appearance in Australia in the 1992 World Cup when they were unluckily denied a place in the finals, South Africa returned for their first full tour of Australia in 30 years in the 1993–94 season. Their capabilities were unknown but after losing their first two matches they recovered to win Australians' respect as a splendidly athletic fielding side, relentlessly competitive, and blessed with a quality pace attack in Allan Donald, Fanie de Villiers and Brian McMillan, whose tour was hampered by injury. Their batting improved as the tour progressed, with Hansie Cronje, Jonty Rhodes, Andrew Hudson, Daryll Cullinan, and Kepler Wessels all playing long innings. Gary Kirston and his half-brother Peter, brought to Australia as replacements for injured players, gave the batting a solidity it lacked early on the tour. Both played spin bowling, which worried team-mates throughout, with slick footwork and sound judgement.

The First Test at Melbourne was drawn after rain sent players from the field on four of the five days. Mark Taylor in his first Test as Australian captain, made 170 after umpires rejected confident appeals against him for lbw. South Africa won the Second Test at Sydney by five runs. Australia held the ascendancy for all bar the last hour thanks to Warne's 12 wickets in the match, but failed miserably in the chase for 117 runs in the final innings. Timid Australian batting after Fanie de Villiers took three wickets in five balls — Damien Martin made six from singles in 59 minutes at the crease — allowed de Villiers and Allan Donald to pull off a startling victory.

Steve Waugh returned after injury for the Third Test in Adelaide and turned in a match-winning double. He scored 164, adding 108 with Border (84) who passed 11 000 runs in Test cricket to lift Australia to 7 declared for 469. He then took four wickets in an hour for only 26 runs to reduce South Africa's response to 273. Australia built their 196-run lead to 320 before Border declared with six men out. McDermott and Warne then bundled South Africa out for 129, taking four wickets each to give Australia victory by 191 runs and level the rubber at a win apiece. Peter Kirsten was fined $750 for dissent when Brian MacMillan and David Richardson were given out lbw while he was batting with them.

The fifth South African tour of Australia produced crowd-pleasing cricket from Jonty Rhodes, a marvellous fieldsman, Hansie Cronje, a world-class allrounder aggressive with bat or ball, fiery pace bowling from Allan Donald, and highly competitive cricket. Injuries dogged South Africa, but the bowling mixture of master spinner Shane Warne dominated the Tests. He averaged a wicket every 58 balls in taking 18 wickets, an exceptional strike rate for a spinner.

South Africa's vulnerability to leg-spin has proved her major weakness on all her five Australian tours. Hordern took 14 wickets in two Tests back in 1910–11, Grimmett 33 wickets in four Tests in 1931–32, Ring 13 wickets in five Tests in 1952–53, Benaud 12 wickets in four Tests in 1963–64, which with Warne's haul means that 90 South African batsmen have lost their wickets to spin in Tests in Australia. A similar pattern prevailed on most Australian tours of South Africa, with Mailey taking 11 wickets in three Tests in 1921–22, Grimmett 44 wickets and O'Reilly 27 in five Tests in 1935–36, McCool 13 wickets in five Tests in 1949–50, Benaud 30 wickets in five Tests in 1957–58. In 1966–67 when South Africa recorded her first home win against Australia, there was no quality leg-spinner in the Australian side. With more than 200 victims to show from their work since Tests between the countries began, Australia's leg-spinners can certainly claim ascendancy.

AUSTRALIA VERSUS ZIMBABWE

Cricket has been played in Zimbabwe, formerly known as Rhodesia, since 1890 when a match was played in a town called Masvingo. The Rhodesian Cricket Union included among its members the Matabeleland Cricket Association, the Mashonoland Cricket Association, and the Hartley District Association whose players travelled vast distances by mule-train for their matches. The Matabele rebellion in 1896 brought large numbers of soldiers into the country, most of them keen on cricket, including the legendary Brigadier-General R.M. Poore, a great swordsman and horseman known as the 'W.G. Grace of the British Army'. Poore later headed the Hampshire and English county batting averages.

Between the wars Rhodesian teams played occasionally in South Africa's Currie Cup tournaments. English teams touring South Africa visited Rhodesia in 1930–31 and 1938–39, and in 1935-n-36 Vic Richardson's Australian team played in Salisbury and Bulawayo. Two Rhodesians, Bob Crisp and D.S. Tomlinson, were included in the South African team which toured England in 1935. From 1946 to 1980 Rhodesian cricket thrived because of regular participation in the Currie Cup, and in that period Rhodesians such as Percy Mansell, Colin Bland, A.D. Pithey, D.B. Pithey, J. du Preez, and A.J. Traicos all played for South Africa.

In 1980, when Zimbabwe became independent, the affiliation with South African cricket ended and in 1981 Zimbabwe became an associate member of the international ruling body, the International Cricket Conference. In 1982, Zimbabwe won the trophy for the ICC's non-Test playing countries, a performance which earned her a place in the World Cup limited over competition. In the 1983 World Cup competition Zimbabwe beat Australia. Zimbabwean tours proved valuable for blooding promising young players, and strong Under 25 teams from the West Indies, India, New Zealand, and New South Wales all toured Zimbabwe. This brought steady improvement in Zimbabwean cricket and in 1991 Australia joined the efforts to boost standards further by sending an Australian XI to tour.

AUSTRALIA IN ZIMBABWE 1991

First-class Results					All Matches				
Matches	Won	Lost	Drawn	Tied	Matches	Won	Lost	Drawn	Tied
2	2	–	–	–	6	5	1	–	–

Date	Venue	Opponent	Results for Australians
Sep 8	Harare	*Zimbabweans	Lost by 6 wkts
Sep 10	Mutare	*Zimbabwe 'B'	Won by 6 wkts
Sep 15	Bulawayo	*Zimbabweans	Won by 35 runs
Sep 16	Bulawayo	Zimbabweans	Won by 10 wkts
Sep 21	Harare	Zimbabweans	Won by 9 wkts
Sep 22	Harare	*Zimbabweans	Won by 8 runs

Player	M	Inn	NO	Runs	HS	50	100	Avrge	Ct/St	Overs	Mdns	Runs	Wkts	Avrge	5wi	10wm	Best
Bevan, MG	2	2	–	74	54	1	–	37.00	–	28.0	6	86	1	86.00	–	–	1/27
Cox, J	1	2	1	14	8	–	–	14.00	–	–	–	–	–	–	–	–	–
Hickey, DJ	2	2	–	35	32	–	–	17.50	–	60.4	12	155	8	19.38	1	–	5/72
Holdsworth, WJ	1	1	–	7	7	–	–	7.00	–	32.0	8	70	1	70.00	–	–	1/17
Law, SG	1	2	–	107	94	1	–	53.50	1	–	–	–	–	–	–	–	–
McIntyre, PE	2	2	–	17	15	–	–	8.50	–	80.0	30	155	5	31.00	–	–	4/42
Moody, TM	2	2	–	226	141	1	1	113.00	5	4.0	1	14	–	–	–	–	–
Nielsen, TJ	2	2	–	22	13	–	–	11.00	6/–	–	–	–	–	–	–	–	–
Reiffel, PR	2	2	1	58	54*	1	–	58.00	1	78.3	19	179	10	17.90	1	–	5/43
Taylor, MA (Capt)	2	3	1	86	41	–	–	43.00	6	–	–	–	–	–	–	–	–
Tucker, RJ	1	2	–	63	62	1	–	63.00	–	2.0	–	8	–	–	–	–	–
Warne, SK	2	3	2	53	35*	–	–	53.00	1	97.4	28	207	11	18.82	1	–	7/49
Waugh, SR	2	2	–	130	119	–	1	65.00	3	27.0	14	21	2	10.50	–	–	2/2

Although the 13-man Australian team was very young, manager John Benaud knew his side oozed with talent, supported by seasoned internationals like Steve Waugh, Tom Moody and the captain Mark Taylor. They lost the opening match, a limited over fixture against Zimbabwe on a turning pitch at Harare, by six wickets because of the wily spin bowling of 46-year-old John Traicos (4 for 20) but went through the rest of the itinerary unbeaten, winning two unofficial Tests and a three-day match with a Zimbabwe B XI and two other limited over games.

Steve Waugh made three centuries on the tour, Paul Reiffel, Dennis Hickey and Wayne Holdsworth did well with the new ball, and the leg spinners Shane Warne and Peter McIntyre befuddled Zimbabwean batsmen. In the second of the official Tests, McIntyre took 4 for 42 in the first innings, Warne 7 for 49 in the second. Ten of Warne's 36 overs were maidens. Michael Bevan, Stuart Law and Rod Tucker all impressed with the bat and Tom Moody completed the trip with 141 v. Zimbabwe at Bulawayo and 85 against Zimbabwe at Harare. David Houghton was the most impressive of the Zimbabweans.

ZIMBABWE IN AUSTRALIA 1994-95

First-class Results					All Matches			
Matches	Won	Lost	Drawn	Tied	Matches	Won	Lost	Drawn	Tied
2	–	1	1	–	19	8	10	1	–

Date	Venue	Opponent	Results for Touring Team
Nov 20	Kalgoorlie	*Western Australia	Lost by 30 runs
Nov 23	Adelaide	*AIS Cricket Academy	Won by 3 wkts
Nov 27	Adelaide	*South Australia	Lost by 7 wkts
Nov 29	Busselton	*Western Australian Country XI	Won by 152 runs
Nov 30	Perth	*Western Australia	Won by 5 runs
Dec 2	Perth	*Australia (L/O Intl)	Lost by 2 wkts
Dec 4	Perth	*Australia 'A' (L/O Intl)	Lost by 5 wkts
Dec 8	Hobart (Bel)	*Australia (L/O Intl)	Lost by 85 runs
Dec 10	Adelaide	*Australia 'A' (L/O Intl)	Lost by 7 wkts
Dec 15	Sydney	*England (L/O Intl)	Won by 13 runs
Dec 17	Launceston	*Tasmania	Lost by 7 wkts
Dec 18	Devonport	Tasmania	Drawn
Dec 22	Yea	*Victorian Country XI	Won by 61 runs
Dec 23	Prahran	*Prahran Invitation XI	Won by 49 runs
Dec 26	Dubbo	*New South Wales Country XI	Won by 82 runs
Dec 29	Maryborough	Queensland	Lost by 4 wkts
Jan 1	Bundaberg	*Queensland	Won by 1 wkt
Jan 4	Beenleigh	*Queensland	Lost by 4 wkts
Jan 7	Brisbane	*England (L/O Intl)	Lost by 26 runs

Player	M	Inn	NO	Runs	HS	50	100	Avrge	Ct/St	Overs	Mdns	Runs	Wkts	Avrge	5wi	10wm	Best
Brain, DH	2	1	–	0	0	–	–	0.00	–	38.5	11	136	5	27.20	–	–	2/45
Butchart, IP	1	1	–	2	2	–	–	2.00	1	5.0	–	31	–	–	–	–	–
Campbell, ADR	2	4	1	10	9	–	–	3.33	1	–	–	–	–	–	–	–	–
Dekker, MH	2	4	–	115	52	1	–	28.75	5	4.0	–	21	–	–	–	–	–
Flower, A (Capt)	2	4	3	223	139*	1	1	223.00	3/1	–	–	–	–	–	–	–	–
Flower, GW	2	4	–	179	63	2	–	44.75	–	–	–	–	–	–	–	–	–
James, WR	1	2	–	18	14	–	–	9.00	3/1	–	–	–	–	–	–	–	–
Martin, GC	2	2	–	15	11	–	–	7.50	1	32.0	10	98	1	98.00	–	–	1/50
Peall, SG	2	1	–	11	11	–	–	11.00	1	39.0	4	138	5	27.60	–	–	4/52
Strang, PA	2	3	3	67	37*	–	–	–	–	33.0	7	98	3	32.67	–	–	2/55
Streak, HH	2	1	–	6	6	–	–	6.00	–	32.4	3	137	1	137.00	–	–	1/45
Whittall, GJ	2	4	–	30	24	–	–	7.50	1	35.0	5	142	3	47.33	–	–	1/20

Zimbabwe's reputation advanced further when they defeated a full England XI by nine runs in the 1991 World Cup at Albury, a defeat which cost England a place in the finals. They repeated the feat on tour in Australia in 1994-95 by defeating England again in a limited overs match on the Sydney Cricket Ground. Zimbabwe made 205, Grant Flower scoring 84 and David Houghton 54, and then restricted England to 192.

Coach John Hampshire, the former England international, rated Zimbabwe's wins over Queensland and Western Australia as more prestigious. The Zimbabweans itinerary bypassed most big cities and took them to play in Kalgoorlie, Busselton, Dubbo, Maryborough, Bundaberg and Beenleigh. 'Beating England was a buzz,' said Hampshire. 'But to beat Western Australia in a day-night one-day game was a major feat. We'd done a lot of travelling and were very, very tired. To lift ourselves for the day-nighter was a fantastic performance. It gave the guys a tremendous amount of confidence.' Only a few weeks later Zimbabwe showed how much that confidence-booster meant when they defeated the crack Pakistani team in a Test match at home.

CHAPTER SIX

GOING HOME

After Australia had beaten England in four Test series in six years, the Marylebone Cricket Club stepped in to prevent further decline in prestige by taking control of cricket tours from English and Australian entrepreneurs. For the next half a century, the MCC arranged programs for national touring teams.

For English cricketers, the crowning achievement in their careers was to receive a letter from Lord's informing them they had been chosen to accompany an MCC team—not England—to tour Australia or wherever.

Pelham Warner led the first MCC sponsored team to Australia in 1903–04, and for the first time English cricket buffs felt confident the best players were in the side, not just those ready to accept a profit-minded promoter's terms. Warner's team restored English confidence by winning the rubber three–two, a gratifying result for aristocrats in the Long Room.

AUSTRALIA IN ENGLAND 1905

	First-class Results					All Matches			
Matches	Won	Lost	Drawn	Tied	Matches	Won	Lost	Drawn	Tied
35	15	3	17	–	38	16	3	19	–

Date	Venue	Opponent	Results for Australians
May 4	Crystal Palace	Gentlemen of England	Drawn
May 8	Nottingham	Nottinghamshire	Drawn
May 11	The Oval	Surrey	Drawn
May 15	Oxford	Oxford University	Won by 200 runs
May 18	Lord's	Gentlemen of England	Won by an inns & 189 runs
May 22	Sheffield	Yorkshire	Won by 174 runs
May 25	Manchester	Lancashire	Won by 244 runs
May 29	Nottingham	ENGLAND (1st Test)	Lost by 213 runs
Jun 1	Cambridge	Cambridge University	Won by 169 runs
Jun 5	Bradford	Yorkshire	Drawn
Jun 8	Lord's	MCC	Drawn
Jun 12	Leicester	Leicestershire	Drawn
Jun 15	Lord's	ENGLAND (2nd Test)	Drawn
Jun 19	Dublin	*Dublin Uni Past & Present	Won by 231 runs
Jun 22	Leyton	Essex	Lost by 19 runs
Jun 26	Birmingham	Warwickshire	Won by an inns & 51 runs
Jun 29	Perth	Gloucestershire	Drawn
Jly 3	Leeds	ENGLAND (3rd Test)	Drawn
Jly 6	Southampton	Hampshire	Won by an inns & 112 runs
Jly 10	Derby	Derbyshire	Won by 105 runs
Jly 13	Bath	Somerset	Drawn

Continued

J. Darling

HOME AND AWAY

Date	Venue	Opponent	Results for Australians
Jly 17	Edinburgh	Scotland	Drawn
Jly 20	Glasgow	*XV of Scotland	Drawn
Jly 24	Manchester	ENGLAND (4th Test)	Lost by an inns & 80 runs
Jly 27	The Oval	Surrey	Won by 22 runs
Jly 31	Hove	Sussex	Won by an inns & 76 runs
Aug 3	Worcester	Worcestershire	Drawn
Aug 7	Cardiff	*South Wales	Drawn
Aug 10	Lord's	Middlesex	Won by 132 runs
Aug 14	The Oval	ENGLAND (5th Test)	Drawn
Aug 17	Northampton	Northamptonshire	Won by an inns & 329 runs
Aug 21	Liverpool	Lancashire	Won by an inns & 67 runs
Aug 24	Canterbury	Kent	Won by an inns & 35 runs
Aug 29	Cheltenham	Gloucestershire	Drawn
Aug 31	Bournemouth	England XI	Won by 1 wkt
Sep 4	Leyton	Essex	Drawn
Sep 7	Scarborough	Cl Thornton's XI	Drawn
Sep 12	Hastings	South of England	Drawn

The 1905 Australians, a strong combination who surrendered the series to a powerful array of England batsmen led by a symbol of old school tie cricket.

Player	State	M	Inn	NO	Runs	HS	50	100	Avrge	Ct/St	Overs	Mdns	Runs	Wkts	Avrge	5wi	10wm	Best
Armstrong, WW	VIC	30	45	7	1902	303*	8	4	50.05	34	990.4	298	2221	122	18.20	9	2	8/50
Cotter, A	NSW	28	40	3	673	48	–	–	18.19	16	735.1	121	2429	119	20.41	9	2	7/15
Darling, J (Capt)	SA	32	51	7	1696	117*	10	2	38.55	22	2.0	–	10	–	–	–	–	–
Duff, RA	NSW	28	44	–	1341	146	8	1	30.48	24	104.5	30	312	9	34.67	–	–	2/43
Gehrs, DRA	SA	21	30	4	510	83	3	–	19.62	19	3.0	–	12	–	–	–	–	–
Gregory, SE	NSW	18	29	3	648	134	2	1	24.92	2	2.1	–	12	–	–	–	–	–
Hill, C	SA	31	48	3	1722	181	9	4	38.27	20	7.0	1	16	–	–	–	–	–
Hopkins, AJY	NSW	28	39	5	996	154	4	1	29.29	17	239.0	53	786	24	32.75	–	–	4/64
Howell, WP	NSW	20	27	8	179	46	–	–	9.42	22	457.5	118	1258	62	20.29	5	–	6/38
Kelly, JJ	NSW	23	30	11	340	74*	1	–	17.88	21/7	–	–	–	–	–	–	–	–
Laver, F	VIC	27	35	6	440	78	1	–	15.17	38	848.1	245	2092	115	18.19	8	3	8/75
McLeod, CE	VIC	28	40	5	597	76	4	–	17.06	13	731.3	208	1807	78	23.17	4	1	5/13
Newland, PM	SA	10	13	6	67	25*	–	–	9.57	11/3	–	–	–	–	–	–	–	–
Noble, MA	NSW	31	46	2	2053	267	13	6	46.66	20	551.5	149	1464	55	26.62	1	–	6/39
Trumper, VT	NSW	30	47	1	1667	110	12	2	36.24	28	2.0	1	4	–	–	–	–	–

Joe Darling took the first Australian team to tour under the new management to England in 1905, the same year that the Australian national control body emerged. All Australians still talked of England as the motherland, the Australian players of 'going home'. Darling encountered a blue-blooded opponent in the new England captain, the Honorable Francis Stanley Jackson, known among cricketers as 'Jacker', who had been Winston Churchill's fagmaster at Harrow, whom he captained to overwhelm Eton before leading Cambridge University to a decisive victory over Oxford University. Jackson, son of Lord Allerton, a member of Cabinet in Lord Salisbury's second government, returned to big cricket after service in the South African war and when Australia won the 1902 series in England was easily the best England batsman.

Between them Darling and Jackson played cricket in

The multi-talented Francis Stanley Jackson, who won seven tosses in a row against Joe Darling's 1905 Australians.

a spirit typical of the late Victorian and Edwardian period and provided some wonderful encounters for what has been called cricket's Golden Age. They were tough and resolute but always highly ethical, spurning any unfair advantage. Jackson played all his county cricket for Yorkshire under Lord Hawke's captaincy and like Len Hutton was destined to captain England but never his county. To the Australians he was the best player in England, a tall, elegant right-handed batsman with rare ability to time cuts and drives, and an accurate right-arm medium pace bowler who varied his pace cleverly and could turn off-breaks sharply.

Jacker boosted the confidence Lord's placed in him by winning seven tosses against Darling in that 1905 summer. Darling became so frustrated by his inability to win a toss, he appeared at Jackson's dressing-room door for the Scarborough Festival match wearing only a towel and offered to wrestle Jackson for first innings. This was the only summer in which Jacker was completely free of business commitments—he never had time to tour Australia—and he made it count. He headed England's batting averages in the Tests with 70.28 and the bowling by taking 13 wickets at a cost of only 15.46. In all first-class matches he made 1359 runs and took 104 wickets in what was later dubbed 'Jackson's Year'.

The 1905 Australians, the twelfth to make the England tour, scored heavily against the counties, Noble compiling six centuries in the season, Armstrong hitting 305 not out against Somerset and 248 against The Gentlemen. Nine of Darling's 15 players made tour centuries and seven scored more than 1000 runs. Denied the chance of batting first in all five Tests, the Australians could not repeat this high scoring in the Tests. Bosanquet, inventor of the googly, swung the First Test England's way by taking 8 for 107 in Australia's second innings after Jacker had led the way by dismissing Noble, Hill and Darling in one over in the first innings.

MacLaren had given England a big lead with his 140 in the second innings opening with a stand of 145 with Tom Hayward (47). Bosanquet's feat in winning a Test for the second time—he did it in Australia in 1903–04—completely vindicated his invention, albeit a ball that only top calibre spinners could master. After winning the First Test by 213 runs, England went on to take the series two–nil when Jackson's 113 set up victory in the Fourth Test, with three Tests drawn. Jackson also made 82 not out in the First Test, 144 in the Third Test and 76 in the Fifth Test, after which he retired from Test cricket.

Cotter bowled very fast all summer and deserved his 119 tour wickets at 20.41, often dismissing quality batsmen. Armstrong took 122 wickets at 18.20 but often irked spectators by bowling leg-breaks down the legside to a packed on-side field. Frank Laver was the big surprise with 115 wickets at 18.19, adapting well to frequent wet pitches while also acting as team manager. But all of this Australian team had difficult curbing free-flowing strokemakers like Jackson, Charles Fry, Archie MacLaren and Johnny Tyldesley in the Tests, with Australia badly handicapped by Victor Trumper's ill-health. Trumper's opening partner Reggie Duff, who previously joked about 'Victor taking me for a run again' as he padded up, this time scored Australia's sole Test century, a lovely 146 in the Fifth Test. Duff was the player Fry said had a 'face like a good looking brown trout but was full of Australian sunshine'.

Both Trumper and Duff later fell on hard times and had to be helped by the New South Wales provident fund for destitute cricketers. Darling retired to concentrate on eradicating rabbits from his Tasmanian property. Jackson became the MP for Howdenshire in Yorkshire, Lieutenant-Colonel of a West Yorkshire Regiment, Governor of Bengal, where an assassin's bullet narrowly missed him, president of the MCC, chairman of England's selectors, chairman of the Unionist Party, and as Sir Stanley Jackson, GCSI, GCIE, financial secretary to the War Office. Cotter toured England successfully in 1909 but refused the Australian Board's terms to return in 1912, and in 1917 skipped guard duty to take part in the Australian Light Horse's charge on Beersheba, only to die of his wounds, aged 34.

AUSTRALIA IN ENGLAND 1909

	First-class Results					All Matches			
Matches	Won	Lost	Drawn	Tied	Matches	Won	Lost	Drawn	Tied
37	11	4	22	–	39	13	4	22	–

Date	Venue	Opponent	Results for Australians
May 6	Nottingham	Nottinghamshire	Won by an inns & 6 runs
May 10	Northampton	Northamptonshire	Won by 9 wkts
May 13	Leyton	Essex	Drawn
May 17	The Oval	Surrey	Lost by 5 runs
May 20	Lord's	MCC	Lost by 3 wkts
May 24	Oxford	Oxford University	Drawn
May 27	Birmingham	ENGLAND (1st Test)	Lost by 10 wkts
May 31	Leicester	Leicestershire	Drawn
Jun 3	Cambridge	Cambridge University	Drawn
Jun 7	Southampton	Hampshire	Won by 6 wkts
Jun 10	Bath	Somerset	Won by 2 wkts
Jun 14	Lord's	ENGLAND (2nd Test)	Won by 9 wkts
Jun 21	Bradford	Yorkshire	Drawn
Jun 26	Manchester	Lancashire & Yorkshire	Drawn
Jun 28	Edinburgh	Scotland	Drawn
Jly 1	Leeds	ENGLAND (3rd Test)	Won by 126 runs
Jly 5	Birmingham	Warwickshire	Drawn
Jly 8	Worcester	Worcestershire	Won by an inns & 112 runs
Jly 12	Perth	Gloucestershire	Won by an inns & 5 runs
Jly 15	The Oval	Surrey	Drawn
Jly 19	Sheffield	Yorkshire	Drawn
Jly 22	Derby	Derbyshire	Won by 10 wkts
Jly 26	Manchester	ENGLAND (4th Test)	Drawn
Jly 29	Hull	Lancashire & Yorkshire	Drawn
Aug 2	Cardiff	*South Wales	Won by 8 wkts
Aug 5	Liverpool	Lancashire	Won by 47 runs
Aug 9	The Oval	ENGLAND (5th Test)	Drawn
Aug 12	Blackpool	England XI	Drawn
Aug 16	Cheltenham	Gloucestershire	Drawn
Aug 19	Canterbury	Kent	Drawn
Aug 23	Lord's	Middlesex	Drawn
Aug 26	Hove	Sussex	Won by 1 wkt
Aug 30	Lord's	MCC	Drawn
Sep 2	Leyton	Essex	Drawn
Sep 7	Staffordshire	MR Bamford's XI	Drawn
Sep 9	Scarborough	Lord Londesborough's XI	Lost by 133 runs
Sep 14	Hastings	South of England	Drawn
Sep 17	Wicklow, Ire.	SH Cochran's XI	Drawn
Sep 27	Inverness	*XIII of Northern Counties	Won by 3 wkts
Oct 5	Glasgow	*West of Scotland	Abandoned

The 1909 Australian team: *back row* Bill Whitty, Albert Cotter, Roger Hartigan, Vernon Ransford, Warren Bardsley, Hanson Carter; *centre* Percy McAlister, Victor Trumper, Bert Hopkins, Monty Noble (capt.), Frank Laver, Warwick Armstrong, Jack O'Connor; *front* Syd Gregory, Charlie Macartney, Barlow Carkeek; *absent* scorer Bill Ferguson, on his first overseas trip. *Melbourne Cricket Club*

Player	State	M	Inn	NO	Runs	HS	50	100	Avrge	Ct/St	Overs	Mdns	Runs	Wkts	Avrge	5wi	10wm	Best
Armstrong, WW	VIC	29	41	8	1451	110*	7	3	43.97	33	857.0	263	1852	113	16.39	9	–	6/35
Bardsley, W	NSW	33	49	4	2072	219	7	6	46.04	11	2.0	–	7	–	–	–	–	–
Carkeek, W	VIC	12	15	4	101	37	–	–	9.18	9/2	–	–	–	–	–	–	–	–
Carter, H	NSW	27	33	7	408	61	1	–	15.69	27/18	–	–	–	–	–	–	–	–
Cotter, A	NSW	26	32	–	335	37	–	–	10.47	12	573.2	68	1862	64	29.09	5	1	6/95
Gregory, SE	NSW	28	39	5	618	74	2	–	18.18	8	15.0	–	84	1	84.00	–	–	1/8
Hartigan, RJ	QLD	19	31	1	400	88	1	–	13.33	23	1.0	–	4	–	–	–	–	–
Hopkins, AJY	NSW	23	28	3	406	56*	2	–	16.24	4	361.1	62	1108	51	21.73	1	–	6/36
Laver, F	VIC	17	18	4	137	17	–	–	9.79	7	480.0	158	999	67	14.91	7	2	8/31
Macartney, CG	NSW	29	37	7	503	51	2	–	16.77	20	480.5	138	1143	64	17.86	3	1	7/58
McAlister, PA	VIC	23	32	5	751	85	3	–	27.81	14	0.2	–	0	1	0.00	–	–	1/0
Noble, MA (Capt)	NSW	31	45	4	1060	131	4	2	25.85	16	343.1	85	864	25	34.56	–	–	3/42
O'Connor, JDA	SA	20	27	7	217	36*	–	–	10.85	9	555.5	154	1433	77	18.61	6	2	7/40
Ransford, VS	VIC	32	44	4	1736	190	4	6	43.40	16	4.0	–	27	1	27.00	–	–	1/15
Trumper, VT	NSW	34	45	2	1435	150	7	3	33.37	19	29.0	2	151	1	151.00	–	–	1/24
Whitty, WJ	SA	25	25	8	132	21	–	–	7.76	8	644.0	192	1551	75	20.68	4	–	5/36

Darling finally decided that after three tours as captain and a fourth as a player his wife deserved more consideration and he headed off to Tasmania to father 15 children and become a fearless but loved independent MP. Monty Noble took over as Australia's captain for the 1909 tour and showed the same consideration for his men, directing religious newcomers to the churches of their choice on the team's arrival in London. The Australians started disastrously, losing three matches in a fortnight and England's selectors made the mistake of under-rating them. Noble remained calm and his team were not beaten again until the 36th match of the 39-match tour.

They lost the First Test by ten wickets in that miserable first month but recovered to win the Second and Third Tests and draw the last two, thus regaining The Ashes.

They were a superb fielding team, and although only Armstrong (113 at 16.39) took more than 100 wickets they bowled well enough to contain an England XI that had declined since 1905 and badly missed Jackson, then in India. Vernon Ransford made a century for Australia in his Test debut at Lord's and his left-hand batting made him a worthy replacement for Darling and Hill. Another left-hander, Warren Bardsley, hit the tour's highest score, 219, against Essex at Leyton, when he and Ransford (174) put on 355 runs in 200 minutes. Bardsley was the only Australian to pass 2000 runs (2092 at 46.04). Charlie Macartney's left-arm spinners won the Leeds Test for Australia (11 for 85) and gave him 64 tour wickets. But Bardsley was the Australian hero, finishing his first tour of England with centuries in each innings of the Fifth Test at The Oval.

English critics found numerous excuses for their beaten team but *Wisden's* Sydney Pardon had it right when he said they badly under-estimated the merit of a splendidly captained Australian side. This was the first Australian team accompanied by scorer Bill Ferguson, who spent 57 years in all travelling with Australian teams. Ferguson was paid £2 a week towards his expenses for the tour, a job he accepted when he went to dentist Noble's surgery to have a tooth extracted. Ferguson's score-books revolutionised the art of scoring and his diagrams of big innings by Australia's opponents helped captains plan field placings. Noble married Ferguson's sister when he was 40 and Ellen Ferguson 20.

AUSTRALIA IN ENGLAND 1912

First-class Results					All Matches				
Matches	Won	Lost	Drawn	Tied	Matches	Won	Lost	Drawn	Tied
36	9	8	19	–	37	9	8	20	–

Date	Venue	Opponent	Results for Australians
May 6	Nottingham	Nottinghamshire	Lost by 6 wkts
May 9	Northampton	Northamptonshire	Won by an inns & 64 runs
May 13	Leyton	Essex	Won by an inns & 132 runs
May 16	The Oval	Surrey	Won by 7 wkts
May 20	Lord's	MCC	Won by 5 wkts
May 23	Oxford	Oxford University	Won by 10 wkts
May 28	Manchester	SOUTH AFRICA (1st Test)	Won by an inns & 88 runs
May 30	Birmingham	Warwickshire	Drawn
Jun 3	Lord's	Middlesex	Drawn
Jun 6	Cambridge	Cambridge University	Drawn
Jun 11	Bradford	Yorkshire	Drawn
Jun 13	Manchester	Lancashire	Lost by 24 runs
Jun 17	The Oval	Surrey	Lost by 21 runs
Jun 20	Taunton	Somerset	Won by 10 wkts
Jun 24	Lord's	ENGLAND (2nd Test)	Drawn
Jun 27	Leyton	Essex	Drawn
Jly 1	Sheffield	Yorkshire	Drawn
Jly 4	Liverpool	Lancashire	Lost by 8 wkts
Jly 8	Edinburgh	Scotland	Won by 296 runs
Jly 11	Bristol	Scotland	Drawn
Jly 15	Lord's	SOUTH AFRICA (3rd Test)	Won by 10 wkts
Jly 18	Leicester	Leicestershire	Drawn
Jly 22	Southampton	Hampshire	Lost by 8 wkts
Jly 25	Hove	Sussex	Drawn
Jly 29	Manchester	ENGLAND (4th Test)	Drawn
Aug 1	Derby	Derbyshire	Drawn
Aug 5	Nottingham	SOUTH AFRICA (5th Test)	Drawn
Aug 9	Sunderland	*Durham	Drawn
Aug 12	Worcester	Worcestershire	Drawn
Aug 15	Cheltenham	Gloucestershire	Drawn
Aug 19	The Oval	ENGLAND (6th Test)	Lost by 244 runs
Aug 23	Cardiff	*South Wales	Abandoned
Aug 27	Norwich	England XI	Drawn
Aug 31	Canterbury	Kent	Drawn
Sep 2	The Oval	Surrey & Middlesex XI	Lost by 10 wkts
Sep 5	Scarborough	Lord Londesborough's XI	Drawn
Sep 9	Hastings	South of England	Drawn
Sep 12	Wicklow, Ire.	CB Fry's XI	Lost by 8 wkts

The 1912 team in England, often described as the worst Australia ever sent overseas: *back row* W. Crouch (manager), Roy Minnett, Harold Webster, Charles Kelleway, Edgar Mayne, Sid Emery, Dave Smith, Bill Whitty, Gervys Hazlitt; *seated* Warren Bardsley, John McLaren, Jimmy Matthews, Syd Gregory (capt.), Claude Jennings, Charlie Macartney, Barlow Carkeek.

Player	State	M	Inn	NO	Runs	HS	50	100	Avrge	Ct/St	Overs	Mdns	Runs	Wkts	Avrge	5wi	10wm	Best
Bardsley, W	NSW	36	52	6	2365	184*	9	8	51.41	22	–	–	–	–	–	–	–	–
Carkeek, W	VIC	25	29	12	155	27	–	–	9.12	33/8	–	–	–	–	–	–	–	–
Emery, SH	NSW	24	28	8	251	37*	–	–	12.55	14	458.1	77	1565	66	23.71	5	2	7/58
Gregory, SE (Capt)	NSW	34	47	2	1055	150	3	2	23.44	5	–	–	–	–	–	–	–	–
Hazlitt, GR	NSW	29	37	8	219	35*	–	–	7.55	13	788.3	215	1890	98	19.29	4	–	6/105
Jennings, CB	SA	32	50	4	1037	82	7	–	22.54	15	–	–	–	–	–	–	–	–
Kelleway, CE	NSW	34	48	7	1281	114	6	2	31.24	26	441.5	123	1140	47	24.26	2	–	5/33
Macartney, CG	NSW	33	49	1	2187	208	8	6	45.56	19	337.0	110	656	38	17.26	2	–	6/54
Matthews, TJ	VIC	28	36	4	584	93	2	–	18.25	15	627.3	163	1647	85	19.38	4	–	7/46
Mayne, ER	SA	25	43	3	766	85	3	–	19.15	10	10.0	–	35	–	–	–	–	–
McLaren, JW	QLD	11	16	1	132	40	–	–	8.80	6	190.3	33	603	27	22.33	–	–	4/45
Minnett, RB	NSW	28	41	5	722	65*	3	–	20.56	6	304.2	80	966	40	24.15	2	–	6/29
Smith, DSM	VIC	16	24	2	292	100	–	1	13.27	6	4.0	–	22	1	22.00	–	–	1/22
Webster, HW	SA	11	13	5	131	26	–	–	16.37	15/3	–	–	–	–	–	–	–	–
Whitty, WJ	SA	30	36	9	282	33	–	–	10.44	5	866.3	281	1971	109	18.08	5	1	7/40

This was widely rated the worst-ever Australian team when it was picked and achieved nothing on tour of England and North America to prove that assessment wrong. Trumper, Hill, Cotter, Carter, Ransford and Armstrong all refused to tour because the Australian Board of Control double-crossed the players. The Board broke promises made when it was founded in 1905 that it would allow touring teams to appoint their own managers and handed the job to the inexperienced Queenslander G.S. Crouch. The players wanted Frank Laver, who had admirably managed the 1905 and 1909 teams in England and made a useful replacement for injured players. Under Crouch, the team behaved so badly the Board appointed a special committee on their return to investigate tour misdemeanours. The committee cited four players—Syd Gregory, Barlow Carkeek, Dave Smith and Jimmy Matthews—to attend its enquiry, but their report to the Board was never released.

Lacking a bowler with the penetration of Cotter or his predecessor Ernie Jones, the Australians conceded big scores to strong England sides. Left-arm swing bowler Bill Whitty took 109 wickets at 18.08 and Gervys Rignold Hazlitt dismissed 98 batsmen with his right-hand off-breaks at 19.29 each, but the team won only nine of their 36 first-class matches, lost eight and left 19 unfinished. On the crossing from Ireland to England, the ship's captain ordered that no more liquor be served the Australians, and on the voyage home Edgar Mayne refused to share a cabin with a team-mate. On the manager's recommendation, the Board introduced a rule giving it the right to refuse a player's selection for an Australian team for reasons other than cricket. The fuss aroused by players' larrikinism denied leg-spinner Matthews the accolades he deserved for his amazing two hat-tricks in one day in the opening match of the Triangular series against South Africa. Syd Gregory, who had come out of retirement to make his eighth tour of England at the age of 42 to help out the desperate Board of Control, could not muster enough discipline from this rabble to prevent their defeat by four counties, Nottinghamshire, Lancashire, combined Middlesex–Surrey, and Hampshire, in addition to their three defeats by England XIs. Ten of the tourists played in Bermuda and America before returning home.

Australian captain Syd Gregory, left, tossing with England captain Charles Fry, before an England–Australia Test in the 1912 Triangular series.

AUSTRALIA IN ENGLAND 1921

First-class Results					All Matches				
Matches	Won	Lost	Drawn	Tied	Matches	Won	Lost	Drawn	Tied
34	21	2	11	–	39	23	2	14	–

Date	Venue	Opponent	Results for Australians
Apr 30	Leicester	Leicestershire	Won by an inns & 152 runs
May 4	Attleborough	L Robinson's XI	Drawn
May 7	The Oval	Surrey	Won by an inns & 55 runs
May 11	Bradford	Yorkshire	Drawn
May 14	Portsmouth	The Services	Won by 198 runs
May 18	Leyton	Essex	Won by an inns & 75 runs
May 21	Lord's	MCC	Won by 3 wkts
May 25	Oxford	Oxford University	Drawn
May 28	Nottingham	ENGLAND (1st Test)	Won by 10 wkts
Jun 1	Cambridge	Cambridge University	Won by an inns & 14 runs
Jun 4	Lord's	Middlesex	Won by 8 wkts
Jun 8	Bristol	Gloucestershire	Drawn
Jun 11	Lord's	ENGLAND (2nd Test)	Won by 8 wkts
Jun 15	Southampton	Hampshire	Drawn
Jun 18	The Oval	Surrey	Won by 78 runs
Jun 22	Northampton	Northamptonshire	Won by an inns & 484 runs
Jun 25	Nottingham	Nottinghamshire	Won by an inns & 517 runs
Jun 29	Birmingham	Warwickshire	Drawn
Jly 2	Leeds	ENGLAND (3rd Test)	Won by 219 runs
Jly 6	Manchester	Lancashire	Won by an inns & 8 runs
Jly 9	Glasgow	*West of Scotland	Drawn
Jly 12	Perth	*Scotland	Drawn
Jly 14	Edinburgh	*Scotland	Drawn
Jly 16	Sunderland	*Durham	Won by 10 wkts
Jly 20	Sheffield	Yorkshire	Won by 175 runs
Jly 23	Manchester	ENGLAND (4th Test)	Drawn
Jly 27	Southend	Essex	Won by an inns & 88 runs
Jly 30	Swansea	Glamorgan	Drawn
Aug 3	Liverpool	Lancashire	Drawn
Aug 6	Birmingham	Warwickshire	Won by an inns & 61 runs
Aug 10	Canterbury	Kent	Drawn
Aug 13	The Oval	ENGLAND (5th Test)	Drawn
Aug 20	Cheltenham	Gloucestershire	Won by an inns & 136 runs
Aug 24	Taunton	Somerset	Won by an inns & 58 runs
Aug 27	Eastbourne	England XI	Lost by 28 runs
Aug 31	Hove	Sussex	Won by 197 runs
Sep 3	Hastings	South of England	Won by an inns & 46 runs
Sep 8	Scarborough	CI Thornton's XI	Lost by 33 runs
Sep 13	Whitehaven	*Cumberland	Won by 5 wkts

One of the great Australian Test teams, which won the first three Tests against England in 1921 inside three days: *back row* Warren Bardsley, Jack Ryder, 'Stork' Hendry, Jack Gregory, Edgar Mayne, Tom Andrews, Syd Smith (manager); *seated* Arthur Mailey, Ted McDonald, Herbie Collins, Warwick Armstrong (capt.), Charlie Macartney, Hanson Carter, Johnnie Taylor; *front* 'Nip' Pellew, Bert Oldfield. Andrews and Carter were funeral parlour directors.

Player	State	M	Inn	NO	Runs	HS	50	100	Avrge	Ct/St	Overs	Mdns	Runs	Wkts	Avrge	5wi	10wm	Best
Andrews, TJE	NSW	30	41	4	1212	132	7	1	32.75	14	26.0	–	136	1	136.00	–	–	1/23
Armstrong, WW (Capt)	VIC	30	37	8	1213	182*	4	3	41.83	21	733.1	271	1444	100	14.44	8	1	7/55
Bardsley, W	NSW	30	41	4	2005	209	10	8	54.18	8	2.0	–	13	–	–	–	–	–
Carter, H	NSW	17	18	1	355	57	1	–	20.88	26/12	–	–	–	–	–	–	–	–
Collins, HL	NSW	24	32	–	953	162	3	3	29.78	17	76.0	26	184	1	184.00	–	–	1/26
Gregory, JM	NSW	27	33	2	1135	107	8	3	36.61	37	655.4	126	1924	116	16.59	8	2	7/52
Hendry, HSTL	NSW	23	26	7	534	56*	4	–	28.10	28	393.1	103	969	38	25.50	–	–	4/30
Macartney, CG	NSW	31	41	2	2317	345	6	8	59.41	5	143.0	58	243	8	30.38	–	–	3/64
Mailey, AA	NSW	28	30	10	233	46*	–	–	11.65	32	800.0	103	2595	134	19.37	7	1	10/66
Mayne, ER	SA	13	15	1	457	157*	2	1	32.64	5	5.0	2	8	–	–	–	–	–
McDonald, EA	VIC	26	27	6	257	36	–	–	12.23	10	809.2	158	2284	138	16.55	9	3	8/41
Oldfield, WAS	NSW	18	20	5	357	123	–	1	23.80	29/21	–	–	–	–	–	–	–	–
Pellew, CE	SA	27	37	3	848	146	2	2	24.94	9	41.0	13	91	2	45.50	–	–	1/4
Ryder, J	VIC	23	29	6	825	124*	4	1	35.86	14	193.0	35	492	18	27.33	–	–	4/72
Taylor, JM	NSW	27	35	2	1019	143	6	1	30.87	8	8.0	1	26	1	26.00	–	–	1/25

Despite Australia's five–nil defeat of England under his leadership in 1920–21, Warwick Armstrong scraped in as captain of the 1921 side for England by only one vote. Armstrong's disrespect for Board of Control strongman Ernie Bean was well-known but Bean's efforts to deprive him of the captaincy just failed. Armstrong had the advantage of leading a team with express bowlers Jack Gregory and Ted McDonald to open the attack, at the time a tactical first that was to have far-reaching influence on selection committees right round the cricket world.

The 1921 Australians deservedly rank as one of the greatest of all cricket teams. Thanks to the successful 1919 tour by the First AIF team, which provided five of his players, Armstrong found Australia had recovered from World War I faster than England. On his fourth tour of England, Armstrong's main problem was in deciding which four players to drop for the Tests. Apart from his devastating pace bowlers, he had medium pacers (Ryder, Hendry), spinners (Mailey, Macartney, Collins and himself) at his disposal, supported by some of the best outfielders (Pellew, Bardsley and Taylor), superb slip catchers (Gregory, Hendry), and two masterful keepers (Carter, Oldfield). The batting was so strong the Australians hit 32 centuries but had only eight made against them. Six of his players had captained their own states so their grasp of tactics was virtually automatic, though some of them did not rank Armstrong's captaincy with that of Trott, Noble, or Collins.

Armstrong shone, however, in demanding privileges for his players. On the voyage to England he informed his men that the lack of rest days before each Test in the itinerary the Australian Board had negotiated was intolerable. He got them to breach their tour contracts and on arrival in England persuaded Oxford University, Gloucestershire and Warwickshire to play their matches with Australia over two days instead of three. Properly rested, the Australians swept to victory in the first three Tests inside three days.

They went 34 matches without defeat until a side specially chosen by former England captain Archie MacLaren inflicted defeat by 28 runs at Eastbourne in the fifth last match of the tour. MacLaren had boasted throughout the summer that he could pick an all-amateur side to beat Australia and he did so after his team was dismissed for 43 runs in 75 minutes in their first innings. Michael Falcon took 6 for 67 to restrict Australia's lead to 131, and when the England XI batted again, 153 by South African Aubrey Faulkner lifted the second innings total to 326, leaving Australia with 196 to get. Clement Gibson, the right-arm fast-medium bowler born in Argentina, took 6 for 64 to help Falcon and Faulkner dismiss Australia for 167. Ten days later against C.I. Thornton's XI at Scarborough the Australian batting failed again in the second innings and they were sent back for 162 at the last minute to lose by 33 runs for only their second defeat in 38 matches. To their credit, the Australian Board forgot members' differences with Armstrong and paid all 15 players a bonus of £300 each on their return home.

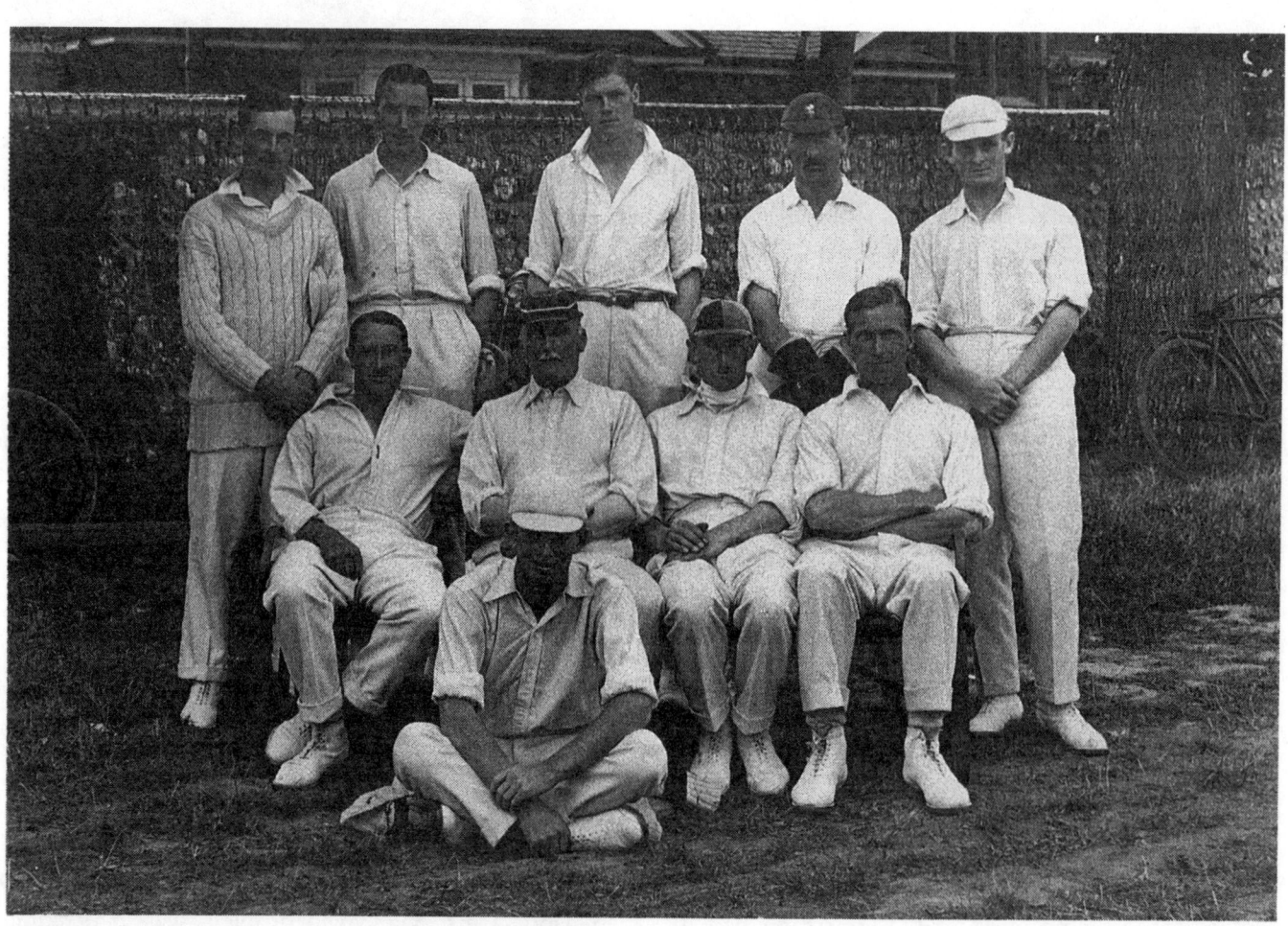

A rare photograph of the only team to beat the 1921 Australians, the England XI that won by 28 runs: Hubert (later Sir Hubert) Ashton, C.H. Gibson, A.P.F. Chapman, G.E.C. Wood, G. Ashton; *middle* G.A. Faulkner, A.C. MacLaren (capt.), G.N. Foster, M. Falcon; *front* C.T. Ashton; *absent* W. Brearley. *Roger Mann*

AUSTRALIA IN ENGLAND 1926

	First-class Results					All Matches			
Matches	Won	Lost	Drawn	Tied	Matches	Won	Lost	Drawn	Tied
33	9	1	23	–	40	12	1	27	–

Date	Venue	Opponent	Results for Australians
Apr 28	Maidenhead	*Minor Counties	Drawn
May 1	Leicester	Leicestershire	Drawn
May 5	Leyton	Essex	Drawn
May 8	The Oval	Surrey	Drawn
May 12	Southampton	Hampshire	Won by 10 wkts
May 15	Lord's	MCC	Drawn
May 19	Cambridge	Cambridge University	Drawn
May 22	Oxford	Oxford University	Won by an inns & 13 runs
May 26	Bristol	South of England	Drawn
May 29	Lord's	Middlesex	Drawn
Jun 2	Birmingham	North of England	Drawn
Jun 5	Bradford	Yorkshire	Drawn
Jun 9	Sunderland	*Durham	Won by an inns & 81 runs
Jun 12	Nottingham	ENGLAND (1st Test)	Drawn
Jun 16	Sheffield	Yorkshire	Drawn
Jun 19	Manchester	Lancashire	Won by an inns & 77 runs
Jun 23	Chesterfield	Derbyshire	Drawn
Jun 26	Lord's	ENGLAND (2nd Test)	Drawn
Jun 30	Northampton	Northamptonshire	Won by an inns & 147 runs
Jly 3	Nottingham	Nottinghamshire	Won by an inns & 136 runs
Jly 7	Worcester	Worcestershire	Won by 176 runs
Jly 10	Leeds	ENGLAND (3rd Test)	Drawn
Jly 14	Liverpool	Lancashire	Drawn
Jly 17	Glasgow	*West of Scotland	Won by an inns & 61 runs
Jly 20	Perth	*Eastern Districts	Won by 6 wkts
Jly 21	Edinburgh	*Scotland	Drawn
Jly 24	Manchester	ENGLAND (4th Test)	Drawn
Jly 28	The Oval	Surrey	Drawn
Jly 31	Swansea	Glamorgan	Won by 224 runs
Aug 4	Birmingham	Warwickshire	Drawn
Aug 7	Cheltenham	Gloucestershire	Won by 9 wkts
Aug 11	Lord's	*XV of Public Schools	Drawn
Aug 14	The Oval	ENGLAND (5th Test)	Lost by 289 runs
Aug 21	Taunton	Somerset	Won by 56 runs
Aug 25	Canterbury	Kent	Drawn
Aug 28	Hove	Sussex	Drawn
Sep 1	Folkestone	England XI	Drawn
Sep 4	Chiswick	*Civil Service	Drawn
Sep 8	Scarborough	C I Thornton's XI	Drawn
Sep 11	Blackpool	England XI	Drawn

The 1926 Australians who surrendered The Ashes by losing the Fifth Test after four draws: *back row* Jack Ellis, 'Stork' Hendry, Jack Gregory, Jack Ryder, Arthur Richardson, Sam Everett, Syd Smith (manager); *seated* Arthur Mailey, Clarrie Grimmett, Warren Bardsley, Herbie Collins (capt.), Charlie Macartney, Tom Andrews, Johnnie Taylor; *front* Bill Woodfull, Bill Ponsford, Bert Oldfield.

Player	State	M	Inn	NO	Runs	HS	50	100	Avrge	Ct/St	Overs	Mdns	Runs	Wkts	Avrge	5wi	10wm	Best
Andrews, TJE	NSW	28	37	5	1234	164	9	1	38.56	24	80.0	16	240	7	34.28	1	–	6/109
Bardsley, W	NSW	27	33	3	1424	193*	4	5	47.46	8	–	–	–	–	–	–	–	–
Collins, HL (Capt)	NSW	22	27	1	779	99	6	–	29.96	11	71.0	21	169	6	28.16	–	–	3/39
Ellis, JL	VIC	13	15	5	322	43	–	–	32.20	21/23	–	–	–	–	–	–	–	–
Everett, SC	NSW	13	10	1	116	59	1	–	12.88	8	197.3	35	557	17	32.76	–	–	3/75
Gregory, JM	NSW	26	30	6	843	130	1	2	35.12	24	423.4	77	1158	36	32.16	–	–	4/53
Grimmett, CV	SA	24	21	2	263	41	–	–	13.84	17	834.3	251	1857	105	17.68	7	1	7/67
Hendry, HSTL	VIC	7	9	1	315	81	4	–	39.37	3	49.0	12	117	1	117.00	–	–	1/8
Macartney, CG	NSW	27	33	4	1561	160	5	6	53.82	4	559.3	242	873	49	17.81	3	–	6/63
Mailey, AA	NSW	27	23	6	117	21	–	–	6.88	16	816.0	153	2437	126	19.34	12	4	9/86
Oldfield, WAS	NSW	21	21	5	303	43*	–	–	18.93	20/19	–	–	–	–	–	–	–	–
Ponsford, WH	VIC	21	26	4	901	144	2	3	40.95	8	–	–	–	–	–	–	–	–
Richardson, AJ	SA	25	30	8	728	100	4	1	33.09	8	573.5	234	966	49	19.71	3	1	6/28
Ryder, J	VIC	28	35	7	966	109	4	3	34.50	8	363.0	91	847	23	36.82	1	–	6/74
Taylor, JM	NSW	27	36	2	760	95	4	–	22.35	6	–	–	–	–	–	–	–	–
Woodfull, WM	VIC	27	34	5	1672	201	6	8	57.65	17	–	–	–	–	–	–	–	–

Herbie Collins succeeded Armstrong as Australia's captain at the age of 32. He was the only bookmaker ever appointed to the leadership, a left-handed batsman and orthodox spinner renowned for his skill with coins whether it was in a two-up ring or in deciding who batted first in Tests. He was an inveterate gambler who could locate baccarat or poker games within hours of his team's arrival at an unknown hotel. He won seven out of 11 of his Test tosses. In 1924–25, when Collins won his third successive toss, England captain Arthur Gilligan knelt down on Adelaide Oval and delighted spectators by making a mock inspection of the coin Collins used. The public knew Collins had learnt his skill in tossing in army two-up games in France when he was a trooper charged with driving truck loads of shells up to front line gunners.

Deprived of the bowling of McDonald—who had settled in Lancashire—and unable to use Gregory for more than a few overs because of his dicky knee, Collins had to fall back on spin from Mailey, Grimmett and himself in England in 1926. With this limited attack he did well to draw the first four Tests. England regained The Ashes by winning the Fifth by 289 runs when the selectors replaced Carr with Chapman as England's captain and brought back Rhodes at the age of 48. His 4 for 44 in Australia's second innings proved decisive and Chapman's athletic fielding set a standard for his team to follow. On a rain-affected pitch the clever batting of Hobbs and Sutcliffe gave England a 172-run start to their second innings, an advantage Australia could not overcome when faced with Rhodes on a drying pitch. Woodfull, on his first tour, topped the averages with 1672 runs at 57.65 in a team that had eight century-makers but only two bowlers who took 100 wickets, Grimmett (105 at 17.68) and Mailey (126 at 19.34).

AUSTRALIA IN ENGLAND 1930

First-class Results					All Matches				
Matches	Won	Lost	Drawn	Tied	Matches	Won	Lost	Drawn	Tied
31	11	1	18	1	33	12	1	19	1

Date	Venue	Opponent	Results for Australians
Apr 30	Worcester	Worcestershire	Won by an inns & 165 runs
May 3	Leicester	Leicestershire	Drawn
May 7	Leyton	Essex	Won by 207 runs
May 10	Sheffield	Yorkshire	Drawn
May 14	Liverpool	Lancashire	Drawn
May 17	Lord's	MCC	Drawn
May 21	Chesterfield	Derbyshire	Won by 10 wkts
May 24	The Oval	Surrey	Drawn
May 28	Oxford	Oxford University	Won by an inns & 158 runs
May 31	Southampton	Hampshire	Won by an inns & 8 runs
Jun 4	Lord's	Middlesex	Won by 5 wkts
Jun 7	Cambridge	Cambridge University	Won by an inns & 134 runs
Jun 13	Nottingham	ENGLAND (1st Test)	Lost by 93 runs
Jun 18	The Oval	Surrey	Drawn
Jun 21	Manchester	Lancashire	Drawn
Jun 27	Lord's	ENGLAND (2nd Test)	Won by 7 wkts
Jly 2	Bradford	Yorkshire	Won by 10 wkts
Jly 5	Nottingham	Nottinghamshire	Drawn
Jly 11	Leeds	ENGLAND (3rd Test)	Drawn
Jly 16	Edinburgh	Scotland	Drawn
Jly 23	Sunderland	*Durham	Abandoned
Jly 25	Manchester	ENGLAND (4th Test)	Drawn
Jly 30	Taunton	Somerset	Won by an inns & 158 runs
Aug 2	Swansea	Glamorgan	Drawn
Aug 6	Birmingham	Warwickshire	Drawn
Aug 9	Northampton	Northamptonshire	Drawn
Aug 16	The Oval	ENGLAND (5th Test)	Won by an inns & 39 runs
Aug 23	Bristol	Gloucestershire	Tied
Aug 27	Canterbury	Kent	Drawn
Aug 30	Hove	Sussex	Drawn
Sep 3	Folkestone	England XI	Drawn
Sep 6	Lord's	*HDG Leveson–Gower's XI	Drawn
Sep 10	Scarborough	England XI	Drawn

The lowly rated 1930 Australians who shocked English fans by regaining The Ashes: *back row* W.L. Kelly (manager), Archie Jackson, Tim Wall, Ted a'Beckett, Percy Hornibrook, Alec Hurwood, Clarrie Grimmett, Tom Howard (treasurer); *seated* Alan Fairfax, Bill Ponsford, Vic Richardson, Bill Woodfull (capt.), Allan Kippax, Don Bradman, Charlie Walker; *front* Stan McCabe, Bert Oldfield.

Player	State	M	Inn	NO	Runs	HS	50	100	Avrge	Ct/St	Overs	Mdns	Runs	Wkts	Avrge	5wi	10wm	Best
a'Beckett, EL	VIC	17	21	5	397	67*	2	–	24.81	15	343.0	112	628	20	31.40	–	–	3/83
Bradman, DG	NSW	27	36	6	2960	334	5	10	98.66	12	76.0	12	301	12	25.08	–	–	3/35
Fairfax, AG	NSW	22	27	6	536	63	3	–	25.52	21	535.4	150	1218	41	29.70	1	–	6/54
Grimmett, CV	SA	26	23	3	237	50	1	–	11.85	11	1013.1	262	2425	144	16.84	15	5	10/37
Hornibrook, PM	QLD	26	26	8	232	59*	1	–	12.88	21	819.2	240	1804	96	18.79	9	3	7/42
Hurwood, A	QLD	20	19	1	188	61	1	–	10.44	12	354.0	115	752	28	26.85	1	–	5/111
Jackson, A	NSW	26	35	3	1097	118	8	1	34.28	10	5.0	–	8	–	–	–	–	–
Kippax, AF	NSW	23	32	7	1451	158	9	4	58.04	7	25.3	2	91	4	22.75	–	–	1/13
McCabe, SJ	NSW	26	33	2	1012	96	7	–	32.64	14	281.0	69	723	26	27.80	–	–	4/25
Oldfield, WAS	NSW	16	16	4	225	43*	–	–	18.75	22/11	–	–	–	–	–	–	–	–
Ponsford, WH	VIC	24	33	4	1425	220*	6	4	49.13	11	1.0	–	6	–	–	–	–	–
Richardson, VY	SA	26	32	1	832	116	2	2	26.83	22/3	1.0	–	8	–	–	–	–	–
Walker, CW	SA	16	14	5	43	10*	–	–	4.77	11/14	–	–	–	–	–	–	–	–
Wall, TW	SA	22	19	6	107	40*	–	–	8.23	10	619.2	111	1638	56	29.25	1	–	5/60
Woodfull, WM (Capt)	VIC	23	26	1	1434	216	6	6	57.36	8	–	–	–	–	–	–	–	–

Schoolmaster Bill Woodfull took a collection of virtually untried players to England (following the unceremonious sacking of Collins and manager Syd Smith) into a series against an English side that had won the previous two rubbers. Against all the odds, Woodfull moulded them into a winning combination and brought back The Ashes. He did it with enormous help from 22-year-old Bowral lad Don Bradman, who scored 2960 runs at 98.66 on the tour and 974 in the Tests at an average of 139.14, including 232 in the crucial Fifth Test, won by Australia on their captain's birthday.

Grimmett was again a match-winner, his subtle mix of leg-breaks, top-spinners and googlies dismissing 144 batsmen at a cost of only 16.84 each. In a team of six century-makers, 20-year-old Stan McCabe failed to get one although he was better to watch than any of his colleagues. He had a top score of 96. At Trent Bridge in the First Test McCabe was batting brilliantly with Bradman and they seemed certain to win the Test for Australia when Sydney Copley, 24, a member of the Notts groundstaff, ran a long way and dived full-length, rolling over but coming up with possession retained, to dismiss McCabe. Copley went into the Notts First XI a week later but never again played in a first-class match. He had only taken the field in the Test because Larwood had a stomach upset and none of the selected England XI were available. Copley's catch turned the match and England won by 93 runs after Australia made 335 chasing 429 for victory.

The other curiosity of the tour was the match between Australia and Gloucestershire, which ended in a tie after Australia were set 118 to win and were dismissed for 117. This was the first tie in the history of first-class cricket in England and came after the Australian openers, Archie Jackson and McCabe, put on 59 runs before they were separated. Charlie Parker, the third highest wicket-taker England has produced with 3278 victims—only Tich Freeman and Rhodes had more—dismissed Bradman twice in this match, taking 3 for 72 in the first innings and 7 for 54 in the second. Wally Hammond's second innings 89 ended up a crucial factor in the result. Parker was the player who is said to have ruined his chances of appearing in more than one Test by punching selector 'Plum' Warner on the nose when they met in a lift.

The Gloucestershire team that played the historic tie against the 1930 Australians: *back row* R.G. Ford (12th man), B.S. Bloodworth (scorer), A.E. Dipper; *third row* E.J. Stevens, C.C. Dacre, R.A. Sinfield, W.R. Hammond; *second row* W.L. Neale, C.J. Barnett, H. Smith; *front* C.W.L. Parker, B.H. Lyon (capt.), F.J. Seabrook, T.W. Goddard. Parker took ten wickets, Goddard seven. Hammond made 89. *Roger Mann*

AUSTRALIA IN ENGLAND 1934

	First-class Results					All Matches		
Matches	Won	Lost	Drawn	Tied	Matches	Won	Lost	Drawn	Tied
30	13	1	16	–	34	15	1	18	–

Date	Venue	Opponent	Results for Australians
May 2	Worcester	Worcestershire	Won by an inns & 297 runs
May 5	Leicester	Leicestershire	Drawn
May 9	Cambridge	Cambridge University	Won by an inns & 163 runs
May 12	Lord's	MCC	Drawn
May 16	Chelmsford	Essex	Won by an inns & 93 runs
May 19	Oxford	Oxford University	Won by an inns & 33 runs
May 23	Southampton	Hampshire	Drawn
May 26	Lord's	Middlesex	Won by 10 wkts
May 30	The Oval	Surrey	Drawn
Jun 2	Manchester	Lancashire	Drawn
Jun 8	Nottingham	ENGLAND (1st Test)	Won by 238 runs
Jun 13	Northampton	Northamptonshire	Drawn
Jun 16	Lord's	Gentlemen of England	Won by 8 wkts
Jun 22	Lord's	ENGLAND (2nd Test)	Lost by an inns & 38 runs
Jun 27	Taunton	Somerset	Won by an inns & 77 runs
Jun 30	The Oval	Surrey	Won by 6 wkts
Jly 6	Manchester	ENGLAND (3rd Test)	Drawn
Jly 11	Chesterfield	Derbyshire	Won by 9 wkts
Jly 14	Sheffield	Yorkshire	Drawn

Continued

The 1934 Australians in England, and for the second tour running, Woodfull's men regained The Ashes: *back row* Bill Ferguson, Clarrie Grimmett, Bill Brown, Hans Ebeling, Harold Busby (manager), Bill O'Reilly, Tim Wall, Leslie Fleetwood-Smith, W.C. Bull (treasurer); *seated* Ernie Blomley, Arthur Chipperfield, Don Bradman, Bill Woodfull (capt.), Allen Kippax, Len Darling, Bill Ponsford; *front* Ben Barnett, Stan McCabe, Bert Oldfield.

HOME AND AWAY

Date	Venue	Opponent	Results for Australians
Jly 20	Leeds	ENGLAND (4th Test)	Drawn
Jly 25	Sunderland	*Durham	Drawn
Jly 27	Edinburgh	Scotland	Drawn
Aug 1	Bristol	Gloucestershire	Drawn
Aug 4	Swansea	Glamorgan	Drawn
Aug 8	Birmingham	Warwickshire	Drawn
Aug 11	Nottingham	Nottinghamshire	Drawn
Aug 15	Aldershot	*Army	Won by 8 wkts
Aug 18	The Oval	ENGLAND (5th Test)	Won by 562 runs
Aug 25	Hove	Sussex	Won by an inns & 35 runs
Aug 29	Canterbury	Kent	Drawn
Sep 1	Folkestone	England XI	Drawn
Sep 5	The Oval	*Minor Counties	Drawn
Sep 8	Scarborough	England XI	Won by an inns & 48 runs
Sep 14	Forres	*North of Scotland	Won by an inns & 20 runs

Player	State	M	Inn	NO	Runs	HS	50	100	Avrge	Ct/St	Overs	Mdns	Runs	Wkts	Avrge	5wi	10wm	Best
Barnett, BA	VIC	18	20	6	470	92	2	–	33.57	19/12	1.0	–	3	1	3.00	–	–	1/3
Bradman, DG	NSW	22	27	3	2020	304	6	7	84.16	9	–	–	–	–	–	–	–	–
Bromley, EH	VIC	18	20	1	312	56	1	–	16.42	20	72.5	12	245	5	49.00	–	–	2/14
Brown, WA	NSW	24	36	2	1308	119	6	5	38.47	9	–	–	–	–	–	–	–	–
Chipperfield, AG	NSW	22	26	4	899	175	4	2	40.86	15	197.5	46	595	12	49.58	–	–	3/19
Darling, LS	VIC	25	31	1	1022	117	4	2	34.06	14	123.3	31	325	9	36.11	–	–	2/9
Ebeling, HI	VIC	21	19	1	265	41	–	–	14.72	16	635.0	200	1290	62	20.80	1	–	5/28
Fleetwood-Smith, LO	VIC	20	13	6	24	7*	–	–	3.42	10	713.5	160	2036	106	19.20	12	3	7/40
Grimmett, CV	SA	21	20	3	255	39	–	–	15.00	8	985.3	308	2159	109	19.80	9	1	7/109
Kippax, AF	NSW	19	23	4	961	250	7	1	50.57	4	5.0	1	13	–	–	–	–	–
McCabe, SJ	NSW	26	37	7	2078	240	7	8	69.26	19	305.3	71	794	21	37.80	–	–	4/24
O'Reilly, WJ	NSW	19	18	9	237	30*	–	–	26.33	7	870.0	320	1858	109	17.04	7	3	9/38
Oldfield, WAS	NSW	15	16	3	295	67	1	–	22.69	22/19	–	–	–	–	–	–	–	–
Ponsford, WH	VIC	22	27	4	1784	281*	7	5	77.56	11	–	–	–	–	–	–	–	–
Wall, TW	SA	16	21	3	84	24	–	–	9.33	4	475.2	95	1290	42	30.71	1	–	6/74
Woodfull, WM (Capt)	VIC	22	27	3	1268	228*	6	3	52.83	4	–	–	–	–	–	–	–	–

This was a peace-making tour after the remarkable events of the Bodyline tour in 1932–33 by Jardine's side in Australia. The Australian attack was badly lacking an opening bowler of any hostility, but Grimmett, O'Reilly and Fleetwood-Smith, astutely handled by Woodfull, hoodwinked England's best batsmen often enough to do the job. All three took more than 100 wickets on the tour, O'Reilly 109 at 17.04, Grimmett 109 at 19.80, and Fleetwood-Smith 106 at 19.20, in a team that fielded superbly and had a wonderful asset in keeper Bert Oldfield at his best. Bradman again headed the averages, this time with 2020 runs at 84.16, top score 304, which was 40 below his best in 1930.

Australian batsmanship probably reached its all-time best in the Fifth Test at The Oval when Bradman and Ponsford followed their stand of 388 in the previous Test by adding 451 for Australia's second wicket. Ponsford made 266, Bradman 244, Australia 701, and Woodfull's youngsters won the match by 562 runs. This was Ponsford's last Test and he announced his retirement soon after hitting his own wicket. Australia had scored 574 runs while he was at the crease. For a team that was demoralised in the previous Bodyline rubber, this was a gratifying revival, but more importantly, it restored good relations between the teams.

AUSTRALIA IN ENGLAND 1938

Australia arrived in England, the first touring team captained by Bradman, with their hopes of Ernie McCormick justifiably high. McCormick, a Melbourne jeweller, had been a big success in South Africa on the tour led by Vic Richardson although the need to use spin on matting wickets restricted his chances. He was a bowler of unusual technique, who marked out his run as though he needed help from engineers, beginning with a series of skips, followed by 20 running strides, arms stiff at his sides, and when he got it together as he usually did in Australia, his line and lift were intimidating even to class batsmen. Without swinging his arms, he generated pace from his powerful 6 ft (183 cm) tall frame that had all batsmen flinching. But in England it all went terribly wrong. Umpire Baldwin no-balled him for overstepping eight times in his first over, and 35 times in 20

The 1938 Australian team to England: *back row* Bill Jeanes (manager), Sid Barnes, Bill Brown, Ernie McCormick, Tim Wall, Bill O'Reilly, Leslie Fleetwood-Smith, Frank Ward, Bill Ferguson (scorer); *seated* Jack Fingleton, Merv Waite, Stan McCabe, Don Bradman (capt.), Ben Barnett, Arthur Chipperfield, Cyril Badcock; *front* Lindsay Hassett, Charlie Walker.

overs. Ernie told team-mates not to worry after lunch because Baldwin was hoarse. But umpires gave him no peace and after sending down 54 no-balls in his first 48 overs of the tour he went past the century in the tenth match. Team-mates tried to help by putting down their caps or handkerchiefs at key points in McCormick's approach run, but even bowling medium-pace off a six-stride run he was no-balled. Some demented statistician calculated that batsmen scored off 49 of his century of no-balls. Billy Brown got him to pump his arms instead of keeping them stiff and this helped.

Although they never got on well together, Bradman was forced to rely on O'Reilly as his main strike bowler because of McCormick's problems, and Big Bill responded by getting all the good England batsmen out, and at Leeds took ten wickets in a thrilling Test to clinch Australia's retention of The Ashes. This was the match in which Lindsay Hassett, rain threatening and an appeal against the light justified, got Australia home with 33 runs more vital than any century. Australia won by five wickets just before a torrential downpour enveloped the scene.

McCabe had put Australia into this position with a legendary innings of 232 at Nottingham which saved the First Test. England scored 8 for 658 declared and Australia was fighting for a draw at 6 for 194 when McCabe set about the bowling, finishing with 72 runs out of the 77 runs scored while he was with last-man Fleetwood-Smith, and lifting Australia to a safe total of 411. Bradman was so moved by the McCabe innings he called to players in the dressing-room not to miss it. When McCabe came in, Bradman wrote later, he was shaking like a young racehorse.

The tour ended with Australia holding The Ashes but England far from disgraced following a Fifth Test in which Len Hutton passed Bradman's Test record of 344 before he was out at 364. England won by a record margin of an innings and 579 runs. Australia made 201 and 123 in reply to England's 7 for 903 declared on a wicket so dead O'Reilly claimed it had been doped. 'Where's the groundsman's hut?' he said after bowling all day without any semblance of turn. 'I'd like to shoot the bastard.' Neither Bradman nor Fingleton could bat in either innings because of injury in a match that always threatened disaster for Australia after part-timers McCabe and Merv Waite opened the bowling. Wicket-keeper Ben Barnett worsened Australia's problems by missing easy stumpings, one when Hutton was stranded metres down the pitch on 87. The match ended for Bradman when he was carried off with a broken ankle. World War II began the following year.

First-class Results					All Matches				
Matches	Won	Lost	Drawn	Tied	Matches	Won	Lost	Drawn	Tied
29	15	2	12	–	35	20	2	13	–

Date	Venue	Opponent	Results for Australians
Apr 30	Worcester	Worcestershire	Won by an inns & 77 runs
May 4	Oxford	Oxford University	Won by an inns & 487 runs
May 7	Leicester	Leicestershire	Won by an inns & 163 runs
May 11	Cambridge	Cambridge University	Won by an inns & 425 runs
May 14	Lord's	MCC	Drawn
May 18	Northampton	Northamptonshire	Won by an inns & 77 runs
May 21	The Oval	Surrey	Drawn
May 25	Southampton	Hampshire	Drawn
May 28	Lord's	Middlesex	Drawn
Jun 1	Bristol	Gloucestershire	Won by 10 wkts
Jun 4	Southend	Essex	Won by 97 runs
Jun 10	Nottingham	ENGLAND (1st Test)	Drawn
Jun 15	Lord's	Gentlemen of England	Won by 282 runs
Jun 18	Manchester	Lancashire	Drawn
Jun 24	Lord's	ENGLAND (2nd Test)	Drawn
Jun 29	Chesterfield	Derbyshire	Won by an inns & 234 runs
Jly 2	Sheffield	Yorkshire	Drawn
Jly 8	Manchester	ENGLAND (3rd Test)	Abandoned
Jly 13	Birmingham	Warwickshire	Won by an inns & 93 runs
Jly 16	Nottingham	Nottinghamshire	Won by 412 runs
Jly 22	Leeds	ENGLAND (4th Test)	Won by 5 wkts
Jly 27	Taunton	Somerset	Won by an inns & 218 runs
Jly 30	Swansea	Glamorgan	Drawn
Aug 4	Broughty Ferry	*Scotland	Drawn
Aug 6	Glasgow	*Scotland	Won by 61 runs
Aug 8	Sunderland	*Durham	Won by 179 runs
Aug 10	The Oval	Surrey	Drawn
Aug 13	Canterbury	Kent	Won by 10 wkts
Aug 17	Aldershot	*Army	Won by an inns & 67 runs
Aug 20	The Oval	ENGLAND (5th Test)	Lost by an inns & 579 runs
Aug 27	Hove	Sussex	Drawn
Aug 31	Blackpool	England XI	Won by 10 wkts
Sep 3	Folkestone	England XI	Drawn
Sep 10	Scarborough	England XI	Lost by 10 wkts
Sep 15	Belfast	*Gentlemen of Ireland	Won by 61 runs
Sep 16	Dublin	*Gentlemen of Ireland	Won by an inns & 33 runs

Player	State	M	Inn	NO	Runs	HS	50	100	Avrge	Ct/St	Overs	Mdns	Runs	Wkts	Avrge	5wi	10wm	Best
Badcock, CL	SA	24	39	4	1604	198	9	4	45.82	14	2.0	–	10	–	–	–	–	–
Barnes, SG	NSW	13	19	2	720	94	5	–	42.35	9/4	44.0	4	116	2	58.00	–	–	1/32
Barnett, BA	VIC	22	29	4	737	120*	4	1	29.48	8/23	–	–	–	–	–	–	–	–
Bradman, DG (Capt)	SA	20	26	5	2429	278	5	13	115.66	8	3.0	2	6	–	–	–	–	–
Brown, WA	NSW	25	37	5	1854	265*	7	5	57.93	14	3.0	–	10	–	–	–	–	–
Chipperfield, AG	NSW	16	18	3	424	104*	2	1	28.26	12	54.1	18	155	6	25.83	–	–	2/12
Fingleton, JHW	NSW	23	32	2	1141	124	2	4	38.03	17/3	–	–	–	–	–	–	–	–
Fleetwood-Smith, LO	VIC	20	20	9	100	16*	–	–	9.09	8	554.5	98	1719	88	19.53	5	1	8/98
Hassett, AL	VIC	24	32	3	1589	220*	6	5	54.79	18	30.0	9	78	1	78.00	–	–	1/4
McCabe, SJ	NSW	23	33	2	1124	232	6	2	36.25	17	214.0	53	523	14	37.35	–	–	4/28
McCormick, EL	VIC	18	15	4	49	12	–	–	4.45	9	335.0	53	1136	34	33.41	1	–	6/58
O'Reilly, WJ	NSW	20	17	3	224	42	–	–	16.00	2	709.4	213	1726	104	16.59	9	2	8/104
Waite, MG	SA	24	30	3	684	77	3	–	25.33	15	647.1	183	1454	56	25.96	4	–	7/101
Walker, CW	SA	9	9	4	175	42	–	–	35.00	7/7	–	–	–	–	–	–	–	–
Ward, FA	SA	19	17	5	162	31	–	–	13.50	8	526.2	99	1773	92	19.27	8	2	7/51
White, ES	NSW	19	19	7	290	52	1	–	24.16	11	375.0	148	708	30	23.60	–	–	3/8

The First AIF cricket team in England: *back row* C.S. Winning, E.J. Long, C.T. Docker, J.M. Gregory, C.B. Willis; *seated* J.M. Taylor, E. Bull, H.L. Collins (capt.), E. Cameron, W.L. Trenerry, W.A. Oldfield. They had only four losses in 28 matches.

CHAPTER SEVEN

THE SERVICES XIs

At the end of World War I, service chiefs found themselves with thousands of war-weary men in Europe and not enough ships to get them all home to Australia. The Australian Sports Board was formed to keep the troops active in rugby, rowing, tennis and cricket competitions, usually for cups presented by King George V. By far the Sports Board's most ambitious ventures were in cricket, which began with matches between services but quickly spread to the foundation of an elite Australian XI charged with touring English counties to help revive the sport. Units all over Europe sent their best players to Salisbury Plain and other centres for exhaustive trials.

Initially, Captain Charles Kelleway from the Glebe club in Sydney, one of the few successes in Australia's 1912 side in England, was named captain of this First AIF team. Kelleway, born at Lismore, NSW, was a noted stonewaller who had been in the NSW team since 1907–08 and had made his Test debut against South Africa in Sydney in 1910. He was a cross-grained character, prone to quarrelling with curators, and after six matches Field Marshal Birdwood, GOC Australian forces, sacked him and made Lance-Corporal Herbie Collins, that chain-smoking, gambling night owl, leader of a side that included Major Cyril Docker, Captains Clarence Pellew, Carl Willis and William Trenerry, and Lieutenant Jack Gregory. Collins was on six shillings a day, plus what he could earn at two-up, but he moulded the AIF XI into a team that defeated the MCC at Lord's and lost only four of their 28 matches.

Collins ended up with a 'Test' batting average of 45 but he had virtually no strokes to show for it. He was the master of the anonymous nudge and the label-free dab, a left-hander who mistrusted deliveries outside his off stump and lacked driving prowess but somehow compiled 32 first-class centuries. Ray Robinson said there was an implacable trench-warfare approach in Collins' batting that drove spectators to the nearest bar and exasperated bowlers. Incongruously, the teams he led were known for their sparkling cricket.

From their first match under Collins, the AIF XI ignored reference to a player's rank and quickly became a happy combination. The MCC originally wanted the team to play a Test match against England to attract crowds back to big cricket but forgot the idea when Jack Massie dropped out because of his war wounds, Charles Macartney because of the death of his father, and the doctors Roy Park and E.P. Barbour because of the need to return home early and re-establish their medical practices. Despite these withdrawals, the MCC soon realised their mistake when Gregory began terrorising good county batsmen and the AIF beat Lancashire and Yorkshire in successive matches.

Gregory was a spectacular allrounder of the highest quality who captained the Shore school's first teams in rugby, cricket and athletics but had not advanced past North Sydney third grade when he joined up. He bounded in to bowl, all exuberant strength, leaping high in his delivery stride in what became known as his 'Kangaroo Hop', and he could destroy a side in two or three overs. Against the powerful Yorkshire side he took three wickets in an over to finish with 6 for 91 and give the AIF a 41-run lead. In the second innings he bowled with frightening pace to dismiss Wilfred Rhodes, Roy Kilner, Herb Sutcliffe and Emmott Robinson, and then hit Yorkshire's captain David Burton in the face to end his part in the match. Chasing 170 to win, the AIF were 9 for 116 when Gregory decided to hit and produce victory over England's 1919 county champions. The unbeaten last wicket stand yielded 54 runs.

1919 AUSTRALIAN IMPERIAL FORCES IN ENGLAND

First-class Results					All Matches				
Matches	Won	Lost	Drawn	Tied	Matches	Won	Lost	Drawn	Tied
28	12	4	12	–	32	13	4	15	–

Date	Venue	Opponent	Results for Australians
May 14	Attleborough	L Robinson's XI	Drawn
May 17	Leyton	Essex	Won by an inns & 114 runs
May 21	Cambridge	Cambridge University	Won by an inns & 239 runs
May 26	Lord's	Middlesex	Drawn
May 29	Oxford	Oxford University	Drawn
May 31	The Oval	Surrey	Drawn
Jun 5	Lord's	MCC	Won by 10 wkts
Jun 9	Hove	Sussex	Drawn
Jun 12	Manchester	Lancashire	Won by an inns & 157 runs
Jun 16	Sheffield	Yorkshire	Won by 1 wkt
Jun 20	Southampton	Hampshire	Drawn
Jun 23	Lord's	Gentlemen of England	Lost by an inns & 133 runs
Jun 26	Northampton	Northamptonshire	Won by 196 runs
Jun 30	Glasgow	*Western Scotland	Won by an inns & 560 runs
Jly 2	Edinburgh	*Scottish Union	Drawn
Jly 4	Glasgow	*Scotland	Drawn
Jly 7	West Hartlepool	*Durham	Drawn
Jly 11	Leicester	Leicestershire	Drawn
Jly 14	Derby	Derbyshire	Lost by 36 runs
Jly 16	Heraford	HK Foster's XI	Drawn
Jly 18	Worcester	Worcestershire	Won by an inns & 203 runs
Jly 21	Birmingham	Warwickshire	Won by an inns & 38 runs
Jly 24	Nottingham	Nottinghamshire	Drawn
Jly 31	The Oval	Surrey	Drawn
Aug 4	Hove	Sussex	Won by an inns & 54 runs
Aug 7	Canterbury	Kent	Drawn
Aug 21	Southend	Essex	Won by 309 runs
Aug 27	Clifton	Gloucestershire	Drawn
Aug 29	Taunton	Somerset	Won by 95 runs
Sep 1	Hastings	South of England	Lost by 122 runs
Sep 4	Portsmouth	South of England	Won by 10 wkts
Sep 8	Scarborough	CI Thornton's XI	Lost by 2 wkts

After 32 matches in England, 28 of them first-class, with 12 wins, 12 draws and the four defeats, all the players were keen to get home to their families but their reputation was so high the Australian Minister of Defence stepped in and ordered them to play ten matches in South Africa on their way home. The Sports Board appointed the former Essendon footballer Ernest Cameron as manager for this tour, which had been underwritten by tycoon Sir Abe Bailey. On sun-baked South African pitches, Gregory was a sensation, scoring runs at an almost feverish rate and skittling scared batsmen. After a rapid 50 against Transvaal, he took three wickets in an over and then returned with the bat to make 86 more runs. At Durban against Natal he took 9 for 32 and ran out the other batsman, and in the return match against Natal at Maritzburg he took 7 for 21.

South African critics named Collins, however, as the AIF XI's finest player, despite Gregory's feats. Collins took wickets regularly with his subtle spinners and at Johannesburg against a South African XI made a magnificent 235 of his team's 441. The *Cape Times* said the AIF emphatically demonstrated their superiority and revealed South Africa's weaknesses. The AIF remained undefeated in South Africa, winning 6 and drawing 2 of their eight first-class matches. They were asked to play three more first-class matches when they arrived home, with the team taking half the takings and the Board of Control paying their expenses and a £1 a day for

Player	M	Inn	NO	Runs	HS	50	100	Avrge	Ct/St	Overs	Mdns	Runs	Wkts	Avrge	5wi	10wm	Best
Bull, EA	16	23	2	395	42	–	–	18.81	4	7.0	1	27	–	–	–	–	–
Collins, HL (Capt)	27	44	2	1615	127	8	5	38.45	19	726.5	164	1750	106	16.51	6	2	8/31
Docker, CT	13	17	7	214	52*	1	–	21.40	12	198.2	35	576	27	21.33	2	–	5/34
Gregory, JM	25	36	4	942	115	4	1	29.43	44	821.0	124	2386	131	18.21	9	2	7/56
Heath, HFT	1	–	–	–	–	–	–	–	–	3.0	–	11	–	–	–	–	–
Kelleway, CE	6	9	–	505	168	3	2	56.11	6	196.5	38	548	18	30.44	1	–	7/47
Lampard, AW	24	35	3	821	112	3	1	25.66	14	517.2	70	1601	69	23.20	3	–	9/42
Long, EJ	16	19	9	110	14*	–	–	11.00	19/12	–	–	–	–	–	–	–	–
Love, HSB	1	2	–	2	2	–	–	1.00	–	–	–	–	–	–	–	–	–
Murray, JT	22	34	1	793	133	5	1	24.03	15	15.0	2	61	1	61.00	–	–	1/15
Oldfield, WAS	13	19	7	382	82*	4	–	31.83	16/10	–	–	–	–	–	–	–	–
Pellew, CE	24	40	7	1260	195*	4	4	38.18	10	12.0	4	50	–	–	–	–	–
Stirling, WS	26	35	3	538	62	3	–	16.81	17	378.5	83	963	44	21.89	2	–	5/26
Taylor, JM	25	39	2	1187	146	6	3	31.24	22	2.0	–	8	–	–	–	–	–
Trenerry, WL	24	37	3	961	82	9	–	28.26	11	67.4	4	221	7	31.57	–	–	2/5
Willis, CB	27	44	4	1652	156*	10	4	41.30	14	6.0	–	29	–	–	–	–	–
Winning, CS	19	24	11	174	30	–	–	13.38	14	472.4	110	1164	51	22.82	3	–	6/30

An AIF XI taking the field for a match against the English Army at Lord's in July 1917: wicket-keeper Ted Long, umpire (obscured), E.P. Barbour, Cyril Docker, Jack Murray, Charlie Macartney and Charles Kelleway, who was later sacked as captain by his Field Marshal. Barbour and Macartney had to go home before the AIF team's tour began.

1919/20 AUSTRALIAN IMPERIAL FORCES IN SOUTH AFRICA

First-class Results					All Matches				
Matches	Won	Lost	Drawn	Tied	Matches	Won	Lost	Drawn	Tied
8	6	–	2	–	10	8	–	2	–

Date	Venue	Opponent	Results for Australians
Oct 18	Cape Town	Western Province	Won by 2 wkts
Oct 25	Johannesburg	Transvaal	Drawn
Nov 1	Durban	Natal	Won by 310 runs
Nov 7	Pietermaritzburg	Natal	Won by an inns & 42 runs
Nov 11	Maritzburg	*Natal Colleges XV	Won by 95 runs
Nov 15	Johannesburg	Transvaal	Won by an inns & 14 runs
Nov 21	Johannesburg	South Africans	Won by 8 wkts
Nov 29	Johannesburg	South Africans	Won by an inns & 128 runs
Dec 6	Cape Town	Western Province	Drawn
Dec 12	Cape Town	*College XV	Won by 229 runs

Player	State	M	Inn	NO	Runs	HS	50	100	Avrge	Ct/St	Overs	Mdns	Runs	Wkts	Avrge	5wi	10wm	Best
Bull, EA	NSW	3	5	–	87	32	–	–	17.40	2	–	–	–	–	–	–	–	–
Collins, HL (Capt)	NSW	8	12	–	607	235	3	1	50.58	5	326.5	97	641	39	16.43	2	–	6/55
Docker, CT	NSW	7	9	2	82	45	–	–	11.71	2	129.2	40	269	17	15.82	2	–	5/37
Gregory, JM	NSW	8	11	–	410	86	4	–	37.27	15	228.0	49	613	47	13.04	5	2	9/32
Lampard, AW	VIC	8	12	2	363	73	4	–	36.30	3	135.4	17	426	24	17.75	2	1	7/71
Long, EJ	NSW	1	1	1	1	1*	–	–	–	–	–	–	–	–	–	–	–	–
Murray, JT	SA	6	7	1	72	41*	–	–	12.00	6	–	–	–	–	–	–	–	–
Oldfield, WAS	NSW	7	10	3	220	47	–	–	31.43	15/4	–	–	–	–	–	–	–	–
Pellew, CE	SA	8	13	–	361	62	2	–	27.76	4	–	–	–	–	–	–	–	–
Stirling, WS	SA	5	7	2	72	27	–	–	14.40	4	59.5	19	140	6	23.33	1	–	5/29
Taylor, JM	NSW	6	8	–	185	81	2	–	23.12	4	–	–	–	–	–	–	–	–
Trenerry, WL	NSW	8	13	–	403	74	3	–	31.00	7	22.0	5	49	3	16.33	–	–	3/28
Willis, CB	VIC	7	11	2	340	94	2	–	37.78	3	–	–	–	–	–	–	–	–
Winning, CS	NSW	6	7	3	54	24	–	–	13.50	5	120.5	37	240	5	48.00	–	–	3/108

incidentals. They defeated Victoria by six wickets, played a draw against Queensland, and wound up their tour by beating NSW by 203 runs. Collins and Gregory both made two centuries in Australia and Carl Willis scored a fifth.

Collins shocked Melbourne Cricket Club diehards when he won his customary toss and sent Victoria in to bat, which appeared unwise on a good batting pitch against a powerful batting lineup. Collins had the last laugh, as he usually did, when Gregory took 7 for 22 in his debut on Australian soil and had Victoria out for 116. The AIF responded with 311 and only had to make 76 in their second innings for a handsome win. Seventy-four years after they walked from the field in Sydney at the conclusion of their last match, the achievements of the First AIF team remain an indisputable testimony of their quality. They won 20 of their 39 first-class matches in three countries and lost only four, using players who had been through a brutal war and deserved to be recuperating from the wounds some of them carried. They left Australia the nucleus of a marvellous Test team by developing players like Oldfield, Gregory, Taylor, Pellew and old poker-faced Herbert Leslie ('Horseshoe') Collins.

AUSTRALIAN SERVICES TEAM 1945–46

1945 AUSTRALIAN SERVICES IN ENGLAND

First-class Results					All Matches				
Matches	Won	Lost	Drawn	Tied	Matches	Won	Lost	Drawn	Tied
6	3	2	1	–	48	24	9	15	–

Date	Venue	Opponent	Results for Australians
Apr 28	Eastbourne	*The Saffrons	Drawn
May 4	Eastbourne	*London Counties	Abandoned
May 9	Dulwich	*PS Wanderers	Won by 10 wkts
May 12	Lord's	*British Empire XI	Won by 6 wkts
May 19	Lord's	England XI	Won by 6 wkts
May 21	Cardiff	*Glamorgan	Won by 56 runs
May 23	Dover	*Dover Wanderers	Lost by 2 wkts
May 26	High Wycombe	*High Wycombe	Won by 83 runs
May 27	High Wycombe	*Buckinghamshire XII	Won by 4 wkts
May 29	Hove	*Empire XI	Won by 54 runs
Jun 2	Gloucester	*RAF	Lost by 16 runs
Jun 2	Eastbourne	*Buccaneers	Won by 1 wkt
Jun 6	Manchester	*Lancashire	Drawn
Jun 9	Birmingham	*LN Constantine's XI	Won by an inns & 145 runs

Continued

Towards the end of World War II Australian Prime Minister John Curtin and his senior soldier Field Marshal Blamey found themselves at Lord's in between important conferences with the Churchill government. Curtin looked out on the pitch and claimed it was not English, but belonged to the British Empire. Alongside him, crafty old 'Plum' Warner commented that England and Australia had a duty to restore international cricket on pitches such as Lord's when the war was won. Warner had always believed a mistake had been made in not staging Tests between England and Herbie Collins' First AIF side and did not want that error repeated. The result was the staging of 'Victory Tests', with Blamey promising to make as many leading Australians available as possible, given that 'we still have to beat the Japanese'.

This was how Gunner Lindsay Hassett and other

HOME AND AWAY

Date	Venue	Opponent	Results for Australians
Jun 9	Eastbourne	*Sussex Cricket Association	Won by 158 runs
Jun 13	Eastbourne	*Services XI	Won by 10 wkts
Jun 16	Eastbourne	*RAAF	Won by 6 wkts
Jun 16	Lord's	*RAF	Drawn
Jun 23	Sheffield	England XI	Lost by 41 runs
Jun 30	Lord's	*South of England	Drawn
Jun 30	Eastbourne	*New Zealand XI	Won by 10 wkts
Jly 1	Oxford	*Oxford & District	Drawn
Jly 7	Eastbourne	*HDG Leveson–Gower's XI	Drawn
Jly 7	Lord's	*Army	Won by 183 runs
Jly 11	Bradford	*Yorkshire	Drawn
Jly 14	Lord's	England XI	Won by 4 wkts
Jly 15	Gravesend	*Gravesend Sunday Club	Won by 83 runs
Jly 21	Coventry	*Coventry and District XI	Drawn
Jly 23	Bramall Lane	*Yorkshire	Drawn
Jly 25	Sunderland	*Durham	Won by 145 runs
Jly 26	Chichester	*Sussex	Drawn
Jly 26	Selkirk	*Scottish Services	Won by 33 runs
Jly 27	Greenock	*Greenock	Drawn
Jly 28	Westcliff	*Metropolitan Police	Won by 74 runs
Jly 28	Glasgow	*Scotland	Won by 59 runs
Aug 1	Portsmouth	*Royal Navy	Drawn
Aug 6	Lord's	England XI	Drawn
Aug 7	Birmingham	*Birmingham Festival XI	Drawn
Aug 11	Northampton	*Northamptonshire	Lost by 24 runs
Aug 12	High Wycombe	*GO Allen's XI	Won by 145 runs
Aug 16	Blackpool	*North of England	Lost by an inns & 89 runs
Aug 18	Manchester	*RAF	Lost by 44 runs
Aug 20	Manchester	England XI	Lost by 6 wkts
Aug 31	Nottingham	*Nottinghamshire	Won by 103 runs
Sep 5	Scarborough	Leverson–Gower's XI	Won by an inns & 108 runs
Sep 9	Kingston	*Surrey	Lost by 3 wkts
Sep 12	Hove	*Sussex	Won by 3 wkts
Sep 15	Middlesbrough	*Combined Counties	Won by 191 runs

The Australian Services team which defeated England at Lord's in the first Victory Test: *standing* Keith Carmody, Keith Miller, Albert Cheetham, Jack Pettiford, Cec Pepper, Reg Willims; *seated* Charlie Price, Bob Cristofani, Lindsay Hassett (capt.), Stan Sismey, Dick Whitington.

Player	M	Inn	NO	Runs	HS	50	100	Avrge	Ct/St	Overs	Mdns	Runs	Wkts	Avrge	5wi	10wm	Best
Carmody, DK	3	6	–	99	42	–	–	16.50	3	–	–	–	–	–	–	–	–
Cheetham, AG	3	6	1	42	18	–	–	8.40	1	75.1	11	213	7	30.42	–	–	3/47
Cristofani, DR	3	4	1	164	110*	–	1	54.66	–	83.3	15	213	14	15.21	2	–	5/49
Ellis, RS	6	8	5	14	9*	–	–	4.66	2	223.3	60	440	23	19.13	2	1	5/24
Hassett, AL (Capt)	6	11	–	296	77	2	–	26.90	7	0.1	–	1	–	–	–	–	–
Miller, KR	6	11	3	514	118	3	2	64.25	2	137.0	25	306	10	30.60	–	–	3/42
Pepper, CG	6	10	1	417	168	2	1	46.33	9	222.3	44	613	20	30.65	–	–	4/60
Pettiford, J	3	5	–	145	39	–	–	29.00	2	39.0	2	139	6	23.16	–	–	3/62
Price, CFT	3	5	1	61	35	–	–	15.25	1	35.4	4	99	7	14.14	–	–	3/18
Roper, AW	1	1	–	10	10	–	–	10.00	2	7.0	1	30	–	–	–	–	–
Sismey, SG	6	9	–	260	78	2	–	28.88	10/7	–	–	–	–	–	–	–	–
Stanford, RM	4	6	1	127	49	–	–	25.40	1	–	–	–	–	–	–	–	–
Whitington, RS	6	11	–	294	79	2	–	26.72	4	2.0	–	8	–	–	–	–	–
Williams, RG	6	8	2	90	53	1	–	15.00	1	172.0	41	459	12	38.25	–	–	3/109
Workman, JA	4	7	–	122	63	1	–	17.42	2	–	–	–	–	–	–	–	–

splendid cricketers found themselves withdrawn from battle units in New Guinea and other places and instructed to join a special force charged with rehabilitating prisoners of war as they were released from European prison camps and free to play a bit of cricket. The cricketers were shipped to England via New York, where they were asked to march in a ticker-tape victory parade after Blamey had been careful not to upset General Douglas Macarthur by insisting on too many cricketers joining the unit. This was why Arthur Morris, Ray Lindwall, Colin McCool and other stars missed out.

Hassett faced similar problems to Collins. Wisely, he rejected offers of an Army commission, and let his record as a Test cricketer silence the RAAF men who believed Squadron-Leader Keith Carmody deserved the Services XI captaincy. In Keith Miller he had a dynamic fast bowler just as Collins had had in Gregory, and in Stan Sismey he had a polished wicket-keeper only slightly below Oldfield's class, and in Charlie Price, Cec Pepper and Bob Cristifani he had a very useful crop of spinners. (Sismey's deputy in England was Colin Bremner, one of a small group of Australians to play first-class cricket but never in their own country.) Dick Whitington, Jack Pettiford, Jack Cheetham, Ross Stanford and Jimmy Workman never surrendered their wickets without a fight, and in Carmody, Hassett's team had an opener of flair who repeatedly confused opening bowlers with his lifted, driving sweep shots and superb cutting. The five Victory Tests severely challenged Hassett's lot but they provided crowds with some spectacular cricket opposed to sides that included Hutton, Compton, Hammond, Ames, Edrich, Griffiths, Wright and other English heroes.

Miller was dynamic. He took wickets galore by generating genuine pace from a shortish run and outthinking well-set batsmen, played an array of classical strokes that had even his opponents applauding, and mixed in some of the longest hits ever seen on English grounds. 'Miller batting from the front foot at Lord's was one of the greatest sights in cricket,' said New Zealander Martin Donnelly, who joined the Dominions team that

Lindsay Hassett's Services team in India, wearing garlands of flowers presented by admiring fans. Hassett is standing in the middle, in shorts.

played England. Miller hit 7 sixes in that match, one of them landing on top of the broadcasting box above England's dressing-room. Oldtimers in the pavilion claimed it went higher than Albert Trott's famous blow. Miller's 185 took 165 minutes, slowed by the time it took to find the ball after his sixes.

The Australians won two, lost two and drew one of the five Victory Tests and in the process restored the popularity of big cricket among the British public.

On the way home they were instructed to play 10 matches in India, which imposed a great strain on their gastric systems and enthusiasm for cricket after years away from their families. They played three major matches against India, losing one and drawing two, and won two of their seven other first-class matches. They began in style with Pettiford scoring 124, Carmody 113, Hassett 53, and Pepper 95 against All India to reach an imposing 531. All India followed-on but Hazare, Merchant and Amarnath contrived to save the match. The second representative match was also drawn but All India won the third by six wickets, despite Hassett's 143 and Pepper's 87. Without opening bowlers R.G. Williams and Albert Cheetham, the Australians tried ten bowlers in India's innings of 525, Modi scoring 203, Amarnath 113.

Flying home across the Indian Ocean in an aircraft heavily weighted by cricket gear, souvenirs and service uniforms, the Australians found themselves in the hands of Army public-relations officer Captain Bert Oldfield, the vestryman at St Andrew's Cathedral, Sydney, who informed them they were required to play matches against each of the states. The players decided they had no option but to agree to this pitiless demand on their family loyalties and stamina but arranged for key men to miss matches in their home states.

They drew with Western Australia and in Adelaide found themselves in an incident that could have changed the entire future of Australian cricket. Bradman, physically drained and recovering from complaints that had seen him invalided out of the Army, was testing his fitness to continue in big cricket when he was deceived by Cec Pepper's 'flipper', the googly that hurries on. All the Services players in position to judge believed Bradman was plumb leg-before-wicket but umpire Jack Scott gave him not out. Pepper could not believe it and abused both Bradman and Scott, who reported Pepper's ill behaviour to administrators. Pepper missed a place he deserved in the Australian team to New Zealand and assumed he was not wanted by Australia's selectors. He went off to spend the rest of his career in England, leaving Bradman to a glorious career climax that could have all been different had Scott given him out.

Hassett's Services team broke up after their last match in Hobart against Tasmania. They had lost to Victoria and New South Wales, and played draws against Western Australia, Queensland and Tasmania, and their failure to win against any of the states brought the team and the players a completely unfair rating. They had, in fact, produced a match-winner in Keith Ross Miller, just as the First AIF XI had done with Jack Gregory.

HOME AND AWAY

The first official New Zealand team which played New South Wales in February 1894. The captain, L.A. Cuffe, wearing a braided blazer, is in the middle of the centre row.

CHAPTER EIGHT

TELEVISION TO THE RESCUE
Australia and New Zealand

Australia played only 32 Tests against New Zealand up to the end of the 1994–95 season, fewer than against any country except Sri Lanka (7). This is an extraordinary statistic considering that Australia has played Test cricket since 1877, and has played 286 Tests against England (including the 1971 Test in Melbourne, which the Australian Cricket Board ruled was a Test although a ball was not bowled. *Wisden* says it was not a Test and has one Test less, 285), 81 against the West Indies, 50 against India, 59 against South Africa, and 37 against Pakistan.

Before television demonstrated the charismatic qualities of Richard Hadlee, Martin Crowe and other New Zealanders, Australian programmers were always fearful of Australia–New Zealand Tests series losing money. The Australian Board of Control had been disappointed by takings in their initial Tests against South Africa and the West Indies and were too protective of the Board's reserves to risk matches against a country that appeared to lack crowd-pulling players. England could afford to encourage New Zealand cricketers but the Australian Board's treasury could not support such a luxury.

Australia's attitude appeared likely to change when the countries met at Wellington in March 1946 in their first official Test, but Australia's one-sided victory by an innings and 103 runs against opponents who managed only 96 runs in two innings (42 and 54) proved disastrous for New Zealand. Australia did not even bother to get the International Cricket Conference to recognise it as an official Test until March 1948, and the countries did not meet again in a bonafide Test until 1973–74.

Television changed everything, and its exploitation of big cricket has brought New Zealand into the growing family of cricket nations. The Hadlees, Lance Cairns and his robust hitting, Danny Morrison's energetic pace bowling, and recently Ken Rutherford and Martin Crowe's batting have all had rich appeal to Australians, and the delay in recognising the calibre of her cricketers has made New Zealanders keener to defeat Australia than any of the other cricket nations. The Trevor Chappell underarm ball that deprived New Zealand of a sporting chance to score the six runs needed off the last ball of a 1980–81 match, and incidents like Merv Hughes jostling Mark Greatbatch and spitting on the pitch in 1993 only intensify New Zealanders' eagerness to upset Australia. 'We would rather beat Australia than any other country,' said captain Martin Crowe after the countries shared the 1993 rubber.

Cricket between Australia and New Zealand began in 1878 when Dave Gregory took the first Australian team to tour England to New Zealand to raise funds to pay for their boat fares. The pill-box hats and sashes of the pioneer Australians were first seen at Invercargill when Australia, in her first international match, met a local Twenty-Two. Australia made 267, Invercargill 89 and 39, Australia winning by an innings and 139 runs. Charles Bannerman, who had made Australia's first Test century (165 retired hurt) in 1877, also made the first century for Australia (125) in New Zealand in that match.

Two years later, when the second Australian team stopped off on their way home from England, Billy Murdoch backed himself to score more runs than the entire Canterbury team. He won his bet and Australia won the match by an innings and 100 runs, with a first innings total of 323. Twenty-Two of Wanganui were the only side to beat this Australian team in their nine matches.

The Mayor of Hobart, George Davies (1883–84), 'Tup' Scott (1886–87), J.C. Davis (1889–90 and 1893–94), and

Les Cobcroft (1895–96) all took state or Australian teams to New Zealand. The star of Davis' 1889–90 New South Wales team, right-arm fast bowler Sydney Callaway, returned to New Zealand permanently after appearing in three Tests for Australia. Callaway, a tall man of soldierly bearing with a Kitchener moustache, took 167 wickets in 24 first-class matches in New Zealand, finding the damp pitches there more to his liking in matches for Canterbury, New Zealand, and the South Island. Callaway's success led to other Australians going to New Zealand to coach and join provincial teams. One of these was dashing Harry Graham, who had made a century at Lord's. Harry first visited New Zealand with a Melbourne Cricket Club XI in 1899 and went back to play for Otago from 1903 to 1907, and for New Zealand in two unofficial 'Tests' against Australia.

Ossie Hitchcock captained the first Queensland team to tour New Zealand in 1896–97, the same summer that Harry Trott took the ninth Australian team to New Zealand for five matches on their way home from England and America. The twelfth Australian team also played in New Zealand, this time before they toured England. By 1909–10 New Zealand standards had improved enough for all seven matches against an Australian team led by Warwick Armstrong to be played on level terms.

Public interest in cricket was building up in New Zealand, and in 1913–14 the New Zealand-born tycoon Sir Arthur Sims judged that his homeland would advance further through a visit by a team of great players who had outplayed the best sides in England. Sims' party had 16 matches in New Zealand, eight of them first-class, and in one of these Victor Trumper played what oldtimers rated the best innings ever seen in New Zealand. Trumper took only 180 minutes to score 283, adding 483 with Sims (184 not out), for the eighth wicket. They put on 50 in 12 minutes at one stage. This was Trumper's last hurrah, for he died of Bright's Disease in 1915, aged 37.

Classy left-hander Vernon Ransford, whose Test career ended when he joined Clem Hill, 'Tibby' Cotter, Hanson Carter, Warwick Armstrong, and Trumper in refusing to tour England in 1912 under the terms offered by the Board of Control, took a Victoria team to New Zealand in 1920–21. Charlie Macartney, who had appeared for Otago in 1909–10, led a New South Wales team back to New Zealand in 1923–24.

These tours encouraged New Zealand to send her first team to England in 1927 under the captaincy of Tom Lowry, an aggressive right-hand batsman who could keep wicket or field brilliantly close to the stumps, and bowl useful spinners. Lowry promoted Ken James to take over as the team's keeper so that he could concentrate on

Sir Arthur Sims with the Australian team he took to New Zealand in 1914: *back row* Les Cody, Frank Laver, L. Black, Dr Charles Dolling, Arthur Mailey, W. McGregor, Bill Ferguson (scorer-baggage master), Victor Trumper, Colin McKenzie; *middle* Mrs M.A. Noble, Monty Noble, Sir Arthur Sims, Warwick Armstrong, Mrs W. Armstrong; *front* J.N. Crawford, 'Gar' Waddy, Vernon Ransford, Herbie Collins.

The 1931 New Zealand team to England, the first to be granted Test status: *back row* I.B. Cromb, J.L. Kerr, K.C. James, R.O. Talbot, G.L. Weir, W.E. Merritt, A.M. Matheson; *centre* J.E. Mills, M.L. Page, T.C. Lowry (capt.), C.F.W. Allcott, C.S. Dempster; *front* R.C. Blunt, H.G. Vivian. They did so well in their initial Test, they were rewarded with two extra Tests.

captaincy and batting. He scored 1277 runs at 38.69 on the tour of 26 matches, with four centuries, and although his team were not given a Test they defeated five of England's first-class counties. Stewart Dempster, a hard-hitting right-hander and superb fieldsman, headed the New Zealand averages with 1430 runs at 44.68, and the quality of New Zealand's batting when Lowry and Dempster were partners earned New Zealand a three-day Test with England on their second tour in 1931.

New Zealand played 32 matches and in a very wet summer had 23 draws. Captained by Lowry, 33, New Zealand staged a spirited recovery in their first Test after an opening day collapse that saw them lose eight wickets for 92 runs after reaching 2 for 132. Faced with a deficit of 230 when Ames (137) and Allen (122) put on 246 for the eighth wicket for England, New Zealand declared at 9 for 469 in their second innings, Dempster recording their first Test century, 120, followed by 104 from Milford ('Curly') Page. England were 5 for 146, chasing 240 to win, when time ran out.

This marvellous debut in Test cricket by New Zealand was rewarded with two more Tests. English officials decided to cancel New Zealand's scheduled matches against Surrey and Lancashire and replace them with Tests. Centuries by Herbert Sutcliffe (117), Duleepsinhji (109) and Hammond (100 not out) took England to 4 declared for 416 in the Second Test at The Oval. New Zealand then had to bat between showers and were bundled out for 193 and 197, England winning by an innings and 26 runs. The Third Test at Old Trafford did not start until the third day because of rain and was declared a draw after Sutcliffe made 109 not out.

Despite their success in England, New Zealand did not attract an invitation to play a Test against Australia. But they played Tests at home in 1931–32 against South Africa, and in 1932–33 against England without success, and returned to England in 1937 for a three Test series which England won 1–0 with two draws. World War II arrived without an invitation from Australia to end 60 years of matches in New Zealand with a Test. Australian Board of Control delegates argued that New Zealand standards did not justify such a step. The break-through came in 1945–46, but with unfortunate results for New Zealand.

AUSTRALIA IN NEW ZEALAND 1946–1974

1945/46 AUSTRALIANS

First-class Results					All Matches			
Matches	Won	Lost	Drawn	Tied	Matches	Won	Lost	Drawn	Tied
5	5	–	–	–	5	5	–	–	–

Date	Venue	Opponent	Results for Australians
Mar 1	Auckland	Auckland	Won by an inns & 180 runs
Mar 8	Christchurch	Canterbury	Won by an inns & 35 runs
Mar 15	Dunedin	Otago	Won by 8 wkts
Mar 22	Wellington	Wellington	Won by an inns & 160 runs
Mar 29	Wellington	NEW ZEALAND (Only Test)	Won by an inns & 103 runs

In 1946 William Alfred Brown, son of a Toowoomba farmer, took a powerful Australian side through five matches, all of them first-class, in New Zealand without defeat. They beat Auckland, Canterbury, Otago, and Wellington by wide margins and in the match against New Zealand at Basin Reserve, Wellington, routed New Zealand for 42 and 54 to win by an innings and 103 runs. *Wisden* recognised this match as a Test immediately, but it took the Australian Board of Control two years to

Player	State	M	Inn	NO	Runs	HS	50	100	Avrge	Ct/St	Overs	Mdns	Runs	Wkts	Avrge	5wi	10wm	Best
Barnes, SG	NSW	5	5	–	264	107	1	1	52.80	5	340	12	92	9	10.22	–	–	3/0
Brown, WA (Capt)	NSW	5	6	–	443	137	2	2	73.83	3	–	–	–	–	–	–	–	–
Dooland, B	SA	3	3	–	19	15	–	–	6.33	4	469	7	160	5	32.00	–	–	3/16
Hamence, RA	SA	3	4	1	74	46	–	–	24.66	1	88	2	32	–	–	–	–	–
Hassett, AL	VIC	5	5	–	351	121	1	2	70.20	3	40	–	21	–	–	–	–	–
Johnson, IW	VIC	4	4	2	98	28*	–	–	49.00	3	556	11	179	8	22.37	–	–	4/47
Lindwall, RR	NSW	4	4	–	30	22	–	–	7.50	4	958	31	259	9	28.77	–	–	2/35
McCool, CL	QLD	4	5	1	148	75	1	–	37.00	5	468	13	184	7	26.28	–	–	2/50
Meuleman, KD	VIC	5	6	–	230	69	3	–	38.33	1	–	–	–	–	–	–	–	–
Miller, KR	VIC	4	4	–	257	139	–	1	64.25	2	146	8	27	5	5.40	–	–	2/6
O'Reilly, WJ	NSW	4	3	2	8	7*	–	–	8.00	–	1090	41	297	28	10.60	2	–	5/14
Tallon, D	QLD	5	5	2	123	38*	–	–	41.00	9/1	–	–	–	–	–	–	–	–
Toshack, ERH	NSW	2	1	–	8	6	–	–	4.00	2	1168	61	238	23	10.34	2	–	6/40

The 1946 Australian team that defeated New Zealand in their first official Test: *back row* W. Watts (scorer), Don Tallon, Keith Miller, Bill O'Reilly, Ernie Toshack, Bruce Dooland, Ron Hamence, E.C. Yeomans (manager); *seated* Ian Johnson, Col McCool, Lindsay Hassett, Bill Brown (capt.), Sid Barnes, Ken Meuleman, Ray Lindwall.

advise the International Cricket Conference that the match had Test status.

The one-sided victories by a side that included legendary players like Keith Miller, Lindsay Hassett, Bill O'Reilly, Sid Barnes, Ray Lindwall and Don Tallon, convinced Australia's top officials they were correct in not playing regular Tests against New Zealand, and it was 27 years before the countries met in another Test. This overlooked the fact that O'Reilly and Toshack on a rain-affected pitch were capable of bundling any side out cheaply. Toshack had 4 for 12 and 2 for 6, O'Reilly 5 for 14 and 3 for 19 in his last Test, ending his representative career by throwing his boots through the dressing-room window in Wellington.

Brown returned to New Zealand in 1949–50 as captain of an Australian Second XI, with the first team touring South Africa, but the Australian Board of Control refused to give the Australia–New Zealand match Test status. When Alan Davidson produced his celebrated double by taking 10 for 29 and 158 not out against Wairarapa, Australian officials said it merely confirmed the low standard of New Zealand cricket. The Australians won nine of their 14 matches—eight by an innings—and

1949/50 AUSTRALIANS

First-class Results					All Matches				
Matches	Won	Lost	Drawn	Tied	Matches	Won	Lost	Drawn	Tied
5	3	–	2	–	14	9	–	5	–

Date	Venue	Opponent	Results for Australians
Feb 15	Wellington	*Hutt Valley	Drawn
Feb 17	Auckland	Auckland	Drawn
Feb 22	Hamilton	*Waikato	Drawn
Feb 25	New Plymouth	*Taranaki	Won by an inns & 113 runs
Feb 28	Wanganui	*Wanganui	Won by an inns & 111 runs
Mar 3	Christchurch	Canterbury	Won by 10 wkts
Mar 7	Timaru	*South Canterbury	Drawn
Mar 10	Dunedin	Otago	Won by an inns & 356 runs
Mar 14	Invercargill	*Southland	Won by an inns & 37 runs
Mar 17	Dunedin	New Zealanders	Drawn
Mar 22	Palmerston North	*Manawatu	Won by an inns & 83 runs
Mar 25	Napier	*Hawkes Bay	Won by an inns & 140 runs
Mar 29	Masterton	*Wairarapa	Won by an inns & 466 runs
Apr 1	Wellington	Wellington	Won by an inns & 85 runs

Player	State	M	Inn	NO	Runs	HS	50	100	Avrge	Ct/St	Overs	Mdns	Runs	Wkts	Avrge	5wi	10wm	Best
Brown, WA (Capt)	QLD	5	5	–	272	184*	–	1	54.40	2	1.0	–	2	–	–	–	–	–
Burke, JW	NSW	5	7	2	204	68*	2	–	40.80	1	6.0	1	24	3	8.00	–	–	3/24
Davidson, AK	NSW	3	3	–	19	13	–	–	6.33	9	84.0	23	163	9	18.11	–	–	4/24
Driver, WG	WA	4	5	1	114	41	–	–	28.50	1	–	–	–	–	–	–	–	–
Duldig, LD	SA	4	4	–	80	37	–	–	20.00	2	–	–	–	–	–	–	–	–
Howard, R	VIC	5	5	–	246	141	1	1	49.20	–	–	–	–	–	–	–	–	–
Iverson, JB	VIC	5	4	4	29	24*	–	–	–	3	125.1	32	279	21	13.29	1	–	6/47
Johnson, LJ	VIC	5	5	1	103	61	1	–	25.75	2	118.2	31	247	22	11.33	2	–	6/20
Meuleman, KD	VIC	5	7	1	287	92	3	–	47.83	1	–	–	–	–	–	–	–	–
Puckett, CW	WA	2	1	–	31	31	–	–	31.00	1	69.0	23	111	7	15.85	1	–	5/24
Ridings, PL	SA	2	2	–	8	7	–	–	4.00	–	15.0	5	22	1	22.00	–	–	1/6
Ring, DT	VIC	5	5	–	126	60	1	–	25.20	4	178.0	55	428	27	15.85	2	–	7/88
Tallon, D	QLD	5	5	1	262	116	1	1	65.50	14/7	–	–	–	–	–	–	–	–

TELEVISION TO THE RESCUE

The 1949-50 Australian team to New Zealand, played five matches but no Tests. *Back row* W. Watts (scorer), Jimmy Burke, Doug Ring, Jack Iverson, Charlie Puckett, Alan Davidson, Roy Howard, G.A. Davies (manager); *seated* Ken Meuleman, Wally Driver, Don Tallon, Len Johnson, Bill Brown (capt.), Phil Ridings, Lance Duldig, Stan Sismey.

remained unbeaten. They had two draws and three wins in the five first-class matches.

Ian Craig captained two Australian teams to New Zealand, but without any Tests in the itineraries. In 1956-57, Craig's team won five of their seven first-class matches. They had two draws and a win in the representative matches against New Zealand XI. Financial results from these tours did not encourage the Australian Board to include Tests in the next tour of 1959-60, when Australia won four of their nine matches and had five draws.

New Zealand moved nearer to Test recognition by winning one of the four representative matches against Les Favell's Australian tourists in 1967, with the other three drawn. Tougher opposition restricted Favell's team of promising youngsters blended with seasoned players to two wins in ten matches on pitches they found too slow for heavy scoring. Similar results came in 1970 when Sam Trimble's Australians won only two of their eight matches and had six draws, including the two representative matches. Both tours served Australia well in developing players like Greg Chappell, Dennis Lillee and Paul Sheahan. (See Appendix for summaries.)

The 1959-60 Australian team in New Zealand, unbeaten in nine matches: *back row* Brian Booth, Barry Fisher, John Shaw, Jack Potter; *middle* Frank Misson, Ian Quick, John Lill, Grahame Thomas, Keith Salter; *front* H.C. Smith (manager), Ron Gaunt, Bob Simpson, Ian Craig (capt.), Len Maddocks, John Martin, T. Bird (scorer).

1956/57 AUSTRALIANS

Matches	First-class Results Won	Lost	Drawn	Tied	All Matches Matches	Won	Lost	Drawn	Tied
7	5	–	2	–	12	7	–	5	–

Date	Venue	Opponent	Results for Australians
Feb 15	Christchurch	Canterbury	Won by 5 wkts
Feb 20	Invercargill	*Southland	Drawn
Feb 22	Dunedin	Otago	Won by an inns & 102 runs
Feb 27	Timaru	*Combined Minor Associations	Won by an inns & 18 runs
Mar 1	Christchurch	New Zealanders	Drawn
Mar 5	Masterton	*Wairarapa	Won by an inns & 217 runs
Mar 8	Wellington	New Zealanders	Drawn
Mar 13	Gisborne	*Poverty Bay	Drawn
Mar 16	Auckland	Auckland	Won by an inns & 54 runs
Mar 20	Hamilton	*Waikato	Drawn
Mar 23	New Plymouth	Central Districts	Won by 10 wkts
Mar 29	Auckland	New Zealanders	Won by 10 wkts

Player	State	M	Inn	NO	Runs	HS	50	100	Avrge	Ct/St	Overs	Mdns	Runs	Wkts	Avrge	5wi	10wm	Best
Benaud, R	NSW	6	8	2	323	113	1	1	53.83	3	285.2	93	618	32	19.31	1	–	6/79
Burge, PJP	QLD	7	10	2	310	105	1	1	38.75	2	–	–	–	–	–	–	–	–
Craig, ID (Capt)	NSW	6	9	1	308	123*	1	1	38.50	4	–	–	–	–	–	–	–	–
Drennan, J	SA	6	6	2	77	28*	–	–	19.25	1	148.3	57	275	22	12.50	–	–	4/7
Favell, LE	SA	6	10	1	354	71	3	–	39.33	3	–	–	–	–	–	–	–	–
Gaunt, RA	WA	5	5	1	49	19*	–	–	12.25	4	135.4	28	346	14	24.71	–	–	4/54
Harvey, RN	VIC	6	10	1	448	161	2	2	49.77	4	29.0	9	44	1	44.00	–	–	1/9
Jarman, BN	SA	7	7	–	72	33	–	–	10.28	12/5	–	–	–	–	–	–	–	–
Kline, LF	VIC	6	6	1	37	13	–	–	7.40	2	145.4	39	386	15	25.73	–	–	3/19
Martin, JW	NSW	4	5	1	87	29	–	–	21.75	5	96.5	29	214	15	14.26	1	–	6/46
Meckiff, I	VIC	4	3	1	2	1*	–	–	1.00	4	123.1	47	217	20	10.85	1	–	5/48
O'Neill, NC	NSW	4	4	1	218	102*	1	1	72.66	4	–	–	–	–	–	–	–	–
Simpson, RB	WA	6	9	3	271	75	2	–	45.16	7	–	–	–	–	–	–	–	–
Watson, WJ	NSW	4	7	–	23	12	–	–	3.28	2	–	–	–	–	–	–	–	–

AUSTRALIA IN NEW ZEALAND 1973-74 TO 1982

1973/74 AUSTRALIANS

First-class Results					All Matches			
Matches	Won	Lost	Drawn	Tied	Matches	Won	Lost	Drawn	Tied
7	2	1	4	–	11	6	1	4	–

Date	Venue	Opponent	Results for Australians
Feb 17	Wellington	*Wellington	Won by 32 runs
Feb 18	Christchurch	Canterbury	Drawn
Feb 22	Auckland	Auckland	Drawn
Feb 25	Hamilton	Northern Districts	Won by an inns & 236 runs
Mar 1	Wellington	NEW ZEALAND (1st Test)	Drawn
Mar 8	Christchurch	NEW ZEALAND (2nd Test)	Lost by 5 wkts
Mar 15	Dunedin	Otago	Drawn
Mar 22	Auckland	NEW ZEALAND (3rd Test)	Won by 297 runs
Mar 28	New Plymouth	*Central Districts	Won by 2 wkts
Mar 30	Dunedin	*New Zealand (L/O Intl)	Won by 7 wkts
Mar 31	Christchurch	*New Zealand (L/O Intl)	Won by 31 runs

Ian Chappell with the 1974 Australian team in New Zealand, a full-strength outfit which shared a three-Test series: *back row* Greg Chappell, Ashley Mallett, Max Walker, Ashley Woodcock; *middle* Ian Davis, Geoff Dymock, Gary Gilmour, Ray Bright, Kerry O'Keeffe; *seated* Doug Walters, Keith Stackpool, Fred Bryant (manager), Ian Chappell (capt.), Rod Marsh, Ian Redpath.

Player	State	M	Inn	NO	Runs	HS	50	100	Avrge	Ct/St	Overs	Mdns	Runs	Wkts	Avrge	5wi	10wm	Best
Bright, RJ	VIC	4	4	1	52	28	–	–	17.33	2	66.2	26	175	8	21.87	–	–	2/6
Chappell, GS	QLD	6	10	2	592	247*	1	2	74.00	8	59.6	10	186	8	23.25	–	–	4/31
Chappell, IM (Capt)	SA	7	11	–	625	145	1	3	56.81	15	9.0	2	20	–	–	–	–	–
Davis, IC	NSW	7	12	1	283	63*	2	–	25.72	4	–	–	–	–	–	–	–	–
Dymock, G	QLD	4	4	2	24	12	–	–	12.00	1	144.0	33	369	16	23.06	–	–	3/40
Gilmour, GJ	NSW	4	5	–	124	57	1	–	24.80	1	95.7	22	300	20	15.00	1	–	5/64
Mallett, AA	SA	6	8	1	42	11	–	–	6.00	1	137.5	42	391	22	17.77	1	–	5/76
Marsh, RW	WA	7	12	1	338	70	1	–	30.72	21/2	–	–	–	–	–	–	–	–
O'Keeffe, KJ	NSW	6	8	2	177	99*	1	–	29.50	4	97.0	21	296	14	21.14	1	–	5/69
Redpath, IR	VIC	6	10	1	560	159*	5	1	62.22	1	–	–	–	–	–	–	–	–
Stackpole, KR	VIC	6	11	–	172	44	–	–	15.63	5	–	–	–	–	–	–	–	–
Walker, MHN	VIC	5	8	2	79	23	–	–	13.16	1	167.6	46	483	20	24.15	–	–	4/39
Walters, KD	NSW	6	10	2	376	104*	2	2	47.00	3	27.0	2	106	3	35.33	–	–	2/18
Woodcock, AJ	SA	3	5	–	99	54	1	–	19.80	3	–	–	–	–	–	–	–	–

Old labels about second-string teams were discarded when Ian Chappell took a full-strength Australian team on an 11-match New Zealand tour at the end of the 1973–74 summer. It proved a historic tour for both countries, attracted large crowds who were thoroughly entertained, and was a financial success. Crowd behaviour was poor in the Christchurch Test, and a fascinating match was further marred by a clash between Glenn Turner and Ian Chappell that ended with New Zealand demanding an apology from Ian Chappell, which was never given.

The First Test at Wellington was a triumph for the Chappell brothers, who both scored centuries in each innings. Greg's 380 runs in the match (247 not out and 133) was a record for most runs in a Test, five runs ahead of Andy Sandham's world record (325 and 50) for England against the West Indies at Kingston, Jamaica, in 1929–30. Ian made 145 and 121. The brothers put on 264 for the third wicket in the first innings, captivating spectators with their handsome stroke-play. New Zealand responded with a record stand of 229 for the fourth wicket in their first innings between Bevan Congdon (132) and Brian Hastings (101), and with the Chappells continuing their grand form in the second innings a draw was inevitable in a match that produced 1455 runs.

The Second Test at Christchurch gave New Zealand her first win over Australia at the sixth meeting of the countries, and only her eighth victory in 113 Tests against all countries. Victory over Australia left only England to be beaten by New Zealand. The five-wicket defeat of Australia was due to the batting of Glenn Maitland Turner, who became the first New Zealander to score a century in each innings of a Test, 101 and 110. This was the decisive contribution in a match that saw the initiative change in almost every session and ended in what veteran New Zealand critic Dick Brittenden called 'New Zealand's greatest cricket occasion'. This time the Hadlee brothers, Richard and Dayle, grabbed the headlines by taking 12 wickets between them. Ten days later Australia squared the rubber by defeating New Zealand by 297 runs at Auckland. Eighteen wickets fell on the first day when Walters gave Australia the ascendancy with a brave century (104 not out). The match ended two days early.

Three years later, when Greg Chappell led Australia on an eight-match tour that included two Tests, Walters was again the hero. He batted for 394 minutes in the First Test at Christchurch to score 250, the highest of his 15 Test centuries, adding 217 for the seventh wicket with Gary Gilmour (101). New Zealand appeared certain of defeat when they began the last hour at 8 for 268,

The lowest point in Australia-New Zealand cricket, with Trevor Chappell bowling the last ball of the 1980-81 one-day match under-arm to prevent Brian McKechnie, a Rugby international, from trying for six runs New Zealand required to win.

chasing 350, but Dayle Hadlee stayed with Congdon (107 not out) to thwart Australia. Australia won the Second Test in this 1977 series by ten wickets, their fifth win in nine matches against New Zealand when Lillee (5 for 51 and 6 for 72) took his 150th Test wicket in his 37th Test. (See Appendix for summary.)

Greg Chappell's batting may have won him many admirers in New Zealand but when he went back as captain of the Australian team in 1982, he found himself the villain, following his instruction to his brother Trevor to bowl the last ball of a limited over match in Melbourne underarm. The celebrated underarm delivery deprived Brian McKechnie of all chance of scoring the six runs needed to win, a long shot anyway, but New Zealand fans rightly believed it violated all the normal standards of fair play. Chappell had to live with fans heckling him all the way as he went out to bat and with a fan who rolled a lawn bowl on to the field to remind him of his poor judgement. Rain prevented a result in the First Test at Wellington and the Second Test at Auckland produced New Zealand's second win over Australia. Australia could not overcome superb bowling by Richard Hadlee after Bruce Edgar's 161 gave New Zealand a 177-run lead.

New Zealanders forgot all their animosity towards Greg Chappell, however, when he produced one of his finest innings to score 176 out of Australia's 353 in the Third Test at Christchurch. Lillee, Thomson and Alderman then bowled Australia to an eight-wicket triumph by dismissing New Zealand for 149 and 272.

1981/82 AUSTRALIANS

First-class Results					All Matches			
Matches	Won	Lost	Drawn	Tied	Matches	Won	Lost	Drawn	Tied
5	1	1	3	–	11	4	4	3	–

Date	Venue	Opponent	Results for Australians
Feb 13	Auckland	*New Zealand (L/O Intl)	Lost by 46 runs
Feb 14	Hamilton	*Northern Districts	Lost by 24 runs
Feb 17	Dunedin	*New Zealand (L/O Intl)	Won by 6 wkts
Feb 20	Wellington	*New Zealand (L/O Intl)	Won by 8 wkts
Feb 22	Napier	North Island	Drawn
Feb 26	Wellington	NEW ZEALAND (1st Test)	Drawn
Mar 4	Nelson	*Nelson–Marlborough	Won by 63 runs
Mar 6	Christchurch	NZCC PrAsiAent's XI	Drawn
Mar 9	New Plymouth	*Central Districts	Lost by 1 wkt
Mar 12	Auckland	NEW ZEALAND (2nd Test)	Lost by 5 wkts
Mar 19	Christchurch	NEW ZEALAND (3rd Test)	Won by 8 wkts

Player	State	M	Inn	NO	Runs	HS	50	100	Avrge	Ct/St	Overs	Mdns	Runs	Wkts	Avrge	5wi	10wm	Best
Alderman, TM	WA	5	4	4	6	5*	–	–	–	2	136.5	37	362	12	30.16	–	–	3/35
Border, AR	QLD	5	5	–	91	38	–	–	18.20	2	20.3	5	52	4	13.00	–	–	3/20
Bright, RJ	VIC	2	1	–	27	27	–	–	27.00	1	42.0	10	156	2	78.00	–	–	1/66
Chappell, GS (Capt)	QLD	5	6	2	317	176	1	1	79.25	4	35.0	10	58	1	58.00	–	–	1/30
Dyson, J	NSW	4	6	2	124	33	–	–	31.00	1	3.0	–	18	1	18.00	–	–	1/18
Hughes, KJ	WA	5	5	–	115	66	1	–	23.00	3	2.0	1	3	1	3.00	–	–	1/3
Laird, BM	WA	4	6	1	155	39	–	–	31.00	1	–	–	–	–	–	–	–	–
Lillee, DK	WA	4	3	–	21	9	–	–	7.00	2	79.0	23	183	7	26.14	–	–	3/13
Marsh, RW	WA	5	4	1	59	33	–	–	19.66	7	–	–	–	–	–	–	–	–
Pascoe, LS	NSW	1	1	–	1	1	–	–	1.00	–	29.0	3	110	3	36.66	–	–	2/53
Thomson, JR	QLD	5	4	–	51	25	–	–	12.75	–	109.0	39	238	8	29.75	–	–	4/51
Wood, GM	WA	5	7	–	388	100	3	1	55.42	4	–	–	–	–	–	–	–	–
Yardley, B	WA	5	4	–	42	25	–	–	10.50	3	150.2	50	462	17	27.17	–	–	4/80

AUSTRALIA IN NEW ZEALAND 1985-86 TO 1994-95

Allan Border succeeded Greg and Ian Chappell as Australia's captain for New Zealand tours from the mid-1980s and found victory no easier to secure than his predecessors. Stunned by a 2–1 loss to New Zealand at home, Border hoped to square counts by winning the three-Test series. He was now fully aware of how detrimental to the Test team the rebel tours to South Africa and the retirement of Lillee, Marsh and Greg Chappell had been. Somehow he had to mould a floundering group into winners, despite the presence in the New Zealand team of the great bowler Richard Hadlee.

At Wellington in the First Test Hadlee took his 300th Test wicket, but Greg Matthews lifted Australia to 435 with a fine 130. Jeremy Coney made 101 not out in New Zealand's reply before rain forced a draw. The Second Test at Christchurch was also drawn after Border made a century in each innings, 140 and 114 not out, the second time he had achieved this feat. Before the rain Martin Crowe limited Australia's lead to 25 with a brave knock for 137, interrupted when he left the field to have ten stitches inserted in a cut in his jaw inflicted by Bruce Reid. Off-spinner John Bracewell routed Australia for 103 in their second innings in the Third Test at Auckland after Australia led by 56 runs in the first innings. Bracewell's 6 for 32 meant New Zealand only had to score 160 to clinch the rubber and they did this for the loss of only two wickets. Border was so disgusted with Australia's failure to win more than one of their five matches on this 1985–86 trip he threatened to resign.

Border returned to New Zealand in March 1990 with a full-strength Australian team that had played 15 Tests without defeat. New Zealand had only narrowly escaped defeat in Perth during that Australian summer when Mark Greatbatch batted all the final day and once again Border was eager to square accounts. New Zealand destroyed Australian hopes, winning the only Test by nine wickets because of Richard Hadlee's 5 for 39 in Australia's first innings and Bracewell's 6 for 85 in the second. Dismissed for 110 and 269, Australia left New Zealand 181 to win and John Wright's 117 not out made light of the task. Peter Taylor, who hit 87 in Australia's second innings and excelled himself in the one-day matches, returned home after a splendid tour to find himself omitted from the New South Wales team for the Sheffield Shield final. The 1990 victory gave New Zealand her fifth win in 21 Tests against Australia and produced Richard Hadlee's 3000th Test run and his 300th Test wicket, a double matched only by Ian Botham, Imran Khan and Kapel Dev.

Border's third tour of New Zealand with an Australian team in 1992–93 proved the culmination of a season of setbacks after promising starts. The Australians had lost the series against the West Indies after leading one–nil with two Tests left. This time they won the First Test at Christchurch convincingly, had a moral victory in the Second Test at Wellington when rain prevented a result, and ended up sharing the rubber when New Zealand won the Third Test in Auckland. New Zealand recalled their oldest (at 39), most experienced batsman, left-hander John Wright, for his final series, and he did the job for them by batting for nine and a half hours in Wellington and five and a half hours in Auckland.

New Zealand started so badly, in losing the First Test, Martin Crowe offered to stand down as captain. Sir Richard Hadlee and coach Warren Lees joined in the criticism of New Zealand's lack of guts. The Australians by contrast were a happy outfit, with captain Allan Border passing Sunil Gavaskar to become Test cricket's highest-ever run-scorer by scoring 88 in the First Test. Border had taken 139 Tests and 240 innings to reach 10,123 at an average of 51.32. It was the 84th time he had passed 50, and in 25 of these innings he went on

The 1993 Australian team in New Zealand, which shared a three-Test rubber: *back row* Errol Alcott (physio), Shane Warne, Mark Waugh, Paul Reiffel, Merv Hughes, Tim May, Steve Waugh, Damien Martin, Justin Langer; *front* Craig McDermott, Ian Healy, Ian McDonald (manager), Allan Border (capt.), Bob Simpson (coach), Mark Taylor, David Boon.

1992/93 AUSTRALIANS

First-class Results					All Matches				
Matches	Won	Lost	Drawn	Tied	Matches	Won	Lost	Drawn	Tied
4	2	1	1	–	10	5	4	1	–

Date	Venue	Opponent	Results for Australians
Feb 16	New Plymouth	New Zealand Board XI	Won by 9 wkts
Feb 22	Nelson	*New Zealand President's XI	Lost by 3 wkts
Feb 25	Christchurch	NEW ZEALAND (1st Test)	Won by an inns & 60 runs
Mar 4	Wellington	NEW ZEALAND (2nd Test)	Drawn
Mar 12	Auckland	NEW ZEALAND (3rd Test)	Lost by 5 wkts
Mar 19	Dunedin	*New Zealand (L/O Intl)	Won by 129 runs
Mar 21	Christchurch	*New Zealand (L/O Intl)	Won by 1 wkt
Mar 24	Wellington	*New Zealand (L/O Intl)	Lost by 88 runs
Mar 27	Hamilton	*New Zealand (L/O Intl)	Lost by 3 wkts
Mar 28	Auckland	*New Zealand (L/O Intl)	Won by 3 runs

Player	State	M	Inn	NO	Runs	HS	50	100	Avrge	Ct/St	Overs	Mdns	Runs	Wkts	Avrge	5wi	10wm	Best
Boon, DC	TAS	3	4	–	125	53	1	–	31.25	3	1.0	1	0	–	–	–	–	–
Border, AR (Capt)	QLD	4	5	–	189	88	2	–	37.80	4	28.0	14	34	1	34.00	–	–	1/8
Healy, IA	QLD	4	5	1	173	87*	2	–	43.25	13/1	–	–	–	–	–	–	–	–
Hughes, MG	VIC	4	5	1	127	45	–	–	31.75	1	171.2	55	405	19	21.32	–	–	4/21
Langer, JL	WA	4	6	1	214	89	2	–	42.80	2	–	–	–	–	–	–	–	–
Martyn, DR	WA	2	3	–	84	74	1	–	28.00	–	1.0	1	0	–	–	–	–	–
May, TBA	SA	1	1	–	1	1	–	–	1.00	–	33.0	6	83	–	–	–	–	–
McDermott, CJ	QLD	3	4	1	27	10	–	–	9.00	1	125.0	36	326	13	25.08	–	–	3/54
Reiffel, PR	VIC	4	5	–	84	49	–	–	16.80	2	142.4	47	367	12	30.58	1	–	5/78
Taylor, MA	NSW	4	6	–	193	82	2	–	32.17	12	4.0	2	15	–	–	–	–	–
Warne, SK	VIC	4	5	2	51	22*	–	–	17.00	1	187.5	81	337	19	17.74	–	–	4/8
Waugh, ME	NSW	3	3	–	25	13	–	–	8.33	2	18.0	6	45	1	45.00	–	–	1/12
Waugh, SR	NSW	4	6	1	250	75	2	–	50.00	2	55.0	21	108	5	21.60	–	–	2/21

to Test centuries. Australians were also delighted at the long spells bowled by Shane Warne without losing hostility. He bowled 53 maidens in his 99 overs in the first two Tests.

Mark Taylor's 82 and Border's 88 lifted Australia to 485 in the first innings of the First Test, setting up victory by an innings and 60 runs. Martin Crowe's 98 gave New Zealand a 31-run first innings lead in the Second Test but at 3 for 30 they were in trouble in the second innings until Wright began his long salvaging knock. Australia dropped Mark Waugh for Damien Martyn in the Third Test. New Zealand only required 201 to win in the final innings after Danny Morrison (6 for 37) routed Australia for 139 on the first day. They got them for the loss of five wickets, with Ken Rutherford confirming his emergence as a batsman of stature by adding 58 not out to his 57 and 102 in the First Test. Australia played ten matches in all on the tour, winning five, losing four and playing one draw. They won two of the four first-class matches in this program, losing one and leaving one unfinished, a disappointment for experts who forecast they would remain undefeated.

The Third Test at Eden Park, Auckland, proved a hot-tempered tussle with Mark Greatbatch jousting with Merv Hughes in an epic of glares and profanities between two bulky characters who swapped snorts and at one point buffeted each other. After Hughes and Greatbatch bumped into each other match referee Javed Burki was asked if the code of good behaviour had been breached. Burki chuckled and replied: 'They were just enjoying themselves.' One commentator applauded this and added that it was not a time to invoke the Marquis of Queensberry rules.

Australia went to New Zealand in February 1995 for a four-match limited over tournament spread over 16 days to celebrate the centenary of the New Zealand Cricket Council. The Australians were without Craig McDermott, Michael Slater and Damien Fleming, but won their way to the final by defeating South Africa and New Zealand in the preliminary rounds. They lost to India, whose batsmen scored freely from the Australian spinners, before comfortably winning the final against New Zealand.

Only Ken Rutherford (46) troubled Australia as New Zealand struggled to 9 for 137 in 50 overs from Reiffel (2 for 14), Mark Waugh (1 for 38), Warne (2 for 21), May (3 for 19), McGrath and Blewett. Australia then made 4 for 138 off 31.1 overs, with Taylor contributing 44, Mark Waugh 46.

1994/95 AUSTRALIANS

First-class Results					All Matches				
Matches	Won	Lost	Drawn	Tied	Matches	Won	Lost	Drawn	Tied
–	–	–	–	–	4	3	1	–	–

Date	Venue	Opponent	Results for Australians
Feb 15	Wellington	*South Africa (L/O Intl)	Won by 3 wkts
Feb 19	Auckland	*New Zealand (L/O Intl)	Won by 27 runs
Feb 22	Dunedin	*India (L/O Intl)	Lost by 5 wkts
Feb 26	Auckland	*New Zealand (L/O Intl)	Won by 6 wkts

NEW ZEALAND TEAMS IN AUSTRALIA

New Zealand's disastrous defeat by Australia in 1946 discouraged Board of Control treasurers from sanctioning further Tests between the countries until New Zealand fully justified Test status. This imposed a long, hard standards build-up on New Zealand, which had to be content with periodic visits to Australia on their way to or from other overseas tours. A New Zealand team played three Australian states in 1954 on their way back from South Africa. They defeated Western Australia and South Australia and had a draw against Victoria. Sutcliffe scored 142 in Perth and 117 in Melbourne. In 1961–62 New Zealand lost to South Australia and Western Australia and drew with Western Australia on their way home from another South African tour in which they had just shared the Test series. Six summers later Barry Sinclair's New Zealand side suffered defeat by South Australia and New South Wales and played draws against Queensland and Victoria. By 1969–70, when New Zealand won a limited over competition in Australia, they were winning Tests often enough to no longer be denied, despite the occasional loss of valuable players to English counties. (See Appendix for summaries included not here.)

The 1967-68 New Zealand team in Australia: *back row* R.S. Cunis, M.G. Burgess, B.R. Taylor, B.A.G. Murray, T.W. Jarvis, K. Thomson, R.J. Harford; *seated* B.W. Yuile, B.E. Congdon, V. Pollard, J.A. Ongley (manager), B.W. Sinclair (capt.), J.C. Alabaster, R.C. Motz; *inset* R.O. Collinge.

The 1969-70 New Zealand team in Australia: *back row* D.R. Hadlee, M.G. Burgess, K.J. Wadsworth, H.J. Howarth, B.F. Hastings, G.M. Turner, R.S. Cunis, G.E. Vivian; *seated* R.O. Collinge, B.J. Paterson (manager), G.T. Dowling (capt.), B.W. Sinclair, B.E. Congdon.

NEW ZEALAND IN AUSTRALIA 1973-74

	First-class Results					All Matches			
Matches	Won	Lost	Drawn	Tied	Matches	Won	Lost	Drawn	Tied
9	2	5	2	–	13	5	6	2	–

Date	Venue	Opponent	Results for Touring Team
Nov 30	Melbourne	Victoria	Drawn
Dec 5	Newcastle	*Newcastle & District	Won by 5 wkts
Dec 7	Sydney	New South Wales	Lost by 7 wkts
Dec 14	Brisbane	Queensland	Lost by an inns & 2 runs
Dec 16	Brisbane	*Queensland	Lost by 71 runs
Dec 19	Canberra	*Australian Capital Territory	Won by 78 runs
Dec 21	Adelaide	South Australia	Lost by 5 wkts
Dec 29	Melbourne	AUSTRALIA (1st Test)	Lost by an inns & 25 runs
Jan 5	Sydney	AUSTRALIA (2nd Test)	Drawn
Jan 12	Launceston	Tasmania	Won by 94 runs
Jan 15	Hobart (TCA)	*Tasmania	Won by 4 wkts
Jan 19	Perth	Western Australia	Won by 4 wkts
Jan 26	Adelaide	AUSTRALIA (3rd Test)	Lost by an inns & 57 runs

The initial Test between Australia and New Zealand in Australia went to Australia by an innings and 25 runs after Keith Stackpole (122) hit the first century in these contests. Australia made 462, New Zealand 237 and 200. The Second Test was drawn after centuries for New Zealand by John Parker (108) and John Morrison (117). Rod Marsh set up victory for Australia in the Third Test at Adelaide with an innings of 132, his second Test century, after Doug Walters softened up the New Zealand bowling with an aggressive 94. Dymock clinched a trip to New Zealand immediately after this series by taking 5 for 58 to finish New Zealand off. Overall New Zealand selectors handicapped their side by not sending a

Player	M	Inn	NO	Runs	HS	50	100	Avrge	Ct/St	Overs	Mdns	Runs	Wkts	Avrge	5wi	10wm	Best
Alabaster, GD	3	3	–	69	29	–	–	23.00	1	80.2	16	292	9	32.44	–	–	3/32
Andrews, B	4	6	2	43	17	–	–	10.75	1	70.0	6	350	9	38.88	1	–	5/85
Cairns, BL	6	8	2	52	29	–	–	8.66	4	141.0	20	526	20	26.30	1	–	5/55
Campbell, KO	4	8	3	64	20	–	–	12.80	11/1	–	–	–	–	–	–	–	–
Coney, JV	6	12	1	271	64*	–	–	24.63	7	–	–	–	–	–	–	–	–
Congdon, BE (Capt)	9	18	1	463	113	1	1	27.23	1	93.3	9	365	10	36.50	–	–	4/52
Hadlee, RJ	7	11	–	197	49	–	–	17.90	2	170.7	18	728	16	45.50	–	–	4/33
Hadlee, DR	9	16	4	242	47*	–	–	20.16	3	213.5	19	908	26	34.92	–	–	4/52
Hastings, BF	9	18	1	561	139*	2	1	33.00	6	–	–	–	–	–	–	–	–
Morrison, JFM	8	16	–	475	117	2	1	29.68	6	1.0	0	3	–	–	–	–	–
O'Sullivan, DR	8	13	4	97	26*	–	–	10.77	1	161.5	27	585	14	41.78	1	–	5/148
Parker, JM	8	16	1	627	140*	3	1	41.80	5	0.6	–	10	–	–	–	–	–
Shrimpton, MJF	6	12	2	426	106	1	2	42.60	2	37.5	2	170	7	24.28	–	–	3/31
Turner, GM	6	10	1	265	106*	–	1	29.44	3	–	–	–	–	–	–	–	–
Wadsworth, KJ	6	11	1	357	80	3	–	35.70	18/1	–	–	–	–	–	–	–	–

genuinely fast bowler or a specialist wrist spinner, restricting captain Bevan Congdon to medium-pacers and finger-spinners. New Zealand beat Tasmania and Western Australia, but lost to NSW, Queensland and South Australia.

The 1973–74 New Zealand team in Australia: *back row* J.F. Morrison, K.O. Campbell, B.L. Cairns; *middle* D.R. O'Sullivan, M.J.F. Shrimpton, B. Andrews, J.V. Coney, R.J. Hadlee, G.D. Alabaster; *front* D.R. Hadlee, K.R. Wadsworth, B.E. Congdon (capt.), R.A. Vance (manager), G.M. Turner, B.F. Hastings, J.M. Parker.

NEW ZEALAND IN AUSTRALIA 1980-81

Programmers gave New Zealand a tricky task in asking them to switch frequently from one-day matches to Tests, and in the Tests the visitors found foolish ways of getting out. At Brisbane in the First Test New Zealand were 3 for 193 and seemingly set for a big total when Parker dragged a ball from outside the off on to his stumps and started a collapse that saw seven wickets fall for 32 runs. Graeme Wood's 111 led Australia to a ten-wicket triumph. Australia then took the three-Test rubber by winning the Second Test in Perth by eight wickets, thanks to Lillee's match bag of 7 for 77. Pascoe and Hogg also bowled well but Marsh was the unlucky player, falling at 91, when within sight of his fourth Test century. The Third Test at Melbourne featured big crowds and the recall of players leaving the field in the general belief that Jim Higgs had been caught by the keeper to end the innings. Walters was 77 not out. The umpire then explained he had no-balled the bowler, Lance Cairns, for excessive use of the bouncer. Play continued until Walters was bowled by Jeremy Coney for 107, but the incident cost New Zealand 69 minutes and 42 runs. Set to score 193 in 145 minutes, New Zealand were 6 for 128 when time ran out.

NEW ZEALAND IN AUSTRALIA 1982-83

Likeable Geoff Howarth, who had done well in the Surrey XI in England, again found himself asked to switch from limited-over cricket to Tests in another Australian tour arranged by ledger-keepers. Even worse,

they were asked to play two first-class matches and two one-day games but not Tests, then go home for Christmas for further one-day matches. They were reinforced for the first time in six years by Glenn Turner, probably the most professional cricketer ever developed by New Zealand, whose impatience with New Zealand officials sent him off to Worcestershire. There were three declarations in New Zealand's match against Victoria before it ended in a tie, with fewer than 100 people watching. New Zealand then played the first first-class match in Queensland outside Brisbane at Salter Oval in Bundaberg. Almost 7000 spectators paid to watch Kepler Wessels (129), Robbie Kerr (102) and Allan Border (104) make centuries, with New Zealand scoring 304 in reply to Queensland's 3 for 403 declared because of Howarth's 138. New Zealand appeared certain of defeat until they were saved by their oldest player, John Morrison, who made 78 not out.

Champagne celebrations followed New Zealand's historic 1983 first-ever win over England by five wickets at Leeds. *Back row* John Bracewell, Martin Crowe, Ewen Chatfield, Jeff Crowe, Ian Smith; *front* Alan (later Sir Alan) Wright (manager), John Wright, Geoff Howarth (capt.), Lance Cairns, Richard Hadlee, Jeremy Coney.

NEW ZEALAND IN AUSTRALIA 1985-86

New Zealand visited Australia briefly to help Victoria celebrate their 150th anniversary in 1985, in a one-day tournament that was soon forgotten, before returning for a six-match first-class visit laughingly called a 'full tour' by administrators who produced the Trans-Tasman Trophy. The New Zealanders were sent to Townsville and Carrara for matches against Queensland country sides, and then played South Australia and Queensland before the first of three Tests. The itinerary gave New Zealand a chance to prepare properly and make the Tests a genuine contest for the first time and they made history by winning the series two–one.

The majestic Richard Hadlee was the difference between the two sides from the first day in Brisbane. He took 9 for 52 to bundle Australia out in their first innings for 179. Centuries from John Reid (108) and Martin Crowe (188) and an innings of 54 by Richard Hadlee, studded with hefty blows, took New Zealand to 553 when Coney declared. Border compiled a typically gusty 152 not out in Australia's second innings but only the extrovert Greg Matthews gave him support and when Matthews went for 115, New Zealand went on to their first victory in Australia by an innings and 41 runs. Hadlee finished with 15 for 123.

Amid widespread discussion about Hadlee's line and length and the inevitability of umpires granting his lbw appeals, Matthews scored another century, 111, for NSW against the tourists, before the Second Test. New Zealand escaped with a draw when NSW captain Dirk Welham refused to enforce the follow-on. Leg-spinner Bob Holland's match haul of 10 for 174 won the Second Test for Australia by four wickets, which sent the teams to Perth for the decider with a win apiece. The pitch was tailor-made for Hadlee, who took 5 for 65 and 6 for 90 in another wonderful exhibition of subtle, accurate fast–medium bowling, seldom straying from or around the batsman's off stump. Bruce Edgar's dour 74 and a sparkling 71 from Martin Crowe gave New Zealand an advantage Hadlee exploited to the full.

NEW ZEALAND IN AUSTRALIA 1987-88

Martin Crowe captained New Zealand in Australia for this six-match tour which *Wisden* said was the 17th visit by a New Zealand team but only the fourth to be granted Test matches in Australia. The New Zealanders came straight from the World Cup limited-over competition in India to a strange program of day/night matches mingled with first-class fixtures. They beat Western Australia in the night game at Perth and then overwhelmed the reigning WA Sheffield Shield holders by an innings and 96 runs in less than three days. After a comfortable win over a South Australian Country XI at Renmark they were put in to bat on a green strip against South Australia in Adelaide and went down by three wickets.

Australia won the first of the three-Test series by nine wickets at the Gabba in Brisbane, Boon's 143 turning the match. The Second Test on a dead pitch produced some sound batting from Jones (150) and Crowe (137) and a double century by Border (205) but Border took the honours when he passed Bradman's Test aggregate of 6996 runs and next day overtook Greg Chappell's 7110 runs. The Third Test in Melbourne provided a thrilling finish with Australia's last pair, Craig McDermott and Mike Whitney, holding out for 4.5 overs to deprive New Zealand of a shared series. Hadlee bowled the final over and by failing to dismiss Whitney missed his chance for the Test bowling record. Earlier New Zealand batsman Andrew Jones was given out caught by keeper Greg Dyer when television replays clearly showed the ball bounced out of Dyer's gloves before he regathered it and claimed the catch. Within a few months, Dyer lost his Test and state team places.

NEW ZEALAND IN AUSTRALIA 1989-90

This was an absurd four-match tour over three weeks which the New Zealand Cricket Council should never have sanctioned. The dates were dictated by Kerry Packer's Channel Nine who opposed international cricket being played within Australia when they were televising the Commonwealth Games from Auckland. The Australian Cricket Board had booked Pakistan to tour but found the Pakistanis had double booked and were committed to play in India. The leading New Zealand players were right in rejecting the idea of substituting for Pakistan but their council over-ruled them.

With little preparation the New Zealanders lost a limited-over match to Western Australia, played draws against Western Australia and South Australia over four days, and then played out a draw over five days in the Test on a lively WACA pitch. David Boon's 200 in Australia's first innings of 9 declared for 521 appeared to set up victory for Australia, who forced New Zealand to follow on, but Mark Greatbatch batted for 462 minutes to save New Zealand, ending on 146 not out after the slowest first-class century ever recorded in Australia at that time.

NEW ZEALAND IN AUSTRALIA 1993-94

New Zealand's hopes of extending such a well-drilled team as Australia disappeared when their captain Martin Crowe flew home after the first Test because of a knee injury, for Crowe was the one New Zealand batsman capable of subduing Australia's most hostile bowlers, Craig McDermott and Shane Warne. Stop-gap captain Ken Rutherford, Tony Blain and Mark Greatbatch struggled hard to lift New Zealand's batting displays but without the prolific strokeplay of Crowe only Andrew Jones proved consistent, averaging 54.00 in the three Tests. Not one New Zealand bowler averaged under 50 runs per wicket and Danny Morris, New Zealand's main strike bowler, took only three wickets for 140.7 runs apiece in the three Tests.

Injuries worsened New Zealand's plight. Willie Watson damaged a hamstring muscle in the First Test, Chris Cairns injured a heel which prevented him playing in the Second Test, Morrison struggled with a groin muscle injury sustained before he left home. After playing a draw in the First Test at Perth, where Andrew Jones (143) and Ian Healy (113 not out) hit centuries, New Zealand suffered heavy defeats in the Second Test at Hobart and the Third Test at Brisbane.

The Second Test lasted little more than three days, with David Boon (106) and Michael Slater (168) taking advantage of missed chances to lift Australia to 3 for 329 after a day's play. Mark Waugh (111) and Allan Border (60) stepped up the scoring next day, Border declaring at 6 for 544. May and Warne then combined to dismiss New Zealand for 161. Following on, New Zealand were out for the same score, 161, leaving Australia winners by an innings and 222 runs, the heaviest defeat ever sustained in Tests by New Zealand. Warne took the last four wickets for three runs to finish with 9 for 67 in the match. May took 7 for 110 (5 for 65 and 2 for 45).

The Third Test was another disaster for New Zealand. Chasing New Zealand's first innings of 233, Australia took the lead by stumps on the second day and went on to a massive 6 declared for 607, Border (105) and Steve Waugh (147 not out) pummelling bowling rendered inept by the top order batsmen. Warne joined the slaughter with 74 not out. He then took 4 for 59 to go with his 4 for 66 in the first innings and complete the rubber with 15 wickets at 16.94. This time Australia won by an innings and 96 runs.

For New Zealanders the only comforting results on the entire tour were the unexpected defeats of New South Wales at Newcastle by three wickets and South Australia at Adelaide by seven wickets after Richard de Groen, who had joined the side for the injured Watson, took five wickets in the match. Major disappointment of the tour was Greatbatch, who made only 67 runs in six Test innings.

1993/94 NEW ZEALANDERS

First-class Results					All Matches				
Matches	Won	Lost	Drawn	Tied	Matches	Won	Lost	Drawn	Tied
7	2	3	2	–	16	5	9	2	–

Date	Venue	Opponent	Results for Touring Team
Oct 19	Caversham	*ACB Chairman's XI	Lost by 6 wkts
Oct 21	Perth	Western Australia	Lost by an inns & 9 runs
Oct 27	North Sydney	*AIS Cricket Academy	Lost by 110 runs
Oct 29	Newcastle	New South Wales	Won by 3 wkts
Nov 4	Launceston	Tasmania	Drawn
Nov 12	Perth	AUSTRALIA (1st Test)	Drawn
Nov 19	Adelaide	South Australia	Won by 7 wkts
Nov 26	Hobart (Bel)	AUSTRALIA (2nd Test)	Lost by an inns & 222 runs
Dec 3	Brisbane	AUSTRALIA (3rd Test)	Lost by an inns & 96 runs
Dec 11	Adelaide	*South Africa (L/O Intl)	Abandoned
Dec 12	Adelaide	*Australia (L/O Intl)	Lost by 8 wkts
Dec 16	Melbourne	*Australia (L/O Intl)	Lost by 3 runs
Dec 18	Hobart (Bel)	*South Africa (L/O Intl)	Won by 4 wkts
Jan 8	Brisbane	*South Africa (L/O Intl)	Won on run rate
Jan 11	Sydney	*Australia (L/O Intl)	Won by 13 runs
Jan 14	Perth	*South Africa (L/O Intl)	Lost by 5 wkts
Jan 19	Melbourne	*Australia (L/O Intl)	Lost by 51 runs

Player	M	Inn	NO	Runs	HS	50	100	Avrge	Ct/St	Overs	Mdns	Runs	Wkts	Avrge	5wi	10wm	Best
Blain, TE	7	12	5	280	45*	–	–	40.00	14/1								
Cairns, CL	4	7	–	215	78	1	–	30.71	2	126.0	19	484	11	44.00	1	–	5/105
Crowe, MD (Capt)	4	8	1	238	105	–	1	34.00	3	–							
de Groen, RP	3	4	2	12	6	–	–	6.00	1	123.0	40	313	8	39.13	–	–	3/50
Doull, SB	5	7	–	36	24	–	–	5.14	3	137.4	16	485	16	30.31	1	–	6/55
Greatbatch, MJ	5	9	–	216	65	2	–	24.00	2	–							
Harris, CZ	2	4	2	20	15*	–	–	10.00	–	6.0	2	33	–	–	–	–	–
Haslam, MJ	2	–	–	–	–	–	–	–	–	57.0	8	149	4	37.25	–	–	3/64
Jones, AH	6	12	–	610	143	4	1	50.83	3	8.0	–	32	–	–	–	–	–
Morrison, DK	5	9	4	109	46*	–	–	21.80	2	192.0	28	614	11	55.82	1	–	6/54
Patel, DN	6	12	2	158	50	1	–	15.80	6	179.0	23	663	14	47.36	1	–	6/87
Pocock, BA	7	14	–	259	60	1	–	18.50	6	7.0	1	27	–	–	–	–	–
Rutherford, KR	7	13	–	528	86	5	–	40.62	10	–							
Su'a, ML	6	10	2	162	56	1	–	20.25	–	178.4	23	620	14	44.29	–	–	4/84
Watson, W	3	2	1	4	4	–	–	4.00	1	93.0	29	231	5	46.20	–	–	2/51
White, DJ	1	2	2	15	14*	–	–	–	–	–							
Young, BA	4	8	–	185	53	1	–	23.13	4	–							

CHAPTER NINE

MCC IN AUSTRALIA 1903–04 TO 1936–37

After a brief visit from Lord Hawke's XI in 1902–03 on their way home from a full tour of New Zealand, England returned for a full tour of Australia in 1903–04. This was the first visit to Australia by a team under the control of the Marylebone Cricket Club, who now believed national prestige was at stake in England v. Australia Tests. They picked a pillar of amateurism, Pelham Francis Warner, born in Trinidad where his father was Attorney-General, but educated at Rugby and Oxford, to captain the side, although he was not at the time captain of his county, Middlesex. Warner, a pale, frail-looking figure, had made 132 not out in his Test debut against South Africa at Johannesburg in 1898–99, but had been out of the England XI for four years. For the first time, the professionals in his team stayed at the same hotels in Australia as the amateurs.

'Plum' Warner, born in Trinidad where his father was Attorney-General, shown in 1895, when he won his first Blue for cricket at Oxford. He managed Jardine's infamous Bodyline tour team in Australia.

1902/03 LORD HAWKE'S TEAM

First-class Results					All Matches				
Matches	Won	Lost	Drawn	Tied	Matches	Won	Lost	Drawn	Tied
3	–	2	1	–	3	–	2	1	–

Date	Venue	Opponent	Results for Touring Team
Mar 13	Melbourne	Victoria	Lost by 7 wkts
Mar 20	Sydney	New South Wales	Drawn
Mar 27	Unley	South Australia	Lost by 97 runs

Player	M	Inn	NO	Runs	HS	50	100	Avrge	Ct/St	Overs	Mdns	Runs	Wkts	Avrge	5wi	10wm	Best
Bosanquet, BJT	3	5	–	168	57	3	–	33.60	5	70.1	1	342	8	42.75	1	–	6/153
Burnup, CJ	3	6	1	188	103	–	1	37.60	2	32.0	4	132	2	66.00	–	–	1/15
Dowson, EM	3	5	–	272	86	3	–	54.40	1	69.0	10	198	8	24.65	–	–	3/62
Fane, FL	3	5	–	131	47	–	–	26.20	1	–	–	–	–	–	–	–	–
Hargreave, S	3	5	1	16	5	–	–	4.00	2	74.1	13	192	2	96.00	–	–	1/32
Johnson, PR	3	5	2	115	54	1	–	38.33	4	–	–	–	–	–	–	–	–
Stanning, J	3	5	–	82	38	–	–	16.40	1	–	–	–	–	–	–	–	–
Taylor, TL	3	5	–	164	105	1	1	32.80	5/1	–	–	–	–	–	–	–	–
Thompson, JG	3	5	2	101	38	–	–	33.67	–	142.0	26	406	19	21.34	1	1	9/85
Trott, AE	3	5	–	34	17	–	–	6.80	2	114.5	15	482	12	40.17	1	–	6/88
Warner, PF (Capt)	3	6	1	156	47	–	–	31.20	1	–	–	–	–	–	–	–	–

ENGLAND IN AUSTRALIA 1903-04

	First-class Results					All Matches			
Matches	Won	Lost	Drawn	Tied	Matches	Won	Lost	Drawn	Tied
14	9	2	3	–	20	10	2	8	–

Date	Venue	Opponent	Results for Touring Team
Nov 7	Adelaide	South Australia	Drawn
Nov 13	Melbourne	Victoria	Won by an inns & 71 runs
Nov 20	Sydney	New South Wales	Won by an inns & 10 runs
Nov 27	Brisbane	Queensland	Won by 6 wkts
Dec 2	West Maitland	*XVIII of Northern District	Drawn
Dec 4	Newcastle	*XV of Newcastle	Drawn
Dec 11	Sydney	AUSTRALIA (1st Test)	Won by 5 wkts
Dec 19	Melbourne	*XVIII Juniors of Melbourne	Won by an inns & 99 runs
Dec 26	Bendigo	*XVIII of Bendigo	Drawn
Jan 1	Melbourne	AUSTRALIA (2nd Test)	Won by 185 runs
Jan 8	Ballarat	*XVIII of Ballarat	Drawn
Jan 15	Adelaide	AUSTRALIA (3rd Test)	Lost by 216 runs
Jan 25	Hobart (TCA)	Tasmania	Drawn
Jan 29	Launceston	Tasmania	Drawn
Feb 5	Melbourne	Victoria	Won by 8 wkts
Feb 12	Sydney	New South Wales	Won by 278 runs
Feb 19	Bathurst	*XV of Bathurst	Drawn
Feb 26	Sydney	AUSTRALIA (4th Test)	Won by 157 runs
Mar 5	Melbourne	AUSTRALIA (5th Test)	Lost by 218 runs
Mar 12	Adelaide	South Australia	Won by 9 wkts

The Sixteenth England team to Australia, the first to be sponsored by the MCC, lost £1500 on the venture but returned home with The Ashes. The captain, Pelham ('Plum') Warner is in the middle of the front-row of this team shot, with B.J.T. Bosanquet, inventor of the bosie or googly, on his right.

Player	M	Inn	NO	Runs	HS	50	100	Avrge	Ct/St	Overs	Mdns	Runs	Wkts	Avrge	5wi	10wm	Best
Arnold, EG	10	15	3	167	34	–	–	13.92	13	359.1	102	884	46	19.22	–	–	4/8
Bosanquet, BJT	12	19	3	587	124*	2	2	36.69	12	276.5	23	1011	37	27.32	2	–	6/45
Braund, LC	11	17	–	395	102	1	1	23.26	17	272.1	58	729	37	19.70	3	–	8/18
Drummond, G	1	1	–	1	1	–	–	1.00	–	5.0	–	21	–	–	–	–	–
Fielder, A	7	8	3	59	23	–	–	11.80	4	138.1	42	323	14	23.07	–	–	3/35
Foster, RE	13	22	4	821	287	2	1	45.61	15	7.0	2	34	1	34.00	–	–	1/34
Hayward, TW	11	17	–	785	157	5	2	46.18	4	14.0	5	27	–	–	–	–	–
Hirst, GH	12	18	1	569	92	5	–	33.47	7	358.1	88	881	36	24.47	2	–	5/37
Knight, AE	10	16	2	444	104	1	1	31.71	2	14.0	2	43	2	21.50	–	–	2/34
Lilley, AFA	11	16	3	226	91*	1	–	17.38	16/13	7.0	2	23	–	–	–	–	–
Relf, A	9	12	2	167	31	–	–	16.70	13	128.4	42	302	10	30.20	–	–	3/48
Rhodes, W	14	18	7	239	49*	–	–	21.73	13	444.3	115	1055	65	16.23	7	2	8/68
Strudwick, H	6	5	–	53	21	–	–	10.60	14/9	5.0	2	6	–	–	–	–	–
Tyldesley, JT	13	22	2	670	97	7	–	33.50	7	8.0	1	28	–	–	–	–	–
Warner, PF (Capt)	14	24	1	694	79	6	–	30.17	5	10.0	3	28	–	–	–	–	–

Warner's 16th English touring team was not highly rated because the amateurs C.B. Fry, F.S. Jackson, A.C. MacLaren, G.L. Jessop, L.C. Palairet, E.M. Dowson, H. Martyn and R.H. Spooner, and the professionals S.F. Barnes and W.H. Lockwood, all declined invitations to join the team. But they were unbeaten in the six matches before the First Test in Sydney where Reggie Foster, who could not afford the time to play county cricket regularly, made a famous 287. This was the highest score in Test cricket until Andy Sandham made 325 in 1929–30 against the West Indies, later lifted to 365 by Gary Sobers. Foster's score is still the best by a player in his first Test. He batted for 419 minutes after Monty Noble had scored an impressive 133 for Australia. Foster's score lifted England to a 577 total and enabled them to defeat Australia by five wickets, despite a brilliant 185 not out from Victor Trumper in Australia's second innings. Foster made 214 of his runs in a day, which took the gloss from Trumper's century in 94 minutes. Foster retired with a chill in the Second Test at Melbourne on 49 and could not bat in the second innings. Rain upset the match after England made 221 on the first day, and the Australians could not handle the wet-pitch specialist Wilfred Rhodes, who took 15 wickets for 124 runs and had eight catches dropped off his bowling.

Down two–nil, Australia made a spirited recovery by winning the Third Test in Adelaide by 216 runs. England won the rubber in the Fourth Test in Sydney by 157 runs when Warner finally gave Bosanquet, the inventor of the googly, his chance. Bosanquet's 6 for 51 in Australia's second innings included a spell of 5 for 12. Australia introduced 'Tibby' Cotter, the Sydney Grammar School express bowler, in the Fifth Test and his 6 for 40 in the first innings led to Australia winning by 218 runs, Hugh Trumble finishing his first-class career with a hat-trick. Warner, in a tribute to Trumble, called him a great camel. Johnny Douglas claimed Trumble should not have been allowed on cricket fields when his proper place was in the trees. In retrospect, Warner's reclaiming of The Ashes was due to Australia's selectors failing to bring in Cotter until the last Test.

ENGLAND IN AUSTRALIA 1907-08

	First-class Results					All Matches			
Matches	Won	Lost	Drawn	Tied	Matches	Won	Lost	Drawn	Tied
18	7	4	7	–	19	7	4	8	–

Date	Venue	Opponent	Results for Touring Team
Oct 26	Perth	Western Australia	Won by an inns & 134 runs
Nov 9	Adelaide	South Australia	Won by an inns & 183 runs
Nov 15	Melbourne	Victoria	Drawn
Nov 22	Sydney	New South Wales	Won by 408 runs
Nov 30	Brisbane	Queensland	Won by an inns & 44 runs
Dec 6	Brisbane	Australian XI	Drawn
Dec 13	Sydney	AUSTRALIA (1st Test)	Lost by 2 wkts
Dec 21	South Melbourne	Victorian XI	Drawn
Dec 26	Bendigo	*XVIII of Bendigo	Drawn
Jan 1	Melbourne	AUSTRALIA (2nd Test)	Won by 1 wkt
Jan 10	Adelaide	AUSTRALIA (3rd Test)	Lost by 245 runs
Jan 18	Launceston	Tasmania	Won by 120 runs
Jan 24	Hobart (TCA)	Tasmania	Drawn
Feb 1	Melbourne	Victoria	Won by 330 runs
Feb 7	Melbourne	AUSTRALIA (4th Test)	Lost by 308 runs
Feb 14	Sydney	New South Wales	Drawn
Feb 21	Sydney	AUSTRALIA (5th Test)	Lost by 49 runs
Mar 2	Adelaide	South Australia	Drawn
Mar 13	Perth	Western Australia	Drawn

The 1907-08 England team in Australia, photographed during their first match in Perth against Western Australia. This was the first time an English team ever played in Western Australia. England won by an innings and 134 runs, thanks to an innings of 133 by their acting captain Frederick Fane, shown in the centre of the front-row in pads. Directly behind him, hands in pockets, is Jack Crawford, who later played for South Australia with great success.

Player	M	Inn	NO	Runs	HS	50	100	Avrge	Ct/St	Overs	Mdns	Runs	Wkts	Avrge	5wi	10wm	Best
Barnes, SF	12	19	4	342	93	1	–	22.80	3	534.0	148	1185	54	21.94	5	1	7/60
Blythe, C	11	14	1	145	27*	–	–	11.15	6	393.2	97	935	41	22.80	3	1	6/48
Braund, LC	16	25	3	783	160	2	2	35.59	25	434.5	63	1644	50	32.88	3	–	7/117
Crawford, JN	16	24	1	610	114	3	1	26.52	15	566.0	115	1663	66	25.20	4	–	5/40
Fane, FL	16	24	1	774	133	3	2	33.65	6	–	–	–	–	–	–	–	–
Fielder, A	10	16	8	134	50*	1	–	16.75	4	418.5	73	1208	50	24.16	4	1	6/27
Gunn, G	11	18	3	817	122*	2	4	54.47	11	16.0	5	43	1	43.00	–	–	1/16
Hardstaff, J sr	17	28	2	1360	135	10	3	52.31	5	29.0	7	86	2	43.00	–	–	1/12
Hayes, EG	11	14	–	230	98	1	–	16.43	9/1	46.0	1	193	5	38.60	–	–	2/35
Hobbs, JB	13	22	1	876	115	6	2	41.71	8	39.0	8	128	4	32.00	–	–	2/14
Humphries, J	10	13	1	92	16	–	–	7.67	18/4	–	–	–	–	–	–	–	–
Hutchings, KL	17	28	–	953	126	6	1	34.04	23	63.5	11	279	3	93.00	–	–	1/5
Jones, AO (Capt)	11	15	1	518	119	3	1	37.00	18	–	–	–	–	–	–	–	–
Rhodes, J	17	27	8	929	119	5	2	48.89	8	429.1	106	1069	31	34.48	1	–	5/73
Young, RA	10	15	–	260	59	1	–	17.33	16/7	–	–	–	–	–	–	–	–

Australia regained The Ashes in England in 1905 and at the end of that tour Joe Darling and his manager Frank Laver recommended that the MCC not accept further invitations to tour Australia until the differences between the Australian Board of Control and leading players were settled. The MCC took this advice and declined to tour Australia in 1906–07 and toured instead in 1907–08, with the Nottinghamshire allrounder Arthur Owen Jones as captain. Jones hit 1000 runs in a season nine times and had just won the County championship for Nottinghamshire. (He is rated as the greatest English fieldsman in any position by English expert Bill Frindall.) His team ran into so many injuries he was glad to call on his Notts teammate George Gunn, who was in Australia for his health.

Australia reversed the four–nil defeat by Warner's side by winning all the Tests except the Second when a wild throw by Hazlitt led to Australia's one-wicket defeat. Hill made 160 in the Third Test despite a queasy stomach which forced him to leave the field several times and vomit beside the pitch. He put on 243 for the eighth wicket in Australia's second innings with Roger Hartigan. Saunders, a left-arm spinner with a corkscrew approach to the crease, spun the ball viciously to bowl Australia to victory in both the Fourth (9 for 104) and Fifth Tests (8 for 196).

The great Yorkshire allrounder Wilfred Rhodes, one of the few successes of A.O. Jones' losing 1907-08 touring side. Australia won the series four-one.

ENGLAND IN AUSTRALIA 1911-12

Matches	First-class Results Won	Lost	Drawn	Tied	Matches	All Matches Won	Lost	Drawn	Tied
14	11	1	2	–	18	12	1	5	–

Date	Venue	Opponent	Results for Touring Team
Nov 10	Adelaide	South Australia	Won by an inns & 194 runs
Nov 17	Melbourne	Victoria	Won by 49 runs
Nov 24	Sydney	New South Wales	Drawn
Dec 1	Brisbane	Queensland	Won by 7 wkts
Dec 6	Toowoomba	*Toowoomba	Won by an inns & 134 runs
Dec 8	Brisbane	Australian XI	Drawn
Dec 15	Sydney	AUSTRALIA (1st Test)	Lost by 146 runs
Dec 26	Bendigo	*XV of Bendigo	Drawn
Dec 30	Melbourne	AUSTRALIA (2nd Test)	Won by 8 wkts
Jan 5	Geelong	*XV of Geelong	Drawn
Jan 12	Adelaide	AUSTRALIA (3rd Test)	Won by 7 wkts
Jan 19	Ballarat	*XV of Ballarat	Drawn
Jan 23	Launceston	Tasmania	Won by 8 wkts
Jan 26	Hobart (TCA)	Tasmania	Won by an inns & 95 runs
Feb 2	Melbourne	Victoria	Won by 8 wkts
Feb 9	Melbourne	AUSTRALIA (4th Test)	Won by an inns & 225 runs
Feb 16	Sydney	New South Wales	Won by 8 wkts
Feb 23	Sydney	AUSTRALIA (5th Test)	Won by 70 runs

The 1911-12 England team in Australia: *back row* H. Strudwick, S.P. Kinneir, E.J. Smith, F.E. Woolley, J. Ironmonger, C.P. Mead, J.W. Hearne, W. Hitch, J. Vine; *front* S.F. Barnes, W. Rhodes, J.W.H.T. Douglas, P.F. Warner (capt.), F.R. Foster, J.B. Hobbs, W. Gunn. They easily defeated a disorganised Australia, whose star players were preoccupied by feuds with administrators.

Player	M	Inn	NO	Runs	HS	50	100	Avrge	Ct/St	Overs	Mdns	Runs	Wkts	Avrge	5wi	10wm	Best
Barnes, SF	13	14	3	126	35	–	–	11.45	7	472.2	118	1231	59	20.86	4	–	5/44
Douglas, JWHT (Capt)	12	15	3	416	140	–	2	34.67	5	316.5	74	803	37	21.70	2	–	5/46
Foster, FR	13	19	1	641	158	3	2	35.61	7	485.1	110	1252	62	20.19	5	–	7/36
Gunn, G	9	15	2	665	106	6	1	51.15	8	–	–	–	–	–	–	–	–
Hearne, JW	13	22	4	808	143	4	2	44.89	5	168.3	16	701	14	50.07	–	–	4/66
Hitch, JW	8	9	2	79	33*	–	–	11.29	3	159.4	23	548	27	20.30	–	–	4/41
Hobbs, JB	11	18	1	943	187	2	3	55.47	8	18.1	3	62	5	12.40	–	–	4/25
Iremonger, J	6	7	–	57	31	–	–	8.14	4	159.5	45	397	12	33.08	1	–	5/52
Kinneir, SP	5	8	–	219	63	1	–	27.38	1	–	–	–	–	–	–	–	–
Mead, CP	13	18	2	531	98	3	–	33.19	5	–	–	–	–	–	–	–	–
Rhodes, W	14	24	4	1098	179	5	4	54.90	11	62.0	9	234	–	–	–	–	–
Smith, EJ	7	9	–	124	47	–	–	13.78	16/2	–	–	–	–	–	–	–	–
Strudwick, H	7	7	3	68	28	–	–	17.00	13/4	–	–	–	–	–	–	–	–
Vine, J	8	9	2	78	36	–	–	11.14	4	38.1	5	182	4	45.50	–	–	2/36
Warner, PF	1	1	–	151	151	–	1	151.00	–	–	–	–	–	–	–	–	–
Woolley, FE	14	18	4	781	305*	1	2	55.79	14	147.1	27	503	17	29.59	–	–	3/71

Pelham Warner captained this team in their first match against South Australia but then fell ill after scoring 151. Johnny Douglas took over as England captain and won wide popularity at a time when Australian cricket was in turmoil. Warner was dismayed by the animosity the dispute between leading players and the Australian Board of Control generated and urged the MCC to suspend further visits until reason prevailed. At a Test selectors' meeting in Sydney Australian captain Clem Hill had a fist fight with Peter McAlister that lasted 20 minutes. The season ended with six of Australia's finest players refusing to go to England in 1912 under the Board of Control's terms. Warner pleaded with all six—Hill, Carter, Armstrong, Ransford, Cotter, and Trumper—to change their minds, but they all dropped out of the tour.

In this atmosphere, the form of the Australians slumped and England had a decisive four–one series win. Foster (32 wickets at 21.62) and Barnes (34 at 22.88) bowled England to victory after Australia's googly expert 'Ranji' Hordern's 12 wickets had swung the First Test Australia's way. Once Hobbs, Rhodes, Hearne, Douglas and Woolley worked out Hordern's googly technique, England scored heavily. For Hill, Trumper, Cotter and Ransford the rubber proved a sad end to outstanding Test careers. England went home with The Ashes, but Warner knew the forthcoming Triangular tournament involving England, South Africa and Australia was doomed to failure without the Australian stars.

ENGLAND IN AUSTRALIA 1920-21

Matches	First-class Results Won	Lost	Drawn	Tied	Matches	All Matches Won	Lost	Drawn	Tied
13	5	6	2	–	22	9	6	7	–

Date	Venue	Opponent	Results for Touring Team
Oct 30	Perth	*Western Australia	Drawn
Nov 5	Adelaide	South Australia	Won by an inns & 55 runs
Nov 12	Melbourne	Victoria	Won by an inns & 59 runs
Nov 19	Sydney	New South Wales	Lost by 6 wkts
Nov 27	Brisbane (Ex)	Queensland	Won by an inns & 41 runs
Dec 3	Brisbane	Australian XI	Drawn
Dec 8	Toowoomba	*Toowoomba	Won by an inns & 119 runs
Dec 14	Sydney	*New South Wales Colts XII	Drawn
Dec 17	Sydney	AUSTRALIA (1st Test)	Lost by 377 runs
Dec 27	Bendigo	*XV of Bendigo	Won by an inns & 264 runs
Dec 31	Melbourne	AUSTRALIA (2nd Test)	Lost by an inns & 91 runs
Jan 7	Ballarat	*XV of Ballarat	Won by an inns & 143 runs
Jan 14	Adelaide	AUSTRALIA (3rd Test)	Lost by 119 runs
Jan 25	Hamilton	*XVI of Hamilton	Drawn
Jan 28	Geelong	*XV of Geelong	Drawn
Feb 4	Melbourne	Victoria	Won by 7 wkts
Feb 11	Melbourne	AUSTRALIA (4th Test)	Lost by 8 wkts
Feb 18	Sydney	New South Wales	Drawn
Feb 25	Sydney	AUSTRALIA (5th Test)	Lost by 9 wkts
Mar 4	Albury	*XV of Albury	Drawn
Mar 7	Benalla	*XVII of Benalla	Won by an inns & 101 runs
Mar 11	Adelaide	South Australia	Won by an inns & 63 runs

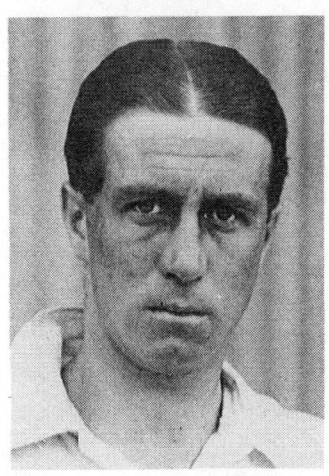

The England captain in 1920-21 encountered powerful opposition, but this did not prevent J.W.H.T. ('Johnny Won't Hit Today') Douglas earning great popularity. He later drowned at sea trying to save his father.

Player	M	Inn	NO	Runs	HS	50	100	Avrge	Ct/St	Overs	Mdns	Runs	Wkts	Avrge	5wi	10wm	Best
Dolphin, A	5	5	1	9	6*	–	–	2.25	9/8	–	–	–	–	–	–	–	–
Douglas, JWHT (Capt)	13	18	4	816	133*	6	2	58.29	6	260.2	33	918	27	34.00	2	–	7/98
Fender, PGH	9	13	1	325	60	3	–	27.08	7	233.0	17	983	32	30.72	4	1	7/75
Hearne, JW	6	7	–	434	182	3	1	62.00	3	147.5	29	407	11	37.00	–	–	3/63
Hendren, EH	12	20	1	1178	271	7	3	62.00	10	3.0	1	15	–	–	–	–	–
Hitch, JW	3	3	–	24	19	–	–	8.00	1	55.0	5	176	5	35.20	–	–	4/28
Hobbs, JB	12	19	1	924	131	1	4	51.33	6	14.0	3	35	–	–	–	–	–
Howell, H	8	10	5	22	6	–	–	4.40	1	248.0	32	856	17	50.35	–	–	4/81
Makepeace, H	9	16	1	449	117	3	1	29.93	–	–	–	–	–	–	–	–	–
Parkin, CH	11	16	1	134	36	–	–	8.93	3	406.0	62	1344	43	31.26	2	–	8/55
Rhodes, W	12	19	–	730	210	2	2	38.42	6	184.3	41	479	18	26.61	1	–	6/39
Russell, AC	10	15	1	818	201	3	3	58.43	7	–	–	–	–	–	–	–	–
Strudwick, H	8	13	3	80	24	–	–	8.00	19/2	–	–	–	–	–	–	–	–
Waddington, A	5	8	2	82	51*	1	–	13.67	2	122.0	25	327	7	46.71	–	–	3/63
Wilson, ER	7	8	–	124	56	1	–	15.50	2	135.0	40	290	8	36.25	–	–	2/18
Woolley, FE	13	20	2	619	138	4	1	34.39	13	391.3	105	1051	31	33.90	–	–	4/27

Boosted by the success of the First AIF team and the talent this side developed, Australia recovered quickly from World War I, whereas England took years to replace the generation of cricketers lost to the war. After a draw in Perth, Johnny Douglas's team defeated South Australia and Victoria in an impressive start, but went down to New South Wales by six wickets. Macartney and Collins warned England of what was ahead with a 244-run stand when New South Wales were set 44 to win. From then on Australian batsmen plundered the weak England bowling. Collins hit 104, Armstrong 158 in the First Test, Pellew 116, Gregory 100 in the Second Test, Collins 162, Kelleway 147, Armstrong 121, Pellew 104 in the Third Test, Armstrong 123 not out in the Fourth Test, and Macartney 170 in the Fifth Test, and despite Hobbs' two centuries Australia won the series five-nil. Through all England's six defeats in a tour of 22 matches—all on level terms for the first time but only 13 of them first-class—Douglas's popularity remained undiminished. Most Australian cricket fans felt they had lost a close relative when he died trying to save his father in a shipping accident in 1930. Even Archie MacLaren, who had a four-match spin around Australia with an MCC 'A' side to prepare for a full tour of New Zealand, did not match Douglas's popularity, admired though MacLaren was for his spectacular hitting.

ENGLAND IN AUSTRALIA 1924-25

	First-class Results					All Matches			
Matches	Won	Lost	Drawn	Tied	Matches	Won	Lost	Drawn	Tied
17	7	6	4	–	23	8	6	9	–

Date	Venue	Opponent	Results for Touring Team
Oct 17	Perth	Western Australia	Drawn
Oct 22	Perth	*Western Australian Colts	Drawn
Oct 25	Perth	Western Australia	Won by an inns & 190 runs
Oct 31	Kalgoorlie	*Goldfields Association XV	Drawn
Nov 7	Adelaide	South Australia	Won by 9 wkts
Nov 14	Melbourne	Victoria	Lost by 6 wkts
Nov 21	Sydney	New South Wales	Won by 3 wkts
Nov 29	Brisbane (Ex)	Queensland	Drawn
Dec 4	Brisbane (Ex)	Australian XI	Drawn
Dec 9	Toowoomba	*Toowoomba	Won by an inns & 126 runs
Dec 13	Sydney	*Australian Juniors XII	Drawn
Dec 19	Sydney	AUSTRALIA (1st Test)	Lost by 193 runs
Jan 1	Melbourne	AUSTRALIA (2nd Test)	Lost by 81 runs
Jan 10	Ballarat	*Ballarat XV	Drawn
Jan 16	Adelaide	AUSTRALIA (3rd Test)	Lost by 11 runs
Jan 27	Launceston	Tasmania	Won by 119 runs
Jan 30	Hobart (TCA)	Tasmania	Won by an inns & 136 runs
Feb 6	Melbourne	Victoria	Won by an inns & 271 runs
Feb 13	Melbourne	AUSTRALIA (4th Test)	Won by an inns & 29 runs
Feb 21	Sydney	New South Wales	Drawn
Feb 27	Sydney	AUSTRALIA (5th Test)	Lost by 307 runs
Mar 6	West Maitland	*Northern District	Drawn
Mar 13	Adelaide	South Australia	Lost by 10 wkts

The twentieth England team to tour Australia went down four–one in The Ashes series, despite the side's abundant talent: *back row* H. Howell, R.K. Tyldesley, A.P.F. Chapman, F.C. Toone (manager), M.W. Tate, W.W. Whysall, J.L. Bryan; *centre* F.E. Woolley, J.W. Hearne, J.W.H.T. Douglas, A.E.R. Gilligan (capt.), J.B. Hobbs, E.H. Hendren, H. Strudwick; *front* R. Kilner, A.P. Freeman, H. Sutcliffe, A. Sandham.

Player	M	Inn	NO	Runs	HS	50	100	Avrge	Ct/St	Overs	Mdns	Runs	Wkts	Avrge	5wi	10wm	Best
Bryan, JL	8	10	1	300	72	2	–	33.33	4	8.0	–	57	–	–	–	–	–
Chapman, APF	13	19	1	625	92	4	–	34.72	10	21.2	3	82	4	20.50	–	–	2/33
Douglas, JWHT	8	11	2	239	62	3	–	26.56	4	100.1	10	393	6	65.50	–	–	2/25
Freeman, AP	9	14	4	157	50*	1	–	15.70	12/1	325.0	45	1209	40	30.23	2	–	6/47
Gilligan, AER (Capt)	15	24	4	357	138	1	1	17.85	9	289.7	32	1075	28	38.39	–	–	4/12
Hearne, JW	11	17	1	513	193	2	1	32.06	9	258.7	30	979	30	32.63	2	–	5/17
Hendren, EH	14	22	3	1233	168	7	3	64.89	13	9.1	–	61	1	61.00	–	–	1/27
Hobbs, JB	10	17	1	865	154	5	3	54.06	–	8.0	–	37	–	–	–	–	–
Howell, H	7	9	4	28	9	–	–	5.60	–	121.4	6	453	15	30.20	1	–	6/96
Kilner, R	12	19	1	448	103	3	1	24.89	5	375.1	57	1007	40	25.18	3	1	6/145
Sandham, A	12	19	–	866	137	6	3	45.58	3	4.1	–	25	–	–	–	–	–
Strudwick, H	11	14	4	70	22	–	–	7.00	22/9	3.0	–	9	1	9.00	–	–	1/9
Sutcliffe, H	12	18	–	1250	188	4	5	69.44	6	6.0	–	25	–	–	–	–	–
Tate, MW	14	20	2	339	44	–	–	18.83	7	502.2	93	1464	77	19.01	7	2	7/74
Tyldesley, R	10	12	2	150	39	–	–	15.00	8	246.0	31	908	22	41.27	1	–	6/83
Whysall, WW	11	17	–	566	101	3	1	33.29	16/2	2.0	–	9	–	–	–	–	–
Woolley, FE	10	17	–	737	149	3	2	43.35	10	169.0	24	549	13	42.23	–	–	4/77

Arthur Gilligan matched Douglas's appeal but a blow he took over the heart before his team reached Australia lessened his effectiveness as a bowler. This, coupled with the punishment Australians handed out to match-winning leg-spinner 'Tich' Freeman, left the task of dismissing Australia largely to Maurice Tate. He took 77 first-class wickets on the tour, 38 of them in the Tests, and although Herbert Sutcliffe played some masterly innings (734 runs in the Tests), Australia's all-round strength produced a four–one series win. For England, the high spot of the tour came when they ended Australia's sequence of 16 Tests without defeat by winning the Fourth Test by an innings and 29 runs. The eight-ball overs used in this rubber undoubtedly helped Australia more than England, with spinners Mailey, Hartkoff, Arthur Richardson and Grimmett getting through a lot of overs. Sutcliffe's Test knocks of 115, 176, 127 and 143, were often tedious, but of great value to his side.

The start of the legendary Hobbs–Sutcliffe partnerships, Grimmett's 11 wickets on debut (5 for 45 and 6 for 37), and Collins's shrewd leadership of Australia were all fuel for cricket's connoisseurs in a memorable summer. But the grace with which Gilligan accepted defeat should not be forgotten.

Hobbs and Sutcliffe, in the Second Test at Melbourne in January 1925, in their memorable 283-run opening stand in response to Australia's total of 600. Australia won by 81 runs.

ENGLAND IN AUSTRALIA 1928-29

	First-class Results				All Matches			
Matches	Won	Lost	Drawn	Tied	Matches	Won	Lost	Drawn	Tied
17	8	1	8	–	24	10	1	13	–

Date	Venue	Opponent	Results for Touring Team
Oct 18	Perth	Western Australia	Drawn
Oct 26	Adelaide	South Australia	Drawn
Nov 1	Melbourne	Victoria	Drawn
Nov 9	Sydney	New South Wales	Drawn
Nov 16	Sydney	Australian XI	Won by 8 wkts
Nov 24	Brisbane (Ex)	Queensland	Won by an inns & 17 runs
Nov 30	Brisbane (Ex)	AUSTRALIA (1st Test)	Won by 675 runs
Dec 8	Warwick	*Combined Country XI	Won by an inns & 169 runs
Dec 14	Sydney	AUSTRALIA (2nd Test)	Won by 8 wkts
Dec 21	Newcastle	*Newcastle & Hunter District	Drawn
Dec 29	Melbourne	AUSTRALIA (3rd Test)	Won by 3 wkts
Jan 7	Geelong	*XII of Geelong	Drawn
Jan 9	Bendigo	*XIII of Bendigo	Drawn
Jan 12	Launceston	Tasmania	Won by an inns & 116 runs
Jan 18	Hobart (TCA)	Tasmania	Won by an inns & 64 runs
Jan 25	Adelaide	South Australia	Drawn
Feb 1	Adelaide	AUSTRALIA (4th Test)	Won by 12 runs
Feb 9	Ballarat	*XIII of Ballarat	Drawn
Feb 15	Sydney	New South Wales	Drawn
Feb 21	Bathurst	*Western District	Won by an inns & 111 runs
Feb 25	Goulburn	*XIII of Southern District	Drawn
Mar 1	Melbourne	Victoria	Drawn
Mar 8	Melbourne	AUSTRALIA (5th Test)	Lost by 5 wkts
Mar 21	Perth	Australian XI	Drawn

Percy Chapman with his England team in Australia in 1928-29, which won The Ashes series by four-one: *back row* Visitor, M. Leyland, G. Duckworth, D.R. Jardine, J.C. White, J.B. Hobbs, C.P. Mead, M.W. Tate, S.J. Staples, E. Tyldesley, E.H. Hendren, W.R. Hammond, L.E.G. Ames; *front* A.P. Freeman, G. Geary, A.P.F. Chapman (capt.), H. Sutcliffe, H. Larwood.

Player	M	Inn	NO	Runs	HS	50	100	Avrge	Ct/St	Balls	Mdns	Runs	Wkts	Avrge	5wi	10wm	Best
Ames, LEG	8	8	3	295	100*	1	1	59.00	8/10	–	–	–	–	–	–	–	–
Chapman, APF (Capt)	14	17	1	533	145	2	1	33.31	23	–	–	–	–	–	–	–	–
Duckworth, G	9	13	6	84	39*	–	–	12.00	17/4	8	–	7	–	–	–	–	–
Freeman, AP	10	7	3	42	17	–	–	10.50	1	2328	32	1136	35	32.45	3	–	5/51
Geary, G	12	16	3	215	66	1	–	16.53	7	2688	103	956	37	25.84	3	–	5/35
Hammond, WR	13	18	1	1553	251	1	7	91.35	10/3	1594	50	661	11	60.09	–	–	3/53
Hendren, EH	12	17	1	1033	169	4	3	64.56	11	120	2	57	–	–	–	–	–
Hobbs, JB	11	18	1	962	142	7	2	56.58	2	–	–	–	–	–	–	–	–
Jardine, DR	12	19	1	1168	214	3	6	64.88	5	112	2	67	2	33.50	–	–	1/0
Larwood, H	13	14	–	367	79	2	–	26.21	8	2714	61	1254	40	31.35	2	–	7/51
Leyland, M	12	17	3	614	137	2	3	43.85	7	742	12	357	4	89.25	–	–	2/37
Mead, CP	10	14	3	460	106	4	1	41.72	3	8	–	11	–	–	–	–	–
Sutcliffe, H	11	16	–	852	135	5	2	53.25	4	32	1	18	–	–	–	–	–
Tate, MW	13	17	1	322	59	2	–	20.12	8	4060	174	1329	44	30.20	1	–	5/35
Tyldesley, E	12	16	2	509	81	5	–	36.35	4	–	–	–	–	–	–	–	–
White, JC	15	18	7	137	30	–	–	12.45	7	5213	223	1471	65	22.63	5	1	8/126

Few cricketers have matched Percy Arthur Frank Chapman's dislike for negative cricket. A tall, loose-limbed left-hander with exceptionally long arms, he introduced spectacular athleticism to English cricket. His catching in the gully was remarkable, his powerful hitting a crowd-thriller, and he changed easily from bowling fast–medium to spin in a manner matched only by Australia's Bill Johnston. He brought to Australia an outstanding team, with Wally Hammond, Patsy Hendren, Duleepsinhji and Maurice Leyland providing batting support for openers Hobbs and Sutcliffe, and Larwood, Tate, George Geary and 'Farmer' White a consistently hostile attack.

England won the First Test, Brisbane's introduction to international cricket, by 675 runs when Australia were trapped on a 'sticky' wicket. Don Bradman made 18 and 1 in his debut on a type of pitch he had never before encountered and was dropped from the Second Test for Otto Nothling, an international Rugby fullback of

Brisbane's first Test at the Agricultural Society's Exhibition Ground in 1928, brought disaster for Australia. Jack Gregory broke down in what proved his last Test, Kelleway could not bat because of food poisoning. Two batsmen short, this Australian team was beaten by 675 runs, scoring only 66 in their second innings: *back row* A.F. Kippax, R.K. Oxenham (12th man), W.H. Ponsford; *centre* C. Kelleway, J.M. Gregory, H.S.T.L. Hendry, H. Ironmonger; *front* W.A.S. Oldfield, C.V. Grimmett, J. Ryder (capt.), D.G. Bradman, W.M. Woodfull.

German descent. England won the Second Test by eight wickets, thanks to Hammond's 251 in a first innings total of 636. Reinstated, Bradman made 112 in the Third Test but could not prevent England's three-wicket triumph that clinched the rubber. Hammond made 119 not out and 177 in the Fourth Test, but Archie Jackson's brilliant 164 on debut reduced England's winning margin to only 12 runs. The Fifth Test in Melbourne lasted eight days and despite centuries by Hobbs (142) and Leyland (137), Australia won by five wickets. Woodfull's 102 and Bradman's 123 helped boost the match aggregate to 1178 runs. This was the sole loss by Chapman's team in 24 matches. The following season (1929–30), an MCC team led by Harold Gilligan played five first-class matches against the states on their way to a full tour of New Zealand, defeating Western Australia and South Australia, losing to Victoria and Queensland, and playing a draw with New South Wales.

ENGLAND IN AUSTRALIA 1932-33

First-class Results					All Matches				
Matches	Won	Lost	Drawn	Tied	Matches	Won	Lost	Drawn	Tied
17	10	1	5	1	22	10	1	10	1

Date	Venue	Opponent	Results for Touring Team
Oct 21	Perth	Western Australia	Drawn
Oct 27	Perth	Combined XI	Drawn
Nov 4	Adelaide	South Australia	Won by an inns & 128 runs
Nov 11	Melbourne	Victoria	Won by an inns & 83 runs
Nov 18	Melbourne	Australian XI	Drawn
Nov 25	Sydney	New South Wales	Won by an inns & 44 runs
Dec 2	Sydney	AUSTRALIA (1st Test)	Won by 10 wkts
Dec 10	Wagga Wagga	*Southern District	Drawn
Dec 16	Launceston	Tasmania	Won by an inns & 126 runs
Dec 23	Hobart (TCA)	Tasmania	Drawn
Dec 30	Melbourne	AUSTRALIA (2nd Test)	Lost by 111 runs
Jan 7	Bendigo	*Victorian Country XIII	Drawn
Jan 13	Adelaide	AUSTRALIA (3rd Test)	Won by 338 runs
Jan 21	Ballarat	*Victorian Country XIII	Drawn
Jan 26	Sydney	New South Wales	Won by 4 wkts
Feb 1	Toowoomba	*Queensland Country XII	Drawn
Feb 4	Brisbane	Queensland	Won by an inns & 61 runs
Feb 10	Brisbane	AUSTRALIA (4th Test)	Won by 6 wkts
Feb 18	Newcastle	*Northern District	Drawn
Feb 23	Sydney	AUSTRALIA (5th Test)	Won by 8 wkts
Mar 3	Melbourne	Victoria	Tied
Mar 10	Adelaide	South Australia	Drawn

The twenty-second England team in Australia: *back row* G. Duckworth, T.B. Mitchell, Nawab of Pataudi, M. Leyland, H. Larwood, E. Paynter, W. Ferguson (scorer); *centre* P.F. Warner (manager), L.E.G. Ames, H. Verity, W. Voce, W.E. Bowes, F.R. Brown, M.W. Tate, R.C.N. Palairet (assistant manager); *front* H. Sutcliffe, R.E.S. Wyatt, D.R. Jardine (capt.), G.O. Allen, W.R. Hammond. They won the rubber four-one with the infamous Bodyline tactics that brought cricket close to disaster.

Player	M	Inn	NO	Runs	HS	50	100	Avrge	Ct/St	Balls	Mdns	Runs	Wkts	Avrge	5wi	10wm	Best
Allen, GOB	12	16	–	397	66	1	–	24.81	14	1673	42	899	39	23.05	1	–	5/69
Ames, LEG	15	21	1	604	107	5	1	30.20	16/8	128	1	51	1	51.00	–	–	1/25
Bowes, WE	10	10	5	38	20	–	–	7.60	1	1626	22	838	30	27.93	–	–	4/18
Brown, FR	8	12	1	186	35	–	–	16.90	7	846	15	427	18	23.72	–	–	4/81
Duckworth, G	7	9	3	89	27*	–	–	14.83	12/3	–	–	–	–	–	–	–	–
Hammond, WR	12	18	1	948	203	5	3	55.76	14	1394	38	578	20	28.90	1	–	6/43
Jardine, DR (Capt)	13	19	2	628	108*	3	1	36.94	15	104	3	42	–	–	–	–	–
Larwood, H	10	13	2	258	98	2	–	23.45	3	1689	45	817	49	16.67	3	1	6/38
Leyland, M	13	21	1	880	152*	4	2	44.00	3	101	1	55	1	55.00	–	–	1/13
Mitchell, TB	9	8	1	28	10	–	–	4.00	7	972	21	492	25	19.68	2	1	6/70
Nawab of Pataudi sr	10	13	–	623	166	1	4	47.92	2	–	–	–	–	–	–	–	–
Paynter, E	11	16	3	538	102	3	1	41.38	5	272	7	71	5	14.20	–	–	3/40
Sutcliffe, H	13	19	1	1318	194	6	5	73.22	4	24	–	18	–	–	–	–	–
Tate, MW	5	8	4	157	94*	1	–	39.25	2	775	16	309	12	25.79	–	–	4/53
Verity, H	13	17	3	300	54*	1	–	21.42	17	2332	119	698	44	15.86	3	1	7/37
Voce, W	10	15	6	143	46	–	–	15.89	7	1775	33	866	32	27.06	1	–	5/85
Wyatt, RES	16	25	2	883	78	8	–	38.39	8	140	2	74	1	74.00	–	–	1/15

In stark contrast to their other post–World War I captains—Douglas, Gilligan and Chapman—England appointed a cross-grained, resolute, stuffed-shirt captain, Douglas Robert Jardine, for what proved the most contentious of all cricket tours. Jardine's tactics in ordering his pace bowlers Voce and Larwood to bowl deliberately at the body with a packed legside field threatened the whole future of international cricket and involved governors and diplomats in finding a solution. The extent of Jardine's disregard for cricket ethics continues to emerge. Publication, after Allen's death in 1989, of letters which 'Gubby' Allen wrote to his parents during the tour, must surely have convinced English critics of the validity of Australian complaints that Jardine's tactics were loathsome.

Bodyline, as Jardine's form of attack was branded, was conceived solely to combat the prodigious run-scoring by Don Bradman in England in 1930. Bradman made 974

MCC IN AUSTRALIA

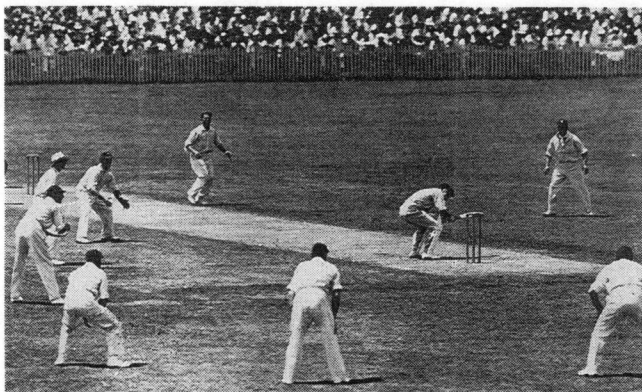

'Gubby' Allen, who refused to bowl to Bodyline fields, rushes to assist Bert Oldfield after Oldfield was struck on the head in Adelaide. Oldfield missed the rest of the Test through a skull fracture.

Bodyline was dependent on these field placings, with batsmen unable to defend themselves against deliveries aimed at their torsoes, with only one man on the offside and the rest waiting for deflections on the legside.

The front page of *Smith's Weekly* demonstrates Australian anger over Jardine's tactics.

runs in five Tests at an average of 139.14, including 232 in the Fifth Test, but in a few moments on a drying pitch at The Oval, near the end of the tour, George Duckworth noticed Bradman flinch against Larwood's rearing deliveries. Duckworth reported this to Jardine, who then devised Bodyline and used it to win the rubber in Australia four–one. Close friendships were broken, charges of poor sportsmanship abounded, and the series ended with the entire Australian team refusing to go to the wharf to see England off. Unfortunately, Australia's anger over Jardine's tactics overshadowed Larwood's magnificent bowling and England's tie against Victoria in her 21st tour match, the first by an overseas team in Australia.

The Bodyline debate reached its bitter peak during the Third Test in Adelaide, when the Australian Board of Control sent a clumsily worded cable to the MCC at Lord's accusing Jardine's team of unsportsmanlike behaviour. England's manager, Pelham Warner, who we now know despised Jardine but did not challenge his tactics, was summoned to meetings with diplomats. The Australian Prime Minister became involved at a time when Australia was seeking a renewal of loans from England to continue its emergence from the Depression. Finally, the Australian Board retracted its accusations about England's sportsmanship, but it took a major peace-making effort by Woodfull and his players in the rubber that followed to patch up the damage Jardine had done.

Larwood, the villain of the Bodyline series, was so moved by the warmth of his SCG reception when he was unluckily out for 98 in the Fifth Test, he migrated to Australia. His decision was hastened by the hostile welcome home he received in England from people who accused Australians of squealing.

ENGLAND IN AUSTRALIA 1936-37

Matches	First-class Results Won	Lost	Drawn	Tied	Matches	All Matches Won	Lost	Drawn	Tied
17	5	5	7	–	25	7	5	13	–

Date	Venue	Opponent	Results for Touring Team
Oct 16	Perth	Western Australia	Won by an inns & 180 runs
Oct 22	Perth	Combined XI	Drawn
Oct 28	Clare	*Clare Country XI	Won by 9 wkts
Oct 30	Adelaide	South Australia	Won by 105 runs
Nov 6	Melbourne	Victoria	Drawn
Nov 13	Sydney	New South Wales	Lost by 135 runs
Nov 20	Sydney	Australian XI	Drawn
Nov 27	Brisbane	Queensland	Drawn
Dec 4	Brisbane	AUSTRALIA (1st Test)	Won by 322 runs
Dec 12	Ipswich	*Queensland Country XI	Drawn
Dec 18	Sydney	AUSTRALIA (2nd Test)	Won by an inns & 22 runs
Dec 26	Newcastle	*New South Wales Country XI	Drawn
Jan 1	Melbourne	AUSTRALIA (3rd Test)	Lost by 365 runs
Jan 9	Launceston	Tasmania	Won by an inns & 4 runs
Jan 12	Launceston	*Tasmania	Drawn
Jan 15	Hobart (TCA)	Combined XI	Drawn
Jan 22	Adelaide	South Australia	Drawn
Jan 29	Adelaide	AUSTRALIA (4th Test)	Lost by 148 runs
Feb 6	Geelong	*Victorian Country XI	Drawn
Feb 10	Canberra	*Southern New South Wales	Won by an inns & 140 runs
Feb 13	Sydney	New South Wales	Lost by 105 runs
Feb 19	Melbourne	Victoria	Drawn
Feb 26	Melbourne	AUSTRALIA (5th Test)	Lost by an inns & 200 runs
Mar 5	Benalla	*Victorian Country XII	Drawn
Mar 8	Sydney	*Combined Universities	Drawn

The twenty-third England team to Australia in 1936–37, which accomplished a peace-making mission but lost The Ashes: *back row* W. Ferguson (scorer), L.B. Fishlock, T.S. Worthington, A.E. Fagg, J. Hardstaff, R. Howard (manager); *centre* T.H. Wade, H. Verity, C.J.B. Barnett, K. Farnes, W.H. Copson, J.M. Sims, W. Voce; *front* L.E.G. Ames, W.R. Hammond, R.W.V. Robins, G.O. Allen (capt.), R.E.S. Wyatt, M. Leyland, G. Duckworth.

Player	M	Inn	NO	Runs	HS	50	100	Avrge	Ct/St	Overs	Mdns	Runs	Wkts	Avrge	5wi	10wm	Best
Allen, GOB (Capt)	12	18	3	380	68	5	–	25.33	12	246.7	20	997	38	26.24	2	–	6/53
Ames, LEG	12	20	–	682	109	4	1	34.10	23/3	2.0	–	14	1	14.00	–	–	1/1
Barnett, CJ	15	25	–	1375	259	5	5	55.00	6	10.0	1	24	2	12.00	–	–	1/3
Copson, WH	6	8	5	34	10*	–	–	11.33	3	131.7	15	467	20	23.35	–	–	4/32
Duckworth, G	5	5	2	31	15*	–	–	10.33	10/2	–	–	–	–	–	–	–	–
Fagg, A	10	17	1	399	112	1	1	24.93	7	–	–	–	–	–	–	–	–
Farnes, K	10	13	5	20	8*	–	–	2.50	6	230.7	26	845	41	20.61	1	–	6/96
Fishlock, LB	10	17	2	318	91	1	–	21.20	6	–	–	–	–	–	–	–	–
Hammond, WR	12	20	2	1205	231*	4	5	66.94	9	164.3	17	516	21	24.57	2	–	5/39
Hardstaff, J jr	16	28	3	850	110	6	1	34.00	5	2.0	–	23	–	–	–	–	–
Leyland, M	12	22	4	902	126	4	3	50.11	3	23.3	–	119	2	59.50	–	–	1/1
Robins, RWV	12	16	–	297	61	2	–	18.56	4	154.3	8	638	16	39.87	–	–	4/63
Sims, JM	10	12	1	86	18*	–	–	7.82	10	229.1	12	945	38	24.87	2	–	5/37
Verity, H	11	20	2	164	31	–	–	9.11	10	361.2	94	861	28	30.75	1	–	5/50
Voce, W	12	18	7	74	16*	–	–	6.72	5	292.5	28	1052	35	30.06	1	1	6/41
Wade, TH	2	3	–	10	10	–	–	3.33	–/1	–	–	–	–	–	–	–	–
Worthington, TS	11	20	1	409	89	2	–	21.52	9	79.0	7	333	4	83.25	–	–	1/8
Wyatt, RES	9	13	1	409	106	2	1	34.08	3	9.0	–	71	1	71.00	–	–	1/40

After a short visit from an England team led by Errol Holmes on their way to New Zealand in 1935–36, 'Gubby' Allen captained a team charged with restoring amicable relations with Australia. This was a major task, which Allen, the one bowler who had refused to bowl to Jardine's packed legside fields on the Bodyline tour, accomplished with a mixture of entertaining cricket, charm, and a strict adherence to good fellowship. Bradman had taken over from Woodfull as Australia's captain and in his initial Test found Australia caught on another Brisbane 'sticky' wicket. Jack Fingleton hit his fourth successive Test century in Australia's first innings but on a gluepot in the second innings was one of four Australian ducks in a total of 58. England went to a two–nil lead by winning the Second Test in Sydney, thanks to Hammond's 231 and a thunderstorm that brought Australia's dismissal for 80 runs, with Badcock absent ill.

This was the innings in which the immortal Bill O'Reilly topscored for Australia with 37 not out, hitting sixes he never let anyone forget.

Both sides were caught on another 'sticky' in the Third Test at Melbourne, but Bradman won the match by sending in tail-enders while the pitch dried. 'Chuck' Fleetwood-Smith could not believe it when he was instructed to open Australia's second innings. 'You can't hit the ball on a normal pitch, so there is no way you can make contact on that monster,' said Bradman, who went to the crease when Australia were 5 for 97 and proceeded to make 270, sharing a 346-run partnership with Fingleton (136) who went in at No. 6 instead of opening. Australia won an absorbing Test—which attracted a record 350,534 spectators—by 365 runs, levelled the series in Adelaide when Fleetwood-Smith disposed of danger-man Hammond, and went on to retain The Ashes which Woodfull's men had regained in England in 1934, by overwhelming England in the Fifth Test. After two successive ducks, Bradman made 810 runs in the rubber at an average of 90.00. A total of 943,513 people watched Australia's recovery. Allen's team did the job of peace-making but won only five of their 17 first-class matches, losing five, with seven drawn.

Bradman led this team in December 1936 in his first Test as Australian captain: *back row* A.G. Chipperfield, E.L. McCormick, M.W. Sievers, W.J. O'Reilly, F.A. Ward; *front* R.H. Robinson, L.P.J. O'Brien, S.J. McCabe, D.G. Bradman, J.H. Fingleton, W.A. Oldfield. O'Brien withdrew and was replaced by Cyril Badcock. Caught on a sticky wicket, Australia were dismissed for 58, losing by 322 runs.

HOME AND AWAY

The first Indian team to go overseas, the Parsees, who visited England in 1886, won 19 of their 28 matches. The *London Graphic* commented: 'After the drubbing from our Australian cousins next we will be knocked into a cricketing cocked hat by descendants of the Fireworshippers of Persia.' *Marylebone Cricket Club*

CHAPTER TEN

ASIA AWAKES

Cricket began in India among the traders and sailors in port, and later English garrison soldiers on the flat areas of the vast, triangular sub-continent below the Himalayas amused themselves by playing cricket. The first recorded match was on a beach in western India in 1721 when a sailor named Downing wrote that he and his fellow crewmen from a boat lying off the Gulf of Cambay 'diverted ourselves' playing cricket.

British adventurers introduced pastimes from their homeland, mostly ill-suited to the prevailing heat, soon after they seized power and ran up the Union Jack. Polo, soccer, squash racquets and boxing were novelties, but the sports that took hold with Indians were cricket and field hockey. Squash was for the members of exclusive clubs in the larger cities but cricket and hockey could be played on the open fields. The Calcutta Cricket Club, founded in 1792, is the second oldest cricket club in the world, and only five years younger than England's MCC, which did not move to Lord's until 1814. For this reason most of India's early cricket history centres around Calcutta. Today Eden Gardens in that city is one of the world's major Test venues, although Calcutta does not match other big Indian cities in supplying Test cricketers.

The Australian Board of Control was too busy, fighting for survival against players who preferred entrepreneurs to sponsor overseas tours, to be concerned with Indian cricket until after World War II. They heard about Sir Stanley Jackson's favourable reactions while he was Governor of Bengal, and of Lord Hawke's and Lord Harris's excitement at the rapid advance of Indian cricket. Matches between Indian cities like Poona and Bombay and even the tour of England by the Parsees in 1886 were only briefly reported.

The adoption of cricket by wealthy Indian princes,

In 1880, two years after Test cricket began in Australia, this Bombay XI met Poona in Bombay, players wearing pill-box hats.

the first tour of England by an All-Indian team in 1932, and the introduction of the Ranji Trophy, a competition for all Indian states, in 1934, failed to impress Australian administrators brought up under the White Australia policy. They admired the talents of Prince Ranjitsinhji when Joe Darling approved his selection to play for England against Australia in 1896 and later delighted in his exquisite timing and daring strokeplay when he toured Australia with Stoddart's team in 1897–98. Kumar Sri Duleepsinhji on the 1929–30 England tour of Australia and the Nawab of Pataudi, the only Indian to play Tests for both India and England, were similarly admired.

Australia's sometimes lofty view of Indian cricket certainly receives a jolt when charismatic Indian cricketers like Gavaskar, Chandrasekar, Bedi, Shastri,

Mankad, Merchant and Azharuddin frustrate Australia's Test teams. The special flair Ranjitsinhji, Duleepsinhji, and the Nawab of Pataudi brought to the game, and carried on by Sachin Tendulkar, Vinod Kambli and Anil Kumble when India outplayed England in 1993 deserves support. India, in fact, offers cricket a rich crop of talent that is exciting to watch, occasionally producing artists like Gundappa Viswanath, whose stroke play remains etched in the memory. Vishy, as he was known, was an all-India hero, with media coverage of his exploits reaching unprecedented peaks. He was humble, genial, sportsmanlike and his wristy strokes gave pleasure to millions in much the same manner that Trumper charmed all who watched him.

The all-Indian team photographed in England in 1932: *back row* Lall Singh, P.E. Palia, Jahangir Khan, Mohomed Nizar, Amar Singh, B.E. Kapadia, S.R. Godamba, Ghulam Mahomed, J.G. Navle; *centre* Syed Wazir Ali, C.K. Nayudu, S. Nazir Ali, Joginder Singh, K.S.G. of Limbdi, H.H. the Maharajah R.S. Porbander; *front* Nacomel Jecomel, S.H.M. Colah, N.D. Marshall. Jahangir Khan was Imran Khan's father.

INDIA IN AUSTRALIA 1947–48

	First-class Results					All Matches			
Matches	Won	Lost	Drawn	Tied	Matches	Won	Lost	Drawn	Tied
14	2	7	5	–	20	5	7	8	–

Date	Venue	Opponent	Results for Touring Team
Oct 17	Perth	Western Australia	Drawn
Oct 24	Adelaide	South Australia	Drawn
Oct 30	Melbourne	Victoria	Drawn
Nov 7	Sydney	New South Wales	Lost by an inns & 48 runs
Nov 14	Sydney	Australian XI	Won by 47 runs
Nov 21	Brisbane	Queensland	Lost by 24 runs
Nov 28	Brisbane	AUSTRALIA (1st Test)	Lost by an inns & 226 runs
Dec 6	Warwick	*Queensland Country XI	Drawn
Dec 12	Sydney	AUSTRALIA (2nd Test)	Drawn
Dec 20	Bathurst	*Western District of NSW	Won by 104 runs
Dec 27	Canberra	*Southern District of NSW	Drawn
Jan 1	Melbourne	AUSTRALIA (3rd Test)	Lost by 233 runs
Jan 10	Hobart (TCA)	Tasmania	Won by an inns & 139 runs
Jan 15	Launceston	Tasmania	Drawn
Jan 20	Mount Gambier	*South Australian Country XI	Won by an inns & 106 runs
Jan 23	Adelaide	AUSTRALIA (4th Test)	Lost by an inns & 16 runs
Jan 31	Mildura	*Victorian Country XI	Won by an inns & 24 runs
Feb 6	Melbourne	AUSTRALIA (5th Test)	Lost by an inns & 177 runs
Feb 14	Geelong	*Victorian Country XI	Drawn
Feb 20	Perth	Western Australia	Lost by 6 runs

The 1947–48 Indian team in Australia, with the captain Lala Amarnath seated in the middle of the centre row. Vinoo Mankad, who twice sent back Billy Brown for backing up too far at the bowler's end and gave his name to this form of dismissal, is on the left in the front row. *Sports Star, Madras*

Player	M	Inn	NO	Runs	HS	50	100	Avrge	Ct/St	Overs	Mdns	Runs	Wkts	Avrge	5wi	10wm	Best
Adhikari, HR	13	23	2	450	65	1	–	21.42	4	1.0	–	4	–	–	–	–
Amarnath, L (Capt)	14	23	3	1162	228*	1	5	58.10	3	276.5	38	853	30	28.43	–	–	4/78
Elahi, A	7	11	–	137	46	–	–	12.45	1	119.5	9	527	8	65.88	–	–	3/175
Hazare, VS	13	23	1	1056	145	4	4	48.00	9	198.7	16	819	13	63.00	–	–	4/29
Irani, JK	7	12	3	94	43	–	–	10.44	12/2	–	–	–	–	–	–	–	–
Kishenchand, G	12	20	3	418	75*	2	–	24.58	4	3.0	–	7	–	–	–	–	–
Mahomad, G	11	21	1	387	85	2	–	19.35	2	13.0	–	57	1	57.00	–	–	1/25

Player	M	Inn	NO	Runs	HS	50	100	Avrge	Ct/St	Overs	Mdns	Runs	Wkts	Avrge	5wi	10wm	Best
Mankad, MH	13	24	1	889	116*	5	3	38.65	11	494.5	79	1595	61	26.15	4	1	8/84
Nayudu, CS	9	16	4	198	58	1	–	16.50	3	72.0	2	394	1	394.00	–	–	1/30
Phadkar, DG	8	13	3	417	123	3	1	41.70	2	128.2	11	524	16	32.75	–	–	4/59
Rangachari, CR	7	10	6	8	4*	–	–	2.00	4	152.0	15	582	20	29.10	1	–	6/45
Rangnekar, KM	9	16	–	173	43	–	–	10.81	6	–	–	–	–	–	–	–	–
Ranvirsinhji, MS	2	3	–	37	27	–	–	12.33	1	–	–	–	–	–	–	–	–
Sarwate, CT	12	21	–	444	128	1	1	21.14	5	189.2	11	782	18	43.44	–	–	4/55
Sen, P	7	11	2	81	38	–	–	9.00	11/3	–	–	–	–	–	–	–	–
Singh, R	4	7	–	52	24	–	–	7.42	–	–	–	–	–	–	–	–	–
Sohoni, SW	6	10	2	97	31	–	–	12.12	3	94.0	9	380	8	47.50	–	–	4/89

Indian captain Lala Amarnath, who scored his country's first Test century, declined Australia's suggestion to cover pitches for the first India v. Australia Tests in Australia. This decision severely handicapped a touring team already weakened by the withdrawal of fine players like Fazal Mahmood, Amir Elahi, Vijay Merchant and Rusi Modi, following the partition of India two months before they arrived. Their country was in turmoil, free at last from British rule, but with Hindus and Muslims slaughtering each other with mindless ferocity. The half-strength Indian team arrived to take on one of the finest teams of all time led by the greatest run-scorer the game has known.

Bradman won the toss in four of the five Tests and in two of them India had the worst of batting conditions. Heavy rain saturated the 'Gabba pitch in the First Test after Bradman had scored 185 in his initial Test against India and Australia had made 8 declared for 382. Two days later Ernie Toshack took 5 for 2 in 19 balls on an unplayable sticky wicket. India followed on and Toshack took 6 for 29, tumbling India out for 98 to give Australia victory by an innings and 226 runs. The Second Test was drawn because of rain in Sydney after Mankad ran out non-striker Bill Brown for illegally backing-up. Bradman made a century in each innings (132 and 127 not out) of the Third Test at Melbourne, which Australia won by 233 runs, despite Mankad's 116. The humiliation continued in the Fourth Test at Adelaide, with Bradman's 201, and 198 not out from Hassett and 112 from Barnes taking Australia to 674, enough to clinch victory by an innings and 16 runs, Lindwall taking 7 for 38 in the final innings. Australia took the series four–nil by winning the Fifth Test at Melbourne by an innings and 177 runs, Harvey scoring 153, and Australia's bowling taking the last 16 wickets for 147 runs.

The Indians were not as weak as the results suggested. They beat a strong Australian XI by 47 runs in Sydney when Bradman scored his 100th first-class century. Amarnath hit 144 against South Australia, 228 not out against Victoria, 172 against Queensland, 171 against Tasmania, but only 140 of his 1162 tour runs came in Tests.

INDIA IN AUSTRALIA 1967–68

Matches	First-class Results				Matches	All Matches			
	Won	Lost	Drawn	Tied		Won	Lost	Drawn	Tied
9	–	6	3	–	15	4	6	5	–

Date	Venue	Opponent	Results for Touring Team
Nov 22	Harvey	*Western Australian Country XI	Drawn
Nov 25	Perth	Western Australia	Lost by an inns & 20 runs
Dec 1	Adelaide	South Australia	Lost by an inns & 67 runs
Dec 6	Mount Gambier	*South Australian Country XI	Won by 96 runs
Dec 8	Melbourne	Victoria	Drawn
Dec 13	Yallourn	*Victorian Country XI	Won by 2 wkts
Dec 15	Hobart (TCA)	Tasmania	Drawn
Dec 19	Launceston	*Tasmania	Drawn
Dec 23	Adelaide	AUSTRALIA (1st Test)	Lost by 146 runs
Dec 30	Melbourne	AUSTRALIA (2nd Test)	Lost by an inns & 4 runs
Jan 6	Sydney	New South Wales	Drawn
Jan 17	Murgon	*Queensland Country XI	Abandoned
Jan 19	Brisbane	AUSTRALIA (3rd Test)	Lost by 39 runs
Jan 26	Sydney	AUSTRALIA (4th Test)	Lost by 144 runs
Feb 1	Canberra	*Southern NSW Country XI	Won by 5 wkts
Feb 2	Newcastle	*Northern NSW Country XI	Won by 2 wkts

India's first visit to Australia in 20 years started badly when their captain, the Nawab of Pataudi, pulled a hamstring muscle while fielding in the first match. He could not play again until the Second Test when he erred in deciding to bat on a green pitch. The one-eyed Pataudi (he had lost an eye in a car crash) went to the crease with his team on 5 for 25, still hampered by his leg injury. *Wisden* said he 'combined batting genius with courage that warmed the hearts of all'. He had to refuse many singles but managed 75 out of 173 in the first innings and 85 out of 352 in the second. Australia, having already won the First Test in Adelaide by 146 runs, won the Second Test by an innings and four runs.

Pataudi's pluck encouraged his team, whose morale was further boosted when Motganhalli Jaisimha, flown in after Chandra returned home with a leg injury, hit 74 and 101 within a few days of his arrival. The margin

Player	M	Inn	NO	Runs	HS	50	100	Avrge	Ct/St	Overs	Mdns	Runs	Wkts	Avrge	5wi	10wm	Best
Abid Ali, S	8	14	–	447	81	3	–	31.93	6	125.0	13	478	11	43.45	1	–	6/55
Bedi, BS	4	7	2	23	8	–	–	4.60	3	124.0	22	354	7	50.77	–	–	3/73
Borde, CG	9	17	–	295	69	3	–	17.35	6	–	–	–	–	–	–	–	–
Chandrasekhar, BS	6	10	4	32	15	–	–	5.33	1	115.2	7	480	3	160.00	–	–	2/76
Desai, RB	3	5	2	62	17	–	–	20.66	1	49.0	2	221	–	–	–	–	–
Engineer, FM	9	14	–	457	128	1	1	32.64	10/8	–	–	–	–	–	–	–	–
Indrajitsinh, KS	2	3	1	68	47*	–	–	34.00	3/5	–	–	–	–	–	–	–	–
Jaisimha, ML	2	4	–	188	101	1	1	47.00	–	4.0	–	17	1	17.00	–	–	1/17

Continued

HOME AND AWAY

Player	M	Inn	NO	Runs	HS	50	100	Avrge	Ct/St	Overs	Mdns	Runs	Wkts	Avrge	5wi	10wm	Best
Kulkarni, U	6	10	3	24	7	–	–	3.42	–	88.0	6	365	5	73.00	–	–	–
Nadkarni, RG	8	16	3	235	46*	–	–	18.07	1	188.6	52	523	12	43.58	–	–	3/58
Nawab of Pataudi jr (C)	3	6	–	339	85	4	–	56.50	1	–	–	–	–	–	–	–	–
Prasanna, EAS	7	13	2	182	38	–	–	15.16	2	255.6	42	930	34	27.35	3	–	6/104
Sardesai, DN	7	14	–	195	54	1	–	13.22	2	–	–	–	–	–	–	–	–
Saxena, R	3	6	2	67	24	–	–	16.75	–	–	–	–	–	–	–	–	–
Subramanyam, V	5	10	2	184	75	1	–	23.00	3	17.0	–	110	1	110.00	–	–	1/34
Surti, RF	9	17	–	557	88	6	–	32.75	6	208.1	23	921	34	39.60	2	–	5/69
Wadekar, AL	9	18	–	493	107	1	1	27.38	9	–	–	–	–	–	–	–	–

between the teams narrowed, but without a fast bowler Pataudi's team could not contain the experienced Australian batting lineup and Australia won the Third Test by 39 runs at the 'Gabba and the Fourth by 144 runs in Sydney.

India's improvement came too late to save them from a four-nil drubbing by Australia, but gave them their first win outside India when they beat New Zealand in Dunedin by five wickets, despite Dowling's 143. New Zealand won the Second Test at Christchurch by six wickets, thanks to Graham Dowling's 239, but India retaliated to win the Third Test in Wellington by eight because of Ajit Wadekar's 143. Rusi Surti, who made a valuable allround contribution to India's tour with 967 runs and 34 wickets, later played for Queensland.

The 1967-68 Indian team in Australia: *back row* A.N. Ghose (assistant manager), Ghulam Ahmed (manager), V. Subramanyam, Ajit Wadekar, B. Bedi, R. Sasena, Umesh Kulkarni, K. Indrajitsinhji, Abid Ali; *front* Bhagwat Chandrasekar, Erapally Prasanna, S. Dardesia, C. Borde, Nawab of Pataudi (capt.), Bapu Nadkarni, R. Desai, R. Surti, F. Engineer. *Sports Star, Madras*

INDIA IN AUSTRALIA 1977-78

	First-class Results					All Matches			
Matches	Won	Lost	Drawn	Tied	Matches	Won	Lost	Drawn	Tied
11	6	5	–	–	20	12	6	2	–

Date	Venue	Opponent	Results for Touring Team
Nov 2	Port Lincoln	*South Australian Country XI	Won by 192 runs
Nov 4	Adelaide	South Australia	Won by 6 wkts
Nov 9	Hastings	*Victorian Country XI	Won by 5 wkts
Nov 11	Melbourne	Victoria	Won by 6 wkts
Nov 16	Griffith	*South West New South Wales	Won by 7 wkts
Nov 18	Sydney	New South Wales	Won by 6 wkts
Nov 23	Nambour	*Queensland Country XI	Won by 128 runs
Nov 25	Brisbane	Queensland	Won by an inns & 123 runs
Dec 2	Brisbane	AUSTRALIA (1st Test)	Lost by 16 runs
Dec 9	Perth	Western Australia	Lost by 150 runs
Dec 14	Wongan Hills	*Western Australian Country XI	Won by 1 run
Dec 16	Perth	AUSTRALIA (2nd Test)	Lost by 2 wkts
Dec 23	Launceston	*Tasmania	Lost by 3 runs
Dec 24	Hobart (TCA)	Tasmania	Lost by 84 runs
Dec 30	Melbourne	AUSTRALIA (3rd Test)	Won by 222 runs
Jan 7	Sydney	AUSTRALIA (4th Test)	Won by an inns & 2 runs
Jan 14	Newcastle	*Northern New South Wales	Won by 9 wkts
Jan 18	Canberra	*ACT & District	Drawn
Jan 21	Geelong	*Geelong & District	Drawn
Jan 28	Adelaide	AUSTRALIA (5th Test)	Lost by 47 runs

Bishen Bedi, who had shown so much promise bowling in tandem with Prasanna on the previous tour, returned ten years later as captain of a team that faced very special challenges. The Indians arrived with world cricket in turmoil over the decision of 56 outstanding players (later increased to 66) to join media tycoon Kerry Packer and play matches outside the control of traditional administrations. The Indians' matches against Australia needed to produce exciting cricket to maintain faith in the establishment.

Bedi was a member of the Sikh religion, people who, according to Mihir Bose, are made fun of in India by other religions who allege that the Sikhs' habit of gathering the hair to the top of their heads softens their brains. Bedi certainly joked a lot about his cricket but Australians soon realised that beneath his knot of hair was a shrewd cricket brain. His team lacked firepower, just as Australia's official team did without the Packer rebels, but he and Bob Simpson, who made a remarkable

Player	M	Inn	NO	Runs	HS	50	100	Avrge	Ct/St	Overs	Mdns	Runs	Wkts	Avrge	5wi	10wm	Best
Amarnath, S	2	3	–	83	63	1	–	27.66	–	–	–	–	–	–	–	–	–
Amarnath, MB	9	16	1	731	137	3	2	48.73	12	109.0	19	321	11	29.18	–	–	2/12
Bedi, BS	8	11	7	69	26*	–	–	17.25	5	323.7	56	1012	54	18.74	7	2	5/19
Chandrasekhar, BS	10	13	3	12	8	–	–	1.20	6	354.5	49	1221	49	24.91	4	1	6/52
Chauhan, CPS	9	16	–	577	157	1	1	36.06	7	4.0	2	19	–	–	–	–	–
Gaekwad, AD	1	2	–	39	27	–	–	19.50	–	5.0	–	37	–	–	–	–	–
Gavaskar, SM (Capt)	8	14	–	537	127	1	3	38.35	8	3.0	–	14	–	–	–	–	–
Ghavri, KD	7	10	1	162	64	1	–	18.00	7	172.4	22	692	27	25.62	1	1	7/49
Kirmani, SMH	8	12	2	411	59*	3	–	41.10	13/5	–	–	–	–	–	–	–	–
Madan Lal, S	7	12	2	263	88	1	–	26.30	6	142.7	21	487	18	27.05	1	–	5/72
Mankad, AV	8	14	4	508	92	4	–	50.80	7	1.0	–	8	–	–	–	–	–
Patel, BP	7	13	1	319	68	3	–	26.58	6	–	–	–	–	–	–	–	–

Player	M	Inn	NO	Runs	HS	50	100	Avrge	Ct/St	Overs	Mdns	Runs	Wkts	Avrge	5wi	10wm	Best
Prasanna, EAS	9	14	5	122	25*	–	–	13.55	2	261.3	50	711	24	29.62	–	–	4/51
Reddy, BR	3	5	–	28	15	–	–	5.60	9/1	–	–	–	–	–	–	–	–
Vengsarkar, DB	10	18	–	589	78	4	–	32.72	10	–	–	–	–	–	–	–	–
Venkataraghavan, S	5	7	1	115	50	1	–	19.16	1	192.0	31	625	11	56.81	–	–	4/93
Viswanath, GR	10	18	–	655	89	6	–	36.38	9	–	–	–	–	–	–	–	–

return to big cricket after ten years in retirement, provided an appealing series that pulled large crowds. Bedi was assisted by a magnificent right-hand batsman in the Hassett mould, 163 cm (5 ft 4 in) Sunil Gavaskar, a splendid allrounder in Mohinder Amarnath, Lala's youngest son, and Chandra, a spinner of the highest quality.

Bhagwat Chandrasekhar bowled with a right-arm withered by polio that had just enough strength in it to propel a cricket ball the length of the pitch, but not enough to throw from any distance. He was labelled a leg-break bowler but he rarely bowled it. His stock delivery was a googly which skimmed along at around medium pace. His chances were limited because of the presence of Bedi, Prasanna and Venkat in the Indian side but on a fateful day in August 1971 he had bowled India to a series victory over England with 6 for 38 in England's second innings. His team-mates made hard work out of scoring the 174 needed after Chandra's coup but eventually managed it. That was the day India's supporters brought an elephant, by arrangement with Chessington Zoo, to the cricket, and India joined cricket's First Division.

With six players making their Test debuts, Simpson contrived to win the First Test at the 'Gabba by 16 runs. The Second Test was equally tense, Simpson following his 89 in Brisbane with 176, and his 100th Test catch. Australia had to score 338 in the final innings to win and they did it with two wickets left, after Tony Mann, sent in as a night-watchman, made 105. India recovered admirably to win the Third Test at Melbourne by 222 runs and the Fourth in Sydney by an innings and two runs. Chandra's fans did not have an elephant handy, but he won the Third Test by taking 6 for 52 in each innings. He also made a pair to become the first player in history to record a pair four times. Australia won the deciding Fifth Test in Adelaide by 47 runs after India made a thrilling fight of it by reaching 445 in the fourth innings, with 493 required to win.

India did not win the series but they had their first-ever Test victories in Australia, and by defeating strong states they ensured the Tests attracted higher gates than any of Packer's matches. The tour may have lost money, but nowhere near as much as the $4 million Packer was reported to have lost that summer.

INDIA IN AUSTRALIA 1980-81

First-class Results					All Matches				
Matches	Won	Lost	Drawn	Tied	Matches	Won	Lost	Drawn	Tied
8	2	2	4	–	25	8	11	6	–

Date	Venue	Opponent	Results for Touring Team
Nov 22	Perth	Western Australia	Drawn
Nov 25	Perth	*Western Australia	Won on run rate
Nov 27	Geraldton	*Western Australian Country XI	Lost by 6 wkts
Nov 29	Adelaide	South Australia	Lost by 43 runs
Dec 4	Whyalla	*South Australian Country XI	Won by 6 wkts
Dec 6	Melbourne	*Australia (L/O Intl)	Won by 66 runs
Dec 9	Perth	*New Zealand (L/O Intl)	Won by 5 runs
Dec 11	Hobart (TCA)	Tasmania	Drawn
Dec 14	Launceston	*Tasmania	Lost by 3 wkts
Dec 18	Sydney	*Australia (L/O Intl)	Lost by 9 wkts
Dec 21	Brisbane	*New Zealand (L/O Intl)	Lost by 3 wkts
Dec 23	Adelaide	*New Zealand (L/O Intl)	Won by 6 runs
Dec 26	Brisbane	Queensland	Drawn
Jan 2	Sydney	AUSTRALIA (1st Test)	Lost by an inns & 4 runs
Jan 8	Sydney	*Australia (L/O Intl)	Lost by 9 wkts
Jan 10	Melbourne	*New Zealand (L/O Intl)	Lost by 10 wkts
Jan 11	Melbourne	*Australia (L/O Intl)	Lost by 7 wkts
Jan 12	Canberra	*Australian Capital Territory	Drawn
Jan 15	Sydney	*Australia (L/O Intl)	Lost by 27 runs
Jan 18	Brisbane	*New Zealand (L/O Intl)	Lost by 22 runs
Jan 20	Portland	*Victorian Country XI	Won by 64 runs
Jan 23	Adelaide	AUSTRALIA (2nd Test)	Drawn
Jan 30	Geelong	Victoria	Won by 10 wkts
Feb 4	Ballarat	*Victorian Country XI	Drawn
Feb 7	Melbourne	AUSTRALIA (3rd Test)	Won by 59 runs

Player	M	Inn	NO	Runs	HS	50	100	Avrge	Ct/St	Overs	Mdns	Runs	Wkts	Avrge	5wi	10wm	Best
Binny, RMH	5	8	–	91	51	1	–	11.37	1	128.0	19	391	10	39.10	–	–	3/50
Chauhan, CPS	7	13	–	523	97	4	–	40.23	4	32.4	7	69	3	23.00	–	–	3/51
Doshi, DR	6	8	5	29	13*	–	–	9.66	4	332.2	71	802	20	40.10	–	–	4/60
Gavaskar, SM (Capt)	7	13	1	625	157	3	2	52.08	8	–	–	–	–	–	–	–	–
Ghavri, KD	6	9	2	111	51	1	–	15.85	1	161.4	33	522	18	29.00	1	–	5/107
Kapil Dev	6	9	–	112	39	–	–	12.44	5	197.1	38	571	22	25.95	2	–	5/28
Kirmani, SMH	4	6	1	124	43*	–	–	24.80	7/3	–	–	–	–	–	–	–	–
Kirti Azad	4	6	–	157	59	1	–	26.16	2	90.0	22	209	6	34.83	–	–	3/53
Patil, SM	5	10	1	586	174	3	2	65.11	4	39.3	13	94	2	47.00	–	–	2/28
Reddy, B	4	5	1	31	16	–	–	7.75	10/3	–	–	–	–	–	–	–	–
Srinivasan, TE	4	8	2	203	69*	1	–	33.83	2	–	–	–	–	–	–	–	–
Vengsarkar, DB	7	13	1	450	153	2	1	37.50	6	–	–	–	–	–	–	–	–
Viswanath, GR	7	12	–	363	114	1	1	30.25	5	–	–	–	–	–	–	–	–
Yadav, NS	6	7	4	66	20*	–	–	22.00	4	257.4	50	689	18	38.27	–	–	4/143
Yashpal Sharma	6	11	3	378	201*	–	1	47.25	3	11.0	3	21	1	21.00	–	–	1/15
Yograj Singh	4	4	1	38	17	–	–	12.66	3	118.5	32	355	9	39.44	–	–	4/72

Gavaskar returned to Australia for a three-Test series as captain of an experienced side, established as the most successful opener in history. Only Bradman had a better success rate than his 30 centuries in 50 Tests. India had beaten Australia in their previous series in India and with Kapil Dev providing strong support for the spinners, looked an outfit that could challenge any team if they retained the elusive will to win.

Australia outplayed Gavaskar's men for almost all of their three-month tour. The batsmen struggled against the pace of Lillee, Pascoe and Hogg, and the bowlers were unable to prevent heavy scoring by Australia's leading players. Australia won the First Test at Brisbane by an innings and four runs, thanks to Greg Chappell's 204. India were lucky to escape defeat in the Second Test at Adelaide where Hughes made 213, Graeme Wood 125. The Third Test appeared a certain Australian triumph when they needed only 143 to win in the last innings but Dev (5 for 28), Doshi, and Ghavri bowled out Australia for 83, giving India a 59-run win that levelled the rubber.

The previous day India had gone close to forfeiting the series when Gavaskar thought he had edged a ball from Lillee on to his pad and he was given out lbw. Petulantly he ordered his partner Chetan Chauhan to accompany him back to the pavilion. Fortunately, manager S.K. Durrani met them at the gate and ordered Chauhan back. *Indian Cricket* magazine said: 'Honours were even in the end but no pragmatic analysis can escape the conclusion that India got away with a trick, Houdini-style.'

INDIA IN AUSTRALIA 1985-86

First-class Results					All Matches				
Matches	Won	Lost	Drawn	Tied	Matches	Won	Lost	Drawn	Tied
5	1	–	4	–	19	8	7	4	–

Date	Venue	Opponent	Results for Touring Team
Nov 27	Canberra	*Australian Capital Territory	Abandoned
Nov 29	Adelaide	South Australia	Won by 4 wkts
Dec 4	Warrnambool	*Victorian Country XI	Won by 4 wkts
Dec 6	Melbourne	Victoria	Drawn
Dec 13	Adelaide	AUSTRALIA (1st Test)	Drawn
Dec 20	Hobart (TCA)	*Tasmania	Abandoned
Dec 26	Melbourne	AUSTRALIA (2nd Test)	Drawn
Jan 2	Sydney	AUSTRALIA (3rd Test)	Drawn
Jan 11	Brisbane	*New Zealand (L/O Intl)	Won by 5 wkts
Jan 12	Brisbane	*Australia (L/O Intl)	Lost by 4 wkts
Jan 16	Melbourne	*Australia (L/O Intl)	Won by 8 wkts
Jan 18	Perth	*New Zealand (L/O Intl)	Lost by 3 wkts
Jan 21	Sydney	*Australia (L/O Intl)	Lost by 100 runs
Jan 23	Melbourne	*New Zealand (L/O Intl)	Lost by 5 wkts
Jan 25	Adelaide	*New Zealand (L/O Intl)	Won by 5 wkts
Jan 26	Adelaide	*Australia (L/O Intl)	Lost by 36 runs
Jan 28	Adelaide	*Australian Country XI	Won by 5 wkts
Jan 31	Melbourne	*Australia (L/O Intl)	Won by 6 wkts
Feb 2	Launceston	*New Zealand (L/O Intl)	Won on run rate
Feb 5	Sydney	*Australia (L/O Intl)	Lost by 11 runs
Feb 9	Melbourne	*Australia (L/O Intl)	Lost by 7 wkts

Player	M	Inn	NO	Runs	HS	50	100	Avrge	Ct/St	Overs	Mdns	Runs	Wkts	Avrge	5wi	10wm	Best
Amarnath, MB	5	7	2	297	138	–	1	59.40	1	16.0	4	37	–	–	–	–	–
Azharuddin, M	5	6	1	245	77	2	–	49.00	4	–	–	–	–	–	–	–	–
Binny, RMH	3	3	–	82	44	–	–	27.33	–	39.0	14	91	2	45.50	–	–	1/24
Chetan Sharma	3	3	1	148	67	2	–	74.00	6	72.0	9	257	5	51.40	–	–	4/55
Gavaskar, SM	4	5	1	360	172	–	2	90.00	3	–	–	–	–	–	–	–	–
Ghai, RS	1	1	1	0	0*	–	–	–	1	13.0	3	40	1	40.00	–	–	1/40
Kapil Dev (Capt)	4	5	–	223	88	2	–	44.60	6	153.0	42	356	18	19.77	1	–	8/106
Kirmani, SMH	4	4	–	69	35	–	–	17.25	8/2	–	–	–	–	–	–	–	–
Kulkarni, RR	1	–	–	–	–	–	–	–	–	11.0	1	27	–	–	–	–	–
Malhotra, AO	1	2	–	79	67	1	–	39.50	1	–	–	–	–	–	–	–	–
More, KS	1	1	1	35	35*	–	–	–	1/1	–	–	–	–	–	–	–	–
Shastri, RJ	4	3	–	92	49	–	–	30.66	1	258.0	85	495	14	35.35	–	–	4/87
Sivaramakrishnan, L	4	2	–	19	15	–	–	9.50	8	120.4	12	427	11	38.81	–	–	3/75
Srikkanth, K	5	7	–	342	116	2	1	48.85	5	–	–	–	–	–	–	–	–
Vengsarkar, DB	5	7	2	187	75	1	–	37.40	2	–	–	–	–	–	–	–	–
Yadav, NS	5	4	2	67	41	–	–	33.50	1	245.1	85	478	19	25.15	1	–	5/99

Gavaskar relinquished the captaincy to concentrate on a batting slump, allowing Kapil Dev to bring India on another short series against a seriously weakened Australian XI. India remained undefeated but failed to win a Test, their five first-class matches producing only one win—against South Australia—the only match not upset by rain.

Gavaskar scored his 31st Test century in the drawn First Test at Adelaide after retiring to have a forearm injury treated. India should have won the Second Test in Melbourne, which was drawn, but Dev made a tactical blunder in not attacking Border (163) in a 64-run last wicket stand with Dave Gilbert. Rain and the Indians' lack of urgency allowed Australia to escape. The Third Test was also drawn, despite an Indian run feast that saw them declared at 4 for 600 in their first innings. Gavaskar made 172, Srikkanth 116, Amarnath 138 on a Sydney pitch that had never previously produced an Indian century. Australia scored 396 and followed on. At 6 for 119, with seven overs left, they appeared in danger but Bright and Ritchie held out.

Gavaskar had his most successful visit to Australia, scoring 352 runs in the Tests at 117.33. But for India the lack of bowling support for Dev was fully exposed. The gap created by the retirement of Bedi, Prasanna, Chandra and Doshi had still to be filled. For Australia, Boon's two centuries (123 and 131) were the main salvation.

The Tamil Nadu team which won the Ranji trophy—Indian equivalent of the Sheffield Shield—in 1988 visited Perth in November that year for one match against Western Australia. Despite the presence of great names like Chandra and Venkat they lost by an innings and 51 runs. Marsh (209) and Veletta (166 not out) had an opening stand of 374 in 363 minutes for WA.

INDIA IN AUSTRALIA 1991–92

Matches	First-class Results Won	Lost	Drawn	Tied	Matches	All Matches Won	Lost	Drawn	Tied
7	1	5	1	–	29	7	19	2	1

Date	Venue	Opponent	Results for Touring Team
Nov 17	Caversham	*ACB Chairman's XI	Lost by 29 runs
Nov 18	Perth	*Western Australia	Lost by 9 wkts
Nov 21	Wagga Wagga	*New South Wales Country XI	Won by 8 wkts
Nov 23	Lismore	New South Wales	Lost by an inns & 8 runs
Nov 29	Brisbane	AUSTRALIA (1st Test)	Lost by 10 wkts
Dec 6	Perth	*West Indies (L/O Intl)	Tied
Dec 8	Perth	*Australia (L/O Intl)	Won by 107 runs
Dec 10	Hobart (Bel)	*Australia (L/O Intl)	Lost by 8 wkts
Dec 14	Adelaide	*West Indies (L/O Intl)	Won by 10 runs
Dec 15	Adelaide	*Australia (L/O Intl)	Lost by 6 wkts
Dec 17	Canberra	*Prime Minister's XI	Lost by 75 runs
Dec 20	Brisbane	Queensland	Won by 39 runs
Dec 26	Melbourne	AUSTRALIA (2nd Test)	Lost by 8 wkts
Jan 2	Sydney	AUSTRALIA (3rd Test)	Drawn
Jan 11	Brisbane	*West Indies (L/O Intl)	Lost by 6 wkts
Jan 14	Sydney	*Australia (L/O Intl)	Lost by 9 wkts
Jan 16	Melbourne	*West Indies (L/O Intl)	Won by 5 wkts
Jan 18	Melbourne	*Australia (L/O Intl)	Lost by 88 runs
Jan 20	Sydney	*Australia (L/O Intl)	Lost by 6 runs
Jan 25	Adelaide	AUSTRALIA (4th Test)	Lost by 38 runs
Feb 1	Perth	AUSTRALIA (5th Test)	Lost by 300 runs
Feb 9	Benalla	*Victoria	Lost by 33 runs
Feb 11	South Melbourne	*Australian Country XI	Lost on run rate
Feb 16	Adelaide	*AIS Cricket Academy	Won by 88 runs
Feb 22	Perth	*England (WC L/O Intl)	Lost by 9 runs
Feb 28	Mackay	*Sri Lanka (WC L/O Intl)	No result
Mar 1	Brisbane	*Australia (WC L/O Intl)	Lost by 1 run
Mar 4	Sydney	*Pakistan (WC L/O Intl)	Won by 43 runs
Mar 15	Adelaide	*South Africa (WC L/O Intl)	Lost by 6 wkts

Player	M	Inn	NO	Runs	HS	50	100	Avrge	Ct/St	Overs	Mdns	Runs	Wkts	Avrge	5wi	10wm	Best
Azharuddin, M (Capt)	7	13	1	340	106	1	1	28.33	6	–	–	–	–	–	–	–	–
Banerjee, ST	3	4	2	15	12	–	–	7.50	2	71.0	10	288	8	36.00	–	–	3/47
Ganguly, S	2	3	–	57	29	–	–	19.00	1	10.0	–	48	–	–	–	–	–
Hirwani, ND	2	2	1	6	6*	–	–	6.00	2	65.0	6	206	6	34.33	–	–	2/53
Kapil Dev	6	10	–	245	80	2	–	24.50	4	306.0	76	699	26	26.88	2	–	5/97
Manjrekar, SV	7	12	1	312	110	–	1	26.00	1	0.5	–	4	–	–	–	–	–
More, KS	4	8	1	155	67*	1	–	22.14	10/1	–	–	–	–	–	–	–	–
Pandit, CS	3	4	–	158	127	–	1	39.50	12/1	–	–	–	–	–	–	–	–
Prabhakar, M	6	11	1	270	64	2	–	27.00	3	270.5	62	723	20	36.15	1	–	5/101
Raju, SLV	5	9	2	86	31	–	–	12.29	2	223.3	51	595	15	39.67	1	–	6/81
Shastri, RJ	4	7	–	336	206	–	1	48.00	–	68.0	12	175	5	35.00	–	–	4/45
Sidhu, NS	3	5	–	102	35	–	–	20.40	1	–	–	–	–	–	–	–	–
Srikkanth, K	6	12	–	152	38	–	–	12.67	8	19.0	3	57	2	28.50	–	–	2/52
Srinath, J	6	11	4	107	24	–	–	15.29	1	221.1	44	605	11	55.00	–	–	3/59
Tendulkar, SR	6	11	1	509	148*	2	2	50.90	5	39.0	10	104	3	34.67	–	–	2/10
Vengsarkar, DB	7	13	1	290	82*	3	–	24.17	4	–	–	–	–	–	–	–	–

Mohammed Azharuddin—a shy, quietly spoken Muslim from the unpretentious region of Hyderabad, who, in 1984 against England, became the first Indian to score centuries in his first three Tests—captained a side that contrived to keep its potential hidden. Only the 18-year-old Sachin Tendulkar lived up to the hopes of selectors, delighting audiences in all his six matches with his happy temperament and confidence in scoring 509 runs at 50.90, with two centuries. The Indians were handicapped by Azharuddin's batting failures and lack of quality in their customary strength, spin bowling.

Australia won the rubber four–nil. They won the First Test in Brisbane by ten wickets because of pace bowlers McDermott and Hughes, and the Second Test in Melbourne because of Bruce Reid's 12 for 126. Australia lost her dominance in the Third Test at Sydney and the Fourth at Adelaide with India outplaying the home side for long periods without pressing home their advantage. India squandered Shastri's 206 and Tendulkar's 148 not out in the Third Test when dogged defence by Border and Hughes forced a draw, with defeat threatening Australia. The Fourth Test went to Australia by 38 runs. This was after a re-emergence of Azharuddin's talents yielded a century (106) that promised victory, before he was bowled by McDermott. Australia reasserted its dominance in the Fifth Test at Perth when Boon scored his third century of the series (129, 135 and 107) and Mike Whitney had his best Test figures of 7 for 27.

Azharuddin said his players were not lacking in confidence and skill but failed to match Australia's will to win, the trait Bill O'Reilly said was missing from Indian cricket back in 1967–68.

TARRANT'S TEAM IN INDIA 1935-36

	First-class Results					All Matches			
Matches	Won	Lost	Drawn	Tied	Matches	Won	Lost	Drawn	Tied
16	9	3	4	–	22	10	3	9	–

Date	Venue	Opponent	Results for Australians
Nov 5	Rajkot	West India States	Won by 6 wkts
Nov 9	Jamnagar	*Jamnagar	Drawn
Nov 12	Ahmedabad	*Gujerat	Won by an inns & 86 runs
Nov 15	Ajmer	C India & Rajputana	Won by 7 wkts
Nov 22	Karachi	Sind	Won by an inns & 90 runs
Nov 28	Poona	*Maharastra	Drawn
Nov 30	Bombay	Bombay Presidency	Drawn
Dec 5	Bombay	All India	Won by 9 wkts
Dec 11	Allahabad	*United Provinces	Drawn
Dec 14	Indore	Central India	Drawn
Dec 20	Nagpur	CP & Berar	Won by an inns & 107 runs
Dec 26	Calcutta	*Cooch Behar XI	Drawn
Dec 27	Calcutta	Bengal & Assam	Won by 9 wkts
Dec 31	Calcutta	All India	Won by 8 wkts
Jan 5	Amritsar	Southern Punjab	Won by an inns & 62 runs
Jan 10	Lahore	All India	Lost by 68 runs
Jan 15	Patiala	Patiala	Drawn
Jan 19	Delhi	Cricket Club of India	Drawn
Jan 29	Secunderabad	Moin–ud–dowlah	Lost by an inns & 115 runs
Feb 2	Madras	Madras Presidency	Won by 1 wkt
Feb 6	Madras	All India	Lost by 33 runs
Feb 10	Bangalore	*Mysore	Drawn

The first Australian team to tour India, organised by champion allrounder Frank Tarrant for the Maharajah of Patiala: *back row* H. Tarrant, A. Allsopp, H.S.T.L. Hendry, L.E. Nagel, O.W. Bill, H. Ironmonger, F.J. Bryant; *centre* H.S.B. Love, J.L. Ellis, C.G. Macartney, F.A. Tarrant, J. Ryder (capt.), R.K. Oxenham, T.W. Leather; *front* R.O.G. Morrisby, H.H. Alexander, F. Mair.

Player	M	Inn	NO	Runs	HS	50	100	Avrge	Ct/St	Overs	Mdns	Runs	Wkts	Avrge	5wi	10wm	Best
Alexander, HH	11	13	4	42	12	–	–	4.66	3	152.2	27	437	16	27.31	1	–	5/64
Allsopp, AH	3	5	–	122	51	1	–	24.40	5	–	–	–	–	–	–	–	–
Bill, OW	11	17	3	522	118+	–	2	37.28	7	–	–	–	–	–	–	–	–
Bryant, FJ	15	25	1	613	155	1	1	25.54	7	–	–	–	–	–	–	–	–
Davis, JH	2	4	1	5	4*	–	–	1.66	–	–	–	–	–	–	–	–	–
Ellis, JL	9	11	4	156	53*	1	–	22.28	12/19	–	–	–	–	–	–	–	–
Hendry, HSTL	15	22	1	400	92	2	–	19.04	14	90.0	24	207	7	29.57	–	–	2/12
Hon HH Patiala	1	1	–	15	15	–	–	15.00	–	8.0	1	40	2	20.00	–	–	2/40
Ironmonger, H	2	2	–	4	4	–	–	2.00	–	57.5	16	177	7	25.28	1	–	5/70
Leather, TW	13	18	4	214	46*	–	–	15.28	5	311.3	69	781	47	16.61	3	–	5/27
Love, HSB	13	19	1	369	82	1	–	20.50	19/11	–	–	–	–	–	–	–	–
Macartney, CG	10	14	1	283	85	1	–	21.76	3	209.5	62	555	31	17.90	2	–	6/41
Mair, F	14	19	5	244	48	–	–	17.42	6	298.0	41	1135	56	20.26	3	–	5/43
Morrisby, ROG	14	22	2	811	145	5	2	40.55	4	–	–	–	–	–	–	–	–
Nagel, LE	10	13	1	107	31	–	–	8.91	5	179.4	42	499	20	24.95	1	–	5/24
Oxenham, RK	11	15	2	225	44*	–	–	20.45	7	303.3	140	555	75	7.40	8	4	7/13
Ryder, J (Capt)	16	23	2	776	115	2	2	36.95	12	60.5	16	206	7	29.42	–	–	2/39
Tarrant, FA	2	3	–	39	32	–	–	13.00	1	26.0	2	117	4	29.25	–	–	2/34
Tarrant, LB	1	1	1	16	16*	–	–	–	1	–	–	–	–	–	–	–	–
Warne, FB	3	4	–	64	27	–	–	16.00	–	8.0	1	31	2	15.50	–	–	1/15

Australians only played cricket in India on private tours between the two World Wars. In 1935–36, they were even discouraged from doing this when the Board of Control objected to the inclusion of veteran Test players in the team Melbourne-born allrounder Frank Tarrant took to India with all costs paid by the Maharajah of Patiala. The Board had an official team touring South Africa at that time and refused to allow Woodfull, Ponsford and others to enjoy their retirement on an Indian tour, arguing that they might be needed in South Africa if players were hurt. Tarrant, who took 1506 first-class wickets at 17.52 and scored 1000 runs in an English season nine times, had been visiting India since 1911.

In the face of an angry public outcry the Board relented and allowed Charlie Macartney, who had not played Test cricket since 1926, 'Stork' Hendry, who last played for Australia in 1928–29, 'Dainty' Ironmonger, who quit in 1931–32 and was in his 53rd year, and Ron Oxenham, whose brief Test career had ended in 1930–31, to tour under the captaincy of Jack Ryder, who was 46 and had last played Test cricket in 1928–29. The Board barred Hugh Chilvers, who played 34 times for New South Wales as Bill O'Reilly's legspin deputy, on the grounds that he might be required in South Africa and so denied Chilvers the only chance he ever had of an overseas trip.

Despite their age, gastric problems which sent several players to hospital, and the intense heat, Tarrant's team did well. They won the first two 'internationals' against All India by eight wickets and nine wickets respectively. India recovered to win the last two 'internationals' and share the series. Considering the hardships of long distance train and ship journeys in the years before regular air travel, Tarrant's amazing mixture of old players excelled themselves by winning ten of their 22 matches in India and losing only three, with the rest drawn. On the trip to India they beat an All-Ceylon XI by an innings.

Tarrant, Western Australian Test player Ernie Bromley, and the Victorian right-hand batsman Willie Scaife, who hailed from Tarrant's Fitzroy club, later travelled to India to coach, with all expenses again paid by the Maharajah of Patialia, but another Australian team did not visit India until Lindsay Hassett's Services side arrived in 1945–46 on their way home from a successful tour of England.

AUSTRALIA IN INDIA 1956

Matches	First-class Results Won	Lost	Drawn	Tied	Matches	All Matches Won	Lost	Drawn	Tied
3	2	–	1	–	3	2	–	1	–

Date	Venue	Opponent	Results for Australians
Oct 19	Madras	INDIA (1st Test)	Won by an inns & 5 runs
Oct 26	Bombay	INDIA (2nd Test)	Drawn
Nov 2	Calcutta	INDIA (3rd Test)	Won by 94 runs

Player	State	M	Inn	NO	Runs	HS	50	100	Avrge	Ct/St	Overs	Mdns	Runs	Wkts	Avrge	5wi	10wm	Best
Benaud, R	NSW	3	4	–	53	24	–	–	13.25	–	169.5	52	388	23	16.87	3	1	7/72
Burge, PJP	QLD	3	4	–	198	83	2	–	49.50	4	–	–	–	–	–	–	–	–
Burke, JW	NSW	3	4	–	183	161	–	1	45.75	3	29.0	7	70	4	17.50	–	–	4/37
Craig, ID	NSW	2	3	–	82	40	–	–	27.33	1	–	–	–	–	–	–	–	–
Crawford, WPA	NSW	3	3	1	53	34	–	–	26.50	1	68.0	25	103	7	14.71	–	–	3/28
Davidson, AK	NSW	1	1	–	16	16	–	–	16.00	1	23.0	10	42	1	42.00	–	–	1/24
Harvey, RN	VIC	3	4	–	253	140	1	1	63.25	10	1.0	1	0	–	–	–	–	–
Johnson, IW (Capt)	VIC	2	3	–	79	73	1	–	26.33	1	50.0	22	78	3	26.00	–	–	1/15
Langley, GRA	SA	2	2	2	11	10*	–	–	–	2/1	–	–	–	–	–	–	–	–
Lindwall, RR	QLD	3	4	1	92	48*	–	–	30.67	1	114.1	45	199	12	16.58	1	–	7/43
Mackay, KD	QLD	3	4	–	87	29	–	–	21.75	2	51.2	20	74	3	24.67	–	–	3/27
Maddocks, LV	VIC	1	1	1	8	8*	–	–	–	4/–	–	–	–	–	–	–	–	–
McDonald, CC	VIC	2	3	–	32	29	–	–	10.67	2	–	–	–	–	–	–	–	–
Rutherford, JW	WA	1	1	–	30	30	–	–	30.00	–	6.0	2	15	1	15.00	–	–	1/11
Wilson, JW	SA	1	–	–	–	–	–	–	–	–	36.0	17	64	1	64.00	–	–	1/25

Ian Johnson's Australians, the 22nd team to tour England, arrived in India in a despondent mood. They had failed to regain The Ashes in England—lost in 1953 by Hassett's side—and been defeated in their first-ever Test against Pakistan on the mat in Karachi. Several players were carrying injuries or encountering gastic woes, but they escaped the enteric fever that had sent Arthur Allsopp to hospital for two months in 1935–36.

Lindwall retired with a stomach complaint after bowling five overs in the First Test at Madras, but Benaud's 7 for 72 gave Australia an advantage which Lindwall exploited when he recovered. His second innings coup of 7 for 43 gave Australia victory by an innings and five runs. Lindwall took over captaincy of a team of crocks for the Second Test at Bombay, with Miller, Johnson and Archer injured, Davidson affected by stomach trouble, Crawford carrying a strained hip, Wilson a pulled muscle, and Benaud unable to bowl for part of the game through illness. Harvey (140) and Burke (161) lifted Australia to 523, a lead of 272 but Umrigar saved India by batting for six hours for 78. Benaud's match bag of 11 for 105 (6 for 52 and 5 for 53) gave Australia a 94-run win in the Third Test at Calcutta, 35 of the 39 wickets that fell going to spin bowlers. Most of the Australians felt like pioneers who had ventured into an unknown region of ancient palaces, princes with vast harems, bizarre cooking, prohibition, untrained umpires, and riotous mobs, and they were happy to leave with a two–nil margin after a month sullied by hundreds of visits to toilets.

AUSTRALIA IN INDIA 1959–60

Matches	First-class Results Won	Lost	Drawn	Tied	Matches	All Matches Won	Lost	Drawn	Tied
7	2	1	4	–	7	2	1	4	–

Date	Venue	Opponent	Results for Australians
Dec 12	Delhi	INDIA (1st Test)	Won by an inns & 127 runs
Dec 19	Kanpur	INDIA (2nd Test)	Lost by 119 runs
Dec 27	Ahmedabad	President's XI	Drawn
Jan 1	Bombay	INDIA (3rd Test)	Drawn
Jan 9	Bangalore	Combined Indian Uni's	Drawn
Jan 13	Madras	INDIA (4th Test)	Won by an inns & 55 runs
Jan 23	Calcutta	INDIA (5th Test)	Drawn

Before Richie Benaud's team left for the first full official tour of India—stopping first in Pakistan—Benaud organised special net practice at which jute matting was pulled tight over turf pitches to simulate conditions expected on the tour. They took with them gallons of fruit juice manager Sam Loxton got from a Melbourne brewery and the sneaking hope that 'Slasher' Mackay, only recently recruited to the bowling dodge, would prove a surprise on the mat with his medium-pacers.

Norman O'Neill's batting dominated the tour, his stroke-making all round the wicket justifying the glowing

Player	State	M	Inn	NO	Runs	HS	50	100	Avrge	Ct/St	Overs	Mdns	Runs	Wkts	Avrge	5wi	10wm	Best
Benaud, R (Capt)	NSW	7	9	2	101	25	–	–	14.42	7	346.2	151	631	31	20.35	2	–	5/43
Burge, PJP	QLD	4	4	–	256	157	1	1	64.00	1	–	–	–	–	–	–	–	–
Davidson, AK	NSW	6	7	1	103	41	–	–	17.16	7	261.0	88	474	30	15.80	2	1	7/93
Favell, LE	SA	6	7	1	436	112	2	2	72.66	4	10.0	3	63	2	31.50	–	–	1/14
Grout, ATW	QLD	6	7	2	266	101	1	1	53.20	15/3	16.0	1	74	2	37.00	–	–	1/29
Harvey, RN	NSW	6	8	–	392	114	1	2	49.00	7	45.0	18	93	4	23.25	–	–	2/24
Jarman, BN	SA	2	4	1	42	28	–	–	14.00	5/2	9.5	1	52	2	26.00	–	–	1/17
Kline, LF	VIC	4	5	2	32	14	–	–	10.66	6	142.0	57	295	13	22.69	–	–	4/42
Lindwall, RR	QLD	4	2	1	11	10	–	–	11.00	–	114.2	31	302	8	38.62	–	–	2/44
Loxton, SJE	VIC	1	1	–	33	33	–	–	33.00	–	6.0	2	32	–	–	–	–	–
Mackay, KD	QLD	6	7	1	199	89	2	–	33.16	2	100.0	38	158	9	17.88	–	–	3/37
McDonald, CC	VIC	7	9	–	214	53	1	–	23.77	2	11.0	3	51	–	–	–	–	–
Meckiff, I	VIC	7	6	4	68	45*	–	–	34.00	2	192.0	55	412	12	34.75	–	–	4/79
O'Neill, NC	NSW	7	7	–	660	284	–	3	94.28	3	24.0	1	106	1	106.00	–	–	1/37
Rorke, GF	NSW	1	2	1	7	7	–	–	3.50	1	23.0	9	38	2	19.00	–	–	2/30
Stevens, GB	SA	3	5	–	171	96	1	–	34.20	2	12.0	2	54	3	18.00	–	–	2/16

assessments of his skills. He hit three centuries on a difficult, exhausting tour, highest score 284 against the Indian President's XI at Ahmedabad. Fresh from his first century in Tests, 134 in the Second Test against Pakistan in Lahore, he added three more in the Tests v. India, and had an average of 94.28 from his seven first-class matches. With Harvey providing helpful advice, Benaud moulded Australia into a fine team, enhancing the reputation he had earned by regaining The Ashes from England in Australia in 1958–59.

Australia won the First Test at Delhi by an innings and 127, the high class spin bowling of Benaud and Kline forcing home the advantage won by the batting of Harvey (114) and Mackay. Benaud's match figures of 8 for 76 included 3 for 0 in the first innings. India countered by winning the Second Test at Kanpur, her first-ever success against Australia, by 119 runs on a newly laid turf pitch. Off-spinner Jasu Patel, brought in to exploit the pitch, took 9 for 69 in Australia's first innings and amid wild excitement routed Australia again with 5 for 55 in the second innings. The Third Test at Bombay was drawn after Harvey (102) and O'Neill (163) had a third-wicket stand of 207. Popular Les Favell made his sole Test century (101) and Davidson took his 100th Test wicket during Australia's Fourth Test win by an innings and 55 runs at Madras, where sawdust was rolled into the pitch to make it last. India left Australia to score 203 in 150 minutes to win the Fifth Test at Calcutta. They settled for a draw, sore from the gamma globulin injections they received from team doctor Ian McDonald to prevent a hepatitis outbreak worsening. Hepatitis contracted on the tour ended the careers of Gordon Rorke and Gavin Stevens. Rorke, a strapping 101.6 kg, 196 cm (16 stone, 6 ft 5 in) fast bowler, had to be sent home before the tour ended, three stone lighter than when he left. Stevens, a strongly built right-hand batsman was also invalided home, emaciated and weak, and took almost three years to regain his strength. Kline and Mackay were confirmed hepatitis victims, but struggled through the tour.

AUSTRALIA IN INDIA 1964

	First-class Results					All Matches			
Matches	Won	Lost	Drawn	Tied	Matches	Won	Lost	Drawn	Tied
3	1	1	1	–	3	1	1	1	–

Date	Venue	Opponent	Results for Australians
Oct 2	Madras	INDIA (1st Test)	Won by 139 runs
Oct 10	Bombay	INDIA (2nd Test)	Lost by 2 wkts
Oct 17	Calcutta	INDIA (3rd Test)	Drawn

The 24th Australian team to England played three Tests in India and one in Pakistan on their way home. Wearied by a 36-match tour, a team that had been rebuilt after the retirement of Benaud, Harvey and Davidson had to dig deep to avoid staleness and preserve keenness. Simpson, Sydney-born son of a Scottish soccer professional who worked in Frank Packer's printing room after migrating to Australia, had opening stands of 66,

Player	State	M	Inn	NO	Runs	HS	50	100	Avrge	Ct/St	Overs	Mdns	Runs	Wkts	Avrge	5wi	10wm	Best
Booth, BC	NSW	3	5	–	112	74	1	–	22.40	2	35.0	17	58	2	29.00	–	–	2/33
Burge, PJP	QLD	3	5	–	164	80	2	–	32.80	2	–	–	–	–	–	–	–	–
Connolly, AN	VIC	2	3	2	0	0*	–	–	0.00	–	48.3	17	100	6	16.67	–	–	3/24
Cowper, RM	VIC	2	4	1	119	81	1	–	39.67	2	23.0	3	56	–	–	–	–	–
Grout, ATW	QLD	1	2	–	12	12	–	–	6.00	4/–	–	–	–	–	–	–	–	–
Hawke, NJN	SA	1	2	1	1	1*	–	–	1.00	–	50.0	20	81	4	20.25	–	–	2/26
Jarman, BN	SA	2	3	–	79	78	1	–	26.33	4/1	–	–	–	–	–	–	–	–
Lawry, WM	VIC	3	6	1	284	68	3	–	56.80	–	–	–	–	–	–	–	–	–
Martin, JW	NSW	2	4	–	75	39	–	–	18.75	–	90.0	28	213	5	42.60	–	–	2/63
McKenzie, GD	WA	3	5	1	56	27	–	–	14.00	1	108.3	26	214	13	16.46	1	1	6/58
O'Neill, NC	NSW	2	2	–	40	40	–	–	20.00	2	16.0	6	60	1	60.00	–	–	1/41
Redpath, IR	VIC	2	3	1	42	32*	–	–	21.00	2	2.0	1	1	–	–	–	–	–
Sellers, RHD	SA	1	1	–	0	0	–	–	0.00	1	5.0	1	17	–	–	–	–	–
Simpson, RB (Capt)	NSW	3	6	–	292	77	3	–	48.67	8	82.0	31	151	6	25.17	–	–	4/45
Veivers, TR	QLD	3	5	–	143	74	2	–	28.60	1	163.4	56	269	11	24.45	–	–	4/68

ASIA AWAKES

91, 35, 59, 97 and 115 with Lawry which virtually safeguarded Australia from defeat in the India Tests. He followed with 153 and 115 in the Test against Pakistan. McKenzie added 13 wickets to his growing Test tally, but the work-horse of the tour was Tom Veivers, whom a London newspaper said resembled a koala in a gum tree. Tom bowled 163 overs in India and a further 46 in Pakistan. He had just set a record by bowling 51 overs unchanged in the Fourth Test against England.

Australia won the First Test at Madras by 139 runs, overcoming an innings of 128 not out from the Nawab of Pataudi. India won the Second Test at Bombay by two wickets to level the rubber, thanks to further watchful batting by 'Tiger' Pataudi (86 and 53). Rain prevented play on the last two days of the Third Test at Calcutta, leaving the series level at a win apiece.

AUSTRALIA IN INDIA 1969-70

	First-class Results					All Matches			
Matches	Won	Lost	Drawn	Tied	Matches	Won	Lost	Drawn	Tied
10	5	1	4	–	10	5	1	4	–

Date	Venue	Opponent	Results for Australians
Oct 31	Poona	West Zone	Drawn
Nov 4	Bombay	INDIA (1st Test)	Won by 8 wkts
Nov 11	Jaipur	Central Zone	Won by an inns & 32 runs
Nov 15	Kanpur	INDIA (2nd Test)	Drawn
Nov 22	Jullundur	North Zone	Drawn
Nov 28	Delhi	INDIA (3rd Test)	Lost by 7 wkts
Dec 6	Gauhati	East Zone	Won by 96 runs
Dec 12	Calcutta	INDIA (4th Test)	Won by 10 wkts
Dec 20	Bangalore	South Zone	Drawn
Dec 24	Madras	INDIA (5th Test)	Won by 77 runs

Player	State	M	Inn	NO	Runs	HS	50	100	Avrge	Ct/St	Overs	Mdns	Runs	Wkts	Avrge	5wi	10wm	Best
Chappell, IM	SA	9	15	3	675	164	2	2	56.25	15	26.0	11	61	3	20.33	–	–	1/7
Connolly, AN	VIC	9	11	4	132	30*	–	–	18.86	4	324.2	100	622	25	24.88	–	–	4/31
Freeman, EW	SA	6	9	–	105	29	–	–	11.67	4	136.0	35	312	17	18.35	1	–	6/63
Gleeson, JW	NSW	6	7	2	55	22	–	–	11.00	2	282.4	105	561	22	25.50	1	–	5/23
Irvine, JT	WA	4	6	–	65	30	–	–	10.83	3	4.0	4	0	–	–	–	–	–
Jordon, RC	VIC	4	5	1	60	23	–	–	15.00	2/5	–	–	–	–	–	–	–	–
Lawry, WM (Capt)	VIC	9	16	4	550	120	2	1	45.83	4	1.0	–	6	–	–	–	–	–
Mallett, AA	SA	8	9	4	38	11*	–	–	7.60	4	412.5	170	773	45	17.17	5	2	7/38
Mayne, LC	WA	5	8	–	157	72	1	–	19.67	3	150.4	41	332	15	22.13	–	–	4/67
McKenzie, GD	WA	7	9	1	105	24*	–	–	13.12	8	269.0	87	546	25	21.84	2	–	6/67
Redpath, IR	VIC	10	16	–	373	77	3	–	23.32	13	6.0	4	9	–	–	–	–	–
Sheahan, AP	VIC	9	13	3	333	114	1	1	33.30	3	6.0	4	5	–	–	–	–	–
Stackpole, KR	VIC	8	16	2	478	61	1	–	39.14	12	80.2	31	196	5	39.20	–	–	1/0
Taber, HB	NSW	7	10	–	167	53	1	–	16.70	14/2	–	–	–	–	–	–	–	–
Walters, KD	NSW	9	14	2	507	102	4	1	42.25	7	21.0	3	50	2	25.00	–	–	1/1

Bill Lawry's team endured one of the most argumentative, incident-packed tours in cricket history, 10 matches of disputed umpires' decisions, crowds lighting fires in the stands, clashes between police and demonstrators, bottle and stone throwing at the grounds and at the players' hotels, and bricks smashing their bus windows. All this plus the customary gastric troubles imposed a lot of stress on the captaincy of Melbourne plumber and pigeon-fancier Bill Lawry. Some members of the Australian Board of Control considered Lawry showed the strain of 15 years of big cricket and they sacked him midway through the following Australian summer.

Indian spectators were fired by their team's defeat of the West Indies the previous season at home, and only the size of the grounds restricted crowds to between 25,000 and 50,000. Some paid a month's wages to get in, others walked 32 kilometres to the Test venues, all of them eager to see glamorous players like Ian Chappell, Paul Sheahan, Doug Walters, Keith Stackpole, and Lawry, the man dubbed an Australian Pinocchio, against spinners like Bedi, Prasanna and Venkat. The ensuing disturbances included a riot at Bombay where police tried to drag spectators from the field as bottles and chairs landed around the outfield. Smoke shrouded the ground from fires lit in the stands.

At Calcutta a clash between groups in the crowd saw people pelted by bottles and refuse invade the ground to escape. As police tried to clear the field, Lawry was alleged to have hit a cameraman, who ventured near the pitch, with the bat. At the team's hotel police had to clear a path with their batons through a stone-throwing mob for the Australians. That night McKenzie and Redpath, mildest of men, were accused of assaulting reporters who tried to join the team dinner. At Bangalore spectators pelted South Zone fieldsmen with coconut husks, apple cores and orange peel, forcing an early finish.

The Tests developed into a contest between spinners, with Ashley Mallett emerging on top for Australia with 28 wickets in five Tests. Prasanna took 26 and Bedi 21 for India. The First Test aroused a public outcry before a ball was bowled when India's selectors omitted their third off-spinner Venkataraghavan. India could not believe it and finally swing bowler Subroto Guha stood down to let Venkat play. He appeared in all five Tests. The First Test was typical of a hard-fought series, with India scoring 271, to which Australia responded with 345, Stackpole scoring 103. Connolly, Gleeson and Mallett combined to dismiss India for 137, leaving Australia 64 to win. Play continued despite a riot in the last hour of the fourth day, Australia winning by eight wickets.

The Second Test at Kanpur was drawn and India levelled the rubber, taking the Third Test by seven wickets. Bedi had 5 for 37, Prasanna 5 for 42. Australia then made the series secure by winning the Fourth Test at Calcutta by ten wickets, Chappell batting superbly in punishing Prasanna before Bedi dismissed him for 99. Australia then confirmed their superiority by winning the Fifth Test at Madras by 77 runs. Mallett took 5 for 91 and 5 for 53 in supporting Walters' (102) century.

AUSTRALIA IN INDIA 1979–80

First-class Results					All Matches				
Matches	Won	Lost	Drawn	Tied	Matches	Won	Lost	Drawn	Tied
11	–	3	8	–	11	–	3	8	–

Date	Venue	Opponent	Results for Australians
Sep 1	Srinagar	North Zone	Drawn
Sep 6	Hyderabad	South Zone	Drawn
Sep 11	Madras	INDIA (1st Test)	Drawn
Sep 19	Bangalore	INDIA (2nd Test)	Drawn
Sep 27	Nagpur	Central Zone	Drawn
Oct 2	Kanpur	INDIA (3rd Test)	Lost by 153 runs
Oct 9	Ahmedabad	West Zone	Drawn
Oct 13	Delhi	INDIA (4th Test)	Drawn
Oct 21	Cuttack	East Zone	Lost by 4 wkts
Oct 26	Calcutta	INDIA (5th Test)	Drawn
Nov 3	Bombay	INDIA (6th Test)	Lost by an inns & 100 runs

Player	State	M	Inn	NO	Runs	HS	50	100	Avrge	Ct/St	Overs	Mdns	Runs	Wkts	Avrge	5wi	10wm	Best
Border, AR	NSW	10	19	–	748	162	3	2	39.36	5	87.2	20	207	7	29.57	–	–	3/32
Darling, WM	SA	9	13	1	304	82	2	–	25.33	2	–	–	–	–	–	–	–	–
Dymock, G	QLD	8	10	2	156	53	1	–	19.50	–	290.4	68	738	32	23.06	2	1	7/67
Higgs, JD	VIC	10	11	4	42	11	–	–	6.00	1	351.0	110	953	29	32.86	1	–	7/143
Hilditch, AMJ	NSW	10	19	1	507	85	4	–	28.16	9	–	–	–	–	–	–	–	–
Hogg, RM	SA	9	13	2	95	19	–	–	8.63	3	248.2	54	747	20	37.35	–	–	4/66
Hughes, KJ (Capt)	WA	10	19	3	858	126	6	2	53.62	9	–	–	–	–	–	–	–	–
Hurst, AG	VIC	4	3	1	6	6*	–	–	3.00	1	102.4	26	224	6	37.33	1	–	5/33
Lawson, GF	NSW	1	1	–	3	3	–	–	3.00	1	22.0	9	23	3	7.66	–	–	2/1
Porter, GD	WA	4	5	3	30	13	–	–	15.00	4	78.0	21	192	1	192.00	–	–	1/25
Sleep, PR	SA	6	10	1	175	64	2	–	19.44	2	131.1	24	442	14	31.57	1	–	5/71
Whatmore, DF	VIC	9	17	–	411	77	3	–	24.17	20	12.4	4	25	3	8.33	–	–	1/00
Wood, GM	WA	6	10	–	138	33	–	–	13.80	2	15.0	4	32	4	8.00	–	–	3/18
Wright, KJ	WA	10	17	6	252	55*	2	–	22.90	20/3	–	–	–	–	–	–	–	–
Yallop, GN	VIC	10	19	4	729	167	5	1	48.60	6/1	41.0	3	146	1	146.00	–	–	1/21
Yardley, B	WA	5	8	2	173	61*	1	–	28.83	1	237.0	74	555	17	32.64	–	–	4/91

To overcome primitive kitchens on this arduous tour, Kim Hughes' Australians seconded their own chef from Lahore's Intercontinental Hotel to buy their food and prepare it under the direction of team medico, Dr Paul Koenig. Accommodation remained spartan, with three, four or more players sharing bedrooms in some of the more remote cities. Wayne Phillips, Greg Ritchie and Allan Border bought fireworks in the Old Lahore markets to entertain the bored players.

Mike Coward in his book *Cricket Beyond The Bazaar* said that the high jinks with the fireworks helped a team that was hopelessly outclassed in aptitude and attitude cope with an alien and sometimes intimidating environment. The Australian Cricket Board was more interested in maintaining good relations with their Indian counterpart than in the abject quality of the Australians' cricket and at the end of the tour fined Border, whose batting was one of the sole tour joys, $600 for breaching his tour agreement by writing a colourful article on the trip.

The dismal displays by the Australians in their last campaign before the ACB settlement with Packer showed how much the national side had deteriorated. Interruptions such as that in Karachi where players retreated under a hail of rocks and vegetables were almost a welcome relief from the 11 matches which Australia got through without a win. Eight of the 15 Australians had never toured before and against a background of floods and bloody demonstrations by religious and political activists, the newcomers simply failed to perform. Only Hughes, Border and Yallop showed any mastery of the technique for playing spin from Doshi, Yadav and Venkat or the medium pace of Kapil Dev.

Apart from the expected gastric problems—partially

solved by travelling with a team chef—manager Bob Merriman had to cope with abnormal injury problems. Hurst had to be sent home after a back injury failed to respond to treatment. His replacement Geoff Lawson had little time to settle. Yardley was prone to accident and illness, Hogg had breathing trouble with his asthma. Coupled with all this the tour was held when the monsoon season had not ended and the first two Tests were played on wet pitches. The First Test at Kanpur, the Second at Bangalore, the Fourth at Delhi, and the Fifth at Calcutta were drawn. India had a historic first series victory by winning the Third Test at Kanpur by 153 runs, and the Sixth at Bombay by an innings and 100 runs. Australia were also beaten by East Zone, ranked the weakest team they encountered.

AUSTRALIA IN INDIA 1986-87

First-class Results					All Matches			
Matches	Won	Lost	Drawn	Tied	Matches	Won	Lost	Drawn	Tied
7	–	–	6	1	13	2	3	7	1

Date	Venue	Opponent	Results for Australians
Aug 30	Bangalore	President's XI	Drawn
Sep 3	Gwalior	Bombay	Drawn
Sep 7	Jaipur	*India (L/O Intl)	Lost by 7 wkts
Sep 9	Srinagar	*India (L/O Intl)	Won by 3 wkts
Sep 12	Chandigarh	Indian Under 25s	Drawn
Sep 18	Madras	INDIA (1st Test)	Tied
Sep 24	Hyderabad	*India (L/O Intl)	No Result
Sep 26	Delhi	INDIA (2nd Test)	Drawn
Oct 2	New Delhi	*India (L/O Intl)	Lost by 3 wkts
Oct 5	Ahmedabad	*India (L/O Intl)	Lost by 52 runs
Oct 7	Rajkot	*India (L/O Intl)	Won by 7 wkts
Oct 10	Baroda	Delhi	Drawn
Oct 15	Bombay	INDIA (3rd Test)	Drawn

Player	State	M	Inn	NO	Runs	HS	50	100	Avrge	Ct/St	Overs	Mdns	Runs	Wkts	Avrge	5wi	10wm	Best
Boon, DC	TAS	6	8	1	476	122	3	1	68.00	4	2.0	1	5	–	–	–	–	–
Border, AR (Capt)	QLD	5	6	1	320	106	2	1	64.00	4	13.0	3	41	–	–	–	–	–
Bright, RJ	VIC	7	6	1	66	30	–	–	13.20	3	174.5	30	564	13	43.38	1	–	5/94
Davis, SP	VIC	2	2	2	3	3*	–	–	–	1	48.4	12	175	5	35.00	–	–	3/52
Dyer, GC	NSW	3	3	–	208	106	1	1	69.33	3/–	–	–	–	–	–	–	–	–
Gilbert, DR	NSW	5	4	2	152	117	–	1	76.00	–	107.0	23	367	11	33.36	–	–	4/92
Jones, DM	VIC	7	9	1	438	210	1	1	54.75	2	10.0	2	35	2	17.50	–	–	1/0
Marsh, GR	WA	6	8	–	328	139	–	2	41.00	4	–	–	–	–	–	–	–	–
Matthews, GRJ	NSW	6	6	1	263	99	1	–	52.60	1	179.0	29	601	20	30.05	2	1	5/103
McDermott, CJ	QLD	5	3	–	62	23	–	–	20.66	2	99.0	13	355	7	50.71	–	–	3/85
Reid, BA	WA	5	4	3	18	12*	–	–	18.00	–	116.0	18	394	7	56.28	–	–	2/34
Ritchie, GM	QLD	6	6	–	291	124	1	1	48.50	7	–	–	–	–	–	–	–	–
Veletta, MRJ	WA	3	4	1	76	26	–	–	25.33	3	–	–	–	–	–	–	–	–
Waugh, SR	NSW	6	7	3	227	82	2	–	56.75	4	97.0	15	367	10	36.70	–	–	4/71
Zoehrer, TJ	WA	5	4	1	123	52*	1	–	41.00	8/2	1.0	–	8	–	–	–	–	–

This became a famous tour when the First Test at Chidambaram Stadium at Chepauk in Madras ended in cricket's second tie. The first tie between Australia and the West Indies in Brisbane in 1960 had taken 84 years and 498 Tests, but this tie came in the 1053rd Test only 26 years later. In Brisbane the spectators always knew the outcome would be close, but in Madras the dramatic finish came after India had been outplayed for three days and only narrowly escaped the follow-on.

Border, who had threatened to quit as captain six months before in New Zealand unless Australia's effort improved, knew Australia had won only three of their last 24 Tests and lost 12 as they began batting in stifling heat. Boon and Jones put on 158 for the second wicket before Boon departed for 122. Jones batted on into the second day, extending his first Test century to Australia's first double century against India, undeterred by umpire Dara Dotiwala's request to change from spiked shoes to ripple soles to preserve the pitch. Mike Coward takes up the story:

As Jones reached 150 his body began to shut down. Time and again he drew away from the wicket, pitched forward, and, body shaking, disgorged the fluids and mineral replacements brought to him. Twice he feigned being sick as he urinated in his flannels . . . too embarrassed to tell a soul he had lost control of his bodily functions. When he was not vomiting he was racked with the pain of leg and stomach cramps as his dehydrated body ground to a halt. Remarkably, his batting did not suffer, defying all reason.

The more his distress increased, the harder Jones hit the ball. At the other end Border opted to goad Jones into continuing when he said he couldn't. 'Okay then. I'll get someone tough out here who can stick it out,' said Border. Jones reacted angrily and struck out at almost every delivery that followed. He reached 200 after seven hours 15 minutes and when he was finally out for 210 he had hit 27 fours and two sixes. His partnership

HOME AND AWAY

with Border had added 178, of which Border had made 64. Jones went to hospital to be placed on a saline drip, his body dehydrated, but later returned to field in this extraordinary match.

Australia declared at 7 for 574. India narrowly averted the follow-on by scoring 397 in reply, thanks to Kapil Dev's 119 and dubious umpiring by show pony Dara Dotiwala. Australia declared at 5 for 170 in their second innings, leaving India 348 to win. When the final 20 overs began, India needed 118 with seven wickets in hand. They moved steadily towards their target until only

18 were required from the last 30 deliveries. Then Chetan Sharma, Kiren More and Shival Yadav were dismissed, with India four runs short and nine wickets down. Shastri took two and a single to bring the scores level. Maninder Singh blocked the fourth ball with difficulty and was given out lbw by umpire Vikram Raju off the fifth, giving Greg Matthews his second five-wicket haul of the match. The other two Tests were drawn, with masseur–ambulance man Errol Alcott Australia's hero in a shared rubber.

AUSTRALIA VERSUS PAKISTAN

Among Western-world cricket buffs, the idea persists that cricket in India and Pakistan lacks charm. The problems imposed by gastric disorders, umpiring difficulties, volatile crowds, racial disturbances and poor pitches take the challenge out of tours of the subcontinent for too many English, Australian and New Zealand cricketers.

Pakistan has largely overcome Western condescension by matching the world's best players on tour and are even more formidable at home. They owe a lot to the founder of Pakistan cricket, Abdul Hafeez Kardar, popularly known as Hafeez, who brought the experience he gained in first-class cricket with Oxford University and Warwickshire to his homeland and became Pakistan's first captain and a dynamic figure in its cricket administration. Fazal Mahmood, the Mohammad brothers, and later Intikhab Alam, Majid Khan, Imran Khan, Asif Iqbal and

Javed Miandad followed Kardar's example and in the early 1990s Wasim Akram took over as Pakistan's captain at the age of 26. His deputy, Waqar Younis, took his 100th Test wicket only eight weeks after his 21st birthday. Their success as an opening bowling twosome has sometimes made it difficult for Pakistan's spinners to get a bowl.

Pakistan's progress is remarkable in that it has been accomplished in such a short time. Pakistan, created by the partition of India in August 1947, first put a Test team into the field in India in October 1952 when they met India in a five Test series. India won 2–1 with three Tests drawn. They played their first Test on Pakistan soil against India in 1960, but after a dull series resulted in a stalemate with all five Tests drawn, political issues prevented them playing India again for 18 years. In that period the other cricket nations came to Pakistan's rescue.

AUSTRALIA IN PAKISTAN 1959–60

First-class Results					All Matches				
Matches	Won	Lost	Drawn	Tied	Matches	Won	Lost	Drawn	Tied
4	3	–	1	–	4	3	–	1	–

Date	Venue	Opponent	Results for Australians
Nov 13	Dacca	PAKISTAN (1st Test)	Won by 8 wkts
Nov 21	Lahore	PAKISTAN (2nd Test)	Won by 7 wkts
Nov 28	Rawalpindi	President's XI	Won by 3 wkts
Dec 4	Karachi	PAKISTAN (3rd Test)	Drawn

Player	State	M	Inn	NO	Runs	HS	50	100	Avrge	Ct/St	Overs	Mdns	Runs	Wkts	Avrge	5wi	10wm	Best
Benaud, R (Capt)	NSW	3	4	1	84	29	–	–	28.00	2	224.0	94	380	18	21.11	1	–	5/93
Burge, PJP	QLD	3	4	–	32	16	–	–	8.00	3	0.1	–	0	1	0.00	–	–	1/0
Davidson, AK	NSW	3	3	1	90	47	–	–	45.00	2	148.5	34	298	12	24.83	–	–	4/42
Favell, LE	SA	4	7	–	86	32	–	–	12.28	3	1.0	–	1	–	–	–	–	–
Grout, ATW	QLD	3	3	1	98	66*	1	–	49.00	8/4	–	–	–	–	–	–	–	–
Harvey, RN	NSW	4	8	1	319	96	2	–	45.57	9	24.0	6	66	3	22.00	–	–	2/23
Jarman, BN	SA	1	2	–	0	0	–	–	0.00	3/1	–	–	–	–	–	–	–	–
Kline, LF	VIC	2	2	1	0	0*	–	–	0.00	1	70.0	31	123	9	13.66	1	–	7/75
Lindwall, RR	QLD	3	4	–	39	23	–	–	9.75	–	83.0	24	162	7	23.14	–	–	4/27
Mackay, KD	QLD	4	5	–	118	40	–	–	23.60	2	134.4	60	205	10	20.50	1	–	6/42
McDonald, CC	VIC	3	5	1	154	44*	–	–	38.50	1	–	–	–	–	–	–	–	–
Meckiff, I	VIC	3	3	1	4	2*	–	–	2.00	1	71.5	18	160	7	22.85	–	–	3/29
O'Neill, NC	NSW	4	8	4	281	134	1	1	70.25	2	24.0	7	72	2	36.00	–	–	1/31
Rorke, GF	NSW	1	1	1	5	5*	–	–	–	1	19.0	9	27	6	4.50	1	–	5/26
Stevens, GB	SA	3	6	–	59	28	–	–	9.83	1	–	–	–	–	–	–	–	–

Three years elapsed after Pakistan's shock defeat of Ian Johnson's 1956 Australian team before the countries met again. Richie Benaud's 1959–60 team, thrown into a Test at Dacca without warm-up matches, took the wise path of sending Pakistan in to bat when they won the toss, seeking time to study conditions on the mat. To Benaud's delight the surface proved ideal for the unheralded medium-pacer Ken ('Slasher') Mackay. He could not find the deviation Fazal achieved but he cut the ball enough to worry all batsmen and clean bowled Hanif Mohammad, who made the world record first-class score of 499 for Karachi against Bahawalpur the previous summer.

Australia replied to Pakistan's modest 200 with 225, Harvey contributing 96, Grout 66. Mackay then bowled superbly to take 6 for 42 off 45 overs, 27 of which were maidens, to set up an Australian triumph. With Pakistan all out for 134, Australia won by eight wickets. Back on turf for the Second Test at Lahore, Australia won convincingly by seven wickets. Norm O'Neill made 134 in Australia's first innings of 391 and only a long knock by Saeed Ahmed (166) in Pakistan's second innings delayed Australia's win. The Third Test at Karachi was drawn after Pakistan batted all the first day to reach 5 for 104, again on the mat. Neither side could score quickly enough to force a result, Intikhab Alam providing the sole highlight by taking a wicket (McDonald's) with his first ball in Test cricket. Even Hanif's second innings 101 not out could not arouse applause.

Australia won the other tour match by beating a President's XI at Rawalpindi by three wickets, which gave them a record of three wins and a draw on the four-match tour in which Neil Harvey made 319 runs at 45.57. Benaud headed the bowling with 18 wickets at 21.11.

AUSTRALIA IN PAKISTAN 1979–80

First-class Results					All Matches			
Matches	Won	Lost	Drawn	Tied	Matches	Won	Lost	Drawn	Tied
5	–	1	4	–	5	–	1	4	–

Date	Venue	Opponent	Results for Australians
Feb 22	Rawalpindi	President's XI	Drawn
Feb 27	Karachi	PAKISTAN (1st Test)	Lost by 7 wkts
Mar 6	Faisalabad	PAKISTAN (2nd Test)	Drawn
Mar 13	Multan	Governor's XI	Drawn
Mar 18	Lahore	PAKISTAN (3rd Test)	Drawn

The 1979–80 Australian team in Pakistan: *standing* scorer, D.W. Hookes, G.R. Beard, G.N. Yallop, D.K. Lillee, M.F. Malone, G.F. Lawson, J.J.M. Wiener, G. Dymock, masseur; *seated* R.J. Bright, R.W. Marsh, K.J. Hughes, F.W. Bennett (manager), G.S. Chappell (capt.), A.R. Border, B.M. Laird.

Player	State	M	Inn	NO	Runs	HS	50	100	Avrge	Ct/St	Overs	Mdns	Runs	Wkts	Avrge	5wi	10wm	Best
Beard, GR	NSW	5	9	1	206	64*	1	–	25.75	1	84.1	32	214	4	53.50	–	–	3/13
Border, AR	NSW	5	9	3	674	178	1	3	112.33	7	8.0	4	31	–	–	–	–	–
Bright, RJ	VIC	5	9	2	129	52	1	–	18.42	3	230.2	72	558	29	19.24	4	2	7/87
Chappell, GS (Capt)	QLD	3	5	–	381	235	2	1	76.20	3	34.0	9	74	3	24.66	–	–	3/49
Dymock, G	QLD	4	5	1	44	26	–	–	11.00	–	71.0	17	188	4	47.00	–	–	3/59
Hookes, DW	SA	3	6	–	10	5	–	–	1.66	4	–	–	–	–	–	–	–	–
Hughes, KJ	WA	5	9	–	220	88	2	–	24.44	1	10.0	2	24	–	–	–	–	–
Laird, BM	WA	5	9	–	202	67	2	–	22.44	2	2.0	1	3	–	–	–	–	–
Lawson, GF	NSW	2	3	1	19	14	–	–	9.50	2	41.0	15	107	6	17.83	–	–	4/46
Lillee, DK	WA	3	4	2	18	12*	–	–	9.00	1	102.0	19	303	3	101.00	–	–	3/114
Malone, MF	WA	2	3	2	3	1*	–	–	3.00	1	35.0	11	123	1	123.00	–	–	1/36
Marsh, RW	WA	5	8	–	201	71	2	–	25.12	7/–	12.0	2	55	–	–	–	–	–
Wiener, JM	VIC	4	7	–	189	93	1	–	27.00	1	5.0	1	19	–	–	–	–	–
Yallop, GN	VIC	4	6	–	283	172	–	1	47.16	1	5.0	–	29	–	–	–	–	–

After Bob Simpson's Australians had played a draw in their only Test in Pakistan in 1964–65, Greg Chappell took an Australian team to Pakistan for five matches in 1979–80. New heroes had emerged in the Pakistan XI to lessen the burden of the Mohammad family and in the First Test at Karachi Australia found the batting of Taslim Arif (58), Javed Miandad (40) and Majid Khan too strong to overcome, going down by seven wickets. Left-arm orthodox spinners Iqbal Qasim (11) and Ray Bright (10) accounted for 21 of the 28 wickets that fell in the match.

The other two Tests were drawn, the Second Test after Greg Chappell and Graham Yallop put on 217 for the fourth wicket, Chappell finishing with 235, Yallop 172. Taslim Arif made 210 not out for Pakistan, Miandad 106 not out in an unfinished 223 third-wicket stand. All 11 Australians had a bowl, Rodney Marsh forsaking his wicket-keeping duties for 10 overs that yielded 51 runs without a wicket. Allan Border made a century in each innings of the Third Test at Lahore, 150 not out and 153, Pakistan using ten bowlers. The other match against a Governor's XI was drawn, giving Chappell's tourists a record of four draws and one defeat.

AUSTRALIA IN PAKISTAN 1982-83

	First-class Results					All Matches			
Matches	Won	Lost	Drawn	Tied	Matches	Won	Lost	Drawn	Tied
6	–	3	3	–	9	–	5	4	–

Date	Venue	Opponent	Results for Australians
Sep 12	Rawalpindi	BCCP Patron's XI	Drawn
Sep 16	Multan	Pakistan XI	Drawn
Sep 20	Hyderabad	*Pakistan (L/O Intl)	Lost by 59 runs
Sep 22	Karachi	PAKISTAN (1st Test)	Lost by 9 wkts
Sep 30	Faisalabad	PAKISTAN (2nd Test)	Lost by an inns & 3 runs
Oct 8	Faisalabad	*Pakistan (L/O Intl)	Lost by 28 runs
Oct 10	Sialkot	BCCP Invitation XI	Drawn
Oct 14	Lahore	PAKISTAN (3rd Test)	Lost by 9 wkts
Oct 22	Karachi	*Pakistan (L/O Intl)	No result

Player	State	M	Inn	NO	Runs	HS	50	100	Avrge	Ct/St	Overs	Mdns	Runs	Wkts	Avrge	5wi	10wm	Best
Alderman, TM	WA	3	2	–	7	7	–	–	3.50	1	68.0	12	260	4	65.00	–	–	2/144
Border, AR	QLD	6	11	1	259	59	2	–	25.90	6	28.0	9	77	4	19.25	–	–	2/14
Bright, RJ	VIC	5	7	2	55	32*	–	–	11.00	1	137.0	43	363	12	30.25	1	–	5/40
Callen, IW	VIC	2	1	1	1	1*	–	–	–	–	20.0	3	60	4	15.00	–	–	2/15
Dyson, J	NSW	6	10	1	361	87	3	–	40.11	–	–	–	–	–	–	–	–	–
Hughes, KJ (Capt)	WA	6	11	1	396	101*	2	1	39.60	2	0.1	–	6	–	–	–	–	–
Laird, BM	WA	5	10	–	258	60	1	–	25.80	6	–	–	–	–	–	–	–	–
Lawson, GF	NSW	4	7	1	106	57*	1	–	17.66	–	134.3	23	364	15	24.26	1	–	5/32
Marsh, RW	WA	4	7	–	83	32	–	–	11.85	5/2	–	–	–	–	–	–	–	–
Phillips, WB	SA	2	3	–	118	92	1	–	39.33	1/1	–	–	–	–	–	–	–	–
Ritchie, GM	QLD	5	9	2	294	106*	1	1	42.00	2	–	–	–	–	–	–	–	–
Sleep, PR	SA	3	5	1	38	29	–	–	9.50	–	56.2	7	247	1	247.00	–	–	1/159
Thomson, JR	QLD	4	8	3	67	18	–	–	13.40	1	89.0	13	352	3	117.33	–	–	1/16
Wood, GM	WA	6	10	1	343	85	3	–	38.11	2	–	–	–	–	–	–	–	–
Yardley, B	WA	5	7	–	111	40	–	–	15.85	2	119.0	26	443	5	88.60	–	–	2/136

Kim Hughes took Australia to Pakistan for six matches, three of them Tests, three summers later. This was a disastrous trip for Australia, Pakistan winning the rubber three–nil. An apparently well-balanced Australian team was outplayed by Pakistan, who were superbly led by Imran Khan. Leg-spinner Abdul Qadir took 22 wickets in the three Tests, repeatedly confusing Australia's batsmen, often pitching into rough created by pace bowlers. None of Australia's bowlers could match his hostility.

The tour opened with a draw against the Patron's XI at Rawalpindi, where Kim Hughes made 101 not out. Pakistan won the First Test at Karachi by nine wickets, Qadir taking 5 for 76 in Australia's second innings. Centuries by Mansoor Akhtar (111) and Zaheer Abbas (126) set up Pakistan's victory by an innings and three runs in the Second Test at Faisalabad, where Qadir took 11 wickets. Qadir's four wickets in the Third Test at Lahore were costly (188 runs), but centuries from Moshin Khan (135) and Javed Miandad (138) gave Pakistan a big advantage, which they never surrendered, winning by nine wickets to complete the clean sweep. Beaten in the Tests, Australia could not secure a win in the one-day matches and finished the six-week tour without a single victory.

AUSTRALIA IN PAKISTAN 1988-89

	First-class Results					All Matches			
Matches	Won	Lost	Drawn	Tied	Matches	Won	Lost	Drawn	Tied
6	–	1	5	–	7	–	2	5	–

Date	Venue	Opponent	Results for Australians
Sep 5	Lahore	BCCP Patron's XI	Drawn
Sep 9	Quetta	Baluchistan Governor's XI	Drawn
Sep 15	Karachi	PAKISTAN (1st Test)	Lost by an inns & 188 runs
Sep 23	Faisalabad	PAKISTAN (2nd Test)	Drawn
Oct 2	Peshawar	NW Frontier Governor's XI	Drawn
Oct 7	Lahore	PAKISTAN (3rd Test)	Drawn
Oct 14	Lahore	*Pakistan (L/O Intl)	Lost on more wkts lost

Player	State	M	Inn	NO	Runs	HS	50	100	Avrge	Ct/St	Overs	Mdns	Runs	Wkts	Avrge	5wi	10wm	Best
Boon, DC	TAS	5	8	–	258	76	2	–	32.25	11	–	–	–	–	–	–	–	–
Border, AR (Capt)	QLD	4	7	3	266	113*	1	1	66.50	4	28.0	11	48	–	–	–	–	–
Dodemaide, AIC	VIC	4	5	1	46	19	–	–	11.50	1	139.1	40	293	13	22.54	–	–	4/46

▶

Player	State	M	Inn	NO	Runs	HS	50	100	Avrge	Ct/St	Overs	Mdns	Runs	Wkts	Avrge	5wi	10wm	Best
Healy, IA	QLD	6	8	2	117	29*	–	–	19.50	10/2	–	–	–	–	–	–	–	–
Jones, DM	VIC	5	9	1	143	60	1	–	17.88	1	9.0	3	21	–	–	–	–	–
Marsh, GR	WA	5	8	1	475	136	3	2	67.85	7	–	–	–	–	–	–	–	–
May, TBA	SA	4	4	1	33	14	–	–	11.00	–	163.0	46	430	14	30.71	–	–	4/97
McDermott, CJ	QLD	3	1	–	16	16	–	–	16.00	–	64.0	7	291	6	48.50	–	–	3/51
Reid, BA	WA	4	5	1	37	20	–	–	9.25	1	140.4	29	407	20	20.35	–	–	4/100
Siddons, JD	VIC	2	2	–	68	60	1	–	34.00	1	–	–	–	–	–	–	–	–
Sleep, PR	SA	4	4	1	120	52	1	–	40.00	2	81.5	23	322	11	29.27	–	–	4/65
Taylor, PL	NSW	5	7	3	254	83	3	–	63.50	2	115.0	32	318	10	31.80	–	–	4/78
Veletta, MRJ	WA	3	5	1	155	72*	1	–	38.75	2	–	–	–	–	–	–	–	–
Waugh, SR	NSW	6	9	–	160	59	1	–	17.78	4	126.0	33	362	4	90.50	–	–	1/15
Wood, GM	WA	6	8	2	314	91	3	–	52.33	3	–	–	–	–	–	–	–	–

Allan Border took Australia on a similar tour of Pakistan six seasons later, but once again Australia went without a win. They gave an improved account of themselves in the Tests, going down one–nil, but the lack of penetration by the bowlers proved fatal. The batsmen scored well, Geoff Marsh contributing 475 runs at 67.85, Graeme Wood, David Boon and Border all making runs and Peter Taylor surprising with a tour batting average of 63.50, topscore 83.

After draws against the Patrons XI at Lahore and against the Governor's XI at Quetta, Australia lost the First Test at Karachi by an innings and 188 runs. Javed Miandad rescued Pakistan with a fine 211 after they lost 2 for 21 in the first innings. Thereafter Pakistan controlled the match, Asif Iqbal taking nine wickets. Border's 113 not out in the Second Test at Faisalabad failed to prevent a draw. At Lahore the Third Test also limped to a draw after rain ended Australian hopes of forcing a win. The Australian fielding throughout this tour was disgraceful, with the players apparently allowing themselves to be upset by poor umpiring and sub-standard pitches, which at one stage attracted threats of the tour being abandoned. Manager Col Egar quickly stifled these moves but went to the Pakistan Board with protests about the umpires and the insulting language of the Pakistani players.

AUSTRALIA IN PAKISTAN 1994-95

	First-class Results					All Matches			
Matches	Won	Lost	Drawn	Tied	Matches	Won	Lost	Drawn	Tied
4	–	1	3	–	10	5	2	3	–

Date	Venue	Opponent	Results for Australians
Sep 23	Rawalpindi	President's XI	Drawn
Sep 28	Karachi	PAKISTAN (1st Test)	Lost by 1 wkt
Oct 5	Rawalpindi	PAKISTAN (2nd Test)	Drawn
Oct 12	Lahore	*South Africa (L/O Intl)	Won by 6 wkts
Oct 14	Multan	*Pakistan (L/O Intl)	Won by 7 wkts
Oct 18	Faisalabad	*South Africa (L/O Intl)	Won by 22 runs
Oct 22	Rawalpindi	*Pakistan (L/O Intl)	Lost by 9 wkts
Oct 24	Peshawar	South Africa (L/O Intl)	Won by 3 wkts
Oct 30	Lahore	*Pakistan (L/O Intl)	Won by 64 runs
Nov 1	Lahore	PAKISTAN (3rd Test)	Drawn

Australia in Pakistan 1994-95: *standing* Errol Alcott (physio), Shane Warne, Phil Emery, Michael Bevan, Glenn McGrath, Jo Angel, Gavin Robertson, Damien Fleming, Michael Slater; *seated* Tim May, Mark Waugh, David Boon, Col Egar (manager), Mark Taylor (capt.), Bob Simpson (coach), Steve Waugh, Justin Langer, Craig McDermott.

Player	State	M	Inn	NO	Runs	HS	50	100	Avrge	Ct/St	Overs	Mdns	Runs	Wkts	Avrge	5wi	10wm	Best
J Angel	WA	2	3	–	20	8	–	–	6.67	1	80.1	11	306	6	51.00	–	–	3/54
MG Bevan	NSW	4	6	1	343	91	4	–	68.60	5	10.0	–	60	1	60.00	–	–	1/21
DC Boon	TAS	4	6	2	250	114*	–	2	62.50	5	3.0	1	9	–	–	–	–	–
PA Emery	NSW	1	1	1	8	8*	–	–	–	5/1	–	–	–	–	–	–	–	–
DW Fleming	VIC	1	–	–	–	–	–	–	–	–	48.0	5	161	7	23.00	–	–	4/75
IA Healy	QLD	3	5	1	184	58	2	–	46.00	14/1	–	–	–	–	–	–	–	–
JL Langer	WA	1	1	–	69	69	1	–	69.00	–	–	–	–	–	–	–	–	–
TBA May	SA	3	4	1	12	10	–	–	4.00	–	111.0	29	294	7	42.00	–	–	3/69
CJ McDermott	QLD	3	3	1	50	29	–	–	25.00	2	129.0	20	458	10	45.80	–	–	4/74
GD McGrath	NSW	3	4	–	4	3	–	–	1.00	–	111.3	24	326	17	19.18	1	1	6/49
MJ Slater	NSW	4	7	–	285	110	1	1	40.71	1	1.1	–	4	1	4.00	–	–	1/4
MA Taylor (Capt)	NSW	4	7	1	111	69	1	–	18.50	4	3.0	1	11	1	11.00	–	–	1/11
SK Warne	VIC	4	5	–	73	33	–	–	14.60	2	210.4	59	598	23	26.00	2	–	6/136
ME Waugh	NSW	4	5	–	277	71	4	–	55.40	3	30.0	3	106	2	53.00	–	–	2/63
SR Waugh	NSW	3	4	1	224	98	3	–	74.67	4	38.0	8	90	1	90.00	–	–	1/28

Three months after Australia completed a seven-week tour of Pakistan in late 1994, allegations emerged that turned the tour into one of the most discussed of all time. The tour programme finished with Australia failing to win one of the three Tests after dropping 13 catches and forfeiting winning positions in all three games. The cricket was absorbing, with Pakistan winning the First Test by the narrowest of margins (one wicket). Inzamum-Ul-Haq and Mushtaq Ahmed added 57 runs for the 10th wicket in the final innings to salvage Pakistan's 39-year unbeaten record at Karachi by one wicket. England's Dickie Bird said it was the finest match he ever umpired. Bird's signal of four leg-byes gave Pakistan the match when Pakistan needed three to win and two to tie off the last ball.

Australian wicket-keeper Ian Healy thought he cost Australia the match when he missed a difficult stumping chance off the last delivery. Healy lost sight of a low, skidding Shane Warne leg-break with Inzamum out of his crease. TV replays later showed the ball had not come off Inzamum's leg as Bird signalled but had missed everything. Australia dominated the Test for four and a half days but were thwarted by the highest last wicket stand to win a match in the 117-year history of Test cricket. Mark Taylor, Australia's 39th Test captain and the first since Ian Craig in 1957 to begin his reign offshore, made a pair in this match.

At Rawalpindi in the Second Test Victorian Damien Fleming, who had taken four other hat-tricks in junior and Melbourne club cricket, became the first Australian to take a hat-trick on his Test debut by dismissing Aamir Malik, Inzamum and Salim Malik with successive balls. Pakistan avoided defeat by scoring 537 in their second innings after following on 261 runs behind. Taylor dropped Salim Malik at 20 and he went on to 237.

After another draw in the Third Test at Lahore gave Pakistan the series one–nil, Taylor blamed his team's failure to break through at crucial periods for Australia's failure to end their 36-year run without a win in Pakistan. Injuries and sloppy catching were major factors, too. 'We just couldn't pinpoint why we were dropping them,' said coach Bob Simpson. McDermott (infected toe), Fleming (shoulder tear), McGrath (thigh injury), Warne (neck strain) and Healy (broken thumb) kept physiotherapist Errol Alcott busy. Healy and Steve Waugh (shoulder damage) flew home early. Phil Emery, flown to Lahore to replace Healy in the Third Test, took five catches and made a stumping in his Test debut but also dropped Salim Malik 38 runs before he was out for 143.

For the sixth series in 18 months Warne was Australia's leading wicket taker, matching Richie Benaud's record 18 wickets in three Tests in 1959–60. Michael Bevan proved a fine replacement for Border at No. 5. Michael Slater was Australia's top scorer with 244 runs at 48.80. But all this proved academic stuff two months later when the *Sydney Morning Herald*'s respected cricket writer Phil Wilkins disclosed that gamblers had attempted to influence match results by offering bribes to Australian players. Initially, Shane Warne and Tim Warne were named as gamblers' targets, but within days Mark Waugh also became involved.

Wilkins said Warne and May were offered $70,000 each to throw the First Test, Mark Waugh $134,000 to throw his wicket away. All the players immediately rejected the approaches, but did not report it to the team management for fear of reprisals. Team manager Col Egar had not learned of the bribe offers until the Third Test at Lahore. In India — centre of cricket bookmaking — newspapers told of star players whose lifestyles had dramatically improved. In Pakistan team manager Intikhab Alam said that after Australia's tour he asked his players to swear on the Koran before touring Zimbabwe that they were not involved in gambling. With the International Cricket Council examining all aspects of the bribery charges, ramifications of Australia's tour appear certain to be far reaching.

PAKISTAN IN AUSTRALIA 1964–65 TO 1992–93

Pakistan played six matches on their initial tour of Australia in 1964–65, four of them first-class. The Test at Melbourne and the other three first-class matches were drawn, with Hanif Mohammad scoring 104 and 93 to topscore for his side in each innings of the Test He then kept wicket throughout the match in place of Abdul Kadir, who was injured while batting. Arif Butt's 6 for 89 was the best bowling feat on debut for Pakistan to that time. Unbeaten in serious matches, Pakistan lost three limited over matches before travelling to New Zealand.

Australia won all three Tests against Pakistan in 1972–73 under the captaincy of Ian Chappell whose batsmen all scored heavily against Intikhab Alam's bowlers. Ian Chappell (196) and Rod Marsh (118) made centuries in the First Test at Adelaide, Ian Redpath (135), Greg Chappell (116 not out), Paul Sheahan (127), and John Benaud (142) centuries in the Second Test in Melbourne, and Max Walker won the Third Test at Sydney by taking 6 for 15 in Pakistan's second innings.

The First Test of the 1976–77 Pakistan v. Australia series in Adelaide was drawn despite centuries from Ian Davis (105), Doug Walters (197) and Zaheer Abbas (101). Australian batsmen found Mushtaq Mohammad's bowlers to their liking again in Melbourne where they ran up a total of 8 declared for 517, thanks to 82 from Turner, 121 from Greg Chappell and 168 by Cosier. This set Australia on the way to victory by 348 runs, Lillee chiming in with 10 for 135. Against all the odds Pakistan levelled the series by winning their first-ever Test in Australia, Imran Khan and Safraz Nawaz combining to bundle Australia out for 180 in their second innings in the Third Test at Sydney. Asif Iqbal gave Pakistan a 149-run first innings lead with an innings of 120, including a match-winning 115 sixth-wicket stand with Miandad (57).

Pakistan had another remarkable win over Australia in the first of two Tests in 1978–79 when Safraz took 9 for 86 in Melbourne. The Test was marred by a tantrum from Rodney Hogg who smashed down his stumps when given run out as he left the crease before the ball

ASIA AWAKES

Intikhab Alam, Pakistan's captain in Australia in 1972-73, proved a classy leg-spinner and a handy late order batsman.

Mushtaq Mohammed (fourth in line), who took over from Intikhab as Pakistan's skipper, was badly handicapped by the lack of genuine strike bowlers.

was dead. Majid Khan's 108 gave Pakistan a big lead which a century from Border (105) and 84 from Kim Hughes could not overtake, Pakistan winning by 71 runs. Australia made amends by winning the Second Test in Perth by seven wickets. Allan Hurst took 4 for 61 and 5 for 94 and, with Geoff Dymock and Rodney Hogg providing fine support, overcame a Pakistan side for which Miandad (129 not out) and Asif Iqbal (134 not out) hit centuries.

Miandad returned to Australia as captain of the 1981-82 Pakistan tourists. His batsmen found Lillee in devastating form in the first two Tests, Australia winning by 286 runs in Perth and by ten wickets in Brisbane. Lillee took 15 wickets in these wins but in the Third Test at Melbourne failed to take a wicket in conceding 104 runs. Only Graeme Wood (100) made headway against Pakistan's bowling and Pakistan provided a major upset yet again by winning by an innings and 82 runs.

Imran Khan took over as Pakistan's captain for the next four series in Australia. But Pakistan officials erred in appointing him captain in 1983-84 as he could not bowl and was only able to bat in the last two of the five Tests because of a stress fracture to his left shin. Zaheer Abbass, who had originally been named to lead the side, refused to take over as Pakistan's captain in Imran's place. Sarfraz Nawar was flown in as a replacement after his suspension, for attacking selectors who initially omitted him from the side, had been lifted.

Pakistan lost two of the five Tests and were also defeated by Western Australia, and had to be content with wins over South Australia, Victoria and Tasmania. They also lost eight and won four of the non-first-class matches, including four limited over matches to Australia. Three drawn Tests added to Pakistan's poor tour record. Australia played up to six left-handed batsmen in the Test sides to combat Abdul Qadir, which forced him to bowl round the wicket and neutralised his googly. Pakistan's big success was Qasim Omar, who showed pluck against Australia's pace bowling, and Moshin Khan who made 149 in the Third Test and 152 in the Fourth Test.

Imran was fit again when Pakistan returned in 1988-89 but he bowled only 3.2 overs in the one-match visit. He was in far better shape the following summer when he appeared in four of Pakistan's six matches, but the wicket-taking was left mainly to Wasim Akram (17 at 18.71), Tauseef Ahmed (10 at 35.80) and Waqar Younis (10 at 49.60). Australia won the First Test at Melbourne by 92 runs, thanks to some clever bowling by Alderman (8 for 135) and a fine century by Mark Taylor (101). Australia won eight lbw appeals in the match, six of them from Alderman. The Second Test at Adelaide was drawn. Wasim produced a brilliant allround display, scoring 52 from 89 balls, then taking 5 for 100, and following it with his maiden first-class century, 123 in 244 minutes, lifting Pakistan's score from 5 for 90 to 6 for 281 in a fine stand with Imran (136). Dean Jones made 116 and 121 not out for Australia. Rain ruined the Third Test in Sydney, which also ended in a draw, leaving Australia winners of the rubber one–nil. The Pakistanis were also defeated on this tour by Western Australia and Victoria. Pakistan paid a high penalty for their key bowler Abdul Qadir returning home before the Tests began, ostensibly because of a damaged finger but almost certainly on grounds of temperament.

Imran made his last visit to Australia for one match in 1991–92 for the World Cup. Pakistan played two first-class matches to prepare for the Cup matches, and were held to a draw by Victoria in Bendigo and a draw by Tasmania in Devonport. They went on to win the World Cup in a thrilling final against England.

Javed Miandad replaced Imran as the Pakistani captain for their 1992–93 Australian trip, which was aimed mainly at the World Series one-day matches. They played only one first-class match in Australia but went to New Zealand over Christmas for a Test and some one-day fixtures. They beat Queensland in their sole first-class appearance, thanks to innings of 102 not out and 125 not out from Asif Mujtaba, the man who hit a six in Hobart to tie a one-day match against Australia. Wasim Akram occasionally took over the captaincy from Miandad and many people saw in his aggressive approach a new face of Pakistani cricket. (See Appendix for summaries.)

AUSTRALIA VERSUS SRI LANKA

Australia played a leading part in Sri Lanka's struggle to achieve Test status, granted by the International Cricket Conference in 1981. Australian teams travelling to and from England by sea played frequent matches in Sri Lanka, encouraging Sri Lankan enthusiasts to improve their standards. The 1884 Australians led by Billy Murdoch played an Eighteen of Ceylon, with F.L. Shand, a former Harrow School fast bowler taking 5 for 42 in Australia's innings of 75. The Ceylon XVIII, all Englishmen working in Ceylon's tea industry, made only 49 in reply before the Australians had to return to their ship. The Reverend E.F. Waddy took an Australian side made up of State and Test players on a nine-match tour of Ceylon in 1913–14. The Australians won five and drew the rest of their matches, Rupert Minnett proving the all round star. None of the matches were recognised as first-class. The team played in Colombo, Galle, Kandy, Anuradhpura, and Darrawella. In 1934 F.C. ('Derrick') de Saram became the first Sri Lankan to score a century against Australia when he made 128 for Oxford University against Woodfull's team in England. He handled the bowling of Grimmett, Fleetwood-Smith and Ebeling without discomfort and later showed his innings was no fluke by scoring a century against Gloucestershire. At least five Sri Lankan-born cricketers have appeared in first-class cricket in Australia, starting with George Bailey, a member of the first Australian touring team in England in 1878, Patrick McCarthy (WA), Malcolm Franke (Queensland), Gamini Goonesena (NSW), and Davenell Whatmore (Victoria). (See Appendix for summaries.)

AUSTRALIA IN SRI LANKA 1969–70 TO 1992–93

After Lindsay Hassett's Australian Services team won their only match in Ceylon in 1945–46, Bill Lawry took Australia on a four-match visit in 1969–70, all of which were drawn. Kim Hughes' 1980–81 side also played a draw in their match in Colombo in 1980–81. Greg Chappell's 1982–83 Australians won the initial Test between the countries by an innings and 38 runs at Kandy, and drew their other first-class match against a President's XI. They lost two, won one and drew one of their limited over matches.

Sri Lanka's improvement on their 1982–83 and 1984–85 Australian tours was rewarded in 1992–93 when Australia played eight matches in Sri Lanka under Border's captaincy. The program included three Tests and the Sri Lankans distinguished themselves by forcing Australia to a close 16-run margin in the First Test at Colombo. They repeated this form with draws in the Second Test at Colombo and the Third Test at Moratuwa. The Sri Lankans' batting was bright and enterprising and their bowlers reduced one of Australia's batting stars, Mark Waugh, to a shadow of his normal self, Waugh's ducks contributing to his poor tour average of 32.33. The wickets of all the Australian bowlers cost at least 20 runs apiece. Later in 1992–93 the Sri Lankans showed their form against Australia was indicative of their improvement by beating England at home in a Test for the first time. (See Appendix for summaries.)

AUSTRALIA IN MALAYA 1927

A strong Australian team that included five Test stars played nine matches in Malaya in 1927 under the captaincy of Charlie Macartney, and sustained one of the most surprising defeats ever by an Australian lineup. Their defeat at Kuala Lumpur between 3 and 6 June by a Malayan XI ranks with Australia's unlikely defeats by America in 1912 and 1913 and with the 1963 loss to The Netherlands by Bill Lawry's team just after they had defeated England for The Ashes.

The Australian team included Tommy Andrews, Bill Woodfull, Bert Oldfield, Ernie Mayne and Macartney, all of whom had enjoyed Test triumphs, pace bowler Sam Everett, who toured England with the 1926 Australians, state representatives Ted Adams and Mick Bardsley (NSW) and Hugh Gamble (Victoria and Queensland), supported by the useful grade cricketers E.F. Rofe and J.P. Sullivan.

Malaya scored 108 and then bundled Australia out for 85, thanks to a 7 for 42 bowling blitz by Dr P.H. Hennessy. Leading by 23 runs on the first innings, Malaya reached 158 in their second innings, and dismissed Australia for 142, Dr Hennessy taking three more wickets to finish with 10 for 72. Bill Woodfull, at the peak of his career, topscored for Australia with 36 before brilliant fielding ran him out. This was the only match Macartney's team lost on a tour in which Woodfull topped the batting averages with 610 runs at 76.25, and Macartney headed the bowling averages with 54 wickets at 5.66. (See Appendix for summaries.)

Charlie Macartney's Australian XI in Malaya in 1927: *back row* R. Bardsley, J. Sullivan, official, H.S. Gamble, official, E.F. Rofe, E.W. Adams; *front* W.A. Oldfield, W.M. Woodfull, C.G. Macartney, official, official, T.J.E. Andrews, E.R. Mayne, S.C. Everett.

CHAPTER ELEVEN

WEST INDIAN FIGHT-BACK

Australia won 11 of the first 15 Tests against the West Indies and suffered only two defeats. Tests between the countries began in 1930–31 when Cambridge blue 'Jackie' Grant brought the first West Indies team to Australia for a 14-match tour, but it was not until 1964–65 that the West Indies won a rubber against Australia at home. The West Indies did not win a series in Australia until 1979–80. Since then the West Indies have staged a recovery, and at the end of the 1995 Caribbean tour by Mark Taylor's team the West Indies had reduced the margin to five wins. The countries have now played 81 Tests, Australia winning 32, the West Indies 27, with 21 drawn and one tied, a great West Indian fight-back.

The West Indian recovery after a disastrous start has been a triumph for the cricket skills of the West Indians, and the outcome of a marked improvement in temperament. The early West Indian teams had a decided tendency to panic under pressure, often when victory was near, but the recent West Indian teams have been coldly efficient. They have learned how to win and their stars enjoy the challenge of tight finishes. Under the rule which allows them a new ball every 85 overs and the luxury of including four fast bowlers, they are likely to overcome Australia's four-win lead, a commendable achievement for a competitor who was only granted Test match status in 1928.

The record of West Indian cricketers has been built against an unlikely background. The islands from which her players are taken have no central government, and the West Indian Board of Control is almost continually strapped for cash. The first postwar Australian tour by the West Indian team captained by John Goddard lost money in 1951–52, despite the presence of Frank Worrell, Everton Weekes, Clyde Walcott, Sonny Ramadhin and Alf Valentine.

Neither of the first two West Indian teams to go overseas appealed to the English public, though the batting of Lebrun Constantine, son of a slave, plantation foreman and father of the legendary Sir Learie Constantine impressed in his innings of 113 at Lord's against the MCC in 1900, and George Challenor's 108 versus Nottinghamshire in 1906 was full of good strokes. The failure of these teams to excite cricket fans who had

The West Indian team to tour England in 1906 failed to arouse public interest that followed later teams: *back row* T.C. Learmond, J.J. Cameron, C.K. Bancroft, C.S. Morrison; *centre* S.G. Smith, L.S. Constantine, P.A. Goodman, R. Ollivierre; *front* G. Challoner, O.H. Leyne, J.E. Parker, H.B.G. Austin (capt.), C.P. Cumberbatch, A.E.A. Harrigan, *absent* T. Burton. *Marylebone Cricket Club*

plenty of county cricket heroics to watch disappointed the influential English players, R.S. Lucas, Lord Hawke and Arthur Priestley. They had toured the West Indies in 1895 and 1897 and returned with promising reports of the islands' abundance of cricket talent.

Wisden's assessment of both the 1900 and 1906 English tours by the West Indies was that they undertook programs that were too ambitious. The pioneering 1900 team captained by Pelham Warner's brother, R.S.A. Warner, won only five of their 17 matches, lost eight, and played four draws. The 1906 visitors, captained by H.B.G. Austin, won only seven of their 19 matches, with 10 losses and two draws. Neither side recovered from heavy defeats by Dr W.G. Grace's London Counties XI in their first matches.

Learie Constantine played alongside his father for Trinidad in 1922 and later that year toured England with the third West Indian team, showing flashes of the brilliance that won him fame from the time the West Indies entered Test cricket in 1928. He made 1381 runs at 34.52, took 107 wickets at 22.95, and took 33 catches on that 1928 tour, some of them catches no other cricketer could have reached. England won all three Tests in that series by an innings. The West Indies did better against England at home in 1929–30, sharing the four-Test rubber by winning the Third Test by 289 runs, their first-ever Test victory, after George Headley made a century in each innings (114 and 112). This enabled them to share the series, each side finishing with a win, and their other Tests producing draws.

WEST INDIES IN AUSTRALIA 1930-31

First-class Results					All Matches				
Matches	Won	Lost	Drawn	Tied	Matches	Won	Lost	Drawn	Tied
14	4	8	2	–	16	5	8	3	–

Date	Venue	Opponent	Results for Touring Team
Nov 21	Sydney	New South Wales	Lost by 4 wkts
Nov 28	Melbourne	Victoria	Lost by an inns & 254 runs
Dec 5	Adelaide	South Australia	Lost by 10 wkts
Dec 12	Adelaide	AUSTRALIA (1st Test)	Lost by 10 wkts
Dec 20	Launceston	Tasmania	Won by an inns & 50 runs
Dec 24	Hobart (TCA)	Tasmania	Drawn
Jan 1	Sydney	AUSTRALIA (2nd Test)	Lost by an inns & 172 runs
Jan 10	Brisbane (Ex)	Queensland	Won by 219 runs
Jan 16	Brisbane (Ex)	AUSTRALIA (3rd Test)	Lost by an inns & 217 runs
Jan 24	Newcastle	*Combined Country of NSW	Won by an inns & 1 run
Jan 29	Geelong	*Combined Country of Victoria	Drawn
Jan 31	Melbourne	Victoria	Drawn
Feb 7	Adelaide	South Australia	Lost by 1 wkt
Feb 13	Melbourne	AUSTRALIA (4th Test)	Lost by an inns & 122 runs
Feb 21	Sydney	New South Wales	Won by 86 runs
Feb 27	Sydney	AUSTRALIA (5th Test)	Won by 30 runs

Learie Constantine, later knighted, shows why he was regarded as one of the most spectacular of cricketers in this session at the Sydney Cricket Ground nets in 1930-31.

Player	M	Inn	NO	Runs	HS	50	100	Avrge	Ct/St	Overs	Mdns	Runs	Wkts	Avrge	5wi	10wm	Best
Barrow, I	9	15	1	245	45	–	–	17.50	15/3	–	–	–	–	–	–	–	–
Bartlett, EL	8	13	1	208	84	1	–	17.33	2	–	–	–	–	–	–	–	–
Birkett, LS	11	20	1	499	128*	1	1	26.26	10	51.0	2	205	2	102.50	–	–	1/16
Constantine, LN	13	23	0	708	100	5	1	30.78	21	257.0	25	950	47	20.21	3	–	6/25
de Caires, FI	4	7	–	165	76	2	–	23.58	2	4.0	–	20	1	20.00	–	–	1/20
Francis, GR	11	17	4	92	16*	–	–	7.07	7	250.6	38	840	29	28.97	–	–	4/48
Grant, GC (Capt)	13	24	4	739	102	5	1	36.95	11	1.0	–	1	–	–	–	–	–
Griffith, HC	12	17	4	92	17	–	–	7.07	4	309.4	42	1107	31	35.71	–	–	4/50
Headley, GA	13	25	1	1066	131	4	4	44.41	7	7.0	–	39	–	–	–	–	–
Hunte, ER	5	9	2	135	29	–	–	19.28	6/3	–	–	–	–	–	–	–	–
Martin, FR	13	24	2	606	123*	2	1	27.54	2	332.2	46	950	21	45.24	–	–	3/35
Roach, CA	14	26	–	637	104	3	1	24.50	10	11.0	1	63	–	–	–	–	–
Scott, OC	12	19	5	251	67*	1	–	17.92	–	292.2	10	1325	40	33.13	2	–	5/63
Sealy, JED	8	13	4	334	92	2	–	37.11	11	25.0	2	127	2	63.50	–	–	1/4
St Hill, EL	4	6	1	16	9	–	–	3.20	2	113.3	10	477	16	29.81	–	–	4/57
Wight, OS	4	6	–	45	22	–	–	7.50	1	–	–	–	–	–	–	–	–

With only seven Tests behind them, the West Indies undertook their initial Australian tour with a team heavily dependent on fast bowlers. Spinners who would have been invaluable in the prevailing conditions were left at home. They were further handicapped by the appointment of Jack Grant, winner of blues at Cambridge in 1929 and 1930, as captain. Neither Grant nor his deputy,

Lionel Birkett, had any experience of international cricket. Despite Constantine's spectacular hitting and fielding and his lively pace bowling and the stroke-play of Headley, the West Indians were outclassed by a splendidly led, well-balanced Australian team who won all the first four Tests by wide margins.

With their tour a shambles after appalling batting

WEST INDIAN FIGHT-BACK

collapses to Grimmett, Hurwood, Oxenham and Ironmonger, the West Indies staged an astonishing recovery to win the Fifth Test by 30 runs. Big Herman Griffith set up this triumph when he bowled Bradman, who had made 223 and 152 in his previous two Test innings, before he had scored. Centuries by Freddie Martin (123) and Headley (105) gave the West Indies enough runs for their bowlers to exploit a 'sticky' wicket.

The first West Indian cricket team to tour Australia suffered from poor captaincy and inexperience but they beat Australia in one of the 1930-31 Tests: *back row* G. Headley, C.A. Roach, E.A.C. Hunts, De Caires, O.C. Scott, O.S. Wright, L. Barrow, E.L. St Hill; *seated* R.C. Griffith, N.N. Constantine, J.E. Seheult (manager), G.C. Grant (capt.), R.H. Mallett (manager), L. Birkett, F.R. Martin, E.J. Bartlett, G. Francis; *front* J.E.D. Sealey. *Marylebone Cricket Club*

WEST INDIES IN AUSTRALIA 1951-52

The 1951-52 West Indies team in Australia: *back row* K.R. Ramadhin, K.R. Richards, D. Atkinson, S.C. Guillen, J. Trim, W. Ferguson; *centre* C.A. Merry (manager), A.F. Rae, A.L. Valentine, C.L. Walcott, P.E. Jones, R.E. Marshall, W. Ferguson (scorer); *front* R.J. Christiani, F.M. Worrell, G.E. Gomez, J.D. Goddard (capt.), J.B. Stollmeyer, E.D. Weekes.

	First-class Results				All Matches				
Matches	Won	Lost	Drawn	Tied	Matches	Won	Lost	Drawn	Tied
13	4	8	1	–	15	5	8	2	–

Date	Venue	Opponent	Results for Touring Team
Oct 26	Newcastle	*New South Wales Country XI	Won by 8 wkts
Oct 30	Townsville	*Queensland Country XI	Drawn
Nov 3	Brisbane	Queensland	Lost by 10 wkts
Nov 9	Brisbane	AUSTRALIA (1st Test)	Lost by 3 wkts
Nov 16	Sydney	New South Wales	Lost by 24 runs
Nov 23	Melbourne	Victoria	Drawn
Nov 30	Sydney	AUSTRALIA (2nd Test)	Lost by 7 wkts
Dec 7	Adelaide	South Australia	Lost by 227 runs
Dec 14	Perth	Western Australia	Lost by 1 wkt
Dec 22	Adelaide	AUSTRALIA (3rd Test)	Won by 6 wkts
Dec 31	Melbourne	AUSTRALIA (4th Test)	Lost by 1 wkt
Jan 8	Launceston	Tasmania	Won by 10 wkts
Jan 12	Hobart (TCA)	Tasmania	Won by an inns & 43 runs
Jan 18	Melbourne	Victoria	Won by 4 wkts
Jan 25	Sydney	AUSTRALIA (5th Test)	Lost by 202 runs

Player	M	Inn	NO	Runs	HS	50	100	Avrge	Ct/St	Overs	Mdns	Runs	Wkts	Avrge	5wi	10wm	Best
Atkinson, DE	7	12	2	99	23	–	–	9.90	1	109.3	19	353	17	20.76	–	–	4/26
Christiani, RJ	10	19	2	626	107*	3	1	36.82	3	–	–	–	–	–	–	–	–
Ferguson, W	7	10	1	133	52	1	–	14.78	4	152.0	12	642	16	40.13	1	–	6/45
Goddard, JD (Capt)	9	15	2	325	57*	1	–	25.00	6	129.4	27	342	7	48.86	–	–	1/55
Gomez, GF	10	19	2	535	97*	4	–	31.47	6	187.7	37	510	27	18.89	1	1	7/55
Guillen, SC	8	12	4	114	23	–	–	14.25	22/8	–	–	–	–	–	–	–	–
Jones, PE	7	9	3	71	46	–	–	11.83	5	154.0	25	482	9	53.56	–	–	3/57
Marshall, RE	8	14	–	368	114	–	1	26.29	4	73.5	16	230	6	38.33	–	–	4/70
Rae, AF	10	17	–	541	171	1	2	31.82	3	–	–	–	–	–	–	–	–
Ramadhin, S	8	12	5	33	16*	–	–	4.71	3	324.3	76	928	22	42.18	1	–	5/90
Rickards, KR	6	9	–	226	59	1	–	25.11	1	–	–	–	–	–	–	–	–
Stollmeyer, JB	11	20	–	529	104	2	1	26.45	9	31.0	3	138	6	23.00	–	–	3/52
Trim, J	4	7	1	27	8	–	–	4.50	–	72.0	7	250	15	16.67	2	1	7/80
Valentine, AL	10	17	5	48	14	–	–	4.00	4	417.7	79	1301	53	24.55	5	1	7/52
Walcott, CL	10	19	1	751	186	5	2	41.72	10/3	–	–	–	–	–	–	–	–
Weekes, EC	9	16	–	422	70	3	–	26.38	8	2.0	1	3	–	–	–	–	–
Worrell, FMM	9	17	2	619	160*	2	2	41.27	9	142.5	19	484	25	19.36	1	–	6/38

Twenty years after their initial tour, the West Indies returned to Australia, with John Goddard leading a confident, ebullient side that had just beaten England three–one in a four-Test series. Australia had defeated England in 1948 and South Africa in 1949-50 and the series was looked upon as a contest for world supremacy.

The Australians took a long, careful look at Ramadhin and Valentine, the spinners who had upset England, before they won the First Test by three wickets and thereafter made them pay heavily for their wickets. Hassett made 132, Miller 129 to help win the Second Test by seven wickets, before the West Indies caused a major

151

surprise by winning the Third Test by six wickets. This was only Australia's second defeat in 29 matches since World War II and stemmed from a first innings rout in which Frank Worrell (6 for 38) and Goddard bundled Australia out for 82. Australia recovered to win both the Fourth and Fifth Tests and take the series four–one. Ring and Bill Johnston, the last-wicket pair, put on 38 runs to win the Fourth Test by one wicket.

WEST INDIES IN AUSTRALIA 1960–61

First-class Results					All Matches				
Matches	Won	Lost	Drawn	Tied	Matches	Won	Lost	Drawn	Tied
14	4	5	4	1	22	10	5	5	2

Date	Venue	Opponent	Results for Touring Team
Oct 25	Bunbury	*Western Australian Country XI	Won by an inns & 94 runs
Oct 28	Perth	Western Australia	Lost by 94 runs
Nov 4	Perth	Australian XI	Drawn
Nov 11	Adelaide	South Australia	Drawn
Nov 18	Melbourne	Victoria	Won by an inns & 171 runs
Nov 25	Sydney	New South Wales	Lost by an inns & 119 runs
Dec 2	Brisbane	Queensland	Drawn
Dec 9	Brisbane	AUSTRALIA (1st Test)	Tied
Dec 16	Gympie	*Queensland Country XI	Won by an inns & 25 runs
Dec 20	Newcastle	*Northern New South Wales XI	Won by an inns & 96 runs
Dec 23	Sydney	New South Wales	Lost by an inns & 97 runs
Dec 30	Melbourne	AUSTRALIA (2nd Test)	Lost by 7 wkts
Jan 5	Hobart (TCA)	Combined XI	Won by 139 runs
Jan 9	Launceston	Tasmania	Won by 6 wkts
Jan 13	Sydney	AUSTRALIA (3rd Test)	Won by 222 runs
Jan 20	Ballarat	*Victorian Country XI	Won by an inns & 97 runs
Jan 23	Berri	*South Australian Country XI	Won by an inns & 235 runs
Jan 27	Adelaide	AUSTRALIA (4th Test)	Drawn
Feb 3	Canberra	*Australian Universities	Drawn
Feb 6	Goulburn	*Southern NSW Country XI	Won by 9 wkts
Feb 10	Melbourne	AUSTRALIA (5th Test)	Lost by 2 wkts
Feb 18	Canberra	*Prime Minister's XI	Tied

The 1960–61 West Indian team in Australia: *back row* P. Lashley, C. Watson, C.W. Smith, T.W. Dewdney, W. Hall, J. Hendriks, L. Gibbs, E. Alves (physio); *centre* G.E. Gomez (manager), K.T. Ramadhin, F.C.M. Alexander, F.M. Worrell (capt.), G. Sobers, A.L. Valentine, M. Marshall (assistant manager); *front* C.C. Hunte, R.B. Kanhai, J. Solomon, S. Nurse.

Player	M	Inn	NO	Runs	HS	50	100	Avrge	Ct/St	Overs	Mdns	Runs	Wkts	Avrge	5wi	10wm	Best
Alexander, FCM	10	19	5	734	108	6	1	52.42	31/1	–	–	–	–	–	–	–	–
Dewdney, DT	6	9	3	61	37*	–	–	10.16	–	71.0	9	296	5	59.20	–	–	2/28
Gibbs, LR	9	14	1	156	43	–	–	23.00	6	373.2	93	922	34	27.11	2	–	5/66
Hall, WW	12	18	–	218	50	1	–	21.11	1	260.4	22	1109	40	27.72	1	–	5/63
Hendriks, JL	4	7	1	191	82	3	–	31.83	5/5	–	–	–	–	–	–	–	–
Hunte, CC	11	20	–	731	110	3	2	36.55	17	4.0	–	16	1	16.00	–	–	1/16
Kanhai, RB	11	18	1	1093	252	4	4	64.29	4	–	–	–	–	–	–	–	–
Lashley, PD	9	15	–	291	69	1	–	19.40	6	–	–	–	–	–	–	–	–
Marshall, M	1	1	1	1	1*	–	–	–	–	–	–	–	–	–	–	–	–
Nurse, SM	10	18	–	498	97	3	–	27.66	7	–	–	–	–	–	–	–	–
Ramadhin, KT	7	12	1	93	16*	–	–	8.45	–	170.3	17	631	24	26.29	3	1	5/37
Smith, OC	11	21	–	560	59	2	–	26.66	5/2	–	–	–	–	–	–	–	–
Sobers, GS	12	22	–	804	168	3	3	36.54	23	356.0	45	1209	34	35.55	2	–	5/63
Solomon, JS	11	21	3	476	65	2	–	26.44	7	15.0	3	67	1	67.00	–	–	1/22
Valentine, AL	11	16	9	27	10*	–	–	3.85	6	376.7	74	1126	39	28.87	2	–	5/33
Watson, CD	7	9	4	57	16*	–	–	11.20	5	126.0	11	469	13	36.07	–	–	4/30
Worrell, FMM (Capt)	12	22	3	818	82	10	–	43.05	4	242.3	42	748	22	34.00	1	–	5/53

Frank Worrell's team produced memorable events with an exhilarating brand of cricket. They boosted attendances at a time when the ultra-cautious approach that characterised Len Hutton's reign as England's captain had brought an alarming crowd decline, and from October to February sustained an aggressive attitude that captivated the entire cricket fraternity. Worrell's stewardship of some marvellously talented players culminated in a world record crowd and a ticker-tape farewell from grateful Australians.

Western Australia defeated them in the first match of the tour, but after draws against an Australian XI and against South Australia, Rohan Kanhai led them on a run-feast with a chanceless 252 that crushed Victoria and set the pattern for the rest of the tour. At Brisbane in the First Test Gary Sobers' thrilling 132 was matched by Norm O'Neill's 181. Australia's powerful batting lineup needed only 233 to win in the fourth innings but Wes Hall ripped through the early batting. At 6 for 92 Australia refused to abandon the run-chase and Benaud and Davidson attacked. They took the score to 226 and appeared in sight of an easy win when Joe Solomons ran out Davidson for 80. The last over began with Australia requiring six runs, with three wickets in hand. It looked a simple task but two wickets fell and last man Lindsay Kline arrived with the scores level, and two balls left. Kline swatted the first delivery for what appeared the winning run but Solomons gathered at square leg and with only one stump to aim at hit the wicket. Three dismissals in the final over created wild confusion but when reality returned cricket's first tied Test was confirmed. It had taken 498 Tests to produce and was the 16th West Indies v. Australia contest.

From then on Worrell and Benaud encouraged the two talented teams to play bright, positive cricket. Australia won the Second Test in Melbourne, West Indies the Third Test in Sydney and after a breath-taking draw in Adelaide in the Fourth Test, they reached Melbourne all-square for the deciding Fifth Test. Melbourne virtually stopped work for five days and all round Australia fans hovered near their radios, following the ebb and flow of another thriller. On the second day a world record 90,800 people attended the match. Australia did not win until the fifth day, however, when their ninth wicket pair scampered for a bye and victory by two wickets, after a match studded with incidents. Bails were mysteriously dislodged by players' caps or found in front of the stumps, umpires Egar and Hoy had frequently to confer over appeals, and the run-out king Joe Solomons was twice run out himself.

WEST INDIES IN AUSTRALIA 1968-69

First-class Results					All Matches				
Matches	Won	Lost	Drawn	Tied	Matches	Won	Lost	Drawn	Tied
15	4	5	6	–	23	9	5	9	–

Date	Venue	Opponent	Results for Touring Team
Oct 22	Kalgoorlie	*Western Australian Country XI	Won by an inns & 155 runs
Oct 26	Perth	Western Australia	Won by 6 wkts
Nov 2	Perth	Combined XI	Lost by 7 wkts
Nov 8	Adelaide	South Australia	Lost by 10 wkts
Nov 15	Melbourne	Victoria	Drawn
Nov 22	Sydney	New South Wales	Won by 9 wkts
Nov 28	Murgon	*Queensland Country XI	Won by 6 wkts
Nov 29	Brisbane	Queensland	Drawn
Dec 6	Brisbane	AUSTRALIA (1st Test)	Won by 125 runs
Dec 13	Mackay	*Queensland Country XI	Drawn
Dec 16	Mildura	*Victorian Country XI	Drawn
Dec 19	Adelaide	South Australia	Drawn
Dec 26	Melbourne	AUSTRALIA (2nd Test)	Lost by an inns & 30 runs
Jan 3	Sydney	AUSTRALIA (3rd Test)	Lost by 10 wkts
Jan 9	Narrandera	*New South Wales Country XI	Won by 6 wkts
Jan 11	Hobart (TCA)	Tasmania	Drawn
Jan 16	Launceston	Combined XI	Won by 10 wkts
Jan 21	Loxton	*South Australian Country XI	Won by 8 wkts
Jan 24	Adelaide	AUSTRALIA (4th Test)	Drawn
Jan 31	Melbourne	Victoria	Drawn
Feb 5	Wangaratta	*Victorian Country XI	Won by 9 wkts
Feb 7	Newcastle	*Northern NSW Country XI	Drawn
Feb 11	Gunnedah	*New South Wales Country XI	Abandoned
Feb 14	Sydney	AUSTRALIA (5th Test)	Lost by 382 runs

Player	M	Inn	NO	Runs	HS	50	100	Avrge	Ct/St	Overs	Mdns	Runs	Wkts	Avrge	5wi	10wm	Best
Butcher, BF	12	23	1	1191	172	4	5	54.13	7	35.0	1	200	6	33.33	–	–	4/58
Camacho, SG	9	18	2	512	102	2	1	32.00	8	3.0	–	22	–	–	–	–	–
Carew, MC	11	22	4	787	90	7	–	42.35	12	130.3	21	474	10	47.40	–	–	3/49
Davis, CA	8	14	–	236	69	1	–	16.85	1	156.3	11	644	21	30.66	2	–	7/106
Edwards, RM	9	11	3	101	28*	–	–	12.62	1	170.7	16	808	14	57.71	–	–	4/13
Findlay, TM	7	10	1	192	59	1	–	21.33	15/3	–	–	–	–	–	–	–	–
Fredericks, RC	13	26	2	935	136	4	1	38.95	15	–	–	–	–	–	–	–	–
Gibbs, LR	10	14	8	32	17	–	–	5.33	7	420.3	77	1312	36	36.44	1	–	5/88
Griffith, CC	8	12	1	132	27	–	–	12.00	2	160.6	14	795	20	39.75	–	–	4/52
Hall, WW	9	14	2	179	78	1	–	14.91	1	218.6	23	966	30	32.20	1	–	5/48
Hendriks, JL	8	14	3	142	37*	–	–	12.90	14/5	–	–	–	–	–	–	–	–
Holford, DAJ	10	17	5	404	80	2	–	33.66	11	229.4	25	999	17	58.76	–	–	3/43
Kanhai, RB	11	21	1	847	174*	3	2	43.72	4	1.0	–	10	–	–	–	–	–
King, LA	6	7	2	100	39*	–	–	20.00	2	117.4	16	417	8	52.12	–	–	3/83
Lloyd, CH	13	22	1	799	129	5	1	38.04	7	56.0	6	217	4	54.25	–	–	2/17
Nurse, SM	12	21	1	694	137	3	1	34.70	10	1.4	–	12	–	–	–	–	–
Sobers, GS (Capt)	10	17	2	1011	132	3	5	67.40	13	310.1	49	1120	36	31.11	2	–	6/73

Some of Gary Sobers' star-studded side left Australia with their reputations in tatters after a young, comparatively inexperienced Australian team took the series three–one. The West Indian bowling lost all hostility by the end of a 23-match program that included 15 first-class games.

The West Indies lost two of their first three matches and although they recovered to beat New South Wales and win the First Test, the hammering Hall, Griffiths, David Holford and Lance Gibbs took placed too much work on Sobers and detracted from his batting. For Australia,

Ian Chappell began with 117, 50 and 165, although his run-getting deserted him in the Fifth Test. Doug Walters had by then become Australia's hero, with innings of 76, 118, 110, 50, 242 and 103. Walters was the first batsman to hit four 100s in a series against the West Indies, usually going to the crease after Lawry, Stackpole, Redpath and Ian Chappell had given Australia handy starts. Lawry had scores of 105, 205, 62, 89, and 151 in the Fifth Test when he and Walters put on 336 for the fourth wicket.

Sobers tried hard to rally his side but their capitulation to a young team demonstrated the mistake of selectors who persevered for too long with fading veterans. Sobers calculated that his team dropped 30 catches in the five Tests. The Australian catching was first-class throughout, and played a big part in winning the Second, Third and Fifth Tests.

WEST INDIES IN AUSTRALIA 1975-76

First-class Results					All Matches				
Matches	Won	Lost	Drawn	Tied	Matches	Won	Lost	Drawn	Tied
13	3	6	4	–	21	8	7	6	–

Date	Venue	Opponent	Results for Touring Team
Oct 29	Adelaide	*South Australian Colts	Won by 7 wkts
Oct 31	Adelaide	South Australia	Drawn
Nov 5	Bendigo	*Victorian Country XI	Won by 8 wkts
Nov 7	Melbourne	Victoria	Drawn
Nov 12	Dubbo	*Western NSW Country XI	Won by 8 wkts
Nov 14	Sydney	New South Wales	Won by 52 runs
Nov 19	Cairns	*Queensland Country XI	Drawn
Nov 21	Brisbane	Queensland	Won by an inns & 90 runs
Nov 28	Brisbane	AUSTRALIA (1st Test)	Lost by 8 wkts
Dec 6	Perth	Western Australia	Lost by 115 runs
Dec 12	Perth	AUSTRALIA (2nd Test)	Won by an inns & 87 runs
Dec 20	Adelaide	*Australia (L/O Intl)	Lost by 5 wkts
Dec 21	Adelaide	South Australia	Drawn
Dec 26	Melbourne	AUSTRALIA (3rd Test)	Lost by 8 wkts
Jan 3	Sydney	AUSTRALIA (4th Test)	Lost by 7 wkts
Jan 10	Newcastle	*Northern New South Wales	Won by an inns & 19 runs
Jan 13	Canberra	*ACT & Southern NSW	Drawn
Jan 16	Hobart (TCA)	Tasmania	Drawn
Jan 19	Launceston	*Tasmania	Won by 117 runs
Jan 23	Adelaide	AUSTRALIA (5th Test)	Lost by 190 runs
Jan 31	Melbourne	AUSTRALIA (6th Test)	Lost by 165 runs

Player	M	Inn	NO	Runs	HS	50	100	Avrge	Ct/St	Overs	Mdns	Runs	Wkts	Avrge	5wi	10wm	Best
Baichan, L	7	11	1	328	72	2	–	32.80	4	–	–	–	–	–	–	–	–
Boyce, KD	9	12	1	263	95*	2	–	29.22	3	173.2	20	764	23	33.21	1	–	5/72
Fredericks, RC	12	22	–	728	169	3	2	33.09	8	29.0	1	159	2	79.50	–	–	1/29
Gibbs, LR	9	15	9	71	15	–	–	11.83	5	291.5	57	818	17	48.11	1	–	5/102
Greenidge, CG	7	13	–	290	76	3	–	22.30	4	1.0	1	0	–	–	–	–	–
Holder, VA	7	11	1	112	24	–	–	11.20	1	192.2	15	902	26	34.69	1	–	5/108
Holding, MA	7	13	1	226	62	2	–	18.83	4	179.5	16	826	19	43.47	1	–	6/60
Inshan Ali	6	8	1	121	29	–	–	17.28	6	150.7	21	562	22	25.54	2	1	6/36
Julien, BD	8	13	2	279	78	1	–	25.36	5	167.4	20	711	20	35.55	–	–	3/32
Kallicharran, AI	12	21	1	730	101	7	1	36.50	6	11.1	2	81	3	27.00	–	–	1/7
Lloyd, CH (Capt)	11	19	1	776	149	3	3	43.11	10	20.0	5	61	1	61.00	–	–	1/5
Murray, DL	10	18	–	555	66	4	–	30.83	28/1	–	–	–	–	–	–	–	–
Murray, DA	3	4	1	67	23*	–	–	22.33	10/2	–	–	–	–	–	–	–	–
Padmore, AL	4	5	3	34	20	–	–	17.00	2	146.5	31	509	12	42.41	–	–	3/52
Richards, IVA	12	21	2	1107	175	4	4	58.26	11	30.4	2	143	2	71.50	–	–	2/42
Roberts, AME	9	14	–	144	32	–	–	10.28	1	235.7	26	893	35	25.51	1	–	7/54
Rowe, LG	10	17	–	434	107	2	1	25.52	5	3.0	–	19	–	–	–	–	–

Critics hailed the clash between Australia and this West Indies side as a virtual world championship and it attracted enough interest for the Australian Cricket Board to extend the rubber to six Tests. The West Indies relied on Andy Roberts and 21-year-old Michael Holding to supply their pace bowling but they were overshadowed by Lillee and Thomson at their peak. They not only took wickets regularly but they also forced the West Indian batting stars to retire frequently for repairs. The series yielded only one West Indian opening partnership of more than 50 runs, though Viv Richards made 1107 runs on his first Australian tour.

Australia's five–one triumph was an outstanding performance by a fine team. The bruising and nasty knocks they absorbed ended West Indies reliance on spin and began their long-standing preference for a four-pronged pace bowling battery. Thomson took 29 wickets in the six Tests, Lillee 27 after missing the Fourth Test.

Walker and Gilmour gave Lillee and Thomson strong support, whereas Bernard Julien and Keith Boyce disappointed in backing up Roberts and Holding. The big difference between the teams, however, was that the Australians flourished under pressure but the West Indies, without Worrell or Goddard to steady them, lacked composure. The Australian top order batsmen all made important contributions. Ian Chappell made 440 runs at 44.90, including 156 in the Second Test. Ian Redpath made three Test 100s, Greg Chappell three, Alan Turner one, Rick McCosker one, and altogether Australians hit 17 centuries in the season against the visitors. Ian Chappell became the fourth Australian to score more than 5000 Test runs and also became the first Australian to take 100 Test catches.

The main solace for a badly beaten West Indian side was Roy Fredericks' whirlwind 169 in Perth, where he hit his first 50 in 45 minutes off 33 balls, 100 in 116 minutes off 71 balls, and hit a six and 27 fours. Lance Gibbs took his 300th Test wicket in this match, matching a feat only Fred Trueman had achieved.

WEST INDIES IN AUSTRALIA 1979-80

First-class Results					All Matches				
Matches	Won	Lost	Drawn	Tied	Matches	Won	Lost	Drawn	Tied
7	5	1	1	–	21	13	5	3	–

Date	Venue	Opponent	Results for Touring Team
Nov 11	Geelong	*Geelong & District	Drawn
Nov 16	Adelaide	South Australia	Won by 9 wkts
Nov 23	Devonport	Tasmanian Invitation XI	Won by 260 runs
Nov 27	Sydney	*Australia (L/O Intl)	Lost by 5 wkts
Nov 28	Sydney	*England (L/O Intl)	Lost by 2 runs
Dec 1	Brisbane	AUSTRALIA (1st Test)	Drawn
Dec 9	Melbourne	*Australia (L/O Intl)	Won by 80 runs
Dec 11	Yea	*Victorian Country XI	Drawn
Dec 14	Launceston	Tasmania	Won by an inns & 61 runs
Dec 19	Toowoomba	*Queensland Country XI	Won by 4 wkts
Dec 21	Sydney	*Australia (L/O Intl)	Lost by 7 runs
Dec 23	Brisbane	*England (L/O Intl)	Won by 9 wkts
Dec 29	Melbourne	AUSTRALIA (2nd Test)	Won by 10 wkts
Jan 5	Perth	Western Australia	Lost by 8 wkts
Jan 8	Perth	*Western Australia	Won by 4 wkts
Jan 12	Melbourne	*England (L/O Intl)	Abandoned
Jan 14	Canberra	*ACT & District	Won by 121 runs
Jan 16	Adelaide	*England (L/O Intl)	Won by 107 runs
Jan 18	Sydney	*Australia (L/O Intl)	Lost by 9 runs
Jan 20	Melbourne	*England (L/O Intl)	Won by 2 runs
Jan 22	Sydney	*England (L/O Intl)	Won by 8 wkts
Jan 26	Adelaide	AUSTRALIA (3rd Test)	Won by 408 runs

The 1979-80 West Indian team in Australia: *standing* D.L. Haynes, M.D. Marshall, C.L. King, C.E. Croft, J. Garner, M.A. Holding, H.A. Gomez, D.R. Parry, D. Waight (physio); *seated* D.A. Murray, I.V.A. Richards, A.I. Kallicharran, W.V. Rodriguez (manager), C.H. Lloyd (capt.), D.L. Murray, L.G. Rowe, A.M.E. Roberts, C.G. Greenidge.

Player	M	Inn	NO	Runs	HS	50	100	Avrge	Ct/St	Overs	Mdns	Runs	Wkts	Avrge	5wi	10wm	Best
Croft, CEH	6	7	3	22	12	–	–	5.50	–	217.0	36	688	29	23.72	2	–	5/49
Garner, J	7	8	3	187	60	1	–	37.40	8	230.1	48	641	32	20.03	1	–	5/43
Gomes, HA	3	5	2	225	137*	1	1	75.00	1	2.0	–	15	–	–	–	–	–
Greenidge, CG	6	11	1	308	76	1	–	30.80	13	–	–	–	–	–	–	–	–
Haynes, DL	6	12	2	298	58	1	–	29.80	5	–	–	–	–	–	–	–	–
Holding, MA	4	5	1	24	11	–	–	6.00	3	140.0	32	407	18	22.61	–	–	4/27
Kallicharran, AI	6	10	2	554	138	–	1	69.25	7	24.2	1	40	1	40.00	–	–	1/6
King, CL	4	8	2	206	92	1	–	34.33	1	79.0	22	196	6	32.66	–	–	2/9
Lloyd, CH (Capt)	6	9	–	315	121	1	1	35.00	6	–	–	–	–	–	–	–	–
Marshall, MD	2	3	1	39	23*	–	–	19.50	–	52.0	14	144	7	20.57	–	–	3/66
Murray, DA	2	3	–	51	23	–	–	17.00	5	–	–	–	–	–	–	–	–
Murray, DL	6	7	1	224	103	–	1	37.33	22/1	–	–	–	–	–	–	–	–
Parry, DR	3	3	–	104	41	–	–	34.66	–	126.4	23	399	11	36.27	–	–	3/66
Richards, IVA	5	6	–	592	140	4	2	98.66	6	5.0	1	9	–	–	–	–	–
Roberts, AME	5	5	–	89	54	1	–	17.80	3	168.3	32	453	18	25.16	–	–	4/25
Rowe, LG	6	9	–	289	82	2	–	32.11	3	–	–	–	–	–	–	–	–

Four years after their five–one drubbing, the West Indians returned with a far superior fast bowling battery in Garner, Holding, Roberts and Croft and in a three-Test series they triumphed two–nil with the other Test drawn. All the West Indian bowlers had been thoroughly blooded by two years of cricket with Packer's World Series rebels and despite some resolute batting from Bruce Laird, Greg Chappell, Allan Border and Kim Hughes, Australia could not match heavy scoring by Vivian Richards, Alvin Kallicharran, Gordon Greenidge and Clive Lloyd. Lillee badly missed Thomson's support, although Geoff Dymock proved a whole-hearted trier. The Australians found the bowling of England's new ball exponents a much easier proposition in the three-Test series staged in the same summer, defeating England three–nil. The Ashes were not at stake.

WEST INDIES IN AUSTRALIA 1981-82

First-class Results					All Matches				
Matches	Won	Lost	Drawn	Tied	Matches	Won	Lost	Drawn	Tied
7	4	1	2	–	24	16	5	3	–

Date	Venue	Opponent	Results for Touring Team
Nov 13	Adelaide	South Australia	Won by 226 runs
Nov 18	Mildura	*Victorian Country XI	Drawn
Nov 21	Melbourne	*Pakistan (L/O Intl)	Won by 18 runs
Nov 24	Sydney	*Australia (L/O Intl)	Lost by 7 wkts
Nov 27	Sydney	New South Wales	Won by 9 wkts
Dec 2	Orange	*New South Wales Country XI	Won by 54 runs
Dec 5	Adelaide	*Pakistan (L/O Intl)	Lost by 8 runs
Dec 7	Hobart (TCA)	Tasmania	Drawn
Dec 11	Brisbane	Queensland	Won by an inns & 92 runs
Dec 16	Caloundra	*Queensland Country XI	Won by 68 runs
Dec 19	Perth	*Pakistan (L/O Intl)	Won by 7 wkts
Dec 20	Perth	*Australia (L/O Intl)	Won by 8 wkts
Dec 26	Melbourne	AUSTRALIA (1st Test)	Lost by 58 runs
Jan 2	Sydney	AUSTRALIA (2nd Test)	Drawn
Jan 10	Melbourne	*Australia (L/O Intl)	Won by 5 wkts
Jan 12	Sydney	*Pakistan (L/O Intl)	Won by 7 wkts
Jan 16	Brisbane	*Pakistan (L/O Intl)	Won on run rate
Jan 17	Brisbane	*Australia (L/O Intl)	Won by 5 wkts
Jan 19	Sydney	*Australia (L/O Intl)	Lost on run rate
Jan 23	Melbourne	*Australia (L/O Intl)	Won by 86 runs
Jan 24	Melbourne	*Australia (L/O Intl)	Won by 128 runs
Jan 26	Sydney	*Australia (L/O Intl)	Lost by 46 runs
Jan 27	Sydney	*Australia (L/O Intl)	Won by 18 runs
Jan 30	Adelaide	AUSTRALIA (3rd Test)	Won by 5 wkts

The 1981-82 West Indian team in Australia: *standing* M.D. Marshall, D.L. Haynes, J.P. Dujon, H. Joseph, C.E. Croft, J. Garner, S.T. Clarke, F.F.A. Bacchus, H.A. Gomes, A. Logie, J. Waight (physio); *seated* D.A. Murray, A.M.E. Roberts, G.S. Camacho (manager), C.H. Lloyd (capt.), I.V.A. Richards, C.G. Greenidge, M.A. Holding.

Player	M	Inn	NO	Runs	HS	50	100	Avrge	Ct/St	Overs	Mdns	Runs	Wkts	Avrge	5wi	10wm	Best
Bacchus, SFAF	6	10	2	319	85	4	–	39.87	4	–	–	–	–	–	–	–	–
Clarke, ST	4	3	–	19	14	–	–	6.33	–	89.0	18	261	9	29.00	–	–	3/28
Croft, CEH	6	8	4	48	34	–	–	12.00	3	251.5	43	673	18	37.38	–	–	3/78
Dujon, PJL	5	8	2	332	104*	1	1	55.33	16	–	–	–	–	–	–	–	–
Garner, J	5	7	–	50	18	–	–	7.14	4	165.3	51	372	23	16.17	2	–	5/45
Gomes, HA	7	10	2	712	200*	2	3	89.00	1	72.0	13	169	5	33.80	–	–	2/20
Greenidge, CG	5	8	–	179	66	2	–	22.37	3	–	–	–	–	–	–	–	–
Haynes, DL	6	11	–	383	139	2	1	34.81	3	–	–	–	–	–	–	–	–
Holding, MA	6	7	–	56	24	–	–	8.00	3	214.3	49	535	32	16.71	4	1	6/62
Joseph, H	2	2	–	11	7	–	–	5.50	1	91.0	25	217	5	43.40	–	–	3/45
Lloyd, CH (Capt)	5	8	1	394	77*	5	–	56.28	3	–	–	–	–	–	–	–	–
Logie, AL	3	4	–	81	43	–	–	20.25	–	–	–	–	–	–	–	–	–
Marshall, MD	2	2	–	66	66	1	–	33.00	–	46.0	14	105	11	9.54	1	–	5/31
Murray, DA	4	6	2	139	72	1	–	34.75	20/–	–	–	–	–	–	–	–	–
Richards, IVA	7	11	1	436	121	3	1	43.60	4	120.5	28	304	6	50.66	1	–	5/88
Roberts, AME	4	5	1	103	42	–	–	25.75	1	147.0	44	318	13	24.46	–	–	4/43

Any lingering doubts about the financial viability of Australia–West Indian matches ended in this summer. More than 355,000 watched the three Tests played by the West Indies, compared with 90,000 who watched the three Australia–Pakistan Tests. Australia were fortunate to share the rubber with the West Indies, sneaking home by 58 runs in the First Test at Brisbane, despite Michael Holding's 11 wickets for 107, thanks to Dennis Lillee's retaliatory 10 for 127 and Hughes' 100 not out. This ended a West Indies run of 15 Tests without defeat. A big improvement in the West Indies' batting made success harder in the remaining Tests. John Dyson saved Australia from defeat in the Second Test at Sydney by batting for 377 minutes for 127 not out. Yardley's career-best figures of 7 for 98 went unrewarded because of the West Indies' 117-run first innings lead. A convincing five-wicket win, built on Larry Gomez' 124 not out and the searing pace of Holding (8 for 142) and Garner (5 for 56 in the second innings), allowed Lloyd's men to retain the Frank Worrell trophy.

WEST INDIES IN AUSTRALIA 1984-85

	First-class Results					All Matches			
Matches	Won	Lost	Drawn	Tied	Matches	Won	Lost	Drawn	Tied
11	4	2	5	–	33	23	4	6	–

Date	Venue	Opponent	Results for Touring Team
Oct 19	Brisbane	Queensland	Drawn
Oct 24	Loxton	*South Australian Country XI	Won by 7 wkts
Oct 26	Adelaide	South Australia	Drawn
Oct 31	Corrigin	*Western Australian Country XI	Won by 81 runs
Nov 2	Perth	Western Australia	Won by 9 wkts
Nov 9	Perth	AUSTRALIA (1st Test)	Won by an inns & 112 runs
Nov 16	Sydney	New South Wales	Lost by 71 runs
Nov 23	Brisbane	AUSTRALIA (2nd Test)	Won by 8 wkts
Nov 30	Melbourne	Victoria	Drawn
Dec 7	Adelaide	AUSTRALIA (3rd Test)	Won by 191 runs
Dec 14	Devonport	Tasmania	Drawn
Dec 19	Echuca	*Victorian Country XI	Won by 64 runs
Dec 22	Melbourne	AUSTRALIA (4th Test)	Drawn
Dec 30	Sydney	AUSTRALIA (5th Test)	Lost by an inns & 55 runs
Jan 6	Melbourne	*Australia (L/O Intl)	Won by 7 wkts
Jan 10	Hobart (TCA)	*Sri Lanka (L/O Intl)	Won by 8 wkts
Jan 12	Brisbane	*Sri Lanka (L/O Intl)	Won by 90 runs
Jan 13	Brisbane	*Australia (L/O Intl)	Won by 5 wkts
Jan 15	Sydney	*Australia (L/O Intl)	Won by 5 wkts
Jan 17	Sydney	*Sri Lanka (L/O Intl)	Won by 65 runs
Jan 20	Melbourne	*Australia (L/O Intl)	Won by 65 runs
Jan 22	Canberra	*Prime Minister's XI	Won by 15 runs
Jan 23	Canberra	*Australian Capital Territory	Won by 8 wkts
Jan 26	Adelaide	*Sri Lanka (L/O Intl)	Won by 8 wkts
Jan 27	Adelaide	*Australia (L/O Intl)	Won by 6 wkts
Jan 29	Albany	*Western Australian Country XI	Won by 11 runs
Feb 2	Perth	*Sri Lanka (L/O Intl)	Won by 82 runs
Feb 6	Sydney	*Australia (L/O Intl)	Lost by 26 runs
Feb 10	Melbourne	*Australia (L/O Intl)	Won by 4 wkts
Feb 12	Sydney	*Australia (L/O Intl)	Won by 7 wkts
Feb 19	Sydney	*New Zealand (L/O Intl)	No result
Feb 27	Melbourne	*Sri Lanka (L/O Intl)	Won by 8 wkts
Mar 6	Melbourne	*Pakistan (L/O Intl)	Lost by 7 wkts

The 1984-85 West Indian team in Australia: *standing* D. Waight (physio), J.P. Dujon, E.A.E. Baptiste, R.A. Harper, W.W. Davis, R.S. Gabriel, M.D. Marshall, R.B. Richardson, A.L. Logie; *seated* C.W. Smith (assistant manager), J. Garner, W.W. Daniel, W. Hall (manager), C.H. Lloyd (capt.), I.V.A. Richards, M.A. Holding, D.L. Haynes, H.A. Gomes; *absent* T.R. Payne, C.G. Greenidge.

Player	M	Inn	NO	Runs	HS	50	100	Avrge	Ct/St	Overs	Mdns	Runs	Wkts	Avrge	5wi	10wm	Best
Baptiste, EAE	4	6	–	107	54	1	–	17.83	1	121.2	28	350	11	31.81	–	–	4/67
Davis, WW	5	7	2	110	50	1	–	22.00	1	117.4	24	421	8	52.62	–	–	3/58
Dujon, PJL	9	13	2	536	151*	1	2	48.72	27/–	7.0	3	43	1	43.00	–	–	1/43
Garner, J	8	9	4	58	17	–	–	11.60	3	237.4	58	668	25	26.72	–	–	4/19
Gomes, HA	10	15	3	621	127	3	2	51.75	2	68.0	17	137	3	45.66	–	–	1/0
Greenidge, CG	9	15	–	469	95	3	–	31.26	9	3.0	–	7	–	–	–	–	–
Harper, RA	6	9	1	104	38*	–	–	13.00	7	253.5	56	658	17	38.70	1	–	5/72
Haynes, DL	10	17	1	635	155	5	1	39.68	5	6.0	–	27	–	–	–	–	–
Holding, MA	6	7	–	49	31	–	–	7.00	6	161.3	40	410	20	20.50	1	–	6/21
Lloyd, CH (Capt)	10	16	2	732	114	5	1	52.28	7	–	–	–	–	–	–	–	–
Logie, AL	5	7	–	250	134	–	1	35.71	–	10.0	1	29	1	29.00	–	–	1/29
Marshall, MD	7	9	2	212	57	2	–	30.28	4	267.3	59	699	36	19.41	4	1	5/38
Payne, TRO	3	5	–	93	55	1	–	18.00	9	–	–	–	–	–	–	–	–
Richards, IVA	10	17	1	606	208	2	2	37.87	9	94.0	26	175	7	25.00	–	–	4/18
Richardson, RB	10	17	1	557	145	3	2	34.81	14	10.0	1	40	–	–	–	–	–
Walsh, CA	9	10	6	55	18*	–	–	13.75	2	311.1	58	946	37	25.56	2	–	6/119

After an argumentative visit to play 18 limited over matches in 1983-84, the West Indies returned for the fourth time in six seasons for a program of traditional cricket. They emphatically reversed their heavy defeat in 1975-76 by winning three of the five Tests comfortably. For Lloyd, in his farewell series, and the other survivors from 1975-76, their dominance was only briefly satisfying. After retaining the Frank Worrell trophy by taking a three-nil lead in the Tests, they reached the Fifth Test in Sydney confronted by critics' claims that they were vulnerable against spin. New South Wales had beaten them on the same pitch a month earlier when Murray Bennett's left-arm spin and Bob Holland's right-arm leg-breaks accounted for 13 wickets. The critics were vindicated when Bennett and Holland repeated the dose on a pitch helpful to spin, and Australia won by an innings and 55 runs. Bennett and Holland took a further 13 wickets, forcing Lloyd to leave the Test arena a loser. Later Lloyd agreed the omission of the West Indies' best spinner, Roger Harper, was a blunder, but Kepler Wessels' 173 was just as vital to Australia.

WEST INDIES IN AUSTRALIA 1988-89

First-class Results					All Matches				
Matches	Won	Lost	Drawn	Tied	Matches	Won	Lost	Drawn	Tied
11	4	2	5	–	23	11	7	5	–

Date	Venue	Opponent	Results for Touring Team
Oct 26	Perth	*Western Australia	Lost by 4 wkts
Oct 28	Perth	Western Australia	Lost by 7 wkts
Nov 4	Adelaide	South Australia	Won by an inns & 20 runs
Nov 11	Sydney	New South Wales	Drawn
Nov 18	Brisbane	AUSTRALIA (1st Test)	Won by 9 wkts
Nov 25	Melbourne	Victoria	Drawn
Dec 2	Perth	AUSTRALIA (2nd Test)	Won by 169 runs
Dec 10	Adelaide	*Pakistan (L/O Intl)	Won by 89 runs
Dec 13	Sydney	*Australia (L/O Intl)	Won by 1 run
Dec 15	Melbourne	*Australia (L/O Intl)	Won by 34 runs
Dec 17	Hobart (Bel)	*Pakistan (L/O Intl)	Won by 17 runs
Dec 19	Hobart (Bel)	Tasmania	Drawn
Dec 24	Melbourne	AUSTRALIA (3rd Test)	Won by 285 runs
Jan 1	Perth	*Pakistan (L/O Intl)	Won by 7 wkts
Jan 5	Melbourne	*Australia (L/O Intl)	Lost by 8 runs
Jan 7	Brisbane	*Pakistan (L/O Intl)	Lost by 55 runs
Jan 12	Sydney	*Australia (L/O Intl)	Lost by 61 runs
Jan 14	Melbourne	*Australia (L/O Intl)	Lost by 2 runs
Jan 16	Sydney	*Australia (L/O Intl)	Won by 92 runs
Jan 18	Sydney	*Australia (L/O Intl)	Won by 8 wkts
Jan 20	Brisbane	Queensland	Drawn
Jan 26	Sydney	AUSTRALIA (4th Test)	Lost by 7 wkts
Feb 3	Adelaide	AUSTRALIA (5th Test)	Drawn

Player	M	Inn	NO	Runs	HS	50	100	Avrge	Ct/St	Overs	Mdns	Runs	Wkts	Avrge	5wi	10wm	Best
Ambrose, CEL	7	11	1	168	44	–	–	16.80	3	266.5	54	729	32	22.78	1	–	5/72
Arthurton, KLT	5	8	1	182	72	2	–	26.00	3	26.0	2	71	–	–	–	–	–
Benjamin, WKM	5	6	2	141	50	1	–	35.25	5	121.0	24	361	8	45.13	–	–	2/33
Bishop, IR	5	7	2	64	20	–	–	12.80	1	120.0	17	408	10	40.80	1	–	5/27
Dujon, PJL	10	16	1	390	53*	1	–	26.00	19/1	1.0	–	1	–	–	–	–	–
Greenidge, CG	9	16	2	800	213	4	2	57.14	5	–	–	–	–	–	–	–	–
Harper, RA	6	10	3	267	82	2	–	38.14	7	201.4	35	580	11	52.73	1	–	5/78
Haynes, DL	9	17	1	787	143	4	3	49.19	8	1.0	–	3	–	–	–	–	–
Hooper, CL	11	18	–	507	83	3	–	28.17	9	210.4	40	537	16	33.56	1	–	5/33
Logie, AL	10	16	2	601	134	2	2	42.93	10	–	–	–	–	–	–	–	–
Marshall, MD	7	11	1	129	31	–	–	12.90	1	243.0	52	651	18	36.17	1	–	5/29
Patterson, BP	9	13	4	73	18*	–	–	8.11	1	229.1	33	786	22	35.73	1	–	5/39
Richards, IVA (Capt)	7	11	1	683	146	4	3	68.30	5	168.1	20	440	8	55.00	–	–	3/78
Richardson, RB	10	17	1	766	122	2	3	47.88	12	–	–	–	–	–	–	–	–
Walsh, CA	7	10	5	80	30*	–	–	16.00	2	218.5	39	621	23	27.00	–	–	4/62
Williams, D	4	5	–	38	14	–	–	7.60	5/1	–	–	–	–	–	–	–	–

Vivian Richards proved a surprisingly dour captain, never prepared to admonish his players for their slow over rates or the arguments with umpires and Australians that marred this five-Test tour. His attitude and the conduct of his manager Clive Lloyd, who supported slow over rates, proved costly to the West Indians. They were docked $22,000 from their Test winnings for failures in reaching the set 90 overs a day. Richards belittled the game by saying winning was more important than money. In a series in which West Indian bowlers were called almost 250 times for over-stepping, boredom drove spectators away. The West Indies' strategy of bouncing the ball into the rib cage or forcing batsmen to absorb repeated blows in overs sprinkled with bouncers gave them wins in the first three Tests.

The Australian resurgence Border had long been chasing began in the Fourth Test, when Border shocked himself and spectators by taking 7 for 46 and 4 for 50. Australia won by seven wickets but by then the West Indies had killed interest so much only 83,729 watched over five days. Every day of the Fifth Test produced rows over umpiring decisions and heated clashes among players. This time only 58,479 attended. Twenty-four days of Test cricket attracted 325,000 fans at a daily rate of 13,500-odd, but with Pakistan joining in, 15 one-day matches drew 500,000 people at a daily rate of 33,000, strong evidence that the West Indies needed to look at the tedium imposed by their Test tactics.

WEST INDIES IN AUSTRALIA 1992–93

Matches	First-class Results				Matches	All Matches			
	Won	Lost	Drawn	Tied		Won	Lost	Drawn	Tied
8	3	1	2	–	22	13	5	4	–

Date	Venue	Opponent	Results for Touring Team
Nov 2	Caversham	*ACB Chairman's XI	Won by 7 wkts
Nov 4	Perth	*Western Australia	Won by 28 runs
Nov 6	Perth	Western Australia	Won by 236 runs
Nov 12	Canberra	*Prime Minister's XI	Lost by 3 runs
Nov 14	Hobart (Bel)	Australian XI	Drawn
Nov 20	Sydney	New South Wales	Drawn
Nov 27	Brisbane	AUSTRALIA (1st Test)	Drawn
Dec 4	Perth	*Pakistan (L/O Intl)	Lost by 5 wkts
Dec 6	Perth	*Australia (L/O Intl)	Won by 9 wkts
Dec 8	Sydney	*Australia (L/O Intl)	Lost by 14 runs
Dec 12	Adelaide	*Pakistan (L/O Intl)	Won by 4 runs
Dec 15	Melbourne	*Australia (L/O Intl)	Lost by 4 runs
Dec 17	Sydney	*Pakistan (L/O Intl)	Won by 133 runs
Dec 19	Bendigo	Victoria	Abandoned
Dec 26	Melbourne	AUSTRALIA (2nd Test)	Lost by 139 runs
Jan 2	Sydney	AUSTRALIA (3rd Test)	Drawn
Jan 9	Brisbane	*Pakistan (L/O Intl)	Won by 9 wkts
Jan 10	Brisbane	*Australia (L/O Intl)	Won by 7 runs
Jan 13	Newcastle	*Australian Country XI	Won by 51 runs
Jan 16	Sydney	*Australia (L/O Intl)	Won by 25 runs
Jan 18	Melbourne	*Australia (L/O Intl)	Won by 4 wkts
Jan 23	Adelaide	AUSTRALIA (4th Test)	Won by 1 run
Jan 30	Perth	AUSTRALIA (5th Test)	Won by an inns & 25 runs

Player	M	Inn	NO	Runs	HS	50	100	Avrge	Ct/St	Overs	Mdns	Runs	Wkts	Avrge	5wi	10wm	Best
Adams, JC	6	10	3	258	77*	2	–	36.86	4	50.0	5	183	2	91.50	–	–	1/2
Ambrose, CEL	7	11	2	51	16	–	–	5.67	1	315.3	87	689	38	18.13	3	1	7/25
Arthurton, KLT	7	12	2	598	157*	3	2	59.80	6	10.0	2	22	–	–	–	–	–
Benjamin, KCG	3	4	2	32	15	–	–	16.00	2	67.0	11	211	6	35.17	–	–	3/27
Bishop, IR	6	9	1	92	35	–	–	11.50	1	240.3	45	617	26	23.73	1	–	6/40
Cummins, AC	3	4	1	21	14*	–	–	7.00	–	91.0	14	302	5	60.40	–	–	3/73
Haynes, DL	7	12	–	356	79	3	–	29.67	4	–	–	–	–	–	–	–	–
Hooper, CL	7	13	2	460	124	2	1	41.82	7	313.2	57	803	22	36.50	1	–	5/72
Lara, BC	7	12	–	586	277	4	1	48.83	9	2.0	–	4	–	–	–	–	–
Logie, AL	3	5	–	168	99	1	–	33.60	3	–	–	–	–	–	–	–	–
Murray, JR	4	5	1	122	49*	–	–	30.50	21	–	–	–	–	–	–	–	–
Patterson, BP	3	3	–	6	6	–	–	2.00	–	73.0	4	304	6	50.67	–	–	2/23
Richardson, RB (Capt)	7	12	–	550	109	4	1	45.83	5	3.0	1	8	–	–	–	–	–
Simmons, PV	8	14	–	570	110	1	3	40.71	11	63.0	14	182	2	91.00	–	–	2/34
Walsh, CA	6	10	3	42	17	–	–	6.00	1	199.1	45	542	13	41.69	–	–	4/91
Williams, D	4	7	–	66	23	–	–	9.43	14/1	–	–	–	–	–	–	–	–

After a fleeting trip to Hobart for a match with an Australian XI in 1991–92, Richie Richardson's team returned the following summer for a tour of eight first-class matches, plus the usual round of one-day fixtures. The tour proved of absorbing interest, with Richardson's candour and media-relations a major contribution. Australia had the best of a drawn First Test in Brisbane, and won the Second Test in Melbourne handsomely when a new hero emerged in leg-spinner Shane Warne (7 for 52). Both teams exceeded 500 runs in their first innings in the drawn Third Test at Sydney, where Brian Lara's 277 ended in a tragic run out when he appeared to have Gary Sobers' West Indian record of 365 not out in his keeping.

The Fourth Test in Adelaide provided thrills galore, culminating in Australia's one-run defeat, the narrowest winning margin in the 1211-match history of Test cricket. Veteran Desmond Haynes saved it for the West Indies when he made a marvellous stop at short leg from a McDermott shot that appeared certain to bring a tie or even an Australian win. McDermott was then given out, dodging a Courtney Walsh bouncer that appeared to touch his gloves as it went through to keeper Junior Murray. Months later, after countless viewings of replays, McDermott remained adamant he did not touch the ball.

With the series level at one–all, the West Indies went to Perth for the decider on a pitch that was ideal for Ambrose, Bishop and Walsh. Ambrose bowled one of the finest spells of fast bowling ever seen in Australia to claim 7 for 25 in Australia's first innings. Trailing by 203 runs, Australia never looked like avoiding defeat. This time Bishop's 6 for 40 clinched victory for the West Indies and a two–one series win, leaving Border lamenting victories that escaped him in Brisbane and Adelaide.

AUSTRALIA IN THE WEST INDIES

Australia has toured the West Indies seven times, and after 34 Tests in the Caribbean, has won 11, the West Indies 12, with 13 drawn. The first Australian touring team, captained by Ian Johnson in 1954–55, and Ian Chappell's 1972–73 team were the only Australian teams to remain unbeaten. Johnson's team was the first overseas team to win a rubber in the West Indies, but his batsmen did not have to face the bouncer-laden attacks nor wear the helmets and protective pads forced on later Australian sides. The 1994–95 Australians ended 23 years of disappointment.

AUSTRALIA IN THE WEST INDIES 1954-55

	First-class Results					All Matches			
Matches	Won	Lost	Drawn	Tied	Matches	Won	Lost	Drawn	Tied
9	5	–	4	–	11	6	–	5	–

Date	Venue	Opponent	Results for Australians
Mar 19	Kingston	Jamaica	Drawn
Mar 26	Kingston	WEST INDIES (1st Test)	Won by 9 wkts
Apr 4	Port-of-Spain	Trinidad	Drawn
Apr 11	Port-of-Spain	WEST INDIES (2nd Test)	Drawn
Apr 20	Georgetown	Guyana	Won by an inns & 134 runs
Apr 26	Georgetown	WEST INDIES (3rd Test)	Won by 8 wkts
May 7	Bridgetown	Barbados	Won by 3 wkts
May 14	Bridgetown	WEST INDIES (4th Test)	Drawn
May 26	Grenada	*Windward Islands	Drawn
Jun 1	Antigua	*Leeward Islands	Won by an inns & 219 runs
Jun 6	Montego Bay	*Combined XI	Abandoned
Jun 11	Kingston	WEST INDIES (5th Test)	Won by an inns & 82 runs

The first Australian team in the West Indies, 1954-55: *standing* L.E. Favell, L.V. Maddocks, J.C. Hill, R.G. Archer, T.J. Burge (manager), P.J.P. Burge, A.K. Davidson, W. Atson, C.C. McDonald; *seated* R.N. Harvey, W.A. Johnston, A.R. Morris, I.W. Johnson (capt.), K.R. Miller, R.R. Lindwall, R. Benaud, G.R. Langley.

Player	State	M	Inn	NO	Runs	HS	50	100	Avrge	Ct/St	Overs	Mdns	Runs	Wkts	Avrge	5wi	10wm	Best
Archer, RG	QLD	8	11	1	478	128	3	1	47.80	13	221.0	47	687	18	27.61	–	–	3/37
Benaud, R	NSW	8	11	1	446	121	3	1	44.60	9	240.4	57	671	21	31.95	–	–	4/15
Burge, PJP	QLD	5	8	–	310	177	1	1	38.75	4	–	–	–	–	–	–	–	–
Davidson, AK	NSW	3	4	2	70	34*	–	–	35.00	3	63.1	9	207	4	51.75	–	–	2/24
Favell, LE	SA	5	8	–	287	72	3	–	35.87	3	–	–	–	–	–	–	–	–
Harvey, RN	VIC	8	12	2	789	204	2	3	78.90	3	12.0	–	67	–	–	–	–	–
Hill, JC	VIC	4	4	2	32	22*	–	–	16.00	3	147.3	53	379	18	21.11	2	1	5/15
Johnson, IW (Capt)	VIC	8	9	2	200	66	2	–	28.57	4	233.2	75	667	23	29.00	1	–	7/44
Johnston, WA	VIC	6	5	3	14	6	–	–	7.00	2	121.0	21	406	8	50.75	–	–	3/97
Langley, GRA	SA	5	5	2	118	53	1	–	39.33	17/4	–	–	–	–	–	–	–	–
Lindwall, RR	QLD	7	9	2	227	118	–	1	32.42	2	237.4	36	802	28	28.64	2	–	6/41
Maddocks, LV	VIC	4	7	3	181	83	2	–	45.25	7/4	–	–	–	–	–	–	–	–
McDonald, CC	VIC	7	12	1	583	127	3	2	53.00	1	–	–	–	–	–	–	–	–
Miller, KR	NSW	8	11	–	577	147	–	3	52.45	1	244.2	51	792	26	30.46	1	–	6/107
Morris, AR	NSW	7	11	2	577	157	2	2	52.45	1	4.0	1	12	–	–	–	–	–
Watson, W	NSW	6	10	1	389	122	2	1	43.66	2	5.0	–	22	–	–	–	–	–

The Australians arrived with their supporters worried that their batting failures in the series just ended against England at home might be repeated. West Indian misgivings hung on whether the tour could be concluded without the ugly scenes and rancour of the previous tour by Hutton's England XI. On easy-paced pitches, before crowds eager to be entertained, the Australians corrected technical failures evident against England and scored a vast number of runs in a style that made them one of the most popular outfits to visit the Caribbean.

Australia won the First, Third and Fifth Tests to take the series three–nil, a remarkable feat considering that Clyde Walcott hit five Test centuries against them, including two in both the Second and Fifth Tests. Walcott's 827 runs (at 82.70) in the Tests, the highest-ever aggregate in a Test series for the West Indies, was 177 runs more than Australia's best run-scorer Neil Harvey (650 at 108.33), who hit three Test centuries. Miller also hit three Test 100s and shared 40 Test wickets with Lindwall. In the Fifth Test, McDonald (127), Harvey (204), Miller (109), Archer (128) and Benaud (121, including 100 in 78 minutes) took Australia to 8 declared for 758 after two wickets fell for seven runs. Jamaican J.K. Holt needed police protection leaving the field after dropping three vital catches in the Fourth Test at Bridgetown. At the time Test star Leslie Hylton was about to be hanged for the murder of his wife. Next day a poster at the ground read: 'Hang Holt, not Hylton', but it didn't save Hylton.

AUSTRALIA IN THE WEST INDIES 1964-65

	First-class Results					All Matches			
Matches	Won	Lost	Drawn	Tied	Matches	Won	Lost	Drawn	Tied
11	3	2	6	–	16	4	3	9	–

Date	Venue	Opponent	Results for Australians
Feb 20	Kingston	*Jamaica Colts	Won by an inns & 5 wkts
Feb 24	Kingston	Jamaica	Won by an inns & 6 runs
Mar 3	Kingston	WEST INDIES (1st Test)	Lost by 179 runs
Mar 12	St Kitt's	Leeward Islands	Won by an inns & 31 runs
Mar 17	Port-of-Spain	*Trinidad Colts	Drawn
Mar 20	Port-of-Spain	Trinidad	Drawn
Mar 26	Port-of-Spain	WEST INDIES (2nd Test)	Drawn
Apr 3	Georgetown	*British Guyana Colts	Drawn
Apr 7	Georgetown	British Guyana	Drawn
Apr 14	Georgetown	WEST INDIES (3rd Test)	Lost by 212 runs
Apr 24	Bridgetown	*Barbados Colts	Drawn
Apr 28	Bridgetown	Barbados	Drawn
May 5	Bridgetown	WEST INDIES (4th Test)	Drawn
May 14	Port-of-Spain	WEST INDIES (5th Test)	Won by 10 wkts
May 22	Grenada	Windward Islands	Drawn
May 27	Tobago	*Tobago	Lost by 3 runs on 1st inns

The 1964-65 Australian team in the West Indies: *back row* S.C. Trimble, P.J. Allan, G.D. McKenzie, B.K. Shepherd, N.J.N. Hawke, L.C. Mayne, R.M. Cowper, D.J. Sincock, G. Thomas, P.I. Philpott; *seated* B.N. Jarman, W.M. Lawry, R.B. Simpson (capt.), R.J. Parish (manager), B.C. Booth, N.C. O'Neill, A.T.W. Grout.

Player	State	M	Inn	NO	Runs	HS	50	100	Avrge	Ct/St	Overs	Mdns	Runs	Wkts	Avrge	5wi	10wm	Best
Allan, PJ	QLD	4	3	–	15	9	–	–	5.00	4	65.0	8	209	5	41.80	1	–	5/33
Booth, BC	NSW	9	14	1	417	117	3	1	32.08	9	37.0	8	106	1	106.00	–	–	1/30
Cowper, RM	VIC	10	15	1	854	188	2	4	61.00	7	108.0	31	291	8	36.35	–	–	3/32
Grout, ATW	QLD	6	6	–	83	35	–	–	13.83	16/4	–	–	–	–	–	–	–	–
Hawke, NJN	SA	9	12	4	192	46*	–	–	24.00	6	277.0	64	681	32	21.28	1	1	6/72
Jarman, BN	SA	5	6	–	122	65	1	–	20.33	8/9	–	–	–	–	–	–	–	–
Lawry, WM	VIC	9	15	3	791	210	5	2	65.92	1	–	–	–	–	–	–	–	–
Mayne, LC	WA	8	9	4	38	11*	–	–	7.76	3	209.0	28	616	24	25.66	–	–	4/43
McKenzie, GD	WA	8	8	2	57	20	–	–	9.50	4	349.0	80	924	25	36.96	1	–	5/33
O'Neill, NC	NSW	7	10	1	617	125	2	3	68.55	1	106.0	25	318	13	24.53	–	–	4/41
Philpott, PI	NSW	9	11	2	147	34	–	–	16.33	6	449.0	99	1207	49	24.63	2	–	6/86
Shepherd, BK	WA	7	9	–	264	76	1	–	29.33	6	4.0	1	8	–	–	–	–	–
Simpson, RB (Capt)	NSW	9	14	1	784	201	3	3	60.31	19	213.0	49	521	12	43.42	–	–	4/83
Sincock, DJ	SA	6	5	1	68	18	–	–	17.00	5	156.0	22	568	18	31.55	–	–	4/82
Thomas, G	NSW	10	15	4	450	110*	3	1	40.91	5	1.0	–	7	–	–	–	–	–
Trimble, SC	QLD	4	6	2	262	155	1	1	52.40	2	3.0	–	13	–	–	–	–	–

Although Charlie Griffith's suspect bowling dominated the headlines, the bowling of Wes Hall won the First Test and the off-breaks of Lance Gibbs won the Third Test. Bob Simpson did well to rally a team sidetracked by the Griffith controversy to make a fighting draw of the Fourth Test and convincingly win the Fifth Test, but the two outstanding West Indian bowling displays swung the series. Hall took 5 for 60 and 4 for 45 in the first of these at Kingston and probably never bowled better. Gibbs followed his first innings 3 for 51 with 6 for 29 to initiate a dispiriting Australian collapse in a game that only started after a childish dispute over the appointment of umpires.

Simpson and Lawry put on 382 for the first wicket in the Fourth Test at Bridgetown. Both went on to double centuries, Lawry 210, Simpson 201, but a vintage Kanhai innings (129) and a double century from Seymour Nurse (201) nullified the advantage Australia had won in scoring 6 for 650 declared. Norm O'Neill topped the Australian first-class averages with 617 runs in seven matches. He was also the loudest critic of umpires who refused to call Griffith for chucking. The Australian Board of Control fined O'Neill for articles he wrote in the London *Daily Mail* on Griffith's alleged throwing but O'Neill later was supported by tour comments from former Australian captain Richie Benaud.

AUSTRALIA IN THE WEST INDIES 1972-73

First-class Results					All Matches				
Matches	Won	Lost	Drawn	Tied	Matches	Won	Lost	Drawn	Tied
12	7	–	5	–	15	10	–	5	–

Date	Venue	Opponent	Results for Australians
Feb 1	Kingston	*University of West Indies	Won by 86 runs
Feb 3	Kingston	Jamaica	Won by 5 wkts
Feb 9	Montego Bay	West Indies President's XI	Won by 7 wkts
Feb 16	Kingston	WEST INDIES (1st Test)	Drawn
Feb 24	Antigua	Leeward Islands	Drawn
Mar 1	Bridgetown	Barbados	Won by 9 wkts
Mar 6	Bridgetown	*Combined Youth XI	Won by an inns & 2 runs
Mar 9	Bridgetown	WEST INDIES (2nd Test)	Drawn
Mar 17	Pointe-a-Pierre	Trinidad	Drawn
Mar 23	Port-of-Spain	WEST INDIES (3rd Test)	Won by 44 runs
Mar 31	Georgetown	Guyana	Won by 40 runs
Apr 6	Georgetown	WEST INDIES (4th Test)	Won by 10 wkts
Apr 14	Grenada	Windward Islands	Won by 5 wkts
Apr 18	Tobago	*Tobago	Won by 111 runs
Apr 21	Port-of-Spain	WEST INDIES (5th Test)	Drawn

Deprived of the services of Lillee, Massie and Mallett, key bowlers in the revival he had orchestrated, Ian Chappell excelled by clearly beating the West Indies at home two-nil, with three Tests drawn, and going through a 15-match tour (12 of them first-class) undefeated. This was an impressive victory, made possible by the temperament of the Australians and their will to win. They were faced with some formidable opposition from Lloyd, Kanhai, Fredericks and Gibbs, and had to improvise with Walker and Hammond as opening bowlers after Lillee broke down, and Chappell set a resolute example for his players who responded remarkably well. Walker took 26 wickets in the Tests at 20.73 apiece, lumbering up for 271 overs of his big swingers.

Player	State	M	Inn	NO	Runs	HS	50	100	Avrge	Ct/St	Overs	Mdns	Runs	Wkts	Avrge	5wi	10wm	Best
Benaud, J	NSW	8	16	2	404	77	2	–	28.85	9	26.0	8	76	3	25.33	–	–	2/12
Chappell, GS	SA	10	17	1	1110	154	7	4	69.37	13	213.3	66	469	13	36.07	–	–	4/57
Chappell, IM (Capt)	SA	9	16	2	862	209	3	3	61.57	9	28.0	9	78	1	78.00	–	–	1/17
Edwards, R	WA	12	20	–	627	74	6	–	31.35	3	–	–	–	–	–	–	–	–
Hammond, JR	SA	10	11	3	95	28*	–	–	11.87	5	307.5	70	958	34	28.17	1	–	5/73
Jenner, TJ	SA	10	14	5	234	48*	–	–	26.00	3	347.3	76	1026	36	28.50	1	–	5/90
Lillee, DK	WA	5	6	1	59	36	–	–	11.80	–	68.0	16	238	5	47.60	–	–	4/21
Marsh, RW	WA	10	16	1	592	97	5	–	39.46	25/3	3.0	2	3	–	–	–	–	–
Massie, RAL	WA	6	6	2	36	14*	–	–	9.00	2	181.4	45	530	18	29.44	1	–	7/52
O'Keeffe, KJ	NSW	10	15	6	324	76*	1	–	36.00	11	297.0	80	743	20	37.15	–	–	4/53
Redpath, IR	VIC	10	20	2	661	83	6	–	36.72	7	8.0	1	36	–	–	–	–	–
Stackpole, KR	VIC	9	16	2	702	168	3	2	50.14	12	57.1	16	130	6	21.66	–	–	2/22
Walker, MHN	VIC	9	9	2	97	29	–	–	13.85	1	375.0	107	840	41	20.48	4	–	6/94
Walters, KD	NSW	10	16	4	834	112	6	3	69.50	3	53.2	10	165	7	23.57	1	–	5/66
Watkins, JR	NSW	4	6	4	20	10*	–	–	10.00	3	78.0	6	336	10	33.60	–	–	4/110

The 1972-73 Australian team in the West Indies: *back row* T.J. Jenner, R. Edwards, J.R. Hammond, D.K. Lillee, M.H.N. Walker, J. Benaud, R.A.L. Massie, K.J. O'Keeffe, J.R. Watkins; *seated* K.D. Walters, I.R. Redpath, I.M. Chappell (capt.), W.L. Jacobs (manager), K.R. Stackpole, R.W. Marsh, G.S. Chappell.

AUSTRALIA IN THE WEST INDIES 1977–78

Matches	First-class Results Won	Lost	Drawn	Tied	Matches	All Matches Won	Lost	Drawn	Tied
11	5	3	3	–	13	6	4	3	–

Date	Venue	Opponent	Results for Australians
Feb 17	St Kitt's	Leeward Islands	Won by 183 runs
Feb 22	Antigua	*West Indies (L/O Intl)	Lost by 132 runs
Feb 25	Port-of-Spain	Trinidad	Won by 6 wkts
Mar 3	Port-of-Spain	WEST INDIES (1st Test)	Lost by an inns & 106 runs
Mar 11	Bridgetown	Barbados	Drawn
Mar 17	Bridgetown	WEST INDIES (2nd Test)	Lost by 9 wkts
Mar 25	Georgetown	Guyana	Drawn
Mar 31	Georgetown	WEST INDIES (3rd Test)	Won by 3 wkts
Apr 7	Grenada	Windward Islands	Won by 52 runs
Apr 12	St Lucia	*West Indies (L/O Intl)	Won by 2 wkts
Apr 15	Port-of-Spain	WEST INDIES (4th Test)	Lost by 198 runs
Apr 22	Kingston	Jamaica	Won by 2 wkts
Apr 28	Kingston	WEST INDIES (5th Test)	Drawn

Player	State	M	Inn	NO	Runs	HS	50	100	Avrge	Ct/St	Overs	Mdns	Runs	Wkts	Avrge	5wi	10wm	Best
Callen, IW	VIC	6	9	1	79	31	–	–	9.87	3	144.2	24	552	11	50.18	–	–	3/77
Clark, WM	WA	7	12	2	21	8	–	–	2.10	5	250.4	51	723	31	23.32	2	1	7/26
Cosier, GJ	QLD	6	10	1	222	114*	1	–	24.66	4	70.0	16	228	4	57.00	–	–	2/65
Darling, WM	SA	8	15	–	492	123	1	2	32.80	3	1.0	–	7	–	–	–	–	–
Higgs, JD	VIC	9	14	10	20	4*	–	–	5.00	2	354.0	90	933	42	22.21	3	1	6/71
Hughes, KJ	WA	2	4	–	98	43	–	–	24.50	3	1.0	1	0	1	0.00	–	–	1/0
Laughlin, TJ	VIC	6	10	1	239	62	1	–	26.55	4	162.4	40	605	19	31.84	2	–	5/101
Ogilvie, AD	QLD	6	11	–	295	65	2	–	26.81	6	1.0	–	4	–	–	–	–	–
Rixon, SJ	NSW	10	18	3	279	54	1	–	18.60	22/8	1.0	–	1	–	–	–	–	–
Serjeant, CS	WA	10	18	1	604	124	1	2	35.52	15	–	–	–	–	–	–	–	–
Simpson, RB (Capt)	NSW	9	16	1	471	113	1	2	31.40	9	185.3	40	583	16	36.43	–	–	4/56
Thomson, JR	QLD	8	12	3	58	19*	–	–	6.44	3	186.2	34	679	24	28.29	1	–	6/77
Toohey, PM	NSW	6	11	–	567	122	4	1	51.54	5	–	–	–	–	–	–	–	–
Wood, GM	WA	10	19	–	779	126	5	2	41.00	11	1.0	–	5	–	–	–	–	–
Yallop, GN	VIC	8	15	3	660	118*	5	1	55.00	9	3.0	1	8	–	–	–	–	–
Yardley, B	WA	10	18	5	295	74	1	–	22.69	12	347.3	91	890	41	21.70	2	–	5/64

Administrative decisions over which he had no control imposed big handicaps on Bob Simpson's team from the outset and it was obvious they could not be overcome. The Australian Board of Control refused to include players who joined Packer, but the West Indian Board picked Packer players, reasoning that none of them had ever refused to play for their country. Simpson's team comprised the best of what was left after the 28 Australians who signed with Packer had been discarded. They opposed the unchanged elite of West Indian cricket on their own grounds before volatile crowds, prone to demonstrations, with umpires who perpetually upset experienced overseas visitors.

Armed guards patrolled the grounds with their dogs while the Australians practised. Australians returned to their dressing-room to find their bats stuck down toilets. Rocketing inflation had made prices for cool drinks, razor blades and other simple items prohibitive. On the field Clive Lloyd's professionals overwhelmed the raw tourists, winning the First Test by an innings and the Second Test by nine wickets after the now-familiar barrage of bouncers. Relief came when Packer's WSC players withdrew from the series after a row with officials. Kallicharan took over a West Indian team with six new caps and from then on an even contest ensued. Australia won the Third Test following centuries by Serjeant (124) and Wood (126) before the West Indies clinched the rubber by winning the Fourth Test. With only their pride at stake the Australians were deprived of an upset victory in the Fifth Test when spectators invaded the field after Vanburn Holder was given out caught. The West Indies had only one wicket left, with 38 deliveries to be bowled, but the umpire Ralph Gosein refused to go out among the brick-throwers who forced players and cricket writers to barricade themselves inside their dressing-rooms.

HOME AND AWAY

AUSTRALIA IN THE WEST INDIES 1983-84

	First-class Results					All Matches			
Matches	Won	Lost	Drawn	Tied	Matches	Won	Lost	Drawn	Tied
10	1	3	6	–	15	2	6	7	–

Date	Venue	Opponent	Results for Australians
Feb 18	St Kitt's	Leeward Islands	Won by 204 runs
Feb 24	Georgetown	Guyana	Drawn
Feb 29	Albion	*West Indies (L/O Intl)	Lost by 8 wkts
Mar 2	Georgetown	WEST INDIES (1st Test)	Drawn
Mar 9	Pointe-a-Pierre	Trinidad & Tobago	Drawn
Mar 14	Port-of-Spain	*West Indies (L/O Intl)	Won by 4 wkts
Mar 16	Port-of-Spain	WEST INDIES (2nd Test)	Drawn
Mar 24	Bridgetown	Barbados	Drawn
Mar 30	Bridgetown	WEST INDIES (3rd Test)	Lost by 10 wkts
Apr 7	Antigua	WEST INDIES (4th Test)	Lost by an inns & 36 runs
Apr 14	Castries	Windward Islands	Drawn
Apr 19	Castries	*West Indies (L/O Intl)	Lost by 7 wkts
Apr 23	Montego Bay	*Jamaica	Drawn
Apr 26	Kingston	*West Indies (L/O Intl)	Lost by 9 wkts
Apr 28	Kingston	WEST INDIES (5th Test)	Lost by 10 wkts

Player	State	M	Inn	NO	Runs	HS	50	100	Avrge	Ct/St	Overs	Mdns	Runs	Wkts	Avrge	5wi	10wm	Best
Alderman, TM	WA	6	8	5	41	21*	–	–	13.66	4	203.3	37	654	15	43.60	–	–	3/47
Border, AR	QLD	8	15	4	825	113	6	2	75.00	3	10.1	2	35	1	35.00	–	–	1/27
Hogan, TG	WA	8	14	2	248	42*	–	–	20.66	1	281.1	58	869	22	39.50	1	–	5/95
Hogg, RM	VIC	6	9	2	101	52	1	–	14.42	2	164.4	15	569	15	37.93	2	–	6/77
Hookes, DW	SA	9	18	2	623	103*	4	1	38.93	4	42.0	–	215	4	53.75	–	–	3/114
Hughes, KJ (Capt)	WA	9	18	1	486	73	3	–	28.58	9	–	–	–	–	–	–	–	–
Jones, DM	VIC	5	10	–	336	95	3	–	33.60	2	19.3	1	74	2	37.00	–	–	1/10
Lawson, GF	NSW	6	10	2	132	35*	1	–	16.50	1	199.0	29	768	14	54.85	–	–	3/59
Maguire, JN	QLD	6	8	2	59	19	–	–	9.83	3	210.0	38	645	26	24.80	–	–	4/57
Matthews, GRJ	NSW	5	8	2	188	54	1	–	31.33	4	150.0	27	472	9	52.44	–	–	2/63
Phillips, WB	SA	9	18	3	475	120	3	1	31.66	16	–	–	–	–	–	–	–	–
Rackemann, CG	QLD	4	4	1	25	12	–	–	8.33	2	149.0	17	546	19	28.73	2	–	6/105
Ritchie, GM	QLD	10	18	–	494	99	4	–	27.44	6	2.0	–	10	1	10.00	–	–	1/4
Smith, SB	NSW	7	12	–	479	127	1	3	39.91	5	1.0	–	5	–	–	–	–	–
Wessels, KC	QLD	4	7	1	333	126*	2	1	55.50	3	4.0	–	14	–	–	–	–	–
Wood, GM	WA	2	4	–	167	76	2	–	41.75	–	–	–	–	–	–	–	–	–
Woolley, RD	TAS	6	9	4	236	56*	2	–	47.20	11/1	–	–	–	–	–	–	–	–

Kim Hughes's team faced similar problems when they toured the West Indies four years later, with Packer's rebels still unavailable. They resisted the bouncer-barrage to escape with draws in the first two Tests, but were heavily defeated in the last three Tests by a splendid side at the peak of their powers after successful tours of India and Australia. The Australians were badly battered. Kepler Wessels flew home with a knee injury, Graeme Wood broke a finger in the Third Test, Steve Smith had his finger broken in the Fifth Test. Hogg, Rackemann and Lawson were asked to bowl despite injuries.

Nothing should detract from the wonderful cricket played by this exceptional West Indian team, however, for they outshone Australia in every department. Only Border enhanced his reputation among the Australians, top-scoring in five of his ten Test innings and scoring 521 runs at 74.42, compared with his next best team-mate Wayne Phillips' 258 runs at 25.80. Outplayed and buffeted, some of the Australians foolishly resorted to arguing over umpires' decisions.

The 1983-84 Australians in the West Indies: *standing* G. Dymock (assistant manager), S. Smith, W.W.B. Phillips, D.M. Jones, J.N. Maguire, T.G. Hogan, C.G. Rackemann, T.M. Alderman, G.M. Ritchie, G.R.J. Matthews, R.D. Woolley; E. Alcott (physio); *seated* G.M. Wood, R.M. Hogg, K.J. Hughes (capt.), C. Egar (manager), A.R. Border, D.W. Hookes, G.F. Lawson; *inset* K.C. Wessels.

AUSTRALIA IN THE WEST INDIES 1990-91

First-class Results					All Matches				
Matches	Won	Lost	Drawn	Tied	Matches	Won	Lost	Drawn	Tied
10	2	2	6	–	19	10	3	6	–

Date	Venue	Opponent	Results for Australians
Feb 16	St Kitt's	West Indies President's XI	Drawn
Feb 21	Kingston	Jamaica	Won by an inns & 137 runs
Feb 26	Kingston	*West Indies (L/O Intl)	Won by 35 runs
Mar 1	Kingston	WEST INDIES (1st TEST)	Drawn
Mar 9	Port-of-Spain	*West Indies (L/O Intl)	Won by 45 runs
Mar 10	Port-of-Spain	*West Indies (L/O Intl)	Lost by 7 wkts
Mar 13	Bridgetown	*West Indies (L/O Intl)	Won by 37 runs
Mar 15	Pointe-a-Pierre	Trinidad & Tobago	Drawn
Mar 17	Pointe-a-Pierre	*Trinidad & Tobago	Won by 26 runs
Mar 20	Georgetown	*West Indies (L/O Intl)	Won by 6 wkts
Mar 23	Georgetown	WEST INDIES (2nd Test)	Lost by 10 wkts
Mar 30	St Vincent	West Indies Under 23s	Drawn
Apr 5	Port-of-Spain	WEST INDIES (3rd Test)	Drawn
Apr 13	Bridgetown	West Indies Cricket Board XI	Drawn
Apr 19	Bridgetown	WEST INDIES (4th Test)	Lost by 343 runs
Apr 27	Antigua	WEST INDIES (5th Test)	Won by 157 runs
May 9	Bermuda	*St George's Cricket Club	Won by 18 runs
May 11	Bermuda	*Bermuda Cricket Board Pres. XI	Won by 34 runs
May 12	Bermuda	*Bermuda	Won by 93 runs

Player	State	M	Inn	NO	Runs	HS	50	100	Avrge	Ct/St	Overs	Mdns	Runs	Wkts	Avrge	5wi	10wm	Best
Alderman, TM	WA	5	4	2	2	2	–	–	1.00	5	117.4	22	346	9	38.44	1	–	5/40
Boon, DC	TAS	10	14	1	456	109*	2	2	35.07	6	–	–	–	–	–	–	–	–
Border, AR (Capt)	QLD	8	13	2	386	59	1	–	35.09	1	84.0	24	214	8	26.75	1	–	5/68
Healy, IA	QLD	7	10	–	187	53	1	–	18.70	15/–	–	–	–	–	–	–	–	–
Hughes, MG	VIC	10	13	1	77	21	–	–	6.41	5	304.5	54	1052	37	28.43	1	–	5/36
Jones, DM	VIC	9	12	1	348	81	2	–	31.63	7	4.0	1	9	–	–	–	–	–
Marsh, GR	WA	8	13	–	264	94	2	–	20.30	6	–	–	–	–	–	–	–	–
Matthews, GRJ	NSW	4	4	1	122	95*	1	–	40.66	1	106.5	21	370	8	46.25	–	–	4/57
McDermott, CJ	QLD	6	9	1	35	17*	–	–	4.37	2	209.5	40	608	28	21.71	1	–	5/80
Reid, BA	WA	5	5	1	3	2	–	–	0.75	1	160.1	28	527	16	32.93	–	–	4/76
Taylor, MA	NSW	10	14	–	777	144	5	3	55.50	6	–	–	–	–	–	–	–	–
Taylor, PL	QLD	5	6	1	89	33	–	–	17.80	4	154.0	45	382	15	25.46	1	–	5/37
Veletta, MRJ	WA	4	4	–	28	14	–	–	7.00	9/1	–	–	–	–	–	–	–	–
Waugh, SR	NSW	6	7	2	229	96*	2	–	45.80	1	78.0	16	234	3	78.00	–	–	3/76
Waugh, ME	NSW	9	12	2	522	139*	2	2	52.20	13	93.2	21	271	12	22.58	–	–	4/80
Whitney, MR	NSW	4	5	2	11	6	–	–	3.66	–	150.0	28	445	14	31.78	2	–	6/42

The Australians failed to follow in the Tests the aggressive approach that gave them limited over superiority. Geoff Marsh, Mark Waugh, Dean Jones, and even David Boon and Allan Border found the Tests hard going. But the team's major disappointment was the abject failure of Bruce Reid. Always injury-prone, he had a miserable tour and Border's lack of a top-class strike bowler helped the West Indian batsmen sustain their ascendancy. Matthews failed to worry top-quality batsmen with his right-arm off-spin, Merv Hughes was revealed as just a plucky stock bowler, leaving Craig McDermott to carry the attack far too often. By contrast the West Indies had four splendid bowlers, Ambrose, Marshall, Patterson and Walsh and a very handy off-spinner in Carl Hooper. Long before the West Indies went to a series winning two–nil lead by taking the Fourth Test, the Australian XI looked in need of rebuilding. Mark Waugh salvaged some Australian pride with a lovely 130 not out which set up Australia's 157-run win in the Fifth Test.

McDermott came through the series with an enhanced reputation, taking 24 wickets at 23.50, and bowled very few loose deliveries. He deserved better support than he received from Merv Hughes, whose 19 wickets cost 31 each. Bruce Reid's failure to find fitness and anything like his Australian form gave both McDermott and captain Allan Border problems neither could surmount. Neither side batted consistently but the West Indian tail invariably managed to add handy runs, whereas the Australian tail regularly flopped.

Both captains admitted they were ignorant of the law under which Dean Jones was wrongly run out in the Second Test. Jones was bowled by a no-ball from Courtney Walsh, but did not hear the umpire's call. He headed for the pavilion believing he was out, only to see Hooper rush up from slips, gather the ball, and uproot the middle stump. Border called to Jones to get back but before he reached the crease umpire C.E. Cumberbatch had answered appeals for a runout by giving Jones out. This was a clear breach of the rule that disallows such a ruling 'unless the batsman attempts a run'. The West Indies won this Test and the fourth, Australia the fifth, and with the first and the third drawn after rain the West Indies took the series 2–1.

AUSTRALIA IN THE WEST INDIES 1994-95

First-class Results					All Matches				
Matches	Won	Lost	Drawn	Tied	Matches	Won	Lost	Drawn	Tied
7	3	1	3	–	16	8	5	3	–

Date	Venue	Opponent	Results for Australians
Mar 5	Bridgetown	*Barbados Second XI	Won by 52 runs
Mar 8	Bridgetown	*West Indies (L/O Intl)	Lost by 6 runs
Mar 11	Port-of-Spain	*West Indies (L/O Intl)	Won by 26 runs
Mar 12	Port-of-Spain	*West Indies (L/O Intl)	Lost by 133 runs
Mar 15	St Vincent	*West Indies (L/O Intl)	Lost on run rate
Mar 18	Georgetown	*West Indies (L/O Intl)	Lost by 5 wkts
Mar 20	Georgetown	Guyana	Won by an inns & 61 runs
Mar 25	St Lucia	West Indies Cricket Board XI	Drawn
Mar 31	Bridgetown	WEST INDIES (1st Test)	Won by 10 wkts
Apr 8	Antigua	WEST INDIES (2nd Test)	Drawn
Apr 15	St Kitt's	West Indies Cricket Board XI	Drawn
Apr 21	Port-of-Spain	WEST INDIES (3rd Test)	Lost by 9 wkts
Apr 29	Kingston	WEST INDIES (4th Test)	Won by an inns & 53 runs
May 11	Bermuda	*St George's Cricket Club	Won by 53 runs
May 13	Bermuda	*Bermuda Cricket National	Won by 32 runs
May 14	Bermuda	*Bermuda Select XI	Won by 18 runs

Player	State	M	Inn	NO	Runs	HS	50	100	Avrge	Ct/St	Overs	Mdns	Runs	Wkts	Avrge	5wi	10wm	Best
Blewett, GS	SA	7	9	–	353	116	2	1	39.22	5	19.0	5	49	1	49.00	–	–	1/25
Boon, DC	TAS	6	8	–	190	67	1	–	23.75	4	–	–	–	–	–	–	–	–
Healy, IA	QLD	7	9	2	202	74*	1	–	28.86	13/2	–	–	–	–	–	–	–	–
Julian, BP	WA	6	7	–	80	31	–	–	11.43	2	107.0	21	351	18	19.50	1	–	5/54
Langer, JL	WA	2	2	–	55	55	1	–	27.50	4	1.0	–	11	–	–	–	–	–
May, TBA	SA	2	2	1	24	24*	–	–	24.00	–	67.1	17	194	6	32.33	–	–	4/73
McGrath, GD	NSW	6	6	2	8	4	–	–	2.00	–	168.4	45	515	24	21.46	3	–	6/47
Ponting, RT	TAS	1	1	–	19	19	–	–	19.00	1	–	–	–	–	–	–	–	–
Rackemann, CG	QLD	1	1	–	0	0	–	–	0.00	–	35.0	5	121	4	30.25	–	–	3/68
Reiffel, PR	VIC	6	7	2	80	23	–	–	16.00	5	129.4	36	374	15	24.93	–	–	4/47
Slater, MJ	NSW	7	10	1	291	90	2	–	32.33	4	3.0	–	20	–	–	–	–	–
Taylor, MA (Capt)	NSW	7	10	1	222	62	2	–	24.67	11	–	–	–	–	–	–	–	–
Warne, SK	VIC	6	6	–	51	23	–	–	8.50	5	178.0	46	553	23	24.04	–	–	4/70
Waugh, ME	NSW	7	9	1	418	126	3	1	52.25	6	36.0	9	146	4	36.50	–	–	2/39
Waugh, SR	NSW	6	8	3	510	200	4	1	102.00	7	37.0	8	100	8	12.50	–	–	2/14

Australia overcame severe handicaps in a memorable show of team spirit to defeat the West Indies by two Tests to one. They did it with a team that did not bear comparison with Australia's best, had a history of collapsing under pressure, lacked the services of leading strike bowlers, Craig McDermott and Damien Fleming, and had just been whipped four–one in a limited over series. Australia lost all four tosses in the series, disappointed with the bat in all bar two Test innings, and had their coach Bob Simpson in hospital at crucial stages, but managed to triumph over a West Indian team well past its peak.

Their success stemmed from the captaincy of Mark Taylor and the brilliance of fielding which restricted the West Indies to a top score of 265 in the four Tests. Some astonishing catches prevented partnerships developing and regularly ended the innings of West Indian batting stars. Taylor had Glenn McGrath, Paul Reiffel and Brendon Julian bowl to a tight line on the off stump and let the uneven bounce of the West Indian pitches do the rest. All three produced performances above their previous standards.

The resolution of the Australians never faltered, and even players struggling for form managed to produce days when they made important contributions to the team's overall success. Greg Blewett failed in the first three Tests but delivered a knockout blow to the West Indies with his classy 69 in the Fourth Test. David Boon's flow of big scores ended but he made up for it with vital catches, none more important than his high, left-hand grab to send dangerman Brian Lara back in the First Test. Ian Healy generally struggled for runs but his 74 not out in the First Test assured an Australian victory. Shane Warne's domination of batsmen wavered yet he still managed 15 wickets in the rubber.

The West Indies were strangely listless, unable to lift their performance to match Australia's spirited challenge as they had in the past, and in the end they were soundly defeated. Richie Richardson made their only century but he was left without support in this long, disciplined innings. His bowlers depended entirely on bouncers to dislodge the Australians and were helped in this tactic by umpires who refused to prevent the illegal delivery of more than two bouncers an over. Once the Australians absorbed the punishment, they were unworried by an attack sadly lacking in variety or ideas.

Above all this remarkable series belonged to the allround skills and mental toughness of Steve Waugh. He batted, bowled and fielded in a manner that inspired all his colleagues and lifted himself to a very high place among the great Australian allrounders. There have been few better Test innings by an Australian than his 200 in the final Test and he capped it all with a magnificent catch in the gully shortly afterwards. That catch sent the West Indies down the path to defeat and ended this long domination of world cricket.

The Australian team in the West Indies, 1994-95: *standing* Erroll Alcott (physio), Shane Warne, Ricky Ponting, Tim May, Glenn McGrath, B. Julian, Carl Rackermann, Paul Reiffel, Michael Slater, Greg Blewett, Mike Walsh (scorer); *seated* Justin Langer, Steve Waugh, Bob Simpson (coach), Ian Healy, Mark Taylor, Jack Edwards (manager), David Boon, Mark Waugh.

Kerry Packer, left, leaves the London High Court after a hearing with the deposed England captain Tony Greig. Packer's success in this case cost establishment cricket more than $600,000 in legal costs. *Patrick Eagar*

CHAPTER TWELVE

THE PACKER REVOLT AND OTHER REBELLIONS

The two-season rebellion in 1977 and 1978 against established cricket, which saw 66 players from all the major cricket nations join colourful promotions underwritten by media tycoon Kerry Packer, had been building up for years. The Australian Cricket Board claimed it paid Test players all the money it could afford, but the leading players disagreed. Every time they looked up from the field at the vast crowds they attracted, the players' discontent increased.

Sid Barnes had refused to join the Australian team's tour of South Africa in 1945–50 because he could not afford to go for the Board's £450 out-of-pocket allowance. Even before he became Australian captain Ian Chappell was openly bitter about the Board's match payments to Test players. As captain of South Australia in 1970–71 his proposed introduction of a provident fund to prevent experienced players like Ken Cunningham and John Causby retiring was summarily rejected. When Ian and his brother Greg went to South Africa to play in the Double Wicket competition in 1972 Board officials sent a message to the sponsors not to pay them too much.

Kerry Packer found when he applied in 1976 for the rights to televise big matches on his Channel 9 network that the delay in answering his bid ran into months, at the end of which he was curtly told the Board had given all rights to the Australian Broadcasting Commission.

Packer was simmering with annoyance at this treatment when John Cornell, manager of top-rating comedian Paul Hogan, popped into his office and informed him of the players' long-standing anger over their poor match fees. Packer realised the Board was unaware that Test cricket was a highly marketable product. There had been virtually no attempt to find sponsors for state or Australian teams, no professional promotion to attract crowds. Marketing of big cricket was, to Board delegates, a strange idea, like the long hair malcontents such as Chappell favoured.

Packer's determination to spare no expense in making World Series Cricket (WSC) succeed surprised even his staff, but it was no surprise to those who knew how the Packer family loved a scrap. He was not content with signing up 28 leading Australian players, but built his stable to 66 elite cricketers by attracting the best from the West Indies, India, Pakistan, England, New Zealand, and South Africa. The reigning England captain Tony Greig, West Indian captain Clive Lloyd, Pakistani greats Imran Khan, Majid Khan and Javed Miandad, and New Zealand hero Richard Hadlee all joined WSC. Offered the chance to make $30,000 a year and have all expenses paid, the cream of the world's cricket talent rushed to sign up and make their financial future secure. Johnny Gleeson and Bob Cowper joined the WSC management committee without fees.

The cricket establishment in the 1977–78 season forced Packer's matches off grounds like Melbourne and Sydney Cricket Grounds, and other venues where people were accustomed to watching big cricket. The rebels were consigned to outlying suburban football grounds, but Packer's ingenious wicket-maker John Maley designed a portable pitch that could be carried round in trucks and dropped into place in a few hours. When the International Cricket Conference banned all WSC players from Tests Packer went to court and after a 31-day hearing won a London High Court ruling that the ban was an unreasonable restraint of trade. This left the ICC and England's Test and County Cricket Board with more than $300,000 to pay in legal fees.

Kerry Packer shows the stance at the crease he first learnt as a pupil at Geelong Grammar, one of Australia's most exclusive schools. He is now Australia's richest man. *Patrick Eagar*

Packer lost an estimated $4 million in the first year of WSC, but from the time the New South Wales Government changed the law to allow him on to Sydney Cricket Ground, and thanks to massive light towers, WSC was a success. Packer himself appeared on commercial radio programs promoting night cricket and when the lights went on at the SCG, crowds broke down fences in their eagerness to get in. Packer was so elated he asked ground staff to throw open the gates and let latecomers in free, but an estimated 55,000 people paid to get in and watch Ian Chappell lead the Australian XI on to the field for the first match under lights.

Packer's Australians were divided into two teams. The players in form appeared in 'Super Tests' against Rest of The World and West Indian sides captained by Tony Greig and Clive Lloyd. The cricket these matches produced was of the highest quality, with opposing players reaching deep into their reserves of stamina, pluck, and technical know-how. Bouncers flew, players broke fingers and sustained heavy bruising in matches of competitive intensity which critics in England have never understood. The second string teams toured country centres and gave clinics in schools, and this was how Duggie Walters found himself back in the bush.

After two seasons, with established cricket losing money at an alarming rate and WSC thriving, the Australian Board of Control sought permission from the ICC to negotiate a settlement with Packer. ICC president Charles Palmer gave them this right—reportedly after a

Twenty-three of the 26 Australians who joined Kerry Packer's World Series Cricket in 1977-78: *back row* Dennis Lillee, Martin Kent, Ray Bright, David Hookes, Richie Robinson, Max Walker, Ian Redpath, Kerry O'Keefe; *middle* Rick McCosker, Graham McKenzie, Wayne Prior, Ashley Mallett, Len Pascoe, Mick Malone, Ian Davis, Gary Gilmour; *front* Trevor Chappell, Doug Walters, Greg Chappell, Ian Chappell, Rod Marsh, Bruce Laird, Ross Edwards.

meeting with Packer at which he disclosed the extent of his wealth to Palmer—and the ACB appointed Ray Steele and Bob Parish to represent WSC at a peace conference. The terms of the settlement have never been released, but the cricket that emerged ended the ACB's crippling losses and showed them how to promote big cricket professionally.

Teams in coloured clothing, cricket under lights using two white balls and microphones in the side of the stumps, attracted large, enthusiastic audiences and over the next two decades the ACB distributed more than $25 million to Australian states as their share of Australian cricket's affluence. Major firms queued to sponsor state and Australian teams, tours for Australian Under-17 and Under-19 teams were paid for by willing sponsors, and a Cricket Academy for Australia's most promising youngsters was set up. A staff of more than 20 people, some of them highly trained in marketing and finance, are on the ACB staff in Jolimont Street, Melbourne. Just up the street lies the Melbourne Cricket Ground, with a stand that can hold 30,000 people—more than the entire population of Richie Richardson's homeland, Antigua (27,000 inhabitants)—and can attract more than $2 million in a single night with its Packer-style cricket.

To those who watched those gripping 'Super Tests' in the two summers of WSC, the ICC's failure to accept the players' performances as part of their first-class career records remains an injustice. The Packer revolt now looks more and more like Australian cricket's grand awakening, with the agony it imposed followed by a show business-style exploitation of its assets. Traditionalists may not enjoy the commercialising this entails, but it is clear the game will never be the same.

AUSTRALIAN REBELS ON TOUR 1985-86 AND 1986-87

Apart from the 28 players who rebelled against the Australian Cricket Board by appearing for two summers with Kerry Packer's WSC promotions, numerous top-class Australian cricketers have gone on tours outside the Board's jurisdiction. Australia's first 11 tours of England were arranged by the players. Edgar Mayne took an Australian side to America in 1913 for 53 matches. The Reverend 'Mick' Waddy organised matches in five Sri Lankan centres in 1914. Frank Tarrant's Australians played 22 matches in India in 1935. Arthur Mailey promoted a US tour by Australians in 1932. Australians went to India, New Zealand and South Africa in Commonwealth XIs, with the Wanderers, the Cavaliers, or Derrick Robins' XIs, all of them outside the Australian Board's control.

By far the most publicised players to go overseas, however, were the sixteen who toured South Africa in

The Australians who defied the Australian Cricket Board and the Australian government's anti-apartheid policy by touring South Africa in 1985-86 and 1986-87: *back row* S.B. Smith, T.V. Hohns, P.I. Faulkner, R.J. McCurdy, T.A. Alderman, C.G. Rackemann, J.N. Maguire, M.D. Haysman, T.G. Hogan, R.M. Hogg, Dr F. Polese; *front* M.D. Taylor, J. Dyson, K.J. Hughes (capt.), B. Francis (manager), G.N. Yallop, S.J. Rixon, G. Shipperd.

1985–86 and 1986–87 in open defiance of the Australian government and the Australian Board's anti-apartheid policy. All the players had previously represented their states, most of them were in line for Test selection, and they chose tours that were reported to have earned them $200,000 each. The Australian Board began court action against the players they had under contract, but dropped this and negotiated a settlement with the South African Cricket Union when they were advised that legal costs could be more than $600,000. The Board believed it had a good case but mindful of Packer's success in England's High Court decided not to take the risk with money that could be used on cricket development at home. All 16 players were banned from appearing for their states for two years and for Australia for three years, but these bans did not worry those with agreements to play in England. Kim Hughes could not play for Western Australia during the period of the ban but his state team-mate Terry Alderman played for Kent while Hughes was sueing the Western Australian Cricket Association for the right to play club cricket.

Most Australians believed the South African rebels were right to place the financial security of their families ahead of their Test ambitions. At first Australian sports fans believed the violent clashes between police and anti-apartheid demonstrators seen in Australia during the Springbok Rugby tour would be repeated at the rebels' matches in South Africa. There was speculation about how the African police methods would compare with the behaviour of Australian police who dragged demonstrators across barbed wire barricades and stood inside Rugby grounds putting out smoke bombs with garbage-tin lids. When the expected demonstrations did not occur in South Africa, however, the public lost interest. Australian reporters sent to South Africa to cover the matches were home before Christmas that first year.

Dr Ali Bacher, chief executive of the South African Cricket Union, used the traditional right of host countries to declare first-class the two rebel tours and other tours by international XIs in the 15 years South Africa was ostracised from big cricket. Statisticians around the world accepted this ruling, but in January 1993 the ruling body of world cricket, the International Cricket Conference, contradicted Ali Bacher and ruled that none of the matches in South Africa for those 15 years were first-class. This meant that none of the performances by Australia's 16 rebel tourists, nor those by Richie Benaud, Graham Gooch, John Gleeson, Greg Chappell, Dennis Lillee, Max Walker, Derek Underwood, Glenn Turner, Lawrence Rowe, Gordon Greenidge, Phil Edmonds or Younis Ahmed could be included in their career records. The confusion this caused among statisticians throughout the cricket world, who had already accepted Ali Bacher's assurances of first-class status, is likely to take years to unravel.

Those cricketers led by Kim Hughes were enthusiastically received by South African officials and crowds. They conducted clinics for black kids eager to learn basic

The International Wanderers team that toured South Africa in 1974-75: *back* J.N. Shepherd, R.E. East, G.R.J. Roope, B.C. Franis, M.J. Smith, G.G.W. Johnstone, R.A. Woolmer, Younis Ahmed, masseur; *centre* J.A. Snow, J.H. Edrich, B.B. Close (capt.), D.H. Robins (patron), L.E.G. Ames (manager), J.T. Murray, J.W. Gleeson; *front* P.G. Lee, J.K. Lever, R.W. Tolchard. They did a great deal to keep first-class cricket going in South Africa during the years of the apartheid ban.

Australian rebels Terry Alderman, left, and Carl Rackemann enjoying a cup of tea and a yarn with Graeme Pollock and Dr Ali Bacher, chief executive of the South African Cricket Union.

skills, and on the field found themselves facing very strong opposition. They won only four of the 22 matches played under first-class rules, suffered five losses, and had 13 draws. They hit 23 centuries, but found difficulty in restricting rival elevens to low totals.

All the rebel tours helped keep cricket going in South Africa in the years of the anti-apartheid ban, which as Bob Hawke said, was not designed to bring South Africa to its knees but to its senses. Most of the rebels ruined their Test prospects by going and it is churlish now for the International Cricket Council to pretend their matches were not first class, for they met every first-class condition. The development work they began in black ghettoes is now being carried on by white and black administrators.

CHAPTER THIRTEEN

THE OLD ENEMY

Since international touring became popular among top-class cricketers in the 1860s, 37 England teams have made extensive Australian tours. Others have popped in for a few matches on their way to or from New Zealand or to celebrate various centenaries. Official MCC sides have sometimes played in Australia on their way to or from other countries, but the visits by full-strength England teams every four years have become an important feature of Australian sport.

England has made 14 extended tours of Australia since World War II, compared with 14 tours of England by official Australian sides. More than half Australia's international cricket has been played against England (286 Tests out of the 552 Australia have played). At the end of Australia's 1993 tour of England, the two countries had played 151 Tests in England. No wonder Australian cricket buffs call England the 'Old Enemy'. To take the field against England remains the crowning ambition of all Australian cricketers, an honour unmatched by playing against any other cricket nation.

This unique international rivalry began in the days of small ships when players endured rough ocean voyages, continued through the era of luxury liners, and now starts with 24-hour jet flights that take all the fun out of tour preparations. English cricketers no longer look rested and sun-tanned when they arrive. Some appear decidedly queasy, relieved to tread firm ground, and yet to get to know their team-mates. Unquestionably air travel imposes problems on captains and managers eager to build team spirit, previously solved on long, restful voyages, deck cricket and balmy partying.

Australia got off to a fine start after World War II, thanks to the Services side. England, hard hit by the loss of Test players in the war, toured before there was time to recover. The heavy defeat sustained by Hammond's team took years to overcome. It was not until 1951 that England won a Test in Melbourne, and it was not until 1953 that England regained The Ashes which Australia had held for 18 years 362 days.

Australia and England have both undergone slumps in their standards of play in the 116 years since their contests began. This has never lessened the expectations of supporters of both teams when the next series comes round because the record shows numerous series wins by the underdogs. Recoveries by badly beaten sides are only a Test match away. Even the most partisan Australian fans chuckled with disbelief at the end of the 1936–37 season when the chairman of the Australian Board of Control, Dr Allen Robertson, said: 'I doubt whether England will ever produce a team to make an even go with Australian cricketers. . . In my lifetime they are not going to produce a team equal to ours.'

Given the persistent vagaries of Test cricket, this was arrant nonsense. Within a year England made a fool of Dr Robertson by inflicting the heaviest defeat in Test history on Australia, with Len Hutton surpassing Bradman's world record of 334, scoring 364 out of a total of 7 declared for 903, enough to defeat Australia by an innings and 579 runs.

ENGLAND IN AUSTRALIA 1946–47

	First-class Results					All Matches			
Matches	Won	Lost	Drawn	Tied	Matches	Won	Lost	Drawn	Tied
17	1	3	13	–	25	4	3	18	–

Date	Venue	Opponent	Results for Touring Team
Oct 2	Northam	*Northam & District	Won by an inns & 215 runs
Oct 7	Fremantle	*Western Australian Colts	Drawn
Oct 11	Perth	Western Australia	Drawn
Oct 17	Perth	Combined XI	Drawn
Oct 22	Port Pirie	*South Australian Country XI	Won by an inns & 308 runs
Oct 25	Adelaide	South Australia	Drawn
Oct 31	Melbourne	Victoria	Won by 244 runs
Nov 9	Melbourne	Australian XI	Drawn
Nov 15	Sydney	New South Wales	Drawn
Nov 22	Brisbane	Queensland	Drawn
Nov 29	Brisbane	AUSTRALIA (1st Test)	Lost by an inns & 332 runs
Dec 7	Gympie	*Queensland Country XI	Drawn
Dec 13	Sydney	AUSTRALIA (2nd Test)	Lost by an inns & 33 runs
Dec 21	Newcastle	*New South Wales Country XI	Drawn
Dec 27	Canberra	*NSW Southern District	Drawn
Dec 30	Bendigo	*Victorian Country XI	Won on 1st innings
Jan 1	Melbourne	AUSTRALIA (3rd Test)	Drawn
Jan 10	Hobart (TCA)	Combined XI	Drawn
Jan 15	Launceston	Tasmania	Drawn
Jan 24	Adelaide	South Australia	Drawn
Jan 31	Adelaide	AUSTRALIA (4th Test)	Drawn
Feb 11	Ballarat	*Victorian Country XI	Drawn
Feb 14	Melbourne	Victoria	Drawn
Feb 21	Sydney	New South Wales	Drawn
Feb 28	Sydney	AUSTRALIA (5th Test)	Lost by 5 wkts

England in Australia 1946–47: *back row* J. Langridge, D.C.S. Compton, T.G. Evans, L. Hutton; *centre* D.V.P. Wright, C. Washbrook, J.T. Ikin, A.V. Bedser, R. Pollard, T.P.B. Smith, R. Howard (manager); *front* W. Voce, P.A. Gibb, N.W.D. Yardley, W.R. Hammond (capt.), W.J. Edrich, L.B. Fishlock, J. Hardstaff Jnr.

Player	M	Inn	NO	Runs	HS	50	100	Avrge	Ct/St	Overs	Mdns	Runs	Wkts	Avrge	5wi	10wm	Best
Bedser, AV	11	17	3	214	51	1	–	15.28	6	399.3	56	1359	28	48.54	–	–	3/40
Compton, DCS	15	25	3	1432	163	8	5	65.09	9	83.2	11	311	6	51.83	–	–	2/46
Edrich, WJ	14	21	2	881	119	6	1	46.37	9	235.0	25	949	22	43.14	–	–	4/26
Evans, TG	11	16	5	224	41*	–	–	20.36	22/4	–	–	–	–	–	–	–	–
Fishlock, LB	7	12	1	299	57	3	–	27.18	4	1.0	–	3	–	–	–	–	–
Gibb, PA	9	14	1	199	37*	–	–	15.30	10/1	1.0	–	14	–	–	–	–	–
Hammond, WR (Capt)	10	14	–	633	208	1	2	45.21	10	3.0	–	8	–	–	–	–	–
Hardstaff, J jr	8	13	1	471	155	3	1	39.25	3	14.0	1	50	3	16.67	–	–	3/24
Hutton, L	14	21	3	1267	151*	8	3	70.38	5	21.0	1	132	2	66.00	–	–	1/8
Ikin, JT	16	24	3	590	71	4	–	28.10	17	107.0	8	481	13	37.00	–	–	4/51
Langridge, J	5	3	1	130	100	–	1	65.00	2	100.0	15	297	7	42.43	–	–	3/60
Pollard, R	9	7	3	45	12*	–	–	11.25	5	233.0	45	735	13	56.54	–	–	2/23
Smith, TPB	7	8	–	154	46	–	–	19.25	5	234.6	14	993	30	33.10	2	1	9/121
Voce, W	8	9	1	116	28	–	–	14.50	3	179.4	34	660	11	60.00	–	–	4/125
Washbrook, C	15	25	–	891	124	4	3	35.64	4	–	–	–	–	–	–	–	–
Wright, DVP	12	16	5	76	20	–	–	6.90	5	395.4	39	1699	51	33.31	2	1	7/105
Yardley, NWD	16	23	4	614	70	5	–	32.31	9	134.7	16	443	15	29.53	–	–	3/19

The Australian Board of Control invited England to tour immediately after VJ-Day. Dr Bert Evatt, deputy Prime Minister and Australian Minister for Foreign Affairs, made a diplomatic deal out of it, urging the MCC not to delay, with national morale at stake. England had lost their great left-arm spin bowler Hadley Verity, who died of wounds in Italy, and hostile fast bowler Ken Farnes, killed in an RAF training accident, and many of their fine pre-war players were past their best, but they put together a party which left Southampton for Australia in the RMS *Stirling Castle* at the end of August 1946. 'Doc' Evatt told the owners of the *Stirling Castle* the safe arrival of Wally Hammond's team was vital to Australia's recovery and the captain rushed the ship to Australia in 24 days without any of the customary refuelling stops. Additional warm-up games had to be arranged by surprised hosts as the *Stirling Castle* docked in Fremantle.

Australia's prospects in the Tests centred around Bradman's fitness. He had been invalided out of the Army with fibrositis after failing an RAAF pilot's test because of his below-average eyesight. Having almost died from a ruptured appendix back in 1934, he knew the folly of over-estimating his strength. He announced he would only resume Test cricket if he came through matches for South Australia satisfactorily immediately after the war. He survived a controversial lbw appeal when Cec Pepper hit him on the pad in the Services XI v. South Australia match. He went to Brisbane for the First Test still under a cloud, despite the satisfaction of making his 100th first-class century against India in 1947–48.

When he was on 28, 38-year-old Bradman was given not out in response to a 'catch' in the gully by Jack Ikin. Hammond never forgave Bradman for not walking, but Hassett, who was batting with Bradman, was sure it was a 'bump ball'. Bradman went on to 187, adding 276 for the third wicket with Hassett. Australia made 645 and won by an innings and 332 runs, after England had to bat on a pitch twice flooded by rain. Fifteen England wickets fell in 3 hours 30 minutes.

Barnes and Bradman both made 234 in the Second Test, Australia winning by an innings and 33 runs. The Third Test was the first draw in Australia since 1881–82. Morris and Compton both scored centuries in each innings of the drawn Fourth Test before Australia took the rubber three–nil in winning the Fifth Test by five wickets. The great Wally Hammond handed the England captaincy to Norman Yardley after the Fourth Test, a broken, dejected figure after 33 Tests. Bradman and his fine team went on to glory in 1948 by touring England undefeated.

Jack Ikin, the Lancashire allrounder who believed he caught Bradman for 28. A confident England appeal was disallowed and Bradman went on to 187, a score that sustained Bradman's comeback from serious wartime injury.

ENGLAND IN AUSTRALIA 1950-51

	First-class Results					All Matches			
Matches	Won	Lost	Drawn	Tied	Matches	Won	Lost	Drawn	Tied
16	5	4	7	–	25	7	4	14	–

Date	Venue	Opponent	Results for Touring Team
Oct 14	Northam	*Western Australian Country XI	Drawn
Oct 16	Perth	*Western Australian Colts	Won by an inns & 149 runs
Oct 20	Perth	Western Australia	Drawn
Oct 27	Adelaide	South Australia	Won by 7 wkts
Nov 3	Melbourne	Victoria	Drawn
Nov 10	Sydney	New South Wales	Drawn
Nov 17	Newcastle	*New South Wales Country XI	Drawn
Nov 20	Lismore	*NSW Northern District	Drawn
Nov 24	Brisbane	Queensland	Drawn
Dec 1	Brisbane	AUSTRALIA (1st Test)	Lost by 70 runs
Dec 8	Toowoomba	*Queensland Country XI	Drawn
Dec 12	Canberra	*Southern District of NSW	Drawn
Dec 15	Sydney	Australian XI	Drawn
Dec 22	Melbourne	AUSTRALIA (2nd Test)	Lost by 28 runs
Dec 30	Sydney	New South Wales	Drawn
Jan 5	Sydney	AUSTRALIA (3rd Test)	Lost by an inns & 13 runs
Jan 13	Hobart (TCA)	Tasmania	Won by 9 wkts
Jan 19	Launceston	Combined XI	Won by 10 wkts
Jan 24	Renmark	*South Australian Country XI	Won by an inns & 25 runs
Jan 27	Adelaide	South Australia	Won by 152 runs
Feb 2	Adelaide	AUSTRALIA (4th Test)	Lost by 274 runs
Feb 10	Melbourne	Victoria	Drawn
Feb 16	Geelong	*Victorian Country XI	Drawn
Feb 19	Euroa	*Victorian Country XI	Drawn
Feb 23	Melbourne	AUSTRALIA (5th Test)	Won by 8 wkts

England in Australia 1950-51: *back row* W. Ferguson (scorer), R. Berry, A.J. McIntyre, T.E. Bailey, W.G.A. Parkhouse, W.E. Hollies; *centre* J.G. Dewes, D.S. Sheppard, J.J. Warr, A.V. Bedser, D.B. Close, R.T. Simpson, D.V.P. Wright; *front* M.A. Green (manager), C. Washbrook, D.C.S. Compton, F.R. Brown (capt.), L. Hutton, T.G. Evans, J.H. Nash (treasurer).

Player	M	Inn	NO	Runs	HS	50	100	Avrge	Ct/St	Overs	Mdns	Runs	Wkts	Avrge	5wi	10wm	Best
Bailey, TE	9	12	3	209	125	–	1	23.22	7	190.1	34	624	25	24.96	1	–	5/54
Bedser, AV	11	14	3	131	42	–	–	11.91	9	352.3	58	1010	51	19.80	3	1	5/46
Bedser, EA	1	1	–	2	2	–	–	2.00	–	12.0	1	39	–	–	–	–	–
Berry, R	7	6	3	32	13	–	–	10.67	3	124.5	21	479	11	43.55	–	–	3/34
Brown, FR (Capt)	11	16	1	349	79	2	–	23.27	7	207.6	20	808	28	28.86	–	–	4/26
Close, CB	9	13	3	231	108*	–	1	23.10	9	98.2	9	475	13	36.54	–	–	3/81
Compton, DCS	12	21	5	882	142	2	4	55.13	11	84.4	8	415	11	37.73	–	–	3/32
Dewes, JG	10	15	2	399	117	2	1	30.69	6	–	–	–	–	–	–	–	–

Continued

HOME AND AWAY

Player	M	Inn	NO	Runs	HS	50	100	Avrge	Ct/St	Overs	Mdns	Runs	Wkts	Avrge	5wi	10wm	Best
Evans, TG	12	18	3	325	49	–	–	21.67	22/8	–	–	–	–	–	–	–	–
Hollies, WE	9	9	6	19	5*	–	–	6.33	3	211.0	26	858	21	40.86	–	–	4/7
Hutton, L	12	21	4	1199	156*	5	5	70.52	18	0.7	–	4	1	4.00	–	–	1/4
McIntyre, AJ	5	7	1	64	32*	–	–	10.67	4/5	–	–	–	–	–	–	–	–
Parkhouse, WGA	7	11	1	371	92	2	–	37.10	3	–	–	–	–	–	–	–	–
Sheppard, DS	10	16	1	308	67*	1	–	20.53	2	–	–	–	–	–	–	–	–
Simpson, RT	13	24	1	995	259	2	3	43.26	7	–	–	–	–	–	–	–	–
Statham, JB	2	4	1	37	18	–	–	12.33	–	36.0	6	109	3	36.33	–	–	1/16
Tattersall, R	3	5	–	37	14	–	–	7.40	2	89.5	19	309	7	44.14	–	–	3/95
Washbrook, C	14	23	1	804	112	5	1	36.55	6	2.0	–	8	2	4.00	–	–	2/8
Warr, JJ	9	10	–	84	23	–	–	8.40	5	251.6	24	870	23	37.83	–	–	4/47
Wright, DVP	10	13	4	64	29	–	–	7.11	1	229.5	17	1076	33	32.61	2	–	7/60

Freddie Brown, born at Lima, Peru, in 1910, was in his 40th year and enjoying a hot bath at Lord's after batting for Gentlemen against The Players when 'Plum' Warner came into the dressing-room and offered him the captaincy of England's team to tour Australia in 1950–51. Brown, who had toured Australia 18 years before in Jardine's team without appearing in a Test, rescued selectors anxious to sustain the job as an amateurs-only appointment, by accepting. Australians who had abhorred Jardine's harlequin cap, loved Brown's knotted kerchief and pipe because they recognised the fibre of the leg-spinner who had been taken prisoner at Tobruk. Australia won the first four Tests but there was pleasure right round Australia—and particularly among the Australians Hassett led at home for the first time—when Brown inspired his team to win the Fifth Test after a memorable 156 not out by Reg Simpson. Len Hutton's 1199 runs at 70.52 headed the England averages and shaped events to come.

ENGLAND IN AUSTRALIA 1954–55

First-class Results					All Matches			
Matches	Won	Lost	Drawn	Tied	Matches	Won	Lost	Drawn	Tied
17	8	2	7	–	23	13	2	8	–

Date	Venue	Opponent	Results for Touring Team
Oct 11	Bunbury	*Western Australian Country XI	Drawn
Oct 15	Perth	Western Australia	Won by 7 wkts
Oct 22	Perth	Combined XI	Won by an inns & 62 runs
Oct 29	Adelaide	South Australia	Won by 21 runs
Nov 5	Melbourne	Australian XI	Drawn
Nov 12	Sydney	New South Wales	Drawn
Nov 19	Brisbane	Queensland	Drawn
Nov 26	Brisbane	AUSTRALIA (1st Test)	Lost by an inns & 154 runs
Dec 4	Rockingham	*Queensland Country XI	Won by an inns & 12 runs
Dec 8	Canberra	*Prime Minister's XI	Won by 31 runs
Dec 10	Melbourne	Victoria	Drawn
Dec 17	Sydney	AUSTRALIA (2nd Test)	Won by 38 runs
Dec 27	Newcastle	*NSW Northern District XI	Won by 9 wkts
Dec 31	Melbourne	AUSTRALIA (3rd Test)	Won by 128 runs
Jan 8	Hobart (TCA)	Combined XI	Drawn
Jan 13	Launceston	Tasmania	Won by 243 runs
Jan 18	Mount Gambier	*South Australian Country XI	Won by an inns & 177 runs
Jan 21	Adelaide	South Australia	Won by an inns & 143 runs
Jan 28	Adelaide	AUSTRALIA (4th Test)	Won by 5 wkts
Feb 5	Yallourn	*Victorian Country XI	Won by an inns & 26 runs
Feb 11	Melbourne	Victoria	Drawn
Feb 18	Sydney	New South Wales	Lost by 45 runs
Feb 25	Sydney	AUSTRALIA (5th Test)	Drawn

England in Australia in 1954-55: *back row* G. Duckworth (baggage master), K.V. Andrew, P.J. Loader, T.W. Graveney, F.H. Tyson, H.W. Dalton (scorer); *centre* J.H. Wardle, R.T. Simpson, J.V. Wilson, R. Appleyard, J. McConnon, J.B. Statham, M.C. Cowdrey, C.G. Howard (manager); *front* T.E. Bailey, W.J. Edrich, P.B.H. May, L. Hutton (capt.), D.C.S. Compton, A.V. Bedser, T.G. Evans.

Player	M	Inn	NO	Runs	HS	50	100	Avrge	Ct/St	Overs	Mdns	Runs	Wkts	Avrge	5wi	10wm	Best
Andrew, KV	7	9	2	63	28*	–	–	9.00	13/1	–	–	–	–	–	–	–	–
Appleyard, R	10	13	7	74	19*	–	–	12.33	8	187.1	50	519	26	19.96	1	–	5/46
Bailey, TE	12	17	2	508	88	5	–	33.86	5	201.1	32	689	33	20.88	–	–	4/53
Bedser, AV	7	11	2	85	30	–	–	9.44	3	207.7	33	659	24	27.46	1	–	5/57
Compton, DCS	11	16	2	799	182	3	3	57.07	3	16.0	1	101	2	50.50	–	–	1/21
Cowdrey, MC	13	24	–	890	110	5	2	37.08	11	7.0	–	63	1	63.00	–	–	1/25
Edrich, WJ	10	16	–	274	88	1	–	17.12	5	8.0	2	53	–	–	–	–	–
Evans, TG	10	16	2	243	40	–	–	17.35	30/4	–	–	–	–	–	–	–	–
Graveney, TW	11	15	1	519	134	–	2	37.07	16	6.0	–	34	1	34.00	–	–	1/34
Hutton, L (Capt)	12	21	2	959	145*	5	2	50.47	6	0.6	–	2	1	2.00	–	–	1/2
Loader, PJ	9	10	1	70	22	–	–	7.78	6	204.2	30	721	34	21.21	1	–	6/22
May, PBH	14	23	3	931	129	3	4	46.55	12	–	–	–	–	–	–	–	–
McConnon, JE	5	7	1	85	22	–	–	14.16	2	75.1	18	267	8	33.38	–	–	2/37
Simpson, RT	12	21	2	518	136	1	1	27.26	5	3.4	1	5	2	2.50	–	–	2/5
Statham, JB	10	12	4	98	25	–	–	12.25	4	244.4	40	778	38	20.47	2	–	6/23
Tyson, FH	11	17	2	181	31*	–	–	12.06	3	296.0	44	1002	51	19.65	4	1	7/27
Wardle, JH	14	18	2	291	63	1	–	18.18	6	269.7	57	832	37	22.49	2	–	5/79
Wilson, JV	9	15	2	271	72	2	–	20.84	10	19.1	1	90	4	22.50	–	–	1/11

Hutton became the first-ever professional captain of an England touring team and he made sure he gave the diehard traditionalists who opposed his appointment no reason to condemn him. His approach as the first MCC captain was cautious, his eagerness to play attractive cricket non-existent ('Blame the yawns on Hutton,' wrote his old adversary Arthur Morris). Spectators had learned the wisdom of enduring boredom in the Third Test, which began with the teams one–all.

This was a massive England triumph, in which too many missed perhaps the most explosive exhibitions of fiery pace bowling of all time when Frank ('Typhoon') Tyson took 6 for 15 from 51 balls to finish with 7 for 27. England's three–one series victory, their first series win in Australia since 1932–33, brought urgent pleas for Australia to rebuild.

ENGLAND IN AUSTRALIA 1958-59

First-class Results					All Matches				
Matches	Won	Lost	Drawn	Tied	Matches	Won	Lost	Drawn	Tied
17	4	4	9	–	20	7	4	9	–

Date	Venue	Opponent	Results for Touring Team
Oct 17	Perth	Western Australia	Drawn
Oct 24	Perth	Combined XI	Drawn
Oct 31	Adelaide	South Australia	Won by 9 wkts
Nov 7	Melbourne	Victoria	Won by 87 runs
Nov 14	Sydney	New South Wales	Drawn
Nov 21	Sydney	Australian XI	Won by 345 runs
Nov 28	Brisbane	Queensland	Drawn
Dec 5	Brisbane	AUSTRALIA (1st Test)	Lost by 8 wkts
Dec 13	Hobart (TCA)	Tasmania	Drawn
Dec 18	Launceston	Combined XI	Drawn
Dec 24	Adelaide	South Australia	Drawn
Dec 31	Melbourne	AUSTRALIA (2nd Test)	Lost by 8 wkts
Jan 9	Sydney	AUSTRALIA (3rd Test)	Drawn
Jan 17	Melbourne	Victoria	Won by 9 wkts
Jan 23	Sydney	New South Wales	Drawn
Jan 30	Adelaide	AUSTRALIA (4th Test)	Lost by 10 wkts
Feb 7	Wangaratta	*Victorian Country XI	Won by 9 wkts
Feb 9	Wagga Wagga	*Southern New South Wales	Won by 7 wkts
Feb 10	Canberra	*Prime Minister's XI	Won by 4 wkts
Feb 13	Melbourne	AUSTRALIA (5th Test)	Lost by 9 wkts

England in Australia 1958-59: *back row* D.E. Montague (physio), C.A. Milton, W. Watson, P.E. Richardson, R. Swetman, G. Duckworth (baggage master); *centre* G.A. Lock, J.B. Statham, P.J. Loader, R. Subba Row, T.W. Graveney, F.H. Tyson, F.S. Trueman; *seated* F.R. Brown (manager), T.E. Bailey, M.C. Cowdrey, P.B.H. May (capt.), T.G. Evans, J.C. Laker, E.D.R. Eagar (assistant manager).

Player	M	Inn	NO	Runs	HS	50	100	Avrge	Ct/St	Overs	Mdns	Runs	Wkts	Avrge	5wi	10wm	Best
Bailey, TE	13	22	3	501	71*	4	–	26.36	5	181.0	31	516	10	51.60	–	–	2/36
Cowdrey, MC	15	26	5	957	100*	6	2	45.57	15	6.3	–	42	1	42.00	–	–	1/17
Dexter, ER	7	12	1	154	38	–	–	14.00	–	53.0	4	204	3	68.00	–	–	2/45
Evans, TG	7	10	–	124	55	2	–	12.40	8/3	–	–	–	–	–	–	–	–
Graveney, TW	14	25	4	931	177*	7	1	44.33	15	18.0	1	86	1	86.00	–	–	1/39
Laker, JC	10	13	3	107	22*	–	–	10.70	1	282.1	63	655	38	17.23	3	1	5/31
Loader, PJ	8	10	7	31	11*	–	–	10.33	1	169.7	30	507	26	19.50	–	–	4/23
Lock, GRA	10	15	1	173	44	–	–	12.35	2	335.1	66	973	33	29.48	2	–	6/29
May, PBH (Capt)	13	22	1	1197	140	5	5	57.00	4	–	–	–	–	–	–	–	–
Milton, CA	12	24	3	658	116	3	1	31.33	11	4.0	–	33	–	–	–	–	–
Mortimore, J	7	7	2	115	44*	–	–	23.00	2	122.0	24	335	8	41.87	–	–	2/27
Richardson, PE	14	26	–	688	88	6	–	26.46	3	–	–	–	–	–	–	–	–
Statham, JB	9	12	5	131	36*	–	–	18.71	4	209.1	30	549	28	19.60	2	–	7/47
Subba Row, R	7	11	2	314	83	3	–	34.88	1	–	–	–	–	–	–	–	–
Swetman, R	10	16	3	318	76	2	–	24.46	15/1	–	–	–	–	–	–	–	–
Trueman, FS	12	16	1	266	53	2	–	17.73	11	265.1	30	824	37	22.27	2	–	5/42
Tyson, FH	11	13	–	140	33	–	–	10.76	1	241.7	38	735	21	35.00	–	–	4/55
Watson, W	8	13	–	386	141	–	1	26.69	3	–	–	–	–	–	–	–	–

Peter May's tourists survived persistent rancour. Their matches aroused weekly arguments about Australia's alleged 'chuckers', rival bowlers with pronounced drag, and heated argument among reporters who claimed they could detect rule-breaking arm actions from 300 metres away. The series led to an international conference on bowlers who threw, and the introduction of the law which prevents fast-bowlers from over-stepping the batting crease. The bowlers who caused this uproar, Ian Meckiff and Gordon Rorke, had brief international careers.

In the First Test Trevor Bailey batted for 357 minutes to reach 50 and 458 minutes to make 68 before Mackay relieved the torment by bowling him. Australia deserved to win after Bailey scored from only 40 of the 425 balls he faced. Davidson's three wickets in an over clinched the Second Test. After a draw in the Third Test Australia regained The Ashes by winning the Fourth Test, thanks to McDonald's 170 and Benaud's match bag of 9 for 173. Justice was done when Bailey achieved spectacles in the Fifth Test, which Australia won to take the series four–nil.

ENGLAND IN AUSTRALIA 1962-63

First-class Results					All Matches				
Matches	Won	Lost	Drawn	Tied	Matches	Won	Lost	Drawn	Tied
15	4	3	8	–	26	12	3	11	–

Date	Venue	Opponent	Results for Touring Team
Oct 16	Kalgoorlie	*Western Australian Country XI	Drawn
Oct 19	Perth	Western Australia	Won by 10 wkts
Oct 26	Perth	Combined XI	Lost by 10 wkts
Nov 2	Adelaide	South Australia	Drawn
Nov 9	Melbourne	Australian XI	Drawn
Nov 14	Griffith	*New South Wales Country XI	Won by 7 wkts
Nov 16	Sydney	New South Wales	Lost by an inns & 80 runs
Nov 23	Brisbane	Queensland	Drawn
Nov 26	Toowoomba	*Queensland Country XI	Won by 7 wkts
Nov 30	Brisbane	AUSTRALIA (1st Test)	Drawn
Dec 7	Townsville	*Queensland Country XI	Won by an inns & 120 runs
Dec 10	Bendigo	*Victorian Country XII	Drawn
Dec 12	Shepparton	*Victorian Country XII	Won by 6 wkts
Dec 14	Melbourne	Victoria	Won by 5 wkts
Dec 20	Port Lincoln	*South Australian Country XI	Won by 10 wkts
Dec 22	Adelaide	South Australia	Drawn
Dec 29	Melbourne	AUSTRALIA (2nd Test)	Won by 7 wkts
Jan 4	Launceston	Combined XI	Won by 313 runs
Jan 11	Sydney	AUSTRALIA (3rd Test)	Lost by 8 wkts
Jan 18	Newcastle	*New South Wales Country XI	Won by 145 runs
Jan 25	Adelaide	AUSTRALIA (4th Test)	Drawn
Feb 1	Melbourne	Victoria	Drawn
Feb 6	Canberra	*Prime Minister's XI	Won by 3 runs
Feb 8	Dubbo	*New South Wales Country XI	Drawn
Feb 11	Tamworth	*New South Wales Country XI	Won by 10 wkts
Feb 15	Sydney	AUSTRALIA (5th Test)	Drawn

The England team in Australia 1962-63: *back row* P.H. Parfitt, A.C. Smith, F.J. Titmus, J.D.F. Larter, B.R. Knight, T.W. Graveney, L.J. Coldwell, the Rev. D.S. Sheppard, A.V. Bedser; *front* J.T. Murray, G. Pullar, D.A. Allen, E.R. Dexter (capt.), J.B. Statham, the Duke of Norfolk (manager), R. Illingworth, F.S. Trueman, M.C. Cowdrey, K.F. Barrington.

Player	M	Inn	NO	Runs	HS	50	100	Avrge	Ct/St	Overs	Mdns	Runs	Wkts	Avrge	5wi	10wm	Best
Allen, DA	9	9	3	119	32*	–	–	19.83	5	290.2	89	690	29	23.79	2	–	5/43
Barrington, KF	13	22	5	1451	219*	7	5	85.35	12	121.2	17	523	10	52.30	–	–	4/35
Coldwell, LJ	7	7	3	12	4	–	–	3.00	5	201.5	27	706	15	47.06	1	–	6/49
Cowdrey, MC	12	24	3	1028	307	6	2	48.95	9	–	–	–	–	–	–	–	–
Dexter, ER (Capt)	13	24	1	1023	102	9	1	44.47	11	185.2	17	711	18	39.50	–	–	4/8
Graveney, TW	11	18	4	737	185	2	2	52.64	13	9.0	2	36	2	18.00	–	–	2/2
Illingworth, R	8	12	3	248	65*	2	–	27.55	5	186.5	34	611	12	50.91	–	–	3/11
Knight, BR	8	14	4	431	108	4	1	43.10	1	128.4	15	506	11	46.00	–	–	3/65
Larter, JDF	7	2	1	4	4*	–	–	4.00	1	186.4	17	700	29	24.13	–	–	4/24
Murray, JT	5	7	3	60	24*	–	–	15.00	9/1	–	–	–	–	–	–	–	–
Parfitt, PH	10	17	1	305	80	1	–	19.06	7	–	–	–	–	–	–	–	–
Pullar, G	10	19	1	564	132	4	1	31.33	–	9.0	–	38	–	–	–	–	–
Sheppard, DS	12	23	–	913	113	8	1	39.69	8	–	–	–	–	–	–	–	–
Smith, AC	10	13	3	257	55	1	–	25.70	27/1	–	–	–	–	–	–	–	–
Statham, JT	9	11	2	96	30	–	–	10.66	6	290.5	34	1043	33	31.60	–	–	4/49
Titmus, FJ	12	17	5	503	137*	2	1	41.91	8	394.4	79	1134	34	33.35	2	–	7/79
Trueman, FS	9	11	–	179	38	–	–	16.27	8	229.3	19	773	30	25.76	1	–	5/62

A noble challenge for The Ashes by an England team managed by the Duke of Norfolk and captained by 'Lord Ted' Dexter did not eventuate. Dexter found himself without penetrative bowlers, despite persistent efforts to keep Fred Trueman's mind on the job and only David Allen took more than 50 wickets on the 26-match tour. Three England batsmen made more than 1000 runs on the tour and eight of the 16 players hit centuries but the ineffectiveness of the bowlers nullified their efforts. The Tests produced three draws and a win to each side, Australia retaining The Ashes which Benaud's team had won in England in 1961. Trueman paved the way to England's win in the Second Test by taking 8 for 147 and Davidson set up Australia's success in the Third Test with match figures of 9 for 79. Barrington became the fifth batsman since Joe Darling in 1897–98 to reach a Test century with a six, by lifting the ball into the crowd in the drawn Fourth Test in Adelaide. Harvey retired after taking six catches in the drawn Fifth Test, which took his career total to 64, a great achievement for a cover point fieldsman.

ENGLAND IN AUSTRALIA 1965-66

First-class Results					All Matches				
Matches	Won	Lost	Drawn	Tied	Matches	Won	Lost	Drawn	Tied
15	5	2	8	–	24	13	2	8	–

Date	Venue	Opponent	Results for Touring Team
Oct 27	Moora	*Western Australian Country XI	Won by 82 runs
Oct 29	Perth	Western Australia	Won by 9 runs
Nov 5	Perth	Combined XI	Drawn
Nov 12	Adelaide	South Australia	Won by 6 wkts
Nov 17	Hamilton	*Victorian Country XI	Won by 6 wkts
Nov 19	Melbourne	Victoria	Lost by 32 runs
Nov 24	Euroa	*Victorian Country XI	Abandoned
Nov 26	Sydney	New South Wales	Won by 9 wkts
Dec 3	Brisbane	Queensland	Drawn
Dec 8	Beaudesert	*Queensland Country XI	Won by 7 wkts
Dec 10	Brisbane	AUSTRALIA (1st Test)	Drawn
Dec 17	Canberra	*Prime Minister's XI	Won by 2 wkts
Dec 18	Bathurst	*New South Wales Country XI	Won by 5 wkts
Dec 20	Albury	*New South Wales Country XI	Won by 6 wkts
Dec 22	Mount Gambier	*South Australian Country XI	Won by 8 wkts
Dec 23	Adelaide	South Australia	Won by 6 wkts
Dec 30	Melbourne	AUSTRALIA (2nd Test)	Drawn
Jan 7	Sydney	AUSTRALIA (3rd Test)	Won by an inns & 93 runs
Jan 14	Newcastle	*Northern NSW Country XI	Won by 10 wkts
Jan 19	Launceston	Tasmania	Drawn
Jan 22	Hobart (TCA)	Combined XI	Drawn
Jan 28	Adelaide	AUSTRALIA (4th Test)	Lost by an inns & 9 runs
Feb 4	Sydney	New South Wales	Drawn
Feb 11	Melbourne	AUSTRALIA (5th Test)	Drawn

England in Australia 1965-66: *back row* J.T. Ikin (assistant manager), D.J. Brown, J.D.F. Larter, K. Higgs, J. Jennings (physio); *centre* P.H. Parfitt, G. Boycott, W.E. Russell, R.W. Barber, I.J. Jones, B.R. Knight, J.H. Edrich; *seated* J.M. Parks, F.J. Titmus, M.C. Cowdrey, M.J.K. Smith (capt.), S.C. Griffith (manager), K.F. Barrington, D.A. Allen, J.T. Murray.

Player	M	Inn	NO	Runs	HS	50	100	Avrge	Ct/St	Overs	Mdns	Runs	Wkts	Avrge	5wi	10wm	Best
Allen, DA	11	12	5	181	54*	2	–	28.85	8	374.7	89	1077	29	37.13	–	–	4/24
Barber, RW	13	22	2	1001	185	3	3	50.05	10	176.1	8	873	10	87.30	–	–	2/33
Barrington, KF	11	17	3	946	158	7	3	67.57	10	32.5	1	149	6	24.83	–	–	4/24
Boycott, G	10	17	2	720	156	6	1	48.00	3	45.0	6	214	3	71.33	–	–	2/32
Brown, DJ	9	11	1	113	27	–	–	11.30	–	221.0	45	900	29	31.03	1	–	5/63
Cowdrey, MC	12	20	4	834	108	6	2	52.12	10	1.0	–	7	–	–	–	–	–
Edrich, JH	12	21	1	977	133	4	3	48.85	5	–	–	–	–	–	–	–	–
Higgs, K	10	7	4	30	12*	–	–	10.00	3	279.3	28	980	24	40.83	–	–	3/35
Jones, IJ	11	8	2	30	16	–	–	5.00	3	294.6	34	1231	34	36.20	2	–	6/118
Knight, BR	6	9	2	370	94	3	–	52.85	1	151.7	16	512	14	36.57	–	–	4/84
Larter, JDF	5	3	–	7	4	–	–	2.33	4	99.2	12	411	12	34.25	–	–	4/49
Murray, JT	7	10	1	255	110	1	1	28.33	12/3	3.0	–	19	–	–	–	–	–
Parfitt, PH	8	15	1	307	87	1	–	21.92	9	48.2	5	217	3	72.33	–	–	1/32
Parks, JM	9	13	3	652	107*	6	1	65.20	19/6	–	–	–	–	–	–	–	–
Russell, WE	8	14	4	580	110	2	2	58.00	3	4.0	–	16	–	–	–	–	–
Smith, MJK (Capt)	13	22	5	792	112*	4	2	46.58	19	3.0	–	9	–	–	–	–	–
Titmus, FJ	10	12	4	528	80*	6	–	66.00	7	420.3	90	1109	36	30.80	2	–	6/65

England entrusted Michael John Knight Smith, one of the most prolific run-scorers in modern cricket, with the captaincy of a team very strong in batting but on Australian pitches unable to dismiss the opposition for low scores. Smith's side was full of crowd-pleasers, chief among them Fred Titmus, who finished top wicket-taker with 36 tour wickets but at a cost of 30.80. There were seven totals of more than 400 in the Tests, which ended with each side winning a match and three draws. Bob Cowper scored Australia's only triple century in a home Test (307) in the Fifth Test, after batting for 727 minutes, the longest first-class innings in Australia. Doug Walters, in his debut series, was the Australian hero with innings of 155 and 115 in his first two Tests. Bob Simpson (225) and Bill Lawry (119) put on 244 in the Test Australia won. Boycott (84) and Barber (185) opened with 234, in the Test England won. A dour rubber cried out for more enterprising batting.

ENGLAND IN AUSTRALIA 1970-71

First-class Results					All Matches				
Matches	Won	Lost	Drawn	Tied	Matches	Won	Lost	Drawn	Tied
15	3	1	11	–	25	10	2	13	–

Date	Venue	Opponent	Results for Touring Team
Oct 28	Port Pirie	*South Australian Country XI	Won by 10 wkts
Oct 30	Adelaide	South Australia	Drawn
Nov 4	Horsham	*Victorian Country XI	Won by 7 wkts
Nov 6	Melbourne	Victoria	Lost by 6 wkts
Nov 13	Sydney	New South Wales	Drawn
Nov 18	Warwick	*Queensland Country XI	Won on 1st innings
Nov 20	Brisbane	Queensland	Drawn
Nov 25	Redlands Bay	*Queensland Country XI	Won by 7 wkts
Nov 27	Brisbane	AUSTRALIA (1st Test)	Drawn
Dec 5	Perth	Western Australia	Drawn
Dec 9	Narrogin	*Western Australian Country XI	Won by 5 wkts
Dec 11	Perth	AUSTRALIA (2nd Test)	Drawn
Dec 18	Adelaide	South Australia	Drawn
Dec 23	Hobart (TCA)	Tasmania	Won by 9 wkts
Dec 27	Launceston	Combined XI	Drawn
Dec 31	Melbourne	AUSTRALIA (3rd Test)	Drawn
Jan 5	Melbourne	*Australia (L/O Intl)	Lost by 5 wkts
Jan 7	Wagga Wagga	*New South Wales Country XI	Won by 9 wkts
Jan 9	Sydney	AUSTRALIA (4th Test)	Won by 299 runs
Jan 16	Newcastle	*Northern New South Wales	Drawn
Jan 21	Melbourne	AUSTRALIA (5th Test)	Drawn
Jan 29	Adelaide	AUSTRALIA (6th Test)	Drawn
Feb 6	Canberra	*Southern New South Wales	Abandoned
Feb 8	Sydney	*Western Australia	Drawn
Feb 9	Parkes	*New South Wales Country XI	Won by 7 wkts
Feb 12	Sydney	AUSTRALIA (7th Test)	Won by 62 runs

England in Australia 1970-71: *back row* B.L. D'Oliviera, K. Shuttleworth, G.G.A. Saulez (scorer), D. Wilson, P. Lever, A. Ward; *centre* A.P.E. Knott, K.W.R. Fletcher, B.W. Luckhurst, D.L. Underwood, J.H. Hampshire, R.W. Taylor; *front* B.W. Thomas (physio), J.A. Snow, M.C. Cowdrey, R. Illingworth (capt.), J.H. Edrich, G. Boycott, D.G. Clark (manager); R.G.D. Willis joined the team as a replacement.

Player	M	Inn	NO	Runs	HS	50	100	Avrge	Ct/St	Overs	Mdns	Runs	Wkts	Avrge	5wi	10wm	Best
Boycott, G	13	22	6	1535	173	7	6	94.94	6	4.4	–	31	1	31.00	–	–	1/23
Cowdrey, MC	11	16	1	412	101	2	1	27.47	3	24.0	–	127	3	42.33	–	–	2/46
D'Oliveira, BL	12	17	3	707	162*	2	3	50.50	6	189.0	33	567	12	36.38	1	–	7/40
Edrich, JH	13	21	5	1097	130	7	3	68.56	6	–	–	–	–	–	–	–	–
Fletcher, KWR	11	19	1	596	80	5	–	33.11	7	40.3	2	232	5	46.40	–	–	3/43
Hampshire, JH	8	13	2	363	156*	2	1	33.00	8	9.0	–	53	–	–	–	–	–
Illingworth, R (Capt)	13	18	4	479	53	1	–	34.21	4	243.0	60	781	20	39.05	–	–	3/39
Knott, APE	11	15	5	342	73	2	–	34.20	24/4	–	–	–	–	–	–	–	–
Lever, P	13	10	1	120	36	–	–	10.91	6	270.2	38	871	22	39.59	–	–	4/17
Luckhurst, BW	10	16	2	886	135	3	4	63.29	9	–	–	–	–	–	–	–	–
Shuttleworth, K	8	7	2	72	24	–	–	14.40	5	147.5	18	560	12	46.67	1	–	5/47
Snow, JA	11	10	1	150	38	–	–	16.66	4	306.5	57	1021	38	26.86	2	–	7/40
Taylor, RW	4	5	–	94	31	–	–	18.00	12/4	–	–	–	–	–	–	–	–
Underwood, DL	12	11	4	32	13*	–	–	4.57	8	337.7	82	918	26	35.31	–	–	4/66
Ward, A	2	3	1	15	8*	–	–	7.50	–	38.5	3	166	4	41.50	–	–	2/25
Willis, RGD	8	6	3	64	27	–	–	21.33	4	162.0	35	669	21	31.86	–	–	4/81
Wilson, D	5	2	–	30	19	–	–	15.00	3	95.7	11	338	6	56.33	–	–	3/32

This was the eventful, argumentative series Australians craved, with John Snow, the temperamental son of a vicar, bouncing the ball into Australians' torsos from a curiously low arm action and England flawlessly captained by an obdurate Yorkshireman, Ray Illingworth. Snow gave all the leading Australian batsmen some nasty bruises, without resorting to boring approach-runs and slow-over rates that later featured in West Indian attacks. This was the stuff Michael Parkinson had in mind when he wrote the Australians were the dearest of enemies who would go to any lengths to win—just like Yorkshiremen.

In the midst of this Australia's Board of Control chose to sack their captain Bill Lawry with the rubber undecided and hand control to Ian Chappell. An iron-willed umpire named Lou Rowan, a Queensland policeman, also got involved when Illingworth led England off the field in Sydney. Rowan followed them into the dressing-room and explained that unless they returned immediately they would forfeit the match. Illingworth had thought the fruit and beer cans that spectators threw at his players was sufficient justification for leaving but they returned to win the decisive match by 62 runs in the longest rubber in history. English and Australian administrators had agreed to play this Seventh Test after the Third Test in Melbourne was washed out without a ball bowled.

ENGLAND IN AUSTRALIA 1974-75

Matches	First-class Results Won	Lost	Drawn	Tied	Matches	All Matches Won	Lost	Drawn	Tied
15	5	5	5	–	23	8	9	6	–

Date	Venue	Opponent	Results for Touring Team
Oct 30	Port Lincoln	*South Australian Country XI	Drawn
Nov 1	Adelaide	South Australia	Drawn
Nov 6	Warrnambool	*Victorian Country XI	Drawn
Nov 8	Melbourne	Victoria	Drawn
Nov 13	Canberra	*Australian Capital Territory	Drawn
Nov 15	Sydney	New South Wales	Won by 6 wkts
Nov 20	Nambour	*Queensland Country XI	Abandoned
Nov 22	Brisbane	Queensland	Won by 46 runs
Nov 26	Southport	*South East Queensland	Won by 10 wkts
Nov 29	Brisbane	AUSTRALIA (1st Test)	Lost by 166 runs
Dec 7	Perth	Western Australia	Lost by 120 runs
Dec 11	Geraldton	*Western Australian Country XI	Drawn
Dec 13	Perth	AUSTRALIA (2nd Test)	Lost by 9 wkts
Dec 21	Adelaide	South Australia	Drawn
Dec 26	Melbourne	AUSTRALIA (3rd Test)	Drawn
Jan 1	Melbourne	*Australia (L/O Intl)	Won by 3 wkts
Jan 4	Sydney	AUSTRALIA (4th Test)	Lost by 171 runs
Jan 11	Hobart (TCA)	Tasmania	Drawn
Jan 14	Launceston	Tasmania	Won by an inns & 72 runs
Jan 18	Sydney	New South Wales	Won by 187 runs
Jan 25	Adelaide	AUSTRALIA (5th Test)	Lost by 163 runs
Feb 1	Newcastle	*Northern New South Wales	Won by 4 wkts
Feb 5	Melbourne	*New Zealanders	Won by 66 runs
Feb 8	Melbourne	AUSTRALIA (6th Test)	Won by an inns & 4 runs

England in Australia 1974-75: *back row* F.J. Titmus, D.L. Amiss, G.G. Arnold, D. Lloyd, B.W. Luckhurst, R.W. Taylor, B.W. Thomas (physio); *centre* D.L. Underwood, C.M. Old, R.G.D. Willis, M. Hendrick, P. Lever, K.W.R. Fletcher; *front* A.V. Bedser (manager), M.C. Cowdrey, J.H. Edrich, M.H. Denness (capt.), A.W. Greig, A. Knott, A.C. Smith (assistant manager).

Player	M	Inn	NO	Runs	HS	50	100	Avrge	Ct/St	Overs	Mdns	Runs	Wkts	Avrge	5wi	10wm	Best
Amiss, DL	12	19	–	765	152	4	2	40.26	9	–	–	–	–	–	–	–	–
Arnold, GG	10	10	2	34	14	–	–	4.25	3	280.3	41	956	26	36.76	1	–	5/86
Cowdrey, MC	7	12	1	284	78	1	–	25.81	4	4.0	–	27	2	13.50	–	–	2/27
Denness, MH (Capt)	13	23	3	896	188	3	2	44.80	10	–	–	–	–	–	–	–	–
Edrich, JH	10	15	3	488	70	3	–	40.66	6	–	–	–	–	–	–	–	–
Fletcher, KWR	14	21	3	703	146	4	1	39.05	13	6.0	–	45	–	–	–	–	–
Greig, AW	11	20	2	836	167*	6	2	46.44	18	306.2	52	1121	36	33.69	1	–	5/55
Hendrick, M	6	8	4	61	24*	–	–	15.25	4	130.3	23	452	17	26.58	1	–	5/68
Knott, APE	11	19	3	638	106*	5	1	39.87	41/2	–	–	–	–	–	–	–	–
Lever, P	8	4	1	35	14	–	–	11.66	5	178.7	15	745	24	31.04	1	–	6/38
Lloyd, D	11	18	1	534	80	2	–	31.41	9	6.6	2	25	2	12.50	–	–	2/25
Luckhurst, BW	9	15	1	383	116	2	1	27.35	11	1.0	–	1	1	1.00	–	–	1/1
Old, CM	10	13	2	230	48	–	–	20.90	7	196.7	21	847	32	26.46	1	–	7/59
Taylor, RW	5	4	2	78	27*	–	–	39.00	11/1	–	–	–	–	–	–	–	–
Titmus, FJ	8	12	1	171	61	1	–	15.54	3	239.3	50	710	18	39.44	–	–	3/65
Underwood, DL	11	13	2	206	33	–	–	18.72	1	349.6	82	1066	40	26.65	2	1	7/113
Willis, RGD	9	15	6	108	21	–	–	12.00	5	223.7	29	811	26	31.19	1	–	5/61

Facing one of Australia's best teams, with Dennis Lillee and Jeff Thomson at their peak, England's captain Mike Denness dropped himself from the Fourth Test, John Edrich taking over. This embarrassment for one of the most prolific batsmen in England failed to turn a six-Test series, which Australia clinched in Denness' absence and then went on to take it out four-one, with one draw. To his credit, Denness made 188 in the Sixth, which England won by an innings and four runs. Australia's top order batting under pressure provided fine support for bowling of alarming pace, with all England's batting stars taking a battering.

ENGLAND IN AUSTRALIA 1978-79

	First-class Results				All Matches				
Matches	Won	Lost	Drawn	Tied	Matches	Won	Lost	Drawn	Tied
13	8	2	3	–	26	17	4	5	–

Date	Venue	Opponent	Results for Touring Team
Nov 1	Renmark	*South Australian Country XI	Drawn
Nov 3	Adelaide	South Australia	Lost by 32 runs
Nov 8	Leongatha	*Victorian Country XI	Won by 71 runs
Nov 10	Melbourne	Victoria	Drawn
Nov 15	Canberra	*Australian Capital Territory	Won by 179 runs
Nov 17	Sydney	New South Wales	Won by 10 wkts
Nov 22	Bundaberg	*Queensland Country XI	Won by 132 runs
Nov 24	Brisbane	Queensland	Won by 6 wkts
Dec 1	Brisbane	AUSTRALIA (1st Test)	Won by 7 wkts
Dec 9	Perth	Western Australia	Won by 140 runs
Dec 13	Albany	*Western Australian Country XI	Won by 69 runs
Dec 15	Perth	AUSTRALIA (2nd Test)	Won by 166 runs
Dec 22	Adelaide	South Australia	Drawn
Dec 29	Melbourne	AUSTRALIA (3rd Test)	Lost by 103 runs
Jan 6	Sydney	AUSTRALIA (4th Test)	Won by 93 runs
Jan 13	Sydney	*Australia (L/O Intl)	Drawn
Jan 14	Newcastle	*Northern New South Wales	Won by 9 wkts
Jan 18	Launceston	*Tasmania	Won by 163 runs
Jan 19	Hobart (TCA)	Tasmania	Drawn
Jan 24	Melbourne	*Australia (L/O Intl)	Won by 7 wkts
Jan 27	Adelaide	AUSTRALIA (5th Test)	Won by 205 runs
Feb 3	Melbourne	*Tasmania	Won by 3 wkts
Feb 4	Melbourne	*Australia (L/O Intl)	Lost by 4 wkts
Feb 6	Geelong	*Geelong & District	Won by 48 runs
Feb 7	Melbourne	*Australia (L/O Intl)	Lost by 6 wkts
Feb 10	Sydney	AUSTRALIA (6th Test)	Won by 9 wkts

England in Australia 1978–79, the Fourth Test in Sydney: *back row* D.W. Randall, C.T. Radley, P. Lever, G. Miller, I.T. Botham, P.H. Edmonds, M. Hendrick, J.E. Emburey, G.A. Gooch, D.I. Gower, R.W. Tolchard, G.G.A. Saulez (scorer); *front* B.W. Thomas (physio), G. Boycott, R.G.D. Willis, J.M. Brearley (capt.), D. Insole (manager), R.W. Taylor, C.M. Old, K.R. Barrington (assistant manager). *Patrick Eagar*

Player	M	Inn	NO	Runs	HS	50	100	Avrge	Ct/St	Overs	Mdns	Runs	Wkts	Avrge	5wi	10wm	Best
Botham, IT	9	14	–	361	74	3	–	25.78	14	239.3	44	848	44	19.27	2	–	5/51
Boycott, G	12	23	3	533	90*	4	–	26.65	5	3.0	–	11	–	–	–	–	–
Brearley, JM (Capt)	11	21	5	538	116*	2	1	33.62	11	–	–	–	–	–	–	–	–
Edmonds, PH	7	9	2	115	38*	–	–	16.42	8	149.0	34	397	11	36.09	1	–	5/52
Emburey, JE	9	12	2	101	42	–	–	10.10	9	261.1	73	563	31	18.16	1	–	5/67
Gooch, GA	13	23	1	514	74	3	–	23.36	13	26.0	2	80	1	80.00	–	–	1/16
Gower, DI	12	20	1	623	102	3	1	32.78	7	–	–	–	–	–	–	–	–
Hendrick, M	8	12	4	68	20	–	–	8.50	6	184.4	40	399	28	14.25	1	–	5/11
Lever, JK	6	7	–	67	28	–	–	9.57	–	118.1	18	377	13	29.00	–	–	4/28
Miller, G	11	18	3	398	68*	2	–	26.53	5	277.1	74	607	36	16.86	2	–	6/56
Old, CM	6	6	1	81	40	–	–	16.20	2	138.0	24	452	21	21.52	1	–	6/42
Radley, CT	6	9	–	138	60	1	–	15.33	2	1.0	–	4	–	–	–	–	–
Randall, DW	10	18	2	763	150	4	2	47.68	6	2.0	–	9	–	–	–	–	–
Taylor, RW	10	15	2	230	97	1	–	17.69	35/6	–	–	–	–	–	–	–	–
Tolchard, RW	3	5	1	142	72	2	–	35.50	13	–	–	–	–	–	–	–	–
Willis, RGD	10	13	4	115	24	–	–	12.77	3	210.3	34	696	34	20.47	1	–	5/44

After a brief (two-match) visit by Tony Greig's team for the Centenary Test in 1977, England resumed full-scale touring under Mike Brearley in the second summer of the Packer breakaway. Brearley completed the rout of Australia he had begun in England in 1977 against Greg Chappell's team and by the end of the series had chalked up 11 wins over Australia in 18 months. This was a tribute to Brearley's tactical acumen but certainly not due to his batting skill. Few England captains have contributed so little with bat or ball and retained their job. Graham Yallop, pitchforked into the job because of the Packer defections, was unable to control his players, let alone devise strategies to outwit one of the masters of leadership techniques. Fast bowler Rodney Hogg, one of Australia's new-found heroes, walked off the field during the Adelaide Test without seeking Yallop's permission and often changed his field without consultation. Hogg took 41 wickets in six Tests, five more than Arthur Mailey's record achieved in 1920–21 for an Australian bowler against England. Australia rekindled interest in a one-sided series by winning the Third Test in Melbourne but the public were more attracted to the showmanship of Packer's WSC matches in a depressing summer for traditional cricket. England were efficient and well-managed by Ken Barrington, who phoned each of his players with their instructions on match mornings, but apart from the polished strokeplay of Gower, occasional sparkle from Botham and the antics of Derek Randall, were devoid of crowd appeal. The rubber ended appropriately with a lone trumpeter sounding the Last Post on the Sydney Hill as England clinched her five-one victory, but with very few on hand to hear him.

ENGLAND IN AUSTRALIA 1979-80

First-class Results					All Matches				
Matches	Won	Lost	Drawn	Tied	Matches	Won	Lost	Drawn	Tied
8	3	3	2	–	20	10	7	3	–

Date	Venue	Opponent	Results for Touring Team
Nov 12	Brisbane	Queensland	Drawn
Nov 17	Newcastle	*Northern New South Wales	Won by 9 wkts
Nov 18	Newcastle	*Northern New South Wales	Won by 32 runs
Nov 22	Adelaide	*Combined Universities	Drawn
Nov 28	Sydney	*West Indies (L/O Intl)	Won by 2 runs
Nov 30	Hobart (TCA)	Tasmania	Won by 100 runs
Dec 4	Adelaide	South Australia	Drawn
Dec 8	Melbourne	*Australia (L/O Intl)	Won by 3 wkts
Dec 11	Sydney	*Australia (L/O Intl)	Won by 72 runs
Dec 14	Perth	AUSTRALIA (1st Test)	Lost by 138 runs
Dec 23	Brisbane	*West Indies (L/O Intl)	Lost by 9 wkts
Dec 26	Sydney	*Australia (L/O Intl)	Won by 4 wkts
Dec 28	Brisbane	Queensland	Won by 138 runs
Jan 4	Sydney	AUSTRALIA (2nd Test)	Lost by 6 wkts
Jan 12	Melbourne	*West Indies (L/O Intl)	Abandoned
Jan 14	Sydney	*Australia (L/O Intl)	Won by 2 wkts
Jan 16	Adelaide	*West Indies (L/O Intl)	Lost by 107 runs
Jan 20	Melbourne	*West Indies (L/O Intl)	Lost by 2 runs
Jan 22	Sydney	*West Indies (L/O Intl)	Lost by 8 wkts
Jan 27	Canberra	New South Wales	Won by 8 wkts
Feb 1	Melbourne	AUSTRALIA (3rd Test)	Lost by 8 wkts

England in Australia 1979-80: *back row* G. Miller, P. Willey, M. Hendrick, G.G.A. Saulez (scorer), G. Dilley, I.T. Botham, J.K. Lever; *centre* D.W. Randall, D. Bairstow, D.I. Gower, G.A. Gooch, W. Larkins, R.W. Taylor; *front* B.W. Thomas (physio), D.L. Underwood, R.G.D. Willis, A.V. Bedser (manager), M.J. Brearley (capt.), G. Boycott, K.F. Barrington (assistant manager).

Player	M	Inn	NO	Runs	HS	50	100	Avrge	Ct/St	Overs	Mdns	Runs	Wkts	Avrge	5wi	10wm	Best
Bairstow, DL	2	2	–	13	12	–	–	6.50	2/–	–	–	–	–	–	–	–	–
Botham, IT	5	9	1	217	119*	–	1	27.12	5	193.1	67	426	21	20.28	2	1	6/78
Boycott, G	7	13	3	534	110	3	2	53.40	3	4.0	–	19	–	–	–	–	–
Brearley, JM (Capt)	6	10	1	297	81	3	–	33.00	4	–	–	–	–	–	–	–	–
Dilley, GR	5	6	3	101	38*	–	–	33.66	2	88.1	11	243	7	34.71	–	–	3/40
Emburey, JE	2	3	–	63	50	1	–	21.00	2	111.2	25	282	7	40.28	–	–	3/80
Gooch, GA	6	12	2	582	115	6	1	58.20	8	41.0	11	110	3	36.66	–	–	2/16
Gower, DI	8	14	2	338	98*	3	–	28.16	6	–	–	–	–	–	–	–	–
Hendrick, M	1	1	–	1	1	–	–	1.00	–	4.0	1	14	–	–	–	–	–
Larkins, W	5	9	1	190	90	1	–	23.75	3	6.0	–	15	–	–	–	–	–
Lever, JK	6	6	2	54	22	–	–	13.50	3	192.4	50	475	12	39.58	–	–	4/111
Miller, G	4	6	2	203	71	2	–	50.75	3	106.0	20	268	5	53.60	–	–	2/47
Randall, DW	6	10	–	250	97	1	–	25.00	3	–	–	–	–	–	–	–	–
Stevenson, GB	3	4	1	64	33	–	–	21.33	–	68.0	11	235	9	26.11	–	–	4/44
Taylor, RW	7	10	1	184	47*	–	–	20.44	19/1	–	–	–	–	–	–	–	–
Underwood, DL	5	7	–	87	43	–	–	12.42	5	253.1	80	581	25	23.24	1	1	7/66
Willey, P	6	12	3	269	101*	1	1	29.88	3	111.0	17	332	7	47.42	–	–	3/68
Willis, RGD	4	6	–	21	11	–	–	3.50	–	113.0	30	252	3	84.00	–	–	1/26

Drained of cash after two summers of Packer's WSC, the Australian Cricket Board rushed England back for the second season in a row for a three-Test series. Strengthened by the return of five Packer players, and an inspiring, knowledgeable captain in Greg Chappell, Australia completely reversed the previous year's debacle, defeating England three–nil. Ian Chappell returned to Tests after four years' absence to play under his brother's captaincy in the Second Test, completing 2000 runs against England, and providing another Packer rebel, Derek Underwood, with his 100th wicket against Australia. It was a summer of crazy programming, with Australia also playing three Tests against the West Indies. Only eight of England's 20 matches were first-class, an inadequate preparation for Tests. Faced with such an itinerary, England were justified in refusing to put The Ashes at stake. Lillee had to be persuaded to discard an aluminium bat after facing four balls with it from Botham in the Perth Test. Boycott was left on 99 not out in Perth, Greg Chappell on 98 not out in Sydney, and Gooch was run out for 99 in Melbourne, where a wonderful 119 not out by Botham gave an outplayed England something to cheer about.

ENGLAND IN AUSTRALIA 1982–83

First-class Results					All Matches				
Matches	Won	Lost	Drawn	Tied	Matches	Won	Lost	Drawn	Tied
11	4	3	4	–	23	10	9	4	–

Date	Venue	Opponent	Results for Touring Team
Oct 22	Brisbane	Queensland	Lost by 171 runs
Oct 27	Newcastle	*Northern New South Wales	Won by 10 wkts
Oct 31	Adelaide	South Australia	Drawn
Nov 5	Perth	Western Australia	Won by 1 wkt
Nov 12	Perth	AUSTRALIA (1st Test)	Drawn
Nov 20	Sydney	New South Wales	Won by 26 runs
Nov 26	Brisbane	AUSTRALIA (2nd Test)	Lost by 7 wkts
Dec 4	Melbourne	Victoria	Drawn
Dec 10	Adelaide	AUSTRALIA (3rd Test)	Lost by 8 wkts
Dec 18	Hobart (TCA)	Tasmania	Won by 6 wkts
Dec 22	Launceston	*Tasmania	Won by 4 wkts
Dec 26	Melbourne	AUSTRALIA (4th Test)	Won by 3 runs
Jan 2	Sydney	AUSTRALIA (5th Test)	Drawn
Jan 11	Sydney	*Australia (L/O Intl)	Lost by 31 runs
Jan 13	Melbourne	*New Zealand (L/O Intl)	Lost by 2 runs
Jan 15	Brisbane	*New Zealand (L/O Intl)	Won by 54 runs
Jan 16	Brisbane	*Australia (L/O Intl)	Lost by 7 wkts
Jan 20	Sydney	*New Zealand (L/O Intl)	Won by 8 wkts
Jan 23	Melbourne	*Australia (L/O Intl)	Lost by 5 wkts
Jan 26	Sydney	*Australia (L/O Intl)	Won by 98 runs
Jan 29	Adelaide	*New Zealand (L/O Intl)	Lost by 4 wkts
Jan 30	Adelaide	*Australia (L/O Intl)	Won by 14 runs
Feb 5	Perth	*New Zealand (L/O Intl)	Lost by 7 wkts

England in Australia 1982–83: *back row* T.E. Jesty, A.J. Lamb, V.J. Marks, G. Fowler, G. Cook, D.R. Pringle, N.G. Cowans, C.J. Tavare, E.E. Hemmings, I.J. Gould, R.D. Jackman; *front* G. Miller, I.T. Botham, D.I. Gower, R.G.D. Willis (capt.), R.W. Taylor, D.W. Randall. *Patrick Eagar*

Player	M	Inn	NO	Runs	HS	50	100	Avrge	Ct/St	Overs	Mdns	Runs	Wkts	Avrge	5wi	10wm	Best
Botham, IT	9	18	–	434	65	2	–	24.11	17	319.4	63	1033	29	35.62	–	–	4/43
Cook, G	7	14	1	428	99	4	–	32.92	4	56.0	12	178	8	22.25	–	–	3/47
Cowans, NG	8	13	2	70	36	–	–	6.36	5	223.4	38	745	26	28.65	1	–	6/77
Fowler, G	9	18	–	445	83	4	–	24.72	6	6.0	–	43	2	21.50	–	–	2/43
Gould, IJ	4	5	1	164	73	1	–	32.80	8/2	–	–	–	–	–	–	–	–
Gower, DI	10	19	1	821	114	6	2	45.61	9	–	–	–	–	–	–	–	–
Hemmings, EE	5	9	3	228	95	2	–	38.00	3	323.0	84	789	23	34.30	1	–	5/101
Jackman, RD	4	5	2	88	50*	1	–	29.33	2	88.5	15	272	3	90.66	–	–	2/37
Lamb, AJ	9	18	–	852	117	5	2	47.33	6	1.0	1	0	–	–	–	–	–
Marks, VJ	4	6	–	41	13	–	–	6.83	4	107.0	26	351	3	117.00	–	–	1/39
Miller, G	10	19	4	465	83	2	–	31.00	5	325.0	96	761	27	28.18	–	–	4/63
Pringle, DR	9	16	5	207	47*	–	–	18.81	6	263.3	53	729	22	33.59	–	–	4/66
Randall, DW	9	17	1	732	115	4	1	45.75	11	–	–	–	–	–	–	–	–
Tavare, CJ	10	19	–	489	147	2	1	25.73	4	–	–	–	–	–	–	–	–
Taylor, RW	7	14	5	188	37	–	–	20.88	16/1	–	–	–	–	–	–	–	–
Willis, RGD (Capt)	7	13	5	65	26	–	–	8.12	7	226.0	41	656	28	23.42	1	–	5/66

The umpiring in this rubber was very poor but the teams suffered equally. Australia regained The Ashes England had held since 1977 but it was wrong to blame the two–one margin in Australia's favour on the umpiring. Indeed, but for a flukey catch in the Melbourne Fourth Test won by England, the series could have finished with Australia three-up. Australia won the Second and Third Tests comfortably to take a two–nil lead. Last pair Jeff Thomson and Allan Border put on 70 of the 74 required to win when Thomson tried to hit the boundary that would have given his side victory, edged it, and saw the ball rebound off Tavare's chest, popping up behind his back for Miller to take the catch and give England the match by three runs.

Badly weakened by the suspension of their South Africa rebels, England struggled to find opening batsmen who could handle Australia's pace men Lawson, Thomson, Hogg and Rackemann, although Lillee was absent, sitting out the series after being injured in the First Test, as was Alderman, who dislocated a collarbone in a clash with a spectator. Perth police arrested 26 demonstrators, some of them carrying Union Jacks, in the ugly scenes that marred this match.

ENGLAND IN AUSTRALIA 1986-87

Matches	First-class Results Won	Lost	Drawn	Tied	Matches	All Matches Won	Lost	Drawn	Tied
11	5	3	3	–	30	19	7	4	–

Date	Venue	Opponent	Results for Touring Team
Oct 18	Bundaberg	*Queensland Country XI	Drawn
Oct 22	Lawes	*SE Queensland Country XI	Won by 58 runs
Oct 24	Brisbane	Queensland	Lost by 5 wkts
Oct 29	Wudinna	*South Australian Country XI	Won by 9 wkts
Oct 31	Adelaide	South Australia	Won by 5 wkts
Nov 5	Kalgoorlie	*Western Australian Country XI	Won by 117 runs
Nov 7	Perth	Western Australia	Drawn
Nov 14	Brisbane	AUSTRALIA (1st Test)	Won by 7 wkts
Nov 21	Newcastle	New South Wales	Lost by 8 wkts
Nov 28	Perth	AUSTRALIA (2nd Test)	Drawn
Dec 6	Melbourne	Victoria	Won by 5 wkts
Dec 12	Adelaide	AUSTRALIA (3rd Test)	Drawn
Dec 18	Hobart (TCA)	Tasmania	Won by an inns & 96 runs
Dec 23	Canberra	*Prime Minister's XI	Won by 4 wkts
Dec 26	Melbourne	AUSTRALIA (4th Test)	Won by an inns & 14 runs
Jan 1	Perth	*Australia (L/O Intl)	Won by 37 runs
Jan 3	Perth	*West Indies (L/O Intl)	Won by 19 runs
Jan 5	Perth	*Pakistan (L/O Intl)	Won by 3 wkts
Jan 7	Perth	*Pakistan (L/O Intl)	Won by 5 wkts
Jan 10	Sydney	AUSTRALIA (5th Test)	Lost by 55 runs
Jan 17	Brisbane	*West Indies (L/O Intl)	Won by 6 wkts
Jan 18	Brisbane	*Australia (L/O Intl)	Lost by 11 runs
Jan 22	Sydney	*Australia (L/O Intl)	Won by 3 wkts
Jan 24	Adelaide	*West Indies (L/I Intl)	Won by 89 runs
Jan 26	Adelaide	*Australia (L/O Intl)	Lost by 33 runs
Jan 30	Melbourne	*West Indies (L/O Intl)	Lost by 6 wkts
Feb 1	Melbourne	*Australia (L/O Intl)	Lost by 109 runs
Feb 3	Devonport	*West Indies (L/O Intl)	Won by 29 runs
Feb 8	Melbourne	*Australia (L/O Intl)	Won by 6 wkts
Feb 11	Sydney	*Australia (L/O Intl)	Won by 8 runs

England in Australia 1986-87: *standing* S.P. Austin (scorer), B.N. French, C.J. Richards, P.A. DeFreitas, G.R. Dilley, B.C. Broad, N.A. Foster, G.C. Small, J.J. Whitaker, W.N. Slack, C.W.J. Athey, L.G. Brown (physio); *seated* P.M. Lush (manager), P.H. Edmonds, D.I. Gower, M.W. Gatting (capt.), J.E. Emburey, I.T. Botham, A.J. Lamb, M.J. Stewart (assistant manager).

Player	M	Inn	NO	Runs	HS	50	100	Avrge	Ct/St	Overs	Mdns	Runs	Wkts	Avrge	5wi	10wm	Best
Athey, CWJ	9	16	1	422	96	4	–	28.13	7	4.0	–	25	–	–	–	–	–
Botham, IT	8	14	2	481	138	1	1	40.08	11	182.1	41	496	18	27.55	1	–	5/41
Broad, BC	10	18	2	679	162	1	3	42.43	7	–	–	–	–	–	–	–	–
DeFreitas, PAJ	7	10	2	130	40	–	–	16.25	1	239.0	43	754	22	34.27	–	–	4/44
Dilley, GR	6	6	3	39	32	–	–	13.00	1	231.1	44	685	21	32.61	1	–	5/68
Edmonds, PH	9	10	2	95	27	–	–	11.87	7	428.4	122	929	25	37.16	–	–	3/37
Emburey, JE	9	14	3	279	69	1	–	25.36	6	463.5	131	1023	31	33.00	3	–	7/78
Foster, NA	4	6	2	172	74*	1	–	43.00	4	149.0	40	352	16	22.00	–	–	4/20
French, BN	3	5	2	113	58	1	–	37.66	9/1	–	–	–	–	–	–	–	–
Gatting, MW (Capt)	10	18	–	520	100	3	1	28.88	11	92.0	27	195	9	21.66	–	–	4/31
Gower, DI	9	16	2	508	136	2	1	36.28	4	–	–	–	–	–	–	–	–
Lamb, AJ	10	18	1	534	105	3	1	31.41	11	1.0	1	0	–	–	–	–	–
Richards, CJ	9	14	1	335	133	–	1	25.76	25/3	–	–	–	–	–	–	–	–
Slack, WN	5	9	–	184	89	1	–	20.44	5	–	–	–	–	–	–	–	–
Small, GC	8	11	3	100	26	–	–	12.50	4	258.4	72	626	33	18.96	3	–	5/48
Whitaker, JJ	5	7	–	214	108	–	1	30.57	2	–	–	–	–	–	–	–	–

England took a commanding lead in this series before Australian selectors brought in leg-spinner Peter Sleep and the then unknown red-haired off-spinner Peter Taylor. Faced with turning deliveries, England batsmen who had looked comfortable against pace bowling, suddenly looked uneasy. England won the First Test by seven wickets and the Fourth Test by an innings and 14 runs to regain The Ashes because of dismal Australian batting against Botham and Gladstone Small, cleverly nursed by captain Mike Gatting and managers Peter Lush and Micky Stewart. Taylor gave Sleep admirable support in the Fifth Test, and in a dream debut took 7 for 68 and 2 for 76, twice dismissing Botham cheaply. Sleep's 5 for 72 gave Australia their first win in 15 Tests. England's fielding, for years inferior to Australia's, reached a very high standard in this rubber. Some exciting catches were held, none better than that by Jack Richards, who sprinted 30 metres to catch a miscued hook by McDermott in the Fourth Test.

HOME AND AWAY

ENGLAND IN AUSTRALIA 1990-91

	First-class Results					All Matches			
Matches	Won	Lost	Drawn	Tied	Matches	Won	Lost	Drawn	Tied
11	1	5	5	–	28	8	14	6	–

Date	Venue	Opponent	Results for Touring Team
Oct 25	Caversham	*Western Australia President's XI	Won by 6 wkts
Oct 27	Geraldton	*Western Australian Country XI	Drawn
Oct 30	Perth	*Western Australia Invitation XI	Lost by 3 wkts
Nov 2	Perth	Western Australia	Drawn
Nov 7	Port Pirie	*South Australian Country XI	Won by 111 runs
Nov 9	Adelaide	South Australia	Lost by 6 wkts
Nov 14	Hobart (Bel)	*Tasmania	Won by 8 wkts
Nov 16	Hobart (Bel)	Australian XI	Drawn
Nov 23	Brisbane	AUSTRALIA (1st Test)	Lost by 10 wkts
Nov 29	Adelaide	*AIS Cricket Academy	Won by 5 wkts
Nov 30	Adelaide	*AIS Cricket Academy	Won by 150 runs
Dec 1	Adelaide	*New Zealand (L/O Intl)	Lost by 7 runs
Dec 4	Canberra	*Prime Minister's XI	Lost by 31 runs
Dec 7	Perth	*New Zealand (L/O Intl)	Won by 4 wkts
Dec 9	Perth	*Australia (L/O Intl)	Lost by 6 wkts
Dec 11	Bowral	*Bradman's XI	Lost by 7 wkts
Dec 13	Sydney	*New Zealand (L/O Intl)	Won by 33 runs
Dec 15	Brisbane	*New Zealand (L/O Intl)	Lost by 8 wkts
Dec 16	Brisbane	*Australia (L/O Intl)	Lost by 37 runs
Dec 20	Ballarat	Victoria	Drawn
Dec 26	Melbourne	AUSTRALIA (2nd Test)	Lost by 8 wkts
Jan 1	Sydney	*Australia (L/O Intl)	Lost by 68 runs
Jan 4	Sydney	AUSTRALIA (3rd Test)	Drawn
Jan 10	Melbourne	*Australia (L/O Intl)	Lost by 3 runs
Jan 13	Albury	New South Wales	Lost by 6 wkts
Jan 19	Carrara	Queensland	Won by 10 wkts
Jan 25	Adelaide	AUSTRALIA (4th Test)	Drawn
Feb 1	Perth	AUSTRALIA (5th Test)	Lost by 9 wkts

England in Australia 1990-91: *standing* C.F. Driver (scorer), R.A. Smith, M.A. Atherton, P.C.R. Tufnell, G.C. Small, M.P. Bicknell, C.C. Lewis, A.R.C. Fraser, D.E. Malcolm, A.J. Stewart, J.E. Morris, L.G. Brown (physio); *seated* P.M. Lush (manager), R.C. Russell, E.E. Hemmings, A.J. Lamb, G.A. Gooch (capt.), D.I. Gower, W. Larkins, M.J. Stewart (assistant manager).

Player	M	Inn	NO	Runs	HS	50	100	Avrge	Ct/St	Overs	Mdns	Runs	Wkts	Avrge	5wi	10wm	Best
Atherton, MA	11	22	2	577	114	2	2	28.85	10	79.1	10	330	6	55.00	–	–	3/27
Bicknell, MP	4	6	2	28	17	–	–	7.00	2	120.4	22	409	9	45.44	–	–	3/124
DeFreitas, PAJ	4	8	1	139	54	1	–	19.86	–	126.0	25	353	11	32.09	–	–	4/56
Fraser, ARC	5	8	1	48	24	–	–	6.86	2	237.0	51	596	17	35.06	1	–	6/82
Gooch, GA (Capt)	8	14	1	623	117	5	1	47.92	7	33.0	8	90	2	45.00	–	–	1/23
Gower, DI	10	19	1	578	123	3	2	32.11	3	–	–	–	–	–	–	–	–
Hemmings, EE	3	5	–	19	13	–	–	3.80	2	164.0	46	391	15	26.07	–	–	4/29
Lamb, AJ	8	14	1	757	154	4	3	58.23	10	–	–	–	–	–	–	–	–
Larkins, W	6	12	–	205	64	2	–	17.08	4	–	–	–	–	–	–	–	–
Lewis, CC	3	6	–	181	73	1	–	30.17	3	93.0	8	342	6	57.00	–	–	3/29
Malcolm, DE	10	14	2	52	18	–	–	4.33	3	422.4	78	1269	39	32.54	1	–	7/74
Morris, JE	4	7	–	252	132	–	1	36.00	2	–	–	–	–	–	–	–	–
Newport, PJ	1	2	1	40	40*	–	–	40.00	–	20.0	–	78	1	78.00	–	–	1/56
Russell, RC	8	13	1	168	36	–	–	14.00	27/4	–	–	–	–	–	–	–	–
Small, GC	9	14	3	147	37*	–	–	13.36	8	277.0	63	774	19	40.74	–	–	4/38
Smith, RA	10	19	6	755	108	7	1	58.08	5	–	–	–	–	–	–	–	–
Stewart, AJ	9	17	–	497	95	4	–	29.24	10/–	–	–	–	–	–	–	–	–
Tufnell, PCR	8	10	7	13	8	–	–	4.33	6	318.0	73	887	26	34.12	2	–	5/61

Injuries to their captain Graham Gooch, dominant batsman Allan Lamb, and to their best bowler Angus Fraser, prevented England making an even contest out of this series. Confidence boosted by their triumph in England in 1989, Border's Australians won the series three–nil, although Mark Taylor, Dean Jones and Steve Waugh all failed to repeat the run-getting spree they enjoyed in England. Australia's ascendancy was so marked, however, they could afford to leave out players like Geoff Lawson, Tom Moody and Carl Rackemann and win with plenty in reserve. Splendidly conditioned by coach Bob Simpson and aggressively led by Border, the Australians looked a formidable outfit, equal to the best Australian sides of the past, an assessment the West Indies soon shattered.

Australia won the First Test when Alderman took 6 for 47, his best figures in Australia. Reid's 13 for 138 turned the Second Test into another big Australia win. The Third and Fourth Tests were drawn, with batsmen on both teams scoring freely. Craig McDermott at his very best produced a big Australian win—by nine wickets—in the Fifth Test, taking 8 for 97 and 3 for 60 on a fast Perth pitch that the England bowlers were unable to exploit.

England spared Gooch the pain of touring Australia without a single victory by defeating Queensland by ten wickets at Carrara in the last match of a tour that included 11 first-class games, and 28 matches in all, including 11 one-day matches.

ENGLAND IN AUSTRALIA 1994-95

Matches	First-class Results				Matches	All Matches			
	Won	Lost	Drawn	Tied		Won	Lost	Drawn	Tied
11	3	4	4	–	24	9	11	4	–

Date	Venue	Opponent	Results for Touring Team
Oct 25	Lilac Hill	*ACB Chairman's XI	Won by 7 wkts
Oct 27	Perth	*Western Australia	Lost by 51 runs
Oct 29	Perth	Western Australia	Drawn
Nov 4	Adelaide	South Australia	Won by 4 wkts
Nov 9	Canberra	*Prime Minister's XI	Lost by 2 wkts
Nov 12	Newcastle	New South Wales	Lost by 4 wkts
Nov 18	Hobart (Bel)	Australian XI	Drawn
Nov 25	Brisbane	AUSTRALIA (1st Test)	Lost by 184 runs
Dec 2	Bowral	*Bradman XI	Won by 4 wkts
Dec 4	Canberra	*Australian Capital Territory	Won by 100 runs
Dec 6	Sydney	*Australia (L/O Intl)	Lost by 28 runs
Dec 10	North Sydney	*AIS Cricket Academy	Lost by 5 wkts
Dec 11	North Sydney	*AIS Cricket Academy	Lost by 6 wkts
Dec 13	Melbourne	*Australia 'A'	Won by 31 runs
Dec 15	Sydney	*Zimbabwe (L/O Intl)	Lost by 13 runs
Dec 17	Toowoomba	Queensland	Won by 37 runs
Dec 24	Melbourne	AUSTRALIA (2nd Test)	Lost by 295 runs
Jan 1	Sydney	AUSTRALIA (3rd Test)	Drawn
Jan 7	Brisbane	*Zimbabwe (L/O Intl)	Won by 26 runs
Jan 10	Melbourne	*Australia (L/O Intl)	Won by 37 runs
Jan 12	Sydney	*Australia 'A'	Lost by 29 runs
Jan 20	Bendigo	Victoria	Drawn
Jan 26	Adelaide	AUSTRALIA (4th Test)	Won by 106 runs
Feb 3	Perth	AUSTRALIA (5th Test)	Lost by 329 runs

England in Australia 1994-95: *back row* David Roberts (physiotherapist), P.C.R. Tufnell, S.D. Udal, D. Gough, M.J. McCague, J.E. Benjamin, J.A. Crawley, C. White, S.J. Rhodes, Keith Fletcher (cricket manager); *front* G.P. Thorpe, G.A. Hick, P.A.J. DeFreitas, A.J. Stewart, M.A. Atherton (capt.), G.A. Gooch, M.W. Gatting, D.E. Malcolm, Mike Smith (manager). *Julian Cowan*

Player	M	Inn	NO	Runs	HS	50	100	Avrge	Ct/St	Overs	Mdns	Runs	Wkts	Avrge	5wi	10wm	Best
Atherton, MA (Capt)	10	20	1	755	88	6	–	39.74	8	2.0	–	6	–	–	–	–	–
Benjamin, JE	4	4	–	11	7	–	–	2.75	1	105.5	22	341	6	56.83	–	–	2/36
Crawley, JP	9	15	2	563	91	6	–	43.31	3	–	–	–	–	–	–	–	–
DeFreitas, PAJ	7	13	1	190	88	1	–	15.83	2	299.1	67	852	24	35.50	–	–	4/60
Fraser, ARC	4	6	1	60	27	–	–	12.00	1	157.5	30	504	14	36.00	1	–	5/73
Gatting, MW	9	16	1	532	203*	1	2	35.47	5	–	–	–	–	–	–	–	–
Gooch, GA	10	19	–	685	101	5	1	36.05	3	27.0	7	79	2	39.50	–	–	1/5
Gough, D	5	8	2	114	51	1	–	19.00	5	222.5	44	688	26	26.46	2	–	6/49
Hick, GA	8	15	1	877	172	3	3	62.64	16	61.0	8	224	2	112.00	–	–	1/11
Lewis, CC	2	4	–	68	40	–	–	17.00	3	78.5	14	249	11	22.64	–	–	4/24
Malcolm, DE	8	12	4	91	29	–	–	11.38	1	340.3	55	1133	34	33.32	1	–	6/70
McCague, MJ	4	5	1	29	16	–	–	7.25	3	125.2	21	487	14	34.79	1	–	5/31
Ramprakash, MR	1	2	–	114	72	1	–	57.00	2	19.0	1	74	–	–	–	–	–
Rhodes, SJ	11	19	2	240	50	1	–	14.12	40/6	–	–	–	–	–	–	–	–
Stewart, AJ	5	9	4	291	101*	1	1	58.20	2/–	–	–	–	–	–	–	–	–
Thorpe, GP	10	20	3	756	123	5	1	44.47	9	2.0	1	6	–	–	–	–	–
Tufnell, PCR	9	13	7	12	4*	–	–	2.00	6	384.2	70	1018	27	37.70	1	–	5/71
Udal, SD	2	4	–	30	16	–	–	7.50	1	81.5	4	345	5	69.00	–	–	2/95
White, C	3	5	–	125	46	–	–	25.00	2	60.5	10	195	7	27.86	–	–	3/13

The deterioration in England's cricket standards which began in 1989 continued on the 37th English tour of Australia six years later. By the time Mike Atherton's team returned home after their 18-match tour Australia had won 14 Tests, England two, with six draws, in the most disastrous slump England has known. There had been other lapses, but always defeat had left England with ingredients for recovery. This time Australia's supremacy was so complete there appeared little hope of an English revival. Some commentators asked if the Ashes Tests were worth continuing given the sad displays of Atherton's men. 'Time to Burn The Urn' was typical of experts' reactions.

Atherton agreed it was time for a drastic reappraisal of cricket in England. A Cricket Academy similar to Australia's was essential. The Academy XI coached by Rodney Marsh had in fact badly beaten England twice in one weekend, showing the technical know-how and composure needed when talented players make the jump from club cricket to the first-class arena. England had been expected to lack athleticism once selection of bulky veterans Graham Gooch and Mike Gatting became known, but the team's lack of enthusiasm was completely unexpected. Right round Australia they were made to look slovenly by youngsters eager to work hard and show some bottle.

Injuries compounded Atherton's problems and by the end of the tour England had used 21 players. And it was cruel luck that Devon Malcolm, England's main strike bowler, missed the First Test through a bout of chickenpox and did not regain full fitness until Australia had retained the Ashes. Only Tufnell of the other English bowlers showed any penetration, with Atherton slow to realise Darren Gough's potential. Australia won the First

Test by 184 runs after Slater (176) and Mark Waugh (140) gave Warne runs to play with. Warne took 8–71 in England's second innings and 11 for 110 in the match, McDermott 8 for 143 in two innings. Ian Healy, broken thumb mended, took nine catches.

Warne again wove his spells over leaden-footed batsmen in the Second Test at Melbourne, taking a further nine wickets (6 for 64 and 3 for 16) including a hat-trick, the first of his career. This made him the ninth Australian to secure a Test hat-trick, the first at the MCG for 90 years. Warne dismissed DeFreitas lbw, Gough caught behind and then had Malcolm caught off his glove by Boon, who dived metres to his right to clutch the ball in. Boon had earlier hit his 20th Test century (131), his seventh against England and first in Melbourne. England never appeared likely to make the 388 needed to win after losing 3 for 23 and Australia won by 295 runs. They then wrapped up the Ashes with a draw in the Third Test at Sydney, with second innings centuries by Slater (103) and Taylor rescuing Australia from a first innings collapse for 116.

England showed the best form of their tour to win the Fourth Test in Adelaide thanks to a brilliant display of hitting by DeFreitas, who made 88 off 95 balls with 2 huge sixes and 9 fours. Devon Malcolm (4–39) and Chris Lewis (4–24) then dismissed Australia for 151, 106 short of the 263 runs needed to win. This was only England's second win over Australia since 1989.

At Perth in the Fifth Test McDermott reasserted Australia's authority with 6 for 38 in the final innings, Australia winning by a big margin of 329 runs to take the rubber 4–1.

CHAPTER FOURTEEN

CHAMPION AUSTRALIAN STATE TEAMS

Down the years some magnificent state teams have appeared, some reaching standards even national teams envied. New South Wales before World War I when Trumper opened the innings with Duff and Noble captained the side, and could call on Macartney to bowl spinners in tandem with Mailey, were formidable opponents. Victoria, when Woodfull and Ponsford opened their batting—they had 22 century partnerships, five over 200—and any of the South Australian teams that included Bradman, Badcock, Grimmett and Richardson were very hard to beat. New South Wales with O'Reilly, McCabe, Barnes and Chipperfield, or later during their run of nine successful Shield wins with Morris, Miller, Benaud, Davidson, Burke and Simpson in the team, or Western Australia, when they had nine men picked in an Australian side for England, were outstanding cricket teams. The photographs show a selection of significant state teams.

The New South Wales team that played South Australia in December 1890 at Adelaide Oval: *back row* A.P. Marr, H. Donnan, E.J. Briscoe, J. Portus (manager), J.J. Ferris, E. Moses (manager); *centre* J.P. Wales, S. Callaway, F. Iredale, H. Moses, P.C. Charlton, C.A. Richardson; *front* A. Clarke, S.E. Gregory, A.C. Bannerman. Ferris won the match for his side with 14 wickets, his best figures before he went to join the Gloucestershire XI. He died in the Boer War of enteric fever.

HOME AND AWAY

The South Australian team that defeated Victoria in November 1891 in Adelaide by an innings and 164 runs, when Lyons hit 104, George Giffen 271: *standing* J. Noel, W.F. Giffen, H.L. Haldane; *middle* I.A. Fisher (umpire), H.T. Moore, J.H. Lyons, J. Reedman, C.W. Hayward; *front* A.H. Jarvis, G. Giffen (capt.), F. Jarvis, H. Blinman. South Australia's victory assured a place in the Sheffield Shield competition when it began in 1892-93.

The first Western Australian team to travel east, photographed in Melbourne in April 1893 during their match against Victoria: *back row* R.E. Bush, E. Wilson, W.V. Duffy (player-coach), W. Bateman, A. Moffatt, J.W.C. Bird, T. Brown; *centre* P.L. Hussey, E. Bishop, H.R. Orr (capt.), F.D. North, W. Back; *front* F. Bennett, H. Wilson, E. Randell. They lost to South Australia and Victoria in their first matches on turf. Duffy, born at Doutla Galla (now Tullamarine), was one of Australia's first professional cricketers.

The first South Australian team to visit Perth, from 3 to 6 April 1899, which played the first intercolonial match in Western Australia, now accepted as Western Australia's inaugural first-class match: *back* F. Hack, V. Hugo, N.H. Claxton, R. Homburg, A.G. Thomas; *front* H.O. Day, J. Travers, W.O. Whitridge (manager), A.H. Jarvis (capt.), A.H. Rosman, W. Hewer; *absent* Fred Jarvis. The team's voyage from Adelaide to Fremantle—there was no railway across the Nullarbor— took six days. Western Australia's spinner Bobby Selk took seven wickets in the match but their batsmen were overawed by the occasion and South Australia won by four wickets.

The Victorian team that beat Tasmania by 185 runs on the MCG in January 1900: *back row* R. Drew, E. Bares (umpire), J. Ainslie, W. Perraton; *centre* T. Hastings, R. Mitchell, W. Carlton, W.M. Morgan; *seated* A.S. Carter, W. Bruce (capt.), W. Murray; *front* D. Sutherland. Murray, a Bendigo man without experience in Melbourne club cricket, scored the only century in the game, 104 in 136 minutes with 11 fours.

CHAMPION STATE TEAMS

The South Australian XI that defeated England in Adelaide in November 1901: *back row* C. Hill, J. McKenzie, E. Jones, C. Hack, G. Giffen, E.L. Leak, P. Argall (umpire); *seated* J. Matthews, J. Travers, J. Reedman (capt.), F. Jarvis, B.T. Bailey. Clem Hill virtually beat McLaren's team single-handed, scoring 107 and 80. England were dismissed for 118 and 86 and lost by 233 runs, George Giffen claiming 13 wickets.

The New South Wales team that defeated Tasmania by an innings and 289 runs in Hobart in March 1913: *back row* T. Howard (manager), H.L. Collins, C.L. Tozer, R.J.A. Massie, N.M. Gregg, R.B. Minnett, Hugh Greg (visitor); *seated* L.A. Cody, T.J.E. Andrews, H.V. Hordern, V.T. Trumper, H. Davis, H. Carter; *front* J.D. Scott. Tozer, 12th man in this match, was later murdered by his lover. *Ric Finlay*

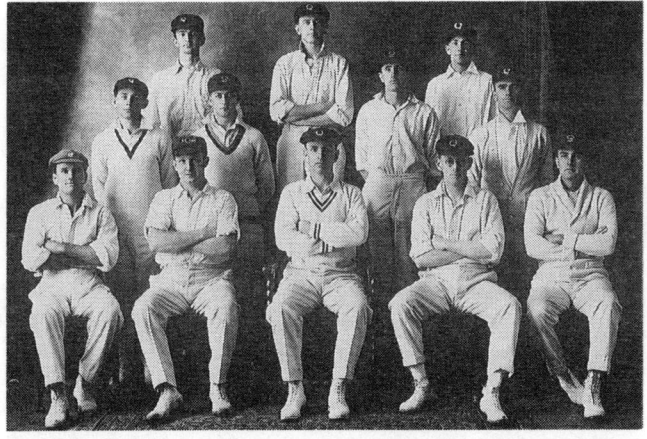

Queensland's first Sheffield Shield team before they made their debut in the competition in Brisbane in December 1926 against New South Wales: *back row* H.D. Noyes, E. Bensted, N. Beeston; *centre* F.J. Gough, F.M. Brew, R. Higgins, R.K. Oxenham; *front* W. Rowe, F.C. Thompson, L. O'Connor (capt.), A.D.A. Mayes, L.E. Oxenham. New South Wales won by eight runs. Five centuries were scored in the match which Queensland's best bowler Percy Hornibrook had to miss because of his dental exams. O'Connor was run out for 196 when a Queensland win appeared likely.

The 1926 New South Wales team that narrowly defeated Queensland in that state's Shield debut: *back row* G. Morgan, H.C. Steele, G. Amos, A.F. Kippax (capt.), J.L. Wall, A. Jackson, R. Osborne, R. McNamee; *front* A. Scanes, L. Wall, D. Seddon, N. Campbell, N.E. Phillips. Kippax scored 127 and 131, and leg-spinner Campbell took 10 wickets in a historic see-sawing match.

Stan McCabe with the crack New South Wales team he captained from 1936 until 1942: *back row* V.E. Jackson, L.J. O'Brien, J.G. Lush, E.C.S. White, A.G. Cheetham, S.G. Barnes; *seated* W.A.S. Oldfield, W.J. O'Reilly, A.G. Chipperfield, S.J. McCabe, J.H. Fingleton, L.C. Hynes. New South Wales won the Sheffield Shield twice in that period despite the presence of Bradman and Grimmett in the South Australian side, and Hassett, Miller and Fleetwood-Smith in the Victorian XI.

The Western Australian team that won the Sheffield Shield at that state's first attempt in 1947-48: *back row* B.A. Rigg, A.R. Edwards, T. O'Dwyer; *middle* C.W. Puckett, W. Langdon, M.U. Herbert, L. Bandy, A.R. Cumming, G.T. Chess; *front* K.B.D. Carmody (capt.), T.M. Outridge, A.D. Watt, R.J. Bryant; *absent* G.D. Robinson. Carmody made 198 in Western Australia's first Shield game to set up victory in Perth versus South Australia.

The New South Wales side that remained basically unchanged in the state's nine successive Sheffield Shield wins between 1953-54 and 1961-62. This is the 1955-56 side: *back row* P.I. Philpott, R.B. Simpson, A.K. Davidson, W.J. Watson; *centre* J.S. Treanor, R. Benaud, W.P.A. Crawford, B.C. Booth; *seated* J.H. de Courcey, K.R. Miller (capt.), J.P. Ross (manager), J.W. Burke, O. Lambert. Only Treanor and Lambert missed Test selection.

Former state wicket-keeper Ray Phillips, captain Allan Border and Trevor Barsby celebrate Queensland's first Sheffield Shield win in 1994-95 after 68 years of failure. *Courier-Mail*

An elated Victorian team after their shock win in the 1990-91 Sheffield Shield competition, with captain Simon O'Donnell, left, holding the famous trophy with the help of Jamie Siddons. Wayne Phillips is directly behind the Shield. Behind them are James Sutherland, Darren Berry, Damien Fleming, Geoff Parker, Darren Lehmann, Paul Jackson, Paul Reiffel, with Garry Watts and Tony Dodemaide behind Siddons. O'Donnell had not long recovered from cancer, but proved an inspiring leader for a team that had finished last the previous season.

AUSTRALIAN STATE TEAMS OVERSEAS

Despite the high costs involved, all Australian states have managed overseas tours. Before the establishment of the Australian Cricket Academy they were regarded as a valuable way of developing promising youngsters. Some tours have been organised as social junkets to celebrate state triumphs, but generally organisers have tried to include first-class fixtures to provide experience for their players and help advance standards in the countries visited.

Since 1883–84 when Tasmania became the first Australian colony to go overseas, New Zealand has been the most favoured venue for state tours. New South Wales has made six visits to New Zealand, two to Zimbabwe, and one to Ceylon before it became Sri Lanka. Victoria has toured New Zealand twice and has also visited England. Queensland has been to New Zealand twice, Tasmania and South Australia once each, while Western Australia went to Madras in 1989 to play the leading Indian club, Tamil Nadu. Some significant state tours follow. (See Appendix for summaries of matches not included here.)

TASMANIA IN NEW ZEALAND 1883–84

	First-class Results					All Matches			
Matches	Won	Lost	Drawn	Tied	Matches	Won	Lost	Drawn	Tied
4	–	3	1	–	7	2	3	2	–

Date	Venue	Opponent	Results for Australians
Feb 1	Dunedin	Otago	Lost by 8 wkts
Feb 7	Christchurch	Canterbury	Lost by 1 wkt
Feb 14	Ashburton	*Ashburton XVIII	Won by 13 runs
Feb 15	Dunedin	Otago	Drawn
Feb 19	Timaru	*South Canterbury	Won by 9 wkts
Feb 22	Christchurch	Canterbury	Lost by 6 runs
Feb 27	Invercargill	*Southland	Drawn

All the Tasmanian players paid their own fares in a six week tour by a team captained by the Mayor of Hobart, John George Davies, who represented Tasmania against four English touring teams between 1873–74 and 1887–88 as a wicketkeeper. Star of the tour was left-arm bowler Tom Kendall who took 7 for 55 to help Australia defeat England in the first-ever Test at Melbourne. In a one-day match against Eighteen of Ashburton, Kendall took 17 for 74.

Player	M	Inn	NO	Runs	HS	50	100	Avrge	Ct/St	Overs	Mdns	Runs	Wkts	Avrge	5wi	10wm	Best
Burn, EJK	4	8	1	74	21*	–	–	10.57	–	333.0	37	62	7	8.86	–	–	2/19
Butler, EH	4	8	–	50	19	–	–	6.25	3	41.0	3	13	–	–	–	–	–
Davies, JG (Capt)	4	8	–	90	42	–	–	11.25	6/3	–	–	–	–	–	–	–	–
Gatehouse, GH	4	8	2	171	62	2	–	28.50	–	–	–	–	–	–	–	–	–
Hale, H	4	8	–	80	38	–	–	10.00	3	603.0	64	199	21	9.48	1	–	6/46
Harris, HVP	4	8	–	172	60	1	–	21.50	1	–	–	–	–	–	–	–	–
Kendall, TK	4	8	2	54	22	–	–	9.00	1	1315.0	143	340	25	13.60	2	–	7/24
Kirby, RG	4	8	1	29	11*	–	–	4.14	2	20.0	2	18	–	–	–	–	–
Mansfield, J	4	8	1	33	8*	–	–	4.71	1	389.0	38	138	6	23.00	–	–	4/45
Sams, LR	4	8	–	49	25	–	–	6.13	–	12.0	–	13	–	–	–	–	–
Sidebottom, WL	4	8	1	114	59	1	–	16.29	2	191.0	9	82	2	41.00	–	–	1/15

NEW SOUTH WALES IN NEW ZEALAND 1889-90

First-class Results					All Matches				
Matches	Won	Lost	Drawn	Tied	Matches	Won	Lost	Drawn	Tied
5	4	–	1	–	7	6	–	1	–

Date	Venue	Opponent	Results for Australians
Jan 30	Auckland	Auckland	Drawn
Feb 7	Christchurch	Canterbury	Won by 109 runs
Feb 13	Oamaru	*Oamaru Club	Won by an inns & 55 runs
Feb 14	Dunedin	Otago	Won by an inns & 66 runs
Feb 18	Timaru	*South Canterbury	Won by 9 wkts
Feb 21	Wellington	Wellington	Won by 8 wkts
Feb 28	Auckland	Auckland	Won by 8 wkts

Player	M	Inn	NO	Runs	HS	50	100	Avrge	Ct/St	Overs	Mdns	Runs	Wkts	Avrge	5wi	10wm	Best
Callaway, ST	5	7	–	63	17	–	–	9.00	–	240.0	89	330	32	10.31	3	1	6/16
Clarke, AE	5	7	–	91	43	–	–	13.00	4	11.0	–	26	2	13.00	–	–	2/12
Cottam, JT	5	9	–	226	62	3	–	25.11	1	36.1	–	98	3	32.67	–	–	2/48
Cowper, G	5	9	2	200	54	1	–	28.57	2	34.0	13	54	3	18.00	–	–	3/7
Davis, J (Capt)	5	9	2	270	57	1	–	38.57	4	–	–	–	–	–	–	–	–
Joseph, J	5	6	1	12	7	–	–	2.00	–	–	–	–	–	–	–	–	–
McGlinchy, WJ	5	9	1	149	34	–	–	18.63	1	160.0	54	268	30	8.93	2	1	6/62
Newell, AL	5	7	4	76	28*	–	–	25.33	2	156.2	51	318	16	19.88	1	–	5/53
Robinson, HJW	5	7	1	111	61*	1	–	18.50	1	–	–	–	–	–	–	–	–
Shepherd, J	5	6	2	61	19*	–	–	15.25	2/1	–	–	–	–	–	–	–	–
Youill, GJ	5	7	–	131	37	–	–	18.71	2	5.0	1	20	–	–	–	–	–

This New South Wales team, captained by J. Coleman Davis, included the Test bowler Syd Callaway, who later settled in New Zealand where he played for Canterbury. New South Wales won six of their seven games, all of them played on level terms. Auckland held them to a draw, after the home captain objected to the umpire accompanying the NSW side. Davis initially refused to withdraw his umpire but did so when the locals threatened not to pay the visitors their guaranteed gate money.

NEW SOUTH WALES IN NEW ZEALAND 1893-94

First-class Results					All Matches				
Matches	Won	Lost	Drawn	Tied	Matches	Won	Lost	Drawn	Tied
7	4	1	2	–	8	4	1	3	–

Date	Venue	Opponent	Results for Australians
Jan 20	Auckland	Auckland	Won by 9 wkts
Jan 24	Napier	Hawke's Bay	Won by an inns & 13 runs
Jan 27	Wellington	Wellington	Drawn
Feb 1	Christchurch	Canterbury	Lost by an inns & 7 runs
Feb 7	Timaru	*South Canterbury XV	Drawn
Feb 10	Dunedin	Otago	Drawn
Feb 15	Christchurch	New Zealanders	Won by 160 runs
Feb 19	Wellington	North Island	Won by 123 runs

J.C. Davis led the second NSW team to New Zealand in 1893-94. Although the New Zealand Cricket Council was not formed until the end of 1894, the first team to officially represent New Zealand played NSW in February of that year. 'Monty' Noble, then 20 years old, was in the NSW team but failed to show the form that later earned him the Australian Test captaincy. NSW defeated New Zealand by 160 runs by dismissing them for 79 when they required 240 to win in the final innings.

Player	M	Inn	NO	Runs	HS	50	100	Avrge	Ct/St	Overs	Mdns	Runs	Wkts	Avrge	5wi	10wm	Best
Austin, SW	7	10	–	163	43	–	–	16.30	1	1747.0	85	612	52	11.77	6	1	8/14
Cowley, OW	7	12	1	266	55	1	–	24.18	6	253.0	16	78	6	13.00	–	–	3/14
Davis, J (Capt)	7	10	3	139	25*	–	–	19.86	2/2	–	–	–	–	–	–	–	–
Gould, JW	7	12	–	232	45	–	–	19.33	3	626.0	16	325	15	21.67	–	–	4/30
Mackenzie, ACK	7	13	–	296	60	1	–	22.77	5	–	–	–	–	–	–	–	–
Miller, DL	7	11	2	86	18	–	–	9.56	5	1407.0	70	482	30	16.07	–	–	4/25
Moore, L	7	12	1	254	68	1	–	23.09	4	64.0	2	25	–	–	–	–	–
Noble, EG	7	11	–	215	51	1	–	23.89	9	–	–	–	–	–	–	–	–
Noble, MA	7	10	1	93	26	–	–	10.33	4	301.0	13	153	4	38.25	–	–	2/16
Searle, J	7	13	6	186	45*	–	–	26.57	7/6	–	–	–	–	–	–	–	–
Walford, SR	7	11	–	121	22	–	–	11.00	3	–	–	–	–	–	–	–	–

CHAMPION STATE TEAMS

NEW SOUTH WALES IN NEW ZEALAND 1895-96

First-class Results					All Matches				
Matches	Won	Lost	Drawn	Tied	Matches	Won	Lost	Drawn	Tied
5	3	1	1	–	5	3	1	1	–

Date	Venue	Opponent	Results for Australians
Dec 14	Christchurch	Canterbury	Won by 6 wkts
Dec 20	Dunedin	Otago	Won by 6 wkts
Dec 26	Wellington	Wellington	Won by 226 runs
Dec 30	Christchurch	New Zealanders	Lost by 142 runs
Jan 7	Auckland	Auckland	Drawn

Player	M	Inn	NO	Runs	HS	50	100	Avrge	Ct/St	Overs	Mdns	Runs	Wkts	Avrge	5wi	10wm	Best
Burton, FJ	4	7	2	78	30	–	–	15.60	7	–	–	–	–	–	–	–	–
Callaway, ST	4	7	–	142	86	1	–	20.28	5	204.2	73	367	40	9.18	5	3	8/98
Cobcroft, LT (Capt)	5	10	1	160	85*	1	–	17.78	–	25.0	2	77	2	38.50	–	–	2/11
Furness, AJ	4	6	2	74	43*	–	–	18.50	3	–	–	–	–	–	–	–	–
Hume, AE	5	8	1	88	36*	–	–	12.57	1	205.2	77	381	17	22.41	1	–	5/34
Noonan, DJ	5	9	3	213	57	1	–	35.50	–	157.5	50	329	20	16.45	2	1	7/95
Poidevin, LOS	4	8	1	286	64	3	–	40.86	1	4.0	–	6	–	–	–	–	–
Pryor, DG	5	10	–	136	35	–	–	13.60	4	–	–	–	–	–	–	–	–
Ridge, FM	4	6	–	98	46	–	–	16.33	–	14.0	5	25	–	–	–	–	–
Shea, M	4	7	1	90	25	–	–	15.00	–	45.1	12	99	4	24.75	–	–	3/6
Wade, FH	5	10	1	145	40*	–	–	16.11	3	22.0	2	68	2	34.00	–	–	2/46
Walford, SR	5	9	–	203	122	–	1	22.56	2	–	–	–	–	–	–	–	–

The NSW team captained by Tom Cobcroft from the Glebe club in Sydney had easy wins over Canterbury, Otago and Wellington before playing New Zealand at Lancaster Park, Christchurch. The NSW team included two outstanding 19-year-olds, Leslie Poidevin and David Noonan. New Zealand won despite protests from the Auckland club that none of their players were in the New Zealand team. Callaway bowled superbly to take 7 for 77 and 8 for 98 but could not prevent New Zealand winning handsomely by 142 runs.

QUEENSLAND IN NEW ZEALAND 1896-97

First-class Results					All Matches				
Matches	Won	Lost	Drawn	Tied	Matches	Won	Lost	Drawn	Tied
5	3	1	1	–	8	4	1	3	–

Date	Venue	Opponent	Results for Australians
Dec 22	Auckland	Auckland	Drawn
Dec 26	Wellington	New Zealanders	Lost by 182 runs
Dec 31	Napier	Hawke's Bay	Won by an inns & 102 runs
Jan 8	Christchurch	Canterbury	Won by 47 runs
Jan 12	Ashburton	*South Canterbury XVIII	Won by 123 runs
Jan 15	Dunedin	Otago	Won by 8 wkts
Jan 20	Invercargill	*Southand XIII	Drawn
Jan 23	Gore	*Eastern District XX	Drawn

Brisbane's powerful Graziers club supplied most of the members of the first Queensland team to go overseas. The Queensland team included Test player S.P. Jones, who made four tours of England before settling in New Zealand. Queensland lost the big match of their tour to New Zealand when Jones was run out in the second innings for a duck. Victory by 183 runs gave New Zealand confidence to plan a tour of Australia.

Player	M	Inn	NO	Runs	HS	50	100	Avrge	Ct/St	Overs	Mdns	Runs	Wkts	Avrge	5wi	10wm	Best
Bradley, WF	5	8	–	148	63	1	–	18.50	4/2	–	–	–	–	–	–	–	–
Byrnes, TJ	4	6	–	39	23	–	–	6.50	1	136.3	47	286	16	17.88	–	–	4/40
Cowley, OW	4	5	–	166	135	–	1	33.20	2	10.0	3	25	–	–	–	–	–
Donahoo, SJ	5	9	1	281	70	2	–	35.13	3	–	–	–	–	–	–	–	–
Hitchcock, OC (Capt)	5	7	3	40	12*	–	–	10.00	3/4	–	–	–	–	–	–	–	–
Hoare, W	5	8	1	112	44	–	–	16.00	6	54.4	12	175	8	21.88	1	–	6/55
Jones, SP	5	8	–	239	85	2	–	29.88	1	22.0	3	87	–	–	–	–	–
Lewis, W	4	6	–	74	43	–	–	14.80	2	37.1	8	152	13	11.69	1	–	6/37
MacDonald, R	4	6	–	223	114	–	1	44.60	4	17.0	1	72	3	24.00	–	–	3/49
McGlinchy, WJ	5	7	–	136	45	–	–	19.43	1	132.0	27	376	22	17.09	2	1	5/63
Miller, DL	4	6	2	37	11*	–	–	9.25	2	113.2	33	254	14	18.14	1	–	5/38
Wilson, R	5	7	1	68	15	–	–	11.33	6	103.4	15	325	20	16.25	1	1	8/35

NEW SOUTH WALES IN CEYLON 1913-14

Matches	First-class Results Won	Lost	Drawn	Tied	Matches	All Matches Won	Lost	Drawn	Tied
–	–	–	–	–	9	8	1	–	–

Date	Venue	Opponent	Results for Australians
Jan 2	Colombo	*Ceylonese XI	Won by 7 wkts
Jan 5	Galle	*Southern Province XVIII	Won by an inns & 146 runs
Jan 6	Colombo	*Ceylonese XI	Lost by 6 wkts
Jan 9	Kandy	*Up Country XI	Won by an inns & 82 runs
Jan 12	Colombo	*Ceylonese XI	Won by 85 runs
Jan 15	Radella	*Dimbula & Dikoya	Won by 51 runs
Jan 19	Anuradhapura	*Anuradhapura XVIII	Won by 155 runs
Jan 21	Colombo	*Combined Colleges XVIII	Won by 76 runs
Jan 22	Colombo	*All Ceylon	Won by 2 wkts

The 1884 Australians captained by Billy Murdoch played a match against Ceylon on their way to England, but the first tour by an Australian team came when the Reverend E.F.('Mick') Waddy took a NSW team to Ceylon just before World War I. (See Chapter 10.)

NEW SOUTH WALES IN NEW ZEALAND 1923-24

Matches	First-class Results Won	Lost	Drawn	Tied	Matches	All Matches Won	Lost	Drawn	Tied
6	5	–	1	–	12	8	–	4	–

Date	Venue	Opponent	Results for Australians
Feb 8	Wellington	Wellington	Drawn
Feb 12	Ashburton	*Ashburton XIII	Won by an inns & 114 runs
Feb 15	Dunedin	Otago	Won by an inns & 327 runs
Feb 19	Oamaru	*North Otago XIII	Drawn
Feb 22	Christchurch	Canterbury	Won by an inns & 276 runs
Feb 26	Timaru	*South Canterbury	Won by an inns & 291 runs
Feb 29	Christchurch	New Zealanders	Won by 8 wkts
Mar 7	Wellington	New Zealanders	Won by an inns & 126 runs
Mar 12	Taranaki	*North Taranaki	Won by an inns & 233 runs
Mar 14	Wanganui	*Wanganui	Drawn
Mar 18	Napier	*East Coast	Drawn
Mar 21	Auckland	Auckland	Won by an inns & 27 runs

Charlie Macartney captained a strong NSW side on this 12-match tour in which NSW ran up some huge scores and were only once dismissed for under 300 runs. Five batsmen averaged over 50 and NSW scored 20 centuries. Seven of their eight wins were by an innings and they twice defeated New Zealand.

Player	M	Inn	NO	Runs	HS	50	100	Avrge	Ct/St	Overs	Mdns	Runs	Wkts	Avrge	5wi	10wm	Best
Andrews, TJE	6	7	1	230	111*	–	1	38.33	2	16.0	3	41	5	8.20	1	–	5/41
Bardsley, R	5	6	1	125	46	–	–	25.00	–	–	–	–	–	–	–	–	–
Bardsley, W	6	7	2	623	200*	5	1	124.00	–	–	–	–	–	–	–	–	–
Everett, SC	5	4	–	25	19	–	–	6.25	1	126.6	15	470	24	19.58	2	–	6/35
Hendry, HSTL	6	7	1	305	110	2	1	50.83	6	153.5	41	419	13	32.23	1	–	8/33
Kippax, AF	6	7	2	461	150*	1	2	92.20	2	–	–	–	–	–	–	–	–
Macartney, CG (Capt)	6	8	1	641	221	2	3	91.57	–	131.4	43	272	13	20.92	–	–	3/26
Mailey, AA	6	5	3	87	57*	1	–	43.50	6	163.3	20	603	37	16.30	4	1	7/108
Mullarkey, DA	5	6	–	90	36	–	–	15.00	2	–	–	–	–	–	–	–	–
Oldfield, WAS	6	6	1	150	56	1	–	30.00	11/7	–	–	–	–	–	–	–	–
Punch, ATE	6	7	–	281	176	1	1	40.14	4	30.0	2	107	10	10.70	–	–	4/24
Ratcliffe, AT	3	3	–	115	56	1	–	38.33	6/5	–	–	–	–	–	–	–	–

VICTORIA IN NEW ZEALAND 1924-25

Matches	First-class Results Won	Lost	Drawn	Tied	Matches	All Matches Won	Lost	Drawn	Tied
6	1	1	4	–	12	4	1	7	–

Date	Venue	Opponent	Results for Australians
Feb 20	Dunedin	Otago	Drawn
Feb 21	Invercargill	*Southland	Won by 10 wkts
Feb 27	Christchurch	Canterbury	Drawn
Mar 3	Oamaru	*North Otago	Drawn
Mar 6	Wellington	Wellington	Lost by 19 runs

Edgar Mayne captained this Victorian team on a 12-match tour which produced four wins for the visitors, defeat by Wellington, and seven draws. The New Zealand Cricket Council were delighted with the £358 tour profit.

CHAMPION STATE TEAMS

Date	Venue	Opponent	Results for Australians
Mar 11	Wanganui	*Wanganui	Won by an inns & 49 runs
Mar 13	Auckland	Auckland	Drawn
Mar 18	Palmerston North	*Manawatu	Won by 9 wkts
Mar 20	Wellington	New Zealanders	Won by 6 wkts
Mar 27	Christchurch	New Zealanders	Drawn
Apr 1	Napier	*Hawkes Bay	Drawn
Apr 3	Gisborne	*Poverty Bay–Waiapu	Drawn

Player	M	Inn	NO	Runs	HS	50	100	Avrge	Ct/St	Overs	Mdns	Runs	Wkts	Avrge	5wi	10wm	Best
Austen, ET	4	7	–	207	82	1	–	29.57	3	–	–	–	–	–	–	–	–
Austin, HM	6	8	–	155	87	1	–	19.37	4	51.4	4	269	7	38.42	–	–	3/97
Ebeling, HI	4	5	1	21	13	–	–	5.25	–	81.0	8	297	11	27.00	–	–	3/38
Ellis, JL	6	9	–	314	103	2	1	34.88	12/3	–	–	–	–	–	–	–	–
Hartkopf, AEV	5	7	2	121	30	–	–	24.20	1	113.2	9	492	18	27.33	1	–	5/65
Liddicut, AE	6	8	1	143	66	1	–	20.42	5	91.0	16	314	13	24.15	–	–	3/31
Mayne, ER (Capt)	6	10	–	162	80	1	–	16.20	5	–	–	–	–	–	–	–	–
Millar, KJ	6	8	2	158	56	1	–	26.33	2	65.0	5	297	9	33.00	–	–	3/47
Ransford, VS	5	5	2	274	106*	–	2	91.33	1	32.3	1	138	6	23.00	1	–	6/38
Wallace, PH	6	8	1	56	36	–	–	8.00	4	151.0	21	501	18	27.83	–	–	4/43
Willis, CB	6	10	–	220	104	–	1	22.00	4	27.0	–	169	3	56.33	–	–	1/17
Woodfull, WM	6	9	5	706	212*	3	3	176.50	3	1.0	–	2	–	–	–	–	–

NEW SOUTH WALES IN NEW ZEALAND 1984–85

	First-class Results					All Matches			
Matches	Won	Lost	Drawn	Tied	Matches	Won	Lost	Drawn	Tied
–	–	–	–	–	1	1	–	–	–

Date	Venue	Opponent	Results for Australians
Jan 6	Wellington	*Wellington	Won by 17 runs

NEW SOUTH WALES IN ZIMBABWE 1985–86

	First-class Results					All Matches			
Matches	Won	Lost	Drawn	Tied	Matches	Won	Lost	Drawn	Tied
2	1	–	1	–	8	5	2	1	–

Date	Venue	Opponent	Results for Australians
Mar 22	Harare	*Zimbabweans	Lost by 4 wkts
Mar 23	Harare	*Zimbabweans	Won by 2 wkts
Mar 26	Mutare	*Zimbabwe Cricket Union Pres. XI	Abandoned
Mar 28	Harare	Zimbabweans	Drawn
Mar 30	Harare	*Zimbabweans	Lost by 2 wkts
Apr 2	Bulawayo	*Zimbabweans	Won by 61 runs
Apr 4	Harare	Zimbabweans	Won by 70 runs
Apr 6	Harare	*Zimbabweans	Won by 4 wkts
Apr 9	Harare	*Zimbabwe Country Districts	Won by 176 runs

Following the successful visit of Young Australia sides, a strong NSW team led by wicket-keeper Greg Dyer played two first class matches and six one-day games in Harare and Bulawayo in 1986.

Player	M	Inn	NO	Runs	HS	50	100	Avrge	Ct/St	Overs	Mdns	Runs	Wkts	Avrge	5wi	10wm	Best
Bayliss, TH	1	2	–	51	46	–	–	25.50	–	–	–	–	–	–	–	–	–
Bower, RJ	2	4	–	46	31	–	–	11.50	–	–	–	–	–	–	–	–	–
Clifford, PS	1	2	–	62	44	–	–	31.00	2	–	–	–	–	–	–	–	–
Done, RP	2	1	1	10	10*	–	–	–	1	44.0	6	182	6	30.33	–	–	4/54
Dyer, GC (Capt)	2	3	2	123	85	1	–	123.00	4/3	–	–	–	–	–	–	–	–
Holland, RG	2	–	–	–	–	–	–	–	2	79.0	24	241	9	26.78	–	–	4/71
O'Neill, MD	2	4	1	221	132	1	1	73.67	1	16.0	4	37	2	18.50	–	–	2/19
Small, SM	2	4	–	58	25	–	–	14.00	2	–	–	–	–	–	–	–	–
Taylor, MA	2	4	–	46	23	–	–	11.50	2	–	–	–	–	–	–	–	–
Taylor, PL	2	2	1	24	12*	–	–	24.00	2	60.1	15	172	13	13.23	1	–	5/39
Waugh, ME	2	4	2	176	83	2	–	88.00	4	43.0	14	110	2	55.00	–	–	1/25
Whitney, MR	2	–	–	–	–	–	–	–	2	56.5	15	127	6	21.17	–	–	3/37

SOUTH AUSTRALIA IN NEW ZEALAND 1986-87

	First-class Results					All Matches			
Matches	Won	Lost	Drawn	Tied	Matches	Won	Lost	Drawn	Tied
–	–	–	–	–	4	4	–	–	–

Date	Venue	Opponent	Results for Australians
Feb 8	New Plymouth	*Central Districts	Won by 61 runs
Feb 9	Palmerston North	*Central Districts	Won by 115 runs
Feb 11	McLean Park	*Central Districts	Won by 6 wkts
Feb 12	Wanganui	*Central Districts	Won by 30 runs

NEW SOUTH WALES IN ZIMBABWE 1987-88

	First-class Results					All Matches			
Matches	Won	Lost	Drawn	Tied	Matches	Won	Lost	Drawn	Tied
2	–	–	2	–	8	5	1	2	–

NSW returned to help replace the competition previously provided by Zimbabwe's participation in South Africa's Currie Cup.

Date	Venue	Opponent	Results for Australians
Sep 5	Harare	*Zimbabweans	Won by 6 wkts
Sep 6	Harare	*Zimbabweans	Won by 6 wkts
Sep 8	Harare	Zimbabweans	Drawn
Sep 12	Bulawayo	*Zimbabweans	Lost by 6 wkts
Sep 13	Bulawayo	*Zimbabweans	Won by 4 runs
Sep 16	Mutare	*Zimbabweans	Won by 4 wkts
Sep 19	Harare	Zimbabweans	Drawn
Sep 20	Harare	*Zimbabweans	Won by 7 wtks

Player	M	Inn	NO	Runs	HS	50	100	Avrge	Ct/St	Overs	Mdns	Runs	Wkts	Avrge	5wi	10wm	Best
Dyer, GC	2	2	–	84	49	–	–	42.00	4/–	–	–	–	–	–	–	–	–
Gilbert, DR	2	1	–	23	23	–	–	23.00	1	58.0	19	130	4	32.50	–	–	3/68
Lawson, GF	1	–	–	–	–	–	–	–	–	19.0	6	48	1	48.00	–	–	1/39
Matthews, GRJ	2	3	1	118	72	1	–	59.00	2	66.0	14	200	6	33.33	–	–	3/61
O'Neill, MD	2	3	1	111	45	–	–	55.50	2	6.0	–	22	–	–	–	–	–
Small, SM	2	2	–	82	74	1	–	41.00	2	–	–	–	–	–	–	–	–
Taylor, MA	2	3	–	71	44	–	–	23.66	–	–	–	–	–	–	–	–	–
Taylor, PL	2	2	1	176	105*	1	1	176.00	1	64.2	22	182	7	26.00	–	–	3/44
Tucker, RJ	1	1	–	5	5	–	–	5.00	1	14.0	5	29	1	29.00	–	–	1/28
Waugh, ME	2	3	1	123	61	1	–	61.50	1	1.0	–	3	–	–	–	–	–
Wellham, DM (Capt)	2	2	1	51	36	–	–	51.00	–	–	–	–	–	–	–	–	–
Whitney, MR	2	2	–	0	0	–	–	0.00	1	55.0	15	122	5	24.40	–	–	3/67

VICTORIA IN NEW ZEALAND 1987-88

	First-class Results					All Matches			
Matches	Won	Lost	Drawn	Tied	Matches	Won	Lost	Drawn	Tied
–	–	–	–	–	2	–	2	–	–

Victoria lost both the limited over matches on this brief visit.

Date	Venue	Opponent	Results for Australians
Nov 6	Auckland	*Auckland	Lost by 2 wkts
Nov 8	Auckland	*Auckland	Lost by 60 runs

QUEENSLAND IN NEW ZEALAND 1987-88

	First-class Results					All Matches			
Matches	Won	Lost	Drawn	Tied	Matches	Won	Lost	Drawn	Tied
–	–	–	–	–	3	3	–	–	–

Queensland's visit was confined to three limited over matches.

Date	Venue	Opponent	Results for Australians
Dec 9	Wellington	*Wellington	Won by losing fewer wkts
Dec 12	Dunedin	*Otago	Won by 6 wkts
Dec 13	Christchurch	*Canterbury	Won by 31 runs

CHAMPION STATE TEAMS

WESTERN AUSTRALIA IN INDIA 1989

Matches	First-class Results Won	Lost	Drawn	Tied	Matches	All Matches Won	Lost	Drawn	Tied
1	–	–	1	–	4	1	2	1	–

A Western Australian team journeyed to Madras in 1989 to return the visit paid to Perth the previous year by the leading Indian club, Tamil Nadu.

Date	Venue	Opponent	Results for Australians
Sep 10	Coimbatore	*Tamil Nadu XI	Lost by 10 runs
Sep 12	Bangalore	*Karnataka State XI	Lost by 7 wkts
Sep 15	Madras	Tamil Nadu	Drawn
Sep 17	Madras	*Tamil Nadu	Won by 29 runs

Player	M	Inn	NO	Runs	HS	50	100	Avrge	Ct/St	Overs	Mdns	Runs	Wkts	Avrge	5wi	10wm	Best
Andrews, WS	1	1	–	89	89	1	–	89.00	1	9.0	–	35	1	35.00	–	–	1/35
Brayshaw, JA	1	1	–	30	30	–	–	30.00	–	7.0	1	31	–	–	–	–	–
Capes, PA	1	1	1	8	8*	–	–	–	1	15.2	1	62	2	31.00	–	–	2/62
Hogan, TG	1	1	–	42	42	–	–	42.00	1	26.0	6	74	–	–	–	–	–
MacLeay, KH	1	1	–	1	1	–	–	1.00	–	10.0	1	66	2	33.00	–	–	2/66
Matthews, CD	1	1	–	19	19	–	–	19.00	–	12.0	1	55	1	55.00	–	–	1/55
Moody, TM	1	1	–	13	13	–	–	13.00	1	8.0	1	15	–	–	–	–	–
Mullally, AD	1	–	–	–	–	–	–	–	–	19.0	4	81	1	81.00	–	–	1/81
Veletta, MRJ	1	1	–	41	41	–	–	41.00	2	–	–	–	–	–	–	–	–
Wood, GM (Capt)	1	1	–	12	12	–	–	12.00	1	–	–	–	–	–	–	–	–
Yardley, B	1	1	1	1	1*	–	–	–	–	17.0	6	73	2	36.50	–	–	2/73

VICTORIA IN ENGLAND 1991

Matches	First-class Results Won	Lost	Drawn	Tied	Matches	All Matches Won	Lost	Drawn	Tied
1	–	–	1	–	4	1	1	2	–

Simon O'Donnell captained Victoria on a short tour of England in 1991 involving one first-class match and four limited over games.

Date	Venue	Opponent	Results for Australians
Sep 16	Durham Uni	*Durham	Lost on run rate
Sep 17	Durham Uni	*Durham	Drawn
Sep 22	Chelmsford	*Essex	Won by 59 runs
Sep 23	Chelmsford	Essex	Drawn

Player	M	Inn	NO	Runs	HS	50	100	Avrge	Ct/St	Overs	Mdns	Runs	Wkts	Avrge	5wi	10wm	Best
Berry, DS	1	2	–	5	4	–	–	2.50	1/1	–	–	–	–	–	–	–	–
Dodemaide, AIC	1	2	–	21	21	–	–	10.50	1	24.0	6	54	2	27.00	–	–	2/54
Fleming, DW	1	1	–	8	8	–	–	8.00	–	25.0	5	88	2	44.00	–	–	2/88
Hughes, MG	1	2	2	72	60*	1	–	–	–	30.3	7	85	1	85.00	–	–	1/85
Jackson, PW	1	1	–	4	4	–	–	4.00	–	18.0	11	50	2	25.00	–	–	2/50
Jones, DM	1	2	–	34	25	–	–	17.00	–	–	–	–	–	–	–	–	–
Lehmann, DS	1	2	–	23	15	–	–	11.50	–	–	–	–	–	–	–	–	–
O'Donnell, SP (Capt)	1	2	–	17	12	–	–	8.50	–	13.0	6	47	1	47.00	–	–	1/47
Parker, GR	1	2	–	1	1	–	–	0.50	–	–	–	–	–	–	–	–	–
Phillips, WN	1	2	–	13	11	–	–	6.50	–	–	–	–	–	–	–	–	–
Ramshaw, DJ	1	2	–	11	11	–	–	5.50	–	–	–	–	–	–	–	–	–

NEW SOUTH WALES IN NEW ZEALAND 1993–94

Matches	First-class Results Won	Lost	Drawn	Tied	Matches	All Matches Won	Lost	Drawn	Tied
–	–	–	–	–	1	1	–	–	–

NSW won their only fixture on a tour aimed at celebrating their Sheffield Shield win.

Date	Venue	Opponent	Results for Australians
Apr 4	Christchurch	*Canterbury	Won by 86 runs

The Prince of Wales (later Edward VII) relaxes in his chair with a cigar after being clean bowled for a duck playing for I Zingari against the Gentlemen of Norfolk. *MCC Library*

A newspaper cartoonist's version of one of cricket's most curious fixtures, the One-Armed versus the One-Legged, played by pensioners at Greenwich in London.

The Jolimonters, a colourful wandering eleven from Melbourne, shown as they prepare for a match in Adelaide in 1880. They went back frequently.

The Rood de Wit club of Haarlem, Holland, in the English cricket uniform they adopted for their matches from 1883. *MCC Library*

CHAPTER FIFTEEN
SPECIAL PURPOSE XIs

Cricket administrators have always had a flair for celebrating, regardless of whether it is for the centenaries of nations or cricket associations, the anniversaries of grounds opening, politicians becoming Prime Ministers, fund-raising, or simply to boast of their important connections. For some the sheer joy of playing cricket is sufficient reason for continuous celebration. The big occasions give cricket administrators a few days in which to remind the public of the game's exalted status, and occasionally produce reunions of heart-warming nostalgia as old heroes who thought they were forgotten meet once again. But even the best-planned special matches can go wrong.

The organisers were delighted when the 24-year-old Prince of Wales (later Edward VII) agreed to play for I Zingari against the Gentlemen of Norfolk at Sandringham on 17 and 18 July 1866, and hoped that bowlers, knowing the Prince was not adept at the sport, would favour him with some easy deliveries to hit. The big crowd wanted to see the Prince make runs but to their horror the Norfolk fast bowler, Wright, scattered his stumps with his second ball. The scorebook recording the Prince's sole appearance in a cricket match was found in a cupboard at St James's Palace. It showed that I Zingari made 277, with R.A. Fitzgerald contributing 101, and had the Gentlemen of Norfolk out for 119 and 60, so at least the Prince's team were not disgraced. The scorebook, now in the possession of the Norfolk County Cricket Club, reads: H.R.H.P. of Wales b. Wright 0.

One of cricket's most curious fixtures, the match between One-Armed and One-Legged Pensioners at Greenwich, London, was first held in 1796. Players on peg-legs celebrated just being alive against opponents who scampered for singles using only one arm. John Arlott wrote that matches such as this were often played in Georgian times, with spectators wagering heavily on the outcome.

Another special cricket event was the October 1811 contest between Hampshire and Surrey women's teams. The Hampshire ladies wore royal purple ribbons; the Surrey ladies, orange and blue. Their match was rather unkindly depicted in an engraving by Thomas Rowlandson, which shows a two-stump wicket, although the middle stump was introduced back in 1776. The women played for a stake of 500 guineas a side and the match was won by Hampshire.

Celebrations around a barrel at the end of a match were not enough for most cricketers. They wanted to travel and find out what conditions were like in other centres. This created what became known as the 'Wandering Elevens', cricket nomads who have gone on travelling for two centuries. One of the earliest recorded touring clubs in Australia were the Jolimonters, an East Melbourne lot that displayed their colourful uniforms in Adelaide in the 1880s. Everybody but the wicket-keeper sported a beard and the Jolimonters included Paddy Horan, the Irish-born allrounder who appeared for Australia in the very first Test against England. The Jolimonters looked very similar to the Rood en Wit club, of Haarlem, Holland, who played in uniforms copied from visiting English teams.

The pioneer Australian teams to England overcame misgivings about their money-grabbing motives by playing several matches for charity. The most famous of these were the Smokers versus Non-Smokers matches, in which players from English and Australian Test teams played alongside each other. The first match was at Lord's at the end of the fourth Australians' 32-match tour in

September 1884. All proceeds went to the Cricketers' Fund Friendly Society. The Non-Smokers made 250, with the giant Australian (6 ft 6 in, 16 st 6 lb [198 cm, 104.3 kg]) George Bonnor scoring 124 out of the 150 runs added while he was at the crease. The Smokers managed a draw by scoring 111 and 152 before time ran out. Highlight of the match was Bonnor's towering six off team-mate Fred Spofforth, who had terrorised English batsmen.

The second match was played at the East Melbourne ground in March 1887 when Non-Smokers scored 803, then the highest score in first-class cricket. Arthur Shrewsbury made 236, William Gunn 150, and the Australian left-hander Billy Bruce 131. The Smokers responded with 356 and followed on. They were on 5 for 135 when time ran out. All the players' performances are included in their first-class records.

By then English cricket was well organised. County cricket provided a living for those who wanted to pursue the game as professionals but they were rigidly divided from their amateur team-mates. Amateurs only met their professional team-mates on the field and they went on to the playing area through different gates. On tour professionals stayed in boarding houses and third-class hotels and the amateurs in the best hotels. Newspapers recorded the scores with 'Mr' and all the initials for the amateurs and just the surnames for the professionals. At net practice amateurs were able to bat for long periods while the professionals did all the donkey work bowling to them.

Every year the best amateur teams played the best professional sides and some wonderful contests ensued. Many of these Gentlemen versus Players matches were as fiercely contested as Test matches, with pride a big factor in the performance of all involved. The mesmerising thing for Australian teams visiting England was the large number of phoney amateurs they encountered. Worst culprit of all was Dr W. G. Grace, who played as an amateur while demanding extortionate appearance fees.

The women cricketers of England joined in the business of making money from the game as professional cricketers. A team calling itself the Original English Ladies Cricketers (OELC) began touring in the 1880s but the agent who promised to pay them £1 15s a week went broke. The OELC sued for payment of their unpaid salaries and for compensation and won their case in the Lord Mayor's court in London in February 1892, but the agent could not pay and the OELC disbanded, with the whole idea of women's professional cricket never to be revived.

The ladies' team were coached during their brief existence at an indoor cricket school in the London suburb of Wandsworth. Among their coaches were Alec and George Hearne, members of a formidable clan who could field an entire field of professionals bearing the Hearne name. Five Hearnes played for England and there were twelve professional cricketers in the family. The Hearnes provided the second instance—after the

The Smokers and Non-Smokers shown with the scoreboard and the record score during their match at East Melbourne in 1887.

The Gentlemen and The Players, the teams that opposed each other at Lord's in 1894, both extremely strong. *The Gentlemen: back row* J. Douglas, J.R. Mason, G.J. Mordaunt, A.C. MacLaren; *centre* Australian S.M.J. Woods, H.T. Hewett, Dr W.G. Grace (capt.), H.W. Bainbridge, F.S. Jackson; *front* G. Macgregor, A.E. Stoddart. *The Players: standing* W. Chatterton, W. Lockwood, J.T. Hearne, W. Flowers, A. Hearne (umpire); *centre* E. Wainwright, A. Ward, W. Gunn (capt.), F. Martin, W. Brockwell; *front* J. Briggs, W. Storer. The matches began in 1806 and ended with the abolition of amateur status after the 1962 season.

Graces—of three brothers playing in the same Test when Alec and George Gibbons Hearne played for England and Frank for South Africa in 1891–92 at Cape Town. Frank Hearne was the first player to represent both England and South Africa in Tests. This was the match in which Billy Murdoch played for England, after previously having appeared for Australia.

The Hearnes' record overshadowed that of the Lucases, who could also field a family team but only had one member, Alfred Perry ('Bunny') Lucas, play for England. Bunny Lucas was an automatic selection for The Gentlemen for several seasons and helped W.G. Grace put on 120 for the second wicket against Australia in 1880 in Test cricket's first century partnership. He visited Australia in 1878–79 with Lord Harris's England team. Nine Lucases played first-class cricket and unlike the Hearnes they were all amateurs.

These were leisurely times, of course, when the financial pressures of playing cricket as an amateur were not as severe as they became later. These were the days when teams of Single Men could play against teams of Single Ladies, with the men handicapped by a rule that they had to bat with broom handles while the ladies used ordinary bats. The Butchers XI played The Bakers XI, and in Australia the Echuca Wharfies XI had regular matches, as did the Barehanded Wolf-Chokers, the Lindfield Funnelwebs, and the Newcastle Ironclads.

In the far corners of the civilised world, British servicemen and British traders played cricket in their spare time. A match between Yokohama's English business community and officers from the British Fleet played a match in Yokohama in 1864, and in 1893 a regular fixture between a China XI and a Japanese XI, both all white men, began in Kobe, one of Japan's major seaports. Boer War prisoners of the British Army played a series of matches after capture, and in the Western Australian gold-mining town of Kalgoorlie prospectors played a Smokers v. Non-Smokers match in 1901.

The first and only women's professional cricket team, who were disbanded in 1890 after their agent could not pay them. They had plans to tour Australia. *Netta Rheinberg*

The Lucas family at Warnham Court, near Horsham in Sussex, with the team they often fielded in social matches in the 1880s. Five of these players appeared in first-class cricket: A.C., A.G., F.M., A.P. and M.P. An A.P. Lucas played Test cricket but was no relation to this family. *Roger Mann*

The Hearnes photographed in 1885 after assembling for a social match: *back row* G.G., J., H., W., W., and G.F. Hearne; *centre* G. senr, T. senr, T. Hearne jnr; *front* F., R., and A. Hearne. Twelve Hearnes played first-class cricket, and five played Test cricket, three in the same Test, A. and G.G. for England and F. for South Africa. *Roger Mann*

The Edrich family team in 1957: *back row* Arthur E., Peter G., George C., Alan W., and John H. Edrich; *front* George H., Bill J., W.A., G.A., Barry G., and B.R. Edrich. *Roger Mann*

THE WANDERING ELEVENS

The Devon Dumplings, founded in 1902, were one of the first cricket clubs in England created for the express purpose of providing non-competitive social matches for amateur gentlemen resident in the county. They retain strong links with the Army, Navy, church and local schools and take teams all over southern England to play, catering in 1993 for 320 players.

The Cryptics, founded at New College, Oxford, in 1910, included Douglas Jardine and several generals among its members, and after World War I took teams to play the British Army of the Rhine (1922), to Oporto in Portugal (1924), Antwerp and Brussels (1925), to The Hague for matches against the Flamingoes (1927), and altogether made 24 overseas tours between the two World Wars. Since World War II they have been back to all those places, and branched out with games in Paris, Kenya, and Berlin. The Cryptics' 976 members include about a dozen ex-Test players, some of them Australian, 20 or more county cricketers, and a sprinkling of noted cricket authors, including E.W. ('Jim') Swanton and John Woodcock. The Yellowhammers, founded by Tunbridge Wells schoolboys in 1909, quickly developed an annual program of matches against The Bluemantles, Sevenoaks Vine, Penhurst Park, Sidcup and the South Saxons. The Free Foresters, founded in the Forest of Arden in 1856, had similar success in quickly building a heavy annual program of matches. Two years after the Foresters, the Band of Brothers CC began, and in 1862 came the Incogniti CC. Gradually a network of such clubs developed through the English counties, the Sussex Martlets, the Hogs of Hampshire, the Somerset Stragglers, and the Dorset Rangers all acquiring surprisingly large membership.

England's exclusive schools and universities followed with their wandering sides. The Eton Ramblers, Uppingham Rovers, Rugby Butterflies, Harrow Wanderers, Old Reptonians, Charterhouse Friars, the Oxford Harlequins and the Cambridge Crusaders all have existed for more than 70 years and retain large membership lists. But by far the most prestigious of all the wandering clubs is I Zingari, which has spread all around the world. The Australian I Zingari club has its headquarters on a private ground at Camden, and there is also a branch in Perth. Many of these clubs play cricket of a very high standard and all of them are highly selective in enrolling members, which is probably why the idea has not taken on in Australia to the same extent.

The wandering clubs have neither sought nor require a control authority, preferring to raise their own funds, find their own grounds and develop their own fixture lists. In 1967 the *Cricketer* magazine started a knockout competition for 32 teams comprising old boys of Britain's public schools who played 50-over matches for The Cricketer Cup. Some of the older clubs for mature adults regarded this as a retrograde step but the competition has survived 26 years of competition and now enjoys the sponsorship of the Moet & Chandon champagne company.

The Cryptics in their blazers in front of the pavilion at Oporto, Portugal, in 1924. They have been back many times.

THE EMUS

The nearest Australia comes to providing a wandering team of its own is the Emus, an organisation aimed at providing opportunities for young bush cricketers. The Emus CC was founded in 1950 by grazier Jim White, who can take pride in the fact that Test cricketers Johnny Gleeson (North Coast), Doug Walters (Upper Hunter) and Rick McCosker (Northern Tablelands) were all first spotted playing for the Emus. Gleeson toured Malaya and New Zealand with the Emus as a wicket-keeper before he became a Test spinner. The Emus operate an ingenious fund-raising scheme by running their own herd of cattle and selling off the progeny. Members donated money to buy the cows and calves in 1967 and were repaid when the calves were sold. The 22 cows and calves in the original herd have grown, and today when the Emus embark on an overseas tour their fares are paid by the herd.

One of the administrators who enthusiastically supports the Emus is the New South Wales Cricket Association president Alan Davidson, himself a former country boy who grew up on an orchard property in the Lisarow district. Alan developed his love for cricket at the feet of his grandfather Paddy Clifton, whose bullock team hauled logs down narrow bush tracks before the turn of the century. From Paddy Clifton Alan learned to crack a stockwhip and imitate the raucous cries of bullock drivers before he discovered how to bowl an outswinger.

Paddy Clifton had five daughters and four sons, and with his brother Roley and later his grandsons, formed the Clifton family cricket team. This family team may not have been as strong as the Lucas, Hearne or Edrich family teams in England but they all had arms like large hams and could hit hard and bowl at express speed, with Arthur Clifton providing leg-breaks and Clem Clifton keeping wicket.

The best known Australian family team, showing Test hero Alan Davidson with his grandfather Paddy Clifton, and the Clifton family XI before a match at Gosford, New South Wales.

SIR JULIEN CAHN'S ELEVEN

This celebrated team organised by the eccentric Nottinghamshire furniture millionaire, Sir Julien Cahn, in the decade before World War II included four outstanding Australian cricketers—Vic Jackson, Harold Mudge, 'Ginty' Lush and Jack Walsh—all of them outstanding in New South Wales teams and not far from Test selection when they joined Sir Julien's XI. They were signed as amateurs and played every week on Sir Julien's private ground in Nottingham, alongside leading players from all the white cricket nations. They received an annual retainer and had all their expenses paid, and were required to go on regular overseas tours. The Australians found themselves at West Bridgeford (down the road from Trent Bridge) staying at Sir Julien's stately home, Stanford Hall. On the field their team-mates include Springboks Bob Crisp and Dennis Morkel, New Zealanders Stuart Dempster and Giff Vivian and the England Test stars Ian Peebles, Walter Robins and Paul Gibb.

Sir Julien, a member of the Magic Circle, entertained them with card tricks and a stunt with a magic phonograph. He had his own seal pool and delighted in the antics of seals Aqua and Ivy as they went through their tricks for the cricketers. Between 1923 and 1941

Sir Julien Cahn's famous team photographed in 1938 not long before war forced their last match: *standing* G. Woolf (manager), E. Watts (Surrey), N. Oldfield (Lancs), J. Hardstaff (Notts), E. Phillipson (Lancs), A. Dyson (Glamorgan), A.G. Lush (NSW), J. Walsh (NSW), E. Astill (assist. manager); *seated* S. Dempster (NZ), H. Mudge (NSW), C. Maxwell (Notts), C. Goodway (Warwick.), Sir Julien Cahn, G.F.H. Heane (Notts, capt.), V.E. Jackson (NSW), P. Smith (Essex).

Sir Julien's teams played 565 matches and lost only 16. They toured Jamaica in 1929, Argentina in 1930, North America and Bermuda in 1933, Ceylon, Malaya and New Zealand in 1939, usually reinforced by England players such as Joe Hardstaff, Buddy Oldfield, Peter Smith and the Lancashire left-hander Eddie Phillipson. Sir Julien appeared in some home games, going to the crease after his butler had pumped up his pneumatic pads. Sir Julien had a wooden fox placed on the ground near the pavilion and when things went badly for his team, which was not often, he would lower the fox's tail.

Sir Julien terminated all contracts and disbanded his team when war broke out, and all the players went home, most to join the services. Sir Julien died in 1944, a month short of his 62nd birthday.

THE KALGOORLIE TEAM

Kalgoorlie's first cricket team, formed in 1896, comprised miners and mining officials who suffered from a lack of net practice and white flannels but lacked nothing in enthusiasm. Several of them had arrived from England at the Victorian port of Geelong, spent their entire savings on bedding, tents and mining gear and then humped the lot more than 3000 kilometres to the Kalgoorlie goldfields in barrows, covering less than 30 kilometres a day over rough, uncharted bushland. They were not the sort of people put off by lack of clothing or equipment and they played their cricket with rare gusto. Later some of them moved to eastern states and qualified as doctors and lawyers or became important civil servants; some of them died serving in World War I.

Kalgoorlie's first cricket team elected the only man in the town with a full set of whites as their captain. Alongside him in the front row is the scorer, whose dog kept him company. The team's umpire did his job with his shotgun handy, an accessory modern umpires no doubt envy.

THE CENTENARY TESTS

The idea of staging a Test match between the teams who introduced Test cricket to the world and inviting all surviving Test players to watch came from Hans Ebeling, president of the Melbourne Cricket Club and a former Australian Test bowler. His brainchild turned out to be the most spectacular event in the history of Australian cricket. After almost three years of painstaking organisation they celebrated 100 years of Test cricket on the ground where it began, with 244 surviving participants of Anglo–Australian Tests in the stands. Only the 26 players who were too old or infirm to travel to Melbourne declined Ebeling's invitation and a week of dinners, lunches and reminiscing made it a memorable venture.

The match on 12 to 17 March 1977 fulfilled all the organisers' highest hopes and ended with Australia the victors by 45 runs, the same margin by which they won the inaugural Test on the same ground in 1877. 'It was an historic triumph and, on a human level, unforgettably reassuring and stimulating,' said John Arlott. Within weeks Jack Ryder, 87 and Percy Fender, 84, had died and before a year was out, Tony Greig, who captained England in the match, had been stripped of the captaincy because of his part in the Packer rebellion.

English authorities made an attempt in 1980 to stage a similar event at Lord's to celebrate the first Test against Australia in England, but this promotion fell surprisingly flat. For a start it was held on the wrong ground—the first Test on English soil 100 years earlier was played at The Oval—and then the weather intervened and prevented the match being played out. Nostalgia reigned again in London hotels and in the Lord's grandstands but for Australians it lacked the sustained drama of the Melbourne Centenary Test. Kim Hughes (117) and Graeme Wood (112) upheld Australia's reputation in helping to build their team's total to 5 for 385 declared, but a draw was always likely after play had been curtailed on the second and third days.

A similar fate befell the Test in Sydney staged to celebrate Australia's Bicentenary, in January and February 1988. Only 103,831 spectators attended the five days of a drawn match, which was at least 100,000 short of the promoters' expectations. Australia followed on after scoring 214, chasing England's 425, and experts agreed that had Australia managed the extra 12 runs which would have avoided the follow-on and forced England to bat again the eventual draw probably would have been averted. As it was, David Boon went on to 185 not out in Australia's second innings of 2 for 328 but by stumps nobody cared.

The players and distinguished guests at Lord's in 1980 for the match celebrating 100 years of Test cricket in England. In the front row are W.J. O'Reilly, L.S. Darling, E.L. a'Beckett, W.H. Ponsford, A. Sandham, R.C. Steele (ACB), P.B.H. May, G.S. Chappell, S.C. Griffith, I.T. Botham, R.J. Parish (ACB), F.G. Mann, H.S.T.L. Hendry, G.O.B. Allen, R.E.S. Wyatt, P.G.H. Fender.

REST OF THE WORLD XI

Matches	First-class Results				Matches	All Matches			
	Won	Lost	Drawn	Tied		Won	Lost	Drawn	Tied
12	5	2	5	–	16	5	3	8	–

Date	Venue	Opponent	Results for Touring Team
Nov 5	Melbourne	Victoria	Drawn
Nov 12	Sydney	New South Wales	Drawn
Nov 19	Brisbane	Queensland	Won by 38 runs
Nov 26	Brisbane	Australia	Drawn
Dec 4	Perth	Western Australia	Won by 72 runs
Dec 10	Perth	Australia	Lost by an inns & 11 runs
Dec 17	Adelaide	South Australia	Lost by an inns & 1 run
Dec 22	Launceston	Tasmania	Won by 8 wkts
Dec 26	Hobart (TCA)	Combined XI	Drawn
Jan 1	Melbourne	Australia	Won by 96 runs
Jan 8	Sydney	Australia	Drawn
Jan 15	Sydney	*Australia	Abandoned
Jan 16	Melbourne	*Australia	Lost by 10 wkts
Jan 19	Canberra	*Southern NSW Country XI	Drawn
Jan 22	Newcastle	*Northern NSW Country XI	Drawn
Jan 28	Adelaide	Australia	Won by 9 wkts

The Rest of the World team which toured Australia in 1971–72: *back row* R.S. Cunis (New Zealand), Zaheer Abbas (Pakistan), S.M. Gavaskar (India), F.M. Engineer (India), R.W. Taylor (England), B.S. Bedi (India), N. Gifford (England); *centre* C.H. Lloyd (West Indies), R.A. Hutton (England), A.W. Greig (South Africa/England), P.M. Pollock (South Africa), Asif Masood (Pakistan), H.M. Ackerman (South Africa); *front* R.B. Kanhai (West Indies), G.S. Sober (West Indies, capt.), W.L. Jacobs (manager), Intikhab Alam (Pakistan), R.G. Pollock (South Africa).

Player	M	Inn	NO	Runs	HS	50	100	Avrge	Ct/St	Overs	Mdns	Runs	Wkts	Avrge	5wi	10wm	Best
Ackerman, HM	7	13	1	449	112	3	1	37.41	10	–	–	–	–	–	–	–	–
Bedi, BS	10	10	4	76	24	–	–	12.66	4	292.1	52	1065	36	32.38	1	–	5/126
Cunis, RS	9	11	2	129	43	–	–	14.34	3	135.0	16	544	9	60.44	–	–	2/59
Engineer, FM	9	14	–	488	192	–	2	34.85	16/1	–	–	–	–	–	–	–	–
Gavaskar, SM	11	20	2	559	95	4	–	31.06	5	1.0	–	4	–	–	–	–	–
Gifford, N	7	10	6	52	19	–	–	13.00	5	146.4	14	540	16	34.12	1	–	5/97
Greig, AW	10	16	2	525	70	6	–	37.50	1	183.6	22	664	26	25.54	1	–	6/30
Hutton, RA	7	10	–	88	41	–	–	8.80	6	89.0	7	370	8	46.25	–	–	2/19
Intikhab Alam	11	16	2	227	73*	1	–	16.21	3	263.3	19	1175	38	30.92	1	–	5/45
Kanhai, RB	6	11	3	525	121*	1	3	65.63	–	3.0	–	14	–	–	–	–	–
Lloyd, CH	6	10	1	370	69	3	–	41.11	2	3.0	–	11	–	–	–	–	–
Asif Masood	7	8	3	40	8	–	–	8.00	3	102.0	13	413	12	34.42	–	–	2/19
Pollock, PM	2	3	–	74	54	1	–	24.66	1	37.0	3	147	2	73.50	–	–	1/16
Pollock, RG	3	5	–	209	136	–	1	41.80	5	–	–	–	–	–	–	–	–
Sobers, GS (Capt)	9	14	4	562	254	–	2	56.20	7	128.6	8	528	13	40.61	–	–	3/67
Taylor, RW	7	11	3	128	51*	1	–	16.00	21/3	–	–	–	–	–	–	–	–
Zaheer Abbas	11	19	–	709	112	5	2	37.31	5	–	–	–	–	–	–	–	–

Towards the end of the European summer of 1971, the Australian Board of Control submitted to sustained political and moral pressures and cancelled the South African tour that had been arranged for the southern summer of 1971–72. The Board secretary Allan Barnes and chairman Sir Donald Bradman hurriedly replaced the Springboks' visit with a tour by a team drawn from all the other leading cricket nations, which became known as the Rest of the World XI. To the great credit of the organisers, who had little time in which to work, the Rest of the World tour was a resounding success and provided Australian fans with some exciting cricket.

The visitors were beset with injuries that often had manager Bill Jacobs struggling to field a side from the 17 players at his disposal. Clive Lloyd was on the danger list and had to be flown home after a shoulder injury, but the players he left in Australia produced some memorable cricket, not least captain Gary Sobers' innings of 254 in which he hit 2 sixes and 35 fours.

Bradman said it was probably the finest innings ever seen in Australia. Graeme Pollock also played an innings of rare power, scoring 136 in the Adelaide match, which enabled the Rest of the World to clinch the series against Australia two–one. Rohan Kanhai hit three superb centuries in these representative matches and headed his team's tour batting averages with 525 runs from 11 innings at 65.62. Tony Greig was a big success as an allrounder.

For Australia, Dennis Lillee confirmed his potential, and in the Perth match routed the Rest of the World by taking 8 for 25, including the last six wickets from 15 balls in which not a run was scored from him. In Sydney Bob Massie demonstrated his talent for swinging the ball, and later performed his 16-wicket haul in a Lord's Test. The Rest of the World XI played 12 first-class matches, five against Australian XIs, winning five, drawing five, and losing to Australia and South Australia.

1988 ABORIGINALS TEAM IN ENGLAND

First-class Results					All Matches				
Matches	Won	Lost	Drawn	Tied	Matches	Won	Lost	Drawn	Tied
–	–	–	–	–	27	15	11	1	–

Date	Venue	Opponent	Results for Australians
May 14	The Oval	*Surrey	Lost by 9 wkts
May 16	Canterbury	*Kent	Lost by 43 runs
May 18	Richmond	*Richmond	Lost by 36 runs
May 19	Motspur Park	*Australia House	Lost by 1 run
May 20	Uxbridge	*Middlesex Clubs	Won by 129 runs
May 21	Osterley	*Indian Gymkhana	Won by 5 wkts
May 23	Hove	*Sussex	Lost by 6 wkts
May 24	Guildford	*Guildford President's XI	Won by 62 runs
May 25	Maidstone	*The Mote Cricket Club	Won by 97 runs
May 27	Farnham	*Farnham	Won by 23 runs
May 28	Southampton	*Sport Aid XI	Won by 6 runs
May 30	Alderney	*Alderney	Won by 174 runs
May 31	Southampton	*Hampshire	Lost by 36 runs
Jun 1	Portsmouth	*Hants Club	Won by 5 wkts
Jun 2	Sutton	*Combined Teams	Won by 30 runs
Jun 4	Monkton Coombe	*Bath Schools	Won by 144 runs
Jun 6	Swansea	*Glamorgan	Lost by 62 runs
Jun 9	Birmingham	*Birmingham & District	Abandoned
Jun 10	Birtles Bowl	*T Hudson's XI	Lost by 114 runs
Jun 11	Middlesbrough	*Middlesbrough Select XI	Lost by 6 runs
Jun 13	Manchester	*Lancashire	Lost by 8 runs
Jun 17	Chatsworth	*Chatsworth House	Won by 173 runs
Jun 18	Cleethorpes	*Humberside	Won by 222 runs
Jun 19	Lincoln	*Lincolnshire	Won by 114 runs
Jun 22	Oxford	*Oxford University	Won by 40 runs
Jun 25	Uxbridge	*Combined Services	Won by 76 runs
Jun 26	Hackney	*CH Lloyd's XI	Won by 7 runs
Jun 29	Lord's	*MCC	Drawn

Averages for All Matches

Player	M	Inn	NO	Runs	HS	50+	Avrge	Overs	Mdns	Runs	Wkts	Avrge
Appoo, S	22	21	–	563	83	5	26.80	75.4	6	337	20	16.85
Bagshaw, P	19	18	4	512	79*	3	36.57	105.0	17	356	16	22.25
Breckenbridge, D	20	19	2	490	86*	3	28.82	–	–	69	3	23.00
Bulger, N	16	14	2	482	73	5	40.16	57.2	7	155	9	17.22
Fry, N	9	9	–	240	76	1	26.66	–	–	91	2	45.50
Gardner, D	15	10	4	89	30	–	14.83	117.0	25	359	12	29.91
Vanderbyl, EG	18	16	5	385	99*	2	35.00	–	–	64	7	9.14
Gregory, P	15	7	2	59	19	–	11.80	120.3	17	368	22	16.72
James, G	18	18	–	285	51	1	15.83	–	–	18	2	9.00
Mainhardt, M	19	15	1	163	40	–	11.64	144.2	19	597	26	22.96
Marks, L	15	7	2	56	22	–	11.20	113.0	12	435	13	33.46
Marsh, J	18	16	4	565	101*	5	47.08	–	–	11	1	11.00
McGuire, J (Capt)	22	21	1	660	110	5	33.00	–	–	22	3	7.33
Monaghan, D	15	4	3	11	9*	–	11.00	127.0	16	529	19	27.84
Pearce, B	18	6	3	34	15*	–	11.33	122.4	22	398	21	18.90
Thompson, D	15	7	–	48	11	–	6.85	105.0	23	317	10	13.78
Williams, M	18	16	5	209	53*	1	19.00	–	–	–	–	–

The second Australian Aboriginal cricketers before they left for their 1988 English tour. They played 27 one-day matches, winning 15, losing 11, and playing one draw, with one abandoned, appearing in many of the places visited by the 1868 Aboriginal team. Manager Mark Ella is on the right, captain John Maguire sixth from the right. *Greg White, Sydney Morning Herald*

HOME AND AWAY

THE FIJIANS IN AUSTRALIA

Australia and Fiji are unlikely to play Test cricket, but there have been several matches between the countries, stretching back to 1905 when Joe Darling's team played a match in Fiji on their way to England. A Fijian team toured Australia in 1908, played matches against South Australia, Victoria, New South Wales and Queensland, and delighted spectators with their barefoot chasing of the ball. They batted with pads but no boots and appeared unconcerned by knocks on the toes.

Charlie Macartney took a team of Australians to Fiji in 1926–27 for an eight-match tour, and in 1959–60 a Fijian team made a 16-match tour of New South Wales cities. Highlight of this tour was a match between the Fijians and New South Wales. The Fijians spurned traditional supplies at the drinks break and instead offered all the players bowls of kava, which Keith Miller said made him unsteady on his feet for a few minutes. One Fijian was hit on the toe by an Alan Davidson yorker but resumed immediately, apparently unaffected by a blow that would have hobbled batsmen in boots. One of the Fijians was an Olympic sprinter and he proved that he had a fair turn of pace by sprinting almost 50 metres to catch a skier from Keith Miller.

The Fijian team in Australia in 1908 when they appeared in four states. Lieutenant E.J. Marsden, wearing a suit, organised the tour and also captained the team, batting at No. 4.

The 1908 Fijian team in Australia usually played their matches barefooted, wearing calf-length skirts or sulus. This shot shows them with their star player Prince Ratu Kadavulevu (white suit), seated next to the tour manager and captain, Lieutenant Marsden. *Jack Pollard Collection*

The strongest team Fiji ever fielded enter the arena in traditional single-file style at Suva in 1948 behind their captain, Englishman Philip Snow. The Governor-General of Fiji, who usually played in the side, Ratu Sir George Cakobau, was absent, having broken a toe batting barefoot during a match in New Zealand.

CHAPTER SIXTEEN

LIMITED-OVER CRICKET

One-day matches in which the duration of each team's innings is restricted or even the size of the opposing sides reduced have been part of cricket since it began. The frenzied rush to get a result has always attracted crowds who enjoy the spectacle of polished strokemakers casting aside the coaching manuals and swinging wildly as the climax nears.

In Australia, many of the first intercolonial matches were followed by novelty matches, particularly when play in the main match ended early. Sometimes the two sides merged in a colonial-born versus British-born encounter, sometimes single wicket matches between individual champions or between the three or four best players from each side were organised. In December 1865, when matches between New South Wales and Victoria were resumed, rivalry between the two colonies was keen enough for Victoria to accept when four professionals from New South Wales challenged the Victorians to a single-wicket match at lunch on the last day. The match ended in a draw but the notion was revived in 1869 when four Victorians challenged New South Wales in Sydney and Melbourne newspapers.

Victoria won this match on Melbourne Cricket Ground from 28 to 30 December 1865, when E. Fowler, T.J.D. Kelly, J. Conway, and T.W.S. Wills scored 72 and 6, to which S. Cosstick, N. Thompson, W. Caffyn and C. Lawrence replied with innings of 52 and 2 for 8. Statistician Alf James says the match attracted 4000 spectators on the first day, 900 on the second day and 200 on the last day. Wills took an hour to score six runs in Victoria's first innings and the New South Wales second innings total of eight runs took 90 minutes to compile.

Victoria repeated their success by beating three New South Wales champions at the Albert Ground in the Sydney suburb of Redfern in April 1869 by one wicket, for a stake of £100 a side. Upset Sydney cricket buffs went to the home of the Gregory family and implored them to restore New South Wales prestige by taking on the Victorians. Dave Gregory, later Australia's first Test captain, agreed and went into serious training for what became a celebrated occasion with his brothers Edward and Charles, rising each morning at dawn to get in a couple of hours' practice before they went to work.

Three thousand Sydneyites watched the match which took three days to complete. The match began on Easter Saturday 1871, and on the first day 96 were scored off the bat from 913 balls. Wills made 13 off 205 balls for Victoria. On the second day there was a sensation when umpire Nat Thompson no-balled Dave Gregory for throwing. Amid uproar, Thompson, a professional born at Birmingham in England, was replaced by William Caffyn, the former Surrey hero. New South Wales won by five runs, with the three Gregory brothers scoring 24 and 30 against innings of 21 and 28 from Victorians J. Conway, S. Cosstick and Wills.

Limited-over cricket or matches between reduced teams continued to entertain spectators in the years of inter-colonial cricket. When district cricket began at the end of the 19th century, rival clubs often challenged each other to friendly Sunday matches. In two World Wars Australian servicemen frequently indulged in limited-over games between units. Australian airmen and soldiers joined their British counterparts in wartime limited-over matches in England, with many of the teams studded with famous names.

Shortened forms of cricket became big business with the introduction of the World Cup in England in 1975, however. The establishment of the Gillette Cup in England in 1963 helped financially struggling county

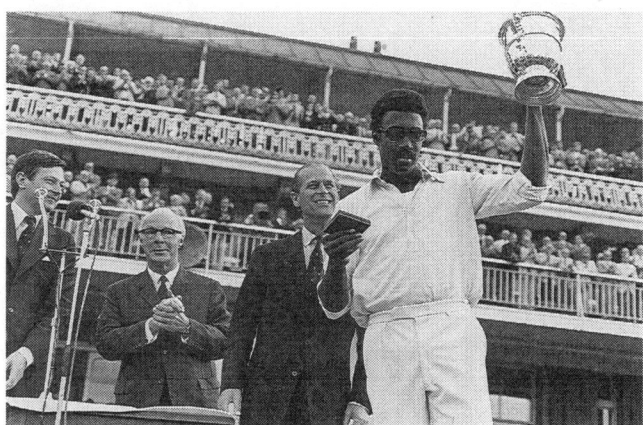

West Indian captain, Clive Lloyd, holds the World Cup aloft after receiving it from the Duke of Edinburgh, following a day-long struggle against Australia in the inaugural final of 1975. *Patrick Eagar*

The Australian team that were runners-up in the first World Cup in 1975: *standing* A.A. Mallett, G.J. Gilmour, D.K. Lillee, J.R. Thomson, A.G. Hurst, M.H.N. Walker, R.B. McCosker, A. Turner; *seated* R. Edwards, K.D. Walters, I.M. Chappell (capt.), manager, G.S. Chappell, R.W. Marsh, B.M. Laird. *Patrick Eagar*

clubs and led to the Prudential insurance group inviting teams to the UK from all over the cricket world. In a tournament of remarkable crowd acceptance Australia reached a dramatic final against the West Indies, but five run outs in the Australian innings led to them falling 17 runs short of the West Indian total of 291 in a 60-over match.

The big breakthrough for limited-over cricket was the introduction of night cricket by Kerry Packer in his two-year battle against established cricket authority. When the lights went on for a WSC night match in Sydney, and 55,000 people crowded in on 28 November 1978, Packer had won his acrimonious two-year feud with traditionalists. Limited-over cricket was established as the most important change to cricket this century. After Australian Cricket Board negotiators Bob Parish and Ray Steele settled the dispute with Packer, limited-over cricket became an integral part of every touring team's itinerary. Shortened matches had been part of these programs since 1970–71 but received only lukewarm acceptance until the lights went on.

Today virtually all the major Australian grounds have lights that allow them to stage limited-over cricket after dark. Two white balls have to be used because of the players' difficulty in sighting the traditional red ball at night and the white balls quickly become sodden and lose shape, but the appeal of limited-over cricket under lights is so great, the Australian Board is anxiously seeking the invention of a high-tech ball that can be seen at night and last at least 100 overs and thus permit parts, if not all, of a Test match to be played at night.

Despite heavy criticism, limited-over cricket continues to gain in popularity. Even the most rabid purists now acknowledge it as the form of cricket modern cricket fans demand. The abbreviated form of the game has attracted a new audience, a noisy, hard-drinking mob who become part of the match with their Mexican waves and their painted signs, but the limited-over matches give them the thrilling finishes they want.

'One-day cricket is injecting a dementia into the souls of those who play it,' wrote the late Bill O'Reilly in the *Sydney Morning Herald*:

> The whole thing is cancerous. For men to whom money is God there is no time to become concerned about what is happening to the proper game. It's sad to see great players swinging wildly. It's character assassination. Even Dennis Lillee did not try to bowl fast in this ridiculous game which is all about containment rather than taking wickets. The bowling is boof-headed rubbish.

The Australian public took little notice of this criticism.

The Australian team surprised the cricket fraternity by winning the fourth World Cup in 1987 against England, after failing in the second and third competitions in 1979 and 1983. Australia succeeded by a combination of brilliant fielding, gutsy batting, scoring 8 for 267 against 249 to beat Pakistan in the semi-finals and then defeating England in the final by scoring 5 for 253 against 8 for 248. This seven-run triumph produced some splendid

Australia's World Cup champions in 1987 photographed in front of the Red Fort at Delhi: *standing* E. Alcott (physio), M.R.J. Veletta, S.R. Waugh, T.B.A. May, B.A. Reid, T.M. Moody, A. Zesers, D.M. Jones, R.B. Simpson (coach); *seated* G.C. Dyer, S.P. O'Donnell, D.C. Boon, A.R. Border (capt.), A. Crompton (manager), G.R. Marsh, C.J. McDermott, P.L. Taylor.

performances from both sides, but none more valuable then David Boon's 75 and Mike Veletta's 45 not out in Australia's innings.

Teams for the 1983 World Cup, with their captains in front: D.A.G. Fletcher (Zimbabwe), Imran Khan (Pakistan), G.P. Howarth (New Zealand), K.M. Hughes (Australia), R.G.D. Willis (England), Kapil Dev (India), C.H. Lloyd (West Indies), L.R.D. Mendis (Sri Lanka). *Patrick Eagar*

Prime Minister Indira Gandhi, with members of India's World Cup champions at a Delhi reception after they returned home in 1983. *Sports Star, Madras*

The competing teams photographed on board H.M.A.S. *Canberra* before the start of the 1992 World Cup, with the Australian players in the foreground in front of the other nine teams, the umpires for the tournament at the stern, and Sydney Harbour Bridge in the background. Pakistan won the final. *Vivian Jenkins*

The limited-over caravan came to Australia and New Zealand in 1991–92 and once again the World Cup produced some shock results. New Zealand surprised by reaching the semi-final against Pakistan after winning seven of their eight matches. South Africa, in their re-introduction to international cricket, were the unlucky team. They went down to England in a semi-final, after winning five of their eight matches, because of a strange rule that prevented them attempting to score the 22 runs they needed to win from 13 balls. Rain then interrupted play.

When the teams returned 21 minutes later, the umpires said that only one over had been lost so South Africa required 22 runs from seven balls. Amid booing, this message was flashed on to the scoreboard, but reserve umpire Steve Woodward then ran out on to the field and announced that umpires Steve Randall and Brian Aldridge had got it wrong and that under the rules South Africa had to score 22 runs off one ball. This was grossly unfair to the South Africans and a blow to the reputation of limited-over cricket.

New Zealand's four-wicket defeat in Auckland by Pakistan came when the Kiwis' bowling, tight and accurate throughout the competition, lost control in the final hour. New Zealand's 262 looked a formidable 50-over target but Javed Miandad talked himself and his team-mates into a high that made it look easy. All of the New Zealand bowlers were hammered, Dipak Patel conceding 50 runs and Chris Harris 72 in their 10 overs; Morrison 55 in nine overs. With both Australia and New Zealand eliminated, fans still packed the Melbourne Cricket Ground for the final. An official crowd of 82,182 was announced as a world record, but this remains doubtful, as Indians are certain larger audiences have watched cricket in Calcutta and other Indian centres. Ian Botham's boast that England would win the World Cup in front of '100,000 convicts' failed to eventuate when Pakistan attacked throughout in an innings of 249. This proved 22 runs too difficult for England and gave Pakistan's captain Imran Khan, at his fifth attempt, the honour of holding the World Cup up for the crowd.

The limited-over critics relented enough to agree that Zimbabwe's defeat of England and Sri Lanka's two wins, despite an itinerary that took them from Mackay in north Queensland to Perth in Western Australia and to the south island of New Zealand, was gratifying stuff for those keen on cricket's development. In Albury Zimbabwe turned giant-killers when its membership of the International Cricket Conference was undecided. They scored 134 after England captain Graham Gooch sent them in to bat and then bundled England out for 125, with Eddo Brandes taking 4 for 21 from his 10 overs and 44-year-old John Traicos allowing only 16 runs off his 10 overs of off-spinners. Sri Lanka's victories over Zimbabwe and South Africa, followed by their defeat of England in 1993 in a home Test, undoubtedly helped their successful application for full membership of ICC.

The limited-over dodge has become far more attractive to administrations eager to exploit anniversaries than five-day Tests. The returns are invariably higher, the weather is a lesser hazard than Tests, which on a one-off basis are difficult to promote. The 1977 Centenary Test was an astonishing success but attempts to repeat it with a Centenary Test at Lord's in 1980 and a Bicentenary Test in Sydney in 1988 fell flat. Big-money sponsors are far more interested in a tournament that brings all the cricket nations together for a month in World Cups.

India demonstrated this in 1989, staging the Nehru Cup to celebrate the birth of India's first Prime Minister and bringing together all the cricket nations, except New Zealand, for a 50-over competition. Unhappily, Indians saw it as an event designed to assist Nehru's grandson, Ranjiv Gandhi, in a forthcoming election and stayed away. Australia failed to reach the semi-finals after defeats by England, Pakistan and India, but took satisfaction from their 99-run defeat of the West Indies, who reached the final, only to go down to Pakistan by four wickets, Wasim Akram swinging the second last ball for six.

New Zealand celebrated her centenary in 1995 with a 10-day limited over tournament involving India, South Africa, Australia and the home team. Australia won the final by six wickets, restricting New Zealand to 137 runs in 50 overs, and scoring the required 138 runs in only 31.1 overs. Tim May won his first ever man-of-the-match award by taking 3–19 off ten overs of off-spin.

Limited-over cricket also enabled the wealthy Arab businessman Abdulrahaman Bukhatir to regularly stage a tournament for leading nations in the middle of the Great Arabian Desert, on the outskirts of the city of Sharjah. Promoting Test cricket in such a location should have been unthinkable but all of the most successful cricket countries have been happy to send their elite players there for an all-expenses-paid fortnight of 50-over matches. Australia first sent a team to Sharjah in 1984–85 to play against teams from England, India and Pakistan, and found that despite the remoteness of the location, the stadium was full for all their four matches and the play was fully televised in Dubai, with recorded highlights relayed to India and Pakistan.

Sharjah in the United Arab Emirates is limited-over cricket's Holy Grail, a cricket venue where sand was removed and replaced by soil carried in by hundreds of lorries. When they filled in the hole, they rolled a turf wicket into the centre, which suffers only from the staff's tendency to over-water it. It's a pitch on which spinners and seamers can extract life. Australia returned in 1986, 1987, 1989, 1990 and 1994, when Mark Taylor led a young side in which Michael Bevan made his international debut, but since then their programs have not been able to fit Sharjah into the top players' schedules. England has encountered the same problem and has twice declined invitations to play in Sharjah in the 1990s because of other tour commitments.

The Australian team that competed in the Nehru Cup in India in 1989: *standing* E.L. Alcott (physio), M.A. Taylor, T.B.A. May, S.P. O'Donnell, T.M. Moody, M.G. Hughes, G.F. Lawson, T.M. Alderman, R.B. Simpson (coach); *seated* P.L. Taylor, D.M. Jones, D.C. Boon, A.R. Border (capt.), A.B. Crompton (manager), G.E.R. Marsh, S.R. Waugh, I.A. Healy; *inset* G.R.J. Matthews.

CHAPTER SEVENTEEN

THE GREATEST TRIP

Of all the overseas trips available to Australian sports heroes, the tour of England by our Test cricketers is by far the best. The cricketers enjoy four months of competition on some idyllic fields, interspersed by visits to intriguing cities, lavish lunches and dinners, meetings with celebrities, the chance to go to bigtime golf, Wimbledon, and hit stage shows. Olympians and football teams are confined to one region and are whisked in and then off home after their events. I have been with them all and found nothing to compare with the England tour by our cricketers.

Touring England has changed, of course, since the first Australian cricketers carried their own cricket bags from match to match. Journeys to matches in lurching horse-drawn coaches and long rides in steam trains have long since gone. No tourist should complain of travel-fatigue once they reach England. Facilities in hotels and at the major grounds have vastly improved, although the uninformative scoreboards remain.

Allan Border led the 32nd Australian team to England in 1993, on a six-Test tour that included matches against 16 counties and a game against Combined Oxford and Cambridge Universities. This time they had a representative from their brewery-sponsors on hand to support their manager, coach and masseur. Unlike early Australian tourists they played teams that were not divided into amateurs and professionals and forced to use their own gates to get on to the field. Their tour pay of at least $70,000 a man plus awards (compared with the $38,000 paid to players on the previous tour in 1989) allowed them to concentrate on cricket without any worries about finding money to send home to their families, pay mortgages, or even about losing their jobs. The Australian Cricket Board paid half their tour pay, sponsors Castlemaine-Perkins (Four X) the rest.

AUSTRALIA IN ENGLAND 1948

First-class Results					All Matches				
Matches	Won	Lost	Drawn	Tied	Matches	Won	Lost	Drawn	Tied
31	23	–	8	–	34	25	–	9	–

Date	Venue	Opponent	Results for Australians
Apr 28	Worcester	Worcestershire	Won by an inns & 17 runs
May 1	Leicester	Leicestershire	Won by an inns & 171 runs
May 5	Bradford	Yorkshire	Won by 4 wkts
May 8	The Oval	Surrey	Won by an inns & 296 runs
May 12	Cambridge	Cambridge University	Won by an inns & 51 runs
May 15	Southend	Essex	Won by an inns & 451 runs
May 19	Oxford	Oxford University	Won by an inns & 90 runs
May 22	Lord's	MCC	Won by an inns & 158 runs
May 26	Manchester	Lancashire	Drawn
May 29	Nottingham	Nottinghamshire	Drawn
Jun 2	Southampton	Hampshire	Won by 8 wkts
Jun 5	Hove	Sussex	Won by an inns & 325 runs
Jun 10	Nottingham	ENGLAND (1st Test)	Won by 8 wkts

Continued

The 1948 Australians in England: *standing* R.N. Harvey, D. Tallon, D. Ring, I.W. Johnson, R. Lindwall, R. Saggers, W.A. Johnston, S.J.E. Loxton, K.R. Miller, E.R. Toshack; *seated* A.R. Morris, C.L. McCool, A.L. Hassett, D.G. Bradman (capt.), W.A. Brown, S.G. Barnes, R.A. Hamence.

Date	Venue	Opponent	Results for Australians
Jun 16	Northampton	Northamptonshire	Won by an inns & 64 runs
Jun 19	Sheffield	Yorkshire	Drawn
Jun 24	Lord's	ENGLAND (2nd Test)	Won by 409 runs
Jun 30	The Oval	Surrey	Won by 10 wkts
Jly 3	Bristol	Gloucestershire	Won by an inns & 363 runs
Jly 8	Manchester	ENGLAND (3rd Test)	Drawn
Jly 17	Lord's	Middlesex	Won by 10 wkts
Jly 22	Leeds	ENGLAND (4th Test)	Won by 7 wkts
Jly 28	Derby	Derbyshire	Won by an inns & 34 runs
Jly 31	Swansea	Glamorgan	Drawn
Aug 4	Birmingham	Warwickshire	Won by 9 wkts
Aug 7	Manchester	Lancashire	Drawn
Aug 11	Sunderland	*Durham	Drawn
Aug 14	The Oval	ENGLAND (5th Test)	Won by an inns & 149 runs
Aug 21	Canterbury	Kent	Won by an inns & 186 runs
Aug 25	Lord's	Gentlemen of England	Won by an inns & 81 runs
Aug 28	Taunton	Somerset	Won by an inns & 374 runs
Sep 1	Hastings	South of England	Drawn
Sep 8	Scarborough	Leverson–Gower's XI	Drawn
Sep 13	Edinburgh	*Scotland	Won by an inns & 40 runs
Sep 17	Aberdeen	*Scotland	Won by an inns & 87 runs

Player	State	M	Inn	NO	Runs	HS	50	100	Avrge	Ct/St	Overs	Mdns	Runs	Wkts	Avrge	5wi	10wm	Best
Barnes, SG	NSW	21	27	3	1354	176	8	3	56.41	19	65.4	26	121	2	60.50	–	–	1/11
Bradman, DG (Capt)	SA	23	31	4	2428	187	8	11	89.92	11	1.0	–	2	–	–	–	–	–
Brown, WA	QLD	22	26	1	1448	200	1	8	57.92	16	3.1	–	16	4	4.00	–	–	4/16
Hamence, RA	SA	19	22	4	582	99	2	–	32.33	9	56.3	13	150	7	21.42	–	–	2/13
Harvey, RN	VIC	22	27	6	1129	126	5	4	53.76	17	10.0	3	29	1	29.00	–	–	1/15
Hassett, AL	VIC	22	27	6	1563	200*	4	7	74.42	23	12.0	–	48	–	–	–	–	–
Johnson, IW	VIC	22	22	4	543	113*	2	1	30.16	23	668.0	228	1562	85	18.37	5	1	7/42
Johnston, WA	VIC	21	18	8	188	29	–	–	18.80	11	850.1	278	1675	102	16.42	6	2	7/81
Lindwall, RR	NSW	22	20	3	411	77	2	–	24.17	14	573.4	139	1349	86	15.68	6	1	6/14
Loxton, SJE	VIC	22	22	5	973	159*	5	3	57.23	13	361.2	92	695	32	21.71	–	–	1/11
McCool, CL	QLD	17	18	3	306	76	3	–	20.40	21	399.4	98	1016	57	17.82	3	–	7/78
Miller, KR	NSW	22	26	3	1088	202*	8	2	47.30	20	429.4	117	985	56	17.58	3	–	6/42
Morris, AR	NSW	21	29	2	1922	290	7	7	71.18	10	35.0	9	91	2	45.50	–	–	1/6
Ring, DT	VIC	19	14	5	150	53	1	–	16.66	12	542.4	155	1309	60	21.81	3	–	5/45
Saggers, RA	NSW	17	12	3	209	104*	–	1	23.22	23/20	–	–	–	–	–	–	–	–
Tallon, D	QLD	14	13	2	283	53	2	–	25.72	29/14	–	–	–	–	–	–	–	–
Toshack, ERH	NSW	15	12	3	78	20*	–	–	8.66	2	502.0	173	1056	50	21.12	4	–	7/81

On the centenary of W.G. Grace's birth the claim that Bradman could be compared with the greatest English cricketers was confirmed when, on his fourth visit to England, he led Australia on an undefeated 34-match tour. His side deservedly ranks among the best Australia has ever assembled. Ten of the 17 players scored centuries, and they accumulated 47 centuries in all. They had only seven centuries scored against them. Seven players made more than 1000 runs and Sam Loxton was just short on 973 after breaking his nose in the last match. Bradman led this scoring orgy with 11 centuries, although his health no longer allowed him to go on to double and triple centuries, and for the fourth time he scored more than 2000 tour runs, this time averaging 89.92. His only disappointment was his dismissal for a duck in his final Test innings when four runs or a not out score would have kept his Test average above 100.

The Australian bowlers dismissed their opponents for under 200 thirty-four times, and for under 100 eight times. Apart from the Tests, no opposing side made 300 against them. They declared at 7 for 774 against Gloucestershire (Morris 290, Loxton 159 not out) to win by 363 runs. They scored 721 runs at Southend in six hours against Essex, a record for a day's play in first-class cricket, and then dismissed Essex twice in a day to win by an innings and 451 runs. Every player in the team thoroughly enjoyed himself and their behaviour set standards seldom matched by all the teams that have followed. *Wisden*'s Reg Hayter calculated that Australia scored 15,120 runs on the tour for the loss of 304 wickets in their first-class matches, at an average of just under 50 runs per wicket, maintaining a fast scoring rate throughout.

Not all their matches were one-sided but when in trouble they showed an ability to fight their way out. At Bradford in their third match 35 wickets fell on a wet pitch. They lost 6 for 31 chasing 60 to win against Yorkshire with Loxton unable to bat through injury, before Tallon and Harvey formed a winning partnership, Harvey hitting a huge six to clinch the match. The Third Test was drawn after Bradman and Morris batted for 100 minutes without changing ends, aware that England's 310-run lead was beyond Australia's reach, Bradman confounding critics, who claimed he could not bat on wet wickets, with his skill. At Leeds in the Fourth Test, they had to overcome opening stands of 168 and 129 by Hutton and Washbrook and then score 404 in 345 minutes to win, a feat they achieved with 15 minutes to spare on a difficult pitch that took spin and lifted. In scoring these runs to retain The Ashes England had last won in 1932–33, the Australian batsmen took guard in holes worn so deep the toes of their boots disappeared from view.

AUSTRALIA IN ENGLAND 1953

First-class Results					All Matches				
Matches	Won	Lost	Drawn	Tied	Matches	Won	Lost	Drawn	Tied
33	16	1	16	–	35	16	1	18	–

Date	Venue	Opponent	Results for Australians
Apr 29	Worcester	Worcestershire	Drawn
May 2	Leicester	Leicestershire	Won by an inns & 154 runs
May 6	Bradford	Yorkshire	Won by an inns & 94 runs
May 9	The Oval	Surrey	Won by an inns & 76 runs
May 13	Cambridge	Cambridge University	Won by an inns & 106 runs
May 16	Lord's	MCC	Drawn
May 20	Oxford	Oxford University	Won by an inns & 86 runs
May 23	Stoke-on-Trent	Minor Counties	Won by an inns & 171 runs
May 27	Manchester	Lancashire	Drawn
May 30	Nottingham	Nottinghamshire	Drawn
Jun 3	Hove	Sussex	Drawn
Jun 6	Southampton	Hampshire	Won by 158 runs
Jun 11	Nottingham	ENGLAND (1st Test)	Drawn
Jun 17	Chesterfield	Derbyshire	Drawn
Jun 20	Sheffield	Yorkshire	Drawn
Jun 25	Lord's	ENGLAND (2nd Test)	Drawn
Jly 1	Bristol	Gloucestershire	Won by 9 wkts
Jly 4	Northampton	Northamptonshire	Won by an inns & 62 runs
Jly 9	Manchester	ENGLAND (3rd Test)	Drawn
Jly 18	Lord's	Middlesex	Drawn
Jly 23	Leeds	ENGLAND (4th Test)	Drawn
Jly 29	The Oval	Surrey	Drawn
Aug 1	Swansea	Glamorgan	Drawn
Aug 5	Birmingham	Warwickshire	Drawn
Aug 8	Manchester	Lancashire	Won by 7 wkts
Aug 12	Southend	Essex	Won by an inns & 212 runs
Aug 15	The Oval	ENGLAND (5th Test)	Lost by 8 wkts
Aug 22	Taunton	Somerset	Drawn
Aug 26	Lord's	Gentlemen of England	Won by 8 wkts
Aug 29	Canterbury	Kent	Won by an inns & 176 runs
Sep 2	Hastings	South of England	Won by an inns & 163 runs
Sep 5	Kingston	Combined Services	Won by an inns & 261 runs
Sep 9	Scarborough	England XI	Won by 2 wkts
Sep 15	Paisley	*Scotland	Drawn
Sep 18	Edinburgh	*Scotland	Drawn

Player	State	M	Inn	NO	Runs	HS	50	100	Avrge	Ct/St	Overs	Mdns	Runs	Wkts	Avrge	5wi	10wm	Best
Archer, RG	QLD	20	25	8	627	108	2	1	36.88	17	395.1	104	955	57	16.75	3	1	7/56
Benaud, R	NSW	22	28	1	748	135	4	1	27.70	18	444.0	103	1273	57	22.33	2	–	7/46
Craig, ID	NSW	23	27	1	429	71*	2	–	16.50	18	4.0	–	23	–	–	–	–	–
Davidson, AK	NSW	23	30	7	944	104*	6	1	41.04	28	506.4	153	1048	50	20.96	–	–	3/10
De Courcy, JH	NSW	24	31	2	1214	204	5	4	41.86	13	4.0	–	28	–	–	–	–	–
Harvey, RN	VIC	25	35	4	2040	202*	5	10	65.80	13	25.0	8	51	4	12.75	–	–	3/9
Hassett, AL (Capt)	VIC	21	30	2	1236	148	6	5	44.14	8	22.0	2	76	3	25.33	–	–	2/24
Hill, JC	VIC	22	19	8	220	51*	1	–	20.00	16	614.5	223	1322	63	20.98	2	–	6/34
Hole, GB	SA	24	33	–	1118	112	8	1	33.87	23	100.0	38	209	4	51.75	–	–	2/3
Johnston, WA	VIC	16	17	16	102	28*	–	–	102.00	6	647.0	206	1541	75	20.54	6	1	6/38
Langley, GRA	SA	18	19	3	273	46	–	–	17.06	34/12	–	–	–	–	–	–	–	–
Lindwall, RR	NSW	23	25	1	400	62	2	–	16.66	12	639.1	179	1394	85	16.40	5	–	5/54
McDonald, CC	VIC	19	24	1	717	125	3	2	31.17	6	–	–	–	–	–	–	–	–
Miller, KR	NSW	24	31	3	1433	262*	5	4	51.17	9	492.2	161	1013	45	22.51	–	–	4/47
Morris, AR	NSW	25	37	3	1302	126*	11	1	38.29	9	6.5	–	30	1	30.00	–	–	1/5
Ring, DT	VIC	19	20	4	252	88	1	–	15.75	10	541.2	162	1353	68	19.89	5	–	5/19
Tallon, D	QLD	15	16	2	169	83*	1	–	12.07	21/6	7.0	3	28	–	–	–	–	–

Hassett's main bowlers were prone to injury and lacked the hostility showed in 1948, but they still had a great chance to retain The Ashes which Australia had held for 19 years. They won 16 of their 35 matches, drew 18, and lost only one, the Fifth Test. They played cricket of great crowd appeal and took home a record profit of more than £100,000 sterling, £55,000 of it from the Tests. In one match, the Second Test at Lord's, the receipt of £57,000 surpassed those of any previous cricket match anywhere in the world. They made 30 centuries—spread among ten of the 17 players—but for the first time in half a century not a single Australian batsman averaged more than 50 in Tests. Only seven centuries were scored against them on the entire tour.

The turning point of the tour came in the Second Test at Lord's when England required 343 to win. Lindwall, still a great bowler, dismissed Hutton and Kenyon, Johnston had Graveney brilliantly caught by Langley to leave England on 3 for 12 with a day to play. Watson, who had been dropped off Ring just before stumps on that score, batted most of the last day to save the match. Compton stayed with him for 95 minutes and then Bailey, last of England's recognised batsmen, stayed for five hours, playing the dead-bat pendulum stroke to every delivery on the stumps. England had no chance of scoring the runs needed but Bailey and Watson slowly extracted the sparkle from Australia's bowling and set up a famous draw. Draws in the Third and Fourth Tests took the teams to the final Test with the deadlock unbroken. There was no complaint from the Australians but Lock's action was decidedly suspect in taking 5 for 45 to bundle Australia out for 162 in their second innings. This left England 132 runs to win and Edrich and Compton steered them home. Hassett was only the second Australian captain (Noble in 1909 was the first) to win every toss in a Test series.

The 1953 Australians in England: *back row* R. Lindwall, A.K. Davidson, D. Ring, J. Hill, G.R. Langley; *centre* G. Hole, R. Archer, W.A. Johnston, K.R. Miller, R. Benaud, D. Tallon; *seated* I.R. Craig, J.H. de Courcy, A.L. Hassett (capt.), G. Davies (manager), A.R. Morris, R.N. Harvey, C. McDonald.

AUSTRALIA IN ENGLAND 1956

Matches	First-class Results Won	Lost	Drawn	Tied	Matches	All Matches Won	Lost	Drawn	Tied
31	9	3	19	–	35	12	3	20	–

Date	Venue	Opponent	Results for Australians
Apr 28	Arundel Castle	*Duke of Norfolk's XI	Won by 3 wkts
May 2	Worcester	Worcestershire	Drawn
May 5	Leicester	Leicestershire	Drawn
May 9	Bradford	Yorkshire	Drawn
May 12	Nottingham	Nottinghamshire	Drawn
May 16	The Oval	Surrey	Lost by 10 wkts
May 19	Cambridge	Cambridge University	Won by 10 wkts
May 23	Manchester	Lancashire	Drawn
May 26	Lord's	MCC	Drawn
May 30	Oxford	Oxford University	Won by 8 wkts
Jun 2	Hove	Sussex	Drawn
Jun 7	Nottingham	ENGLAND (1st Test)	Drawn
Jun 13	Northampton	Northamptonshire	Drawn
Jun 16	Canterbury	Kent	Drawn
Jun 21	Lord's	ENGLAND (2nd Test)	Won by 185 runs
Jun 27	Sheffield	Yorkshire	Drawn
Jun 30	Bristol	Gloucestershire	Won by an inns & 48 runs
Jly 4	Taunton	Somerset	Drawn
Jly 7	Southampton	Hampshire	Drawn
Jly 12	Leeds	ENGLAND (3rd Test)	Lost by an inns & 42 runs
Jly 21	Lord's	Middlesex	Drawn
Jly 26	Manchester	ENGLAND (4th Test)	Lost by an inns & 170 runs
Aug 1	The Oval	Surrey	Drawn
Aug 4	Swansea	Glamorgan	Won by an inns & 11 runs
Aug 8	Birmingham	Warwickshire	Won by an inns & 127 runs
Aug 11	Derby	Derbyshire	Won by 57 runs
Aug 15	Manchester	Lancashire	Drawn
Aug 18	Southend	Essex	Won by an inns & 12 runs
Aug 23	The Oval	ENGLAND (5th Test)	Drawn
Aug 29	Lord's	Gentlemen of England	Drawn
Sep 1	Hastings	England XI	Drawn
Sep 5	Scarborough	TN Pearce's XI	Won by 5 wkts
Sep 8	Newcastle	*Minor Counties	Won by 7 wkts
Sep 12	Glasgow	*Scotland	Drawn
Sep 14	Aberdeen	*Scotland	Won by an inns & 126 runs

Player	State	M	Inn	NO	Runs	HS	50	100	Avrge	Ct/St	Overs	Mdns	Runs	Wkts	Avrge	5wi	10wm	Best
Archer, RG	QLD	22	25	4	649	148	4	1	30.90	29	584.4	179	1353	61	22.18	2	–	6/98
Benaud, R	NSW	23	29	4	871	160	5	1	34.84	16	584.5	182	1337	60	22.28	3	1	6/31
Burge, PJP	QLD	22	26	4	780	131	5	1	35.45	12	2.0	1	2	–	–	–	–	–
Burke, JW	NSW	21	35	7	1339	194	5	4	47.82	5	81.0	34	181	6	30.16	–	–	3/5
Craig, ID	NSW	20	29	5	872	100*	8	1	36.33	8	4.0	1	14	1	14.00	–	–	1/3
Crawford, WPA	NSW	18	15	7	101	19	–	–	12.62	8	343.2	80	836	31	26.96	–	–	4/28
Davidson, AK	NSW	15	13	3	270	75	2	–	27.00	14	238.5	79	585	26	22.50	–	–	4/39
Harvey, RN	VIC	23	32	1	976	225	5	2	31.48	12	6.0	2	24	1	24.00	–	–	1/24
Johnson, IW (Capt)	VIC	23	20	2	193	44	–	–	10.72	4	531.3	162	1348	50	27.16	2	–	6/168
Langley, GRA	SA	16	13	8	112	41	–	–	22.40	37/9	2.0	1	2	–	–	–	–	–
Lindwall, RR	QLD	17	18	6	260	116*	–	1	21.66	6	413.3	119	924	47	19.65	1	–	7/40
Mackay, KD	QLD	20	28	7	1103	163*	7	3	52.52	5	132.0	42	268	8	29.77	–	–	2/32
Maddocks, LV	VIC	17	17	3	201	56	1	–	14.35	31/13	3.0	–	4	1	4.00	–	–	1/4
McDonald, CC	VIC	23	35	–	1202	195	6	2	34.34	4	2.0	–	12	–	–	–	–	–
Miller, KR	NSW	20	29	6	843	281*	4	1	36.65	13	430.0	97	980	50	19.60	4	1	5/29
Rutherford, JW	WA	22	33	5	640	98	3	–	22.85	18	40.0	9	152	3	50.66	–	–	2/29
Wilson, JW	SA	19	11	3	23	8*	–	–	2.87	3	402.4	151	992	43	23.06	3	1	7/40

After sweeping through the Caribbean with a series of fine displays against the West Indies, Australia were expected to triumph against an England team restricted by the old-fashioned adherence to amateur captains. Peter May, a fine cricketer, led England in all five Tests, but lacked the firepower Ian Johnson had at his disposal and the experience of professionals like Washbrook. The English curators levelled things up by preparing pitches ideal for spinners Laker and Lock and the wettest English summer in years destroyed the Australians' confidence.

Jim Laker claimed 63 wickets in the seven matches he had against Australia, including a world record 19 wickets in the Fourth Test at Manchester. Well equipped to face pace from the likes of Statham and Tyson, the Australians floundered on pitches which day after day helped the spinners. All who mixed with the Australians soon realised the tremendous spirit of the 1948 and 1953 sides was missing. Too many leading players failed to give Johnson—the man Sid Barnes called 'Australia's non-playing captain'—their support. The Australians fielded well and in Langley and Maddocks they had very efficient keepers, but the young Englishmen, Cowdrey, May and Sheppard, outplayed the Australian newcomers. Ian Craig had a better tour than in 1953 and Benaud at last started to justify the selectors' faith in him, but only three batsmen, Burke, Mackay and McDonald, completed 1000 runs. England's two–one success was her third successive series win over Australia, who also lost to Surrey, the first county in 44 years to defeat Australia, a result Johnson greeted by presenting Surrey captain Stuart Surridge with his cap.

The 1956 Australians in England: *back row* J.W. Wilson, K.D. Mackay, A.K. Davidson, P.J.P. Burge, W.P.A. Crawford, R. Benaud, R. Archer, R.N. Harvey; *middle* G.R.A. Langley, K.R. Miller, I.W. Johnson (capt.), R.R. Lindwall, C.C. McDonald, J.W. Burke; *front* I.D. Craig, L.V. Maddocks, J.W. Rutherford.

AUSTRALIA IN ENGLAND 1961

First-class Results					All Matches				
Matches	Won	Lost	Drawn	Tied	Matches	Won	Lost	Drawn	Tied
32	13	1	18	–	37	14	2	21	–

Date	Venue	Opponent	Results for Australians
Apr 29	Worcester	Worcestershire	Drawn
May 3	Chesterfield	Derbyshire	Drawn
May 6	Bradford	Yorkshire	Drawn
May 10	Manchester	Lancashire	Won by 4 wkts
May 13	The Oval	Surrey	Won by 10 wkts
May 17	Cambridge	Cambridge University	Won by 9 wkts
May 20	Cardiff	Glamorgan	Drawn
May 24	Bristol	Gloucestershire	Drawn
May 27	Lord's	MCC	Won by 63 runs
May 31	Oxford	Oxford University	Drawn
Jun 3	Hove	Sussex	Drawn
Jun 8	Birmingham	ENGLAND (1st Test)	Drawn
Jun 14	Leicester	Leicestershire	Won by 10 wkts
Jun 17	Canterbury	Kent	Drawn
Jun 22	Lord's	ENGLAND (2nd Test)	Won by 5 wkts
Jun 28	Taunton	Somerset	Drawn
Jly 1	Manchester	Lancashire	Drawn
Jly 6	Leeds	ENGLAND (3rd Test)	Lost by 8 wkts
Jly 13	Blackheath	*Club Cricket Conference	Lost by 8 wkts
Jly 15	Nottingham	Nottinghamshire	Drawn
Jly 19	Northampton	Northamptonshire	Drawn
Jly 22	Lord's	Middlesex	Won by 10 wkts
Jly 27	Manchester	ENGLAND (4th Test)	Won by 54 runs
Aug 2	The Oval	Surrey	Won by 255 runs
Aug 5	Swansea	Glamorgan	Drawn
Aug 9	Birmingham	Warwickshire	Drawn
Aug 12	Sheffield	Yorkshire	Drawn
Aug 17	The Oval	ENGLAND (5th Test)	Drawn
Aug 23	Southend	Essex	Won by 55 runs
Aug 26	Southampton	Hampshire	Won by 5 wkts
Aug 30	Lord's	Gentlemen of England	Drawn
Sep 2	Hastings	England XI	Won by 3 wkts
Sep 6	Scarborough	TN Pearce's XI	Won by 3 wkts
Sep 9	Jesmond	*Minor Counties	Drawn
Sep 12	Edinburgh	*Scotland	Drawn
Sep 15	Belfast	*Ireland	Drawn
Sep 18	Dublin	*Ireland	Won by 282 runs

Player	State	M	Inn	NO	Runs	HS	50	100	Avrge	Ct/St	Overs	Mdns	Runs	Wkts	Avrge	5wi	10wm	Best
Benaud, R (Capt)	NSW	22	32	7	627	80*	3	–	25.08	18	575.5	193	1436	61	23.54	5	–	6/70
Booth, BC	NSW	23	32	3	1279	127*	8	2	44.10	17	12.0	1	37	–	–	–	–	–
Burge, PJP	QLD	24	36	11	1376	181	3	4	55.04	16	3.0	1	13	–	–	–	–	–
Davidson, AK	NSW	20	25	5	607	90	5	–	30.35	15	634.2	182	1517	68	22.30	5	–	6/46
Gaunt, RA	VIC	17	12	6	77	30	–	–	12.83	5	360.2	97	845	40	21.12	1	–	6/50
Grout, ATW	QLD	17	21	3	299	49	–	–	16.61	51/9	–	–	–	–	–	–	–	–
Harvey, RN	NSW	24	35	2	1452	140	5	5	44.00	25	53.3	21	93	4	23.25	–	–	4/8
Jarman, BN	SA	15	14	5	354	85	2	–	39.33	29/14	–	–	–	–	–	–	–	–
Kline, LF	VIC	19	12	2	68	22*	–	–	6.80	12	539.4	168	1519	54	28.12	2	–	5/16
Lawry, WM	VIC	23	39	6	2019	165	7	9	61.18	15	7.0	2	33	1	33.00	–	–	1/24
Mackay, KD	QLD	21	25	3	683	168	3	2	31.04	10	667.2	206	1479	52	28.44	1	–	5/121
McDonald, CC	VIC	17	26	7	913	140	1	4	48.05	2	3.0	–	14	–	–	–	–	–
McKenzie, GD	WA	21	26	8	254	48	–	–	14.11	8	569.2	156	1547	54	28.64	3	–	5/29
Misson, FM	NSW	19	15	3	194	33	–	–	16.16	20	479.3	123	1287	51	25.23	1	–	6/75
O'Neill, NC	NSW	24	37	4	1981	162	11	7	60.03	20	80.5	18	269	6	44.83	–	–	2/44
Quick, IW	VIC	20	18	9	108	18	–	–	12.00	8	541.2	172	1700	50	34.00	–	–	4/107
Simpson, RB	WA	26	44	6	1947	160	8	6	51.23	23	539.4	163	1707	51	33.47	–	–	4/13

Australia retained The Ashes, won amid controversy from Peter May's team in 1958–59, thanks to thrilling victories at Lord's in the 'Battle of The Ridge', and at Manchester, where they recovered from the brink of defeat. These outstanding triumphs were a personal boost for Richie Benaud and completed the turn-around in a career that appeared to be floundering four years earlier. By the end of the tour, his eagerness to fulfill his promise to play attractive cricket made him the most popular Australian captain of modern times. Benaud reached this exalted status despite an inflamed tendon in his right shoulder, which prevented him bowling with any freedom, and the interference of team-manager Syd Webb to stop Benaud speaking freely to fellow journalists.

Australia took a series lead in the Second Test at Lord's, after a drawn First Test, when Bill Lawry batted coolly for six hours on a pitch players claimed had a pronounced ridge in it. Lawry soaked up frequent bruising blows from Statham and Trueman to score 130 and give Australia a 134-run first innings lead. Misson and Davidson then had their turn in dealing out punishment and Grout's brilliant catch to get rid of May off another rising ball clinched victory. Experts armed with theodolites and other gear took charge of the pitch immediately Australia scored the winning runs on a still lively strip.

England won the Third Test at Leeds when Trueman took 5 for 58 and 6 for 30, and appeared to hold a winning advantage three times in the Fourth Test at Old Trafford. On the last day Australia were only 157 runs ahead when last man McKenzie joined Davidson. Davidson hit out defiantly and forced May to take off

The 1961 Australians in England: *back row* B.C. Booth, W.M. Lawry, F.M. Misson, R.A. Gaunt, G.D. McKenzie; *middle* masseur, scorer, B.N. Jarman, I.W. Quick, R. Steele (treasurer), L.F. Kline, N.C. O'Neill, P.J.P. Burge, R.B. Simpson; *front* A.T.W. Grout, A.K. Davidson, R. Benaud (capt.), S.G. Webb (manager), R.N. Harvey, C.C. McDonald, K.D. Mackay.

danger man David Allen by hitting 20 from an Allen over. Davidson went on to a dazzling 77 not out and when Flavell bowled McKenzie for 32, they had put on 98 for the last wicket and deprived England of valuable time. Set to score 256 runs in 210 minutes, England seemed in command when Dexter made 76 in 84 minutes. By bowling round the wicket into Trueman's footmarks, Benaud transformed the match by dismissing Dexter, May, Close and Subba Row and gave Australia their first win at Old Trafford since 1902. The ball with which he bowled May around his legs for a duck swung a marvellous contest Australia's way. England tried hard to level the rubber in the Fifth Test at The Oval but were thwarted by centuries from O'Neill (117) and Burge (181).

AUSTRALIA IN ENGLAND 1964

Bob Simpson lacked Benaud's cavalier approach, but he was a resourceful captain, unwilling to concede England any advantage, despite his limited bowling resources. Burge gave Australia a one-Test lead with a magnificent 160 at Leeds in the Third Test. Thereafter Simpson's skilful handling of his pace bowlers and his own stubborn batting did not give England a chance of drawing level. Simpson batted for 762 minutes in scoring 311, his maiden Test century, in the Fourth Test at Manchester to kill off any likely England challenge. Rain prevented any English hopes that remained in the Fifth Test. Seven Australians made 1000 runs during the tour in which they hit 25 centuries and had 18 scored against them. Lack of a hostile bowler of Davidson's class who could partner McKenzie restricted Australia to 11 wins, and accounted for their three losses and 16 draws. Simpson was forced to give slow bowlers Cowper, Martin and Veivers a lot of work and bowled a lot himself.

First-class Results					All Matches				
Matches	Won	Lost	Drawn	Tied	Matches	Won	Lost	Drawn	Tied
30	11	3	16	–	36	14	4	18	–

Date	Venue	Opponent	Results for Australians
Apr 25	Arundel Castle	*Duke of Norfolk's XI	Won by 4 wkts
Apr 29	Worcester	Worcestershire	Drawn
May 2	Bristol	Gloucestershire	Won by 10 wkts
May 6	Taunton	Somerset	Won by 172 runs
May 9	The Oval	Surrey	Drawn
May 13	Nottingham	Nottinghamshire	Drawn
May 16	Cardiff	Glamorgan	Drawn
May 20	Cambridge	Cambridge University	Drawn
May 23	Lord's	MCC	Won by 9 wkts
May 27	Oxford	Oxford University	Won by an inns & 120 runs
May 30	Manchester	Lancashire	Drawn
Jun 4	Nottingham	ENGLAND (1st Test)	Drawn
Jun 10	Derby	Derbyshire	Drawn
Jun 13	Sheffield	Yorkshire	Drawn
Jun 18	Lord's	ENGLAND (2nd Test)	Drawn
Jun 25	Bedford	*Minor Counties	Won by an inns & 26 runs
Jun 27	Northampton	Northamptonshire	Won by 10 wkts
Jly 2	Leeds	ENGLAND (3rd Test)	Won by 7 wkts
Jly 8	Leicester	Leicestershire	Drawn
Jly 11	Southampton	Hampshire	Drawn
Jly 15	Hove	Sussex	Won by 63 runs
Jly 18	Lord's	Middlesex	Drawn
Jly 23	Manchester	ENGLAND (4th Test)	Drawn
Aug 1	Swansea	Glamorgan	Lost by 36 runs
Aug 5	Birmingham	Warwickshire	Lost by 9 runs
Aug 8	Bradford	Yorkshire	Won by 81 runs
Aug 13	The Oval	ENGLAND (5th Test)	Drawn
Aug 19	Lord's	President MCC XI	Drawn
Aug 22	Southend	Essex	Lost by 6 wkts
Aug 26	Canterbury	Kent	Won by 8 wkts
Aug 29	The Hague	*Holland	Lost by 3 wkts
Sep 2	Hastings	AER Gilligan's XI	Won by 2 wkts
Sep 5	Scarborough	TN Pearce's XI	Won by 7 wkts
Sep 9	Titwood	*Scotland	Drawn
Sep 11	Aberdeen	*Scotland	Drawn
Sep 14	Hove	*Sussex	Won by 66 runs

The 1964 Australians in England: *back row* A.E. James (masseur), N.J.N. Hawke, G.E. Corling, J.W. Martin, R.M. Cowper, A.N. Connolly, D. Sherwood (scorer); *centre* R.H.D. Sellers, T.R. Veivers, J. Potter, J. Ledward (treasurer), G.D. McKenzie, I.R. Redpath, B.N. Jarman; *front* P.J.P. Burge, N.C. O'Neill, R.B. Simpson (capt.), R.O. Steele (manager), B.C. Booth, W.M. Lawry, A.T.W. Grout.

Player	State	M	Inn	NO	Runs	HS	50	100	Avrge	Ct/St	Overs	Mdns	Runs	Wkts	Avrge	5wi	10wm	Best
Booth, BC	NSW	23	36	8	1551	193*	10	3	55.39	12	24.3	4	106	1	106.80	–	–	1/9
Burge, PJP	QLD	23	34	4	1114	160	6	2	37.13	18/1	2.0	–	17	–	–	–	–	–
Connolly, AN	VIC	15	10	6	27	14	–	–	6.75	9	323.5	74	850	28	30.35	–	–	4/29
Corling, GE	NSW	19	13	6	43	6	–	–	6.14	3	575.2	140	1381	44	31.28	1	–	5/59
Cowper, RM	VIC	20	29	4	1287	113	9	3	51.48	25	222.2	59	713	23	31.00	–	–	4/58
Grout, ATW	QLD	18	20	2	303	53	1	–	16.83	34/9	2.0	–	22	1	22.00	–	–	1/22
Hawke, NJN	SA	22	16	6	159	37	–	–	15.90	12	742.0	211	1644	83	19.80	6	–	6/19
Jarman, BN	SA	12	17	2	417	105	1	1	27.80	26/3	3.0	–	7	–	–	–	–	–
Lawry, WM	VIC	24	41	3	1601	121	10	5	42.13	11	6.0	–	32	–	–	–	–	–
Martin, JW	NSW	16	23	4	361	70	1	–	19.00	4	361.1	86	1134	35	32.40	–	–	4/50
McKenzie, GD	WA	22	25	7	290	50	1	–	16.11	14	838.1	217	1976	88	22.45	3	–	7/153
O'Neill, NC	NSW	20	34	4	1369	151	7	4	45.63	10	108.0	21	356	6	59.33	–	–	2/31
Potter, J	VIC	17	27	4	751	78	6	–	31.29	9	140.0	27	436	11	39.63	–	–	3/37
Redpath, IR	VIC	22	37	4	1075	162	4	2	32.57	18	30.0	3	147	3	49.00	–	–	2/33
Sellers, RHD	SA	13	19	8	233	36	–	–	21.18	10	373.5	93	1128	30	37.60	1	–	5/36
Simpson, RB (Capt)	NSW	22	38	8	1714	311	10	5	57.13	36	380.5	103	1033	32	32.28	1	–	5/33
Veivers, TR	QLD	22	28	7	725	79	7	–	34.52	10	754.3	226	1881	52	36.17	1	–	5/85

AUSTRALIA IN ENGLAND 1968

	First-class Results				All Matches			
Matches	Won	Lost	Drawn	Tied	Matches	Won	Lost	Drawn	Tied
25	8	3	14	–	29	10	3	16	–

Date	Venue	Opponent	Results for Australians
May 4	Arundel Castle	*Duke of Norfolk's XI	Drawn
May 8	Worcester	Worcestershire	Abandoned
May 11	Leicester	Leicestershire	Drawn
May 15	Manchester	Lancashire	Drawn
May 18	Lord's	MCC	Drawn
May 22	Northampton	Northamptonshire	Won by 10 wkts
May 25	Cambridge	Cambridge University	Won by 10 wkts
May 29	Taunton	Somerset	Drawn
Jun 1	The Oval	Surrey	Drawn
Jun 6	Manchester	ENGLAND (1st Test)	Won by 159 runs
Jun 12	Birmingham	Warwickshire	Drawn
Jun 15	Hove	Sussex	Won by 5 wkts
Jun 20	Lord's	ENGLAND (2nd Test)	Drawn
Jun 26	Southend	Essex	Won by an inns & 58 runs
Jun 29	Sheffield	Yorkshire	Lost by an inns & 69 runs
Jly 3	Dublin	*Ireland	Won by 6 wkts
Jly 4	Belfast	*Ireland	Won by 121 runs
Jly 6	Nottingham	Nottinghamshire	Drawn
Jly 11	Birmingham	ENGLAND (3rd Test)	Drawn
Jly 17	Bristol	Gloucestershire	Drawn
Jly 20	Lord's	Middlesex	Drawn
Jly 25	Leeds	ENGLAND (4th Test)	Drawn
Jly 31	Chesterfield	Derbyshire	Won by 8 runs
Aug 3	Swansea	Glamorgan	Lost by 79 runs
Aug 7	Torquay	*Minor Counties	Drawn
Aug 10	Southampton	Hampshire	Drawn
Aug 14	Lord's	President MCC XI	Drawn
Aug 17	Canterbury	Kent	Won by 9 wkts
Aug 22	The Oval	ENGLAND (5th Test)	Lost by 226 runs
Aug 31	Lord's	Rest of The World XI	Won by 8 wkts

The 1968 Australians in England: *back row* E.W. Freeman, A.N. Connolly, R.J. Inverarity, D.A. Renneberg, A.P. Sheahan, A.A. Mallett, J.W. Gleeson; *centre* A.E. James (masseur), H.B. Taber, K.D. Walters, I.R. Redpath, I.M. Chappell, L.R. Joslin, D. Sherwood (scorer); *front* N.J.N. Hawke, B.N. Jarman, R.K. Steele (manager), W.M. Lawry (capt.), L.E. Trueman (treasurer), G.D. McKenzie, R.M. Cowper.

Player	State	M	Inn	NO	Runs	HS	50	100	Avrge	Ct/St	Overs	Mdns	Runs	Wkts	Avrge	5wi	10wm	Best
Chappell, IM	SA	20	30	4	1261	202	7	3	48.50	20	214.1	63	529	18	29.38	–	–	4/22
Connolly, AN	VIC	15	18	8	88	22	–	–	8.80	3	553.4	188	1116	55	20.29	1	–	5/72
Cowper, RM	VIC	16	24	4	744	148	5	1	37.20	14	337.0	109	770	32	24.06	1	–	7/42
Freeman, EW	SA	13	14	–	326	116	–	1	23.28	8	289.2	62	829	31	26.74	1	–	5/78
Gleeson, JW	NSW	14	18	3	122	19	–	–	8.13	6	538.1	198	1198	58	20.65	3	–	6/97
Hawke, NJN	SA	14	18	5	267	47	–	–	20.53	11	323.1	90	729	35	20.82	1	–	6/26
Inverarity, RJ	WA	18	30	4	645	88	4	–	24.80	17	8.0	2	34	2	17.00	–	–	2/31
Jarman, BN	SA	13	19	1	184	41	–	–	10.22	21/6	–	–	–	–	–	–	–	–
Joslin, LR	VIC	13	18	2	344	61	2	–	21.50	6	–	–	–	–	–	–	–	–
Lawry, WM (Capt)	VIC	17	23	3	906	135	5	2	45.30	9	–	–	–	–	–	–	–	–
Mallett, AA	SA	13	13	6	106	43	–	–	15.14	4	428.1	115	1245	44	28.29	2	1	7/75
McKenzie, GD	WA	16	18	2	185	50	1	–	11.56	11	523.1	145	1247	40	31.17	–	–	4/25
Redpath, IR	VIC	22	37	3	1474	135	10	4	43.35	24	3.0	–	16	–	–	–	–	–
Renneberg, DA	NSW	14	12	6	27	9	–	–	4.50	3	356.5	72	1010	41	24.63	3	–	8/72
Sheahan, AP	VIC	22	32	3	817	137	2	2	28.17	17	–	–	–	–	–	–	–	–
Taber, HB	NSW	14	16	2	365	81	2	–	26.07	35/4	–	–	–	–	–	–	–	–
Walters, KD	NSW	21	32	2	933	95	8	–	31.10	13	–	–	–	–	–	–	–	–

On his third tour of England, and his first as captain, Bill Lawry was hamstrung by wet weather. From the second match against Worcestershire, the rain followed the Australians, who were prevented from showing their true merit. The wet weather cast such an alarming financial cloud over the tour that manager Bob Parish, at that time chairman of the Australian Board of Control, asked English counties to play one day of their matches against Australia on Sundays. Only Kent agreed and for the first time in England, Australia played on a Sunday on 18 August 1964 at Canterbury. Advance bookings for the last four Tests rescued tour finances.

Australia's inexperienced youngsters won only five of their 17 matches against the first-class counties and although they held on to The Ashes, they were beaten by both Yorkshire and Glamorgan. The Australian bowlers were flattered by their defeat of England by 159 runs in the First Test at Manchester where Bob Cowper's 4 for 48 from 26 overs gave Australia a first innings lead of 192. Australia retained this one-Test lead until the Fifth Test when England belatedly exerted their superiority to win by 226 runs with six minutes to spare. Ian Redpath scored four of the Australians' 13 tour centuries but Lawry's lack of sympathy with his spinners limited their value on pitches that should have been ideal for them.

AUSTRALIA IN ENGLAND 1972

Matches	First-class Results Won	Lost	Drawn	Tied	Matches	All Matches Won	Lost	Drawn	Tied
26	11	5	10	–	37	14	10	13	–

Date	Venue	Opponent	Results for Australians
Apr 22	Arundel Castle	*Duke of Norfolk's XI	Lost by 28 runs
Apr 29	Worcester	Worcestershire	Won by 6 wkts
May 3	Manchester	Lancashire	Drawn
May 8	Bradford	*Yorkshire	Drawn
May 9	Bradford	*Yorkshire	Drawn
May 10	Nottingham	Nottinghamshire	Drawn
May 13	The Oval	Surrey	Drawn
May 17	Southampton	Hampshire	Won by 9 wkts
May 20	Lord's	MCC	Won by 4 wkts
May 24	Bristol	Gloucestershire	Drawn
May 27	Swansea	Glamorgan	Drawn
May 31	Chesterfield	Derbyshire	Drawn
Jun 3	Birmingham	Warwickshire	Drawn
Jun 8	Manchester	ENGLAND (1st Test)	Lost by 89 runs
Jun 14	Oxford	Combined Universities	Won by 10 wkts
Jun 17	Ilford	Essex	Drawn
Jun 22	Lord's	ENGLAND (2nd Test)	Won by 8 wkts
Jun 29	Nottingham	*Cricketers' Association	Lost by 57 runs
Jly 1	Bath	Somerset	Drawn
Jly 5	Leicester	Leicestershire	Won by an inns & 46 runs
Jly 8	Lord's	Middlesex	Won by 5 wkts
Jly 13	Nottingham	ENGLAND (3rd Test)	Drawn
Jly 19	Stoke-on-Trent	Minor Counties	Won by an inns & 26 runs
Jly 22	Hove	Sussex	Lost by 5 wkts
Jly 23	Hove	*Sussex	Drawn
Jly 27	Leeds	ENGLAND (4th Test)	Lost by 9 wkts
Aug 2	Perth	*Scotland	Won by 6 wkts
Aug 5	Northampton	Northamptonshire	Lost by 7 wkts
Aug 10	The Oval	ENGLAND (5th Test)	Won by 5 wkts
Aug 19	Canterbury	Kent	Won by 9 wkts
Aug 24	Manchester	*England (L/O Intl)	Lost by 6 wkts
Aug 26	Lord's	*England (L/O Intl)	Won by 5 wkts
Aug 28	Birmingham	*England (L/O Intl)	Lost by 2 wkts
Aug 30	Manchester	Lancashire	Lost by 9 wkts
Sep 2	Scarborough	TN Pearce's XI	Won by 6 wkts
Sep 3	Scarborough	*TN Pearce's XI	Lost by 13 runs
Sep 5	Scarborough	*TN Pearce's XI	Won by 6 wkts

Player	State	M	Inn	NO	Runs	HS	50	100	Avrge	Ct/St	Overs	Mdns	Runs	Wkts	Avrge	5wi	10wm	Best
Chappell, GS	SA	18	28	10	1260	181	3	4	70.00	26	205.2	51	488	19	25.68	1	–	7/58
Chappell, IM (Capt)	SA	20	34	2	1017	118	6	2	31.78	19	43.5	14	106	10	10.60	–	–	3/1
Colley, DJ	NSW	16	16	3	268	58*	2	–	20.61	5	346.4	73	946	33	28.66	2	–	5/27
Edwards, R	WA	18	26	3	747	170*	3	1	32.47	9	1.2	–	15	–	–	–	–	–
Francis, BC	NSW	18	27	1	772	210	4	2	29.69	5	2.5	–	15	1	15.00	–	–	1/10
Gleeson, JW	NSW	17	12	4	88	30	–	–	11.00	3	354.5	106	1014	44	23.04	2	–	6/21
Hammond, JR	SA	13	6	3	78	36*	–	–	26.00	4	278.0	59	809	26	31.11	1	–	6/15
Inverarity, RJ	WA	21	30	9	553	100*	1	1	26.33	13	353.5	101	983	37	26.56	1	–	5/67
Lillee, DK	WA	14	13	7	30	11*	–	–	5.00	3	456.5	119	1197	53	22.58	3	1	5/58
Mallett, AA	SA	15	13	3	146	29	–	–	14.60	5	427.0	124	1165	41	28.41	3	–	5/59
Marsh, RW	WA	17	24	5	664	91	5	–	34.94	38/7	–	–	–	–	–	–	–	–
Massie, RAL	WA	12	10	1	45	18	–	–	5.00	–	382.1	115	851	50	17.02	4	2	8/53
Sheahan, AP	VIC	17	26	7	788	135*	4	1	41.47	6	4.0	–	19	1	19.00	–	–	1/19
Stackpole, KR	VIC	21	35	5	1309	154*	7	3	43.63	15	63.0	20	164	2	82.00	–	–	1/12
Taber, HB	NSW	12	11	3	180	54	1	–	22.50	22/5	–	–	–	–	–	–	–	–
Walters, KD	NSW	19	29	5	935	154	–	3	38.95	7	35.3	6	117	2	58.50	–	–	1/10
Watson, GD	WA	18	27	2	915	176*	4	2	36.60	7	244.0	64	621	25	24.84	1	–	5/36

Ian Chappell's efforts to rebuild the Australian team after the retirement of Benaud, Simpson, McKenzie, Hawke, Jarman, Cowper and Lawry were rewarded by some tremendous individual displays. Dennis Lillee took 31 wickets in the five Tests and 53 on the tour. Bob Massie, who had been unable to hold a place in Northants Seconds two years earlier, captured 16 for 137 in his Test debut. Although only three batsmen scored more than 1000 runs on the tour, the team had more batting depth than on the previous tour, with most of them chiming in with useful scores. Greg Chappell had a splendid first tour of England, averaging 70.00 runs an innings and scoring 1260 runs, including a century at Lord's in the Second Test and another at The Oval in the Fifth Test. He joined his brother when Australia were 2 for 34 and together they added 200 runs that steered Australia towards 400 and the chance of a win that levelled the series. This was the first time brothers had scored centuries in the same Test innings. The spinners, Mallett and Gleeson, appreciated Ian Chappell's sympathetic captaincy and gave the pace men strong support.

Despite their difficulties against John Snow's fast, rising deliveries and the subtle variations of left-arm spinner Derek Underwood, the Australians hit five Test 100s and for the first time in a five-Test rubber prevented England from scoring any. The fielding reached a high level and long before the tour ended it was clear Australia had found another match-winning keeper in Rodney Marsh, whose acrobatic catching thrilled spectators all over England.

The 1972 Australians in England: *back row* G.D. Watson, A.A. Mallett, R.A.L. Massie, J.R. Hammond, R.W. Marsh; *centre* masseur, B.C. Francis, G.S. Chappell, R. Edwards, F.W. Bennett (assistant manager), A.P. Sheahan, D.J. Colley, D.K. Lillee, D. Sherwood (scorer); *front* H.B. Taber, K.D. Walters, I.M. Chappell (capt.), R.K. Steele (manager), K.R. Stackpole, R.J. Inverarity, J.W. Gleeson.

AUSTRALIA IN ENGLAND 1975

Matches	First-class Results Won	Lost	Drawn	Tied	Matches	All Matches Won	Lost	Drawn	Tied
15	8	2	5	–	21	12	4	5	–

Date	Venue	Opponent	Results for Australians
Jun 1	Lord's	*Middlesex	Won by 24 runs
Jun 7	Leeds	*Pakistan (WC L/O Intl)	Won by 73 runs
Jun 11	The Oval	*Sri Lanka (WC L/O Intl)	Won by 52 runs
Jun 14	The Oval	*West Indies (WC L/O Intl)	Lost by 7 wkts
Jun 18	Leeds	*England (WC L/O Intl)	Won by 4 wkts
Jun 21	Lord's	*West Indies (WC L/O Intl)	Lost by 17 runs
Jun 25	Canterbury	Kent	Lost by 4 wkts
Jun 28	Southampton	Hampshire	Won by 4 wkts
Jly 2	Lord's	MCC	Won by 7 wkts
Jly 5	Swansea	Glamorgan	Won by 7 wkts
Jly 10	Birmingham	ENGLAND (1st Test)	Won by an inns & 85 runs
Jly 16	Hove	Sussex	Drawn
Jly 19	Chesterfield	Derbyshire	Won by an inns & 38 runs
Jly 23	Manchester	Lancashire	Drawn
Jly 26	Leicester	Leicestershire	Lost by 31 runs
Jly 31	Lord's	ENGLAND (2nd Test)	Drawn
Aug 6	Taunton	Somerset	Won by 9 wkts
Aug 9	Northampton	Northamptonshire	Won by 5 wkts
Aug 14	Leeds	ENGLAND (3rd Test)	Drawn
Aug 23	Chelmsford	Essex	Won by 98 runs
Aug 28	The Oval	ENGLAND (4th Test)	Drawn

Player	State	M	Inn	NO	Runs	HS	50	100	Avrge	Ct/St	Overs	Mdns	Runs	Wkts	Avrge	5wi	10wm	Best
Chappell, GS	QLD	12	20	3	762	144	4	2	44.82	17	48.0	16	150	5	30.00	–	–	2/22
Chappell, IM (Capt)	SA	11	19	–	1022	192	4	4	53.78	4	64.3	18	183	6	30.50	–	–	2/30
Edwards, R	WA	12	20	4	675	101	5	1	42.18	3	5.0	–	27	–	–	–	–	–
Gilmour, GJ	NSW	10	14	5	389	102	2	1	43.22	10	225.1	47	789	28	28.17	1	–	6/85
Higgs, JD	VIC	8	2	1	0	0*	–	–	0.00	3	209.1	44	889	27	32.92	1	–	5/96
Hurst, AG	VIC	8	4	1	15	10*	–	–	5.00	4	197.3	49	659	21	31.38	–	–	3/8
Laird, BM	WA	9	17	2	488	127	3	1	32.53	3	2.0	–	7	–	–	–	–	–
Lillee, DK	WA	9	9	4	154	73*	–	–	30.80	1	345.0	107	886	41	21.60	2	1	7/67
Mallett, AA	SA	13	12	8	112	25*	–	–	28.00	13	400.5	118	1225	31	39.51	–	–	4/70
Marsh, RW	WA	12	17	2	469	65*	3	–	31.26	26/2	–	–	–	–	–	–	–	–
McCosker, RB	NSW	11	20	2	1078	127	4	4	59.88	3	–	–	–	–	–	–	–	–
Robinson, RD	VIC	7	9	3	223	41	–	–	37.16	23/7	–	–	–	–	–	–	–	–
Thomson, JR	NSW	10	10	4	186	49	–	–	31.00	5	338.1	88	1059	34	31.14	1	–	5/38
Turner, A	NSW	11	20	1	654	156	1	2	34.42	6	–	–	–	–	–	–	–	–
Walker, MHN	VIC	10	12	3	134	25	–	–	14.88	5	374.1	94	1076	36	29.88	1	–	5/48
Walters, KD	NSW	12	18	5	784	103*	4	3	60.30	13	47.5	9	169	7	24.14	–	–	1/6

The four-Test series between cricket's oldest rivals followed the first World Cup limited-over competition won by the West Indies. The Tests were spoiled by vandals, who damaged the pitch at Leeds, in the Third Test when Rick McCosker was on 95 not out and within sight of a deserved initial Test century. Australia led one–nil and needed 225 to win on the last day, with seven wickets on hand, but the overnight actions of a group campaigning for the release of a prisoner prevented any play. A result may not have been possible because heavy rain fell at 4 p.m. on the last afternoon, but both sides felt cheated of a possible win.

McCosker got his century in the drawn Fourth Test. He made 127 and was involved in a stand of 277 after Australia's first wicket fell for seven runs. By the end of the first day all hope England had of winning and squaring the series had gone with Australia on 1 for 280. Thereafter all England's resources were devoted to saving the match, which they managed with some fine second innings batting, after Lillee, Thomson and Walker had routed them for 191 in their first innings. Bob Woolmer scored 149, leading an England recovery that took them to a second-innings total of 538 after they had followed on 341 behind. The Australians' major problem was in finding an opening partner for Stackpole.

The 1975 Australians in England: *back row* masseur, J.R. Thomson, D.K. Lillee, R.B. McCosker, A.G. Hurst, M.H.N. Walker, A.A. Mallett, R.D. Robinson, J.D. Higgs, D. Sherwood (scorer); *front* G.J. Gilmour, K.D. Walters, R. Edwards, I.M. Chappell (capt.), F.W. Bennett (manager), G.S. Chappell, R.W. Marsh, B.M. Laird, A. Turner.

AUSTRALIA IN ENGLAND 1977

	First-class Results					All Matches			
Matches	Won	Lost	Drawn	Tied	Matches	Won	Lost	Drawn	Tied
22	5	4	13	–	31	8	8	15	–

Date	Venue	Opponent	Results for Australians
Apr 27	Arundel Castle	*Duchess of Norfolk's XI	Won by 20 runs
Apr 30	The Oval	Surrey	Drawn
May 4	Canterbury	Kent	Drawn
May 7	Hove	Sussex	Drawn
May 14	St Helens	Glamorgan	Drawn
May 18	Nath	Somerset	Lost by 7 wkts
May 21	Bristol	Gloucestershire	Won by 173 runs
May 24	Bristol	*Gloucestershire	Won by 6 wkts
May 25	Lord's	MCC	Won by 79 runs
May 28	Worcester	Worcestershire	Drawn
Jun 2	Manchester	*England (L/O Intl)	Lost by 2 wkts
Jun 4	Birmingham	*England (L/O Intl)	Lost by 101 runs
Jun 6	The Oval	*England (L/O Intl)	Won by 2 wkts
Jun 9	Dublin	*Ireland	Drawn
Jun 11	Chelmsford	Essex	Drawn
Jun 16	Lord's	ENGLAND (1st Test)	Drawn
Jun 23	Oxford	*Oxford & Cambridge Uni's	Drawn
Jun 25	Nottingham	Nottinghamshire	Won by an inns & 98 runs
Jun 29	Chesterfield	Derbyshire	Drawn
Jly 2	Scarborough	Yorkshire	Drawn
Jly 7	Manchester	ENGLAND (2nd Test)	Lost by 9 wkts
Jly 16	Northampton	Northamptonshire	Drawn
Jly 20	Birmingham	Warwickshire	Won by 130 runs
Jly 23	Leicester	Leicestershire	Drawn
Jly 28	Nottingham	ENGLAND (3rd Test)	Lost by 7 wkts
Aug 4	Sunderland	*Minor Counties	Lost by 6 wkts
Aug 6	Manchester	Lancashire	Won by 7 wkts
Aug 11	Leeds	ENGLAND (4th Test)	Lost by an inns & 85 runs
Aug 18	Arundel Castle	*Rest of the World	Lost by 3 wkts
Aug 20	Lord's	Middlesex	Drawn
Aug 25	The Oval	ENGLAND (5th Test)	Drawn

This turned into a disastrous tour once it became known at the end of the first month that 13 of the 17 players had signed contracts to join Kerry Packer's breakaway World Series Cricket. Manager Len Maddocks was at pains to explain that the players' Packer agreements had nothing to do with their disappointing displays but *Wisden* undoubtedly had it right in suggesting there was a lot of heresy in what this Australian team did in England.

Lillee, Ian Chappell and Ross Edwards, all Packer signings, were unavailable for the tour and without Lillee, Thomson was not the dominating opening bowler of old. Feeling his way as captain, Greg Chappell had major problems with morale, and once again Doug Walters failed in the matches that counted. Richie Robinson found himself opening Australia's batting in his Test debut, a strange fate for a second-string wicket-keeper. The Australians managed to score 400 in an innings only once on the tour—against the weak Northants bowling. They worsened their problems by dropping vital catches, including Boycott at 22, before he went on to his 100th Test century at Leeds. Nobody was surprised that a combination in such disarray should lose the Tests three–nil.

Player	State	M	Inn	NO	Runs	HS	50	100	Avrge	Ct/St	Overs	Mdns	Runs	Wkts	Avrge	5wi	10wm	Best
Bright, RJ	VIC	14	19	8	287	53*	1	–	26.09	5	333.5	114	794	39	20.35	2	–	5/67
Chappell, GS (Capt)	QLD	16	25	5	1182	161*	2	5	59.10	18	106.0	28	304	6	50.66	–	–	3/45
Cosier, GJ	SA	12	20	1	587	100	4	1	30.89	7	16.0	3	36	–	–	–	–	–
Davis, IC	NSW	13	20	–	608	83	5	–	30.40	5	–	–	–	–	–	–	–	–
Dymock, G	QLD	10	6	5	16	8*	–	–	16.00	2	192.0	54	468	15	31.20	–	–	3/20
Hookes, DW	SA	17	26	1	804	108	6	1	32.16	4	4.0	–	18	1	18.00	–	–	1/17
Hughes, KJ	WA	14	19	–	540	95	5	–	28.42	10	–	–	–	–	–	–	–	–
Malone, MF	WA	10	10	3	95	46	–	–	13.57	4	328.0	95	837	32	26.15	1	–	5/63
Marsh, RW	WA	17	24	2	477	124	2	1	21.68	30/2	1.0	–	6	–	–	–	–	–
McCosker, RB	NSW	18	32	1	737	107	4	1	23.77	20	2.0	1	5	–	–	–	–	–
O'Keeffe, KJ	NSW	13	19	12	355	48*	–	–	50.71	5	335.4	112	1035	36	28.75	–	–	4/21
Pascoe, LS	NSW	11	9	3	44	20	–	–	7.33	–	323.4	79	893	41	21.78	1	–	6/68
Robinson, RD	VIC	14	23	4	715	137*	4	1	37.63	31/3	–	–	–	–	–	–	–	–
Serjeant, CS	WA	15	22	2	663	159	6	1	33.15	2	–	–	–	–	–	–	–	–
Thomson, JR	QLD	16	17	1	130	25	–	–	8.12	3	385.2	84	1207	43	28.06	1	–	4/41
Walker, MHN	VIC	15	17	2	250	78*	1	–	16.66	2	514.0	154	1184	53	22.33	3	–	7/19
Walters, KD	NSW	17	26	1	663	88	3	–	26.52	8	17.0	5	30	–	–	–	–	–

The 1977 Australians looked a dishevelled lot as they arrived at London airport, facing the cameras in casual gear. Here captain Greg Chappell answers media questions with manager Len Maddocks. This unimpressive start proved fitting for a shambles of a tour.

AUSTRALIA IN ENGLAND 1981

	First-class Results					All Matches			
Matches	Won	Lost	Drawn	Tied	Matches	Won	Lost	Drawn	Tied
17	3	3	11	–	26	7	7	12	–

Date	Venue	Opponent	Results for Australians
May 16	Arundel Castle	*Duchess of Norfolk's XI	Lost by 3 wkts
May 20	Southampton	Hampshire	Drawn
May 23	Taunton	Somerset	Drawn
May 27	Swansea	Glamorgan	Drawn
May 30	Bristol	Gloucestershire	Abandoned
Jun 1	Bristol	Gloucestershire	Drawn
Jun 4	Lord's	*England (L/O Intl)	Lost by 6 wkts
Jun 6	Birmingham	*England (L/O Intl)	Won by 2 runs
Jun 8	Leeds	*England (L/O Intl)	Won by 71 runs
Jun 10	Derby	Derbyshire	Drawn
Jun 13	Lord's	Middlesex	Drawn
Jun 18	Nottingham	ENGLAND (1st Test)	Won by 4 wkts
Jun 24	Manchester	*Lancashire	Lost on run rate
Jun 27	Canterbury	Kent	Drawn
Jly 2	Lord's	ENGLAND (2nd Test)	Drawn
Jly 9	Birmingham	*Warwickshire	Drawn
Jly 11	Northampton	Northamptonshire	Drawn
Jly 16	Leeds	ENGLAND (3rd Test)	Lost by 18 runs
Jly 23	Glasgow	*Scotland	Won by 10 runs
Jly 25	Worcester	Worcestershire	Won by 7 wkts
Jly 30	Birmingham	ENGLAND (4th Test)	Lost by 29 runs
Aug 6	The Oval	*Surrey	Abandoned
Aug 8	Chelmsford	Essex	Drawn
Aug 13	Manchester	ENGLAND (5th Test)	Lost by 103 runs
Aug 20	Leicester	*Leicestershire	Won by 68 runs
Aug 22	Hove	Sussex	Won by 7 wkts
Aug 27	The Oval	ENGLAND (6th Test)	Drawn
Sep 2	Cheltenham	*Gloucestershire	Lost by 72 runs

The 1981 Australians in England: *standing* D.I. Adler (physio), J. Dyson, M.F. Kent, G.R. Beard, T.M. Alderman, P. Philpott (coach), G.F. Lawson, D.K. Lillee, R.M. Hogg, D.M. Wellham, D. Sherwood (scorer); *front* G.N. Yallop, R.J. Bright, T.M. Chappell, R.W. Marsh, F.W. Bennett (manager), K.J. Hughes (capt.), A.R. Border, S.J. Rixon, G.M. Wood.

Player	State	M	Inn	NO	Runs	HS	50	100	Avrge	Ct/St	Overs	Mdns	Runs	Wkts	Avrge	5wi	10wm	Best
Alderman, TM	WA	12	11	6	34	12*	–	–	6.80	11	402.5	100	1064	51	20.86	4	–	6/135
Beard, GR	NSW	9	9	2	131	36	–	–	18.71	–	209.1	58	559	16	34.93	–	–	4/92
Border, AR	QLD	13	21	5	807	123*	4	3	50.43	16	24.0	6	65	2	32.50	–	–	1/12
Bright, RJ	VIC	15	18	1	280	42	–	–	16.47	12	473.4	178	1056	40	26.40	2	–	5/57
Chappell, TM	NSW	12	18	2	409	91	2	–	25.56	3	4.0	1	18	–	–	–	–	–
Dyson, J	NSW	13	20	1	582	102	3	1	30.63	2	1.0	–	2	–	–	–	–	–
Hogg, RM	SA	11	8	2	15	6	–	–	2.50	2	217.2	51	657	27	24.33	1	–	6/87
Hughes, KJ (Capt)	WA	15	24	1	679	89	5	–	29.52	8	5.5	2	14	–	–	–	–	–
Kent, MF	QLD	10	15	–	347	92	3	–	23.13	11	–	–	–	–	–	–	–	–
Lawson, GF	NSW	10	9	3	140	38*	–	–	23.33	4	218.1	53	652	25	26.08	2	–	7/81
Lillee, DK	WA	8	11	4	158	40*	–	–	22.57	3	377.4	102	1028	47	21.87	3	1	7/89
Marsh, RW	WA	10	16	1	368	72*	2	–	24.53	26/2	0.2	–	0	1	0.00	–	–	1/0
Rixon, SJ	NSW	8	9	2	146	40	–	–	20.85	20/2	2.0	–	19	–	–	–	–	–
Wellham, DM	NSW	9	13	4	497	135*	1	2	55.22	3	2.0	–	11	1	11.00	–	–	1/11
Whitney, MR	NSW	3	5	–	5	4	–	–	1.00	1	102.0	19	327	11	29.72	1	–	5/60
Wood, GM	WA	15	24	2	690	81	5	–	31.36	8	–	–	–	–	–	–	–	–
Yallop, GN	VIC	14	22	3	624	114	3	1	32.84	8	69.0	14	241	6	40.16	–	–	4/63

Australia outplayed England for much of this astonishing series, before capitulating to the brilliance of one man, Ian Botham, who relinquished the Test captaincy after the first two Tests because it affected his form. England were in difficulty until Mike Brearley, on his record of run-getting against Australia seemingly unworthy of a Test berth, took over the captaincy and freed Botham to produce his own brand of mayhem. Under Brearley, England held catches they had dropped. His appointment coincided with Australia's loss of Lawson and Hogg through injury and Lillee through a bout of pneumonia. This forced Mike Whitney, who had been playing league cricket for Fleetwood, to be drafted into the side.

Despite the absence of Greg Chappell—rebuilding his fitness in Australia—Australia won the First Test by four wickets. The Second Test was drawn. Australia should have won the Third Test after forcing England to follow on but capitulated by 18 runs. Botham began England's recovery with a whirlwind 149 not out, which helped lift the total from 7 for 135 to 356. Willis finished Australia off by taking 8 for 43. Another staggering display by Botham, this time with the ball, cost Australia the Fourth Test by a margin of only 29 runs. Botham took 5 for 11, including a spell of five wickets for one run after taking the ball reluctantly. Australia never recovered from the disaster of two defeats in twelve days in matches where they had the upper hand. England completed the rubber three–one up, with a 103-run win in the Fifth Test against a demoralised and frustrated Australia, who had been so close to a three–nil triumph.

AUSTRALIA IN ENGLAND 1985

First-class Results					All Matches				
Matches	Won	Lost	Drawn	Tied	Matches	Won	Lost	Drawn	Tied
20	4	3	13	–	29	9	5	15	–

Date	Venue	Opponent	Results for Australians
May 5	Arundel	*Duchess of Norfolk's XI	Drawn
May 8	Taunton	Somerset	Won by 233 runs
May 11	Worcester	Worcestershire	Drawn
May 14	Nottingham	*Nottinghamshire	Abandoned
May 16	The Oval	*Surrey	Lost by 6 wkts
May 18	Hove	Sussex	Drawn
May 22	Lord's	MCC	Drawn
May 25	Derby	Derbyshire	Drawn
May 28	Derby	*Derbyshire	Won by 6 wkts
May 30	Manchester	*England (L/O Intl)	Won by 3 wkts
Jun 1	Birmingham	*England (L/O Intl)	Won by 4 wkts
Jun 3	Lord's	*England (L/O Intl)	Lost by 8 wkts
Jun 5	Leeds	Yorkshire	Drawn
Jun 8	Leicester	Leicestershire	Drawn
Jun 13	Leeds	ENGLAND (1st Test)	Lost by 5 wkts
Jun 20	Cambridge	*Oxford & Cambridge Uni's	Won by 79 runs
Jun 22	Southampton	Hampshire	Drawn
Jun 27	Lord's	ENGLAND (2nd Test)	Won by 4 wkts
Jly 6	Chelmsford	Essex	Drawn
Jly 11	Nottingham	ENGLAND (3rd Test)	Drawn
Jly 18	Jesmond	*Minor Counties	Won by 125 runs
Jly 20	Neath	Glamorgan	Drawn
Jly 24	Bristol	Gloucestershire	Won by 170 runs
Jly 27	Northampton	Northamptonshire	Drawn
Aug 1	Manchester	ENGLAND (4th Test)	Drawn
Aug 8	Downpatrick	*Ireland	Drawn
Aug 10	Lord's	Middlesex	Drawn
Aug 15	Birmingham	ENGLAND (5th Test)	Lost by an inns & 118 runs
Aug 24	Canterbury	Kent	Won by 7 wkts
Aug 29	The Oval	ENGLAND (6th Test)	Lost by an inns & 94 runs

Player	State	M	Inn	NO	Runs	HS	50	100	Avrge	Ct/St	Overs	Mdns	Runs	Wkts	Avrge	5wi	10wm	Best
Bennett, MJ	NSW	11	10	3	111	23	–	–	15.85	6	266.4	62	766	16	47.87	–	–	4/39
Boon, DC	TAS	15	20	4	832	206*	3	3	55.46	13	6.0	–	33	–	–	–	–	–
Border, AR (Capt)	QLD	14	21	2	1355	196	1	8	71.31	13	13.0	2	38	–	–	–	–	–
Gilbert, DR	NSW	10	8	3	39	12	–	–	7.80	2	253.2	42	885	21	42.14	–	–	4/41
Hilditch, AMJ	SA	17	27	–	829	119	4	1	30.70	7	7.0	2	29	–	–	–	–	–
Holland, RG	NSW	13	10	1	59	35	–	–	6.55	5	376.0	94	1017	29	35.06	2	–	5/21
Lawson, GF	NSW	13	13	2	154	53	1	–	14.00	1	347.0	61	1165	31	n 37.58	1	–	5/103
Matthews, GRJ	NSW	10	12	3	216	51*	1	–	24.00	3	159.4	34	521	12	43.41	–	–	3/76
McDermott, CJ	QLD	16	14	3	183	53*	1	–	16.63	2	421.5	49	1609	51	31.54	3	–	8/141
O'Donnell, SP	VIC	11	16	5	448	100*	–	1	40.72	5	242.4	47	819	12	68.25	–	–	3/37
Phillips, RB	QLD	7	7	2	130	39	–	–	26.00	13/–	–	–	–	–	–	–	–	–
Phillips, WB	SA	14	22	3	899	128	6	1	47.31	20/1	–	–	–	–	–	–	–	–
Ritchie, GM	QLD	16	23	3	1097	155	4	4	54.85	7	6.3	–	33	1	33.00	–	–	1/22
Thomson, JR	QLD	11	11	6	82	28*	–	–	16.40	2	241.3	33	988	29	34.06	2	–	6/44
Wellham, DM	NSW	10	16	4	669	125*	4	2	55.75	1	–	–	–	–	–	–	–	–
Wessels, KC	QLD	16	26	1	905	156	8	1	36.20	9	32.0	9	79	–	–	–	–	–
Wood, GM	WA	16	25	3	691	172	–	2	31.40	6	–	–	–	–	–	–	–	–

Australian plans for this tour were disrupted when Terry Alderman, Rodney Hogg, Carl Rackemann, Kim Hughes, Graham Yallop, Steve Smith and Michael Haysman, all of them close to selection in the touring party, opted to join a rebel outfit in South Africa. Right at the last moment, Dirk Wellham, Graeme Wood and Wayne Phillips changed their minds after accepting offers to join the rebels, which inevitably led to strain within the Australian side. England on the other hand had the luxury of including their own South African rebels, Gooch, Embury, Willey and Taylor, for the first time in three seasons. The Australians never regained their composure in a six-Test series and their inconsistency left their captain's effort in scoring eight tour 100s go unrewarded. The Australians discovered that the days when every county fielded their best players against them and tried hard to win as a matter of regional pride had gone. The counties rested their stars for the matches against the tourists, who found these matches on ill-prepared pitches inadequately promoted. Programs that previously involved more than 30 first-class matches and that gave players on the fringe of Test selection a chance to press their claims, had been trimmed to 20 first-class games. With the management forced to get their Test players into form, the also-rans sat around for weeks waiting for action.

Somehow Australia held England to a win apiece after four Tests, but they won only four of the 20 first-class matches. England revived to win both the Fifth and Sixth Tests by an innings and emerge three–one victors, but the overall England performance attracted little praise. McDermott was the only Australian bowler to consistently worry quality batsmen, turning in a fine effort by taking 30 Test wickets at the age of 20. Of the other bowlers only Holland showed occasional glimpses of penetration but he mystified all his admirers by not bowling his googly more often. Wood, Boon, Wessels, Phillips and Ritchie all played well at times but lacked consistency. Hilditch began with 119 in the First Test but later became a notorious victim of his hook shot, finding boundary fieldsmen with unerring accuracy.

The 1985 Australians in England: *standing* G.R. Mackay (physio), R.B. Phillips, G.M. Ritchie, D.R. Gilbert, C.J. McDermott, S.P. O'Donnell, M.J. Bennett, R.G. Holland, G.R.J. Matthews, D.M. Wellham, M.P. Ringham (scorer); *seated* G.M. Wood, K.C. Wessels, J.R. Thomson, A.R. Border (capt.), R.F. Merriman (manager), G. Dymock (assistant manager), A.M.J. Hilditch, G.F. Lawson, W.B. Phillips, D.C. Boon.

AUSTRALIA IN ENGLAND

	First-class Results					All Matches			
Matches	Won	Lost	Drawn	Tied	Matches	Won	Lost	Drawn	Tied
20	12	1	7	–	31	20	3	7	1

Date	Venue	Opponent	Results for Australians
May 5	Dartmouth	*League Cricket Conference	Won by 165 runs
May 7	Arundel	*Duchess of Norfolk's XI	Won by 120 runs
May 9	Hove	*Sussex	Lost by 4 wkts
May 11	Lord's	*MCC	Won by 101 runs
May 13	Worcester	Worcestershire	Lost by 3 wkts
May 17	Taunton	Somerset	Drawn
May 20	Lord's	Middlesex	Won by 3 wkts
May 23	Leeds	*Yorkshire	Won by 109 runs
May 25	Manchester	*England (L/O Intl)	Lost by 95 runs
May 27	Nottingham	*England (L/O Intl)	Tied
May 29	Lord's	*England (L/O Intl)	Won by 6 wkts
May 31	Birmingham	Warwickshire	Drawn
Jun 3	Derby	Derbyshire	Won by 11 runs
Jun 8	Leeds	ENGLAND (1st Test)	Won by 210 runs
Jun 14	Manchester	Lancashire	Won by 9 wkts
Jun 17	Northampton	Northamptonshire	Won by 272 runs
Jun 22	Lord's	ENGLAND (2nd Test)	Won by 6 wkts
Jun 28	Oxford	*Oxford & Cambridge Uni's	Won by 99 runs
Jly 1	Neath	Glamorgan	Drawn
Jly 6	Birmingham	ENGLAND (3rd Test)	Drawn
Jly 15	Glasgow	*Scotland	Won by 97 runs
Jly 17	Trowbridge	*Minor Counties	Won by 27 runs
Jly 19	Southampton	Hampshire	Drawn
Jly 22	Bristol	Gloucestershire	Won by an inns & 146 runs
Jly 27	Manchester	ENGLAND (4th Test)	Won by 9 wkts
Aug 2	Nottingham	Nottinghamshire	Won by 196 runs
Aug 5	Leicester	Leicestershire	Won by 9 wkts
Aug 10	Nottingham	ENGLAND (5th Test)	Won by an inns & 180 runs
Aug 16	Canterbury	Kent	Drawn
Aug 19	Chelmsford	Essex	Won by 150 runs
Aug 24	The Oval	ENGLAND (6th Test)	Drawn

Player	State	M	Inn	NO	Runs	HS	50	100	Avrge	Ct/St	Overs	Mdns	Runs	Wkts	Avrge	5wi	10wm	Best
Alderman, TM	WA	11	10	6	38	8	–	–	9.50	5	411.2	103	1095	70	15.64	6	1	6/128
Boon, DC	TAS	17	28	5	1306	151	8	3	56.78	22	1.0	1	0	–	–	–	–	–
Border, AR (Capt)	QLD	16	22	4	979	135	9	1	54.39	18	68.0	21	154	1	154.00	–	–	1/55
Campbell, GD	TAS	11	10	2	87	31	–	–	10.88	3	250.2	50	824	30	27.47	1	–	5/54
Healy, IA	QLD	14	19	4	442	73*	1	–	29.47	33/2	–	–	–	–	–	–	–	–
Hohns, TV	QLD	15	18	4	393	95	2	–	28.07	8	321.4	108	809	26	31.12	–	–	4/87
Hughes, MG	VIC	15	16	4	246	71	1	–	20.50	1	399.0	102	1242	47	26.43	3	–	5/37
Jones, DM	VIC	14	20	3	1510	248	8	5	88.82	8	1.0	–	13	–	–	–	–	–
Lawson, GF	NSW	14	12	2	174	74	1	–	17.40	4	522.3	140	1447	69	20.97	3	–	6/30
Marsh, GR	WA	18	33	4	934	138	2	2	32.21	14	–	–	–	–	–	–	–	–
May, TBA	SA	10	8	3	59	24	–	–	11.80	1	287.5	86	740	28	26.43	–	–	4/43
Moody, TM	WA	12	20	4	564	144*	3	1	35.25	8	63.0	19	151	6	25.17	–	–	4/30
Rackemann, CG	QLD	8	6	1	22	11	–	–	4.40	2	225.5	47	747	32	23.34	1	–	5/65
Taylor, MA	NSW	17	30	1	1669	219	10	3	57.55	24	–	–	–	–	–	–	–	–
Veletta, MRJ	WA	5	8	1	294	134*	1	1	42.00	6	–	–	–	–	–	–	–	–
Waugh, SR	NSW	16	24	8	1030	177*	3	4	64.38	6	176.1	39	571	23	24.83	–	–	3/10
Zoehrer, TJ	WA	7	9	–	259	93	1	–	28.78	16/–	5.0	–	9	1	9.00	–	–	1/9

Allan Border's team lost the first match of their tour against Worcestershire by three wickets. Thereafter their tour was a regular triumph. They became the first team since Bill Woodfull's 1934 side to regain The Ashes in England, by winning the Fourth Test at Old Trafford by nine wickets. This gave Australia 100 wins in Tests against England and 200 wins in all Tests. Their mastery of England's bowling continued in the Fifth Test at Trent Bridge, where they made 6 for 602 declared, after Geoff Marsh and Mark Taylor batted all the first day for 301 without being separated. Their opening stand was worth 329, a record that will take some beating. Taylor went on to 219, Marsh to 138.

Alderman, fully recovered from the shoulder injury suffered in Perth when he retaliated against a thump on the head from a spectator, took 41 wickets in the Tests, exposing weaknesses in technique of those who played across the line of his swinging deliveries. Bowling to batsmen who were unable to play straight consistently, he had 19 favourable leg-before-wicket decisions. Lumbering Merv Hughes bowled without the same deviation or subtlety but even critics of his technique admired his big heart. Trevor Hohns with his leg-spinners, Steve Waugh with his medium-pacers, Geoff Lawson with his clever mixture of swing and accurate pace and Greg Campbell with his medium-paced swing, all gave valuable support.

The batting was always sound and at times brilliant. Mark Taylor joined the select group of great left-handers Australia has sent to England, with 1669 runs, including three centuries. Dean Jones had some exhilarating knocks, five of them producing centuries. David Boon always proved hard to dismiss, and Steve Waugh's four centuries capped his allround value to a fine side that fielded splendidly, were well captained and fully deserved the ticker tape parade a grateful Australian public gave them when they got home.

The 1989 Australians in England: *back row* E. Alcott (physio), T.V. Hohns, T.B.A. May, G.F. Lawson, C.G. Rackemann, T.M. Moody, M.G. Hughes, T.M. Alderman, G.D. Campbell, M.K. Walsh (scorer); *front* R.B. Simpson (coach), T.J. Zoehrer, M.A. Taylor, D.M. Jones, A.R. Border (capt.), L.M. Sawle (manager), G.R. Marsh, D.C. Boon, S.R. Waugh, M.R.J. Veletta, I.A. Healy. *Patrick Eagar*

AUSTRALIA IN ENGLAND 1993

	First-class Results					All Matches			
Matches	Won	Lost	Drawn	Tied	Matches	Won	Lost	Drawn	Tied
21	10	2	9	–	30	18	3	9	–

Date	Venue	Opponent	Results for Australians
Apr 30	Radlett	*England Amateur XI	Won by 94 runs
May 2	Arundel	*Duchess of Norfolk's XI	Won by 7 runs
May 3	Lord's	*Middlesex	Won by 69 runs
May 5	Worcester	Worcestershire	Won by 5 wkts
May 8	Taunton	Somerset	Won by 35 runs
May 13	Hove	Sussex	Drawn
May 16	Northampton	*Northamptonshire	Lost on run rate
May 19	Manchester	*England (L/O Intl)	Won by 4 runs
May 21	Birmingham	*England (L/O Intl)	Won by 6 wkts
May 23	Lord's	*England (L/O Intl)	Won by 19 runs
May 25	The Oval	Surrey	Won by 174 runs
May 29	Leicester	Leicestershire	Won by 97 runs
Jun 3	Manchester	ENGLAND (1st Test)	Won by 179 runs
Jun 9	Birmingham	Warwickshire	Drawn
Jun 12	Bristol	Gloucestershire	Drawn
Jun 17	Lord's	ENGLAND (2nd Test)	Won by an inns & 62 runs
Jun 23	Oxford	Combined Universities	Won by 166 runs
Jun 26	Southampton	Hampshire	Drawn
Jly 1	Nottingham	ENGLAND (3rd Test)	Drawn
Jly 8	Stoke	*Minor Counties	Won by 58 runs
Jly 10	Clontarf	*Ireland	Won by 272 runs
Jly 13	Derby	Derbyshire	Drawn
Jly 17	Durham	Durham	Drawn
Jly 22	Headingley	ENGLAND (4th Test)	Won by an inns & 148 runs
Jly 28	Manchester	Lancashire	Lost by 5 wkts
Jly 31	Neath	Glamorgan	Drawn
Aug 5	Birmingham	ENGLAND (5th Test)	Won by 8 wkts
Aug 11	Canterbury	Kent	Won by 89 runs
Aug 14	Chelmsford	Essex	Drawn
Aug 19	The Oval	ENGLAND (6th Test)	Lost by 161 runs

The 1993 Australians in England: *standing* E. Alcott (physio), S. Warne, M. Slater, T. May, P. Reiffel, M. Hughes, M.K. Walsh (scorer), B. Julian, M. Hayden, M. Waugh, D. Martyn, W. Holdsworth, R.B. Simpson (coach); *front* T. Zoehrer, S. Waugh, M. Taylor, A.R. Border (capt.), D.L. Rundle (manager), D. Boon, C. McDermott, I. Healy. *Patrick Eagar*

Player	State	M	Inn	NO	Runs	HS	50	100	Avrge	Ct/St	Overs	Mdns	Runs	Wkts	Avrge	5wi	10wm	Best
Boon, DC	TAS	14	23	4	1437	164*	2	9	75.63	10/–	–	–	–	–	–	–	–	–
Border, AR (Capt)	QLD	16	21	3	823	200*	4	1	45.72	15/–	65.0	17	177	3	59.00	–	–	1/12
Hayden, ML	QLD	13	21	1	1150	151*	7	3	57.50	9/–	8.4	1	31	1	31.00	–	–	1/24
Healy, IA	QLD	16	20	7	499	102*	3	1	38.38	42/11	–	–	–	–	–	–	–	–
Holdsworth, WJ	NSW	9	3	–	17	12	–	–	5.67	2/–	204.5	32	833	23	36.22	1	–	5/117
Hughes, MG	VIC	14	12	3	299	71	2	–	33.22	3/–	470.2	113	1420	48	29.58	1	–	5/92
Julian, BP	WA	13	17	6	284	66	2	–	25.82	7/–	318.5	57	1158	29	39.93	1	–	5/63
Martyn, DR	WA	12	15	3	838	138*	3	4	69.83	9/1	8.0	2	21	–	–	–	–	–
May, TBA	SA	17	9	5	31	15	–	–	7.75	5/–	562.2	156	1429	53	26.96	1	–	5/89
McDermott, CJ	QLD	6	3	–	42	23	–	–	14.00	3/–	143.0	26	449	6	74.83	–	–	2/36
Reiffel, PR	VIC	13	9	1	181	52	1	–	22.63	3/–	375.4	85	1113	37	30.08	2	–	6/71
Slater, MJ	NSW	17	28	4	1275	152	8	4	53.13	6/–	–	–	–	–	–	–	–	–
Taylor, MA	NSW	15	25	2	972	124	4	3	42.26	25/–	9.0	–	31	1	31.00	–	–	1/4
Warne, SK	VIC	16	15	4	246	47	–	–	22.36	8/–	765.5	281	1698	75	22.64	2	–	5/61
Waugh, ME	NSW	16	25	6	1361	178	9	4	71.63	18/–	121.1	28	403	6	67.17	–	–	3/26
Waugh, SR	NSW	16	21	8	875	157*	2	3	167.31	7/–	73.1	19	229	7	32.71	–	–	2/9
Zoehrer, TJ	WA	8	9	1	115	38	–	–	14.38	17/4	87.2	21	250	12	20.83	–	–	3/16

On seventh and last tour of England and his fourth as captain, Border had the difficult task of reviving a team that had suffered grievous disappointment not long before they left. They narrowly failed to defeat the West Indies in a captivating series, going down by one run in the crucial Fourth Test, which allowed the West Indies to draw level and go on and take the rubber two–one. They had similar chances immediately afterwards to beat New Zealand in New Zealand but again were thwarted. Lifting the morale of a team that included seven players new to touring with the national team in England represented a major chore for Border and coach Bob Simpson. Some of the newcomers had had the benefit of touring England in Australian Under-19 teams or had played for English counties. They looked a splendidly balanced combination with a welcome infusion of youth to replace faded stars. Googly bowler Shane Warne and fast bowler Wayne Holdsworth carried some outstanding form in the tour. Between them Border and Simpson had to blend them into a match-winning unit that could repeat the triumphs of 1989. Warne was a spectacular success from the moment he bowled Mike Gatting with his Test delivery in England, but Holdsworth proved a sorry disappointment. The English opposition was so weak that assessment of Australia's performance was virtually impossible.

CHAPTER EIGHTEEN

THE VERDICT

Comparison of cricket teams from different eras is difficult, and to a few supporters meaningless, even odious, but it is fun and I believe a majority of fans find it irresistible. The achievements of the 33 teams Australia has sent to England, the seven that have gone to the West Indies, the ten to South Africa, the 2 Services XIs, the 14 teams to New Zealand, six to India and eight to Pakistan, and other official sides are all well documented. I believe their performances can, in fact, be evaluated because of what cricketers call the 'balance' of the teams involved.

The requirement that each team comprise the magical number of 11 players places the responsibility for getting the 'balance' right firmly on the selectors. Given that tour results expose selectors' mistakes and that they are often hamstrung by the range of available talent, the great teams still emerge.

These are the teams equipped to meet all the likely challenges, the sides with the players who had the widest spread of skills. Billy Murdoch's 1882 players had to play on rough, ill-prepared wickets, but in the opinion of Dr W.G. Grace, A.G. Steel and Alfred Shaw—all of them wise in assessing the demands on Test XIs—the 1882 team was the best Australia ever sent to England. Harry Altham, who wrote what is still the best history of big cricket, said that only Joe Darling's 1902 side bore comparison with their 1882 predecessors.

Altham's rating is all the more pertinent when one considers Warwick Armstrong's pronouncement after his 1921 team clinched the series (by beating England inside three days in the first three Tests and remaining unbeaten until the serious part of the tour was over): 'The 1902 lot would have beaten my 1921 lads by an innings, with time to spare.' The 1921 team still deserves a very high

Warwick Armstrong, who captained the all-conquering 1921 Australian team in England at a time when the opposition was weak, led with style and gusto. (*below*) Armstrong leading the 1921 Australians out for the first Test at Trent Bridge, closely followed by his vice-captain Herbie Collins and wicket-keeper Hanson Carter.

ranking because they were strong in all departments.

The 1921 Australians were a very powerful batting lineup with Charlie Macartney, Warren Bardsley, Armstrong, Tommy Andrews, Herbie Collins and Johnny Taylor all contributing more than 1000 runs, and nine of the side averaging 30 or more with the bat. They had a fine pair of opening bowlers in Jack Gregory and Ted McDonald, outstanding wicket-keepers in Sammy Carter and Bert Oldfield, and gifted spinners in Armstrong and Mailey. The medium-pace of 'Stork' Hendry and Jack Ryder seldom needed to be used. They were a marvellous fielding side, with Taylor and Pellew a sight to behold in the outfield, and some very smart slips fieldsmen. There was an ideal sprinkling of left and right-handers, players who could get runs quickly in an exciting show of strokeplay or men who could defend dourly if the need arose.

England's selectors were unable to find a combination that could even extend this craftily-led Australian outfit and tried 30 players in a one-sided series. Eleven of the 15 Australians on the tour made centuries, with Macartney's 345 in a day against Nottingham the highspot. McDonald took 150 wickets, Mailey 146, Gregory 120, and Armstrong 106. Armstrong's main problem was who to leave out in the Tests.

Despite the dominance of his team, Armstrong remained firmly of the view that they would not have extended the 1902 team, which had seven batsmen who made tour centuries, Vic Trumper heading the list with 2570 runs and Monty Noble producing the highest score, 285. Clem Hill and Darling were masterly left-handers, Joe Kelly and Carter superb keepers. The team's fast bowler, Ernie Jones, was one of the most alarming new ball bowlers cricket has known, and Hugh Trumble (140) and Jack Saunders (127) both took more than 100 wickets with spin. Noble made 1416 runs and took 98 wickets to outdo the other allrounders and Hill, Duff, Trumper and Bert Hopkins made centuries and took catches that were talked about for generations. As with the 1921 side, the balance was ideal.

Trumper had the luxury of batting on pitches with the approaches uncovered, which guaranteed him an hour or more to make runs before wet pitches dried and bowlers' footholds firmed. This was later denied batsmen like Bradman, McCabe and Jackson, who had to bat on pitches where the approaches were covered and pace bowlers operated with confidence. After costs rocketed and treasurers ruled, pitches were fully covered—Australia's 'sticky' wickets disappeared.

For bowlers, the covering or uncovering of pitches had an enormous affect on their ability to take wickets, but not as big as the changes in the number of balls comprising an over. We have been through four, six and eight ball overs, and it defies belief that all the cricket nations cannot agree the eight-ball over is the most sensible. Even more ridiculous is the adherence to an 85-overs-a-day rule. If six-ball overs are to apply, teams should be asked to bowl 110 overs if we are to provide value for spectators paying high prices for a day's admission.

Both the Australian teams Bill Woodfull captained in England (1930 and 1934) surprised critics by winning the Ashes, but they did so by the sheer weight of runs from Bradman, Ponsford, Woodfull himself, and in 1930 from Kippax and in 1934 from Brown. They fielded brilliantly with Bradman at that stage of his career one of the best ever in any position. But the teams lacked Test quality pace bowling and relied too much on spin, conceeding too many big totals.

In 1948 I watched all five Tests played by Don Bradman's team. This was Bradman's second tour as captain in the England–Australia saga, and came after he had lost his highest Test score record (334) to Len Hutton (364) on the previous tour in 1938. Bradman had been undecided about touring again after a series of physical disorders that resulted in his premature retirement from the Australian Army. Before he took Australia to England he survived a leg-before-wicket appeal against Cec Pepper's flipper in the Services XI match against South Australia, and against England in Brisbane when the English team thought he had been caught in the gully by Jack Ikin. Had the umpires decided against Bradman

Don Bradman chatting with King George VI at Balmoral during the tour of the 1948 team in England, a team Jack Pollard rates Australia's best ever.

THE VERDICT

in either of these matched the history of Australian cricket in the decade after World War II would have changed.

Bradman found himself, with his fortieth birthday approaching, in charge of a team that was accustomed to services discipline, the best of a wonderful crop of cricketers whose careers had been upset by the war. I watched him once at the nets and in an hour and a half not one ball went past his bat. He lacked the artistry of a McCabe or a Greg Chappell but he hit the loose balls hard and his confidence destroyed bowlers' attempts to defeat him.

Bradman's 1948 team remains the only unbeaten Australian side to tour England. They had a devastating opening bowler partnership in Lindwall and Miller, an unsurpassed wicket-keeper in Don Tallon, spin Bradman seldom needed, left-arm bowlers who could open with swing and revert to spin, and an eagerness to do well that produced totals of 300 or more in 27 innings. No county team made 300 against them. They scored 47 first-class centuries between them, and nobody who watched them doubted the great fun they had in defeating England and having a drink with them afterwards.

Australia's 1948 side was so strong Bradman rarely called on leg-spinners Colin McCool and Doug Ring. In 34 matches McCool appeared in only 17 and had only 18 tour innings. With a new ball available after 55 overs, Bradman had no reason to use McCool or Ring any more and although McCool's leg spinners had won Tests and he had a splendid record as a run-getter and slips fielder he did not play in a Test in England.

Although he avoided long innings to avoid excessive strain on a long-standing rib injury, Bradman sustained his career average by scoring a century at better than every third time he batted. The certainty that he could always rely on his own batting gave him an advantage no other Australian captain enjoyed. His 31 innings on the tour yielded 11 centuries and allowed him to head the batting averages with 2428 runs at 89.92. Seven of his team averaged more than 50 runs an innings while only seven centuries were made against them. Only at Manchester, in the Test ruined by rain, did their catching skill falter—Hassett twice dropped Washbrook on the boundary when Washbrook took the bait and hooked Lindwall bouncers—but throughout the tour the team's throwing and gathering was immaculate.

Like the 1882, 1902 and 1921 Australian teams in England, the balance of the 1948 side was faultless. The 1882 Australians were a splendid mixture of powerful hitters (Massie, Bonnor, Horan), stroke-makers (Murdoch, Garrett, Jones), a noted stonewaller (Alick Bannerman), hostile bowlers (Spofforth, Boyle, Palmer, Garrett and Giffen), backed by a great keeper (Blackham). They sustained a very high standard in the field but they only played one Test, and although they upset all forecasts by defeating a full-strength England (by seven runs), they were not sufficiently tested to compare with the other three great teams.

Both the 1921 and 1948 teams faced only one major challenge to their supremacy, the 1921 side after the serious part of the tour was over and they went down to an England XI at Eastbourne by 28 runs, the 1948 team when they were set to score more than 400 runs to win on the last day at Leeds and achieved it. The 1902 Australians had to overcome a tougher path, with every match against a fine England eleven keenly contested. They kept their heads to win an epic Third Test by three runs at Old Trafford and retain The Ashes, a wonderful achievement in a wet summer that gave England an advantage.

Herbie Collins, one of the shrewdest of captains, leading out the New South Wales team against England in 1923-24. Charlie Macartney and Jack Gregory are behind Collins, with keeper Bert Oldfield chatting with Johnny Taylor, and Arthur Mailey hitching up his sweater.

This ability to triumph despite adversity is not always present in even well-balanced cricket teams, but since 1948 it has been displayed by teams led by Richie Benaud, Ian Chappell and to a lesser extent by Allan Border's 1989 team in England. Benaud created a winning combination out of nothing when Australia was in a slump. The 1960–61 series with the West Indies, which he presided over with Frank Worrell, restored Australian prestige and he carried it on against Peter May's England team in England in 1961. Ian Chappell's feat in rebuilding a demoralised Australia in the 1970s deserves similar commendation. His team's five–one defeat of a powerful West Indian team in Australia in 1975–76 was one of Australia's greatest performances.

The balance of Benaud's 1961 team, however, does not stand up to comparison with Australia's 1882, 1902, 1921 and 1948 sides. Apart from Davidson, Benaud and McKenzie, the bowling lacked hostility and often looked pedestrian. Benaud's bowling needed more variety. A talented off-spinner in the Hugh Trumble (1902) or Ashley Mallett (1970s) mould or a skilled bowler of left-arm spin like Charlie Macartney (1921), Bill Johnston and Ernie Toshack (1948) would have benefited his team enormously. Lindsay Kline did the job for Benaud in Australia against the West Indies and in South Africa for Ian Craig in 1957–58, but was not used in a Test in 1961.

Ian Chappell's team in the 1970s was only at its best when both Lillee and Thomson were operating at peak form. Chappell had a splendid cast of supporting bowlers in Walker, Gilmour and Mallett, and seldom needed his own right-arm legspin. The batting, with brother Greg superb, was strong but occasionally upset by the lack of a reliable opening pair. The team's fielding and wicket-keeping were sustained at a high level and like the other great sides had some exciting throwing arms.

None of Border's teams, apart from one brilliant performance in the 1989 series in England, rated comparison with Australia's 1902, 1921, 1948, 1960–61, and 1975–76 sides. Until Shane Warne came along, the Border teams lacked a spinner worth automatic selection. Through no fault of Border's, the middle order batting often failed and the tailenders' presence at the creases was usually brief. The lack of a genuinely hostile opening bowler to partner McDermott left a gap Merv Hughes did not always fill.

Significantly, all the great Australian teams were blessed with wicket-keepers of exceptional skill. Blackham (1882), Kelly (1902), Carter and Oldfield (1921), Tallon (1948), Grout (1960–61), and Marsh (1975–76) were all major contributors to success, offering support Ian Healy now provides for Australian teams after a hesitant start. His brilliant first Test 102 not out at Manchester on the 1993 tour silenced his critics.

Judged on the balance of the teams and the results they achieved my pick as the best-ever Australian side is the 1948 team in England, closely followed in order by the 1902, 1975–76, and 1921 outfits, with the 1960–61 side a distinguished challenger. My choice for the best

Ian Healy. His chanceless century at Manchester in 1993 silenced critics and pressed home a resounding Australian victory.

Australian captain of all time is not nearly as clear-cut because captains of other teams such as Harry Trott (1896), Monty Noble (1909), Bill Woodfull (1930 and 1934 in England), Lindsay Hassett in South Africa in 1949–50, and Herbie Collins with the First AIF and in Australia in 1924–25, all deserve comparison with Murdoch, Darling, Armstrong, Bradman and Ian Chappell.

Clem Hill and Hugh Trumble always maintained Trott was the finest captain they ever played under, intriguing assessments from men who played a lot of cricket with Darling as their leader. Noble regained The Ashes in England after a disastrous defeat in the First Test, and

Jack Pollard's Selections

Best-ever Australian team: the 1948 Australians in England.

Finest Australian captain: Monty Noble, whose 1909 Australians won The Ashes after a heavy first Test defeat. Mark Taylor, fairly new in the job, could be a candidate later.

Best opposing team: the 1905 England team which beat Australia two–nil under the captaincy of F.S. Jackson.

Most formidable opponents: Curtly Ambrose in 1993, closely followed by Garfield Sobers from 1960 to 1969, and by Harold Larwood in 1932–33.

Best allrounder: Keith Miller, often Australia's hero in his 55 Tests. Steve Waugh could challenge Miller if he retains his 1995 form in the West Indies.

Best Australian bowler: W.J. ('Bill') O'Reilly in a close decision over Dennis Lillee, Clarrie Grimmett, and Shane Warne.

Best batsman: Don Bradman — no other cricketer has come close to his feat in scoring a century at better than every third time he batted.

Collins' poker-faced manoeuvres were legendary. Woodfull twice recovered The Ashes in England after they had been lost in the previous series in Australia. Hassett pulled off remarkable wins for Australia, firstly by bluffing South Africa into continung to bat on a wet pitch—and instructing his bowlers not to get them out while conceding few runs—in the Third Test of the 1949–50 rubber after Australia had been routed for 75 in their first innings, and secondly by declaring at 7 for 32 on a Brisbane 'sticky' against Freddie Brown's team in 1950–51.

The acumen of these outstanding captains on the field was as impressive as their relations with their players off it. Harry Trott once opened the bowling with leg-spin because he noticed that W.G. Grace was slow-footed in his bulky mature years. Noble disciplined players who stayed up all night partying by sending them in first next morning, albeit unshaven. Collins sat on the end of their beds discussing tactics with key players at their hotels. Woodfull directed religious newcomers to England to the nearest churches of their faith. Darling extracted fiery spells from pace man Ernie Jones by asking Joe Kelly to stand up on the stumps for a few balls, knowing Jones would be affronted. To get used to batting on wet pitches similar to those in England, Darling had the Adelaide oval curator flood the practice pitches for several days before he left.

Monty (M.A.) Noble.

Harry Trott captained Australia on the last of his four trips to England in 1896, and in eight Tests altogether for five wins and three losses. He was rated an outstanding tactician.

Bradman planned his tactics for the 1948 campaign in Australia months before his team sailed, building on the rule change that gave him a big supply of new balls, drawing on his remarkable memory of English batsmen's strengths and weaknesses. He knew Edrich liked to cut, that Compton often hit his legside shots in the air, and he felt confident that in Miller, Lindwall, Johnston and Toshack he had the bowlers to discomfort Hutton. Toshack's ability to get through his overs economically, while the pace men waited for new balls, became an important part of his plans once he had proved his own fitness by scoring five centuries in six matches against the 1947–48 Indian tourists.

I always thought Bradman knew how to leave graciously when he was out, regardless of whether he had made a century or a duck. There was never any complaint or gesture of dissent towards umpires even when he was the victim of bad decisions. Through 338 first-class innings in which he scored 117 centuries, he was sometimes given out unfairly but these misfortunes were impossible to detect from his reactions in leaving the crease. When Neville Cardus asked him to explain his continuous success, Bradman said: 'Well, I treat every ball as if it were the first ball, whether I've just broken my duck or passed a double century, and I never consider the possibility that anybody can get me out.' No wonder almost two-thirds of his centuries were chanceless, and that 37 times he continued on past 200, and six times past 300.

Australia won four out of five Tests series against England between 1930 and 1948 with Bradman in the team for all matches, and even in the series Australia lost (1932–33) he still headed the Australian averages with 56 runs an innings. When he took over as captain in 1936 he became the only Test leader in history to win a rubber after losing the first two Tests. Even in 1938, when England ran up 7 for 903 declared in the fifth Test, he brought back The Ashes.

As Ray Robinson said, no other captain could go into a series knowing he could score more runs than anybody else, but surely that should not detract from his ranking as a captain. He was a captain who won 11 of his 20 Tests, lost three, had five drawn, and one washed out, and was never tactically outsmarted. His teams always played bright, enterprising cricket, and no Australian captain was ever more aware of the need to score quickly. He averaged 36 runs an hour in his 80 Test innings and while he was at the crease he and his partners exceeded a run a minute, a rate that produced victories when painstaking innings would have brought draws.

It was not in Bradman's nature to join team-mates and opponents at the bar after a day's play. Normally he preferred a cup of tea in his hotel room, but he did join in the champagne-drinking after the 1948 team won The Ashes in a memorable day's batting at Leeds.

It probably would have been more fun to have played under Linsday Hassett, who made friends more easily than any Australian captain. From the days of his captaincy of the Services XI, to the tours of South Africa and England after he succeeded Bradman, Hassett's enjoyment of the leisure hours after a hard day's play was free-wheeling stuff, interspersed with notable pranks and his rendition of 'The Bridle Hanging On The Wall' and other ditties.

Of the recent captains of Australian first-class teams, Geoff Lawson impressed with his eagerness to chase victories instead of allowing New South Wales' matches to drift tamely into draws. He was an unusually thoughtful leader, but unfortunately injuries usually had him fighting for a Test place, instead of staking claims to become the first fast bowler to captain Australia.

Pitch-forked into the job when Kim Hughes made his tearful departure, Border often had only his own batting to rely on. Success was elusive for him but he was never a lucky captain like Benaud, though his leadership had more polish than Ian Chappell's. His record as a fighter never wavered but his teams produced disappointing results until the 1989 and 1993 English tours. It remains an oddity that he has become Test cricket's highest run-scorer using very few shots.

In assessing the performances of Australian touring teams, constant reminders crop up of the importance of a little luck in evenly-fought matches. Joe Darling suggested to Harry Trott in 1896 that the great W.G. Grace was slow-footed because of his increasing bulk—Grace was 48—and proposed that Trott open the bowling with his leg-breaks to expose Grace's footwork.

Shane Warne in the delivery stride demonstrates the powers of concentration that made him a cricket mega-star in England in 1993. His ability to bowl long spells without losing accuracy is remarkable. *Peter Ward, Herald and Weekly Times*

Trott's leg-breaks to open a Test attack caused almost as big a sensation as Shane Warne's delivery that bowled Mike Gatting in 1993. Each time the bowler was fortunate to pitch the leg-break just in the right spot to deceive accomplished batsmen. Trott's delivery did not have the benefit of television replays that Warne's leg-break enjoyed, but keeper Kelly talked about it until the day he died.

The 1993 Australians' margin of superiority should not earn them a place among the great Australian teams, for they were not a well-balanced side, particularly after Craig McDermott went home, presenting England's openers with the weakest attack since McCabe and Waite began our attack in 1938. With a suspect middle order like this they were lucky to encounter such pathetic England bowlers, some of whom would struggle to play first-grade district cricket in Australia. The 1989 Australians faced much sterner opposition and were a far more balanced side, with Trevor Hohns' left-handed batting and allround performance an unsung asset.

Crowds were returning to Test cricket in 1994–95 and performances by the national team improving. Formation of the Australian Cricket Academy, higher pay for Test players, and a massive outlay in school and teenaged cricket had bolstered the game from its lethargy. Taylor's teams did a great job in restoring respect for winning a baggy green cap, but the occasional collapses of the Test team, when they appear certain of winning, is a worrying factor as Australia pushes for top spot among the world's cricket nations.

APPENDIX
HOME...

Apart from tour summaries, the tours recorded here were not major ventures, even though they may have included Test matches.

CRICKET TEAMS IN AUSTRALIA

Season	Touring Team	First-class Results					All Matches					Captain
		Games	W	L	D	T	Games	W	L	D	T	
1861/62	HH Stephenson's	–	–	–	–	–	14	6	3	5	–	HH Stephenson
1863/64	G Parr's	–	–	–	–	–	14	7	2	5	–	G Parr
1873/74	WG Grace's	–	–	–	–	–	15	10	3	2	–	WG Grace
1876/77	J Lillywhite's	3	1	1	1	–	15	5	4	6	–	J Lillywhite
1878/79	Lord Harris's	5	2	3	–	–	13	5	3	5	–	Lord Harris
1881/82	A Shaw's	7	3	2	2	–	18	8	3	7	–	A Shaw
1882/83	Hon IFW Bligh's	7	4	3	–	–	17	9	3	5	–	Hon IFW Bligh
1884/85	A Shrewsbury's	8	6	2	–	–	33	16	2	15	–	A Shrewsbury
1886/87	A Shrewsbury's	10	6	2	2	–	30	12	2	16	–	A Shrewsbury
1887/88	GF Vernon's	8	6	1	1	–	26	11	1	14	–	GF Vernon's
	A Shrewsbury's	7	5	2	–	–	22	14	2	6	–	A Shrewsbury
	Combined England	1	1	–	–	–	1	1	–	–	–	WW Read
1891/92	Lord Sheffield's	8	6	2	–	–	27	12	2	13	–	WG Grace
1894/95	AE Stoddart's	12	8	4	–	–	23	9	4	10	–	AE Stoddart
1897/98	AE Stoddart's	12	4	5	3	–	22	6	5	11	–	AE Stoddart
1898/99	New Zealanders	2	–	2	–	–	4	1	2	1	–	LB Cobcroft
1901/02	AC MacLaren's	11	5	6	–	–	22	8	6	8	–	AC MacLaren
1902/03	Lord Hawke's	3	–	2	1	–	3	–	2	1	–	PF Warner
1903/04	MCC	14	9	2	3	–	20	10	2	8	–	PF Warner
1907/08	MCC	18	7	4	7	–	19	7	4	8	–	AO Jones
1910/11	South Africans	15	6	7	2	–	22	12	7	3	–	PW Sherwell
1911/12	MCC	14	11	1	2	–	18	12	1	5	–	JWHT Douglas
1913/14	New Zealanders	4	1	2	1	–	9	5	2	2	–	D Reese
1920/21	MCC	13	5	6	2	–	22	9	6	7	–	JWHT Douglas
1922/23	MCC	7	–	3	4	–	8	–	3	5	–	AC MacLaren
1924/25	MCC	17	7	6	4	–	23	8	6	9	–	AER Gilligan
1925/26	New Zealanders	4	–	1	3	–	9	3	1	5	–	WR Patrick
1927/28	New Zealanders	1	–	1	–	–	1	–	1	–	–	TC Lowry
1928/29	MCC	17	8	1	8	–	24	10	1	13	–	APF Chapman
1929/30	AHH Gilligan's	5	2	2	1	–	5	2	2	1	–	AHH Gilligan
1930/31	West Indians	14	4	8	2	–	16	5	8	3	–	GC Grant
1931/32	South Africans	16	4	6	6	–	18	6	6	6	–	HB Cameron
1932/33	MCC	17	10	1	5	1	22	10	1	10	1	DR Jardine
1935/36	MCC	6	3	1	2	–	6	3	1	2	–	ERT Holmes
1936/37	MCC	17	5	5	7	–	25	7	5	13	–	GOB Allen
1937/38	New Zealanders	3	–	3	–	–	3	–	3	–	–	ML Page
1946/47	MCC	17	1	3	13	–	25	4	3	18	–	WR Hammond
1947/48	Indians	14	2	7	5	–	20	5	7	8	–	NB Amarnath
1950/51	MCC	16	5	4	7	–	25	7	4	14	–	FR Brown
1951/52	West Indians	13	4	8	1	–	15	5	8	2	–	JDC Goddard
1952/53	South Africans	16	4	3	9	–	23	7	3	13	–	JE Cheetham
1953/54	New Zealanders	3	2	–	1	–	3	2	–	1	–	B Sutcliffe
1954/55	MCC	17	8	2	7	–	23	13	2	8	–	L Hutton
1958/59	MCC	17	4	4	9	–	20	7	4	9	–	PBH May
1960/61	West Indians	14	4	5	4	1	22	10	5	5	2	FMM Worrell
1961/62	New Zealanders	3	–	2	1	–	3	–	2	1	–	JR Reid

Continued

TEAMS IN AUSTRALIA

Season	Touring Team	First-class Results Games	W	L	D	T	All Matches Games	W	L	D	T	Captain
1962/63	MCC	15	4	3	8	–	26	12	3	11	–	ER Dexter
1963/64	South Africans	14	5	3	6	–	28	16	4	8	–	TL Goddard
1964/65	Pakistanis	4	–	–	4	–	4	–	–	4	–	Hanif Mohammad
1965/66	MCC	15	5	2	8	–	23	13	2	8	–	MJK Smith
1967/68	New Zealanders	4	–	2	2	–	7	2	2	3	–	BW Sinclair
	Indians	9	–	6	3	–	15	4	6	5	–	Nawab of Pataudi jr
1968/69	West Indians	15	4	5	6	–	23	9	5	9	–	GS Sobers
1969/70	New Zealanders	3	–	–	3	–	8	3	–	5	–	GT Dowling
1970/71	MCC	15	3	1	11	–	25	10	2	13	–	R Illingworth
	New Zealanders	1	–	–	1	–	2	–	1	1	–	GT Dowling
1971/72	World XI	12	5	2	5	–	16	5	3	8	–	GS Sobers
	New Zealanders	–	–	–	–	–	2	1	1	–	–	RW Morgan
1972/73	Pakistanis	8	2	5	1	–	13	5	6	2	–	Intikhab Alam
	New Zealanders	1	–	–	1	–	3	2	–	1	–	BE Congdon
1973/74	New Zealanders	9	2	5	2	–	13	5	6	2	–	BE Congdon
1974/75	MCC	15	5	5	5	–	23	8	9	6	–	MH Denness
	New Zealanders	–	–	–	–	–	3	3	–	–	–	BE Congdon
1975/76	West Indians	13	3	6	4	–	21	8	7	6	–	CH Lloyd
1976/77	Pakistanis	5	1	2	2	–	5	1	2	2	–	Mushtaq Mohammad
	MCC	2	–	1	1	–	2	–	1	1	–	AW Greig
1977/78	Indians	11	6	5	–	–	20	12	6	2	–	BS Bedi
1978/79	England	13	8	2	3	–	26	17	4	5	–	JM Brearley
	Pakistanis	4	1	1	2	–	5	2	1	2	–	Mushtaq Mohammad
1979/80	West Indians	7	5	1	1	–	21	13	5	3	–	CH Lloyd
	England	8	3	3	2	–	20	10	7	3	–	JM Brearley
1980/81	New Zealanders	7	1	2	4	–	29	14	9	6	–	GP Howarth
	Indians	8	2	2	4	–	25	8	11	6	–	SM Gavaskar
1981/82	Pakistanis	8	2	2	4	–	21	8	8	5	–	Javed Miandad
	West Indians	7	4	1	2	–	24	16	5	3	–	CH Lloyd
1982/83	England	11	4	3	4	–	23	10	9	4	–	RGD Willis
	New Zealanders	2	–	–	1	1	22	13	7	1	1	GP Howarth
	Sri Lankans	2	–	–	2	–	5	1	1	3	–	LRD Mendis
1983/84	Pakistanis	11	3	3	5	–	24	7	11	6	–	Imran Khan
	West Indians	–	–	–	–	–	13	10	2	–	1	CH Lloyd
1984/85	West Indians	11	4	2	5	–	33	24	4	5	–	CH Lloyd
	Sri Lankans	1	1	–	–	–	22	11	11	–	–	LRD Mendis
	England	–	–	–	–	–	3	–	3	–	–	DI Gower
	Indians	–	–	–	–	–	5	5	–	–	–	SM Gavaskar
	Pakistanis	–	–	–	–	–	5	3	2	–	–	Javed Miandad
	New Zealanders	–	–	–	–	–	4	1	2	1	–	GP Howarth
1985/86	New Zealanders	6	2	1	3	–	19	5	7	7	–	JV Coney
	Indians	5	1	–	4	–	19	8	7	4	–	Kapil Dev
1986/87	England	11	5	3	3	–	30	19	7	4	–	MW Gatting
	Pakistanis	–	–	–	–	–	4	2	2	–	–	Imran Khan
	West Indians	1	–	–	1	–	13	4	8	1	–	IVA Richards
1987/88	New Zealanders	6	1	2	3	–	19	8	8	3	–	JJ Crowe
	Sri Lankans	3	–	1	2	–	18	6	9	3	–	RS Madugalle
	England	1	–	–	1	–	2	–	1	1	–	MW Gatting
1988/89	West Indians	11	4	2	5	–	23	11	7	5	–	IVA Richards
	Tamil Nadu	1	–	1	–	–	3	–	3	–	–	S Vasudevan
	Pakistanis	1	–	–	1	–	14	6	7	1	–	Imran Khan
	New Zealanders	–	–	–	–	–	1	–	1	–	–	JG Wright
	Worcestershire	–	–	–	–	–	2	–	2	–	–	PA Neale
1989/90	New Zealanders	3	–	–	3	–	4	–	1	3	–	JG Wright
	Pakistanis	6	–	3	3	–	17	5	9	3	–	Imran Khan
	Sri Lankans	6	–	2	4	–	27	6	14	7	–	A Ranatunga
	Lancashire	–	–	–	–	–	8	3	5	–	–	DP Hughes
1990/91	England	11	1	5	5	–	28	8	14	6	–	GA Gooch
	Wellington	1	–	1	–	–	4	1	1	2	–	EB McSweeney
	New Zealanders	–	–	–	–	–	11	4	7	–	–	MD Crowe
	Lancashire	–	–	–	–	–	6	4	2	–	–	G Flower
1991/92	New Zealanders	–	–	–	–	–	6	4	2	–	–	MD Crowe
	Indians	7	1	5	1	–	29	7	19	2	1	M Azharuddin
	West Indians	1	–	1	–	–	22	12	8	1	1	RB Richardson
	Pakistanis	2	–	–	2	–	14	5	6	3	–	Imran Khan
	South Africans	–	–	–	–	–	12	7	3	2	–	KC Wessels
	Zimbabweans	–	–	–	–	–	6	1	5	–	–	DL Houghton
	Sri Lankans	–	–	–	–	–	7	2	4	1	–	PA de Silva
	England	–	–	–	–	–	9	6	2	1	–	GA Gooch
1992/93	West Indians	8	3	1	4	–	22	13	5	4	–	RB Richardson
	Pakistanis	1	1	–	–	–	12	5	6	–	1	Javed Miandad
	England 'A'	4	–	2	2	–	11	4	4	3	–	MD Moxon
1993/94	New Zealanders	7	2	3	2	–	16	5	9	2	–	MD Crowe
	South Africans	5	1	2	2	–	17	6	9	2	–	KC Wessels
	Indian XI	–	–	–	–	–	3	–	3	–	–	SR Tendulkar
1994/95	England XI	11	3	4	4	–	24	9	11	4	–	MA Atherton
	Zimbabweans	2	–	1	1	–	19	8	10	1	–	A Flower

ENGLAND IN AUSTRALIA

Touring Teams	First-class results					All Matches				
	Games	W	L	D	T	Games	W	L	D	T
England	446	183	114	148	1	891	381	180	329	1
Indians	55	12	26	17	–	139	49	62	27	1
New Zealanders	70	11	27	31	1	205	82	75	47	1
Pakistanis	50	10	16	24	–	138	49	60	28	1
Sri Lankans	12	1	3	8	–	79	26	39	14	–
South Africans	66	20	21	25	–	120	54	32	34	–
West Indians	115	39	40	35	1	268	140	77	47	4
World XI	12	5	2	5	–	16	5	3	8	–
Zimbabweans	2	–	1	1	–	25	9	15	1	–
	828	281	250	294	3	1881	795	543	535	8

ENGLAND TEAMS IN AUSTRALIA

Season	Touring Team	First-class Results					All Matches					Captain
		Games	W	L	D	T	Games	W	L	D	T	
1861/62	HH Stephenson's	–	–	–	–	–	14	6	3	5	–	HH Stephenson
1863/64	G Parr's	–	–	–	–	–	14	7	2	5	–	G Parr
1873/74	WG Grace's	–	–	–	–	–	15	10	3	2	–	WG Grace
1876/77	J Lillywhite's	3	1	1	1	–	15	5	4	6	–	J Lillywhite
1878/79	Lord Harris's	5	2	3	–	–	13	5	3	5	–	Lord Harris
1881/82	A Shaw's	7	3	2	2	–	18	8	3	7	–	A Shaw
1882/83	Hon IFW Bligh's	7	4	3	–	–	17	9	3	5	–	Hon IFW Bligh
1884/85	A Shrewsbury's	8	6	2	–	–	33	16	2	15	–	A Shrewsbury
1886/87	A Shrewsbury's	10	6	2	2	–	30	12	2	16	–	A Shrewsbury
1887/88	GF Vernon's	8	6	1	1	–	26	11	1	14	–	GF Vernon's
1887/88	A Shrewsbury's	7	5	2	–	–	22	14	2	6	–	A Shrewsbury
1887/88	Combined England	1	1	–	–	–	1	1	–	–	–	WW Read
1891/92	Lord Sheffield's	8	6	2	–	–	27	12	2	13	–	WG Grace
1894/95	AE Stoddart's	12	8	4	–	–	23	9	4	10	–	AE Stoddart
1897/98	AE Stoddart's	12	4	5	3	–	22	6	5	11	–	AE Stoddart
1901/02	AC MacLaren's	11	5	6	–	–	22	8	6	8	–	AC MacLaren
1902/03	Lord Hawke's	3	–	2	1	–	3	–	2	1	–	PF Warner
1903/04	MCC	14	9	2	3	–	20	10	2	8	–	PF Warner
1907/08	MCC	18	7	4	7	–	19	7	4	8	–	AO Jones
1911/12	MCC	14	11	1	2	–	18	12	1	5	–	JWHT Douglas
1920/21	MCC	13	5	6	2	–	22	9	6	7	–	JWHT Douglas
1922/23	MCC	7	–	3	4	–	8	–	3	5	–	AC MacLaren
1924/25	MCC	17	7	6	4	–	23	8	6	9	–	AER Gilligan
1928/29	MCC	17	8	1	8	–	24	10	1	13	–	APF Chapman
1929/30	AHH Gilligan's	5	2	2	1	–	5	2	2	1	–	AHH Gilligan
1932/33	MCC	17	10	1	5	1	22	10	1	10	1	DR Jardine
1935/36	MCC	6	3	1	2	–	6	3	1	2	–	ERT Holmes
1936/37	MCC	17	5	5	7	–	25	7	5	13	–	GOB Allen
1946/47	MCC	17	1	3	13	–	25	4	3	18	–	WR Hammond
1950/51	MCC	16	5	4	7	–	25	7	4	14	–	FR Brown
1954/55	MCC	17	8	2	7	–	23	13	2	8	–	L Hutton
1958/59	MCC	17	4	4	9	–	20	7	4	9	–	PBH May
1962/63	MCC	15	4	3	8	–	26	12	3	11	–	ER Dexter
1965/66	MCC	15	5	2	8	–	23	13	2	8	–	MJK Smith
1970/71	MCC	15	3	1	11	–	25	10	2	13	–	R Illingworth
1974/75	MCC	15	5	5	5	–	23	8	9	6	–	MH Denness
1976/77	MCC	2	–	1	1	–	2	–	1	1	–	AW Greig
1978/79	England XI	13	8	2	3	–	26	17	4	5	–	JM Brearley
1979/80	England XI	8	3	3	2	–	20	10	7	3	–	JM Brearley
1982/83	England XI	11	4	3	4	–	23	10	9	4	–	RGD Willis
1984/85	England XI	–	–	–	–	–	3	–	3	–	–	DI Gower
1986/87	England XI	11	5	3	3	–	30	19	7	4	–	MW Gatting
1987/88	England XI	1	–	–	1	–	2	–	1	1	–	MW Gatting
1988/89	Worcestershire	–	–	–	–	–	2	–	2	–	–	PA Neale
1989/90	Lancashire	–	–	–	–	–	8	3	5	–	–	DP Hughes
1990/91	England XI	11	1	5	5	–	28	8	14	6	–	GA Gooch
1990/91	Lancashire	–	–	–	–	–	6	4	2	–	–	G Flower
1991/92	England XI	–	–	–	–	–	9	6	2	1	–	GA Gooch
1992/93	England 'A'	4	–	2	2	–	11	4	4	3	–	MD Moxon
1994/95	England XI	11	3	4	4	–	24	9	11	4	–	MA Atherton
		446	183	114	148	1	891	381	180	329	1	

FIRST-CLASS RESULTS

Opponent	Venue	First Game	Games	W	L	D	T
AUSTRALIA	Melbourne	Mar 15 1877	50	18	24	8	–
	Sydney	Feb 17 1882	49	20	23	6	–
	Adelaide	Dec 12 1884	25	7	13	5	–
	Brisbane (Ex)	Nov 28 1930	1	1	–	–	–
	Brisbane	Feb 10 1933	14	4	7	3	–
	Perth	Dec 11 1970	7	1	3	3	–
			146	51	70	25	–
Australian XIs	Melbourne	Dec 31 1887	8	3	–	5	–
	Sydney	Feb 3 1888	9	7	–	2	–

Continued

ENGLAND IN AUSTRALIA

Opponent	Venue	First Game	Games	W	L	D	T
	Brisbane	Dec 6 1907	3	–	–	3	–
	Brisbane (Ex)	Dec 4 1924	1	–	–	1	–
	Perth	Mar 21 1929	1	–	–	1	–
	Hobart (Bel)	Nov 16 1990	1	–	–	1	–
			23	10	–	13	–
Combined XIs	Brisbane (Ex)	Feb 15 1895	2	1	–	1	–
	Perth	Oct 27 1932	8	1	1	6	–
	Hobart (TCA)	Jan 15 1937	4	–	–	4	–
	Launceston	Jan 19 1951	3	2	–	1	–
			17	4	1	12	–
New South Wales	Redfern	Jan 15 1877	1	–	–	1	–
	Sydney	Dec 9 1881	59	25	16	18	–
	Canberra	Jan 26 1980	1	1	–	–	–
	Newcastle	Nov 21 1986	1	–	1	–	–
	Albury	Jan 13 1991	1	–	1	–	–
			63	26	18	19	–
Queensland	Brisbane (Ex)	Dec 7 1894	4	3	–	1	–
	Brisbane	Nov 27 1903	20	8	3	9	–
	Carrara	Jan 19 1991	1	1	–	–	–
	Caloundra	Feb 19 1993	1	–	–	1	–
			26	12	3	11	–
South Australia	Adelaide	Oct 28 1887	51	22	7	22	–
	Unley	Mar 27 1903	1	–	1	–	–
			52	22	8	22	–
Tasmania	Hobart (TCA)	Jan 25 1904	14	8	–	6	–
	Launceston	Jan 29 1904	12	8	–	4	–
			26	16	–	10	–
Victoria	Melbourne	Feb 21 1879	57	30	9	17	1
	Ballarat	Dec 20 1990	1	–	–	1	–
			58	30	9	18	1
Western Australia	Perth	Oct 26 1907	23	9	1	13	–
Others							
Surrey v The World	Melbourne	Mar 1 1862	1	–	1	–	–
The World v Surrey	Melbourne	Mar 1 1862	1	1	–	–	–
G Parrs v G Andersons	Melbourne	Mar 5 1864	1	–	1	–	–
G Andersons v G Parrs	Melbourne	Mar 5 1864	1	1	–	–	–
Non Smokers v Smokers	East Melbourne	Mar 17 1887	1	–	–	1	–
Smokers v Non Smokers	East Melbourne	Mar 17 1887	1	–	–	1	–

1922/23 MCC

First-class Results					All Matches			
Matches	Won	Lost	Drawn	Tied	Matches	Won	Lost	Drawn	Tied
7	–	3	4	–	8	–	3	5	–

Date	Venue	Opponent	Results for Touring Team
Nov 3	Perth	Western Australia	Drawn
Nov 10	Adelaide	South Australia	Lost by 6 wkts
Nov 17	Melbourne	Victoria	Lost by 2 wkts
Nov 24	Sydney	New South Wales	Lost by 5 wkts
Mar 2	Sydney	New South Wales	Drawn
Mar 7	Melbourne	*Combined Universities	Drawn
Mar 9	Melbourne	Victoria	Drawn
Mar 15	Adelaide	South Australia	Drawn

Player	M	Inn	NO	Runs	HS	50	100	Avrge	Ct/St	Overs	Mdns	Runs	Wkts	Avrge	5wi	10wm	Best
Brand, Hon DF	6	10	1	146	60	1	–	16.22	1	70.0	8	333	9	37.00	–	–	4/43
Calthorpe, Hon FSG	6	11	–	316	110	1	1	28.73	4	96.0	5	510	8	63.75	–	–	4/41
Chapman, APF	7	13	1	782	134*	6	2	65.17	10	20.7	0	99	3	33.00	–	–	1/10
Freeman, AP	7	11	4	121	57	1	–	17.29	4	214.7	25	989	30	32.97	1	–	6/176
Gibson, CH	7	11	4	82	30*	–	–	11.71	3	245.4	28	913	21	43.78	1	–	6/140
Hartley, JC	4	5	1	86	48	–	–	21.50	–	–	–	–	–	–	–	–	–
Hill-Wood, WW	5	10	1	304	122*	1	1	33.78	4	13.0	1	95	–	–	–	–	–
Lowry, TC	5	8	–	118	45	1	–	14.75	3/1	–	–	–	–	–	–	–	–
MacLaren, AC (Capt)	3	6	1	140	54	1	–	28.00	3	–	–	–	–	–	–	–	–
MacLean, JF	5	8	1	96	37	–	–	13.71	5/6	–	–	–	–	–	–	–	–
Swan, HD	1	1	–	0	0	–	–	0.00	–	–	–	–	–	–	–	–	–
Titchmarsh, CH	7	13	2	337	82	3	–	30.64	1	–	–	–	–	–	–	–	–
Tyldesley, H	4	7	–	24	7	–	–	3.43	3	82.0	9	319	12	26.58	1	–	5/100
Wilkinson, WAC	4	8	1	210	64	2	–	21.50	–	–	–	–	–	–	–	–	–
Wilson, G	6	12	2	417	142*	2	1	41.70	2	7.0	–	44	1	44.00	–	–	1/44

ENGLAND IN AUSTRALIA

1929/30 MCC

First-class Results					All Matches			
Matches	Won	Lost	Drawn	Tied	Matches	Won	Lost	Drawn	Tied
5	2	2	1	–	5	2	2	1	–

Date	Venue	Opponent	Results for Touring Team
Oct 31	Perth	Western Australia	Won by 7 wkts
Nov 8	Adelaide	South Australia	Won by 239 runs
Nov 15	Melbourne	Victoria	Lost by 7 wkts
Nov 22	Sydney	New South Wales	Drawn
Nov 29	Brisbane	Queensland	Lost by 5 wkts

Player	M	Inn	NO	Runs	HS	50	100	Avrge	Ct/St	Overs	Mdns	Runs	Wkts	Avrge	5wi	10wm	Best
Allom, MJC	5	8	5	51	18*	–	–	17.00	4	137.7	13	532	17	31.29	1	–	5/26
Barratt, F	4	7	1	78	32	–	–	13.00	1	136.3	13	455	17	26.76	2	–	5/32
Benson, ET	2	3	–	18	14	–	–	6.00	1	–	–	–	–	–	–	–	–
Bowley, EH	2	2	1	79	79*	1	–	79.00	1	24.2	–	127	7	18.14	1	–	5/30
Cornford, W	3	5	2	32	15*	–	–	10.67	7/4	–	–	–	–	–	–	–	–
Dawson, EW	5	10	1	234	83*	1	–	26.00	2	3.0	–	30	–	–	–	–	–
Ducat, A	1	2	–	23	13	–	–	11.50	–	–	–	–	–	–	–	–	–
Duleepsinhji, KS	5	10	1	349	68	3	–	38.78	6	10.0	–	60	1	60.00	–	–	1/8
Earle, GF	3	5	–	82	43	–	–	16.40	2	–	–	–	–	–	–	–	–
Gilligan, AHH (Capt)	5	9	–	265	58	3	–	29.44	–	–	–	–	–	–	–	–	–
Legge, GB	2	4	1	115	47*	–	–	38.33	1	–	–	–	–	–	–	–	–
Nichols, MS	4	7	–	197	82	1	–	28.14	7	101.2	5	407	21	19.38	1	1	8/65
Turnbull, MJ	5	9	1	216	100	–	1	27.00	3	–	–	–	–	–	–	–	–
Woolley, FE	4	7	–	425	219	–	2	60.72	8	66.0	12	270	7	38.57	–	–	4/34
Worthington, TS	5	7	–	111	66	1	–	15.86	2	69.0	6	341	8	42.63	–	–	3/151

1935/36 MCC

First-class Results					All Matches			
Matches	Won	Lost	Drawn	Tied	Matches	Won	Lost	Drawn	Tied
6	3	1	2	–	6	3	1	2	–

Date	Venue	Opponent	Results for Touring Team
Oct 31	Perth	Western Australia	Drawn
Nov 8	Adelaide	South Australia	Won by 36 runs
Nov 15	Melbourne	Victoria	Drawn
Nov 22	Sydney	New South Wales	Lost by 10 wkts
Nov 29	Brisbane	Queensland	Won by an inns & 106 runs
Dec 6	Sydney	Australian XI	Won by 203 runs

Player	M	Inn	NO	Runs	HS	50	100	Avrge	Ct/St	Overs	Mdns	Runs	Wkts	Avrge	5wi	10wm	Best
Barber, W	5	8	–	226	91	1	–	28.25	2	–	–	–	–	–	–	–	–
Baxter, AD	5	7	1	28	9*	–	–	4.67	–	146.0	16	511	17	30.06	1	–	5/61
Griffith, SC	3	4	–	67	35	–	–	16.75	3	–	–	–	–	–	–	–	–
Hardstaff, J jr	6	11	2	634	230*	4	1	70.44	2	2.0	–	3	–	–	–	–	1/3
Holmes, ERT (Capt)	5	9	–	239	80	2	–	26.55	2	42.6	5	135	4	33.75	–	–	1/3
Human, JH	4	7	–	291	118	1	1	41.57	2	15.0	1	50	2	25.00	–	–	1/12
Langridge, J	6	10	3	329	59	2	–	47.00	4	95.5	17	244	10	24.40	–	–	4/53
Lyttelton, CJ	5	9	–	176	42	–	–	19.55	–	15.0	1	47	–	–	–	–	–
Mitchell-Innes, NS	4	7	–	108	58	1	–	15.42	4	3.0	–	7	–	–	–	–	–
Parks, JH	5	9	–	315	72	4	–	35.00	3	75.5	11	225	8	28.13	–	–	3/30
Powell, AG	3	6	1	39	32	–	–	7.80	5	–	–	–	–	–	–	–	–
Read, HD	3	5	1	5	4	–	–	1.25	1	84.0	2	334	10	33.40	–	–	3/81
Sims, JM	6	10	3	150	35	–	–	21.42	3	214.3	14	834	33	25.00	2	–	7/95
Smith, D	6	11	1	361	109	2	1	36.10	8	1.0	–	5	1	5.00	–	–	1/5

1976/77 MCC

First-class Results					All Matches			
Matches	Won	Lost	Drawn	Tied	Matches	Won	Lost	Drawn	Tied
2	–	1	1	–	2	–	1	1	–

Date	Venue	Opponent	Results for Touring Team
Mar 5	Perth	Western Australia	Drawn
Mar 12	Melbourne	AUSTRALIA (Only Test)	Lost by 45 runs

Player	M	Inn	NO	Runs	HS	50	100	Avrge	Ct/St	Overs	Mdns	Runs	Wkts	Avrge	5wi	10wm	Best
Amiss, DL	2	4	–	106	64	1	–	26.50	2	–	–	–	–	–	–	–	–
Barlow, GD	1	2	–	70	60	1	–	35.00	–	–	–	–	–	–	–	–	–
Brearley, JM	2	4	1	174	61	2	–	58.00	2	–	–	–	–	–	–	–	–
Fletcher, KWR	1	2	–	5	4	–	–	2.50	2	–	–	–	–	–	–	–	–

Continued

ENGLAND IN AUSTRALIA

Player	M	Inn	NO	Runs	HS	50	100	Avrge	Ct/St	Overs	Mdns	Runs	Wkts	Avrge	5wi	10wm	Best
Greig, AW (Capt)	2	4	–	72	41	–	–	18.00	4	29.0	3	124	3	41.33	–	–	2/66
Knott, APE	2	4	–	68	42	–	–	17.00	8/–	–	–	–	–	–	–	–	–
Lever, JK	1	2	–	15	11	–	–	7.50	–	33.0	2	131	4	32.75	–	–	2/36
Miller, G	1	2	–	78	56	1	–	39.00	1	5.0	–	29	–	–	–	–	–
Old, CM	2	4	1	25	12	–	–	8.33	1	45.6	6	167	7	23.85	–	–	4/104
Randall, DW	2	4	–	225	174	–	1	56.25	1	–	–	–	–	–	–	–	–
Selvey, MWW	1	1	1	23	23*	–	–	–	–	28.2	2	183	6	30.50	–	–	3/81
Underwood, DL	1	2	–	14	7	–	–	7.00	–	23.6	4	54	4	13.50	–	–	3/16
Willis, RGD	2	2	2	6	5*	–	–	–	1	46.0	2	205	2	102.50	–	–	2/33
Woolmer, RA	2	4	–	78	51	1	–	19.50	–	20.0	3	121	1	121.00	–	–	1/51

1984/85 ENGLAND XI

First-class Results					All Matches			
Matches	Won	Lost	Drawn	Tied	Matches	Won	Lost	Drawn	Tied
–	–	–	–	–	3	–	3	–	–

Date	Venue	Opponent	Results for Touring Team
Feb 17	Melbourne	*Australia (L/O Intl)	Lost by 7 wkts
Feb 26	Sydney	*India (L/O Intl)	Lost by 86 runs
Mar 2	Melbourne	*Pakistan (L/O Intl)	Lost by 67 runs

1987/88 ENGLAND XI

First-class Results					All Matches			
Matches	Won	Lost	Drawn	Tied	Matches	Won	Lost	Drawn	Tied
1	–	–	1	–	2	–	1	1	–

Date	Venue	Opponent	Results for Touring Team
Jan 29	Sydney	AUSTRALIA (Only Test)	Drawn
Feb 4	Melbourne	*Australia (L/O Intl)	Lost by 22 runs

Player	M	Inn	NO	Runs	HS	50	100	Avrge	Ct/St	Overs	Mdns	Runs	Wkts	Avrge	5wi	10wm	Best
Athey, CWJ	1	1	–	37	37	–	–	37.00	2	–	–	–	–	–	–	–	–
Broad, BC	1	1	–	139	139	–	1	139.00	1	–	–	–	–	–	–	–	–
Capel, DJ	1	1	–	21	21	–	–	21.00	–	23.0	7	51	3	17.00	–	–	2/13
Dilley, GR	1	1	–	13	13	–	–	13.00	–	32.1	5	102	3	34.00	–	–	3/54
Emburey, JE	1	1	–	23	23	–	–	23.00	2	68.0	15	155	1	155.00	–	–	1/98
Foster, NA	1	1	–	19	19	–	–	19.00	1	34.0	12	54	2	27.00	–	–	2/27
French, BN	1	1	–	47	47	–	–	47.00	4/–	–	–	–	–	–	–	–	–
Gatting, MW (Capt)	1	1	–	13	13	–	–	13.00	–	–	–	–	–	–	–	–	–
Hemmings, EE	1	1	1	8	8*	–	–	–	–	74.0	18	160	3	53.33	–	–	3/53
Moxon, MD	1	1	–	40	40	–	–	40.00	1	–	–	–	–	–	–	–	–
Robinson, RT	1	1	–	43	43	–	–	43.00	–	–	–	–	–	–	–	–	–

1988/89 WORCESTERSHIRE

First-class Results					All Matches			
Matches	Won	Lost	Drawn	Tied	Matches	Won	Lost	Drawn	Tied
–	–	–	–	–	2	–	2	–	–

Date	Venue	Opponent	Results for Touring Team
Apr 8	Brisbane	*Queensland	Lost by 88 runs
Apr 9	Brisbane	*Queensland	Lost by 133 runs

1989/90 LANCASHIRE

First-class Results					All Matches			
Matches	Won	Lost	Drawn	Tied	Matches	Won	Lost	Drawn	Tied
–	–	–	–	–	8	3	5	–	–

Date	Venue	Opponent	Results for Touring Team
Mar 21	Devonport	*North West Tasmanian XI	Won by 2 wkts
Mar 24	Launceston	*Northern Tasmania XI	Lost by 59 runs
Mar 25	Launceston	*Tasmania	Lost by 6 wkts
Mar 27	Hobart (TCA)	*Tasmanian Cricket Association XI	Won by 7 wkts
Mar 28	Hobart (TCA)	*Tasmanian Under 23s	Won by 5 wkts
Mar 30	Launceston	*Tasmania	Lost by 4 wkts
Apr 1	Launceston	*Tasmania	Lost by 10 wkts
Apr 7	Perth	*Western Australia	Lost by 3 runs

1990/91 LANCASHIRE

	First-class Results					All Matches			
Matches	Won	Lost	Drawn	Tied	Matches	Won	Lost	Drawn	Tied
–	–	–	–	–	6	4	2	–	–

Date	Venue	Opponent	Results for Touring Team
Mar 25	Subiaco	*Subiaco–Floreat	Won by 6 wkts
Mar 26	Dianella	*Mt Lawley	Lost by 8 wkts
Mar 27	Fremantle	*Fremantle	Won by 38 runs
Apr 3	Scarborough	*Scarborough	Won by 7 wkts
Apr 5	Caversham	*Midland–Guildford	Won by 7 runs
Apr 6	Perth	*Western Australia	Lost by 33 runs

1991/92 ENGLAND XI

	First-class Results					All Matches			
Matches	Won	Lost	Drawn	Tied	Matches	Won	Lost	Drawn	Tied
–	–	–	–	–	9	6	2	1	–

Date	Venue	Opponent	Results for Touring Team
Feb 22	Perth	*India (WC L/O Intl)	Won by 9 runs
Feb 27	Melbourne	*West Indies (WC L/O Intl)	Won by 6 wkts
Mar 1	Adelaide	*Pakistan (WC L/O Intl)	No Result
Mar 5	Sydney	*Australia (WC L/O Intl)	Won by 8 wkts
Mar 9	Ballarat	*Sri Lanka (WC L/O Intl)	Won by 106 runs
Mar 12	Melbourne	*South Africa (WC L/O Intl)	Won by 3 wkts
Mar 18	Albury	*Zimbabwe (WC L/O Intl)	Lost by 9 runs
Mar 22	Sydney	*South Africa (WC L/O Intl)	Won by 19 runs
Mar 25	Melbourne	*Pakistan (WC L/O Intl)	Lost by 22 runs

1992/93 ENGLAND 'A'

	First-class Results					All Matches			
Matches	Won	Lost	Drawn	Tied	Matches	Won	Lost	Drawn	Tied
4	–	2	2	–	11	4	4	3	–

Date	Venue	Opponent	Results for Touring Team
Jan 31	Bowral	*New South Wales XI	Lost by 28 runs
Feb 2	Canberra	*Australian Capital Territory	Drawn
Feb 7	Launceston	*Tasmania	Lost by 24 runs
Feb 8	Launceston	Tasmania	Drawn
Feb 14	Melbourne	*AIS Cricket Academy	Won by 81 runs
Feb 19	Caloundra	Queensland	Drawn
Feb 26	Adelaide	South Australia	Lost by 7 wkts
Mar 4	Sydney	New South Wales	Lost by 10 wkts
Mar 10	Alice Springs	*Northern Territory Invitation XI	Won by 6 wkts
Mar 12	Perth	*Western Australia XI	Won by 5 wkts
Mar 14	Perth	*Western Australia XI	Won by 260 runs

Player	M	Inn	NO	Runs	HS	50	100	Avrge	Ct/St	Overs	Mdns	Runs	Wkts	Avrge	5wi	10wm	Best
Boiling, J	2	3	1	10	5*	–	–	5.00	1	87.0	19	232	4	58.00	–	–	3/93
Caddick, AC	2	3	–	16	16	–	–	5.33	–	61.0	18	143	5	28.60	–	–	3/68
Capel, DJ	4	6	1	109	80*	1	–	21.80	1	87.2	8	249	6	41.50	–	–	4/72
Cork, DG	3	4	–	28	22	–	–	7.00	–	54.3	11	164	3	54.67	–	–	2/65
Ilott, MC	2	3	2	38	23*	–	–	38.00	1	76.0	21	187	2	93.50	–	–	2/64
Lathwell, MN	4	7	–	332	175	–	2	47.43	1	–	–	–	–	–	–	–	–
Lloyd, GD	2	4	1	140	60	1	–	46.67	–	–	–	–	–	–	–	–	–
Middleton, TC	4	8	–	88	21	–	–	11.00	1	–	–	–	–	–	–	–	–
Millns, DJ	3	5	1	90	30	–	–	22.50	–	74.5	10	265	1	265.00	–	–	1/103
Moxon, MD (Capt)	3	6	2	194	62	2	–	48.50	1	–	–	–	–	–	–	–	–
Prichard, PR	2	4	–	48	34	–	–	12.00	–	–	–	–	–	–	–	–	–
Roseberry, MA	3	6	1	129	39	–	–	25.80	2	–	–	–	–	–	–	–	–
Russell, RC	4	6	1	103	51*	1	–	20.60	3/1	–	–	–	–	–	–	–	–
Such, PM	3	5	2	18	11*	–	–	6.00	1	106.2	21	271	6	45.17	–	–	3/36
Thorpe, GP	3	5	1	215	96	1	–	53.75	2	2.0	–	6	–	–	–	–	–

NEW ZEALANDERS IN AUSTRALIA

		First-class Results				All Matches				
Season	Touring Team	Games	W	L	D	T	Games	W	L	D	T	Captain
1898/99	New Zealanders	2	–	2	–	–	4	1	2	1	–	LB Cobcroft
1913/14	New Zealanders	4	1	2	1	–	9	5	2	2	–	D Reese
1925/26	New Zealanders	4	–	1	3	–	9	3	1	5	–	WR Patrick
1927/28	New Zealanders	1	–	1	–	–	1	–	1	–	–	TC Lowry
1937/38	New Zealanders	3	–	3	–	–	3	–	3	–	–	ML Page
1953/54	New Zealanders	3	2	–	1	–	3	2	–	1	–	B Sutcliffe
1961/62	New Zealanders	3	–	2	1	–	3	–	2	1	–	JR Reid

NEW ZEALANDERS IN AUSTRALIA

Season	Touring Team	First-class Results					All Matches					Captain
		Games	W	L	D	T	Games	W	L	D	T	
1967/68	New Zealanders	4	–	2	2	–	7	2	2	3	–	BW Sinclair
1969/70	New Zealanders	3	–	–	3	–	8	3	–	5	–	GT Dowling
1970/71	New Zealanders	1	–	–	1	–	2	–	1	1	–	GT Dowling
1971/72	New Zealanders	–	–	–	–	–	2	1	1	–	–	RW Morgan
1972/73	New Zealanders	1	–	–	1	–	3	2	–	1	–	BE Congdon
1973/74	New Zealanders	9	2	5	2	–	13	5	6	2	–	BE Congdon
1974/75	New Zealanders	–	–	–	–	–	3	3	–	–	–	BE Congdon
1980/81	New Zealanders	7	1	2	4	–	29	14	9	6	–	GP Howarth
1982/83	New Zealanders	2	–	–	1	1	22	13	7	1	1	GP Howarth
1984/85	New Zealanders	–	–	–	–	–	4	1	2	1	–	GP Howarth
1985/86	New Zealanders	6	2	1	3	–	19	5	7	7	–	JV Coney
1987/88	New Zealanders	6	1	2	3	–	19	8	8	3	–	JJ Crowe
1988/89	New Zealanders	–	–	–	–	–	1	–	1	–	–	JG Wright
1989/90	New Zealanders	3	–	–	3	–	4	–	1	3	–	JG Wright
1990/91	Wellington	1	–	1	–	–	4	1	1	2	–	EB McSweeney
1990/91	New Zealanders	–	–	–	–	–	11	4	7	–	–	MD Crowe
1991/92	New Zealanders	–	–	–	–	–	6	4	2	–	–	MD Crowe
1993/94	New Zealanders	7	2	3	2	–	16	5	9	2	–	MD Crowe
		70	11	27	31	1	205	82	75	47	1	

FIRST-CLASS RESULTS

Opponent	Venue	First Game	Games	W	L	D	T
AUSTRALIA	Sydney	Jan 5 1974	2	–	1	1	–
	Adelaide	Jan 26 1974	2	–	1	1	–
	Brisbane	Nov 28 1980	3	1	2	1	–
	Perth	Dec 12 1980	3	1	1	1	–
			13	2	6	5	–
New South Wales	Sydney	Feb 24 1899	12	–	8	4	–
Queensland	Brisbane	Dec 19 1913	6	1	2	3	–
	Bundaberg	Dec 18 1982	1	–	–	1	–
			7	1	2	4	–
South Australia	Adelaide	Jan 16 1914	11	1	5	5	–
Tasmania	Hobart (TCA)	Dec 26 1969	1	–	–	1	–
	Launceston	Jan 12 1974	2	1	–	1	–
	Devonport	Dec 18 1987	1	–	–	1	–
			4	1	–	3	–
Victoria	Melbourne	Feb 17 1899	10	1	3	5	1
Western Australia	Perth	Mar 5 1954	6	3	–	3	–

1898/99 NEW ZEALANDERS

First-class Results					All Matches			
Matches	Won	Lost	Drawn	Tied	Matches	Won	Lost	Drawn	Tied
2	–	2	–	–	4	1	2	1	–

Date	Venue	Opponent	Results for Touring Team
Feb 3	Hobart (TCA)	*Southern Tasmania	Drawn
Feb 10	Launceston	*Northern Tasmania	Won by 150 runs
Feb 17	Melbourne	Victoria	Lost by an inns & 132 runs
Feb 24	Sydney	New South Wales	Lost by an inns & 384 runs

Player	M	Inn	NO	Runs	HS	50	100	Avrge	Ct/St	Overs	Mdns	Runs	Wkts	Avrge	5wi	10wm	Best
Ashbolt, F	2	4	–	48	31	–	–	12.00	2	18.0	1	72	–	–	–	–	–
Baker, J	2	4	–	109	56	1	–	27.25	1	3.0	–	16	–	–	–	–	–
Boxshall, C	2	3	1	43	38	–	–	21.50	2	–	–	–	–	–	–	–	–
Cobcroft, LT (Capt)	2	4	1	81	59*	1	–	27.00	–	10.0	1	29	1	29.00	–	–	1/24
Downes, A	2	4	–	6	5	–	–	1.50	3	74.3	20	230	6	38.33	–	–	4/127
Fisher, AH	1	2	–	8	5	–	–	4.00	1	16.0	–	62	–	–	–	–	–
Frankish, FS	2	4	–	51	26	–	–	12.75	1	71.0	10	254	4	63.50	–	–	2/127
Lusk, HB	2	4	–	49	15	–	–	12.25	–	–	–	–	–	–	–	–	–
Mills, G	2	4	–	50	31	–	–	12.50	–	2.0	–	5	1	5.00	–	–	1/5
Reese, D	2	4	–	102	88	1	–	25.50	–	62.0	10	225	4	56.25	–	–	2/112
Sims, A	1	2	–	24	18	–	–	12.00	–	2.0	–	13	–	–	–	–	–
Upham, E	2	4	2	50	31*	–	–	25.00	1	76.0	11	249	3	83.00	–	–	2/135

1913/14 NEW ZEALANDERS

First-class Results					All Matches			
Matches	Won	Lost	Drawn	Tied	Matches	Won	Lost	Drawn	Tied
4	1	2	1	–	9	5	2	2	–

Date	Venue	Opponent	Results for Touring Team
Dec 12	West Maitland	*Northern District No 1	Won by 303 runs
Dec 14	Glen Innes	*Northern District No 2	Won by an inns & 46 runs
Dec 19	Brisbane	Queensland	Won by 12 runs
Dec 26	Sydney	New South Wales	Lost by an inns & 247 runs
Dec	Goulburn	*Southern District	Won by 8 wkts
Dec	Albury	*Albury & Border Association	Won by an inns & 127 runs
Jan 9	Melbourne	Victoria	Lost by an inns & 110 runs
Jan 16	Adelaide	South Australia	Drawn
Jan 21	Melbourne	*Melbourne Cricket Club	Drawn

Player	M	Inn	NO	Runs	HS	50	100	Avrge	Ct/St	Overs	Mdns	Runs	Wkts	Avrge	5wi	10wm	Best
Bennett, JHC	3	5	–	33	16	–	–	6.60	1	87.0	16	268	8	33.50	–	–	3/40
Boxshall, C	4	7	4	22	7	–	–	7.33	–/1	–	–	–	–	–	–	–	–
Carlton, TA	2	4	1	55	22*	–	–	18.33	1	22.0	3	143	1	143.00	–	–	1/79
Hemus, LC	4	8	–	124	46	–	–	15.50	–	3.0	–	8	–	–	–	–	–
Hickmott, RG	4	8	–	94	46	–	–	11.75	3	8.0	–	58	–	–	–	–	–
Patrick, WR	3	6	–	53	27	–	–	6.63	–	–	–	–	–	–	–	–	–
Reese, D (Capt)	4	8	1	307	130*	1	1	43.86	3	56.2	4	246	11	22.36	1	–	7/53
Robinson, CW	4	7	1	84	31	–	–	14.00	2	85.4	9	396	14	28.29	–	–	4/129
Sandman, DM	4	8	2	182	56	2	–	30.33	4	101.3	6	457	14	32.64	1	–	5/41
Snedden, NC	4	8	–	244	88	3	–	30.50	1	16.0	–	93	2	46.50	–	–	2/51
Somervell, RC	1	2	–	–	–	–	–	–	–	2.0	1	14	–	–	–	–	–
Taylor, LG	3	6	–	106	43	–	–	17.67	3	–	–	–	–	–	–	–	–
Tuckwell, BJ	4	8	–	97	33	–	–	12.13	4	2.0	–	15	–	–	–	–	–

1925/26 NEW ZEALANDERS

First-class Results					All Matches			
Matches	Won	Lost	Drawn	Tied	Matches	Won	Lost	Drawn	Tied
4	–	1	3	–	9	3	1	5	–

Date	Venue	Opponent	Results for Touring Team
Dec 4	Brisbane	Queensland	Lost by an inns & 92 runs
Dec 11	Goulburn	*Goulburn	Won by an inns & 156 runs
Dec	Wagga Wagga	*Wagga Wagga	Won by an inns & 53 runs
Dec 18	Melbourne	Victoria	Drawn
Dec 23	Ballarat	*Ballarat	Won by an inns & 71 runs
Dec 26	Adelaide	South Australia	Drawn
Jan 1	Sydney	New South Wales	Drawn
Jan 8	Newcastle	*Newcastle	Drawn
Jan 11	Maitland	*Northern District	Drawn

Player	M	Inn	NO	Runs	HS	50	100	Avrge	Ct/St	Overs	Mdns	Runs	Wkts	Avrge	5wi	10wm	Best
Alcott, CFW	4	7	2	298	116	1	1	59.60	7	117.0	11	396	7	56.57	–	–	2/40
Alloo, AW	4	7	1	65	18*	–	–	10.83	–	39.5	–	155	4	46.25	–	–	3/41
Blunt, RC	4	7	–	275	73	4	–	39.29	1	82.0	1	506	8	63.25	–	–	4/72
Crawford, CG	2	4	2	31	23*	–	–	15.50	1	–	–	–	–	–	–	–	–
Cunningham, WHR	4	5	2	28	16	–	–	9.33	–	124.5	4	635	13	48.85	1	–	5/125
Dacre, CC	4	7	–	243	80	2	–	34.71	3	1.0	–	4	–	–	–	–	–
Gillespie, HD	1	2	–	2	2	–	–	1.00	–	–	–	–	–	–	–	–	–
Hope, RW	2	2	–	5	5	–	–	2.50	–	42.0	–	252	3	84.00	–	–	2/119
James, KC	1	1	–	10	10	–	–	10.00	–	–	–	–	–	–	–	–	–
Lowry, TC	4	7	–	213	123	–	1	30.43	4/3	–	–	–	–	–	–	–	–
McBeath, DJ	2	3	1	21	16	–	–	10.50	–	43.0	5	178	3	59.33	–	–	1/28
Oliver, CJ	4	7	–	218	68	2	–	31.14	1	10.0	–	48	–	–	–	–	–
Patrick, WR (Capt)	4	6	1	196	143	–	1	39.20	–	19.0	–	104	2	52.00	–	–	1/18
Worker, RV	4	7	–	195	89	1	–	27.86	–	–	–	–	–	–	–	–	–

1927/28 NEW ZEALANDERS

First-class Results					All Matches			
Matches	Won	Lost	Drawn	Tied	Matches	Won	Lost	Drawn	Tied
1	–	1	–	–	1	–	1	–	–

Date	Venue	Opponent	Results for Touring Team
Oct 28	Sydney	New South Wales	Lost by 10 wkts

Player	M	Inn	NO	Runs	HS	50	100	Avrge	Ct/St	Overs	Mdns	Runs	Wkts	Avrge	5wi	10wm	Best
Alcott, CFW	1	2	–	54	43	–	–	27.00	–	8.0	–	33	–	–	–	–	–
Blunt, RC	1	2	–	116	63	2	–	58.00	1	12.0	–	83	–	–	–	–	–
Dacre, CC	1	2	–	64	54	1	–	32.00	–	1.0	–	7	–	–	–	–	–
Dempster, CS	1	2	–	35	32	–	–	17.50	–	1.0	–	7	–	–	–	–	–
Henderson, M	1	2	1	25	25*	–	–	25.00	1	13.0	1	76	2	38.00	–	–	2/76

Continued

Player	M	Inn	NO	Runs	HS	50	100	Avrge	Ct/St	Overs	Mdns	Runs	Wkts	Avrge	5wi	10wm	Best
Lowry, TC (Capt)	1	2	–	79	44	–	–	39.50	1/2	–	–	–	–	–	–	–	–
McGirr, HM	1	2	–	22	13	–	–	11.00	1	17.0	3	87	3	29.00	–	–	3/87
Merritt, WE	1	2	1	28	22	–	–	28.00	–	23.2	–	218	5	43.60	1	–	5/118
Mills, JE	1	2	–	28	16	–	–	14.00	–	0.1	–	0	–	–	–	–	–
Oliver, CJ	1	2	–	7	7	–	–	3.50	–	–	–	–	–	–	–	–	–
Page, ML	1	2	–	89	51	1	–	44.50	–	5.0	–	42	–	–	–	–	–

1937/38 NEW ZEALANDERS

First-class Results					All Matches				
Matches	Won	Lost	Drawn	Tied	Matches	Won	Lost	Drawn	Tied
3	–	3	–	–	3	–	3	–	–

Date	Venue	Opponent	Results for Touring Team
Nov 5	Adelaide	South Australia	Lost by 10 wkts
Nov 12	Melbourne	Victoria	Lost by 5 wkts
Nov 19	Sydney	New South Wales	Lost by 8 wkts

Player	M	Inn	NO	Runs	HS	50	100	Avrge	Ct/St	Overs	Mdns	Runs	Wkts	Avrge	5wi	10wm	Best
Carson, WN	1	2	1	67	40*	–	–	67.00	–	11.0	1	33	2	16.50	–	–	2/17
Cowie, JA	2	4	1	18	11	–	–	6.00	–	61.0	8	175	9	19.44	–	–	4/76
Donnelly, MP	2	4	–	40	24	–	–	10.00	2	19.3	1	66	1	66.00	–	–	1/56
Hadlee, WA	2	4	–	104	51	1	–	26.00	–	2.0	–	10	–	–	–	–	–
Kerr, JL	3	6	–	105	41	–	–	17.50	–	1.7	–	10	–	–	–	–	–
Lamason, JR	2	4	–	34	29	–	–	8.50	1	6.0	1	21	–	–	–	–	–
Lowry, TC	1	2	1	8	8*	–	–	8.00	2	–	–	–	–	–	–	–	–
Moloney, DAR	3	6	–	92	42	–	–	15.33	1	48.7	6	194	4	48.50	–	–	2/77
Page, ML (Capt)	1	2	1	41	21*	–	–	41.00	1	–	–	–	–	–	–	–	–
Parsloe, CK	3	6	1	36	15	–	–	7.20	1	63.0	5	243	9	27.00	1	–	5/47
Roberts, AW	2	4	–	19	9	–	–	4.75	2	41.0	9	107	–	–	–	–	–
Tindill, EWT	2	4	1	41	25	–	–	13.67	4	–	–	–	–	–	–	–	–
Vivian, HG	3	6	–	204	66	2	–	34.00	3	97.3	31	263	10	26.30	–	–	4/33
Wallace, MW	3	6	–	246	63	2	–	41.00	–	2.0	–	7	–	–	–	–	–
Weir, GL	3	6	–	78	38	–	–	13.00	2	4.3	–	21	–	–	–	–	–

1953/54 NEW ZEALANDERS

First-class Results					All Matches				
Matches	Won	Lost	Drawn	Tied	Matches	Won	Lost	Drawn	Tied
3	2	–	1	–	3	2	–	1	–

Date	Venue	Opponent	Results for Touring Team
Mar 5	Perth	Western Australia	Won by 184 runs
Mar 12	Adelaide	South Australia	Won by 8 wkts
Mar 19	Melbourne	Victoria	Drawn

Player	M	Inn	NO	Runs	HS	50	100	Avrge	Ct/St	Overs	Mdns	Runs	Wkts	Avrge	5wi	10wm	Best
Beck, JEF	3	6	1	140	85	1	–	28.00	1	1.0	–	5	–	–	–	–	–
Bell, W	1	1	–	7	7	–	–	7.00	1	30.0	1	186	4	46.50	–	–	2/92
Blair, RW	2	2	–	22	22	–	–	11.00	1	58.3	14	192	10	19.20	–	–	4/48
Chapple, ME	1	2	–	49	45	–	–	24.50	–	–	–	–	–	–	–	–	–
Dempster, EW	2	4	–	36	17	–	–	9.00	–	42.0	7	132	5	26.20	1	–	5/95
Leggat, JG	3	6	1	339	121*	2	1	67.80	3	1.0	–	16	–	–	–	–	–
Leggat, IB	1	2	–	17	9	–	–	8.50	3	10.0	1	37	1	37.00	–	–	1/15
MacGibbon, AR	3	5	–	95	40	–	–	19.00	3	86.1	19	236	7	33.72	–	–	3/89
Miller, LSM	2	3	–	220	142	1	1	73.33	2	2.0	–	15	1	15.00	–	–	1/15
Mooney, FLH	3	4	–	97	65	1	–	24.25	13	–	–	–	–	–	–	–	–
Overton, GWF	3	4	4	9	8*	–	–	–	2	78.2	15	228	11	20.73	1	–	7/52
Poore, MB	3	5	–	55	33	–	–	11.00	–	34.0	7	104	2	52.00	–	–	1/6
Reid, JR	3	6	1	335	160	2	1	67.00	6	63.3	13	198	5	39.60	–	–	2/51
Sutcliffe, B (Capt)	3	6	–	480	149	–	3	80.00	2	33.0	1	188	2	94.00	–	–	1/12

1961/62 NEW ZEALANDERS

First-class Results					All Matches				
Matches	Won	Lost	Drawn	Tied	Matches	Won	Lost	Drawn	Tied
3	–	2	1	–	3	–	2	1	–

Date	Venue	Opponent	Results for Touring Team
Oct 12	Perth	Western Australia	Drawn
Mar 2	Adelaide	South Australia	Lost by 6 wkts
Mar 9	Sydney	New South Wales	Lost by 59 runs

NEW ZEALANDERS IN AUSTRALIA

Player	M	Inn	NO	Runs	HS	50	100	Avrge	Ct/St	Overs	Mdns	Runs	Wkts	Avrge	5wi	10wm	Best
Alabaster, JC	2	3	–	6	4	–	–	2.00	2	37.0	2	170	2	85.00	–	–	1/43
Bartlett, GA	3	5	–	79	27	–	–	15.80	2	49.0	4	210	9	23.33	–	–	4/26
Barton, PT	3	6	–	101	34	–	–	16.83	7	–	–	–	–	–	–	–	–
Cameron, FJ	3	5	3	7	5	–	–	3.50	2	88.0	13	289	15	19.26	2	–	7/27
Chapple, ME	3	6	–	166	56	2	–	27.66	4	21.3	5	65	2	32.50	–	–	1/7
Dick, AE	3	6	2	199	127	–	1	49.75	7	–	–	–	–	–	–	–	–
Dowling, GT	3	6	1	215	83*	2	–	43.00	5	1.0	–	8	–	–	–	–	–
Guy, JW	2	4	–	31	19	–	–	7.75	–	–	–	–	–	–	–	–	–
McGregor, SN	3	6	–	94	36	–	–	15.66	1	–	–	–	–	–	–	–	–
Motz, RC	2	3	–	1	1	–	–	0.33		31.0	5	126	4	31.50	–	–	3/53
Reid, JR (Capt)	3	6	–	168	62	1	–	28.00	2	44.7	9	120	5	24.00	–	–	2/45
Sparling, JT	1	2	–	48	42	–	–	24.00		7.0	2	25	1	25.00	–	–	1/25
Yuile, BW	2	4	1	58	31	–	–	19.33		18.0	1	96	3	32.00	–	–	2/38

1967/68 NEW ZEALANDERS

First-class Results					All Matches				
Matches	Won	Lost	Drawn	Tied	Matches	Won	Lost	Drawn	Tied
4	–	2	2	–	7	2	2	3	–

Date	Venue	Opponent	Results for Touring Team
Nov 17	Adelaide	South Australia	Lost by 24 runs
Nov 22	Angaston	*South Australian Country XI	Won by 6 wkts
Nov 24	Melbourne	Victoria	Drawn
Nov 29	Kyabram	*Victorian Country XI	Won by 7 wkts
Dec 1	Brisbane	Queensland	Drawn
Dec 6	Newcastle	*Northern NSW Country XI	Drawn
Dec 8	Sydney	New South Wales	Lost by 131 runs

Player	M	Inn	NO	Runs	HS	50	100	Avrge	Ct/St	Overs	Mdns	Runs	Wkts	Avrge	5wi	10wm	Best
Alabaster, JC	1	2	–	0	0	–	–	0.00	–	5.0	–	31	1	31.00	–	–	1/16
Burgess, MG	3	6	–	182	98*	1	–	45.50	1	1.0	1	0	–	–	–	–	–
Collinge, RO	4	6	1	116	38	–	–	23.20	1	119.7	24	365	11	33.18	–	–	4/54
Congdon, BE	4	8	–	153	59	2	–	19.12	2	8.0	1	24	1	24.00	–	–	1/13
Harford, RI	4	6	4	22	8*	–	–	11.00	12/1	–	–	–	–	–	–	–	–
Jarvis, TW	3	6	–	90	56	1	–	15.00	–	–	–	–	–	–	–	–	–
Motz, RC	4	7	–	132	94	1	–	18.85	–	104.6	14	326	10	32.60	–	–	3/72
Murray, BAG	4	8	–	351	98	3	–	43.87	6	1.0	–	1	–	–	–	–	–
Pollard, V	4	8	–	293	125	1	1	36.62	7	83.1	18	248	10	24.80	–	–	4/38
Sinclair, BW (Capt)	4	8	1	161	64*	1	–	23.00	4	–	–	–	–	–	–	–	–
Taylor, BR	4	7	–	70	37	–	–	10.00	–	94.2	21	325	13	25.00	–	–	3/61
Thomson, K	2	4	–	47	43	–	–	11.75	–	–	–	–	–	–	–	–	–
Yuile, BW	3	6	2	63	28	–	–	15.75	2	57.0	10	166	8	20.75	–	–	3/29

1969/70 NEW ZEALANDERS

First-class Results					All Matches				
Matches	Won	Lost	Drawn	Tied	Matches	Won	Lost	Drawn	Tied
3	–	–	3	–	8	3	–	5	–

Date	Venue	Opponent	Results for Touring Team
Dec 26	Hobart (TCA)	Tasmania	Drawn
Dec 30	Sydney	*New South Wales	Won by 4 wkts
Jan 1	Melbourne	*Victoria	Won by 6 wkts
Jan 3	Ararat	*Victorian Country XI	Abandoned
Jan 5	Echuca	*Victorian Country XI	Won by 105 runs
Jan 6	Benalla	*Combined Australian Universities	Drawn
Jan 9	Melbourne	Victoria	Drawn
Jan 14	Canberra	*Southern NSW Country XI	Drawn
Jan 17	Sydney	New South Wales	Drawn

Player	M	Inn	NO	Runs	HS	50	100	Avrge	Ct/St	Overs	Mdns	Runs	Wkts	Avrge	5wi	10wm	Best
Burgess, MG	3	5	–	129	91	1	–	25.80	1	13.0	1	44	1	44.00	–	–	1/13
Collinge, RO	3	2	–	19	17	–	–	9.50	2	53.0	8	176	7	25.14	–	–	4/42
Congdon, BE	3	6	1	205	53*	1	–	41.00	3	3.0	–	16	–	–	–	–	–
Cunis, RS	3	2	–	20	18	–	–	10.00	–	58.0	5	208	8	26.00	–	–	2/27
Dowling, GT (Capt)	1	2	–	95	57	1	–	47.50	–	–	–	–	–	–	–	–	–
Hadlee, DR	3	3	1	47	21	–	–	23.50	2	45.0	5	234	10	23.40	–	–	4/56
Hastings, BF	3	6	2	126	59*	1	–	31.50	–	–	–	–	–	–	–	–	–
Howarth, HJ	3	3	2	14	9*	–	–	14.00	1	81.0	18	258	8	32.35	1	–	5/32
Morgan, RW	2	3	–	43	34	–	–	14.33	1	–	–	–	–	–	–	–	–
Turner, GM	3	6	–	205	99	2	–	34.16	6	–	–	–	–	–	–	–	–
Vivian, GE	3	5	1	193	137*	–	1	48.25	–	39.0	2	175	3	58.33	–	–	2/62
Wadsworth, KJ	3	5	2	67	39	–	–	22.33	5/1	–	–	–	–	–	–	–	–

NEW ZEALANDERS IN AUSTRALIA

1970/71 NEW ZEALANDERS

Matches	First-class Results Won	Lost	Drawn	Tied	Matches	All Matches Won	Lost	Drawn	Tied
1	–	–	1	–	2	–	1	1	–

Date	Venue	Opponent	Results for Touring Team
Jan 29	Perth	Western Australia	Drawn
Jan 31	Perth	*Western Australia	Lost by 3 wkts

Player	M	Inn	NO	Runs	HS	50	100	Avrge	Ct/St	Overs	Mdns	Runs	Wkts	Avrge	5wi	10wm	Best
Burgess, MG	1	1	1	104	104*	–	1	–	1	5.0	–	35	–	–	–	–	–
Collinge, RO	1	1	–	1	1	–	–	1.00	–	13.0	1	57	1	57.00	–	–	1/44
Congdon, BE	1	1	–	40	40	–	–	40.00	1	18.0	4	57	4	14.25	–	–	4/57
Cunis, RS	1	–	–	–	–	–	–	–	–	20.0	3	69	4	17.25	–	–	4/6
Dowling, GT (Capt)	1	1	–	99	99	1	–	99.00	–	–	–	–	–	–	–	–	–
Howarth, HJ	1	1	–	0	0	–	–	0.00	1	23.0	4	58	–	–	–	–	–
Jarvis, TW	1	1	–	17	17	–	–	17.00	1	2.0	–	17	–	–	–	–	–
Morgan, FW	1	1	–	80	80	1	–	80.00	–	10.0	–	39	–	–	–	–	–
Taylor, BR	1	1	–	31	31	–	–	31.00	–	17.0	–	57	–	–	–	–	–
Turner, GM	1	1	–	8	8	–	–	8.00	–	3.0	2	1	–	–	–	–	–
Wadsworth, KJ	1	1	–	25	25	–	–	25.00	3/–	2.0	–	10	–	–	–	–	–

1971/72 NEW ZEALANDERS

Matches	First-class Results Won	Lost	Drawn	Tied	Matches	All Matches Won	Lost	Drawn	Tied
–	–	–	–	–	2	1	1	–	–

Date	Venue	Opponent	Results for Touring Team
Feb 2	Melbourne	*Victorian Universities	Won by 7 wkts
Feb 4	Melbourne	*Victoria	Lost by 76 runs

1972/73 NEW ZEALANDERS

Matches	First-class Results Won	Lost	Drawn	Tied	Matches	All Matches Won	Lost	Drawn	Tied
1	–	–	1	–	3	2	–	1	–

Date	Venue	Opponent	Results for Touring Team
Jan 14	Adelaide	*South Australia	Won by 53 runs
Jan 16	Adelaide	South Australia	Drawn
Jan 21	Brisbane	*Queensland	Won by 38 runs

Player	M	Inn	NO	Runs	HS	50	100	Avrge	Ct/St	Overs	Mdns	Runs	Wkts	Avrge	5wi	10wm	Best
Andrews, B	1	1	–	12	12	–	–	12.00	–	35.0	4	117	2	58.50	–	–	1/58
Congdon, BE (Capt)	1	2	–	55	33	–	–	27.50	2	3.0	–	20	–	–	–	–	–
Dunning, B	1	2	–	31	17	–	–	15.50	1	–	–	–	–	–	–	–	–
Hadlee, RJ	1	1	–	9	9	–	–	9.00	–	26.0	3	80	1	80.00	–	–	1/32
Hastings, BF	1	2	–	70	46	–	–	35.00	–	–	–	–	–	–	–	–	–
Jordan, AB	1	1	–	0	0	–	–	0.00	1	20.0	1	97	1	97.00	–	–	1/31
O'Sullivan, DR	1	1	–	14	14	–	–	14.00	2	49.0	7	159	8	19.87	–	–	4/73
Redmond, RE	1	2	1	87	49	–	–	87.00	–	–	–	–	–	–	–	–	–
Turner, GM	1	–	–	–	–	–	–	–	–	–	–	–	–	–	–	–	–
Vivian, GE	1	2	2	11	11*	–	–	–	–	–	–	–	–	–	–	–	–
Wadsworth, KJ	1	2	2	74	74*	–	–	–	2/1	–	–	–	–	–	–	–	–

1974/75 NEW ZEALANDERS

Matches	First-class Results Won	Lost	Drawn	Tied	Matches	All Matches Won	Lost	Drawn	Tied
–	–	–	–	–	3	3	–	–	–

Date	Venue	Opponent	Results for Touring Team
Jan 17	Melbourne	*Tasmania	Won by 7 wkts
Feb 2	Melbourne	*Western Australia	Won by 8 wkts
Feb 5	Melbourne	*MCC	Won by 66 runs

1980/81 NEW ZEALANDERS

First-class Results					All Matches				
Matches	Won	Lost	Drawn	Tied	Matches	Won	Lost	Drawn	Tied
7	1	2	4	–	29	14	9	6	–

Date	Venue	Opponent	Results for Touring Team
Oct 31	Melbourne	Victoria	Won by 8 wkts
Nov 5	Traralgon	*Victorian Country XI	Won by 97 runs
Nov 7	Canberra	*Australian Capital Territory	Drawn
Nov 12	Armidale	*Northern New South Wales XII	Won by 84 runs
Nov 14	Brisbane	Queensland	Drawn
Nov 19	Newcastle	*Newcastle & District	Won by 10 wkts
Nov 23	Adelaide	*Australia (L/O Intl)	Won by 3 wkts
Nov 25	Sydney	*Australia (L/O Intl)	Lost by 94 runs
Nov 28	Brisbane	AUSTRALIA (1st Test)	Lost by 10 wkts
Dec 5	Wagga Wagga	*Southern New South Wales	Won by 66 runs
Dec 7	Melbourne	*Australia (L/O Intl)	Lost by 4 wkts
Dec 9	Perth	*India (L/O Intl)	Lost by 5 runs
Dec 12	Perth	AUSTRALIA (2nd Test)	Lost by 8 wkts
Dec 19	Currumain	*Queensland Country XI	Won by 111 runs
Dec 21	Brisbane	*India (L/O Intl)	Won by 3 wkts
Dec 23	Adelaide	*India (L/O Intl)	Lost by 6 runs
Dec 26	Melbourne	AUSTRALIA (3rd Test)	Drawn
Jan 1	Launceston	Tasmania	Drawn
Jan 6	Geelong	*Geelong & District	Won by 9 wkts
Jan 10	Melbourne	*India (L/O Intl)	Won by 10 wkts
Jan 13	Sydney	*Australia (L/O Intl)	Won by 1 run
Jan 15	Bundaberg	*Queensland Country XI	Won by 95 runs
Jan 18	Brisbane	*India (L/O Intl)	Won by 22 runs
Jan 21	Sydney	*Australia (L/O Intl)	No result
Jan 24	Sydney	New South Wales	Drawn
Jan 29	Sydney	*Australia (L/O Intl)	Won by 78 runs
Jan 31	Melbourne	*Australia (L/O Intl)	Lost by 7 wkts
Feb 1	Melbourne	*Australia (L/O Intl)	Lost by 6 runs
Feb 3	Sydney	*Australia (L/O Intl)	Lost by 6 wkts

Player	M	Inn	NO	Runs	HS	50	100	Avrge	Ct/St	Overs	Mdns	Runs	Wkts	Avrge	5wi	10wm	Best
Boock, SL	2	1	–	9	9	–	–	9.00	–	71.0	26	161	4	40.25	–	–	2/95
Bracewell, BP	1	2	–	8	8	–	–	4.00	–	25.0	11	71	–	–	–	–	–
Bracewell, JG	4	6	1	52	24	–	–	10.40	3	104.0	21	283	9	31.44	1	–	5/67
Burgess, MG	7	12	1	371	134	–	1	33.72	2	16.0	4	53	1	53.00	–	–	1/26
Cairns, BL	4	7	–	105	68	1	–	15.00	3	179.3	50	420	15	28.00	1	–	5/87
Chatfield, EJ	3	2	1	4	4*	–	–	4.00	–	149.3	42	326	9	36.22	–	–	3/46
Coney, JV	6	10	2	328	96	4	–	41.00	9	86.3	30	227	5	45.40	–	–	3/28
Edgar, BA	7	13	–	251	51	2	–	19.30	2	–	–	–	–	–	–	–	–
Hadlee, RJ	5	8	2	249	103	1	1	41.50	2	229.3	52	567	27	21.00	3	–	6/57
Howarth, GP (Capt)	5	9	2	369	78*	5	–	52.71	4	1.0	–	1	–	–	–	–	–
Lees, WK	4	6	1	73	25*	–	–	14.60	9	–	–	–	–	–	–	–	–
McEwan, PE	4	8	–	224	87	2	–	28.00	1	13.0	1	40	1	40.00	–	–	1/40
McKechnie, BJ	2	3	–	33	30	–	–	11.00	1	32.0	9	68	1	68.00	–	–	1/26
Parker, JM	7	13	1	240	56	2	–	20.00	8	10.0	–	53	1	53.00	–	–	1/37
Smith, IDS	3	5	–	59	30	–	–	11.80	2	–	–	–	–	–	–	–	–
Snedden, MC	2	3	2	4	3	–	–	4.00	1	70.0	16	210	8	26.25	–	–	4/74
Troup, GB	4	5	3	11	6*	–	–	5.50	–	109.0	25	270	4	67.50	–	–	1/31
Wright, JG	7	13	–	410	106	2	1	31.53	3	2.0	–	15	–	–	–	–	–

1982/83 NEW ZEALANDERS

First-class Results					All Matches				
Matches	Won	Lost	Drawn	Tied	Matches	Won	Lost	Drawn	Tied
2	–	–	1	1	22	13	7	1	1

Date	Venue	Opponent	Results for Touring Team
Dec 8	Horsham	*Victorian Country XI	Won by 7 wkts
Dec 10	Melbourne	Victoria	Tied
Dec 16	Sydney	*New South Wales	Lost by 16 runs
Dec 18	Bundaberg	Queensland	Drawn

Team returned home and a new squad returned to play in the World Series

Date	Venue	Opponent	Results for Touring Team
Jan 7	Geelong	*Geelong & District	Won by 99 runs
Jan 9	Melbourne	*Australia (L/O Intl)	Lost by 8 wkts
Jan 13	Melbourne	*England (L/O Intl)	Won by 2 runs
Jan 15	Brisbane	*England (L/O Intl)	Lost by 54 runs
Jan 18	Sydney	*Australia (L/O Intl)	Won by 47 runs
Jan 20	Sydney	*England (L/O Intl)	Lost by 8 wkts
Jan 22	Melbourne	*Australia (L/O Intl)	Won by 58 runs
Jan 24	Canberra	*Australian Capital Territory	Won by 97 runs
Jan 25	Canberra	*Australian Capital Territory	Won by 6 wkts

Continued

NEW ZEALANDERS IN AUSTRALIA

Date	Venue	Opponent	Results for Touring Team
Jan 26	Canberra	*Australian Capital Territory	Won on run rate
Jan 29	Adelaide	*England (L/O Intl)	Won by 4 wkts
Jan 31	Adelaide	*Australia (L/O Intl)	Won by 47 runs
Feb 2	Northam	*Western Australian Country XI	Won by 58 runs
Feb 5	Perth	*England (L/O Intl)	Won by 7 wkts
Feb 6	Perth	*Australia (L/O Intl)	Lost by 27 runs
Feb 9	Sydney	*Australia (L/O Intl)	Lost on run rate
Feb 13	Melbourne	*Australia (L/O Intl)	Lost by 149 runs

Team returned home and a new team returned to play the Bush-fire Appeal Match

Date	Venue	Opponent	Results for Touring Team
Mar 17	Sydney	*Australia (L/O Intl)	Won by 14 runs

Player	M	Inn	NO	Runs	HS	50	100	Avrge	Ct/St	Overs	Mdns	Runs	Wkts	Avrge	5wi	10wm	Best
Blair, BR	1	2	–	46	27	–	–	23.00	–	–	–	–	–	–	–	–	–
Carrington, MS	1	1	–	10	10	–	–	10.00	1	26.0	2	133	2	66.50	–	–	1/51
Chatfield, EJ	2	1	1	0	0*	–	–	–	1	58.0	16	160	3	53.33	–	–	2/31
Coney, JV	2	4	1	38	18*	–	–	12.66	1	35.0	10	89	1	89.00	–	–	1/29
Crowe, MD	2	4	–	49	27	–	–	12.25	2	13.0	2	37	–	–	–	–	–
Edgar, BA	1	2	–	111	66	1	–	55.50	–	–	–	–	–	–	–	–	–
Howarth, GP (Capt)	2	3	–	253	138	–	2	84.33	1	14.0	2	51	1	51.00	–	–	1/21
Lees, WK	2	3	–	22	19	–	–	7.33	5/1	–	–	–	–	–	–	–	–
Morrison, JFM	2	4	3	197	78*	2	–	197.00	1	41.0	9	144	6	24.00	–	–	4/62
Reid, JF	2	4	–	103	58	1	–	25.75	2	–	–	–	–	–	–	–	–
Robertson, GK	2	3	–	32	18	–	–	10.66	–	43.0	3	206	4	51.50	–	–	1/26
Snedden, MC	1	1	–	3	3	–	–	3.00	–	21.5	5	81	2	40.50	–	–	2/28
Troup, GB	2	3	1	23	21	–	–	11.50	1	45.5	4	158	5	31.60	–	–	2/30

1984/85 NEW ZEALANDERS

First-class Results					All Matches				
Matches	Won	Lost	Drawn	Tied	Matches	Won	Lost	Drawn	Tied
–	–	–	–	–	4	1	2	1	–

Date	Venue	Opponent	Results for Touring Team
Feb 21	Sydney	*West Indies (L/O Intl)	No result
Feb 23	Melbourne	*Sri Lanka (L/O Intl)	Won by 51 runs
Mar 5	Sydney	*India (L/O Intl)	Lost by 7 wkts
Mar 9	Sydney	*West Indies (L/O Intl)	Lost by 6 wkts

1985/86 NEW ZEALANDERS

First-class Results					All Matches				
Matches	Won	Lost	Drawn	Tied	Matches	Won	Lost	Drawn	Tied
6	2	1	3	–	19	5	7	7	–

Date	Venue	Opponent	Results for Touring Team
Oct 18	Townsville	*Queensland Combined XI	Drawn
Oct 22	Carrara	*South Queensland Country XI	Drawn
Oct 26	Adelaide	South Australia	Drawn
Nov 1	Brisbane	Queensland	Drawn
Nov 8	Brisbane	AUSTRALIA (1st Test)	Won by an inns & 41 runs
Nov 15	Sydney	New South Wales	Drawn
Nov 22	Sydney	AUSTRALIA (2nd Test)	Lost by 4 wkts
Nov 30	Perth	AUSTRALIA (3rd Test)	Won by 6 wkts

Team returned home and a new squad returned to play in the World Series

Date	Venue	Opponent	Results for Touring Team
Jan 9	Melbourne	*Australia (L/O Intl)	No Result
Jan 11	Brisbane	*India (L/O Intl)	Lost by 5 wkts
Jan 14	Sydney	*Australia (L/O Intl)	Lost by 4 wkts
Jan 18	Perth	*India (L/O Intl)	Won by 3 wkts
Jan 19	Perth	*Australia (L/O Intl)	Lost by 4 wkts
Jan 22	Canberra	*Prime Minister's XI	Drawn
Jan 23	Melbourne	*India (L/O Intl)	Won by 5 wkts
Jan 25	Adelaide	*India (L/O Intl)	Lost by 5 wkts
Jan 27	Adelaide	*Australia (L/O Intl)	Won by 206 runs
Jan 29	Sydney	*Australia (L/O Intl)	Lost by 99 runs
Feb 2	Launceston	*India (L/O Intl)	Lost by 21 runs

Player	M	Inn	NO	Runs	HS	50	100	Avrge	Ct/St	Overs	Mdns	Runs	Wkts	Avrge	5wi	10wm	Best
Boock, SL	4	3	–	40	37	–	–	13.33	1	202.5	49	560	17	32.94	–	–	4/83
Bracewell, JG	2	3	3	113	83*	1	–	–	3	89.5	27	195	7	27.85	–	–	3/91
Brown, VR	5	8	3	121	36*	–	–	24.20	6	189.0	29	624	14	44.57	–	–	4/75
Cairns, BL	4	3	–	29	25	–	–	9.66	3	145.5	32	389	6	64.83	–	–	2/46
Chatfield, EJ	3	2	–	3	3	–	–	1.50	3	139.0	44	252	8	31.50	–	–	3/33
Coney, JV (Capt)	6	11	2	303	89	1	–	33.66	10	66.0	26	132	3	44.00	–	–	–
Crowe, JJ	6	11	4	252	79*	1	–	36.00	8	–	–	–	–	–	–	–	–

Continued

Player	M	Inn	NO	Runs	HS	50	100	Avrge	Ct/St	Overs	Mdns	Runs	Wkts	Avrge	5wi	10wm	Best
Crowe, MD	4	7	2	562	242*	1	2	112.40	4	21.0	5	55	–	–	–	–	–
Edgar, BA	6	10	–	389	122	3	1	38.90	3	–	–	–	–	–	–	–	–
Franklin, TJ	1	1	–	13	13	–	–	13.00	1	–	–	–	–	–	–	–	–
Hadlee, RJ	5	6	–	151	54	1	–	25.16	3	241.3	65	537	37	14.51	5	2	9/52
McSweeney, EB	1	1	1	26	26*	–	–	–	1/1	–	–	–	–	–	–	–	–
Reid, JF	5	9	–	241	108	–	1	26.77	4	–	–	–	–	–	–	–	–
Smith, IDS	5	7	3	93	28	–	–	23.25	8/2	–	–	–	–	–	–	–	–
Snedden, MC	3	1	–	26	26	–	–	26.00	–	107.0	13	364	6	60.66	–	–	4/88
Wright, JG	6	11	–	331	46	–	–	30.09	4	–	–	–	–	–	–	–	–

1987/88 NEW ZEALANDERS

First-class Results					All Matches			
Matches	Won	Lost	Drawn	Tied	Matches	Won	Lost	Drawn	Tied
6	1	2	3	–	19	8	8	3	–

Date	Venue	Opponent	Results for Touring Team
Nov 18	Perth	*Western Australia	Won by 4 wkts
Nov 20	Perth	Western Australia	Won by an inns & 96 runs
Nov 25	Renmark	*South Australian Country XI	Won by 85 runs
Nov 27	Adelaide	South Australia	Lost by 3 wkts
Dec 4	Brisbane	AUSTRALIA (1st Test)	Lost by 9 wkts
Dec 11	Adelaide	AUSTRALIA (2nd Test)	Drawn
Dec 18	Devonport	Tasmania	Drawn
Dec 23	Canberra	*Prime Minister's XI	Won by 37 runs
Dec 26	Melbourne	AUSTRALIA (3rd Test)	Drawn
Jan 3	Perth	*Australia (L/O Intl)	Won by 1 runs
Jan 5	Sydney	*Sri Lanka (L/O Intl)	Won by 6 wkts
Jan 7	Melbourne	*Australia (L/O Intl)	Lost by 6 runs
Jan 9	Adelaide	*Sri Lanka (L/O Intl)	Won by 4 wkts
Jan 12	Hobart (Bel)	*Sri Lanka (L/O Intl)	Lost by 4 wkts
Jan 16	Brisbane	*Sri Lanka (L/O Intl)	Won by 4 wkts
Jan 17	Brisbane	*Australia (L/O Intl)	Lost by 5 wkts
Jan 20	Sydney	*Australia (L/O Intl)	Lost by 78 runs
Jan 22	Melbourne	*Australia (L/O Intl)	Lost by 8 wkts
Jan 24	Sydney	*Australia (L/O Intl)	Lost by 6 wkts

Player	M	Inn	NO	Runs	HS	50	100	Avrge	Ct/St	Overs	Mdns	Runs	Wkts	Avrge	5wi	10wm	Best
Bracewell, JG	4	7	1	106	41*	–	–	17.66	4	207.5	39	553	18	30.72	1	1	7/98
Chatfield, EJ	4	5	5	12	6*	–	–	–	1	180.0	55	352	8	44.00	–	–	3/52
Crowe, JJ (Capt)	6	11	–	158	36	–	–	14.36	6	–	–	–	–	–	–	–	–
Crowe, MD	5	9	1	715	144	4	3	89.37	4	–	–	–	–	–	–	–	–
Gray, EJ	3	5	1	89	26	–	–	22.25	4	83.0	21	193	5	38.60	–	–	3/60
Hadlee, RJ	5	8	3	151	36	–	–	30.20	1	237.4	63	564	29	19.44	5	2	5/30
Horne, PA	3	5	–	218	125	–	1	43.60	2	–	–	–	–	–	–	–	–
Jones, AH	6	11	–	439	150	2	1	39.90	5	–	–	–	–	–	–	–	–
Morrison, DK	5	6	1	8	5*	–	–	1.60	1	158.3	25	555	16	34.68	–	–	4/86
Patel, DN	6	11	–	374	105	1	1	34.00	3	72.4	16	212	3	70.66	–	–	1/17
Rutherford, KR	4	7	–	133	36	–	–	19.00	4	–	–	–	–	–	–	–	–
Smith, IDS	6	11	2	193	62	1	–	21.44	13/1	–	–	–	–	–	–	–	–
Snedden, MC	2	2	1	8	8*	–	–	8.00	–	64.0	10	171	3	57.00	–	–	2/40
Watson, W	2	3	1	27	27*	–	–	13.50	–	69.2	13	201	8	25.12	–	–	4/42
Wright, JG	5	10	–	383	49	–	–	38.30	3	–	–	–	–	–	–	–	–

1988/89 NEW ZEALANDERS

First-class Results					All Matches			
Matches	Won	Lost	Drawn	Tied	Matches	Won	Lost	Drawn	Tied
–	–	–	–	–	1	–	1	–	–

Date	Venue	Opponent	Results for Touring Team
Apr 4	Perth	*Western Australia	Lost by 40 runs

1989/90 NEW ZEALANDERS

First-class Results					All Matches			
Matches	Won	Lost	Drawn	Tied	Matches	Won	Lost	Drawn	Tied
3	–	–	3	–	4	–	1	3	–

Date	Venue	Opponent	Results for Touring Team
Nov 8	Perth	*Western Australia	Lost by 7 wkts
Nov 10	Perth	Western Australia	Drawn
Nov 17	Adelaide	South Australia	Drawn
Nov 24	Perth	AUSTRALIA (Only Test)	Drawn

NEW ZEALANDERS IN AUSTRALIA

Player	M	Inn	NO	Runs	HS	50	100	Avrge	Ct/St	Overs	Mdns	Runs	Wkts	Avrge	5wi	10wm	Best
Bracewell, BP	1	2	–	17	9	–	–	8.50	2	32.0	8	88	1	88.00	–	–	1/88
Bracewell, JG	1	2	–	104	86	1	–	52.00	–	34.0	6	81	4	20.25	–	–	4/81
Cairns, CL	2	3	–	68	39	–	–	22.66	2	51.0	8	190	4	47.50	–	–	2/22
Crowe, MD	3	5	–	332	143	2	1	66.40	2	–	–	–	–	–	–	–	–
Crowe, JJ	3	5	1	195	109*	–	1	48.75	4	–	–	–	–	–	–	–	–
Greatbatch, MJ	3	5	1	261	146*	1	1	65.25	3	–	–	–	–	–	–	–	–
Jones, AH	1	1	–	13	13	–	–	13.00	1	–	–	–	–	–	–	–	–
Morrison, DK	3	3	2	3	3	–	–	3.00	–	91.1	16	318	8	39.75	–	–	4/71
Patel, DN	2	3	–	27	20	–	–	9.00	–	55.4	13	142	4	35.50	–	–	3/62
Smith, IDS	3	4	–	164	123	–	1	41.00	1/–	–	–	–	–	–	–	–	–
Snedden, MC	2	2	2	46	33*	–	–	–	–	79.0	16	213	7	30.42	–	–	3/85
Vance, RH	3	5	–	79	65	1	–	15.80	–	–	–	–	–	–	–	–	–
Watson, W	3	2	–	4	4	–	–	2.00	–	113.0	20	355	2	177.50	–	–	2/102
Wright, JG (Capt)	3	5	1	170	107*	–	1	42.50	3	–	–	–	–	–	–	–	–

1990/91 WELLINGTON

First-class Results					All Matches				
Matches	Won	Lost	Drawn	Tied	Matches	Won	Lost	Drawn	Tied
1	–	1	–	–	4	1	1	2	–

Date	Venue	Opponent	Results for Touring Team
Nov 12	Canberra	*Australian Capital Territory	Won by 6 wkts
Nov 14	Canberra	*Australian Capital Territory	Drawn
Nov 18	Gosford	*New South Wales Country XI	Drawn
Nov 22	North Sydney	New South Wales	Lost by 160 runs

Player	M	Inn	NO	Runs	HS	50	100	Avrge	Ct/St	Overs	Mdns	Runs	Wkts	Avrge	5wi	10wm	Best
Aiken, JM	1	2	–	56	30	–	–	28.00	–	–	–	–	–	–	–	–	–
Burnett, GP	1	2	–	87	50	1	–	83.50	–	–	–	–	–	–	–	–	–
Cederwall, GN	1	2	–	1	1	–	–	0.50	–	30.4	5	118	3	39.33	–	–	2/30
Davis, WW	1	2	1	4	4	–	–	4.00	–	41.0	6	154	5	30.80	–	–	3/97
Hotter, SJ	1	2	–	8	6	–	–	4.00	1	33.0	5	149	4	37.25	–	–	3/100
Jones, AH	1	2	–	37	27	–	–	18.50	3	10.0	3	25	–	–	–	–	–
Larsen, GR	1	2	–	42	39	–	–	21.00	3	38.0	15	65	1	65.00	–	–	1/32
McSweeney, EB (Capt)	1	2	–	33	33	–	–	16.50	2/1	–	–	–	–	–	–	–	–
Ritchie, TD	1	2	1	75	70*	1	–	75.00	–	–	–	–	–	–	–	–	–
Vance, RH	1	2	–	52	47	–	–	26.00	1	–	–	–	–	–	–	–	–
Williams, BR	1	2	–	37	27	–	–	18.50	–	42.0	11	109	2	54.50	–	–	2/53

1990/91 NEW ZEALANDERS

First-class Results					All Matches				
Matches	Won	Lost	Drawn	Tied	Matches	Won	Lost	Drawn	Tied
–	–	–	–	–	11	4	7	–	–

Date	Venue	Opponent	Results for Touring Team
Nov 27	Wollongong	*New South Wales	Won by 7 wkts
Nov 29	Sydney	*Australia (L/O Intl)	Lost by 61 runs
Dec 1	Adelaide	*England (L/O Intl)	Won by 7 runs
Dec 2	Adelaide	*Australia (L/O Intl)	Lost by 6 wkts
Dec 7	Perth	*England (L/O Intl)	Lost by 4 wkts
Dec 11	Melbourne	*Australia (L/O Intl)	Lost by 39 runs
Dec 13	Sydney	*England (L/O Intl)	Lost by 33 runs
Dec 15	Brisbane	*England (L/O Intl)	Won by 8 wkts
Dec 18	Hobart (Bel)	*Australia (L/O Intl)	Won by 1 run
Jan 13	Sydney	*Australia (L/O Intl)	Lost by 6 wkts
Jan 15	Melbourne	*Australia (L/O Intl)	Lost by 7 wkts

1991/92 NEW ZEALANDERS

First-class Results					All Matches				
Matches	Won	Lost	Drawn	Tied	Matches	Won	Lost	Drawn	Tied
–	–	–	–	–	6	4	2	–	–

Date	Venue	Opponent	Results for Touring Team
Oct 5	Adelaide	*South Australian 2nd XI	Won by 47 runs
Oct 6	Adelaide	*South Australia	Lost by 7 wkts
Oct 8	Adelaide	*South Australia	Won by 7 wkts
Oct 9	Adelaide	*South Australia	Won by 7 wkts
Oct 11	Adelaide	*AIS Cricket Academy	Won by 75 runs
Oct 14	Adelaide	*AIS Cricket Academy	Lost by 7 wkts

SOUTH AFRICANS IN AUSTRALIA

Season	Touring Team	First-class Results					All Matches					Captain
		Games	W	L	D	T	Games	W	L	D	T	
1910/11	South Africans	15	6	7	2	–	22	12	7	3	–	PW Sherwell
1931/32	South Africans	16	4	6	6	–	18	6	6	6	–	HB Cameron
1952/53	South Africans	16	4	3	9	–	23	7	3	13	–	JE Cheetham
1963/64	South Africans	14	5	3	6	–	28	16	4	8	–	TL Goddard
1991/92	South Africans	–	–	–	–	–	12	7	3	2	–	KC Wessels
1993/94	South Africans	5	1	2	2	–	17	6	9	2	–	KC Wessels
		66	20	21	25	–	120	54	32	34	–	

FIRST-CLASS RESULTS

Opponent	Venue	First Game	Games	W	L	D	T
AUSTRALIA	Sydney	Dec 9 1910	6	–	4	2	–
	Melbourne	Dec 31 1910	7	2	5	–	–
	Adelaide	Jan 7 1911	4	2	1	1	–
	Brisbane	Nov 27 1931	3	–	2	1	–
			20	4	12	4	–
Combined XI	Brisbane	Dec 2 1910	1	–	–	1	–
	Sydney	Dec 12 1952	1	–	–	1	–
	Perth	Nov 1 1963	1	–	–	1	–
	Melbourne	Nov 15 1963	1	1	–	–	–
	Hobart (TCA)	Dec 26 1963	1	–	–	1	–
			5	1	–	4	–
New South Wales	Sydney	Nov 18 1910	7	1	3	3	–
Queensland	Brisbane	Nov 25 1910	4	1	1	2	–
South Australia	Adelaide	Nov 5 1910	7	4	1	2	–
Tasmania	Launceston	Jan 17 1911	4	3	–	1	–
	Hobart (TCA)	Jan 20 1911	2	1	–	1	–
			6	4	–	2	–
Victoria	Melbourne	Nov 11 1910	7	1	2	4	–
Western Australia	Perth	Oct 22 1931	5	3	–	2	–

1991/92 SOUTH AFRICANS

First-class Results					All Matches				
Matches	Won	Lost	Drawn	Tied	Matches	Won	Lost	Drawn	Tied
–	–	–	–	–	12	7	3	2	–

Date	Venue	Opponent	Results for Touring Team
Feb 9	Perth	*Western Australia	Lost by 3 wkts
Feb 11	Adelaide	*AIS Cricket Academy	Drawn
Feb 12	Adelaide	*AIS Cricket Academy	Won by 45 runs
Feb 15	Canberra	*Pakistan	Won by 17 runs
Feb 17	Hobart (Bel)	*Tasmania	Won by 7 wkts
Feb 21	Brisbane	*Queensland	Abandoned
Feb 23	Bowral	*Bradman's XI	Drawn
Feb 26	Sydney	*Australia (WC L/O Intl)	Won by 9 wkts
Mar 8	Brisbane	*Pakistan (WC L/O Intl)	Won by 20 runs
Mar 10	Canberra	*Zimbabwe (WC L/O Intl)	Won by 7 wkts
Mar 12	Sydney	*England (WC L/O Intl)	Lost by 3 wkts
Mar 15	Adelaide	*India (WC L/O Intl)	Won by 6 wkts
Mar 22	Sydney	*England (WC L/O Intl)	Lost by 19 runs

WEST INDIANS IN AUSTRALIA

Season	Touring Team	First-class Results					All Matches					Captain
		Games	W	L	D	T	Games	W	L	D	T	
1930/31	West Indians	14	4	8	2	–	16	5	8	3	–	GC Grant
1951/52	West Indians	13	4	8	1	–	15	5	8	2	–	JDC Goddard
1960/61	West Indians	14	4	5	4	1	22	10	5	5	2	FMM Worrell
1968/69	West Indians	15	4	5	6	–	23	9	5	9	–	GS Sobers
1975/76	West Indians	13	3	6	4	–	21	8	7	6	–	CH Lloyd
1979/80	West Indians	7	5	1	1	–	21	13	5	3	–	CH Lloyd
1981/82	West Indians	7	4	1	2	–	24	16	5	3	–	CH Lloyd
1983/84	West Indians	–	–	–	–	–	13	10	2	–	1	CH Lloyd
1984/85	West Indians	11	4	2	5	–	33	24	4	5	–	CH Lloyd
1986/87	West Indians	1	–	–	1	–	13	4	8	1	–	IVA Richards
1988/89	West Indians	11	4	2	5	–	23	11	7	5	–	IVA Richards
1991/92	West Indians	1	–	1	–	–	22	12	8	1	1	RB Richardson
1992/93	West Indians	8	3	1	4	–	22	13	5	4	–	RB Richardson
		115	39	40	35	1	268	140	77	47	4	

WEST INDIANS IN AUSTRALIA

FIRST-CLASS RESULTS

Opponent	Venue	First Game	Games	W	L	D	T
AUSTRALIA	Adelaide	Dec 12 1930	10	5	2	3	–
	Sydney	Jan 1 1931	12	2	8	2	–
	Brisbane (Ex)	Jan 16 1931	1	–	1	–	–
	Brisbane	Nov 9 1951	8	3	2	2	1
	Melbourne	Dec 31 1951	12	2	9	1	–
	Perth	Dec 12 1975	4	4	–	–	–
			47	16	22	8	1
Australian/Combined XIs	Perth	Nov 4 1960	2	–	1	1	–
	Hobart (TCA)	Jan 5 1960	1	1	–	–	–
	Launceston	Jan 16 1969	1	1	–	–	–
	Devonport	Nov 23 1979	1	1	–	–	–
	Hobart (Bel)	Dec 20 1991	2	–	1	1	–
			7	3	2	2	–
New South Wales	Sydney	Nov 21 1930	11	4	5	2	–
Queensland	Brisbane	Jan 10 1931	8	3	1	4	–
	Townsville	Jan 11 1987	1	–	–	1	–
			9	3	1	5	–
South Australia	Adelaide	Dec 5 1930	12	3	4	5	–
Tasmania	Launceston	Dec 20 1930	4	4	–	–	–
	Hobart (TCA)	Dec 24 1930	5	1	–	4	–
	Devonport	Dec 14 1984	1	–	–	1	–
	Hobart (Bel)	Dec 19 1988	1	–	–	1	–
			11	5	–	6	–
Victoria	Melbourne	Nov 28 1930	10	2	1	7	–
Western Australia	Perth	Dec 14 1951	8	3	5	–	–

1983/84 WEST INDIANS

First-class Results					All Matches				
Matches	Won	Lost	Drawn	Tied	Matches	Won	Lost	Drawn	Tied
–	–	–	–	–	13	10	2	–	1

Date	Venue	Opponent	Results for Touring Team
Jan 8	Melbourne	*Australia (L/O Intl)	Won by 27 runs
Jan 12	Melbourne	*Pakistan (L/O Intl)	Lost by 97 runs
Jan 14	Brisbane	*Pakistan (L/O Intl)	Won by 5 wkts
Jan 17	Sydney	*Australia (L/O Intl)	Won by 28 runs
Jan 19	Sydney	*Pakistan (L/O Intl)	Won by 5 wkts
Jan 22	Melbourne	*Australia (L/O Intl)	Won by 26 runs
Jan 28	Adelaide	*Pakistan (L/O Intl)	Won by 1 wkt
Jan 29	Adelaide	*Australia (L/O Intl)	Won by 6 wkts
Feb 4	Perth	*Pakistan (L/O Intl)	Won by 7 wkts
Feb 5	Perth	*Australia (L/O Intl)	Lost by 14 runs
Feb 8	Sydney	*Australia (L/O Intl)	Won by 9 wkts
Feb 11	Melbourne	*Australia (L/O Intl)	Tied
Feb 12	Melbourne	*Australia (L/O Intl)	Won by 6 wkts

1986/87 WEST INDIANS

First-class Results					All Matches				
Matches	Won	Lost	Drawn	Tied	Matches	Won	Lost	Drawn	Tied
1	–	–	1	–	13	4	8	1	–

Date	Venue	Opponent	Results for Touring Team
Dec 30	Perth	*Pakistan (L/O Intl)	Lost by 34 runs
Jan 3	Perth	*England (L/O Intl)	Lost by 19 runs
Jan 4	Perth	*Australia (L/O Intl)	Won by 164 runs
Jan 10	Townsville	*Queensland	Lost by 25 runs
Jan 11	Townsville	Queensland	Drawn
Jan 17	Brisbane	*England (L/O Intl)	Lost by 6 wkts
Jan 20	Melbourne	*Australia (L/O Intl)	Won by 7 wkts
Jan 24	Adelaide	*England (L/O Intl)	Lost by 89 runs
Jan 25	Adelaide	*Australia (L/O Intl)	Won by 16 runs
Jan 28	Sydney	*Australia (L/O Intl)	Lost by 26 runs
Jan 30	Melbourne	*England (L/O Intl)	Won by 6 wkts
Feb 3	Devonport	*England (L/O Intl)	Lost by 29 runs
Feb 6	Sydney	*Australia (L/O Intl)	Lost by 2 wkts

Player	M	Inn	NO	Runs	HS	50	100	Avrge	Ct/St	Overs	Mdns	Runs	Wkts	Avrge	5wi	10wm	Best
Benjamin, WKM	1	2	1	5	4*	–	–	5.00	–	12.0	1	30	–	–	–	–	–
Garner, J	1	1	–	1	1	–	–	1.00	–	10.0	1	19	–	–	–	–	–
Gomes, HA	1	2	1	184	164*	–	1	184.00	–	12.0	1	38	1	38.00	–	–	1/38
Greenidge, CG	1	1	1	16	16*	–	–	–	–	–	–	–	–	–	–	–	–
Harper, RA	1	2	–	138	118	–	1	69.00	–	19.0	5	65	2	32.50	–	–	2/65
Haynes, DL	1	2	–	82	67	1	–	41.00	1	–	–	–	–	–	–	–	–
Holding, MA (Capt)	1	1	–	2	2	–	–	2.00	1	11.0	3	18	3	54.00	–	–	3/18
Logie, AL	1	2	–	61	36	–	–	30.50	1	–	–	–	–	–	–	–	–
Payne, TRO	1	1	1	60	60*	1	–	–	–	–	–	–	–	–	–	–	–
Richardson, RB	1	2	–	10	7	–	–	5.00	–	–	–	–	–	–	–	–	–
Walsh, CA	1	1	1	0	0*	–	–	–	–	17.0	1	57	1	57.00	–	–	1/57

1991/92 WEST INDIANS

First-class Results					All Matches				
Matches	Won	Lost	Drawn	Tied	Matches	Won	Lost	Drawn	Tied
1	–	1	–	–	22	12	8	1	1

Date	Venue	Opponent	Results for Touring Team
Dec 1	Northam	*Western Australian Invitation XI	Won by 66 runs
Dec 4	Perth	*Western Australia	Lost by 7 wkts
Dec 6	Perth	*India (L/O Intl)	Tied
Dec 10	Leongatha	*Victorian Country XI	Won by 45 runs
Dec 12	Melbourne	*Australia (L/O Intl)	Lost by 9 runs
Dec 14	Adelaide	*India (L/O Intl)	Lost by 10 runs
Dec 18	Sydney	*Australia (L/O Intl)	Lost by 51 runs
Dec 20	Hobart (Bel)	Australian XI	Lost by an inns & 93 runs
Dec 26	Cairns	*Queensland XI	Won by 3 wkts
Dec 29	Bundaberg	*Queensland XI	Won by 11 runs
Jan 1	Carrara	*Queensland XI	Won by 7 wkts
Jan 3	Armidale	*New South Wales Country XI	Won by 46 runs
Jan 5	Lismore	*New South Wales	Won by 21 runs
Jan 9	Melbourne	*Australia (L/O Intl)	No result
Jan 11	Brisbane	*India (L/O Intl)	Won by 6 wkts
Jan 12	Brisbane	*Australia (L/O Intl)	Won by 12 runs
Jan 16	Melbourne	*India (L/O Intl)	Lost by 5 wkts
Feb 23	Melbourne	*Pakistan (WC L/O Intl)	Won by 10 wkts
Feb 27	Melbourne	*England (WC L/O Intl)	Lost by 6 wkts
Feb 29	Brisbane	*Zimbabwe (WC L/O Intl)	Won by 75 runs
Mar 13	Berri	*Sri Lanka (WC L/O Intl)	Won by 91 runs
Mar 18	Melbourne	*Australia (WC L/O Intl)	Lost by 57 runs

Player	M	Inn	NO	Runs	HS	50	100	Avrge	Ct/St	Overs	Mdns	Runs	Wkts	Avrge	5wi	10wm	Best
Anthony, HAG	1	2	–	23	15	–	–	11.50	1	21.0	1	107	2	53.50	–	–	2/107
Arthurton, KLT	1	2	–	10	8	–	–	5.00	–	–	–	–	–	–	–	–	–
Best, CA	1	2	–	49	37	–	–	24.50	2	–	–	–	–	–	–	–	–
Cummins, AC	1	2	1	38	23	–	–	38.00	–	26.0	1	80	1	80.00	–	–	1/80
Haynes, DL (Capt)	1	2	–	26	20	–	–	13.00	1	–	–	–	–	–	–	–	–
Haynes, RC	1	2	–	14	13	–	–	7.00	–	27.5	4	106	4	26.50	–	–	4/106
Hooper, CL	1	2	–	37	33	–	–	18.50	1	27.0	1	72	–	–	–	–	–
Lara, BC	1	2	–	93	83	1	–	46.50	–	–	–	–	–	–	–	–	–
Patterson, BP	1	2	–	2	2	–	–	1.00	–	17.0	1	85	2	42.50	–	–	2/85
Wallace, PA	1	2	–	34	21	–	–	17.00	–	–	–	–	–	–	–	–	–
Williams, D	1	2	1	12	8	–	–	12.00	2/–	–	–	–	–	–	–	–	–

INDIANS IN AUSTRALIA

Season	Touring Team	First-class Results					All Matches					Captain
		Games	W	L	D	T	Games	W	L	D	T	
1947/48	Indians	14	2	7	5	–	20	5	7	8	–	NB Amarnath
1967/68	Indians	9	–	6	3	–	15	4	6	5	–	Nawab of Pataudi jr
1977/78	Indians	11	6	5	–	–	20	12	6	2	–	BS Bedi
1980/81	Indians	8	2	2	4	–	25	8	11	6	–	SM Gavaskar
1984/85	Indians	–	–	–	–	–	5	5	–	–	–	SM Gavaskar
1985/86	Indians	5	1	–	4	–	19	8	7	4	–	Kapil Dev
1988/89	Tamil Nadu	1	–	1	–	–	3	–	3	–	–	S Vasudevan
1991/92	Indians	7	1	5	1	–	29	7	19	2	1	M Azharuddin
1993/94	Indian XI	–	–	–	–	–	3	–	3	–	–	SR Tendulkar
		55	12	26	17	–	139	49	62	27	1	

INDIANS IN AUSTRALIA

FIRST-CLASS RESULTS

Opponent	Venue	First Game	Games	W	L	D	T
AUSTRALIA	Brisbane	Nov 28 1947	4	–	4	–	–
	Sydney	Dec 12 1947	6	1	2	3	–
	Melbourne	Jan 1 1948	7	2	4	1	–
	Adelaide	Jan 23 1948	6	–	4	2	–
	Perth	Dec 16 1977	2	–	2	–	–
			25	3	16	6	–
Australian XI	Sydney	Jan 12 1906	1	1	–	–	–
New South Wales	Sydney	Nov 7 1947	3	1	1	1	–
	Lismore	Nov 23 1991	1	–	1	–	–
			4	1	2	1	–
Queensland	Brisbane	Nov 21 1947	4	2	1	1	–
South Australia	Adelaide	Oct 24 1947	5	2	2	1	–
Tasmania	Hobart (TCA)	Jan 10 1948	4	1	1	2	–
	Launceston	Jan 15 1948	1	–	–	1	–
			5	1	1	3	–
Victoria	Melbourne	Oct 30 1947	4	1	–	3	–
	Geelong	Jan 30 1981	1	1	–	–	–
			5	2	–	3	–
Western Australia	Perth	Oct 17 1947	5	–	3	2	–
	Perth (Tamil Nadu)	Nov 4 1988	1	–	–	1	–
			6	–	3	3	–

1984/85 INDIANS IN AUSTRALIA

First-class Results					All Matches				
Matches	Won	Lost	Drawn	Tied	Matches	Won	Lost	Drawn	Tied
–	–	–	–	–	5	5	–	–	–

Date	Venue	Opponent	Results for Touring Team
Feb 20	Melbourne	*Pakistan (L/O Intl)	Won by 6 wkts
Feb 26	Sydney	*England (L/O Intl)	Won by 86 runs
Mar 3	Melbourne	*Australia (L/O Intl)	Won by 8 wkts
Mar 5	Sydney	*New Zealand (L/O Intl)	Won by 7 wkts
Mar 10	Melbourne	*Pakistan (L/O Intl)	Won by 8 wkts

1988/89 TAMIL NADU IN AUSTRALIA

First-class Results					All Matches				
Matches	Won	Lost	Drawn	Tied	Matches	Won	Lost	Drawn	Tied
1	–	1	–	–	3	–	3	–	–

Date	Venue	Opponent	Results for Touring Team
Nov 3	Mandurah	*Western Australian Country XI	Lost by 46 runs
Nov 4	Perth	Western Australia	Lost by an inns & 51 runs
Nov 8	Perth	*Western Australia	Lost by 8 wkts

Player	M	Inn	NO	Runs	HS	50	100	Avrge	Ct/St	Overs	Mdns	Runs	Wkts	Avrge	5wi	10wm	Best
Arun, B	1	2	–	45	24	–	–	22.50	–	18.0	2	75	1	75.00	–	–	1/75
Chandrasekhar, VB	1	2	–	15	9	–	–	7.50	–	–	–	–	–	–	–	–	–
Girish, D	1	2	1	28	14*	–	–	28.00	–	–	–	–	–	–	–	–	–
Prakash, PC	1	2	–	44	37	–	–	22.00	–	–	–	–	–	–	–	–	–
Raman, WV	1	2	–	21	21	–	–	10.50	1	12.0	–	66	–	–	–	–	–
Robin Singh	1	2	–	56	30	–	–	28.00	–	4.0	1	19	–	–	–	–	–
Sivaramakrishnan, V	1	2	–	94	75	1	–	47.00	–	–	–	–	–	–	–	–	–
Sivaramakrishnan, L	1	2	–	16	9	–	–	8.00	1	3.0	–	13	–	–	–	–	–
Vasu, D	1	2	1	39	34	–	–	39.00	–	15.0	2	58	–	–	–	–	–
Vasudevan, S (Capt)	1	2	–	1	1	–	–	0.50	–	23.0	4	80	–	–	–	–	–
Venkataramana, MV	1	2	–	4	2	–	–	2.00	–	26.0	3	116	1	116.00	–	–	1/116

1993/94 INDIANS IN AUSTRALIA

First-class Results					All Matches				
Matches	Won	Lost	Drawn	Tied	Matches	Won	Lost	Drawn	Tied
–	–	–	–	–	3	–	3	–	–

Date	Venue	Opponent	Results for Touring Team
Apr 30	Canberra	*Australian XI	Lost by 6 wkts
May 1	Drummoyne	*Australian XI	Lost by 52 runs
May 3	South Yarra	*Australian XI	Lost by 5 wkts

PAKISTANIS IN AUSTRALIA

Season	Touring Team	First-class Results					All Matches					Captain
		Games	W	L	D	T	Games	W	L	D	T	
1964/65	Pakistanis	4	–	–	4	–	4	–	–	4	–	Hanif Mohammad
1972/73	Pakistanis	8	2	5	1	–	13	5	6	2	–	Intikhab Alam
1976/77	Pakistanis	5	1	2	2	–	5	1	2	2	–	Mushtaq Mohammad
1978/79	Pakistanis	4	1	1	2	–	5	2	1	2	–	Mushtaq Mohammad
1981/82	Pakistanis	8	2	2	4	–	21	8	8	5	–	Javed Miandad
1983/84	Pakistanis	11	3	3	5	–	24	7	11	6	–	Imran Khan
1984/85	Pakistanis	–	–	–	–	–	5	3	2	–	–	Javed Miandad
1986/87	Pakistanis	–	–	–	–	–	4	2	2	–	–	Imran Khan
1988/89	Pakistanis	1	–	–	1	–	14	6	7	1	–	Imran Khan
1989/90	Pakistanis	6	–	3	3	–	17	5	9	3	–	Imran Khan
1991/92	Pakistanis	2	–	–	2	–	14	5	6	3	–	Imran Khan
1992/93	Pakistanis	1	1	–	–	–	12	5	6	–	1	Javed Miandad
		50	10	16	24	–	138	49	60	28	1	

FIRST-CLASS RESULTS

Opponent	Venue	First Game	Games	W	L	D	T
AUSTRALIA	Melbourne	Dec 4 1964	6	2	3	2	–
	Adelaide	Dec 22 1972	3	–	1	3	–
	Sydney	Jan 6 1973	3	1	2	1	–
	Perth	Mar 24 1979	3	–	3	–	–
	Brisbane	Nov 27 1981	2	–	1	1	–
			20	3	10	7	–
Combined XI	Launceston	Dec 18 1972	1	–	–	1	–
New South Wales	Sydney	Dec 11 1964	3	–	–	3	–
	Canberra	Mar 3 1979	1	–	–	1	–
			4	–	–	4	–
Queensland	Brisbane	Nov 27 1964	7	2	–	5	–
South Australia	Adelaide	Dec 18 1983	4	1	–	3	–
Tasmania	Hobart (TCA)	Dec 15 1972	2	2	–	–	–
	Launceston	Jan 1 1982	1	1	–	–	–
	Devonport	Feb 9 1992	1	–	–	1	–
			4	3	–	1	–
Victoria	Melbourne	Nov 24 1972	4	1	2	1	–
	Bendigo	Feb 4 1992	1	–	–	1	–
			5	1	2	2	–
Western Australia	Perth	Nov 18 1972	5	–	4	1	–

1964/65 PAKISTANIS

First-class Results					All Matches				
Matches	Won	Lost	Drawn	Tied	Matches	Won	Lost	Drawn	Tied
4	–	–	4	–	4	–	–	4	1

Date	Venue	Opponent	Results for Touring Team
Nov 27	Brisbane	Queensland	Drawn
Dec 4	Melbourne	AUSTRALIA (Only Test)	Drawn
Dec 11	Sydney	New South Wales	Drawn
Dec 18	Adelaide	South Australia	Drawn

Player	M	Inn	NO	Runs	HS	50	100	Avrge	Ct/St	Overs	Mdns	Runs	Wkts	Avrge	5wi	10wm	Best
Abdul Kadir	2	4	–	83	35	–	–	20.75	1	–	–	–	–	–	–	–	–
Afaq Hussain	1	2	2	21	13*	–	–	–	–	9.0	1	45	–	–	–	–	–
Arif Butt	3	3	–	24	12	–	–	8.00	–	75.2	2	338	13	26.00	1	–	6/89
Asif Iqbal	3	6	1	130	67*	1	–	26.00	2	50.0	2	289	4	72.25	–	–	2/70
Farooq Hamid	2	4	–	29	19	–	–	7.25	–	43.0	2	196	3	65.33	–	–	2/81
Ghulam Abbas	1	2	–	11	9	–	–	5.50	1	–	–	–	–	–	–	–	–
Hanif Mohammad (Capt)	3	4	1	402	110*	2	2	134.00	7/–	–	–	–	–	–	–	–	–
Intikhab Alam	3	5	1	135	61	2	–	33.75	3	46.7	2	220	6	36.66	–	–	4/70
Javed Burki	4	7	–	275	47	–	–	39.28	1	5.0	2	11	–	–	–	–	–
Masod-ul-Hasan	2	3	3	82	50*	1	–	–	–	14.0	1	62	1	62.00	–	–	1/29
Mohammad Ilyas	4	7	–	402	154	–	2	57.42	–	6.0	–	43	–	–	–	–	–
Mufasirul Haq	2	1	1	1	1	–	–	–	–	38.0	–	233	2	116.50	–	–	2/92
Nasim-ul-Ghani	3	5	–	119	31	–	–	23.80	–	29.0	2	142	2	71.00	–	–	1/28
Naushad Ali	2	3	–	130	51	1	–	43.33	4/1	–	–	–	–	–	–	–	–
Pervez Sajjad	2	2	–	14	13	–	–	7.00	–	34.0	1	152	3	50.66	–	–	2/88
Saeed Ahmed	4	7	–	353	105	1	1	50.42	4	31.2	3	121	4	30.25	–	–	3/50
Shafqat Rana	3	5	–	97	44	–	–	19.40	1	–	–	–	–	–	–	–	–

1972/73 PAKISTANIS

First-class Results					All Matches				
Matches	Won	Lost	Drawn	Tied	Matches	Won	Lost	Drawn	Tied
8	2	5	1	–	13	5	6	2	–

Date	Venue	Opponent	Results for Touring Team
Nov 15	Perth	*Western Australian Colts	Drawn
Nov 18	Perth	Western Australia	Lost by 8 wkts
Nov 24	Melbourne	Victoria	Lost by 6 wkts
Nov 28	Shepparton	*Victorian Country XI	Won by 66 runs
Dec 1	Brisbane	Queensland	Won by 163 runs
Dec 6	Roma	*Queensland Country XI	Won by 67 runs
Dec 8	Newcastle	*Northern NSW Country XI	Lost by 2 wkts
Dec 12	Canberra	*Southern NSW Country XI	Won by 127 runs
Dec 15	Hobart (TCA)	Tasmania	Won by an inns & 4 runs
Dec 18	Launceston	Combined XI	Drawn
Dec 22	Adelaide	AUSTRALIA (1st Test)	Lost by an inns & 114 runs
Dec 29	Melbourne	AUSTRALIA (2nd Test)	Lost by 92 runs
Jan 6	Sydney	AUSTRALIA (3rd Test)	Lost by 52 runs

Player	M	Inn	NO	Runs	HS	50	100	Avrge	Ct/St	Overs	Mdns	Runs	Wkts	Avrge	5wi	10wm	Best
Asif Iqbal	8	15	2	449	130	2	1	34.53	4	26.0	1	129	1	129.00	–	–	1/11
Asif Masood	6	10	5	36	24	–	–	7.20	–	135.6	8	726	17	42.70	1	–	5/54
Intikhab Alam	8	14	–	418	68	3	–	29.85	3	157.6	18	802	15	53.46	1	1	8/54
Majid Khan	7	14	1	753	158	3	3	57.92	6	76.0	4	295	4	73.75	–	–	2/88
Masood Iqbal	2	3	2	44	31	–	–	44.00	3/–	–	–	–	–	–	–	–	–
Mohammad Ilyas	1	2	–	11	11	–	–	5.50	–	0.5	–	5	–	–	–	–	–
Mushtaq Mohammad (Capt)	8	15	–	382	121	2	1	25.46	5	66.5	3	345	9	38.33	–	–	3/67
Nasim-ul-Ghani	3	5	1	200	66	3	–	50.00	1	31.0	3	84	3	28.00	–	–	2/28
Pervez Sajjad	2	–	–	–	–	–	–	–	2	51.0	9	212	6	35.33	–	–	3/79
Sadiq Mohammad	7	14	–	453	137	2	1	32/35	5	2.0	–	8	–	–	–	–	–
Saeed Ahmed	6	11	–	332	106	1	1	30.18	6	45.2	5	205	5	41.00	–	–	3/55
Salim Altaf	8	14	7	155	35*	–	–	22.14	3	158.5	14	603	17	35.47	–	–	4/60
Sarfraz Nawaz	5	7	1	61	21	–	–	10.16	3	144.7	22	581	25	23.24	1	1	7/76
Talat Ali	5	9	1	359	129	3	1	44.87	–	–	–	–	–	–	–	–	–
Wasim Bari	6	10	2	107	72	1	–	13.37	14/2	–	–	–	–	–	–	–	–
Zaheer Abbas	6	11	–	487	143	2	2	44.27	6	–	–	–	–	–	–	–	–

1976/77 PAKISTANIS

First-class Results					All Matches				
Matches	Won	Lost	Drawn	Tied	Matches	Won	Lost	Drawn	Tied
5	1	2	2	–	5	1	2	2	–

Date	Venue	Opponent	Results for Touring Team
Dec 18	Perth	Western Australia	Lost by 6 wkts
Dec 24	Adelaide	AUSTRALIA (1st Test)	Drawn
Jan 1	Melbourne	AUSTRALIA (2nd Test)	Lost by 348 runs
Jan 8	Brisbane	Queensland	Drawn
Jan 14	Sydney	AUSTRALIA (3rd Test)	Won by 8 wkts

Player	M	Inn	NO	Runs	HS	50	100	Avrge	Ct/St	Overs	Mdns	Runs	Wkts	Avrge	5wi	10wm	Best
Asif Iqbal	4	7	1	345	152*	–	2	57.50	4	31.0	8	105	3	35.00	–	–	3/52
Asif Masood	1	2	2	0	0*	–	–	–	1	47.0	3	306	2	153.00	–	–	1/45
Haroon Rashid	2	3	1	203	123	1	1	101.50	3	–	–	–	–	–	–	–	–
Imran Khan	5	8	2	199	54*	1	–	33.16	2	171.0	19	741	24	30.87	3	1	6/63
Intikhab Alam	1	1	–	1	1	–	–	1.00	–	24.0	1	162	3	54.00	–	–	3/115
Iqbal Qasim	3	5	2	7	5	–	–	2.33	1	96.0	17	374	11	34.00	–	–	4/84
Javed Miandad	5	9	–	169	64	2	–	18.77	4	62.1	9	258	6	43.00	–	–	3/85
Majid Khan	4	8	1	347	76	2	–	49.57	3	3.7	–	23	1	23.00	–	–	1/10
Mudassar Nazar	2	4	–	69	29	–	–	17.25	–	–	–	–	–	–	–	–	–
Mushtaq Mohammad (Capt)	5	10	3	369	132*	2	1	52.71	4	37.4	4	164	4	41.00	–	–	4/58
Sadiq Mohammad	4	8	–	268	105	1	1	33.50	1	–	–	–	–	–	–	–	–
Salim Altaf	3	5	1	38	21	–	–	9.50	–	56.0	5	309	3	103.00	–	–	2/62
Sarfraz Nawaz	3	4	–	46	29	–	–	11.50	1	95.0	13	418	12	34.83	–	–	3/42
Sikander Bakht	1	–	–	–	–	–	–	–	2	16.1	–	125	3	41.66	–	–	3/79
Taslim Arif	1	2	1	44	40	–	–	44.00	2/–	–	–	–	–	–	–	–	–
Wasim Bari	4	6	–	30	21	–	–	5.00	12/4	–	–	–	–	–	–	–	–
Wasim Raja	1	2	–	120	108	–	1	60.00	–	5.0	1	29	–	–	–	–	–
Zaheer Abbas	4	8	–	412	101	4	1	51.50	8	–	–	–	–	–	–	–	–

1978/79 PAKISTANIS

First-class Results					All Matches				
Matches	Won	Lost	Drawn	Tied	Matches	Won	Lost	Drawn	Tied
4	1	1	2	–	5	2	1	2	–

Date	Venue	Opponent	Results for Touring Team
Mar 3	Canberra	New South Wales	Drawn
Mar 6	Canberra	*New South Wales	Won by 12 runs
Mar 10	Melbourne	AUSTRALIA (1st Test)	Won by 71 runs
Mar 17	Adelaide	South Australia	Drawn
Mar 24	Perth	AUSTRALIA (2nd Test)	Lost by 7 wkts

Player	M	Inn	NO	Runs	HS	50	100	Avrge	Ct/St	Overs	Mdns	Runs	Wkts	Avrge	5wi	10wm	Best
Anwar Khan	2	2	2	18	16*	–	–	–	1	18.0	3	62	3	20.66	–	–	3/61
Ashraf Ali	2	2	–	21	12	–	–	10.50	–/–	–	–	–	–	–	–	–	–
Asif Iqbal	2	4	1	222	134*	–	1	74.00	1	–	–	–	–	–	–	–	–
Haroon Rashid	3	5	1	220	104	1	1	55.00	–	–	–	–	–	–	–	–	–
Imran Khan	2	4	–	90	33	–	–	22.50	1	94.0	23	285	7	40.71	–	–	4/26
Iqbal Qasim	2	2	–	29	17	–	–	14.50	–	38.5	3	127	3	42.33	–	–	3/127
Javed Miandad	4	7	1	325	129*	1	1	54.16	2	8.0	–	38	1	38.00	–	–	1/8
Majid Khan	4	7	–	150	108	–	1	21.42	3	9.0	1	34	–	–	–	–	–
Mohsin Khan	2	3	1	38	14	–	–	19.00	1	–	–	–	–	–	–	–	–
Mudassar Nazar	3	5	1	117	48	–	–	29.25	–	47.0	7	144	3	48.00	–	–	3/48
Mushtaq Mohammad (Capt)	4	6	–	98	36	–	–	16.33	1	18.0	–	77	–	–	–	–	–
Sarfraz Nawaz	3	4	–	66	35	–	–	16.50	1	111.2	21	322	13	24.76	1	1	9/86
Sikander Bakht	4	4	2	5	5*	–	–	2.50	–	56.0	2	228	5	45.60	–	–	4/136
Wasim Raja	1	2	–	41	28	–	–	20.50	–	10.4	–	34	2	17.00	–	–	2/23
Wasim Bari	2	4	1	8	8*	–	–	2.66	6/–	–	–	–	–	–	–	–	–
Zaheer Abbas	3	6	–	267	126	1	1	44.50	1	–	–	–	–	–	–	–	–

1981/82 PAKISTANIS

First-class Results					All Matches				
Matches	Won	Lost	Drawn	Tied	Matches	Won	Lost	Drawn	Tied
8	2	2	4	–	21	8	8	5	–

Date	Venue	Opponent	Results for Touring Team
Oct 23	Perth	Western Australia	Drawn
Oct 30	Brisbane	Queensland	Drawn
Nov 6	Melbourne	Victoria	Drawn
Nov 13	Perth	AUSTRALIA (1st Test)	Lost by 286 runs
Nov 21	Melbourne	*West Indies (L/O Intl)	Lost by 18 runs
Nov 22	Melbourne	*Australia (L/O Intl)	Won by 4 wkts
Nov 23	Canberra	*Australian Capital Territory	Drawn
Nov 27	Brisbane	AUSTRALIA (2nd Test)	Lost by 10 wkts
Dec 3	Port Lincoln	*South Australian Country XI	Won by 8 wkts
Dec 5	Adelaide	*West Indies (L/O Intl)	Won by 8 runs
Dec 6	Adelaide	*Australia (L/O Intl)	Lost by 38 runs
Dec 11	Melbourne	AUSTRALIA (3rd Test)	Won by an inns & 82 runs
Dec 17	Sydney	*Australia (L/O Intl)	Won by 6 wkts
Dec 19	Perth	*West Indies (L/O Intl)	Lost by 7 wkts
Dec 26	Adelaide	South Australia	Drawn
Jan 1	Launceston	Tasmania	Won by 10 wkts
Jan 6	Stawell	*Victorian Country XI	Won by 5 wkts
Jan 9	Melbourne	*Australia (L/O Intl)	Won by 25 runs
Jan 12	Sydney	*West Indies (L/O Intl)	Lost by 7 wkts
Jan 14	Sydney	*Australia (L/O Intl)	Lost by 76 runs
Jan 16	Brisbane	*West Indies (L/O Intl)	Lost on run rate

Player	M	Inn	NO	Runs	HS	50	100	Avrge	Ct/St	Overs	Mdns	Runs	Wkts	Avrge	5wi	10wm	Best
Ashraf Ali	2	4	2	35	17	–	–	17.50	5/–	–	–	–	–	–	–	–	–
Ijaz Faqih	4	6	2	164	61*	1	–	41.00	3	124.4	20	324	9	36.00	–	–	3/32
Imran Khan	6	7	2	244	93*	2	–	48.80	1	281.2	66	686	28	24.50	1	–	5/89
Iqbal Qasim	5	4	1	25	16*	–	–	8.33	5	214.4	56	532	23	23.13	2	–	5/31
Javed Miandad (Capt)	7	11	2	682	158*	4	2	75.77	6	38.0	4	137	1	137.00	–	–	1/20
Majid Khan	6	9	–	264	110	1	1	29.33	5	56.0	13	137	2	68.50	–	–	1/36
Mansoor Akhtar	4	7	–	345	86	3	–	49.28	1	2.0	1	3	–	–	–	–	–
Mohsin Khan	3	5	1	99	43	–	–	24.75	2	–	–	–	–	–	–	–	–
Mudassar Nazar	6	9	1	295	95	2	–	36.87	5	22.0	6	78	–	–	–	–	–
Rizwan-uz-Zaman	6	10	1	431	126	1	2	43.10	1	6.0	1	15	–	–	–	–	–
Salim Malik	3	5	1	159	62	2	–	39.75	1	7.0	1	33	–	–	–	–	–
Sarfraz Nawaz	6	7	–	63	26	–	–	9.00	1	208.0	52	590	12	49.16	–	–	3/11
Sikander Bakht	6	7	4	21	11	–	–	7.00	–	146.3	26	454	10	45.40	–	–	3/93
Tahir Naqqash	4	3	1	39	25*	–	–	19.50	–	81.0	15	272	6	45.33	–	–	4/60
Wasim Raja	7	10	–	239	50	1	–	23.90	2	163.0	30	480	7	68.57	–	–	3/49
Wasim Bari	6	8	1	68	26	–	–	9.71	12/3	2.0	1	1	–	–	–	–	–
Zaheer Abbas	7	9	1	461	117	3	1	57.62	5	–	–	–	–	–	–	–	–

1983/84 PAKISTANIS

First-class Results					All Matches				
Matches	Won	Lost	Drawn	Tied	Matches	Won	Lost	Drawn	Tied
11	3	3	5	–	24	7	11	6	–

Date	Venue	Opponent	Results for Touring Team
Oct 21	Brisbane	Queensland	Drawn
Oct 26	Whyalla	*South Australian Country XI	Won by 9 wkts
Oct 28	Adelaide	South Australia	Won by 7 wkts
Nov 2	Northam	*Western Australian Country XI	Won by 113 runs
Nov 4	Perth	Western Australia	Lost by 6 wkts
Nov 11	Perth	AUSTRALIA (1st Test)	Lost by an inns & 9 runs
Nov 18	Sydney	New South Wales	Drawn
Nov 25	Brisbane	AUSTRALIA (2nd Test)	Drawn
Dec 2	Melbourne	Victoria	Won by 7 wkts
Dec 9	Adelaide	AUSTRALIA (3rd Test)	Drawn
Dec 16	Hobart (TCA)	Tasmania	Won by 42 runs
Dec 21	Griffith	*South-West New South Wales	Won by 8 wkts
Dec 26	Melbourne	AUSTRALIA (4th Test)	Drawn
Jan 2	Sydney	AUSTRALIA (5th Test)	Lost by 10 wkts
Jan 10	Sydney	*Australia (L/O Intl)	Lost by 34 runs
Jan 12	Melbourne	*West Indies (L/O Intl)	Won by 97 runs
Jan 14	Brisbane	*West Indies (L/O Intl)	Lost by 5 wkts
Jan 15	Brisbane	*Australia (L/O Intl)	No result
Jan 19	Sydney	*West Indies (L/O Intl)	Lost by 5 wkts
Jan 21	Melbourne	*Australia (L/O Intl)	Lost by 43 runs
Jan 25	Sydney	*Australia (L/O Intl)	Lost by 87 runs
Jan 28	Adelaide	*West Indies (L/O Intl)	Lost by 1 wkt
Jan 30	Adelaide	*Australia (L/O Intl)	Lost by 70 runs
Feb 4	Perth	*West Indies (L/O Intl)	Lost by 7 wkts

Player	M	Inn	NO	Runs	HS	50	100	Avrge	Ct/St	Overs	Mdns	Runs	Wkts	Avrge	5wi	10wm	Best
Abdul Qadir	10	15	2	223	45	–	–	17.15	–	441.5	78	1413	28	50.46	2	–	7/122
Ashraf Ali	3	5	1	71	39	–	–	17.75	8/1	–	–	–	–	–	–	–	–
Atiq-ur-Rehman	2	–	–	–	–	–	–	–	–	30.0	2	177	2	88.50	–	–	2/115
Azeem Hafeez	9	8	3	22	7	–	–	4.40	3	316.2	62	1217	27	45.07	2	–	5/100
Imran Khan (Capt)	3	6	1	202	83	2	–	40.40	–	–	–	–	–	–	–	–	–
Javed Miandad	10	18	3	952	141*	6	3	63.46	3	21.0	5	80	–	–	–	–	–
Mansoor Akhtar	3	6	3	68	25*	–	–	22.66	2	–	–	–	–	–	–	–	–
Mohammad Nazir	8	8	5	63	20*	–	–	21.00	3	252.5	59	627	16	39.18	–	–	4/73
Mohsin Khan	10	19	–	699	152	2	2	36.78	5	8.0	2	24	–	–	–	–	–
Mudassar Nazar	10	19	1	1071	139	3	5	59.50	9	164.0	26	534	8	66.75	–	–	3/76
Qasim Omar	11	20	2	767	131	3	2	42.61	4	5.0	1	22	1	22.00	–	–	1/22
Rashid Khan	6	8	3	122	45*	–	–	24.40	1	224.0	51	633	12	52.75	–	–	3/129
Salim Malik	4	7	–	306	80	3	–	43.71	2	7.0	1	39	1	39.00	–	–	1/3
Sarfraz Nawaz	4	6	1	104	32	–	–	20.80	2	223.0	55	516	10	51.60	–	–	3/106
Tahir Naqqash	5	6	2	86	29*	–	–	21.50	3	163.3	31	555	15	37.00	–	–	4/80
Wasim Bari	8	11	3	154	73*	1	–	19.25	23/–	–	–	–	–	–	–	–	–
Wasim Raja	7	11	–	268	83	2	–	24.36	4	62.0	15	160	–	–	–	–	–
Zaheer Abbas	8	14	2	448	61	4	–	37.33	3	27.0	5	63	–	–	–	–	–

1984/85 PAKISTANIS

First-class Results					All Matches				
Matches	Won	Lost	Drawn	Tied	Matches	Won	Lost	Drawn	Tied
–	–	–	–	–	5	3	2	–	–

Date	Venue	Opponent	Results for Touring Team
Feb 20	Melbourne	*India (L/O Intl)	Lost by 6 wkts
Feb 24	Melbourne	*Australia (L/O Intl)	Won by 62 runs
Mar 2	Melbourne	*England (L/O Intl)	Won by 67 runs
Mar 6	Melbourne	*West Indies (L/O Intl)	Won by 7 wkts
Mar 10	Melbourne	*India (L/O Intl)	Lost by 8 wkts

1986/87 PAKISTANIS

First-class Results					All Matches				
Matches	Won	Lost	Drawn	Tied	Matches	Won	Lost	Drawn	Tied
–	–	–	–	–	4	2	2	–	–

Date	Venue	Opponent	Results for Touring Team
Dec 30	Perth	*West Indies (L/O Intl)	Won by 34 runs
Jan 2	Perth	*Australia (L/O Intl)	Won by 1 wkt
Jan 5	Perth	*England (L/O Intl)	Lost by 3 wkts
Jan 7	Perth	*England (L/O Intl)	Lost by 5 wkts

1988/89 PAKISTANIS

First-class Results					All Matches				
Matches	Won	Lost	Drawn	Tied	Matches	Won	Lost	Drawn	Tied
1	–	–	1	–	14	6	7	1	–

Date	Venue	Opponent	Results for Touring Team
Dec 1	Cairns	*North Queensland	Won by 96 runs
Dec 3	Mackay	*Queensland	Lost by 4 runs
Dec 4	Mackay	*Queensland	Won by 37 runs
Dec 10	Adelaide	*West Indies (L/O Intl)	Lost by 89 runs
Dec 11	Adelaide	*Australia (L/O Intl)	Lost by 9 wkts
Dec 13	Adelaide	*AIS Cricket Academy	Won by 67 runs
Dec 17	Hobart (Bel)	*West Indies (L/O Intl)	Lost by 17 runs
Dec 19	Sydney	New South Wales	Drawn
Dec 27	Newcastle	*New South Wales Invitation XI	Won by 4 runs
Jan 1	Perth	*West Indies (L/O Intl)	Lost by 7 wkts
Jan 2	Perth	*Australia (L/O Intl)	Won by 38 runs
Jan 7	Brisbane	*West Indies (L/O Intl)	Won by 55 runs
Jan 8	Brisbane	*Australia (L/O Intl)	Lost by 5 wkts
Jan 10	Melbourne	*Australia (L/O Intl)	Lost on run rate

Player	M	Inn	NO	Runs	HS	50	100	Avrge	Ct/St	Overs	Mdns	Runs	Wkts	Avrge	5wi	10wm	Best
Aaqib Javed	1	1	1	0	0*	–	–	–	–	19.0	4	51	2	25.50	–	–	2/28
Abdul Qadir	1	2	1	13	13	–	–	13.00	–	24.0	6	67	–	–	–	–	–
Ijaz Ahmed	1	2	–	46	29	–	–	23.00	–	–	–	–	–	–	–	–	–
Imran Khan (Capt)	1	2	–	35	20	–	–	17.50	–	3.2	1	4	1	4.00	–	–	1/4
Moin-ul-Atiq	1	2	–	41	36	–	–	20.50	–	–	–	–	–	–	–	–	–
Mudassar Nazar	1	2	–	89	66	1	–	44.50	–	–	–	–	–	–	–	–	–
Rameez Raja	1	2	–	29	23	–	–	14.50	2	–	–	–	–	–	–	–	–
Saeed Anwar	1	2	–	53	31	–	–	26.50	–	1.0	–	6	–	–	–	–	–
Salim Yousuf	1	2	–	34	19	–	–	17.00	1/1	–	–	–	–	–	–	–	–
Tauseef Ahmed	1	1	–	10	10	–	–	10.00	–	46.4	9	106	3	35.33	–	–	3/59
Wasim Akram	1	2	–	25	19	–	–	12.50	1	33.4	8	73	5	14.60	–	–	4/40

1989/90 PAKISTANIS

First-class Results					All Matches				
Matches	Won	Lost	Drawn	Tied	Matches	Won	Lost	Drawn	Tied
6	–	3	3	–	17	5	9	3	–

Date	Venue	Opponent	Results for Touring Team
Dec 27	Perth	Western Australia	Lost by an inns & 78 runs
Dec 31	Perth	*Sri Lanka (L/O Intl)	Lost by 3 wkts
Jan 3	Melbourne	*Australia (L/O Intl)	Lost by 7 wkts
Jan 6	Brisbane	Queensland	Drawn
Jan 12	Melbourne	AUSTRALIA (1st Test)	Lost by 92 runs
Jan 19	Adelaide	AUSTRALIA (2nd Test)	Drawn
Jan 26	Melbourne	Victoria	Lost by 59 runs
Jan 31	Canberra	*Prime Minister's XI	Lost by 81 runs
Feb 3	Sydney	AUSTRALIA (3rd Test)	Drawn
Feb 10	Brisbane	*Sri Lanka (L/O Intl)	Won by 5 wkts
Feb 11	Brisbane	*Australia (L/O Intl)	Lost by 67 runs
Feb 13	Sydney	*Australia (L/O Intl)	Won by 5 wkts
Feb 15	Hobart (Bel)	*Sri Lanka (L/O Intl)	Won by 6 wkts
Feb 17	Adelaide	*Sri Lanka (L/O Intl)	Won by 27 runs
Feb 20	Sydney	*Australia (L/O Intl)	Won by 2 runs
Feb 23	Melbourne	*Australia (L/O Intl)	Lost by 7 wkts
Feb 25	Sydney	*Australia (L/O Intl)	Lost by 69 runs

Player	M	Inn	NO	Runs	HS	50	100	Avrge	Ct/St	Overs	Mdns	Runs	Wkts	Avrge	5wi	10wm	Best
Aamir Malik	5	9	–	113	53	1	–	12.56	5	14.0	1	57	2	28.50	–	–	2/57
Aaqib Javed	4	7	2	10	9*	–	–	2.00	2	121.1	30	327	9	36.33	–	–	2/47
Abdul Qadir	2	3	–	51	51	1	–	17.00	1	–	–	–	–	–	–	–	–
Ijaz Ahmed	6	11	–	349	121	1	1	31.73	6	–	–	–	–	–	–	–	–
Imran Khan (Capt)	4	7	1	320	136	1	1	53.33	1	–	–	–	–	–	–	–	–
Javed Miandad	4	7	1	322	77	4	–	53.67	1	–	–	–	–	–	–	–	–
Mansoor Akhtar	3	6	–	127	74	1	–	21.17	2	–	–	–	–	–	–	–	–
Maqsood Rana	1	2	–	7	7	–	–	3.50	1	15.0	2	57	2	28.50	–	–	2/57
Mushtaq Ahmed	2	4	–	51	32	–	–	12.75	2	74.0	18	212	5	42.40	–	–	2/17
Nadeem Ghauri	3	5	1	20	19	–	–	5.00	1	76.0	21	194	7	27.71	–	–	4/59
Rameez Raja	3	5	–	24	9	–	–	4.80	1	–	–	–	–	–	–	–	–
Saeed Anwar	3	6	–	131	44	–	–	21.83	4	14.5	1	35	2	17.50	–	–	2/35
Salim Malik	1	2	1	76	65*	1	–	76.00	–	–	–	–	–	–	–	–	–
Salim Yousuf	6	11	2	265	78	1	–	29.44	12/1	–	–	–	–	–	–	–	–
Shoaib Mohammad	6	11	–	219	52	1	–	19.91	3	–	–	–	–	–	–	–	–
Tauseef Ahmed	4	7	2	99	36	–	–	19.80	–	131.5	26	358	10	35.80	1	–	5/42
Waqar Younus	6	9	2	81	23	–	–	11.57	–	157.0	26	496	10	49.60	–	–	3/84
Wasim Akram	3	5	–	197	123	1	1	39.40	2	135.4	37	318	17	18.71	3	1	6/62

PAKISTANIS IN AUSTRALIA

1991/92 PAKISTANIS

	First-class Results					All Matches			
Matches	Won	Lost	Drawn	Tied	Matches	Won	Lost	Drawn	Tied
2	–	–	2	–	14	5	6	3	–

Date	Venue	Opponent	Results for Touring Team
Feb 4	Bendigo	Victoria	Drawn
Feb 8	Launceston	*Tasmania	Lost by 42 runs
Feb 9	Devonport	Tasmania	Drawn
Feb 13	Canberra	*Australian Capital Territory	Won by 48 runs
Feb 15	Canberra	*South Africa	Lost by 17 runs
Feb 17	North Sydney	*Sri Lanka	Lost by 14 runs
Feb 23	Melbourne	*West Indies (WC L/O Intl)	Lost by 10 wkts
Feb 27	Hobart (Bel)	*Zimbabwe (WC L/O Intl)	Won by 53 runs
Mar 1	Adelaide	*England (WC L/O Intl)	No result
Mar 4	Sydney	*India (WC L/O Intl)	Lost by 43 runs
Mar 8	Brisbane	*South Africa (WC L/O Intl)	Lost by 20 runs
Mar 11	Perth	*Australia (WC L/O Intl)	Won by 48 runs
Mar 15	Perth	*Sri Lanka (WC L/O Intl)	Won by 4 wkts
Mar 25	Melbourne	*England (WC L/O Intl)	Won by 22 runs

Player	M	Inn	NO	Runs	HS	50	100	Avrge	Ct/St	Overs	Mdns	Runs	Wkts	Avrge	5wi	10wm	Best
Aamir Sohail	1	2	1	47	27*	–	–	47.00	1	10.0	5	25	–	–	–	–	–
Aaqib Javed	1	2	2	3	2*	–	–	–	–	29.2	7	71	2	35.50	–	–	1/22
Akram Raza	1	1	1	5	5*	–	–	–	1	14.0	7	15	1	15.00	–	–	1/15
Ijaz Ahmed	2	3	–	67	67	1	–	22.33	1	27.0	7	65	–	–	–	–	–
Imran Khan (Capt)	2	3	–	42	29	–	–	14.00	–	21.0	7	52	–	–	–	–	–
Moin Khan	2	3	2	9	6*	–	–	9.00	2/–	–	–	–	–	–	–	–	–
Mushtaq Ahmed	1	2	–	0	0	–	–	0.00	–	42.0	11	131	4	32.75	–	–	3/75
Rameez Raja	2	4	1	124	50*	2	–	41.33	2	–	–	–	–	–	–	–	–
Salim Jaffar	1	–	–	–	–	–	–	–	–	13.0	2	36	1	36.00	–	–	1/36
Salim Malik	1	2	–	48	26	–	–	24.00	–	–	–	–	–	–	–	–	–
Shahid Saeed	2	3	1	50	40*	–	–	25.00	1	29.4	4	88	3	29.33	–	–	2/39
Wasim Akram	2	3	–	70	30	–	–	23.33	–	43.5	15	73	7	10.43	1	–	5/47
Zahid Fazal	2	3	–	96	47	–	–	32.00	2	–	–	–	–	–	–	–	–

1992/93 PAKISTANIS

	First-class Results					All Matches			
Matches	Won	Lost	Drawn	Tied	Matches	Won	Lost	Drawn	Tied
1	1	–	–	–	12	5	6	–	1

Date	Venue	Opponent	Results for Touring Team
Nov 29	Northam	*Western Australian Invitation XI	Won by 1 run
Dec 1	Perth	*Western Australia	Won by 27 runs
Dec 6	Alice Springs	*Northern Territory Invitation XI	Won by 94 runs
Dec 4	Perth	*West Indies (L/O Intl)	Won by 5 wkts
Dec 10	Hobart (Bel)	*Australia (L/O Intl)	Tied
Dec 12	Adelaide	*West Indies (L/O Intl)	Lost by 4 runs
Dec 13	Adelaide	*Australia (L/O Intl)	Lost by 8 wkts
Dec 17	Sydney	*West Indies (L/O Intl)	Lost by 133 runs
Dec 19	Brisbane	Queensland	Won by 5 wkts
Jan 9	Brisbane	*West Indies (L/O Intl)	Lost by 9 wkts
Jan 12	Melbourne	*Australia (L/O Intl)	Lost by 32 runs
Jan 14	Sydney	*Australia (L/O Intl)	Lost by 23 runs

Player	M	Inn	NO	Runs	HS	50	100	Avrge	Ct/St	Overs	Mdns	Runs	Wkts	Avrge	5wi	10wm	Best
Aamir Sohail	1	2	–	70	65	1	–	35.00	4	6.0	1	32	–	–	–	–	–
Aaqib Javed	1	–	–	–	–	–	–	–	–	22.0	6	72	–	–	–	–	–
Asif Mujtaba	1	2	2	227	125*	–	2	–	2	5.0	1	15	–	–	–	–	–
Ata-ur-Rehman	1	–	–	–	–	–	–	–	1	15.0	4	60	2	30.00	–	–	2/60
Inzamam-ul-Haq	1	2	–	125	83	1	–	62.50	–	–	–	–	–	–	–	–	–
Mushtaq Ahmed	1	1	1	0	0*	–	–	–	–	49.2	5	206	8	25.75	–	–	4/70
Naved Anjum	1	1	–	0	0	–	–	0.00	–	23.0	1	122	1	122.00	–	–	1/107
Rashid Latif	1	2	1	37	19	–	–	37.00	4/1	–	–	–	–	–	–	–	–
Saeed Anwar	1	2	–	85	72	1	–	42.50	1	–	–	–	–	–	–	–	–
Shahid Saeed	1	2	–	97	83	1	–	48.50	–	11.0	–	47	2	23.50	–	–	2/16
Wasim Akram (Capt)	1	1	–	3	3	–	–	3.00	–	40.0	11	88	3	29.33	–	–	2/45

SRI LANKANS IN AUSTRALIA

Season	Touring Team	First-class Results					All Matches					Captain
		Games	W	L	D	T	Games	W	L	D	T	
1982/83	Sri Lankans	2	–	–	2	–	5	1	1	3	–	LRD Mendis
1984/85	Sri Lankans	1	1	–	–	–	22	11	11	–	–	LRD Mendis
1987/88	Sri Lankans	3	–	1	2	–	18	6	9	3	–	RS Madugalle
1989/90	Sri Lankans	6	–	2	4	–	27	6	14	7	–	A Ranatunga
1991/92	Sri Lankans	–	–	–	–	–	7	2	4	1	–	PA de Silva
		12	1	3	8	–	79	26	39	14	–	

FIRST-CLASS RESULTS

Opponent	Venue	First Game	Games	W	L	D	T
AUSTRALIA	Perth	Feb 12 1988	1	–	1	–	–
	Brisbane	Dec 8 1989	1	–	–	1	–
	Hobart (Bel)	Dec 16 1989	1	–	1	–	–
			3	–	2	1	–
New South Wales	Sydney	Feb 10 1983	1	–	–	1	–
	Canberra	Nov 17 1989	1	–	–	1	–
			2	–	–	2	–
South Australia	Adelaide	Dec 1 1989	1	–	–	1	–
Tasmania	Devonport	Feb 14 1983	2	–	–	2	–
	Hobart (Bel)	Jan 23 1988	1	–	–	1	–
			3	–	–	3	–
Victoria	Melbourne	Feb 6 1988	1	–	–	1	–
	Sale	Nov 24 1989	1	–	1	–	–
			2	–	1	1	–
Western Australia	Perth	Dec 31 1984	1	1	–	–	–

1982/83 SRI LANKANS

First-class Results					All Matches				
Matches	Won	Lost	Drawn	Tied	Matches	Won	Lost	Drawn	Tied
2	–	–	2	–	5	1	1	3	–

Date	Venue	Opponent	Results for Touring Team
Feb 3	Melbourne	*Victoria	Drawn
Feb 6	Melbourne	*Victoria	Lost by 6 wkts
Feb 8	Canberra	*Australian Capital Territory	Won by 59 runs
Feb 10	Sydney	New South Wales	Drawn
Feb 14	Devonport	Tasmania	Drawn

Player	M	Inn	NO	Runs	HS	50	100	Avrge	Ct/St	Overs	Mdns	Runs	Wkts	Avrge	5wi	10wm	Best
de Alwis, RG	1	1	–	42	42	–	–	42.00	1	–	–	–	–	–	–	–	–
de Mel, ALF	1	1	1	0	0*	–	–	–	2	18.0	1	73	1	73.00	–	–	1/49
de Silva, DS	1	1	–	65	65	1	–	65.00	1	22.0	3	70	1	70.00	–	–	1/70
Dias, RL	2	3	–	67	27	–	–	22.33	–	–	–	–	–	–	–	–	–
Fernando, ERNS	1	2	–	91	72	1	–	45.50	1	–	–	–	–	–	–	–	–
Goonasekera, Y	1	2	–	34	27	–	–	17.00	2	4.0	–	17	1	17.00	–	–	1/17
Jeganathan, S	2	3	–	98	74	1	–	32.66	2	54.0	14	123	2	61.50	–	–	2/58
John, VB	2	–	–	–	–	–	–	–	–	53.0	10	157	4	39.25	–	–	2/37
Madugalle, RS	2	3	–	68	35	–	–	22.66	–	–	–	–	–	–	–	–	–
Mendis, LRD (Capt)	1	1	–	15	15	–	–	15.00	–	–	–	–	–	–	–	–	–
Ratnayake, RJ	1	–	–	–	–	–	–	–	–	30.0	16	72	3	24.00	–	–	2/34
Ratnayeke, JR	2	3	2	91	64*	1	–	91.00	3	32.0	11	79	6	13.16	–	–	4/34
Silva, SAR	1	2	–	0	0	–	–	0.00	2/–	–	–	–	–	–	–	–	–
Wettimuny, MD	2	3	–	55	31	–	–	18.33	–	6.0	3	9	–	–	–	–	–
Wettimuny, S	1	1	–	9	9	–	–	9.00	–	–	–	–	–	–	–	–	–
Wijesuriya, RGCE	1	1	–	1	1	–	–	1.00	1	5.0	1	20	–	–	–	–	–

1984/85 SRI LANKANS

First-class Results					All Matches				
Matches	Won	Lost	Drawn	Tied	Matches	Won	Lost	Drawn	Tied
1	1	–	–	–	22	11	11	–	–

Date	Venue	Opponent	Results for Touring Team
Dec 31	Perth	Western Australia	Won by 7 wkts
Jan 5	Brisbane	*Queensland	Won by 5 wkts
Jan 6	Brisbane	*Queensland	Won on run rate
Jan 8	Sydney	*Australia (L/O Intl)	Lost by 6 wkts
Jan 10	Hobart (TCA)	*West Indies (L/O Intl)	Lost by 8 wkts
Jan 12	Brisbane	*West Indies (L/O Intl)	Lost by 90 runs
Jan 17	Sydney	*West Indies (L/O Intl)	Lost by 65 runs
Jan 19	Melbourne	*Australia (L/O Intl)	Won by 4 wkts

Continued

SRI LANKANS IN AUSTRALIA

Date	Venue	Opponent	Results for Touring Team
Jan 23	Sydney	*Australia (L/O Intl)	Lost by 3 wkts
Jan 26	Adelaide	*West Indies (L/O Intl)	Lost by 8 wkts
Jan 28	Adelaide	*Australia (L/O Intl)	Lost by 232 runs
Jan 30	Fremantle	*Western Australian Colts	Won by 2 wkts
Feb 2	Perth	*West Indies (L/O Intl)	Lost by 82 runs
Feb 3	Perth	*Australia (L/O Intl)	Lost by 9 wkts
Feb 6	Maryborough	*Central Highlands	Won by 108 runs
Feb 8	Shepparton	*Goulburn Murray Districts	Won by 100 runs
Feb 10	Yea	*Upper Goulburn	Won by 78 runs
Feb 12	Leongatha	*South Gippsland	Won by 4 wkts
Feb 14	Morwell	*Gippsland	Won by 7 wkts
Feb 16	Hastings	*Mornington Peninsula	Won by 150 runs
Feb 23	Melbourne	*New Zealand (L/O Intl)	Lost by 51 runs
Feb 27	Melbourne	*West Indies (L/O Intl)	Lost by 8 wkts

Player	M	Inn	NO	Runs	HS	50	100	Avrge	Ct/St	Overs	Mdns	Runs	Wkts	Avrge	5wi	10wm	Best
de Mel, ALF	1	1	–	0	0	–	–	0.00	1	25.3	3	90	5	18.00	–	–	3/66
de Silva, PA	1	1	–	40	40	–	–	40.00	–	–	–	–	–	–	–	–	–
Dias, RL	1	2	–	57	54	1	–	28.50	2	–	–	–	–	–	–	–	–
John, VB	1	1	1	10	10*	–	–	–	1	30.0	4	88	5	17.60	1	–	5/28
Kuruppu, DSBP	1	2	1	22	21	–	–	22.00	3	–	–	–	–	–	–	–	–
Mendis, LRD (Capt)	1	1	–	67	67	1	–	67.00	–	–	–	–	–	–	–	–	–
Ranatunga, A	1	–	–	–	–	–	–	–	–	8.3	2	20	1	20.00	–	–	1/20
Ratnayake, RJ	1	1	1	18	18*	–	–	–	–	1.0	–	9	–	–	–	–	–
Ratnayeke, JR	1	2	–	22	18*	–	–	22.00	–	27.0	5	91	5	18.20	–	–	3/25
Silva, SAR	1	2	–	52	41	–	–	26.00	1	–	–	–	–	–	–	–	–
Wettimuny, S	1	2	–	19	13	–	–	9.50	1	3.3	–	13	–	–	–	–	–

1987/88 SRI LANKANS

First-class Results					All Matches			
Matches	Won	Lost	Drawn	Tied	Matches	Won	Lost	Drawn	Tied
3	–	1	2	–	18	6	9	3	–

Date	Venue	Opponent	Results for Touring Team
Dec 26	Perth	*Western Australia	Won by 61 runs
Dec 28	Perth	*Western Australia	Drawn
Dec 31	Mandurah	*Western Australian Country XI	Won by 143 runs
Jan 2	Perth	*Australia (L/O Intl)	Lost by 81 runs
Jan 5	Sydney	*New Zealand (L/O Intl)	Lost by 6 wkts
Jan 9	Adelaide	*New Zealand (L/O Intl)	Lost by 4 wkts
Jan 10	Adelaide	*Australia (L/O Intl)	Lost by 81 runs
Jan 12	Hobart (Bel)	*New Zealand (L/O Intl)	Won by 4 wkts
Jan 14	Melbourne	*Australia (L/O Intl)	Lost by 38 runs
Jan 16	Brisbane	*New Zealand (L/O Intl)	Lost by 4 wkts
Jan 19	Sydney	*Australia (L/O Intl)	Lost by 3 wkts
Jan 23	Hobart (Bel)	Tasmania	Drawn
Jan 27	Canberra	*Australian Country XI	Won by 14 runs
Jan 30	Alice Springs	*Northern Territory Invitation XI	Won by 115 runs
Jan 31	Alice Springs	*South Australia	Lost by 6 wkts
Feb 3	Bendigo	*Victorian Country XI	Won by 110 runs
Feb 6	Melbourne	Victoria	Drawn
Feb 12	Perth	AUSTRALIA (Only Test)	Lost by an inns & 108 runs

Player	M	Inn	NO	Runs	HS	50	100	Avrge	Ct/St	Overs	Mdns	Runs	Wkts	Avrge	5wi	10wm	Best
Amalean, KN	1	2	2	7	7*	–	–	–	1	22.2	1	97	4	24.25	–	–	4/97
de Alwis, RG	2	4	1	40	30*	–	–	13.33	4/–	–	–	–	–	–	–	–	–
de Silva, PA	3	5	–	92	69	1	–	18.40	2	22.0	1	81	1	81.00	–	–	1/70
Gurusinha, AP	2	3	–	164	118	–	1	54.67	1	–	–	–	–	–	–	–	–
Jeganathan, S	2	2	2	5	3*	–	–	–	–	34.1	2	124	2	62.00	–	–	2/83
Kaluperuma, SMS	2	3	–	32	26	–	–	10.67	–	26.0	3	108	–	–	–	–	–
Kuruppu, DSBP	3	5	–	65	22	–	–	13.00	1/–	–	–	–	–	–	–	–	–
Labrooy, GF	3	4	–	43	25	–	–	10.75	2	89.5	21	236	10	23.60	1	–	7/71
Madugalle, RS (Capt)	3	5	–	123	56	1	–	24.60	–	–	–	–	–	–	–	–	–
Mahanama, RS	3	5	–	158	51	1	–	31.60	1	–	–	–	–	–	–	–	–
Ramanayake, CPH	3	4	–	33	15	–	–	8.25	1	70.0	9	253	5	50.60	–	–	3/99
Ranatunga, A	3	5	–	191	68	2	–	38.20	1	38.0	6	106	4	26.50	–	–	3/66
Ratnayeke, JR	2	4	1	130	39*	–	–	43.33	–	66.0	11	177	5	35.40	–	–	4/98
Samarasekera, MAR	1	1	–	4	4	–	–	4.00	–	5.5	1	11	–	–	–	–	–

1989/90 SRI LANKANS

	First-class Results					All Matches			
Matches	Won	Lost	Drawn	Tied	Matches	Won	Lost	Drawn	Tied
6	–	2	4	–	27	6	14	7	–

Date	Venue	Opponent	Results for Touring Team
Nov 17	Canberra	New South Wales	Drawn
Nov 24	Sale	Victoria	Lost by an inns & 3 runs
Dec 1	Adelaide	South Australia	Drawn
Dec 8	Brisbane	AUSTRALIA (1st Test)	Drawn
Dec 16	Hobart (Bel)	AUSTRALIA (2nd Test)	Lost by 173 runs
Dec 22	Melbourne	*Victoria	Lost by 109 runs
Dec 23	Hastings	*Victorian Country Cricket League	Lost by 3 wkts
Dec 26	Melbourne	*Australia (L/O Intl)	Lost by 30 runs
Dec 30	Perth	*Australia (L/O Intl)	Lost by 9 wkts
Dec 31	Perth	*Pakistan (L/O Intl)	Won by 3 wkts
Jan 4	Melbourne	*Australia (L/O Intl)	Lost by 73 runs
Jan 6	Devonport	Tasmania	Drawn
Jan 11	Adelaide	*AIS Cricket Academy	Drawn
Jan 14	Port Lincoln	*South Australian Country XI	Won by 25 runs
Jan 27	Bendigo	*Australian Country XI	Drawn
Jan 21	Coffs Harbour	*New South Wales	Lost by 81 runs
Jan 23	South Grafton	*New South Wales Country XI	Won by 3 wkts
Jan 26	Nth Rockhampton	*Queensland	Drawn
Jan 28	Nth Rockhampton	*Queensland	Lost by 7 wkts
Jan 30	Caloundra	*Queensland Country XI	Won by 7 wkts
Feb 2	Perth	*Western Australia	Won by 4 wkts
Feb 4	Perth	*Western Australia	Lost by 65 runs
Feb 6	Brookton	*Western Australian Country XI	Won by 63 runs
Feb 10	Brisbane	*Pakistan (L/O Intl)	Lost by 5 wkts
Feb 15	Hobart (Bel)	*Pakistan (L/O Intl)	Lost by 6 wkts
Feb 17	Adelaide	*Pakistan (L/O Intl)	Lost by 27 runs
Feb 18	Adelaide	*Australia (L/O Intl)	Lost by 7 wkts

Player	M	Inn	NO	Runs	HS	50	100	Avrge	Ct/St	Overs	Mdns	Runs	Wkts	Avrge	5wi	10wm	Best
de Silva, EAR	5	7	1	198	66*	2	–	33.00	4	160.1	29	486	6	81.00	–	–	3/121
de Silva, PA	6	10	–	524	167	4	1	52.40	2	68.0	7	226	3	75.33	–	–	2/65
Gurusinha, AP	5	9	–	295	109	1	1	32.78	7	28.3	4	111	5	22.20	–	–	2/31
Jayasuriya, ST	4	7	2	171	37*	–	–	34.20	–	20.0	3	74	1	74.00	–	–	1/17
Kalpage, RS	1	2	1	10	10*	–	–	10.00	1	1.0	–	6	–	–	–	–	–
Labrooy, GF	5	5	1	43	26*	–	–	10.75	1	167.1	23	652	15	43.47	2	–	5/133
Madurasinghe, MAWR	2	1	–	4	4*	–	–	–	2	60.0	4	208	4	52.00	–	–	4/80
Mahanama, RS	4	7	1	173	85	2	–	28.83	4	1.0	–	3	–	–	–	–	–
Ramanayake, CPH	4	5	4	35	16*	–	–	35.00	1	129.0	13	490	8	61.25	–	–	2/81
Ranatunga, D	5	9	–	197	56	1	–	21.89	1	–	–	–	–	–	–	–	–
Ranatunga, A (Capt)	4	6	–	181	75	1	–	30.17	4	51.0	1	166	3	55.33	–	–	2/17
Ratnayake, RJ	2	4	–	13	5	–	–	3.25	1	83.4	7	318	10	31.80	1	–	6/66
Ratnayake, NLK	1	–	–	–	–	–	–	–	–	21.0	3	45	1	45.00	–	–	1/18
Ratnayeke, JR	5	7	1	244	75	3	–	40.67	4	125.5	13	423	5	84.60	–	–	2/75
Samarasekera, MAR	4	7	1	201	133	–	1	33.50	1	1.0	–	15	–	–	–	–	–
Tillekeratne, HP	4	7	1	143	74	1	–	23.83	5/–	2.0	–	10	–	–	–	–	–
Wickremasinghe, AGD	4	7	1	50	24	–	–	8.33	5/1	–	–	–	–	–	–	–	–
Wijegunawardene, KIW	1	2	1	6	5	–	–	6.00	–	20.0	1	109	–	–	–	–	–

1991/92 SRI LANKANS

	First-class Results					All Matches			
Matches	Won	Lost	Drawn	Tied	Matches	Won	Lost	Drawn	Tied
–	–	–	–	–	7	2	4	1	–

Date	Venue	Opponent	Results for Touring Team
Feb 16	Manly	*President's XI	Won by 8 wkts
Feb 17	North Sydney	*Pakistan	Won by 14 runs
Feb 28	Mackay	*India (L/O Intl)	No Result
Mar 7	Adelaide	*Australia (L/O Intl)	Lost by 7 wkts
Mar 9	Ballarat	*England (L/O Intl)	Lost by 106 runs
Mar 13	Berri	*West Indies (L/O Intl)	Lost by 91 runs
Mar 15	Perth	*Pakistan (L/O Intl)	Lost by 4 wkts

ZIMBABWEANS IN AUSTRALIA

Season	Touring Team	First-class Results					All Matches					Captain
		Games	W	L	D	T	Games	W	L	D	T	
1991/92	Zimbabweans	–	–	–	–	–	6	1	5	–	–	DL Houghton
1994/95	Zimbabweans	2	–	1	1	–	19	8	10	1	–	A Flower
		2	–	1	1	–	25	9	15	1	–	

1991/92 ZIMBABWEANS

First-class Results					All Matches			
Matches	Won	Lost	Drawn	Tied	Matches	Won	Lost	Drawn	Tied
–	–	–	–	–	6	1	5	–	–

Date	Venue	Opponent	Results for Touring Team
Feb 9	Brisbane	*Queensland 2nd XI	Lost by 129 runs
Feb 27	Hobart (Bel)	*Pakistan (L/O Intl)	Lost by 53 runs
Feb 29	Brisbane	*West Indies (L/O Intl)	Lost by 75 runs
Mar 10	Canberra	*South Africa (L/O Intl)	Lost by 7 wkts
Mar 14	Hobart (Bel)	*Australia (L/O Intl)	Lost by 128 runs
Mar 18	Albury	*England (L/O Intl)	Won by 9 runs

APPENDIX
...and AWAY

AUSTRALIAN CRICKETERS ON TOUR

			First-class Results					All Matches					
Season	Touring Team	Country	Games	W	L	D	T	Games	W	L	D	T	Captain
1868	Aboriginals	England	–	–	–	–	–	47	14	14	19	–	C Lawrence
1877/78	Australians	New Zealand	–	–	–	–	–	7	5	1	1	–	DW Gregory
1878	Australians	England	15	7	4	4	–	37	18	7	12	–	DW Gregory
1878/79	Australians	North America	1	–	–	1	–	6	4	–	2	–	DW Gregory
1880	Australians	England	9	4	2	3	–	37	21	4	12	–	WL Murdoch
1880/81	Australians	New Zealand	–	–	–	–	–	10	6	1	3	–	WL Murdoch
1882	Australians	England	33	18	4	11	–	38	23	4	11	–	WL Murdoch
1882/83	Australians	North America	–	–	–	–	–	2	2	–	–	–	WL Murdoch
1883/84	Tasmania	New Zealand	4	–	3	1	–	7	2	3	2	–	JG Davies
1884	Australians	England	31	17	7	7	–	32	18	7	7	–	WL Murdoch
1886	Australians	England	37	9	7	21	–	39	9	8	22	–	HJH Scott
1886/87	Australians	New Zealand	–	–	–	–	–	5	2	–	3	–	HJH Scott
1888	Australians	England	37	17	13	7	–	40	19	14	7	–	PS McDonnell
1889/90	New South Wales	New Zealand	5	4	–	1	–	7	6	–	1	–	J Davis
1890	Australians	England	34	10	16	8	–	38	13	16	9	–	WL Murdoch
1893	Australians	England	31	14	10	7	–	36	18	10	8	–	JM Blackham
1893/94	Australians	North America	2	1	1	–	–	6	4	1	1	–	JM Blackham
	New South Wales	New Zealand	7	4	1	2	–	8	4	1	3	–	J Davis
1895/96	New South Wales	New Zealand	5	3	1	1	–	5	3	1	1	–	LT Cobcroft
1896	Australians	England	34	20	6	8	–	34	20	6	8	–	GHS Trott
1896/97	Australians	North America	3	2	1	–	–	6	4	1	1	–	GHS Trott
	Australians	New Zealand	–	–	–	–	–	5	3	–	2	–	GHS Trott
	Queensland	New Zealand	5	3	1	1	–	8	4	1	3	–	OC Hitchcock
1899	Australians	England	35	16	3	16	–	35	16	3	16	–	J Darling
1902	Australians	England	37	21	2	14	–	39	23	2	14	–	J Darling
1902/03	Australians	South Africa	4	3	–	1	–	6	3	–	3	–	J Darling
1904/05	Australians	New Zealand	4	3	–	1	–	6	4	–	2	–	MA Noble
1905	Australians	England	35	15	3	17	–	38	16	3	19	–	J Darling
1909	Australians	England	37	11	4	22	–	39	13	4	22	–	MA Noble
1909/10	Australians	New Zealand	6	5	–	1	–	9	7	–	2	–	WW Armstrong
1912	Australians	England	36	9	8	19	–	37	9	8	20	–	SE Gregory
1912/13	Australians	North America	2	1	1	–	–	7	5	1	1	–	SE Gregory
1913/14	New South Wales	Ceylon	–	–	–	–	–	9	8	1	–	–	EF Waddy
	Australians	North America	5	4	–	1	–	53	49	1	3	–	A Diamond
	Australians	New Zealand	8	6	–	2	–	16	8	–	8	–	A Sims
1919	AIF Team	England	28	12	4	12	–	32	13	4	15	–	HL Collins
1919/20	AIF Team	South Africa	8	6	–	2	–	10	8	–	2	–	HL Collins
1920/21	Australians	New Zealand	9	6	–	3	–	15	12	–	3	–	VS Ransford
1921	Australians	England	34	21	2	11	–	39	23	2	14	–	WW Armstrong
1921/22	Australians	South Africa	6	4	–	2	–	6	4	–	2	–	HL Collins
1923/24	New South Wales	New Zealand	6	5	–	1	–	12	8	–	4	–	CG Macartney
1924/25	Victoria	New Zealand	6	1	1	4	–	12	4	1	7	–	ER Mayne
1926	Australians	England	33	9	1	23	–	40	12	1	27	–	HL Collins
1927/28	Australians	New Zealand	6	4	–	2	–	13	6	–	7	–	VY Richardson
1930	Australians	England	31	11	1	18	1	33	12	1	19	1	WM Woodfull
1932/33	Australians	North America	–	–	–	–	–	51	46	1	4	–	VY Richardson

Continued

AUSTRALIANS ON TOUR

Season	Touring Team	Country	First-class Results Games	W	L	D	T	All Matches Games	W	L	D	T	Captain
1934	Australians	England	30	13	1	16	–	34	15	1	18	–	WM Woodfull
1935/36	Australians	Ceylon	1	1	–	–	–	1	1	–	–	–	J Ryder
	Australians	India	16	9	3	4	–	22	10	3	9	–	J Ryder
	Australians	South Africa	16	13	–	3	–	16	13	–	3	–	VY Richardson
1938	Australians	England	29	15	2	12	–	35	20	2	13	–	DG Bradman
1945	Services	England	6	3	2	1	–	48	24	9	15	–	AL Hassett
1945/46	Australians	India	8	1	2	5	–	9	1	2	6	–	AL Hassett
	Australians	Ceylon	1	1	–	–	–	1	1	–	–	–	AL Hassett
	Australians	New Zealand	5	5	–	–	–	5	5	–	–	–	WA Brown
1948	Australians	England	31	23	–	8	–	34	25	–	9	–	DG Bradman
1949/50	Australians	South Africa	21	14	–	7	–	25	18	–	7	–	AL Hassett
	Australians	New Zealand	5	3	–	2	–	14	9	–	5	–	WA Brown
1953	Australians	England	33	16	1	16	–	35	16	1	18	–	AL Hassett
1954/55	Australians	West Indies	9	5	–	4	–	12	6	–	6	–	IW Johnson
1956	Australians	England	31	9	3	19	–	35	12	3	20	–	IW Johnson
1956/57	Australians	Pakistan	1	–	1	–	–	1	–	1	–	–	IW Johnson
	Australians	India	3	2	–	1	–	3	2	–	1	–	IW Johnson
	Australians	New Zealand	7	5	–	2	–	12	7	–	5	–	ID Craig
1957/58	Australians	South Africa	20	11	–	9	–	22	11	–	11	–	ID Craig
1959/60	Australians	Pakistan	4	3	–	1	–	4	3	–	1	–	R Benaud
	Australians	India	7	2	1	4	–	7	2	1	4	–	R Benaud
	Australians	New Zealand	6	2	–	4	–	9	4	–	5	–	ID Craig
1961	Australians	England	32	13	1	18	–	37	14	2	21	–	R Benaud
1964	Australians	England	30	11	3	16	–	36	14	4	18	–	RB Simpson
1964/65	Australians	India	3	1	1	1	–	3	1	1	1	–	RB Simpson
	Australians	Pakistan	1	–	–	1	–	1	–	–	1	–	RB Simpson
	Australians	West Indies	11	3	2	6	–	16	4	3	9	–	RB Simpson
1966/67	Australians	South Africa	17	7	5	5	–	24	11	6	7	–	RB Simpson
	Australians	New Zealand	9	1	2	6	–	10	2	2	6	–	LE Favell
1968	Australians	England	25	8	3	14	–	29	10	3	16	–	WM Lawry
1969/70	Australians	Ceylon	1	–	–	1	–	4	1	–	3	–	WM Lawry
	Australians	India	10	5	1	4	–	10	5	1	4	–	WM Lawry
	Australians	South Africa	12	4	4	4	–	12	4	4	4	–	WM Lawry
	Australians	New Zealand	8	2	–	6	–	8	2	–	6	–	SC Trimble
1972	Australians	England	26	11	5	10	–	37	14	10	13	–	IM Chappell
1972/73	Australians	West Indies	12	7	–	5	–	15	10	–	5	–	IM Chappell
1973/74	Australians	New Zealand	7	2	1	4	–	11	6	1	4	–	IM Chappell
1974/75	Australians	North America	–	–	–	–	–	5	2	1	2	–	IM Chappell
1975	Australians	England	15	8	2	5	–	21	12	4	5	–	IM Chappell
1976/77	Australians	New Zealand	6	5	–	1	–	8	5	2	1	–	GS Chappell
1977	Australians	England	22	5	4	13	–	31	8	8	15	–	GS Chappell
1977/78	Australians	West Indies	11	5	3	3	–	13	6	4	3	–	RB Simpson
1979	Australians	England	–	–	–	–	–	6	2	3	1	–	KJ Hughes
1979/80	Australians	India	11	–	3	8	–	11	–	3	8	–	KJ Hughes
	Australians	Pakistan	5	–	1	4	–	5	–	1	4	–	GS Chappell
1980	Australians	England	5	1	2	2	–	8	1	4	3	–	GS Chappell
1980/81	Australians	Sri Lanka	1	–	–	1	–	4	2	1	1	–	KJ Hughes
1981	Australians	England	17	3	3	11	–	26	7	7	12	–	KJ Hughes
1981/82	Australians	New Zealand	5	1	1	3	–	11	4	4	3	–	GS Chappell
1982/83	Australians	Pakistan	6	–	3	3	–	9	–	5	4	–	KJ Hughes
1982/83	Australians	Zimbabwe	2	1	1	–	–	8	7	1	–	–	DM Wellham
	Australians	Sri Lanka	2	1	–	1	–	6	1	2	3	–	GS Chappell
1983/84	Australians	West Indies	10	1	3	6	–	15	2	6	7	–	KJ Hughes
1984/85	Australians	India	–	–	–	–	–	6	4	–	2	–	KJ Hughes
	New South Wales	New Zealand	–	–	–	–	–	1	1	–	–	–	DM Wellham
	Australians	Sharjah	–	–	–	–	–	2	1	1	–	–	AR Border
1985	Australians	England	20	4	3	13	–	29	9	5	15	–	AR Border
1985/86	Australians	Zimbabwe	2	1	–	1	–	9	3	5	1	–	RB Kerr
	Australians	South Africa	10	2	2	6	–	25	10	9	6	–	KJ Hughes
	Australians	New Zealand	5	1	1	3	–	11	5	3	3	–	AR Border
	Australians	Sharjah	–	–	–	–	–	1	–	1	–	–	RJ Bright
1985/86	New South Wales	Zimbabwe	2	1	–	1	–	8	5	2	1	–	GC Dyer
1986/87	Australians	India	7	–	–	6	1	13	2	3	7	1	AR Border
	New South Wales	New Zealand	–	–	–	–	–	2	1	1	–	–	DM Wellham
	Australians	South Africa	12	2	3	7	–	25	8	9	8	–	KJ Hughes
	South Australia	New Zealand	–	–	–	–	–	4	4	–	–	–	DW Hookes
	Australians	Sharjah	–	–	–	–	–	3	–	3	–	–	AR Border
1987/88	New South Wales	Zimbabwe	2	–	–	2	–	8	5	1	2	–	DM Wellham
	Australians	India	–	–	–	–	–	7	6	1	–	–	AR Border
	Australians	Pakistan	–	–	–	–	–	1	1	–	–	–	AR Border
	Victoria	New Zealand	–	–	–	–	–	2	–	2	–	–	DF Whatmore
	Queensland	New Zealand	–	–	–	–	–	3	3	–	–	–	RB Kerr
1988	Aboriginals	England	–	–	–	–	–	27	15	11	1	–	J MacGuire
1988/89	Australians	Pakistan	6	–	1	5	–	7	–	2	5	–	AR Border
1989	Australians	England	20	12	1	7	–	31	20	3	7	1	AR Border
1989/90	Western Australia	India	1	–	–	1	–	4	1	2	1	–	GM Wood
	Australians	India	–	–	–	–	–	5	2	3	–	–	AR Border
	Australians	New Zealand	1	–	1	–	–	6	5	–	1	–	AR Border
	Australians	Sharjah	–	–	–	–	–	4	3	1	–	–	AR Border
1990/91	Australians	West Indies	10	2	2	6	–	19	10	3	6	–	AR Border
1991	Victoria	England	1	–	–	1	–	4	1	1	2	–	SP O'Donnell
1991/92	Australians	Zimbabwe	2	2	–	–	–	6	5	1	–	–	MA Taylor
	Australians	New Zealand	–	–	–	–	–	2	1	1	–	–	AR Border

Continued

AUSTRALIANS IN ENGLAND

Season	Touring Team	Country	First-class Results					All Matches					Captain
			Games	W	L	D	T	Games	W	L	D	T	
1992/93	Australians	Sri Lanka	5	1	–	4	–	8	2	2	4	–	AR Border
	Australians	New Zealand	4	2	1	1	–	10	5	4	1	–	AR Border
1993	Australians	England	21	10	2	9	–	30	18	3	9	–	AR Border
1993/94	Australians	South Africa	6	3	1	2	–	16	7	5	4	–	AR Border
	New South Wales	New Zealand	–	–	–	–	–	1	1	–	–	–	PA Emery
	Australians	Sharjah	–	–	–	–	–	3	2	1	–	–	MA Taylor
1994/95	Australians	Sri Lanka	–	–	–	–	–	3	1	2	–	–	MA Taylor
1994/95	Australians	Pakistan	4	–	1	3	–	10	5	2	3	–	MA Taylor
	Australians	New Zealand	–	–	–	–	–	4	3	1	–	–	MA Taylor
	Cricket Academy	New Zealand	1	1	–	–	–	6	6	–	–	–	NW Ashley
	Australians	West Indies	7	3	1	3	–	16	8	5	3	–	MA Taylor

Touring Teams	First-class results					All Matches				
	Games	W	L	D	T	Games	W	L	D	T
England	961	406	135	419	1	1283	567	202	512	2
New Zealand	140	74	14	52	–	285	163	30	92	–
South Africa	132	69	15	48	–	187	97	33	57	–
India	66	20	11	34	1	100	36	20	43	1
West Indies	70	26	11	33	–	105	46	21	38	–
Pakistan	27	3	7	17	–	38	9	11	18	–
North America	13	8	3	2	–	136	116	6	14	–
Ceylon/Sri Lanka	11	4	–	7	–	36	17	8	11	–
United Arab Emirates (Sharjah)	–	–	–	–	–	13	6	7	–	–
Zimbabwe	10	5	1	4	–	39	25	10	4	–
	1430	615	197	616	2	2222	1082	348	789	3

AUSTRALIAN CRICKET TEAMS IN ENGLAND

Season	Touring Team	First-class Games					All Games					Captain
		P	W	L	D	T	P	W	L	D	T	
1868	Aboriginals	–	–	–	–	–	47	14	14	19	–	C Lawrence
1878	Australians	15	7	4	4	–	37	18	7	12	–	DW Gregory
1880	Australians	9	4	2	3	–	37	21	4	12	–	WL Murdoch
1882	Australians	33	18	4	11	–	38	23	4	11	–	WL Murdoch
1884	Australians	31	17	7	7	–	32	18	7	7	–	WL Murdoch
1886	Australians	37	9	7	21	–	39	9	8	22	–	HJH Scott
1888	Australians	37	17	13	7	–	40	19	14	7	–	PS McDonnell
1890	Australians	34	10	16	8	–	38	13	16	9	–	WL Murdoch
1893	Australians	31	14	10	7	–	36	18	10	8	–	JM Blackham
1896	Australians	34	20	6	8	–	34	20	6	8	–	GHS Trott
1899	Australians	35	16	3	16	–	35	16	3	16	–	J Darling
1902	Australians	37	21	2	14	–	39	23	2	14	–	J Darling
1905	Australians	35	15	3	17	–	38	16	3	19	–	J Darling
1909	Australians	37	11	4	22	–	39	13	4	22	–	MA Noble
1912	Australians	36	9	8	19	–	37	9	8	20	–	SE Gregory
1919	AIF Team	28	12	4	12	–	32	13	4	15	–	HL Collins
1921	Australians	34	21	2	11	–	39	23	2	14	–	WW Armstrong
1926	Australians	33	9	1	23	–	40	12	1	27	–	HL Collins
1930	Australians	31	11	1	18	1	33	12	1	19	1	WM Woodfull
1934	Australians	30	13	1	16	–	34	15	1	18	–	WM Woodfull
1938	Australians	29	15	2	12	–	35	20	2	13	–	DG Bradman
1945	Services	6	3	2	1	–	48	24	9	15	–	AL Hassett
1948	Australians	31	23	–	8	–	34	25	–	9	–	DG Bradman
1953	Australians	33	16	1	16	–	35	16	1	18	–	AL Hassett
1956	Australians	31	9	3	19	–	35	12	3	20	–	IW Johnson
1961	Australians	32	13	1	18	–	37	14	2	21	–	R Benaud
1964	Australians	30	11	3	16	–	36	14	4	18	–	RB Simpson
1968	Australians	25	8	3	14	–	29	10	3	16	–	WM Lawry
1972	Australians	26	11	5	10	–	37	14	10	13	–	IM Chappell
1975	Australians	15	8	2	5	–	21	12	4	5	–	IM Chappell
1977	Australians	22	5	4	13	–	31	8	8	15	–	GS Chappell
1979	Australians	–	–	–	–	–	6	2	3	1	–	KJ Hughes
1980	Australians	5	1	2	2	–	8	1	4	3	–	GS Chappell
1981	Australians	17	3	3	11	–	26	7	7	12	–	KJ Hughes
1985	Australians	20	4	3	13	–	29	9	5	15	–	AR Border
1988	Aboriginals	–	–	–	–	–	27	15	11	1	–	J MacGuire
1989	Australians	20	12	1	7	–	31	20	3	7	1	AR Border
1991	Victoria	1	–	–	1	–	4	1	1	2	–	SP O'Donnell
1993	Australians	21	10	2	9	–	30	18	3	9	–	AR Border
		961	406	135	419	1	1283	567	202	512	2	

FIRST-CLASS RESULTS

Opponent	Venue	First Game	Games	W	L	D	T
ENGLAND	The Oval	Sep 6 1880	32	5	14	12	–
	Manchester	Jly 11 1884	26	6	7	13	–
	Lord's	Jly 21 1884	30	12	5	13	–

Continued

AUSTRALIANS IN ENGLAND

Opponent	Venue	First Game	Games	W	L	D	T
	Nottingham	Jun 1 1899	17	5	3	9	–
	Leeds	Jun 29 1899	21	7	6	8	–
	Birmingham	May 29 1902	9	2	3	4	–
	Sheffield	Jly 3 1902	1	1	–	–	–
			135	38	38	59	–
A Shaw's XI	Leeds	Sep 11 1882	1	1	–	–	–
	The Oval	Sep 18 1882	1	–	–	1	–
			2	1	–	1	–
A Shrewsbury's XI	Holbeck	Sep 10 1888	1	–	1	–	–
	Manchester	Sep 13 1888	1	–	1	–	–
	Nottingham	Jun 26 1893	1	–	1	–	–
			3	–	3	–	–
A Staffordshire's XI	Stoke-on-Trent	Jly 3 1890	1	1	–	–	–
AER Gilligan's XI	Hastings	Sep 2 1964	1	1	–	–	–
Cambridge & Oxford Uni's	Portsmouth	Aug 27 1888	3	–	–	3	–
	Leyton	Aug 7 1890	1	–	–	1	–
	Oxford	Jun 14 1972	2	2	–	–	–
			6	2	–	4	–
Cambridge University	Lord's	Jly 22 1878	1	–	1	–	–
	Cambridge	May 29 1882	23	15	1	7	–
	Portsmouth	Aug 17 1882	1	–	1	–	–
	Hove	Aug 25 1884	1	1	–	–	–
	Leyton	Aug 23 1886	2	–	–	2	–
			28	16	3	9	–
CB Fry's XI	Wicklow, Ireland	Sep 12 1912	1	–	1	–	–
CE De Trafford's XI	Crystal Palace	May 18 1896	1	1	–	–	–
CI Thornton's XI	Chiswick Park	Jly 2 1886	1	–	–	1	–
	Surrey	May 7 1888	1	1	–	–	–
	Scarborough	Sep 4 1893	8	–	3	5	–
			10	1	3	6	–
Combined Services	Kingston	Sep 5 1953	1	1	–	–	–
Derbyshire	Derby	May 17 1880	18	11	1	6	–
	Chesterfield	Jun 23 1926	10	5	–	5	–
			28	16	1	11	–
Durham	Durham	Jly 17 1993	1	–	–	1	–
Earl De La Warr's XI	Bexhill	Jly 30 1896	1	–	1	–	–
England XI	Derby	Aug 14 1882	1	–	–	1	–
	Harrogate	Sep 23 1882	3	2	–	1	–
	Birmingham	May 26 1884	3	2	–	1	–
	Huddersfield	Jly 3 1884	1	–	–	1	–
	Stoke-on-Trent	Jly 26 1886	2	1	–	1	–
	Lord's	Sep 19 1886	4	2	–	2	–
	Hastings	Aug 3 1888	3	2	–	1	–
	Crystal Palace	Aug 23 1888	1	–	1	–	–
	Manchester	Sep 18 1890	2	–	1	1	–
	Eastbourne	May 18 1899	3	2	1	–	–
	Truro	Jly 7 1899	1	1	–	–	–
	Bradford	Jun 26 1902	1	1	–	–	–
	Bournemouth	Aug 31 1905	1	1	–	–	–
	Blackpool	Aug 12 1909	3	1	–	2	–
	Norwich	Aug 27 1912	1	–	–	1	–
	Folkestone	Sep 1 1926	4	–	–	4	–
	Scarborough	Sep 10 1930	4	2	1	1	–
	Sheffield	Jun 23 1945	1	–	1	–	–
			39	17	5	17	–
Essex	Leyton	May 14 1896	14	5	2	7	–
	Southend	Aug 21 1919	9	8	1	–	–
	Chelmsford	May 16 1934	8	3	–	5	–
	Ilford	Jun 17 1972	1	–	–	1	–
			32	16	3	13	–
GN Wyatt's XI	Portsmouth	Aug 19 1886	1	1	–	–	–
Gentlemen of England	Chelsea	Jun 17 1878	1	–	1	–	–
	Scarborough	Sep 9 1878	1	–	–	1	–
	The Oval	Jun 22 1882	3	2	–	1	–
	Lord's	May 29 1884	11	6	2	3	–
	Crystal Palace	May 4 1905	1	–	–	1	–
			17	8	3	6	–
Glamorgan	Swansea	Jly 30 1921	14	3	2	9	–
	Cardiff	May 20 1961	2	–	–	2	–
	St Helens	May 14 1977	1	–	–	1	–
	Neath	Jly 20 1985	3	–	–	3	–
			20	3	2	15	–

Continued

AUSTRALIANS IN ENGLAND

Opponent	Venue	First Game	Games	W	L	D	T
Gloucestershire	Clifton	Sep 5 1878	8	3	1	4	–
	Cheltenham	Aug 18 1884	13	8	1	4	–
	Perth	Jly 10 1890	7	4	–	3	–
	Bristol	Jun 8 1921	16	8	–	7	1
			44	23	2	18	1
Hampshire	Southampton	Jly 6 1896	25	12	1	12	–
HDG Leverson-Gower's XI	Scarborough	Sep 5 1945	2	1	–	1	–
HK Foster's XI	Heraford	Jly 16 1919	1	–	–	1	–
Hurst Park Club	East Molesey	Sep 11 1890	1	–	1	–	–
I Zingari	Scarborough	Sep 7 1882	2	1	–	1	–
Kent	Canterbury	Aug 7 1882	31	13	6	12	–
	Maidstone	Jly 28 1890	1	1	–	–	–
	Gravesend	Jun 22 1893	1	1	–	–	–
			33	15	6	12	–
Lancashire	Manchester	Aug 15 1878	35	14	4	17	–
	Liverpool	Aug 27 1896	9	4	1	4	–
			44	18	5	21	–
Lancashire & Yorkshire	Manchester	Jun 26 1909	1	–	–	1	–
	Hull	Jly 29 1909	1	–	–	1	–
			2	–	–	2	–
Leicestershire	Leicester	Jly 13 1896	24	11	1	12	–
Liverpool & Districts	Liverpool	Jly 31 1882	5	3	–	2	–
London County	Crystal Palace	May 5 1902	1	–	–	1	–
Lord Londesborough's XI	Scarborough	Sep 2 1886	5	1	2	2	–
Lord March's XI	Chichester	Jun 28 1886	1	1	–	–	–
Lord Sheffield's XI	Uckfield	May 12 1884	4	1	2	1	–
	Sheffield Park	May 8 1890	1	1	–	–	–
			5	2	2	1	–
L Robinson's XI	Attleborough	May 14 1919	2	–	–	2	–
MCC	Lord's	May 27 1878	34	14	6	14	–
Middlesex	Lord's	Jun 20 1878	29	16	–	13	–
Midlands Counties XI	Birmingham	Jun 18 1896	2	1	1	–	–
Minor Counties	Stoke-on-Trent	May 23 1953	2	2	–	–	–
MR Bamford's XI	Staffordshire	Sep 7 1909	1	–	–	1	–
Northamptonshire	Northampton	Aug 17 1905	21	13	1	7	–
North of England	Bradford	Sep 20 1880	1	–	–	1	–
	Manchester	Sep 14 1882	7	3	2	2	–
	Nottingham	Sep 1 1884	1	–	1	–	–
	Leeds	Sep 1 1890	1	1	–	–	–
	Birmingham	Jun 2 1926	1	–	–	1	–
			11	4	3	4	–
Nottinghamshire	Nottingham	May 20 1878	35	11	8	16	–
Oxford University	Oxford	May 15 1882	23	17	1	5	–
	Leyton	Jun 11 1888	1	1	–	–	–
	Portsmouth	Jun 19 1899	1	1	–	–	–
			25	19	1	5	–
Players of England	The Oval	Sep 2 1878	5	2	2	1	–
	Chelsea	Sep 11 1878	1	–	–	1	–
	Crystal Palace	Sep 27 1880	1	1	–	–	–
	Sheffield	Jun 30 1884	2	1	1	–	–
	Nottingham	Jun 21 1886	1	–	–	1	–
	Bradford	Sep 6 1886	1	–	–	1	–
	Lord's	Jun 19 1890	2	1	1	–	–
	Leyton	Jly 9 1896	1	1	–	–	–
	Harrogate	Sep 1 1902	1	1	–	–	–
			15	7	4	4	–
President's MCC XI	Lord's	Aug 19 1964	2	–	–	2	–
Rest of the World XI	Lord's	Aug 31 1968	1	1	–	–	–
Scotland	Edinburgh	Jly 11 1912	6	1	–	5	–
Second Class Counties	Birmingham	Aug 21 1893	1	1	–	–	–
SH Cochran's XI	Wicklow, Ireland	Sep 17 1909	1	–	–	1	–
Somerset	Taunton	Aug 21 1882	23	14	–	9	–
	Bath	Jly 13 1905	4	1	1	2	–
			27	15	1	11	–
SOUTH AFRICA	Manchester	May 28 1912	1	1	–	–	–
	Lord's	Jly 15 1912	1	1	–	–	–
	Nottingham	Aug 5 1912	1	–	–	1	–
			3	2	–	1	–
South of England	Chichester	Jun 26 1882	1	1	–	–	–
	Gravesend	Aug 28 1884	2	1	–	1	–
	The Oval	Sep 11 1884	3	1	2	–	–
	Hove	Sep 9 1886	1	–	–	1	–
	Hastings	Sep 16 1886	14	4	3	7	–
	Eastbourne	May 21 1896	1	1	–	–	–
	Crystal Palace	May 8 1899	1	–	–	1	–
	Bournemouth	Sep 12 1902	1	1	–	–	–

Continued

AUSTRALIANS IN ENGLAND

Opponent	Venue	First Game	Games	W	L	D	T
	Portsmouth	Sep 4 1919	1	1	–	–	–
	Bristol	May 26 1926	1	–	–	1	–
			26	10	5	11	–
Surrey	The Oval	Jun 3 1878	50	20	9	21	–
Surrey & Middlesex	The Oval	Sep 2 1912	1	–	1	–	–
Sussex	Hove	Aug 29 1878	33	14	2	17	–
The Lyric Club	Barnes	Jly 31 1890	1	–	1	–	–
The Orleans Club	Twickenham	Jly 8 1878	2	–	–	2	–
The Services	Portsmouth	May 14 1921	1	1	–	–	–
The United XI	Tunbridge Wells	Aug 31 1882	1	–	–	1	–
TN Pearce's XI	Scarborough	Sep 5 1956	4	4	–	–	–
Warwickshire	Birmingham	Aug 3 1896	23	9	1	13	–
Wembly Park XI	Wembly Park	Jun 8 1896	1	1	–	–	–
WG Grace's XI	Crystal Palace	Jly 20 1899	1	–	–	1	–
WH Laverton's XI	Wiltshire	May 15 1890	1	–	1	–	–
Worcestershire	Worcester	Jly 10 1902	20	11	1	8	–
Yorkshire	Huddersfield	May 30 1878	4	1	–	3	–
	Sheffield	Jly 1 1878	23	6	4	13	–
	Dewsbury	Jun 10 1880	2	1	–	1	–
	Bradford	Jun 6 1882	20	8	1	11	–
	Middlesborough	Jly 20 1882	1	1	–	–	–
	Leeds	Jly 10 1893	4	1	1	2	–
	Scarborough	Jly 2 1977	1	–	–	1	–
			55	18	6	31	–

1979 AUSTRALIANS

First-class Results					All Matches			
Matches	Won	Lost	Drawn	Tied	Matches	Won	Lost	Drawn	Tied
–	–	–	–	–	7	2	3	1	–

Date	Venue	Opponent	Results for Australians
May 31	Southall	*Middlesex	Abandoned
Jun 2	Arundel Castle	*New Zealanders	Won by 153 runs
Jun 6	Canterbury	*Kent	Lost by 73 runs
Jun 7	Southampton	*Hampshire	No Result
Jun 9	Lord's	*England (WC L/O Intl)	Lost by 6 wkts
Jun 13	Nottingham	*Pakistan (WC L/O Intl)	Lost by 89 runs
Jun 16	Birmingham	*Canada (WC L/O Intl)	Won by 7 wkts

1980 AUSTRALIANS

First-class Results					All Matches			
Matches	Won	Lost	Drawn	Tied	Matches	Won	Lost	Drawn	Tied
5	1	2	2	–	8	1	4	3	–

Date	Venue	Opponent	Results for Australians
Aug 6	Southampton	Hampshire	Won by 10 wkts
Aug 10	The Oval	Surrey	Lost by 59 runs
Aug 14	Worcester	*Young England	Drawn
Aug 16	Manchester	Lancashire	Drawn
Aug 20	The Oval	*England (L/O Intl)	Lost by 23 runs
Aug 22	Birmingham	*England (L/O Intl)	Lost by 47 runs
Aug 23	Nottingham	Nottinghamshire	Lost by an inns & 76 runs
Aug 28	Lord's	ENGLAND (Only Test)	Drawn

Player	State	M	Inn	NO	Runs	HS	50	100	Avrge	Ct/St	Overs	Mdns	Runs	Wkts	Avrge	5wi	10wm	Best
Border, AR	NSW	4	7	3	321	95	3	–	80.25	3	–	–	–	–	–	–	–	–
Bright, RJ	VIC	3	1	–	21	21	–	–	21.00	1	105.1	40	292	7	41.71	–	–	3/20
Chappell, GS (Capt)	QLD	4	6	–	303	101	2	1	50.50	4	16.0	4	51	2	25.50	–	–	2/32
Dymock, G	QLD	2	1	–	37	37	–	–	37.00	–	42.0	6	184	2	92.00	–	–	1/35
Dyson, J	NSW	3	6	1	66	33	–	–	13.20	–	–	–	–	–	–	–	–	–
Hughes, KJ	VIC	5	9	1	249	117	1	1	31.12	3	–	–	–	–	–	–	–	–
Laird, BM	WA	5	9	1	240	85	3	–	30.00	3	–	–	–	–	–	–	–	–
Lillee, DK	WA	4	4	1	81	33	–	–	27.00	–	116.2	25	391	20	19.55	1	–	6/133
Mallett, AA	SA	4	3	1	49	30*	–	–	24.50	–	77.2	16	282	5	56.40	–	–	2/69
Marsh, RW	WA	5	7	4	172	56	2	–	57.33	11/–	–	–	–	–	–	–	–	–
Pascoe, LS	NSW	4	3	1	8	6	–	–	4.00	1	114.1	14	445	17	26.17	2	–	5/59
Thomson, JR	QLD	3	4	–	42	33	–	–	10.50	3	68.0	15	265	6	44.16	–	–	2/45
Wood, GM	WA	4	7	1	282	112	1	1	47.00	4	–	–	–	–	–	–	–	–
Yallop, GN	VIC	5	7	1	108	45	–	–	18.00	5	–	–	–	–	–	–	–	–

1983 AUSTRALIANS

	First-class Results					All Matches			
Matches	Won	Lost	Drawn	Tied	Matches	Won	Lost	Drawn	Tied
–	–	–	–	–	9	3	5	1	–

Date	Venue	Opponent	Results for Australians
Jun 1	Hove	*Sussex	Abandoned
Jun 2	Hove	*Sussex	Won by 29 runs
Jun 3	Hove	*Sussex	Lost by 7 wkts
Jun 4	Arundel	*New Zealanders	Drawn
Jun 6	Arundel	*New Zealanders	Abandoned
Jun 9	Nottingham	*Zimbabwe (WC L/O Intl)	Lost by 13 runs
Jun 11	Leeds	*West Indies (WC L/O Intl)	Lost by 101 runs
Jun 13	Nottingham	*India (WC L/O Intl)	Won by 162 runs
Jun 16	Southampton	*Zimbabwe (WC L/O Intl)	Won by 32 runs
Jun 18	Lord's	*West Indies (WC L/O Intl)	Lost by 7 wkts
Jun 20	Chelmsford	*India (WC L/O Intl)	Lost by 118 runs

AUSTRALIAN CRICKET TEAMS IN INDIA

Season	Touring Team	First-class Games					All Games					Captain
		P	W	L	D	T	P	W	L	D	T	
1935/36	FA Tarrant's	16	9	3	4	–	22	10	3	9	–	J Ryder
1945/46	Services	8	1	2	5	–	9	1	2	6	–	AL Hassett
1956/57	Australians	3	2	–	1	–	3	2	–	1	–	IW Johnson
1959/60	Australians	7	2	1	4	–	7	2	1	4	–	R Benaud
1964/65	Australians	3	1	1	1	–	3	1	1	1	–	RB Simpson
1969/70	Australians	10	5	1	4	–	10	5	1	4	–	WM Lawry
1979/80	Australians	11	–	3	8	–	11	–	3	8	–	KJ Hughes
1984/85	Australians	–	–	–	–	–	6	4	–	2	–	KJ Hughes
1986/87	Australians	7	–	–	6	1	13	2	3	7	1	AR Border
1987/88	Australians	–	–	–	–	–	7	6	1	–	–	AR Border
1989/90	Western Australia	1	–	–	1	–	4	1	2	1	–	GM Wood
1989/90	Australians	–	–	–	–	–	5	2	3	–	–	AR Border
		66	20	11	34	1	100	36	20	43	1	

FIRST-CLASS RESULTS

Opponent	Venue	First Game	Games	W	L	D	T
INDIA	Madras	Oct 19 1956	6	4	–	1	1
	Bombay	Oct 26 1956	6	1	2	3	–
	Calcutta	Nov 2 1956	5	2	–	3	–
	Delhi	Dec 12 1959	4	1	1	2	–
	Kanpur	Dec 19 1959	3	–	2	1	–
	Bangalore	Sep 19 1979	1	–	–	1	–
			25	8	5	11	1
All India	Bombay	Dec 5 1935	1	1	–	–	–
	Calcutta	Dec 31 1935	1	1	–	–	–
	Lahore	Jan 10 1935	1	–	1	–	–
	Madras	Feb 6 1936	1	–	1	–	–
			4	2	2	–	–
Bengal & Assam	Calcutta	Dec 27 1935	1	1	–	–	–
Bombay	Gwalior	Sep 3 1986	1	–	–	1	–
Bombay Presidency	Bombay	Nov 30 1935	1	–	–	1	–
C.India & Rajputana	Ajmer	Nov 15 1935	1	1	–	–	–
CP & Berar	Nagpur	Dec 20 1935	1	1	–	–	–
Central India	Indore	Dec 14 1935	1	–	–	1	–
Central Zone	Jaipur	Nov 11 1969	1	1	–	–	–
	Nagpur	Sep 27 1979	1	–	–	1	–
			2	1	–	1	–
Combined Indian Uni's	Bangalore	Jan 9 1960	1	–	–	1	–
Cricket Club of India	Delhi	Jan 19 1936	1	–	–	1	–
Delhi	Baroda	Oct 10 1986	1	–	–	1	–
East Zone	Calcutta	Nov 21 1945	1	–	1	–	–
	Gauhati	Dec 6 1969	1	1	–	–	–
	Cuttack	Oct 21 1979	1	–	1	–	–
			3	1	2	–	–
Indian XI	Bombay	Nov 10 1945	1	–	–	1	–
	Calcutta	Nov 25 1945	1	–	–	1	–
	Madras	Dec 7 1945	1	–	1	–	–
			3	–	1	2	–
Indian Under 25's	Chandigarh	Sep 12 1986	1	–	–	1	–

Continued

AUSTRALIANS IN INDIA

Opponent	Venue	First Game	Games	W	L	D	T
Madras Presidency	Madras	Feb 2 1936	1	1	–	–	–
Moin–ud–Dowlah	Secunderabad	Jan 29 1936	1	–	1	–	–
North Zone	Lahore	Oct 28 1945	1	–	–	1	–
	Jullundur	Nov 22 1969	1	–	–	1	–
	Srinagar	Sep 1 1979	1	–	–	1	–
			3	–	–	3	–
Patiala	Patiala	Jan 15 1936	1	–	–	1	–
President's XI	Ahmedabad	Dec 27 1959	1	–	–	1	–
	Bangalore	Aug 30 1986	1	–	–	1	–
			2	–	–	2	–
Prince's XI	Delhi	Nov 1 1945	1	1	–	–	–
Sind	Karachi	Nov 22 1935	1	1	–	–	–
South Zone	Madras	Dec 2 1945	1	1	–	–	–
	Bangalore	Dec 20 1969	1	–	–	1	–
	Hyderabad	Sep 6 1979	1	–	–	1	–
			3	1	–	2	–
Southern Punjab	Amritsar	Jan 5 1936	1	1	–	–	–
Tamil Nadu	Madras	Sep 16 1989	1	–	–	1	–
West India States	Rajkot	Nov 5 1935	1	1	–	–	–
West Zone	Bombay	Nov 6 1945	1	–	–	1	–
	Poona	Oct 31 1969	1	–	–	1	–
	Ahmedabad	Oct 9 1979	1	–	–	1	–
			3	–	–	3	–

1945/46 AUSTRALIAN SERVICES

First-class Results					All Matches			
Matches	Won	Lost	Drawn	Tied	Matches	Won	Lost	Drawn	Tied
8	1	2	5	–	9	1	2	6	–

Date	Venue	Opponent	Results for Australians
Oct 28	Lahore	North Zone	Drawn
Nov 1	Delhi	Prince's XI	Drawn
Nov 6	Bombay	West Zone	Drawn
Nov 10	Bombay	Indian XI	Drawn
Nov 15	Poona	*Indian University	Drawn
Nov 21	Calcutta	East Zone	Lost by 2 wkts
Nov 25	Calcutta	Indian XI	Drawn
Dec 2	Madras	South Zone	Won by 6 wkts
Dec 7	Madras	Indian XI	Lost by 6 wkts

Player	M	Inn	NO	Runs	HS	50	100	Avrge	Ct/St	Overs	Mdns	Runs	Wkts	Avrge	5wi	10wm	Best
Bremner, CD	3	3	2	2	2*	–	–	0.00	1/3	–	–	–	–	–	–	–	–
Carmody, DK	7	12	1	557	113	3	1	58.00	1/1	6.0	1	16	–	–	–	–	–
Cristofani, DR	5	8	1	231	69	2	–	33.00	3	108.0	15	339	12	28.25	–	–	4/46
Ellis, RS	7	7	4	15	10*	–	–	3.66	–	289.3	55	769	21	36.61	–	–	4/21
Hassett, AL (Capt)	6	10	1	769	187	2	4	85.44	6	6.0	–	27	1	27.00	–	–	1/6
Miller, KR	8	13	1	338	106	1	1	28.16	2	119.3	31	306	11	27.81	–	–	3/19
Pepper, CG	6	9	1	314	95	3	–	39.25	6	318.0	50	991	27	36.70	1	–	5/45
Pettiford, J	8	13	1	417	124	–	2	34.75	2	141.0	20	503	9	55.88	–	–	2/45
Price, CFT	6	8	1	188	55	1	–	26.85	3	107.2	13	366	16	22.87	–	–	4/33
Roper, AW	5	6	–	60	28	–	–	10.00	8	90.0	16	257	9	28.55	–	–	2/45
Sismey, SG	4	5	1	49	16*	–	–	12.25	5/2	–	–	–	–	–	–	–	–
Stanford, RM	3	4	–	45	24	–	–	11.25	1	–	–	–	–	–	–	–	–
Whitington, RS	7	12	1	396	155	1	1	36.00	9	10.0	3	35	1	35.00	–	–	1/4
Williams, RG	7	11	4	180	100*	–	1	24.33	4	143.2	28	413	9	42.77	–	–	2/47
Workman, JA	6	11	1	277	76	2	–	27.70	2	–	–	–	–	–	–	–	–

1984/85 AUSTRALIANS

First-class Results					All Matches			
Matches	Won	Lost	Drawn	Tied	Matches	Won	Lost	Drawn	Tied
–	–	–	–	–	6	4	–	2	–

Date	Venue	Opponent	Results for Australians
Sep 28	New Delhi	*India (L/O Intl)	Won by 48 runs
Oct 1	Trivandrum	*India (L/O Intl)	No Result
Oct 3	Jamshedpur	*India (L/O Intl)	No Result
Oct 5	Ahmedabad	*India (L/O Intl)	Won by 7 wkts
Oct 6	Indore	*India (L/O Intl)	Won by 6 wkts
Oct 8	Bombay	*Bombay	Won by 5 wkts

1987/88 AUSTRALIANS IN INDIA

Matches	First-class Results				Matches	All Matches			
	Won	Lost	Drawn	Tied		Won	Lost	Drawn	Tied
–	–	–	–	–	7	6	1	–	–

Date	Venue	Opponent	Results for Australians
Oct 9	Madras	*India (WC L/O Intl)	Won by 1 run
Oct 13	Madras	*Zimbabwe (WC L/O Intl)	Won by 96 runs
Oct 19	Indore	*New Zealand (WC L/O Intl)	Won by 3 runs
Oct 22	New Delhi	*India (WC L/O Intl)	Lost by 56 runs
Oct 27	Chandigarh	*New Zealand (WC L/O Intl)	Won by 17 runs
Oct 30	Cuttack	*Zimbabwe (WC L/O Intl)	Won by 70 runs
Nov 8	Calcutta	*England (WC L/O Intl)	Won by runs

1989/90 AUSTRALIANS IN INDIA

Matches	First-class Results				Matches	All Matches			
	Won	Lost	Drawn	Tied		Won	Lost	Drawn	Tied
–	–	–	–	–	5	2	3	–	–

Date	Venue	Opponent	Results for Australians
Oct 19	Hyderabad	*England (L/O Intl)	Lost by 7 wkts
Oct 21	Madras	*West Indies (L/O Intl)	Won by 99 runs
Oct 23	Bombay	*Pakistan (L/O Intl)	Lost by 66 runs
Oct 25	Goa	*Sri Lanka (L/O Intl)	Won by 28 runs
Oct 27	Bangalore	*India (L/O Intl)	Lost by 3 wkts

AUSTRALIANS IN NORTH AMERICA

Season	Touring Team	First-class Games					All Games					Captain
		P	W	L	D	T	P	W	L	D	T	
1878/79	Australians	1	–	–	1	–	6	4	–	2	–	DW Gregory
1882/83	Australians	–	–	–	–	–	2	2	–	–	–	WL Murdoch
1893/94	Australians	2	1	1	–	–	6	4	1	1	–	JM Blackham
1896/97	Australians	3	2	1	–	–	6	4	1	1	–	GHS Trott
1912/13	Australians	2	1	1	–	–	7	5	1	1	–	SE Gregory
1913/14	Australians	5	4	–	1	–	53	49	1	3	–	A Diamond
1932/33	Australians	–	–	–	–	–	51	46	1	4	–	VY Richardson
1974/75	Australians	–	–	–	–	–	5	2	1	2	–	IM Chappell
		13	8	3	2	–	136	116	6	14	–	

FIRST-CLASS RESULTS

Opponent	Venue	First Game	Games	W	L	D	T
Canada & USA	Toronto	Aug 22 1913	1	1	–	–	–
	Philadelphia	Jly 4 1913	1	1	–	–	–
			2	2	–	–	–
Philadelphia	Philadelphia	Oct 3 1878	11	6	3	2	–

1878/79 AUSTRALIANS IN NORTH AMERICA

Matches	First-class Results				Matches	All Matches			
	Won	Lost	Drawn	Tied		Won	Lost	Drawn	Tied
1	–	–	1	–	6	4	–	2	–

Date	Venue	Opponent	Results for Australians
Oct 1	New York	*XVIII of New York	Won by 5 wkts
Oct 3	Philadelphia	Philadelphia	Drawn
Oct 8	Toronto	*XXII of Canada	Won by 10 wkts
Oct 10	Montreal	*XXII of Quebec	Drawn
Oct 14	Detroit	*XIX of Detroit	Won by an inns & 66 runs
Oct 24	San Francisco	*XXII of San Francisco	Won by an inns & 134 runs

Player	State	M	Inn	NO	Runs	HS	50	100	Avrge	Ct/St	Overs	Mdns	Runs	Wkts	Avrge	5wi	10wm	Best
Allan, FE	VIC	1	1	1	4	4	–	–	0.00	1	38.0	15	50	11	4.55	2	1	6/27
Bailey, GH	TAS	1	2	–	24	24	–	–	12.00	2	4.0	1	5	1	5.00	–	–	1/5
Bannerman, AC	NSW	1	2	–	27	27	–	–	13.50	–	–	–	–	–	–	–	–	–
Bannerman, C	NSW	1	1	–	46	46	–	–	46.00	–	–	–	–	–	–	–	–	–
Blackham, JM	VIC	1	2	1	20	20	–	–	20.00	–/3	–	–	–	–	–	–	–	–
Boyle, HF	VIC	1	1	–	30	30	–	–	30.00	1	19.0	4	39	1	39.00	–	–	1/39
Garrett, TW	NSW	1	1	–	1	1	–	–	1.00	–	13.0	2	26	–	–	–	–	–
Gregory, DW (Capt)	NSW	1	1	–	0	0	–	–	0.00	2	–	–	–	–	–	–	–	–
Horan, TP	VIC	1	2	–	5	5	–	–	2.50	–	10.0	1	24	1	24.00	–	–	1/24
Murdoch, WL	NSW	1	2	1	37	37	–	–	37.00	1	10.0	4	10	–	–	–	–	–
Spofforth, FR	NSW	1	2	–	8	4	–	–	4.00	2	42.3	12	75	6	12.50	1	–	5/24

1882/83 AUSTRALIANS

First-class Results					All Matches				
Matches	Won	Lost	Drawn	Tied	Matches	Won	Lost	Drawn	Tied
–	–	–	–	–	2	2	–	–	–

Date	Venue	Opponent	Results for Australians
Nov 9	New York	*XVIII of New York	Won by Australians
Nov 12	Philadelphia	*XVIII of Philadelphia	Won by Australians

1893/94 AUSTRALIANS

First-class Results					All Matches				
Matches	Won	Lost	Drawn	Tied	Matches	Won	Lost	Drawn	Tied
2	1	1	–	–	6	4	1	1	–

Date	Venue	Opponent	Results for Australians
Sep 29	Philadelphia	Philadelphia	Lost by an inns & 68 runs
Oct 4	New York	*XVIII of New York	Drawn
Oct 6	Philadelphia	Philadelphia	Won by 6 wkts
Oct 11	Boston	*XVIII of Massachusetts	Won by 7 wkts
Oct 16	Toronto	*Canada	Won by an inns & 70 runs
Oct 18	Detroit	*XVIII of Detroit	Won by an inns & 157 runs

Player	State	M	Inn	NO	Runs	HS	50	100	Avrge	Ct/St	Overs	Mdns	Runs	Wkts	Avrge	5wi	10wm	Best
Bannerman, AC	NSW	2	4	2	120	79*	1	–	60.00	1	3.1	2	1	1	1.00	–	–	1/1
Blackham, JM (Capt)	VIC	2	3	–	31	22	–	–	10.33	1/1	–	–	–	–	–	–	–	–
Bruce, W	VIC	2	4	–	26	14	–	–	6.50	2	27.0	4	118	5	23.60	–	–	3/100
Coningham, A	NSW	1	2	–	39	30	–	–	19.50	–	20.0	5	63	1	63.00	–	–	1/63
Giffen, G	SA	2	4	–	102	62	1	–	25.50	3	33.0	7	114	–	–	–	–	–
Giffen, WF	SA	2	3	1	39	19	–	–	19.50	–	–	–	–	–	–	–	–	–
Graham, H	VIC	2	3	–	28	25	–	–	9.33	–	–	–	–	–	–	–	–	–
Gregory, SE	NSW	2	4	1	87	35*	–	–	29.00	–	12.0	5	27	–	–	–	–	–
Lyons, JJ	SA	2	4	–	57	30	–	–	14.25	1	11.0	4	34	–	–	–	–	–
McLeod, RW	VIC	1	1	1	4	4*	–	–	–	–	37.2	14	91	5	18.20	–	–	4/62
Trott, GHS	VIC	2	4	–	89	58	1	–	22.25	1	15.0	3	45	–	–	–	–	–
Trumble, H	VIC	2	3	–	5	4	–	–	1.66	–	100.3	33	200	15	13.33	2	1	7/48

1896/97 AUSTRALIANS

First-class Results					All Matches				
Matches	Won	Lost	Drawn	Tied	Matches	Won	Lost	Drawn	Tied
3	2	1	–	–	6	4	1	1	–

Date	Venue	Opponent	Results for Australians
Sep 18	Philadelphia	Philadelphia	Won by 123 runs
Sep 23	New Jersey	*New Jersey	Won by an inns & 99 runs
Sep 25	Philadelphia	Philadelphia	Won by an inns & 71 runs
Oct 2	Philadelphia	Philadelphia	Lost by an inns & 60 runs
Oct 8	Chicago	*XVIII of Chicago	Won by an inns & 37 runs
Oct 15	San Francisco	*San Francisco	Drawn

Player	State	M	Inn	NO	Runs	HS	50	100	Avrge	Ct/St	Overs	Mdns	Runs	Wkts	Avrge	5wi	10wm	Best
Darling, J	SA	3	5	–	167	77	2	–	33.40	–	–	–	–	–	–	–	–	–
Donnan, H	NSW	2	3	1	39	19	–	–	19.50	1	–	–	–	–	–	–	–	–
Eady, CJ	TAS	1	2	–	3	2	–	–	1.50	–	–	–	–	–	–	–	–	–
Giffen, G	SA	3	5	–	266	96	2	–	53.20	1	98.1	21	259	10	25.90	1	–	5/67
Graham, H	VIC	1	2	–	5	5	–	–	2.50	–	–	–	–	–	–	–	–	–
Gregory, SE	NSW	3	5	–	56	23	–	–	11.20	4	1.0	1	0	–	–	–	–	–
Hill, C	SA	3	5	–	65	42	–	–	13.00	2	2.0	1	7	1	7.00	–	–	1/7
Iredale, FA	NSW	3	5	–	136	67	1	–	27.20	2	–	–	–	–	–	–	–	–
Jones, E	SA	3	5	1	50	30	–	–	12.50	–	86.0	30	151	11	13.73	1	–	5/82
Kelly, JJ	NSW	3	5	1	28	20	–	–	7.00	3/5	–	–	–	–	–	–	–	–
McKibbin, TR	NSW	2	3	1	4	2*	–	–	2.00	1	61.3	17	138	9	15.33	1	–	5/60
Trott, GHS (Capt)	VIC	3	5	–	35	16	–	–	7.00	1	55.0	15	114	11	10.36	1	–	6/39
Trumble, H	VIC	3	5	1	79	46	–	–	19.75	1	63.3	17	164	7	23.43	–	–	4/50

1912/13 AUSTRALIANS

First-class Results					All Matches				
Matches	Won	Lost	Drawn	Tied	Matches	Won	Lost	Drawn	Tied
2	1	1	–	–	7	5	1	1	–

Date	Venue	Opponent	Results for Australians
Sep 27	Philadelphia	Philadelphia	Lost by 2 runs
Oct 2	Livingston	*All New York	Won by 192 runs
Oct 4	Philadelphia	Philadelphia	Won by 45 runs
Oct 7	Haverford	*Philadelphia Colts	Drawn
Oct 12	Hamilton	*All Bermuda	Won by 57 runs
Oct 21	Winnipeg	*Winnipeg XV	Won by 7 wkts
Oct 26	Victoria	*British Colombia XV	Won by 444 runs

Player	State	M	Inn	NO	Runs	HS	50	100	Avrge	Ct/St	Overs	Mdns	Runs	Wkts	Avrge	5wi	10wm	Best
Carkeek, W	VIC	2	4	1	32	28*	–	–	10.67	2	–	–	–	–	–	–	–	–
Ducker, NG		1	2	–	15	9	–	–	7.50	–	–	–	–	–	–	–	–	–
Emery, SH	NSW	2	4	–	61	46	–	–	15.25	–	31.1	3	96	10	9.60	1	–	5/38
Gregory, SE (Capt)	NSW	2	4	–	113	70	1	–	28.25	–	–	–	–	–	–	–	–	–
Kelleway, CE	NSW	2	4	–	14	7	–	–	3.50	–	10.0	2	28	–	–	–	–	–
Matthews, TJ	VIC	2	4	–	37	28	–	–	9.25	3	34.0	8	130	5	26.00	1	–	5/65
Mayne, ER	SA	2	4	–	138	54	2	–	34.50	–	–	–	–	–	–	–	–	–
McLaren, JW	QLD	2	4	1	6	6	–	–	2.00	–	35.0	15	88	5	17.60	–	–	4/29
Penfold, E		1	2	1	0	0*	–	–	0.00	–	–	–	–	–	–	–	–	–
Smith, DBM	VIC	2	4	–	60	45	–	–	15.00	–	–	–	–	–	–	–	–	–
Webster, HW	SA	2	4	–	79	54	1	–	19.75	1	–	–	–	–	–	–	–	–
Whitty, WJ	SA	2	4	1	24	23	–	–	8.00	–	67.0	20	155	19	8.16	2	1	7/45

1913/14 AUSTRALIANS

First-class Results					All Matches				
Matches	Won	Lost	Drawn	Tied	Matches	Won	Lost	Drawn	Tied
5	4	–	1	–	53	49	1	3	–

Date	Venue	Opponent	Results for Australians
May 28	Victoria	*Victoria	Won by an inns & 89 runs
May 30	Victoria	*Victoria & Cowichan	Won by an inns & 191 runs
May 31	Victoria	*British Colombia	Won by an inns & 103 runs
Jun 3	Edmonton	*Edmonton XVIII	Won by 241 runs
Jun 4	Edmonton	*Edmonton XVIII	Drawn
Jun 6	Prince Albert	*Saskatechewan	Won by 394 runs
Jun 7	Prince Albert	*Saskatechewan	Won by 94 runs
Jun 11	Toronto	*Toronto	Won by 242 runs
Jun 13	Montreal	*Montreal	Won by 399 runs
Jun 20	Philadelphia	Philadelphia	Won by an inns & 178 runs
Jun 24	Schenectady	*Schenectady XVIII	Won by 205 runs
Jun 25	Schenectady	*Schenectady XVIII	Won by 54 runs
Jun 27	Haverford	Gentlemen of Philadelphia	Won by 10 wkts
Jun 30	Haverford	Gentlemen of Philadelphia	Drawn
Jly 4	Manheim	USA & Canada	Won by 399 runs
Jly 11	Pittsburgh	*Pittsburgh Field Club XVIII	Won by 80 runs
Jly 12	Pittsburgh	*Pittsburgh Field Club XVIII	Won by 211 runs
Jly 19	Hamilton	*Hamilton	Won by 285 runs
Jly 21	Hamilton	*Hamilton	Won by 240 runs
Jly 22	Hamilton	*All Bermuda	Won by an inns & 114 runs
Jly 24	Hamilton	*Bermuda Coloured Team	Won by an inns & 122 runs
Jly 29	Providence	*Rhode Island XXII	Won by 124 runs
Jly 30	Providence	*Rhode Island XXII	Won by 125 runs
Aug 1	Livingstone	*All New York XV	Won by 9 wkts
Aug 4	Manor Field	*New York Vetrans XIII	Won by 320 runs
Aug 6	Manheim	*Germantown XII	Lost by 3 wkts
Aug 8	Brooklyn	*West Indian Coloured Team	Won by an inns & 139 runs
Aug 12	Ottawa	*Eastern Canada	Won by an inns & 121 runs
Aug 13	Ottawa	*Eastern Canada	Won by 174 runs
Aug 15	Montreal	*Montreal XVI	Won by 85 runs
Aug 16	Montreal	*Montreal XVII	Won by 189 runs
Aug 18	Montreal	*McGill University XVII	Won by 114 runs
Aug 19	Montreal	*McGill University XVIII	Won by 164 runs
Aug 22	Toronto	Canada & USA	Won by an inns & 147 runs
Aug 27	Chicago	*All Chicago XVI	Won by 191 runs
Aug 28	Chicago	*All Chicago XVI	Won by 263 runs
Aug 29	Chicago	*All Chicago XV	Won by 209 runs
Sep 1	Winnipeg	*Winnipeg Cricket Association	Won by an inns & 58 runs
Sep 2	Winnipeg	*Winnipeg Cricket Association	Won by 266 runs
Sep 3	Winnipeg	*Winnipeg Cricket Assoc. XVII	Won by 178 runs
Sep 5	Regina	*Saskatchewan XVIII	Won by 195 runs
Sep 6	Regina	*Saskatchewan XX	Won by 171 runs
Sep 8	Yorkton	*Yorkton XVIII	Won by 197 runs
Sep 9	Yorkton	*Yorkton XVIII	Won by 199 runs
Sep 12	Edmonton	*Edmonton XVIII	Won by 141 runs
Sep 13	Edmonton	*Edmonton XVIII	Won by 94 runs
Sep 15	Calgary	*Calgary XXII	Won by 258 runs
Sep 16	Calgary	*Calgary XV	Won by an inns & 1 run
Sep 20	Vancouver	*Vancouver XV	Won by an inns & 240 runs
Sep 22	Vancouver	*Vancouver XV	Won by 494 runs
Sep 25	Victoria	*Cowichan	Won by an inns & 29 runs
Sep 26	Victoria	*British Colombia Colts XXII	Won by an inns & 46 runs
Sep 27	Victoria	*British Colombia Colts XXII	Drawn

AUSTRALIANS IN NORTH AMERICA

Player	State	M	Inn	NO	Runs	HS	50	100	Avrge	Ct/St	Overs	Mdns	Runs	Wkts	Avrge	5wi	10wm	Best
Arnott, PS	NSW	4	5	1	111	49	–	–	27.75	2	–	–	–	–	–	–	–	–
Bardsley, W	NSW	5	6	2	437	142*	–	3	109.25	1	5.0	–	21	–	–	–	–	–
Campbell, GC	SA	5	5	–	53	28	–	–	10.60	3/6	–	–	–	–	–	–	–	–
Cody, LA	NSW	5	7	1	355	97	3	–	59.17	3	11.0	2	24	2	12.00	–	–	2/24
Collins, HL	NSW	3	4	–	18	9	–	–	4.50	–	–	–	–	–	–	–	–	–
Crawford, JN	SA	5	6	–	147	58	1	–	24.50	9	116.2	21	359	33	10.88	3	–	6/40
Diamond, A (Capt)	NSW	5	5	–	73	31	–	–	14.60	5	–	–	–	–	–	–	–	–
Down, GS	SA	3	3	–	77	47	–	–	25.67	1	–	–	–	–	–	–	–	–
Emery, SH	NSW	5	5	–	126	51	1	–	25.20	2	59.0	4	229	11	20.82	–	–	4/47
Macartney, CG	NSW	5	6	–	329	186*	–	2	54.83	3	75.0	22	180	14	12.86	–	–	4/17
Mailey, AA	NSW	5	5	5	65	27*	–	–	–	5	82.2	12	265	24	11.04	2	–	7/31
Mayne, ER	SA	5	7	1	273	85	2	–	45.50	1	–	–	–	–	–	–	–	–

1932/33 AUSTRALIANS

First-class Results					All Matches				
Matches	Won	Lost	Drawn	Tied	Matches	Won	Lost	Drawn	Tied
–	–	–	–	–	51	46	1	4	–

Date	Venue	Opponent	Results for Australians
Jun 17	Duncan	*Cowichan XVII	Won by 319 runs
Jun 18	Victoria	*Victoria League XV	Won by 181 runs
Jun 20	Victoria	*Victoria League XV	Won by Australians
Jun 22	Vancouver	*BC Mainland League XV	Lost by 18 runs
Jun 23	Vancouver	*BC Mainland League XV	Won by Australians
Jun 25	Vancouver	*BC Mainland League XV	Won by Australians
Jun 29	Toronto	*Toronto XII	Drawn
Jun 30	Toronto	*Toronto XVI	Won by Australians
Jly 1	Toronto	*Eastern Canada	Won by 49 runs
Jly 2	Toronto	*Eastern Canada	Won by Australians
Jly 4	Guelph	*Western Ontario XVIII	Won by Australians
Jly 5	St Katherine's	*Ridley College Past and Present	Drawn
Jly 6	St Katherine's	*Ridley College XVIII	Won by Australians
Jly 7	Montreal	*Montreal XII	Won by Australians
Jly 8	Montreal	*Montreal XVIII	Won by Australians
Jly 9	Montreal	*Montreal XV	Won by Australians
Jly 11	Ottawa	*Ottawa Valley XVI	Won by Australians
Jly 12	Ottawa	*Ottawa Valley XVI	Won by Australians
Jly 14	New York	*New York West Indians	Won by Australians
Jly 15	New York	*New York West Indians	Won by Australians
Jly 17	Staten Island	*New York XV	Won by Australians
Jly 18	Staten Island	*New York XV	Won by Australians
Jly 19	Staten Island	*New York XV	Won by Australians
Jly 21	Detroit	*Detroit XVI	Won by Australians
Jly 22	Windsor	*Border Cities XVI	Won by Australians
Jly 23	Chicago	*Illinois XVIII	Drawn
Jly 24	Chicago	*Illinois XVIII	Won by 5 wkts
Jly 25	Chicago	*Illinois XVIII	Won by 4 wkts
Jly 26	Chicago	*Illinois XVIII	Won by 6 wkts
Jly 28	Winnipeg	*Manitoba XV	Won by Australians
Jly 29	Winnipeg	*Canadian XI	Won by 130 runs
Aug 1	Regina	*Regina XVII	Won by Australians
Aug 2	Moose Jaw	*Moose Jaw XVIII	Won by Australians
Aug 3	Moose Jaw	*Moose Jaw XVIII	Won by Australians
Aug 4	Yorkton	*Yorkton XVIII	Won by Australians
Aug 6	Saskatoon	*Saskatoon XX	Won by Australians
Aug 8	Edmonton	*Edmonton XV	Won by Australians
Aug 9	Edmonton	*Edmonton XVIII	Won by 264 runs
Aug 10	Calgary	*Calgary XVI	Won by Australians
Aug 11	Calgary	*Calgary XVI	Drawn
Aug 13	Vancouver	*British Colombia	Won by an inns & 204 runs
Aug 15	Vancouver	*Vancouver Colts XIX	Won by Australians
Aug 16	Victoria	*Victoria Colts XX	Won by Australians
Aug 17	Victoria	*British Colombia	Won by Australians
Aug 20	San Francisco	*Northern California XV	Won by an inns & 213 runs
Aug 21	San Francisco	*All California XVIII	Won by Australians
Aug 24	Santa Barbara	*Montecito Cricket Club XVIII	Won by Australians
Aug 25	Hollywood	*Hollywood Cricket Club XVIII	Won by Australians
Aug 26	Hollywood	*Hollywood Cricket Club XVIII	Won by Australians
Aug 27	Hollywood	*Hollywood & District XVIII	Won by Australians
Aug 28	Hollywood	*Hollywood XX	Won by Australians

Averages for All Matches

Player	Inn	NO	Runs	HS	Avrge	Runs	Wkts	Avrge
Bramble,	1	–	36	36	36.00	–	–	–
Bradman, DG	51	14	3782	260	102.16	240	24	10.00
Carney, PH	21	8	201	27	15.46	89	2	44.50
Carter, HS	10	5	100	27*	20.00	–	–	–
Carter, W	2	1	1	1	1.00	–	–	–
Fleetwood–Smith, LO	11	3	39	23	4.87	1788	238	7.51
Ives, W	29	12	444	46*	26.11	678	92	7.36
Kippax, AF	43	9	1853	132	54.50	225	20	11.25
Mailey, AA	20	2	236	51*	13.11	1755	203	8.64
McCabe, SJ	47	4	2361	157	54.90	1139	189	6.02
Nutt, RN	41	11	1402	109	46.70	29	–	–
Richardson, VY (Capt)	44	3	1380	147	33.65	103	5	20.60
Rofe, EF	26	6	280	40	14.00	15	–	–
Tolhurst, EK	42	12	1285	117*	42.83	19	–	–
Vaughan,	1	–	14	14	14.00	–	–	–

1974/75 AUSTRALIANS

First-class Results					All Matches			
Matches	Won	Lost	Drawn	Tied	Matches	Won	Lost	Drawn	Tied
–	–	–	–	–	5	2	1	2	–

Date	Venue	Opponent	Results for Australians
May 21	Vancouver	*British Colombia	Won by 153 runs
May 22	Victoria	*Western Canada	Drawn
May 24	Toronto	*Eastern Canada	Lost by 5 wkts
May 25	Toronto	*Ontario	Won by 159 runs
May 27	Toronto	*Toronto Cricket Club	Drawn

AUSTRALIAN CRICKET TEAMS IN NEW ZEALAND

Season	Touring Team	First-class Games					All Games					Captain
		P	W	L	D	T	P	W	L	D	T	
1877/78	Australians	–	–	–	–	–	7	5	1	1	–	DW Gregory
1880/81	Australians	–	–	–	–	–	10	6	1	3	–	WL Murdoch
1883/84	Tasmania	4	–	3	1	–	7	2	3	2	–	JG Davis
1886/87	Australians	–	–	–	–	–	5	2	–	3	–	HJH Scott
1889/90	New South Wales	5	4	–	1	–	7	6	–	1	–	J Davis
1893/94	New South Wales	7	4	1	2	–	8	4	1	3	–	J Davis
1895/96	New South Wales	5	3	1	1	–	5	3	1	1	–	LT Cobcroft
1896/97	Australians	–	–	–	–	–	5	3	–	2	–	GHS Trott
1896/97	Australians	5	3	1	1	–	8	4	1	3	–	OC Hitchcock
1904/05	Australians	4	3	–	1	–	6	4	–	2	–	MA Noble
1909/10	Australians	6	5	–	1	–	9	7	–	2	–	WW Armstrong
1913/14	Australians	8	6	–	2	–	16	8	–	8	–	A Sims
1920/21	Australians	9	6	–	3	–	15	12	–	3	–	VS Ransford
1923/24	New South Wales	6	5	–	1	–	12	8	–	4	–	CG Macartney
1924/25	Victoria	6	1	1	4	–	12	4	1	7	–	ER Mayne
1927/28	Australians	6	4	–	2	–	13	6	–	7	–	VY Richardson
1945/46	Australians	5	5	–	–	–	5	5	–	–	–	WA Brown
1949/50	Australians	5	3	–	2	–	14	9	–	5	–	WA Brown
1956/57	Australians	7	5	–	2	–	12	7	–	5	–	ID Craig
1959/60	Australians	6	2	–	4	–	9	4	–	5	–	ID Craig
1966/67	Australians	9	1	2	6	–	10	2	2	6	–	LE Favell
1969/70	Australians	8	2	–	6	–	8	2	–	6	–	SC Trimble
1973/74	Australians	7	2	1	4	–	11	6	1	4	–	IM Chappell
1976/77	Australians	6	5	–	1	–	8	5	2	1	–	GS Chappell
1981/82	Australians	5	1	1	3	–	11	4	4	3	–	GS Chappell
1984/85	New South Wales	–	–	–	–	–	1	1	–	–	–	DM Wellham
1985/86	Australians	5	1	1	3	–	11	5	3	3	–	AR Border
1986/87	New South Wales	–	–	–	–	–	2	1	1	–	–	DM Wellham
	South Australia	–	–	–	–	–	4	4	–	–	–	DW Hookes
1987/88	Victoria	–	–	–	–	–	2	–	2	–	–	DF Whatmore
	Queensland	–	–	–	–	–	3	3	–	–	–	RB Kerr
1989/90	Australians	1	–	1	–	–	6	5	–	1	–	AR Border
1991/92	Australians	–	–	–	–	–	2	1	1	–	–	AR Border
1992/93	Australians	4	2	1	1	–	10	5	4	1	–	AR Border
1993/94	New South Wales	–	–	–	–	–	1	1	–	–	–	PA Emery
1994/95	Australians	–	–	–	–	–	4	3	1	–	–	MA Taylor
1994/95	Cricket Academy	1	1	–	–	–	6	6	–	–	–	NW Ashley
		140	74	14	52	–	285	163	30	92	–	

FIRST-CLASS RESULTS

Opponent	Venue	First Game	Games	W	L	D	T
NEW ZEALAND	Wellington	Mar 29 1946	6	1	1	4	–
	Christchurch	Mar 8 1974	5	2	1	2	–
	Auckland	Mar 22 1974	5	2	3	–	–
			16	5	5	6	–
Auckland	Auckland	Jan 30 1890	17	11	–	6	–
Canterbury	Christchurch	Feb 7 1884	20	11	4	5	–
Central Districts	New Plymouth	Mar 23 1957	3	1	–	2	–
	Palmerston North	Mar 12 1960	2	–	–	2	–
	Nelson	Feb 8 1977	1	1	–	–	–
			6	2	–	4	–
Hawke's Bay	Napier	Jan 24 1894	3	2	–	1	–
	Nelson	Feb 18 1914	1	1	–	–	–
			4	3	–	1	–
Minor Associations	Wellington	Mar 8 1921	1	1	–	–	–
New Zealand Board XI	New Plymouth	Feb 16 1993	1	1	–	–	–
NZ Emerging Players	Hamilton	Apr 2 1995	1	1	–	–	–
New Zealand Under 23s	Napier	Mar 2 1970	1	1	–	–	–
New Zealanders	Christchurch	Feb 15 1894	10	3	1	6	–
	Wellington	Dec 26 1896	9	4	1	4	–
	Dunedin	Mar 6 1914	5	3	–	2	–
	Auckland	Mar 27 1914	7	3	–	4	–
	New Plymouth	Mar 3 1967	1	–	1	–	–
			32	13	3	16	–
North Island	Wellington	Feb 19 1894	1	1	–	–	–
	Napier	Feb 22 1982	1	–	–	1	–
			2	1	–	1	–
Northern Districts	Hamilton	Mar 21 1967	5	3	–	2	–
NZCC President's XI	Christchurch	Mar 6 1982	1	–	–	1	–
Otago	Dunedin	Feb 1 1884	18	12	1	5	–
Southland	Invercargill	Mar 16 1921	1	–	–	1	–
Wellington	Wellington	Feb 21 1890	14	9	1	4	–

1877/78 AUSTRALIANS

First-class Results					All Matches				
Matches	Won	Lost	Drawn	Tied	Matches	Won	Lost	Drawn	Tied
–	–	–	–	–	7	5	1	1	–

Date	Venue	Opponent	Results for Australians
Jan 9	Invercargill	*Southland XXII	Won by an inns & 139 runs
Jan 12	Dunedin	*Otago XXII	Drawn
Jan 17	Oamaru	*Oamaru XXII	Won by 43 runs
Jan 19	Christchurch	*Canterbury XV	Lost by 6 wkts
Jan 26	Wellington	*Wellington XXII	Won by 9 wkts
Feb 1	Napier	*Hawke's Bay XXII	Won by an inns & 34 runs
Feb 7	Auckland	*Auckland XXII	Won by an inns & 25 runs

1880/81 AUSTRALIANS

First-class Results					All Matches				
Matches	Won	Lost	Drawn	Tied	Matches	Won	Lost	Drawn	Tied
–	–	–	–	–	10	6	1	3	–

Date	Venue	Opponent	Results for Australians
Jan 8	Invercargill	*Southland	Won by an inns * 83 runs
Jan 21	Dunedin	*Otago XXII	Won by 44 runs
Jan 24	Oamaru	*North Otago XXII	Drawn
Jan 26	Timaru	*South Canterbury	Won by an inns & 108 runs
Feb 1	Christchurch	*Canterbury XV	Won by an inns & 100 runs
Feb 5	Wellington	*Wellington XXII	Won by an inns & 21 runs
Feb 9	Nelson	*Nelson XXII	Drawn
Feb 11	Wanganui	*Wanganui XXII	Lost by 10 wkts
Feb 16	Hastings	*Hawke's Bay	Won by an inns & 1 runs
Feb 22	Auckland	*Auckland XXII	Drawn

1886/87 AUSTRALIANS

First-class Results					All Matches				
Matches	Won	Lost	Drawn	Tied	Matches	Won	Lost	Drawn	Tied
–	–	–	–	–	5	2	–	3	–

Date	Venue	Opponent	Results for Australians
Nov 22	Dunedin	*Otago XXII	Won by 6 wkts
Nov 26	Christchurch	*Canterbury XVIII	Drawn
Dec 1	Wellington	*Wellington XXII	Drawn
Dec 4	Napier	*Hawke's Bay	Won by 23 runs
Dec 6	Auckland	*Auckland XXII	Drawn

1896/97 AUSTRALIANS

First-class Results					All Matches				
Matches	Won	Lost	Drawn	Tied	Matches	Won	Lost	Drawn	Tied
–	–	–	–	–	5	3	–	2	–

Date	Venue	Opponent	Results for Australians
Nov 6	Auckland	*Auckland XVIII	Drawn
Nov 12	Wellington	*Wellington XVIII	Drawn
Nov 18	Invercargill	*Southland XVIII	Won by an inns & 69 runs
Nov 21	Dunedin	*Otago XV	Won by 17 runs
Nov 26	Christchurch	*New Zealand XV	Won by 5 wkts

1904/05 AUSTRALIANS

First-class Results					All Matches				
Matches	Won	Lost	Drawn	Tied	Matches	Won	Lost	Drawn	Tied
4	3	–	1	–	6	4	–	2	–

AUSTRALIANS IN NEW ZEALAND

Date	Venue	Opponent	Results for Australians
Feb 10	Auckland	*Auckland XV	Won by an inns & 160 runs
Feb 20	Wellington	*Wellington XV	Drawn
Feb 24	Christchurch	Canterbury	Won by 8 wkts
Mar 3	Dunedin	Otago	Won by an inns & 173 runs
Mar 10	Christchurch	New Zealanders	Drawn
Mar 16	Wellington	New Zealanders	Won by an inns & 358 runs

Player	State	M	Inn	NO	Runs	HS	50	100	Avrge	Ct/St	Overs	Mdns	Runs	Wkts	Avrge	5wi	10wm	Best
Armstrong, WW	VIC	4	4	2	254	126*	1	1	127.00	5	69.5	16	145	21	6.90	2	1	5/25
Cotter, A	NSW	3	3	–	98	44	–	–	32.67	1	75.0	23	138	15	9.20	1	–	5/20
Duff, RA	NSW	4	5	–	172	74	2	–	34.40	1	7.0	3	20	2	10.00	–	–	1/11
Gehrs, DRA	SA	4	4	1	78	45*	–	–	26.00	11	8.0	2	24	–	–	–	–	–
Gregory, SE	NSW	4	4	–	75	61	1	–	18.75	1	–	–	–	–	–	–	–	–
Hill, C	SA	4	5	1	308	129	1	2	77.00	1	–	–	–	–	–	–	–	–
Hopkins, AJY	NSW	3	3	–	40	25	–	–	13.33	3	25.0	12	47	5	9.40	–	–	4/19
Howell, WP	NSW	3	3	1	10	10*	–	–	5.00	2	38.0	21	73	4	18.25	–	–	4/20
Kelly, JJ	NSW	2	2	–	36	28	–	–	18.00	5	–	–	–	–	–	–	–	–
Laver, F	VIC	1	1	–	9	9	–	–	9.00	2	28.1	10	90	7	12.86	1	–	7/66
McLeod, CE	VIC	2	2	–	16	12	–	–	8.00	–	37.5	9	101	7	14.43	1	–	6/51
Newland, PM	SA	2	2	–	71	37	–	–	35.50	–/3	–	–	–	–	–	–	–	–
Noble, MA (Capt)	NSW	4	5	1	102	42	–	–	25.50	3	76.1	21	183	15	12.20	2	1	7/38
Trumper, VT	NSW	4	5	1	436	172	3	1	109.00	3	–	–	–	–	–	–	–	–

1909/10 AUSTRALIANS

First-class Results					All Matches				
Matches	Won	Lost	Drawn	Tied	Matches	Won	Lost	Drawn	Tied
6	5	–	1	–	9	7	–	2	–

Date	Venue	Opponent	Results for Australians
Jan 25	Christchurch	Canterbury	Drawn
Feb 11	Wellington	Wellington	Won by 6 wkts
Feb 18	Auckland	Auckland	Won by an inns & 128 runs
Mar 5	Dunedin	Otago	Won by 10 wkts
Mar 11	Christchurch	New Zealanders	Won by 9 wkts
Mar 16	Palmerston North	*Manawatu XIII	Won by inns & 104 runs
Mar 18	Wanganui	*Wanganui XI	Won by 121 runs
Mar 22	Taranaki	*Taranaki XV	Drawn
Mar 26	Wellington	New Zealanders	Won by 162 runs

Player	State	M	Inn	NO	Runs	HS	50	100	Avrge	Ct/St	Overs	Mdns	Runs	Wkts	Avrge	5wi	10wm	Best
Armstrong, WW (Capt)	VIC	6	8	1	393	149*	3	1	56.14	6	122.3	27	367	16	22.94	–	–	4/56
Bardsley, W	NSW	6	11	2	375	97	2	–	41.67	3	–	–	–	–	–	–	–	–
Dodds, N	TAS	3	5	–	84	53	1	–	16.80	4/1	–	–	–	–	–	–	–	–
Emery, SH	NSW	6	8	2	116	50*	1	–	19.33	3	92.0	15	355	22	16.14	2	–	5/20
Facy, AC	VIC	3	4	1	15	7*	–	–	5.00	–	61.0	12	178	11	16.18	1	–	7/71
Gorry, GR	NSW	5	5	3	25	11*	–	–	12.50	4/6	–	–	–	–	–	–	–	–
Hopkins, AJY	NSW	4	5	–	16	8	–	–	3.20	1	63.3	17	163	9	18.11	–	–	4/34
Kelleway, CE	NSW	6	8	1	187	51	1	–	26.71	5	47.0	10	116	5	23.20	–	–	2/1
Mayne, ER	SA	6	11	2	533	136	2	2	59.22	1	–	–	–	–	–	–	–	–
Simpson, CE	NSW	5	8	1	155	51	1	–	22.14	8	27.4	11	52	1	52.00	–	–	1/5
Smith, DBM	VIC	6	9	1	206	102	–	1	25.75	2	–	–	–	–	–	–	–	–
Warne, TSD	VIC	4	5	2	112	54	1	–	37.33	4	35.1	6	154	7	22.00	1	–	5/37
Whitty, WJ	SA	6	7	1	53	14	–	–	8.83	1	219.0	71	510	42	12.14	3	–	8/27

1913/14 AUSTRALIANS

First-class Results					All Matches				
Matches	Won	Lost	Drawn	Tied	Matches	Won	Lost	Drawn	Tied
8	6	–	2	–	16	8	–	8	–

Date	Venue	Opponent	Results for Australians
Feb 3	Hamilton	*South Auckland XVIII	Drawn
Feb 4	Taranaki	*South Taranaki XVI	Won by 8 wkts
Feb 6	Auckland	Auckland	Won by an inns & 221 runs
Feb 13	Wellington	Wellington	Won by 7 wkts
Feb 18	Nelson	Hawke's Bay	Won by 9 wkts
Feb 20	Gisborne	*Poverty Bay	Drawn
Feb 24	Wanganui	*Wanganui	Drawn
Feb 27	Christchurch	Canterbury	Won by an inns & 364 runs
Mar 3	Temuka	*South Canterbury	Drawn
Mar 6	Dunedin	New Zealanders	Won by 7 wkts
May 11	Invercargill	*Southland	Drawn
Mar 13	Christchurch	Canterbury	Drawn

Continued

Date	Venue	Opponent	Results for Australians
Mar 19	Nelson	*Nelson	Won by 10 wkts
Mar 20	Wellington	Wellington	Drawn
Mar 23	Palmerston North	*Manawatu XV	Drawn
Mar 27	Auckland	New Zealanders	Won by an inns & 113 runs

Player	State	M	Inn	NO	Runs	HS	50	100	Avrge	Ct/St	Overs	Mdns	Runs	Wkts	Avrge	5wi	10wm	Best
Armstrong, WW	VIC	8	8	1	441	128	2	2	63.00	11	312.0	81	789	52	15.17	7	1	7/17
Cody, LA	NSW	6	7	2	160	54	1	–	32.00	3	26.2	5	62	2	31.00	–	–	2/22
Collins, HL	NSW	6	8	–	185	94	1	–	23.13	4	22.0	3	64	2	32.00	–	–	1/12
Crawford, JN	SA	5	5	–	190	134	1	1	38.00	2	140.1	30	388	21	18.48	1	–	5/60
Dolling, CE	SA	7	9	–	263	104	1	1	29.22	–	–	–	–	–	–	–	–	–
Laver, FJ	VIC	4	4	1	21	15*	–	–	7.00	2	103.0	25	274	8	34.25	–	–	4/69
Mailey, AA	NSW	8	7	–	58	23	–	–	8.29	2	151.3	19	570	30	19.00	2	1	8/51
McGregor, W		4	5	2	50	35	–	–	16.67	5/4	–	–	–	–	–	–	–	–
McKenzie, C	VIC	7	7	2	143	40	–	–	28.60	5	49.0	13	121	8	15.13	–	–	4/41
Noble, MA	NSW	7	7	–	201	90	1	–	28.71	9	120.0	32	318	18	17.67	–	–	4/25
Ransford, VS	VIC	4	5	1	283	159	–	2	70.75	–	21.0	6	41	2	20.50	–	–	1/6
Sims, A (Capt)		7	6	2	204	184*	–	1	51.00	5	–	–	–	–	–	–	–	–
Trumper, VT	NSW	7	9	–	628	293	3	1	68.78	4	–	–	–	–	–	–	–	–
Waddy, EL	NSW	8	10	3	480	140	1	2	68.57	4/4	2.0	–	11	1	11.00	–	–	1/11

1920/21 AUSTRALIANS

First-class Results					All Matches				
Matches	Won	Lost	Drawn	Tied	Matches	Won	Lost	Drawn	Tied
9	6	–	3	–	15	12	–	3	–

Date	Venue	Opponent	Results for Australians
Feb 11	Wellington	Wellington	Won by 8 wkts
Feb 15	Palmerston North	*Manawatu	Won by an inns & 73 runs
Feb 18	Auckland	Auckland	Won by an inns & 17 runs
Feb 22	Hamilton	*Waikaot XV	Won by an inns & 96
Feb 25	Napier	Hawke's Bay	Drawn
Mar 1	Masterton	*Wairarapa XV	Won by 10 wkts
Mar 4	Wanganui	*Wanganui XII	Won by an inns & 33 runs
Mar 8	Wellington	Minor Associations	Won by an inns & 6 runs
Mar 11	Christchurch	Canterbury	Won by 7 wkts
Mar 16	Invercargill	Southland	Drawn
Mar 18	Dunedin	Otago	Won by an inns & 12 runs
Mar 23	Ashburton	*Ashburton XV	Won by 10 wkts
Mar 26	Wellington	New Zealanders	Drawn
Apr 1	Auckland	New Zealanders	Won by an inns & 227 runs
Apr 4	Rotorua	*Rotorua XV	Won by 64 runs

Player	State	M	Inn	NO	Runs	HS	50	100	Avrge	Ct/St	Overs	Mdns	Runs	Wkts	Avrge	5wi	10wm	Best
Asher, OP	NSW	6	6	–	49	22	–	–	8.17	3	70.5	7	290	15	19.33	–	–	4/44
Bogle, J	NSW	8	9	1	311	84	3	–	38.86	1	8.0	–	32	4	8.00	–	–	3/27
Forssberg, EEB	NSW	5	5	–	75	52	1	–	15.00	6	40.0	10	125	5	25.00	–	–	1/7
Hornibrook, PM	QLD	7	7	1	27	14	–	–	4.50	7	164.6	33	573	47	12.19	4	2	7/47
Ironmonger, H	VIC	9	9	4	89	36*	–	–	17.80	–	197.7	40	593	45	13.18	4	1	7/36
Kippax, AF	NSW	9	10	2	275	84*	2	–	34.38	8	9.4	3	27	3	9.00	–	–	1/4
Lampard, AW	VIC	9	11	2	501	132	4	1	55.67	4	66.0	3	285	14	20.36	–	–	4/47
Liddicutt, AE	VIC	8	10	2	326	83	2	–	40.75	1	112.7	17	404	15	26.93	–	–	4/54
Pellew, LV	SA	5	5	–	52	17	–	–	10.40	2	9.0	–	29	1	29.00	–	–	1/23
Ransford, VS (Capt)	VIC	8	9	2	497	158	–	3	71.00	11	1.0	–	2	–	–	–	–	–
Ratcliffe, AT	NSW	7	8	–	185	48	–	–	23.13	2/3	–	–	–	–	–	–	–	–
Richardson, VY	SA	9	12	1	420	112	–	1	38.18	8/1	19.0	3	95	5	19.00	–	–	1/18
Waddy, EL	NSW	9	12	–	264	79	1	–	22.00	8	10.0	1	81	–	–	–	–	–

1927/28 AUSTRALIANS

First-class Results					All Matches				
Matches	Won	Lost	Drawn	Tied	Matches	Won	Lost	Drawn	Tied
6	4	–	2	–	13	6	–	7	–

Date	Venue	Opponent	Results for Australians
Feb 17	Wellington	Wellington	Won by 4 wkts
Feb 22	Oamaru	*North Otago	Drawn
Feb 24	Dunedin	Otago	Drawn
Feb 28	Invercargill	*Southland	Drawn
Mar 2	Christchurch	Canterbury	Won by 9 wkts
Mar 7	Hamilton	*Waikato	Drawn
Mar 9	Auckland	Auckland	Won by an inns & 40 runs

Continued

AUSTRALIANS IN NEW ZEALAND

Date	Venue	Opponent	Results for Australians
Mar 14	New Plymouth	*Taranaki	Won by an inns & 177 runs
Mar 15	Nelson	*Nelson, Marlborough & Westland	Drawn
Mar 16	Wanganui	*Wanganui	Won by an inns & 213 runs
Mar 20	Gisborne	*Poverty Bay	Drawn
Mar 23	Auckland	New Zealanders	Drawn
Mar 31	Dunedin	New Zealanders	Won by 7 wkts

Player	State	M	Inn	NO	Runs	HS	50	100	Avrge	Ct/St	Overs	Mdns	Runs	Wkts	Avrge	5wi	10wm	Best
Alexander, WC	SA	4	5	–	166	95	1	–	33.20	2	–	–	–	–	–	–	–	–
Blackie, DD	VIC	6	5	–	9	3	–	–	1.80	7	184.1	53	398	21	18.95	1	–	5/27
Grimmett, CV	SA	6	6	1	136	59	1	–	27.20	4	319.5	65	795	47	16.91	5	1	7/92
Jackson, A	NSW	4	5	1	198	63	1	–	49.50	1	–	–	–	–	–	–	–	–
Kippax, AF	NSW	5	7	1	123	38	–	–	20.50	4	10.1	1	40	–	–	–	–	–
McNamee, RLA	NSW	4	3	–	16	12	–	–	5.33	4	160.0	52	247	15	16.47	1	–	5/12
Morton, FL	VIC	4	3	3	9	6*	–	–	–	–	98.1	26	230	7	32.86	–	–	3/24
Oldfield, WAS	NSW	6	6	–	181	137	–	1	30.17	9/3	–	–	–	–	–	–	–	–
Oxenham, RK	QLD	4	5	1	58	46*	–	–	14.50	2	139.0	41	236	10	23.60	–	–	4/39
Ponsford, WH	VIC	6	9	1	452	148	3	1	56.50	1	–	–	–	–	–	–	–	–
Richardson, VY (Capt)	SA	6	8	2	234	107	1	1	39.00	6	–	–	–	–	–	–	–	–
Schneider, KJ	SA	5	8	1	328	138	2	1	46.86	2	6.0	1	23	–	–	–	–	–
Woodfull, WM	VIC	6	9	3	781	284	2	3	130.17	5	–	–	–	–	–	–	–	–

1959/60 AUSTRALIANS

First-class Results					All Matches				
Matches	Won	Lost	Drawn	Tied	Matches	Won	Lost	Drawn	Tied
6	2	–	4	–	9	4	–	5	–

Date	Venue	Opponent	Results for Australians
Feb 12	Auckland	Auckland	Won by an inns & 109 runs
Feb 16	Hamilton	*Northern Districts	Drawn
Feb 19	Wellington	New Zealanders	Drawn
Feb 24	Nelson	*Nelson, Marlborough, Hutt Valley	Won by an inns & 109 runs
Feb 27	Christchurch	New Zealanders	Drawn
Mar 4	Dunedin	New Zealanders	Won by 8 wkts
Mar 9	Invercargill	*South Island Minor Associations	Won by an inns & 96 runs
Mar 12	Palmerston North	Central Districts	Drawn
Mar 18	Auckland	New Zealanders	Drawn

Player	State	M	Inn	NO	Runs	HS	50	100	Avrge	Ct/St	Overs	Mdns	Runs	Wkts	Avrge	5wi	10wm	Best
Booth, BC	NSW	5	7	–	289	105	1	1	41.28	1	42.0	19	75	3	25.00	–	–	2/29
Craig, ID (Capt)	NSW	5	9	–	256	70	1	–	28.44	4	–	–	–	–	–	–	–	–
Fisher, B	QLD	4	4	1	56	40	–	–	18.66	2	71.2	27	169	6	28.83	–	–	3/54
Gaunt, RA	WA	5	3	3	1	1*	–	–	–	2	198.0	58	423	15	30.13	1	–	5/90
Lill, JC	SA	3	5	–	22	15	–	–	4.40	2	–	–	–	–	–	–	–	–
Maddocks, LV	VIC	6	8	4	286	122*	1	1	71.50	7/3	–	–	–	–	–	–	–	–
Martin, JW	NSW	3	4	1	38	14	–	–	12.66	4	60.0	22	146	6	24.33	–	–	2/31
Misson, FM	NSW	3	4	–	5	2	–	–	1.25	1	127.0	43	212	17	13.17	–	–	4/35
Potter, J	VIC	4	3	–	89	55	1	–	29.66	2	16.0	6	22	–	–	–	–	–
Quick, IW	VIC	6	5	1	66	43	–	–	16.50	4	248.1	93	481	28	17.17	2	1	7/20
Shaw, JH	VIC	5	9	1	323	120	1	1	40.37	5	1.0	–	2	1	2.00	–	–	1/2
Simpson, RB	WA	6	10	3	518	129*	5	1	74.00	8	182.0	66	338	10	33.80	–	–	4/80
Slater, KN	WA	4	3	1	35	22	–	–	17.50	3	156.3	74	234	12	19.83	–	–	4/38
Thomas, G	NSW	4	7	1	162	60	1	–	27.00	9	1.0	–	1	–	–	–	–	–

1966/67 AUSTRALIANS

First-class Results					All Matches				
Matches	Won	Lost	Drawn	Tied	Matches	Won	Lost	Drawn	Tied
9	1	2	6	–	10	2	2	6	–

Date	Venue	Opponent	Results for Australians
Feb 15	Dunedin	*Otago	Won by 6 wkts
Feb 17	Christchurch	Canterbury	Lost by 4 wkts
Feb 21	Wellington	Wellington	Drawn
Feb 24	Auckland	Auckland	Won by 10 wkts
Feb 28	Palmerston North	Central Districts	Drawn
Mar 3	New Plymouth	New Zealanders	Lost by 159 runs
Mar 10	Dunedin	New Zealanders	Drawn
Mar 16	Christchurch	New Zealanders	Drawn
Mar 21	Hamilton	Northern Districts	Drawn
Mar 25	Auckland	New Zealanders	Drawn

AUSTRALIANS IN NEW ZEALAND

Player	State	M	Inn	NO	Runs	HS	50	100	Avrge	Ct/St	Overs	Mdns	Runs	Wkts	Avrge	5wi	10wm	Best
Bitmead, RC	VIC	5	4	1	11	4*	–	–	3.66	2	143.0	58	222	15	14.80	1	–	6/11
Booth, BC	NSW	9	13	1	569	214*	–	2	47.42	8	29.5	9	74	1	74.00	–	–	1/0
Burge, PJP	QLD	9	12	2	379	102	2	1	37.90	8/1	3.0	1	8	–	–	–	–	–
Connolly, AN	VIC	8	8	5	47	16*	–	–	15.66	7	314.5	102	647	24	26.96	2	–	5/61
Cunningham, KJ	SA	8	11	1	345	65	2	–	34.50	4	57.0	15	136	2	68.00	–	–	2/13
Davies, GR	NSW	8	9	–	303	91	2	–	37.00	6	144.0	32	372	20	18.60	–	–	4/20
Favell, LE (Capt)	SA	10	15	–	272	59	1	–	18.13	6	12.0	1	32	–	–	–	–	–
Freeman, EW	SA	7	9	1	161	47	–	–	20.13	3	174.2	40	464	12	38.67	–	–	4/62
Frost, AR	SA	6	8	1	52	27	–	–	7.43	2	132.5	20	334	16	20.87	1	–	5/28
Gleeson, JW	NSW	8	10	4	144	59	1	–	24.00	5	294.3	76	744	26	28.61	–	–	4/53
Jarman, BN	SA	9	12	2	330	127*	1	1	33.00	18/9	11.0	1	25	1	25.00	–	–	1/17
O'Neill, NC	NSW	7	12	1	340	101	1	1	30.91	2	5.0	1	18	–	–	–	–	–
Philpott, PI	NSW	8	10	2	279	89	2	–	34.25	4	227.2	51	587	23	25.52	1	–	5/45
Sheahan, AP	VIC	8	11	1	324	135	1	1	32.40	6	5.0	1	12	–	–	–	–	–

1969/70 AUSTRALIANS

First-class Results					All Matches				
Matches	Won	Lost	Drawn	Tied	Matches	Won	Lost	Drawn	Tied
8	2	–	6	–	8	2	–	6	–

Date	Venue	Opponent	Results for Australians
Feb 20	Christchurch	Canterbury	Drawn
Feb 26	Dunedin	Otago	Won by an inns & 50 runs
Mar 2	Napier	New Zealand Under 23's	Won by an inns & 20 runs
Mar 6	Auckland	New Zealanders	Drawn
Mar 12	Christchurch	New Zealanders	Drawn
Mar 17	Hamilton	Northern Districts	Drawn
Mar 21	New Plymouth	Central Districts	Drawn
Mar 28	Wellington	New Zealanders	Drawn

Player	State	M	Inn	NO	Runs	HS	50	100	Avrge	Ct/St	Overs	Mdns	Runs	Wkts	Avrge	5wi	10wm	Best
Chadwick, D	WA	7	11	–	196	56	1	–	17.81	5	–	–	–	–	–	–	–	–
Chappell, GS	SA	7	11	2	519	94	5	–	57.66	9	74.0	23	185	7	26.43	–	–	2/20
Davies, GR	NSW	7	8	2	351	105*	3	1	58.50	3	39.6	6	138	5	27.60	–	–	4/42
Inverarity, RJ	WA	7	10	1	376	117	1	2	37.60	7	26.0	8	70	5	14.00	1	–	5/28
Jenner, TJ	SA	7	7	1	100	26*	–	–	16.66	–	214.2	52	625	32	19.53	1	–	7/84
Lillee, DK	WA	5	4	3	66	26*	–	–	66.00	4	92.4	16	296	18	16.44	1	–	6/40
Maclean, JA	QLD	7	8	4	122	43*	–	–	30.50	19/–	–	–	–	–	–	–	–	–
O'Keeffe, KJ	NSW	6	5	1	47	28	–	–	11.75	2	171.1	43	511	22	23.23	–	–	4/62
Renneberg, DA	NSW	6	4	2	8	5*	–	–	4.00	4	119.3	24	421	13	32.39	–	–	3/42
Steele, JA	NSW	6	8	1	225	83	1	–	32.14	7/2	–	–	–	–	–	–	–	–
Thomson, AL	VIC	5	4	1	13	6	–	–	4.33	1	110.0	19	357	12	20.75	–	–	3/82
Trimble, SC (Capt)	QLD	7	10	–	555	213	3	1	55.50	5	–	–	–	–	–	–	–	–
Turner, A	NSW	4	6	–	117	34	–	–	19.50	1	–	–	–	–	–	–	–	–
Watson, GD	VIC	7	8	2	142	42*	–	–	22.66	6	102.0	36	235	8	29.37	–	–	2/15

1976/77 AUSTRALIANS

First-class Results					All Matches				
Matches	Won	Lost	Drawn	Tied	Matches	Won	Lost	Drawn	Tied
6	5	–	1	–	8	5	2	1	–

Date	Venue	Opponent	Results for Australians
Jan 30	Christchurch	*Invitation XI	Lost by 6 wkts
Jan 31	Auckland	*Invitation XI	Lost by 12 runs
Feb 1	Hamilton	Northern Districts	Won by 113 runs
Feb 5	Wellington	Wellington	Won by 50 runs
Feb 8	Nelson	Central Districts	Won by 65 runs
Feb 12	Dunedin	Otago	Won by 48 runs
Feb 18	Christchurch	NEW ZEALAND (1st Test)	Drawn
Feb 25	Auckland	NEW ZEALAND (2nd Test)	Won by 10 wkts

Player	State	M	Inn	NO	Runs	HS	50	100	Avrge	Ct/St	Overs	Mdns	Runs	Wkts	Avrge	5wi	10wm	Best
Bright, RJ	VIC	4	4	–	68	30	–	–	17.00	4	105.5	32	366	25	14.64	2	–	5/5
Chappell, GS (Capt)	QLD	5	9	1	333	130	1	1	37.00	8	35.0	8	85	2	42.50	–	–	1/15
Cosier, GJ	SA	5	9	–	308	93	2	–	34.22	3	7.0	1	18	2	9.00	–	–	2/18
Davis, IC	NSW	6	12	1	371	68	3	–	33.72	3	–	–	–	–	–	–	–	–
Gilmour, GJ	NSW	4	5	–	200	101	1	1	40.00	5	56.0	6	292	3	97.33	–	–	1/28
Hughes, KJ	WA	3	6	–	106	76	1	–	17.66	3	–	–	–	–	–	–	–	–
Hurst, AG	VIC	3	2	2	18	18*	–	–	–	3	43.0	8	218	3	72.66	–	–	2/38
Lillee, DK	WA	4	4	1	54	23*	–	–	13.50	3	123.4	24	392	23	17.04	2	1	6/72
Marsh, RW	WA	6	10	3	115	46	–	–	16.42	19/3	–	–	–	–	–	–	–	–

Continued

Player	State	M	Inn	NO	Runs	HS	50	100	Avrge	Ct/St	Overs	Mdns	Runs	Wkts	Avrge	5wi	10wm	Best
McCosker, RB	NSW	5	9	2	415	135*	2	1	59.28	6	–	–	–	–	–	–	–	–
O'Keeffe, KJ	NSW	6	8	1	110	36	–	–	15.71	4	150.3	41	568	35	16.22	5	2	6/50
Turner, A	NSW	5	10	1	184	37	–	–	20.44	6	–	–	–	–	–	–	–	–
Walker, MHN	VIC	5	5	3	49	20	–	–	24.50	1	149.0	32	397	22	18.04	–	–	4/65
Walters, KD	NSW	5	9	4	441	250	2	1	88.20	5	4.0	1	20	1	20.00	–	–	1/20

1985/86 AUSTRALIANS

First-class Results					All Matches				
Matches	Won	Lost	Drawn	Tied	Matches	Won	Lost	Drawn	Tied
5	1	1	3	–	11	5	3	3	–

Date	Venue	Opponent	Results for Australians
Feb 15	Auckland	*Auckland	Won by 6 wkts
Feb 16	Hamilton	Northern Districts	Won by 4 wkts
Feb 21	Wellington	NEW ZEALAND (1st Test)	Drawn
Feb 28	Christchurch	NEW ZEALAND (2nd Test)	Drawn
Mar 6	Nelson	*Nelson	Won by 82 runs
Mar 8	New Plymouth	Central Districts	Drawn
Mar 13	Auckland	NEW ZEALAND (3rd Test)	Lost by 8 wkts
Mar 19	Dunedin	*New Zealand (L/O Intl)	Lost by 30 runs
Mar 22	Christchurch	*New Zealand (L/O Intl)	Lost by 53 runs
Mar 26	Wellington	*New Zealand (L/O Intl)	Won by 3 wkts
Mar 29	Auckland	*New Zealand (L/O Intl)	Won by 44 runs

Player	State	M	Inn	NO	Runs	HS	50	100	Avrge	Ct/St	Overs	Mdns	Runs	Wkts	Avrge	5wi	10wm	Best
Boon, DC	TAS	4	7	1	302	119	2	1	50.33	1	–	–	–	–	–	–	–	–
Border, AR (Capt)	QLD	4	6	1	357	140	1	2	71.40	3	4.0	3	1	–	–	–	–	–
Bright, RJ	VIC	4	7	1	82	21*	–	–	13.67	1	116.2	33	307	9	34.11	1	–	5/42
Davis, SP	VIC	3	3	2	3	2*	–	–	3.00	1	71.0	13	214	3	71.33	–	–	1/23
Gilbert, DR	NSW	2	2	–	15	15	–	–	7.50	–	51.0	11	184	3	61.33	–	–	2/106
Marsh, GR	WA	5	8	1	349	118	–	2	49.86	3	–	–	–	–	–	–	–	–
Matthews, GRJ	NSW	5	8	1	223	130	1	1	31.86	5	153.0	52	388	12	32.33	–	–	4/61
McDermott, CJ	QLD	3	5	–	40	19	–	–	8.00	1	79.3	15	240	6	40.00	–	–	3/61
Phillips, WB	SA	5	9	–	261	62	1	–	29.00	2	2.0	–	6	–	–	–	–	–
Reid, BA	WA	5	6	4	54	28*	–	–	27.00	1	132.4	24	372	13	28.62	–	–	4/25
Ritchie, GM	QLD	5	8	1	292	92	3	–	41.71	1	–	–	–	–	–	–	–	–
Waugh, SR	NSW	5	7	–	124	74	1	–	17.71	4	53.0	12	149	7	21.29	–	–	4/56
Zoehrer, TJ	WA	5	8	–	172	71	1	–	21.50	7/2	–	–	–	–	–	–	–	–

1986/87 NEW SOUTH WALES

First-class Results					All Matches				
Matches	Won	Lost	Drawn	Tied	Matches	Won	Lost	Drawn	Tied
–	–	–	–	–	2	1	1	–	–

Date	Venue	Opponent	Results for Australians
Nov 29	Wellington	*Wellington	Won by 105 runs
Nov 30	Wellington	*Auckland	Lost on run rate

1989/90 AUSTRALIANS

First-class Results					All Matches				
Matches	Won	Lost	Drawn	Tied	Matches	Won	Lost	Drawn	Tied
1	–	1	–	–	6	5	–	1	–

Date	Venue	Opponent	Results for Australians
Mar 3	Christchurch	*India (L/O Intl)	Won by 18 runs
Mar 4	Christchurch	*New Zealand (L/O Intl)	Won by 150 runs
Mar 8	Hamilton	*India (L/O Intl)	Won by 7 wkts
Mar 10	Auckland	*New Zealand (L/O Intl)	Won on run rate
Mar 11	Auckland	*New Zealand (L/O Intl)	Won by 8 wkts
Mar 15	Wellington	NEW ZEALAND (Only Test)	Lost by 9 wkts

Player	State	M	Inn	NO	Runs	HS	50	100	Avrge	Ct/St	Overs	Mdns	Runs	Wkts	Avrge	5wi	10wm	Best
Alderman, TM	WA	1	2	–	5	4	–	–	2.50	–	43.0	17	73	4	18.25	–	–	4/46
Boon, DC	TAS	1	2	–	12	12	–	–	6.00	–	–	–	–	–	–	–	–	–
Border, AR (Capt)	QLD	1	2	1	79	78*	1	–	79.00	1	16.4	8	39	1	39.00	–	–	1/12
Campbell, GD	TAS	1	2	–	4	4	–	–	2.00	–	28.0	5	74	3	24.67	–	–	2/51
Healy, IA	QLD	1	2	–	10	10	–	–	5.00	4/–	–	–	–	–	–	–	–	–

Continued

AUSTRALIANS IN PAKISTAN

Player	State	M	Inn	NO	Runs	HS	50	100	Avrge	Ct/St	Overs	Mdns	Runs	Wkts	Avrge	5wi	10wm	Best
Jones, DM	VIC	1	2	–	20	20	–	–	10.00	–	6.0	3	14	–	–	–	–	–
Marsh, GR	WA	1	2	–	45	41	–	–	22.50	1	–	–	–	–	–	–	–	–
Rackemann, CG	QLD	1	2	1	7	6*	–	–	7.00	–	47.0	21	81	–	–	–	–	–
Taylor, PL	NSW	1	2	–	116	87	1	–	58.00	–	44.0	22	83	3	27.67	–	–	3/44
Taylor, MA	NSW	1	2	–	9	5	–	–	4.50	2	–	–	–	–	–	–	–	–
Waugh, SR	NSW	1	2	–	50	25	–	–	25.00	–	–	–	–	–	–	–	–	–

1991/92 AUSTRALIANS

First-class Results					All Matches			
Matches	Won	Lost	Drawn	Tied	Matches	Won	Lost	Drawn	Tied
–	–	–	–	–	2	1	1	–	–

Date	Venue	Opponent	Results for Australians
Feb 21	Auckland	*Auckland	Won by 62 runs
Feb 22	Auckland	*New Zealand (WC L/O Intl)	Lost by 37 runs

1994/95 AUSTRALIAN CRICKET ACADEMY IN NEW ZEALAND

First-class Results					All Matches			
Matches	Won	Lost	Drawn	Tied	Matches	Won	Lost	Drawn	Tied
1	1	–	–	–	6	6	–	–	–

Date	Venue	Opponent	Results for Australians
Mar 23	Auckland	*Auckland Emerging Players	Won by 7 wkts
Mar 26	Auckland	*Auckland Emerging Players	Won by 7 wkts
Mar 28	Wellington	*Wellington Invitation XI	Won by 378 runs
Mar 31	Wellington	*Wellington Invitation XI	Won by 6 wkts
Apr 2	Hamilton	New Zealand Cricket Academy	Won by 10 wkts
Apr 6	Hamilton	*New Zealand Cricket Academy	Won by 70 runs

(Averages for all matches)

Player	M	Inn	NO	Runs	HS	50	100	Avrge	Ct/St	Overs	Mdns	Runs	Wkts	Avrge	5wi	10wm	Best
Allanby, RA	5	5	2	178	131*	–	1	59.33	3	7.1	–	34	1	34.00	–	–	1/12
Arnold, EMC	4	5	2	95	49*	–	–	31.66	3	41.5	8	161	7	23.00	–	–	3/0
Ashley, NW (Capt)	6	8	1	343	63	4	–	49.00	3	–	–	–	–	–	–	–	–
Baker, RM	6	8	–	335	79	4	–	41.87	1	59.5	13	168	11	15.27	1	–	6/53
Campbell, RJ	6	9	1	438	118	3	1	54.75	10/5	2.0	–	6	1	6.00	–	–	1/6
Glassock, CA	4	5	1	132	72	1	–	33.00	8/2	–	–	–	–	–	–	–	–
Harvey, IJ	6	5	1	147	70	1	–	36.75	4	86.1	28	212	12	17.66	–	–	3/39
Harvey, KM	5	4	–	123	79	1	–	30.75	8	16.1	2	67	4	16.75	–	–	2/9
Howard, C	6	3	–	10	8	–	–	3.33	4	96.3	29	292	21	13.90	1	–	6/37
Lee, B	5	3	2	10	6	–	–	10.00	2	61.0	6	294	10	29.40	–	–	3/46
Swain, BA	5	2	1	26	17*	–	–	26.00	–	61.0	13	207	8	25.87	–	–	3/20
Symonds, A	6	8	3	290	115	1	1	58.00	4	46.0	9	145	1	145.00	–	–	1/16
Wilson, P	2	1	1	15	15*	–	–	–	–	47.0	9	189	7	27.00	–	–	4/27

AUSTRALIAN CRICKET TEAMS IN PAKISTAN

Season	Touring Team	First-class Games					All Games					Captain
		P	W	L	D	T	P	W	L	D	T	
1956/57	Australians	1	–	1	–	–	1	–	1	–	–	IW Johnson
1959/60	Australians	4	3	–	1	–	4	3	–	1	–	R Benaud
1964/65	Australians	1	–	–	1	–	1	–	–	1	–	RB Simpson
1979/80	Australians	5	–	1	4	–	5	–	1	4	–	GS Chappell
1982/83	Australians	6	–	3	3	–	9	–	5	4	–	KJ Hughes
1987/88	Australians	–	–	–	–	–	1	–	1	–	–	AR Border
1988/89	Australians	6	–	1	5	–	7	–	2	5	–	AR Border
1994/95	Australians	4	–	1	3	–	10	5	2	3	–	MA Taylor
		27	3	7	17	–	38	9	11	18	–	

FIRST-CLASS RESULTS

Opponent	Venue	First Game	Games	W	L	D	T
PAKISTAN	Karachi	Oct 11 1956	7	–	5	2	–
	Dacca	Nov 13 1959	1	–	1	–	–
	Lahore	Nov 21 1959	5	1	1	3	–
	Faisalabad	Mar 6 1980	3	–	1	2	–
	Rawalpindi	Oct 5 1994	1	–	–	1	–
			17	2	7	8	–

AUSTRALIANS IN PAKISTAN

Opponent	Venue	First Game	Games	W	L	D	T
BCCP Invitation XI	Sialkot	Oct 10 1982	1	–	–	1	–
BCCP Patron's XI	Rawalpindi	Sep 12 1982	1	–	–	1	–
	Lahore	Sep 5 1988	1	–	–	1	–
			2	–	–	2	–
Governor's XI	Multan	Mar 13 1980	1	–	–	1	–
	Quetta	Sep 9 1988	1	–	–	1	–
			2	–	–	2	–
NW Frontier Province XI	Peshawar	Oct 2 1988	1	–	–	1	–
Pakistan XI	Multan	Sep 16 1982	1	–	–	1	–
President's XI	Rawalpindi	Nov 28 1959	3	1	–	2	–

1956/57 AUSTRALIANS

First-class Results					All Matches			
Matches	Won	Lost	Drawn	Tied	Matches	Won	Lost	Drawn	Tied
1	–	1	–	–	1	–	1	–	–

Date	Venue	Opponent	Results for Australians
Oct 11	Karachi	PAKISTAN (Only Test)	Lost by 9 wkts

Player	State	M	Inn	NO	Runs	HS	50	100	Avrge	Ct/St	Overs	Mdns	Runs	Wkts	Avrge	5wi	10wm	Best
Archer, RG	QLD	1	2	–	37	27	–	–	18.50	–	7.5	3	19	1	19.00	–	–	1/18
Benaud, R	NSW	1	2	–	60	56	1	–	56.00	–	17.0	5	36	1	36.00	–	–	1/36
Burke, JW	NSW	1	2	–	14	10	–	–	7.00	–	–	–	–	–	–	–	–	–
Craig, ID	NSW	1	2	–	18	18	–	–	9.00	–	–	–	–	–	–	–	–	–
Davidson, AK	NSW	1	2	–	40	37	–	–	37.00	–	15.0	9	15	2	7.50	–	–	1/06
Harvey, RN	VIC	1	2	–	6	4	–	–	3.00	1	–	–	–	–	–	–	–	–
Johnson, IW (Capt)	VIC	1	2	1	13	13*	–	–	13.00	1	28.2	5	66	4	16.50	–	–	4/50
Langley, GRA	SA	1	2	1	14	13*	–	–	14.00	3/–	–	–	–	–	–	–	–	–
Lindwall, RR	QLD	1	2	–	2	2	–	–	1.00	1	43.0	16	64	1	64.00	–	–	1/42
McDonald, CC	VIC	1	2	–	20	12	–	–	10.00	1	–	–	–	–	–	–	–	–
Miller, KR	NSW	1	2	–	32	21	–	–	16.00	–	29.0	9	58	2	29.00	–	–	2/40

1964/65 AUSTRALIANS

First-class Results					All Matches			
Matches	Won	Lost	Drawn	Tied	Matches	Won	Lost	Drawn	Tied
1	–	–	1	–	1	–	–	1	–

Date	Venue	Opponent	Results for Australians
Oct 24	Karachi	PAKISTAN (Only Test)	Drawn

Player	State	M	Inn	NO	Runs	HS	50	100	Avrge	Ct/St	Overs	Mdns	Runs	Wkts	Avrge	5wi	10wm	Best
Booth, BC	NSW	1	1	–	15	15	–	–	15.00	1	18.0	6	33	1	33.00	–	–	1/18
Burge, PJP	QLD	1	2	1	82	54	1	–	82.00	–	–	–	–	–	–	–	–	–
Cowper, RM	VIC	1	1	–	16	16	–	–	16.00	–	11.0	3	36	1	36.00	–	–	1/36
Grout, ATW	QLD	1	1	–	0	0	–	–	0.00	5/–	–	–	–	–	–	–	–	–
Hawke, NJN	SA	1	1	1	8	8*	–	–	–	–	26.0	4	104	1	104.00	–	–	1/84
Lawry, WM	VIC	1	2	–	29	22	–	–	14.50	–	–	–	–	–	–	–	–	–
Martin, JW	NSW	1	1	–	26	26	–	–	26.00	–	53.0	15	148	3	49.33	–	–	2/106
McKenzie, GD	WA	1	1	–	2	2	–	–	2.00	2	55.0	14	131	8	16.38	1	–	6/69
Redpath, IR	VIC	1	2	1	59	40*	–	–	59.00	3	1.0	–	14	–	–	–	–	–
Simpson, RB (Capt)	NSW	1	2	–	268	153	–	2	134.00	1	50.0	13	116	1	116.00	–	–	1/47
Veivers, TR	QLD	1	1	–	25	25	–	–	25.00	–	46.0	21	77	2	38.50	–	–	2/44

1987/88 AUSTRALIANS

First-class Results					All Matches			
Matches	Won	Lost	Drawn	Tied	Matches	Won	Lost	Drawn	Tied
–	–	–	–	–	1	1	–	–	–

Date	Venue	Opponent	Results for Australians
Nov 4	Lahore	*Pakistan (WC L/O Intl)	Won by 18 runs

AUSTRALIAN CRICKET TEAMS IN SOUTH AFRICA

Season	Touring Team	First-class Games					All Games					Captain
		P	W	L	D	T	P	W	L	D	T	
1902/03	Australians	4	3	–	1	–	6	3	–	3	–	J Darling
1919/20	AIF Team	8	6	–	2	–	10	8	–	2	–	HL Collins
1921/22	Australians	6	4	–	2	–	6	4	–	2	–	WW Armstrong
1935/36	Australians	16	13	–	3	–	16	13	–	3	–	VY Richardson
1949/50	Australians	21	14	–	7	–	25	18	–	7	–	AL Hassett
1957/58	Australians	20	11	–	9	–	22	11	–	11	–	ID Craig
1966/67	Australians	17	7	5	5	–	24	11	6	7	–	RB Simpson
1969/70	Australians	12	4	4	4	–	12	4	4	4	–	WM Lawry
1985/86	Australians	10	2	2	6	–	25	10	9	6	–	KJ Hughes
1986/87	Australians	12	2	3	7	–	25	8	9	8	–	KJ Hughes
1993/94	Australians	6	3	1	2	–	16	7	5	4	–	AR Border
		132	69	15	48	–	187	97	33	57	–	

FIRST-CLASS RESULTS

Opponent	Venue	First Game	Games	W	L	D	T
SOUTH AFRICA	Johannesburg	Oct 11 1902	16	6	4	6	–
	Cape Town	Nov 8 1902	9	6	1	2	–
	Durban	Nov 5 1921	9	3	2	4	–
	Port Elizabeth	Mar 3 1950	6	2	2	2	–
			40	17	9	14	–
Boland	Stellenbosch	Dec 17 1985	1	–	–	1	
Border	East London	Jan 11 1936	7	5	–	2	
Eastern Province	Port Elizabeth	Jan 7 1936	7	5	1	1	
Griqualand West	Kimberley	Jan 31 1936	5	3	–	2	
NE Transvaal	Benoni	Nov 5 1949	2	1	–	1	
	Pretoria	Feb 4 1950	4	3	–	1	
	Verwoerdburg	Jan 24 1987	1	–	–	1	
			7	4	–	3	
Natal	Durban	Oct 29 1921	8	4	–	4	
	Pietermaritzburg	Feb 24 1950	4	1	1	2	
			12	5	1	6	
Orange Free State	Bloemfontein	Jan 18 1936	7	3	–	4	
President's XI	Pretoria	Nov 29 1985	2	1	1	–	
Rhodesia	Salisbury	Oct 25 1957	2	2	–	–	
	Bulawayo	Nov 5 1966	1	1	–	–	
			3	3	–	–	
South Africa Universities	Cape Town	Mar 8 1958	1	–	–	1	
	Pretoria	Dec 17 1966	1	–	–	1	
	Pietermaritzburg	Jan 13 1987	1	–	–	1	
			3	–	–	3	
South Africans	Salisbury	Nov 19 1949	1	1	–	–	
	Durban	Dec 16 1949	1	–	–	1	
	Johannesburg	Mar 17 1950	1	1	–	–	
	Pretoria	Nov 15 1957	1	1	–	–	
	East London	Dec 2 1966	1	–	1	–	
	Pietermaritzburg	Feb 17 1967	1	–	–	1	
			6	3	1	2	–
South African Inv. XI	Kingsmead	Jan 17 1987	1	–	–	1	
Southern Rhodesia	Bulawayo	Feb 8 1936	2	1	–	1	
Transvaal	Johannesburg	Oct 22 1921	11	7	1	3	–
Western Province	Cape Town	Nov 5 1902	12	8	–	4	–

1985/86 AUSTRALIANS

First-class Results					All Matches				
Matches	Won	Lost	Drawn	Tied	Matches	Won	Lost	Drawn	Tied
10	2	2	6	–	25	10	9	6	–

Date	Venue	Opponent	Results for Australians
Nov 9	Nelspruit	*N Transvaal Cntry Districts	Won by 152 runs
Nov 16	Virginia	*Free State Country Districts	Won by 208 runs
Nov 18	Orkney	*Transvaal Country Districts	Won by 49 runs
Nov 22	Bloemfontein	Orange Free State	Drawn
Nov 27	Pretoria	*Northern Transvaal	Lost by 7 runs
Nov 29	Pretoria	President's XI	Won by 5 wkts
Dec 4	Johannesburg	*Transvaal	Lost by 58 runs
Dec 6	East London	Border	Drawn
Dec 11	Port Elizabeth	*Eastern Province	Won by 5 runs
Dec 13	Port Elizabeth	Eastern Province	Lost by 2 wkts
Dec 17	Stellenbosch	Boland	Drawn
Dec 21	Cape Town	*Western Province	Won by 48 runs
Dec 23	Durban	*Natal	Won by 28 runs
Dec 26	Durban	South Africans	Drawn
Jan 1	Cape Town	South Africans	Drawn
Jan 6	Port Elizabeth	South African Universities	Drawn
Jan 10	Pretoria	Northern Transvaal	Won by 25 runs
Jan 16	Johannesburg	South Africans	Lost by 188 runs
Jan 24	Johannesburg	*South Africans	Won by 46 runs
Jan 26	Durban	*South Africans	Won by 4 wkts
Jan 28	Port Elizabeth	*South Africans	Lost by 72 runs
Jan 30	Cape Town	*South Africans	Lost by 24 runs
Feb 1	Johannesburg	*South Africans	Lost by 5 wkts
Feb 3	Kimberley	*Griqualand West	Lost by 6 wkts
Feb 5	Pretoria	*South Africans	Lost by 6 wkts

AUSTRALIANS IN SOUTH AFRICA

Player	State	M	Inn	NO	Runs	HS	50	100	Avrge	Ct/St	Overs	Mdns	Runs	Wkts	Avrge	5wi	10wm	Best
Alderman, TM	WA	6	6	3	24	19	–	–	8.00	7	200.5	50	499	23	21.70	–	–	4/114
Dyson, J	NSW	8	15	2	577	141	4	1	44.38	7	–	–	–	–	–	–	–	–
Faulkner, PI	TAS	5	8	2	226	109	–	1	37.67	1	107.0	17	333	11	30.27	–	–	3/45
Haysman, MD	SA	8	13	2	326	125*	–	1	29.64	10	22.0	5	84	–	–	–	–	–
Hogan, TG	WA	7	7	–	169	63	2	–	24.14	10	206.0	50	618	16	38.63	1	–	8/86
Hogg, RM	VIC	6	6	2	34	13	–	–	8.50	–	172.0	39	520	21	24.76	1	–	5/83
Hohns, TV	QLD	6	8	–	206	90	1	–	25.75	1	116.5	24	395	9	43.89	–	–	3/69
Hughes, KJ (Capt)	WA	9	16	3	585	116	4	1	45.00	7	–	–	–	–	–	–	–	–
Maguire, JN	QLD	6	7	3	52	20	–	–	13.00	1	183.3	31	547	20	27.35	2	–	5/58
McCurdy, RJ	SA	4	4	1	36	17	–	–	12.00	–	96.0	8	376	14	26.86	1	–	5/85
Rackemann, CG	QLD	7	6	–	31	11	–	–	5.17	1	256.4	32	848	39	21.74	2	1	8/84
Rixon, SJ	NSW	8	11	3	126	28	–	–	15.75	34/2	–	–	–	–	–	–	–	–
Shipperd, G	WA	8	15	1	397	79	2	–	28.36	8/1	–	–	–	–	–	–	–	–
Smith, SB	NSW	6	9	–	394	116	–	2	43.78	2	–	–	–	–	–	–	–	–
Taylor, MD	VIC	9	15	3	668	109	3	3	55.67	7	–	–	–	–	–	–	–	–
Yallop, GN	VIC	7	11	1	272	62	2	–	27.20	3	1.0	1	0	–	–	–	–	–

1986/87 AUSTRALIANS

First-class Results				All Matches				
Matches	Won	Lost	Drawn	Tied	Matches	Won	Lost	Drawn	Tied
12	2	3	7	–	25	8	9	8	–

Date	Venue	Opponent	Results for Australians
Nov 14	Oudsshoorn	*Southern Cape	Won by 131 runs
Nov 15	Oudtshoorn	*Southern Cape Invitation XI	Won by 95 runs
Nov 17	Stellenbosch	*Boland	Won by 2 runs
Nov 18	Stellenbosch	*Boland Invitation XI	Lost by 3 wkts
Nov 21	Bloemfontein	Orange Free State	Drawn
Nov 25	Kimberley	*Griqualand West	Won by 80 runs
Nov 27	Virginia	President's XI	Lost by 3 wkts
Dec 2	East London	Border	Drawn
Dec 6	Verwoerdburg	*South Africans	Lost by 6 wkts
Dec 8	Johannesburg	*South Africans	Drawn
Dec 10	Cape Town	*South Africans	Lost by 8 wkts
Dec 12	Port Elizabeth	Eastern Province	Won by an inns & 84 runs
Dec 17	Durban	*South Africans	Won by 6 wkts
Dec 19	Durban	Natal	Lost by 6 wkts
Dec 24	Johannesburg	South Africans	Lost by 49 runs
Jan 1	Cape Town	South Africans	Drawn
Jan 9	East London	South African Invitation XI	Won by an inns & 46 runs
Jan 13	Pietermaritzburg	South African Universities	Drawn
Jan 17	Durban	South Africans	Drawn
Jan 24	Verwoerdburg	Northern Transvaal	Drawn
Jan 30	Port Elizabeth	South Africans	Drawn
Feb 7	Port Elizabeth	*South Africans	Lost by 6 runs
Feb 10	Cape Town	*South Africans	Lost by 8 wkts
Feb 12	Verwoerdburg	*South Africans	Won by 5 wkts
Feb 14	Johannesburg	*South Africans	Lost by 4 wkts

Player	State	M	Inn	NO	Runs	HS	50	100	Avrge	Ct/St	Overs	Mdns	Runs	Wkts	Avrge	5wi	10wm	Best
Alderman, TM	WA	6	2	–	14	13	–	–	7.00	4	174.0	27	590	18	32.77	–	–	4/24
Dyson, J	NSW	8	12	2	522	198	2	2	52.20	3	1.0	1	0	–	–	–	–	–
Faulkner, PI	TAS	7	9	–	183	55	1	–	20.33	1	123.5	23	353	7	50.42	1	–	5/49
Haysman, MD	SA	9	14	2	738	180	2	3	61.50	14	1.0	1	0	–	–	–	–	–
Hogan, TG	WA	6	7	4	101	34*	–	–	33.66	3	174.0	64	394	10	39.40	–	–	3/28
Hogg, RM	VIC	6	4	–	15	9	–	–	3.75	2	180.0	41	443	22	20.13	1	–	5/97
Hohns, TV	QLD	9	11	3	257	50*	1	–	32.12	8	327.5	81	819	33	24.81	2	–	6/98
Hughes, KJ (Capt)	WA	10	15	1	596	100	3	1	42.57	4	–	–	–	–	–	–	–	–
Maguire, JN	QLD	8	10	2	64	20	–	–	8.00	2	282.2	65	762	33	23.09	2	–	7/46
McCurdy, RJ	SA	7	8	5	24	11*	–	–	8.00	–	263.1	47	815	22	37.04	1	–	6/67
Rackemann, CG	QLD	8	5	1	28	12	–	–	7.00	1	236.4	43	758	16	47.37	–	–	3/54
Rixon, SJ	NSW	9	11	1	268	61	2	–	26.80	34/2	–	–	–	–	–	–	–	–
Shipperd, G	WA	8	12	5	523	110*	5	1	74.71	11/1	–	–	–	–	–	–	–	–
Smith, SB	NSW	9	14	1	769	137	3	3	59.15	5	8.0	1	27	–	–	–	–	–
Taylor, MD	VIC	8	12	1	306	64	2	–	27.81	2	–	–	–	–	–	–	–	–
Wessels, KC	QLD	6	9	1	541	137	1	3	67.62	4	12.0	6	18	1	18.00	–	–	1/18
Yallop, GN	VIC	8	11	2	552	182*	2	1	61.33	5	32.0	8	104	3	34.66	–	–	2/48

AUSTRALIAN CRICKET TEAMS IN SRI LANKA

Season	Touring Team	First-class Games					All Games					Captain
		P	W	L	D	T	P	W	L	D	T	
1913/14	New South Wales	–	–	–	–	–	9	8	1	–	–	Rev RF Waddy
1935/36	FA Tarrant's XI	1	1	–	–	–	1	1	–	–	–	J Ryder
1945/46	Services XI	1	1	–	–	–	1	1	–	–	–	AL Hassett
1969/70	Australians	1	–	–	1	–	4	1	–	3	–	WM Lawry
1980/81	Australians	1	–	–	1	–	4	2	1	1	–	KJ Hughes
1982/83	Australians	2	1	–	1	–	6	1	2	3	–	KJ Hughes
1992/93	Australians	5	1	–	4	–	8	2	2	4	–	AR Border
1994/95	Australians	–	–	–	–	–	3	1	2	–	–	MA Taylor
		11	4	–	7	–	36	17	8	11	–	

FIRST-CLASS RESULTS

Opponent	Venue	First Game	Games	W	L	D	T
SRI LANKA	Kandy	Apr 22 1982	1	1	–	–	–
	Colombo (SSC)	Aug 17 1992	1	1	–	–	–
	Colombo (PIS)	Aug 28 1992	1	–	–	1	–
	Moratuwa	Sep 8 1992	1	–	–	1	–
			4	2	–	2	–
Board President's XI	Moratuwa	Apr 17 1983	1	–	–	1	–
	Kandy	Aug 10 1992	1	–	–	1	–
			2	–	–	2	–
Ceylon	Colombo (SSC)	Oct 25 1935	1	1	–	–	–
	Colombo Oval	Dec 14 1945	2	1	–	1	–
			3	2	–	1	–
Southern Districts XI	Matara	Aug 24 1992	1	–	–	1	–
Sri Lankans	Colombo (PSS)	May 7 1981	1	–	–	1	–

1935/36 AUSTRALIANS IN CEYLON

First-class Results					All Matches				
Matches	Won	Lost	Drawn	Tied	Matches	Won	Lost	Drawn	Tied
1	1	–	–	–	1	1	–	–	–

Date	Venue	Opponent	Results for Australians
Oct 25	Colombo (SSC)	Ceylon	Won by an inns & 127 runs

Player	State	M	Inn	NO	Runs	HS	50	100	Avrge	Ct/St	Overs	Mdns	Runs	Wkts	Avrge	5wi	10wm	Best
Bill, OW	NSW	1	1	–	101	101	–	1	101.00	–	–	–	–	–	–	–	–	–
Ellis, JL	VIC	1	1	–	6	6	–	–	6.00	1/1	–	–	–	–	–	–	–	–
Hendry, HSTL	VIC	1	1	–	8	8	–	–	8.00	1	3.0	3	0	–	–	–	–	–
Ironmonger, H	VIC	1	1	1	0	0*	–	–	–	–	14.0	3	42	3	14.00	–	–	2/23
Leather, TW	VIC	1	1	–	0	0	–	–	0.00	1	7.0	2	23	–	–	–	–	–
Macartney, CG	NSW	1	1	–	53	53	1	–	53.00	–	3.0	2	4	1	4.00	–	–	1/4
Mair, F	NSW	1	1	–	24	24	–	–	24.00	–	12.0	2	44	2	22.00	–	–	2/28
Morrisby, ROG	TAS	1	1	–	2	2	–	–	2.00	–	–	–	–	–	–	–	–	–
Nagel, LE	VIC	1	1	–	40	40	–	–	40.00	–	8.0	2	21	2	10.50	–	–	2/11
Oxenham, RK	QLD	1	1	–	22	22	–	–	22.00	–	17.0	6	48	11	4.36	1	1	9/35
Ryder, J (Capt)	VIC	1	1	–	67	67	1	–	67.00	–	2.0	–	18	1	18.00	–	–	1/18

1945/46 AUSTRALIAN SERVICES

First-class Results					All Matches				
Matches	Won	Lost	Drawn	Tied	Matches	Won	Lost	Drawn	Tied
1	1	–	–	–	1	1	–	–	–

Date	Venue	Opponent	Results for Australians
Dec 14	Colombo	Ceylon	Won by an inns & 44 runs

Player	M	Inn	NO	Runs	HS	50	100	Avrge	Ct/St	Overs	Mdns	Runs	Wkts	Avrge	5wi	10wm	Best
Cristofani, DR	1	1	–	28	28	–	–	28.00	2	6.0	–	18	–	–	–	–	–
Ellis, RS	1	1	1	0	0*	–	–	–	1	21.0	4	48	8	6.00	1	–	5/25
Hassett, AL (Capt)	1	1	–	57	57	1	–	57.00	1	10.0	4	10	2	5.00	–	–	2/10
Miller, KR	1	1	–	132	132	–	1	132.00	1	17.0	4	37	2	18.50	–	–	1/14
Pepper, CG	1	1	–	15	15	–	–	15.00	–	19.3	3	79	5	15.80	–	–	4/46
Pettiford, J	1	1	–	16	16	–	–	16.00	–	5.0	1	20	–	–	–	–	–
Price, CFT	1	1	–	10	10	–	–	10.00	2	4.0	–	21	–	–	–	–	–
Roper, AW	1	1	–	0	0	–	–	0.00	1	10.0	3	9	2	4.50	–	–	2/9
Sismey, SG	1	1	–	3	3	–	–	3.00	1/2	–	–	–	–	–	–	–	–
Stanford, RM	1	1	–	20	20	–	–	20.00	–	–	–	–	–	–	–	–	–
Workman, JA	1	1	–	18	18	–	–	18.00	–	–	–	–	–	–	–	–	–

AUSTRALIANS IN SRI LANKA

1969/70 AUSTRALIANS

First-class Results					All Matches				
Matches	Won	Lost	Drawn	Tied	Matches	Won	Lost	Drawn	Tied
1	–	–	1	–	4	1	–	3	–

Date	Venue	Opponent	Results for Australians
Oct 17	Colombo	*Ceylon Board XI	Drawn
Oct 20	Kandy	*Central Province	*Won by 189 runs
Oct 22	Colombo	*Ceylon Board XI	*Drawn
Oct 23	Colombo	Ceylon	Drawn

Player	State	M	Inn	NO	Runs	HS	50	100	Avrge	Ct/St	Overs	Mdns	Runs	Wkts	Avrge	5wi	10wm	Best
Chappell, IM	SA	1	2	–	35	29	–	–	17.50	–	4.0	–	11	–	–	–	–	–
Gleeson, JW	NSW	1	1	–	0	0	–	–	0.00	–	45.0	9	95	5	19.00	–	–	3/32
Irvine, JT	WA	1	2	–	18	16	–	–	9.00	–	–	–	–	–	–	–	–	–
Jordon, RC	VIC	1	2	1	16	9	–	–	16.00	–/2	–	–	–	–	–	–	–	–
Lawry, WM (Capt)	VIC	1	2	–	82	70	1	–	41.00	1	1.0	–	8	–	–	–	–	–
Mallett, AA	SA	1	1	–	5	5	–	–	5.00	–	32.2	9	63	4	15.75	–	–	3/35
Mayne, LC	WA	1	1	1	2	2*	–	–	–	–	22.0	5	46	2	23.00	–	–	2/19
McKenzie, GD	WA	1	2	1	58	52	1	–	58.00	–	22.0	10	29	3	9.66	–	–	2/8
Redpath, IR	VIC	1	2	–	16	9	–	–	8.00	1	–	–	–	–	–	–	–	–
Stackpole, KR	VIC	1	2	–	44	25	–	–	22.00	1	16.0	7	20	1	20.00	–	–	1/20
Walters, KD	NSW	1	2	–	60	49	–	–	30.00	1	–	–	–	–	–	–	–	–

1980/81 AUSTRALIANS

First-class Results					All Matches				
Matches	Won	Lost	Drawn	Tied	Matches	Won	Lost	Drawn	Tied
1	–	–	1	–	4	2	1	1	–

Date	Venue	Opponent	Results for Australians
May 2	Moratuwa	*Sri Lankans	Won on run rate
May 3	Colombo (SSC)	*Sri Lankans	Lost by 6 wkts
May 5	Colombo (SSC)	*Sri Lankans	Won by 6 runs
May 7	Colombo (PSS)	Sri Lankans	Drawn

Player	State	M	Inn	NO	Runs	HS	50	100	Avrge	Ct/St	Overs	Mdns	Runs	Wkts	Avrge	5wi	10wm	Best
Beard, GR	NSW	1	2	–	13	9	–	–	6.50	–	19.0	3	69	5	13.80	1	–	5/69
Border, AR	QLD	1	2	–	19	19	–	–	9.50	–	3.0	–	4	–	–	–	–	–
Bright, RJ	VIC	1	2	–	1	1	–	–	0.50	–	12.0	2	34	–	–	–	–	–
Dyson, J	NSW	1	2	–	90	68	1	–	45.00	1	–	–	–	–	–	–	–	–
Hogg, RM	SA	1	2	–	7	6	–	–	3.50	–	8.0	–	33	1	33.00	–	–	1/33
Hughes, KJ (Capt)	WA	1	2	–	15	15	–	–	7.50	1	–	–	–	–	–	–	–	–
Kent, MF	QLD	1	2	–	10	6	–	–	5.00	–	–	–	–	–	–	–	–	–
Lawson, GF	NSW	1	2	2	11	9*	–	–	–	–	10.4	3	14	4	3.50	–	–	4/14
Rixon, SJ	NSW	1	2	–	18	14	–	–	9.00	3/1	–	–	–	–	–	–	–	–
Wood, GM	WA	1	2	–	54	28	–	–	27.00	–	–	–	–	–	–	–	–	–
Yallop, GN	VIC	1	2	–	38	25	–	–	19.00	–	2.0	–	9	–	–	–	–	–

1982/83 AUSTRALIANS

First-class Results					All Matches				
Matches	Won	Lost	Drawn	Tied	Matches	Won	Lost	Drawn	Tied
2	1	–	1	–	6	1	2	3	–

Date	Venue	Opponent	Results for Australians
Apr 13	Colombo (PSS)	*Sri Lankans (L/O Intl)	Lost by 2 wkts
Apr 16	Colombo (PSS)	*Sri Lankans (L/O Intl)	Lost by 4 wkts
Apr 17	Moratuwa	Board President's XI	Drawn
Apr 22	Kandy	SRI LANKA (Only Test)	Won by an inns & 38 runs
Apr 29	Colombo (SSC)	*Sri Lankans (L/O Intl)	No result
Apr 30	Colombo (SSC)	*Sri Lankans (L/O Intl)	No result

Player	State	M	Inn	NO	Runs	HS	50	100	Avrge	Ct/St	Overs	Mdns	Runs	Wkts	Avrge	5wi	10wm	Best
Border, AR	QLD	1	1	1	47	47*	–	–	–	3	4.5	–	11	1	11.00	–	–	1/11
Chappell, GS (Capt)	QLD	2	2	–	92	66	1	–	46.00	–	1.0	–	2	–	–	–	–	–
Hogan, TG	WA	2	1	–	10	10	–	–	10.00	1	67.2	15	195	12	16.25	1	–	5/66
Hogg, RM	SA	2	1	–	0	0	–	–	0.00	1	31.0	9	81	5	16.20	–	–	2/17
Hookes, DW	SA	2	2	1	163	143*	–	1	163.00	6	–	–	–	–	–	–	–	–
Lillee, DK	WA	2	1	–	12	12*	–	–	–	1	52.2	12	179	7	25.57	–	–	3/26
Smith, SB	NSW	1	2	–	54	33*	–	–	54.00	–	–	–	–	–	–	–	–	–
Wessels, KC	QLD	2	3	–	199	141	–	1	66.33	1	1.0	1	0	1	0.00	–	–	1/0
Wood, GM	WA	2	3	–	31	14	–	–	10.33	1	–	–	–	–	–	–	–	–
Woolley, RD	TAS	2	1	–	57	57	1	–	57.00	8/–	–	–	–	–	–	–	–	–
Yallop, GN	VIC	2	3	1	171	98	1	–	85.50	1	3.0	1	7	–	–	–	–	–
Yardley, B	WA	2	1	–	14	14	–	–	14.00	1	83.0	20	261	10	26.10	1	–	5/88

1992/93 AUSTRALIANS

First-class Results					All Matches				
Matches	Won	Lost	Drawn	Tied	Matches	Won	Lost	Drawn	Tied
5	1	–	4	–	8	2	2	4	–

Date	Venue	Opponent	Results for Australians
Aug 10	Kandy	Board President's XI	Drawn
Aug 15	Colombo (PSS)	*Sri Lankans (L/O Intl)	Lost by 4 wkts
Aug 17	Colombo (SSC)	SRI LANKA (1st Test)	Won by 16 runs
Aug 24	Matara	Southern District XI	Drawn
Aug 28	Colombo (PIS)	SRI LANKA (2nd Test)	Drawn
Sep 4	Colombo (PIS)	*Sri Lankans (L/O Intl)	Lost on run rate
Sep 5	Colombo (PIS)	*Sri Lankans (L/O Intl)	Won by 5 wkts
Sep 8	Moratuwa	SRI LANKA (3rd Test)	Drawn

Player	State	M	Inn	NO	Runs	HS	50	100	Avrge	Ct/St	Overs	Mdns	Runs	Wkts	Avrge	5wi	10wm	Best
Boon, DC	TAS	5	9	–	235	68	2	–	26.11	3	3.0	–	4	–	–	–	–	–
Border, AR (Capt)	QLD	5	9	–	324	106	1	1	36.00	3	23.0	6	60	1	60.00	–	–	1/28
Dodemaide, AIC	VIC	4	6	3	39	16*	–	–	13.00	1	98.5	31	229	11	20.82	–	–	4/65
Healy, IA	QLD	5	9	3	326	78*	3	–	54.33	9/1	–	–	–	–	–	–	–	–
Jones, DM	VIC	5	9	1	295	100*	2	1	36.88	2	0.5	–	1	1	1.00	–	–	1/1
Martyn, DR	WA	1	2	–	74	61	1	–	37.00	–	–	–	–	–	–	–	–	–
Matthews, GRJ	NSW	4	7	–	340	96	5	–	48.57	3	148.0	33	381	10	38.10	–	–	4/76
McDermott, CJ	QLD	5	7	1	142	58*	1	–	23.67	–	182.0	43	514	16	32.13	–	–	4/53
Moody, TM	WA	5	9	–	106	54	1	–	11.78	4	39.0	7	99	1	99.00	–	–	1/17
Taylor, MA	NSW	4	7	–	161	43	–	–	23.00	2	–	–	–	–	–	–	–	–
Warne, SK	VIC	3	4	–	67	35	–	–	16.75	1	38.1	8	158	3	52.67	–	–	3/11
Waugh, ME	NSW	5	9	–	291	118	2	1	32.33	5	40.0	6	129	2	64.50	–	–	2/77
Whitney, MR	NSW	4	6	4	30	13	–	–	15.00	1	102.0	31	246	9	27.33	–	–	4/34

1994/95 AUSTRALIANS IN SRI LANKA

First-class Results					All Matches				
Matches	Won	Lost	Drawn	Tied	Matches	Won	Lost	Drawn	Tied
–	–	–	–	–	3	1	2	–	–

Date	Venue	Opponent	Results for Australians
Sep 7	Colombo (SSC)	*Pakistan (L/O Intl)	Won by 28 runs
Sep 9	Colombo (PIS)	*India (L/O Intl)	Lost by 31 runs
Sep 13	Colombo (PSS)	*Sri Lanka (L/O Intl)	Lost on run rate

AUSTRALIAN CRICKET TEAMS IN WEST INDIES

		First-class Games					All Games					
Season	Touring Team	P	W	L	D	T	P	W	L	D	T	Captain
1954/55	Australians	9	5	–	4	–	11	6	–	5	–	IW Johnson
1964/65	Australians	11	3	2	6	–	16	4	3	9	–	RB Simpson
1972/73	Australians	12	7	–	5	–	15	10	–	5	–	IM Chappell
1977/78	Australians	11	5	3	3	–	13	6	4	3	–	RB Simpson
1983/84	Australians	10	1	3	6	–	15	2	6	7	–	KJ Hughes
1990/91	Australians	10	2	2	6	–	19	10	3	6	–	AR Border
1994/95	Australians	7	3	1	3	–	16	8	5	3	–	MA Taylor
		70	26	11	33	–	105	46	21	38	–	

FIRST-CLASS RESULTS

Opponent	Venue	First Game	Games	W	L	D	T
WEST INDIES	Kingston	Mar 26 1955	8	3	2	3	–
	Port-of-Spain	Apr 11 1955	10	2	3	5	–
	Georgetown	Apr 26 1955	6	3	2	1	–
	Bridgetown	May 14 1955	7	1	3	3	–
	Antigua	Apr 7 1984	3	1	1	1	–
			34	10	11	13	–
Barbados	Bridgetown	May 7 1955	5	2	–	3	–
Guyana	Georgetown	Apr 20 1955	6	3	–	3	–
Jamaica	Kingston	Mar 19 1955	5	4	–	1	–
Leeward Islands	St Kitt's	Mar 12 1965	3	3	–	–	–
	Antigua	Feb 24 1973	1	–	–	1	–
			5	3	–	1	–
Trinidad	Port-of-Spain	Apr 4 1955	3	1	–	2	–
	Pointe-a-Pierre	Mar 17 1972	3	–	–	3	–
			6	1	–	5	–

▶

Opponent	Venue	First Game	Games	W	L	D	T
WI Cricket Board XI	Bridgetown	Apr 13 1991	1	–	–	1	–
	St Kitt's	Apr 15 1995	2	–	–	2	–
			3	–	–	3	–
WI President's XI	Montego Bay	Feb 9 1973	1	1	–	–	–
	St Lucia	Mar 25 1995	1	–	–	1	–
			2	1	–	1	–
West Indies Under 23's	St Vincent	Mar 25 1991	1	–	–	1	–
Windward Island	Grenada	May 22 1965	3	2	–	1	–
	Castries	Apr 14 1984	1	–	–	1	–
			4	2	–	2	–

AUSTRALIAN CRICKET TEAMS IN ZIMBABWE

Season	Touring Team	First-class Games					All Games					Captain
		P	W	L	D	T	P	W	L	D	T	
1982/83	Young Australians	2	1	1	–	–	8	7	1	–	–	DM Wellham
1985/86	Young Australians	2	1	–	1	–	9	3	5	1	–	RB Kerr
1985/86	New South Wales	2	1	–	1	–	8	5	2	1	–	GC Dyer
1987/88	New South Wales	2	–	–	2	–	8	5	1	2	–	DM Wellham
1991/92	Australian XI	2	2	–	–	–	6	5	1	–	–	MA Taylor
		10	5	1	4	–	39	25	10	4	–	

FIRST-CLASS RESULTS

Opponent	Venue	First Game	Games	W	L	D	T
Zimbabweans	Harare	Apr 1 1983	9	4	1	4	–
	Bulawayo	Sep 16 1991	1	1	–	–	–
			10	5	1	4	–

1982/83 AUSTRALIANS

First-class Results					All Matches			
Matches	Won	Lost	Drawn	Tied	Matches	Won	Lost	Drawn	Tied
2	1	1	–	–	8	7	1	–	–

Date	Venue	Opponent	Results for Australians
Mar 30	Harare	*Zimbabwean Colts	Won by 121 runs
Apr 1	Harare	Zimbabweans	Won by an inns & 54 runs
Apr 6	Mutare	*Zimbabwean Colts	Won by 22 runs
Apr 9	Bulawayo	*Zimbabweans	Won by 4 wkts
Apr 10	Bulawayo	*Zimbabweans	Won on run rate
Apr 12	Harare	*Zimbabwe Country Districts	Won by 137 runs
Apr 14	Harare	Zimbabweans	Lost by 93 runs
Apr 17	Harare	*Zimbabweans	Won by 6 wkts

Player	State	M	Inn	NO	Runs	HS	50	100	Avrge	Ct/St	Overs	Mdns	Runs	Wkts	Avrge	5wi	10wm	Best
Bennett, MJ	NSW	2	3	–	80	35	–	–	26.66	3	53.0	24	113	5	22.60	–	–	2/39
Boon, DC	TAS	2	3	–	274	148	–	2	91.33	3	–	–	–	–	–	–	–	–
Haysman, MD	SA	1	2	–	12	8	–	–	6.00	2	–	–	–	–	–	–	–	–
Kerr, RB	QLD	2	3	–	37	23	–	–	12.33	3	–	–	–	–	–	–	–	–
MacLeay, KH	WA	2	3	–	36	31	–	–	12.00	2	69.1	28	141	5	28.20	–	–	3/27
McCurdy, RJ	VIC	2	3	1	21	20*	–	–	10.50	2	71.0	16	195	13	15.00	–	–	4/37
Phillips, WB	SA	2	3	–	82	58	1	–	27.33	4/–	–	–	–	–	–	–	–	–
Ritchie, GM	QLD	1	1	–	69	69	1	–	69.00	2	–	–	–	–	–	–	–	–
Saunders, SL	TAS	2	3	1	35	17*	–	–	17.50	–	42.4	10	106	3	35.33	–	–	2/30
Shipperd, G	WA	2	3	–	32	16	–	–	10.66	2	–	–	–	–	–	–	–	–
Wellham, DM (Capt)	NSW	2	3	–	24	16	–	–	8.00	–	–	–	–	–	–	–	–	–
Whitney, MR	NSW	2	3	1	5	2	–	–	2.50	–	81.4	25	162	12	13.50	1	–	5/29

1985/86 AUSTRALIANS

First-class Results					All Matches				
Matches	Won	Lost	Drawn	Tied	Matches	Won	Lost	Drawn	Tied
2	1	–	1	–	9	3	5	1	–

Date	Venue	Opponent	Results for Australians
Sep 18	Harare	*Zimbabwe Country Districts	Won by 112 runs
Sep 20	Harare	Zimbabweans	Drawn
Sep 22	Harare	*Zimbabweans	Lost by 3 wkts
Sep 25	Mutare	*Zimbabwe 'B'	Won by 9 wkts
Sep 28	Bulawayo	*Zimbabweans	Lost by 1 wkt
Sep 29	Bulawayo	*Zimbabweans	Lost by 8 wkts
Oct 1	Harare	Zimbabweans	Won by 65 runs
Oct 5	Harare	*Zimbabweans	Lost by 108 runs
Oct 6	Harare	*Zimbabweans	Lost by 23 runs

Player	State	M	Inn	NO	Runs	HS	50	100	Avrge	Ct/St	Overs	Mdns	Runs	Wkts	Avrge	5wi	10wm	Best
Bishop, GA	SA	2	4	1	98	41*	–	–	32.66	1	–	–	–	–	–	–	–	–
Brown, RL	TAS	1	2	2	4	4*	–	–	–	1	22.2	4	90	3	30.00	–	–	3/90
Clifford, PS	NSW	1	2	–	38	29	–	–	19.00	–	–	–	–	–	–	–	–	–
Courtice, BA	QLD	2	4	–	119	59	1	–	29.75	1	–	–	–	–	–	–	–	–
Dimattina, MGD	VIC	2	3	1	83	64*	1	–	41.50	5/–	–	–	–	–	–	–	–	–
Dodemaide, AIC	VIC	2	3	1	77	41	–	–	38.50	1	53.5	12	143	3	47.67	–	–	2/27
Gilbert, DR	NSW	2	2	–	18	14	–	–	9.00	1	68.0	14	215	15	14.33	2	1	7/43
Jones, DM	VIC	2	4	1	192	70	2	–	64.00	1	–	–	–	–	–	–	–	–
Kerr, RB (Capt)	QLD	2	4	–	103	68	1	–	25.75	3	–	–	–	–	–	–	–	–
Reid, BA	WA	2	2	–	14	14	–	–	7.00	–	58.4	12	177	6	29.50	–	–	4/91
Saunders, SL	TAS	2	3	–	101	53	1	–	33.66	2	4.0	1	22	–	–	–	–	–
Veletta, MRJ	WA	1	1	–	4	4	–	–	4.00	4	–	–	–	–	–	–	–	–
Waugh, SR	NSW	1	1	–	30	30	–	–	30.00	–	20.5	2	85	2	42.50	–	–	2/57

AUSTRALIANS CRICKET TEAMS IN UNITED ARAB EMIRATES (SHARJAH)

Date	Australia	Opponent	Total	Result for Australia	Captain
Mar 24 1985	8–178	England	8–177*	Won by 2 wkts	AR Border
Mar 29 1985	139*	India	7–140	Lost by 3 wkts	AR Border
Apr 11 1986	7–202*	Pakistan	2–206	Lost by 8 wkts	RJ Bright
Apr 3 1987	9–176*	Pakistan	4–180	Lost by 6 wkts	AR Border
Apr 6 1987	6–176*	India	3–177	Lost by 7 wkts	GR Marsh
Apr 9 1987	9–219	England	6–230*	Lost by 11 runs	AR Border
Apr 26 1990	5–258*	New Zealand	7–195	Won by 63 runs	AR Border
Apr 30 1990	3–140	Bangladesh	8–134*	Won by 7 wkts	AR Border
May 2 1990	3–332*	Sri Lanka	218	Won by 114 runs	AR Border
May 4 1990	230	Pakistan	7–266*	Lost by 36 runs	AR Border
Apr 14 1994	1–158	Sri Lanka	154*	Won by 9 wkts	MA Taylor
Apr 16 1994	3–208	New Zealand	9–207*	Won by 7 wkts	MA Taylor
Apr 19 1994	9–244*	India	3–245	Lost by 7 wkts	MA Taylor

(* Denotes batted first)

Acknowledgments

The author and publisher would like to thank the following for their help in the production of this book: The Australian Cricket Board (ACB); Stephen Green, curator of the MCC Library at Lord's; Bob Radford, former chief executive of the New South Wales Cricket Association (NSWCA); Ken Jacobs, chief executive of the Victorian Cricket Association; XXXX Brewers and their public relations officer Ray Phillips; Stephen Gibbs, librarian to the NSWCA; the noted cricket photographers Vivian Jenkins and Patrick Eagar; former managers of Australian touring teams Fred Bennett, Bob Merriman, Bill Jacobs and Allan Crompton, chairman of the ACB; Bruce Francis, the manager of the two rebel teams to South Africa; PBL Marketing; and all the players who have allowed me to dip into their personal albums, particularly John Gleeson and Stan Sismey. Roger Mann, the prominent collector of Devon, England, generously granted me free use of his files, as did Phil Derriman in Sydney and the ACB's Public Relations Officer, Ian McDonald. The photographs in the book are from my private collection unless otherwise credited. –J.P.